THE OXFORD HANDBOOK OF
DEUTERONOMY

THE OXFORD HANDBOOK OF
DEUTERONOMY

Edited by
DON C. BENJAMIN

OXFORD
UNIVERSITY PRESS

Oxford University Press is a department of the University of Oxford. It furthers the University's objective of excellence in research, scholarship, and education by publishing worldwide. Oxford is a registered trade mark of Oxford University Press in the UK and certain other countries.

Published in the United States of America by Oxford University Press
198 Madison Avenue, New York, NY 10016, United States of America.

© Oxford University Press 2025

All rights reserved. No part of this publication may be reproduced, stored in a retrieval system, or transmitted, in any form or by any means, without the prior permission in writing of Oxford University Press, or as expressly permitted by law, by license, or under terms agreed with the appropriate reproduction rights organization. Inquiries concerning reproduction outside the scope of the above should be sent to the Rights Department, Oxford University Press, at the address above.

You must not circulate this work in any other form and you must impose this same condition on any acquirer.

CIP data is on file at the Library of Congress

ISBN 978–0–19–027355–2

DOI: 10.1093/oxfordhb/9780190273552.001.0001

Printed by Marquis Book Printing, Canada

Contents

List of Contributors   ix
Introduction   xi
   Don C. Benjamin

SECTION I: LITERARY DEVELOPMENT OF DEUTERONOMY

1. The Literary History of Deuteronomy   3
Anselm C. Hagedorn

2. Near Eastern Practice of Law in Deuteronomy   18
Stephen C. Russell

3. Deuteronomy—Code or Covenant?   33
Anne K. Knafl

4. The Decalogue in Deuteronomy   42
Dominik Markl

5. Blessings and Curses in Deuteronomy   56
Laura Quick

SECTION II: LITERARY MOTIFS IN DEUTERONOMY

6. Monotheism and Deuteronomy   71
Matthew Lynch

7. Space Theory and the *Maqom* (Sanctuary) in Deuteronomy   93
Michaela Geiger

8. Archaeology and the *Maqom* Sanctuary in Deuteronomy   110
Gary P. Arbino

9. Love and Hate in Deuteronomy   131
   FRANCOISE MIRGUET

10. War in Deuteronomy   146
    PEKKA PITKÄNEN

11. Moses and a Prophet Like Moses in Deuteronomy   160
    STEPHEN L. COOK

SECTION III: SOCIAL WORLD OF DEUTERONOMY

12. Israel in Deuteronomy   177
    C. L. CROUCH

13. Women in Deuteronomy   189
    SANDRA JACOBS

14. Deuteronomy and Scribes   204
    JOACHIM L. W. SCHAPER

15. Priests, Levites, and Levitical Priests in Deuteronomy   219
    NATHAN MACDONALD

16. The "Stranger, Fatherless, and Widow" in Deuteronomy   233
    MARK R. GLANVILLE

17. Deuteronomy and the Reigns of Kings Hezekiah and Josiah of Judah   252
    MARVIN A. SWEENEY

18. The Socio-Economic World of Deuteronomy   267
    SANDRA LYNN RICHTER

SECTION IV: INTERTEXTUALITY OF DEUTERONOMY

19. Deuteronomy and the Pentateuch   287
    RICHARD J. BAUTCH

20. Deuteronomy, the Deuteronomistic History, and the Books of Joshua through Kings   310
    RANNFRID I. LASINE THELLE

21. Deuteronomy, Hosea, and the Theory of Northern Origins   328
    BILL T. ARNOLD

22. Deuteronomy and Jeremiah   344
    MARK LEUCHTER

SECTION V: RECEPTION HISTORY OF DEUTERONOMY

23. Deuteronomy in the Texts from the Judean Desert   365
    ARIEL FELDMAN

24. Deuteronomy in the New Testament   384
    MICHAEL LABAHN

25. Deuteronomy and Early Rabbinic Judaism   402
    JOEL GEREBOFF

26. Deuteronomy and Islam   417
    JOHN KALTNER

27. Deuteronomy in African-American Christianity   430
    STEPHEN BRECK REID

28. Latin American Liberation Theology as a Response to Deuteronomy   445
    MERCEDES GARCÍA BACHMANN

29. Disability in Deuteronomy and Its Reception   463
    SARAH J. MELCHER

30. Deuteronomy in the LGBTQIA+ Community   475
    DAVID TABB STEWART

Index   499

Contributors

Gary P. Arbino, Gateway Seminary

Bill T. Arnold, Asbury Theological Seminary

Mercedes Garcia Bachmann, Director of the Institute for Contextual Pastoral Studies for the United Evangelical Lutheran Church of Argentina and Uruguay

Richard J. Bautch, St. Edward's University

Don C. Benjamin, Arizona State University

Stephen L. Cook, Virginia Theological Seminary

C. L. Crouch, Radboud University Nijmegen and University of Pretoria

Ariel Feldman, Brite Divinity School at Texas Christian University

Michaela Geiger, Kirchliche Hochschule Wuppertal

Joel Gereboff, Arizona State University

Mark R. Glanville, Regent College British Columbia

Anselm C. Hagedorn, Universität Osnabrück

Sandra Jacobs, King's College London

John Kaltner, Rhodes College

Anne K. Knafl, The University of Chicago Library

Michael Labahn, Martin-Luther-University Halle-Wittenberg and University of the Free State Bloemfontein

Mark Leuchter, Temple University

Matthew Lynch, Regent College

Nathan MacDonald, University of Cambridge and St John's College Cambridge

Dominik Markl, University of Innsbruck

Sarah J. Melcher, Xavier University

Francoise Mirguet, Arizona State University

Pekka Pitkänen, University of Gloucestershire

Laura Quick, University of Oxford

Stephen Breck Reid, Baylor University

Sandra Lynn Richter, Westmont College

Stephen C. Russell, John Jay College, City University of New York

Joachim L. W. Schaper, University of Aberdeen

David Tabb Stewart, California State University, Long Beach

Marvin A. Sweeney, Claremont School of Theology

Rannfrid I. Lasine Thelle, Wichita State University

Introduction

DON C. BENJAMIN

As the editor, it is my pleasure to introduce you to *The Oxford Handbook of Deuteronomy*. Planning for this handbook began in 2013 with the patient guidance of Steve A. Wiggins, editor for Bibles and Biblical Studies at Oxford University Press. The first chapters were published online in 2020 with the professional and conscientious editing of Preethi Krishnan and her team at SPi Global. Jaishree Srijan and her team at Newgen KnowledgeWorks did the good work on the print edition of the handbook.

Personal experience influences the research we do as scholars. Therefore, feminist biblical critics often introduce their research with intellectual biographies explaining experiences that may influence their work. For example, "I am an observant Jewish daughter, wife, and mother," writes Sarah Jacobs in the introduction to her study of "Terms of Endearment? The Desirable Female Captive and Her Illicit Acquisition" (Jacobs 2012, 238). Here, I will share some personal experiences from *my* journey that significantly influenced my work on the *Oxford Handbook of Deuteronomy*.

When Steve was on a campus visit at Arizona State University to acquire publications, it was a beautiful time of year in Arizona. So, we met for lunch outdoors at a small landmark eatery near campus. When Steve asked me about my projects, I told him that I had received an unexpected invitation to publish a feminist commentary on Deuteronomy. I had written my first book on Deuteronomy (Benjamin 1983). In the intervening years; however, the focus of my research and teaching was much broader, encompassing courses like *Introduction to the Hebrew Bible/Old Testament* (Benjamin 2004; Matthews and Benjamin 2023), *Archaeology and the Bible* (Benjamin 2010), and *Women and the Bible* (Benjamin 2017, 2019). Nonetheless, I accepted the commentary invitation, thinking it would be interesting to see how Deuteronomy studies had changed or remained the same in the intervening thirty years. The form critic in me also thought a commentary on Deuteronomy would create a fitting artistic frame—a *chiasm*—for my academic career.

Then, Steve asked if I had any interest in editing a handbook of Deuteronomy. I also found his invitation intriguing and we eventually agreed to work together. It was the beginning of a productive, professional, and personally enjoyable relationship between the two of us. I have learned much from him throughout the years of collaboration on this project.

A formative experience in my own intellectual biography was studying form criticism and biblical theology with Rolf P. Knierim (1928–2018). Rolf was proud to have been the last graduate student trained by Gerhard von Rad (1901–1971). He was also passionate about the importance of the legal traditions for accurately understanding the Bible. He supervised my dissertation study of legal traditions in Deuteronomy dealing with the administration of justice at the gates of a city. My postgraduate focus moved to social-scientific criticism, using anthropology, archaeology, sociology, and narrative studies to better understand and appreciate the world of the Bible and the Bible itself (Matthews and Benjamin 1993).

When I ask my students how many have wanted to read the Bible cover to cover, I am always inspired by the number who do. Then I ask how many successfully completed the task. Many fewer than those who wanted to. When I ask those who did not complete their task "Why?" most answer: "The stories in Genesis and Exodus were exciting to read, but then I got to legal traditions in Exodus and Leviticus and the census lists and genealogies in Numbers, I just gave up." Most never reached Deuteronomy. Similarly, until I wrote my own commentaries on Deuteronomy, I did not fully appreciate just how important legal traditions are as a window into the social world where the Bible developed (Benjamin 2015, 2021).

Legal traditions are not dry and dated relics of a long-gone culture. They pass on the essence of a culture and how it struggled to resolve the crises of daily life. Problem-solving reveals the values of a culture in action. This handbook can help its readers navigate the Bible's legal traditions and realize what a remarkable source of information about the cultural identity and social world of the people of YHWH it is. Legal traditions like Deuteronomy teach us how the people of YHWH thought about themselves and about their world. They not only describe the cultural identity of the people of YHWH but also show us how this ancient people faced and resolved the challenges of daily life. Readers today will certainly not find that all these ancient resolutions reflect their values today, but the process of problem-solving and crisis resolution in Deuteronomy continues to inspire audiences to take on the challenges of living their values with confidence.

The American Theological Library Association (ATLA) database now lists more than two thousand books and articles on Deuteronomy. This handbook can introduce readers to some significant topics in this thriving conversation and in the rich diversity in the academic community studying Deuteronomy. The contributors to the *Oxford Handbook of Deuteronomy* are specialists in a variety of critical methods for understanding and appreciating biblical traditions. My goal was to assemble a diverse group of scholars from Europe and the Americas. Some are emerging scholars, some are veterans. Some teach at religiously affiliated schools, some at private religiously unaffiliated schools, some at public institutions. Some are classmates from the Claremont Graduate University. Some are my colleagues at Arizona State University and in the Pacific Coast Region of the Society of Biblical Literature. All are remarkable men and women whose work I found enlightening and exciting, but most of all, whose work I found helpful in my own study of Deuteronomy. I hope that those who read the chapters in this handbook will learn as much from the contributors as I have learned from working with them.

Each contributor composed a seven-thousand-word chapter. I asked them to guide readers through the conversation on their topic from Deuteronomy studies using three questions. "Who Began the Conversation?" offers a summary of the scholars who pioneered research on their topic. "What Is the Status of the Conversation?" describes the consensus among scholars on their topic today. "What Is Trending in the Conversation?" profiles their own ongoing research as a new and stimulating example of what is trending in the study of Deuteronomy and shows how their research either continued or redirected the conversation on the topic. Contributors have documented their chapters with secondary literature which they recommend to readers who wish to continue studying their chapter topic.

I divided the handbook into five sections: *Literary Development of Deuteronomy, Literary Motifs in Deuteronomy, Social World of Deuteronomy, Intertextuality of Deuteronomy*, and the *Reception History of Deuteronomy*. This list is, by no means, definitive but only indicative of the rich diversity of scholarship now used to better understand and appreciate Deuteronomy.

The section on the *Literary Development of Deuteronomy* includes chapters like the "Near Eastern Practice of Law in Deuteronomy" by Stephen C. Russell and "Deuteronomy—Code or Covenant?" by Anne K. Knafl. Studies of the genre covenant during the twentieth century, for example, led to a scholarly consensus that Deuteronomy was a covenant whose stipulations were apodictic and case laws. Then research on Neo-Babylonian trial law suggested that the Code of Hammurabi and the Deuteronomic Code do not pass laws to govern a society but instead analyze, explain, and classify laws. If they were intended to provide precedents for legal assemblies, then records of actual trials should cite them, but Mesopotamian trial records do not, even when precedents in the Code of Hammurabi are available (Wells 2008).

The section on *Literary Motifs in Deuteronomy* includes chapters like "Monotheism and Deuteronomy" by Matthew Lynch and "Love and Hate in Deuteronomy" by Francoise Mirguet. Deuteronomy is a major resource for biblical theologians studying monotheism, worship, love-hate language, war, and prophecy. The early twentieth-century scholarly consensus that Deuteronomy marks the birth of biblical monotheism, for example, was pioneered by Julius Wellhausen (1844–1918). For him, and others, *before* Deuteronomy the people of YHWH were *Hebrews*; *after* Deuteronomy the people of YHWH were *Jews* who believed that YHWH was the only divine. Today although the monotheism of Jews, Christians, and Muslims teaches that only one God exists, Deuteronomy teaches henotheism—that the Hebrews have only one divine patron and that *You shall have no other gods before me* (5:7) teaches the fathers of households in ancient Israel not to follow any other divine patron but YHWH (Coogan and Smith 2012).

The section on the *Social World of Deuteronomy* includes chapters like "Women in Deuteronomy" by Sandra Jacobs and "Archaeology and the *Maqom* Sanctuary in Deuteronomy" by Gary P. Arbino. The contrast between the theology of worship in Deuteronomy, for example, and in other biblical traditions is pronounced. Interpretations of Deuteronomy have been driven by an assumption that it centralizes worship of YHWH at a single sanctuary. In other traditions the people of YHWH worship their divine patron at sanctuaries throughout the land. The annals of Hezekiah (2 Kgs. 18:27–37) portray Sennacherib's *Rabshakeh*, claiming that YHWH had sent the Assyrians to punish Hezekiah for destroying the sanctuaries of YHWH. Nonetheless, archaeology now suggests that when Sennacherib invaded Judah, those sanctuaries were intact.

The section on *Intertextuality of Deuteronomy* includes chapters like "Deuteronomy and the Pentateuch" by Richard J. Bautch and "Deuteronomy, Hosea, and the Theory of Northern Origins" by Bill T. Arnold. Intertextuality studies the relationship of Deuteronomy to the books that precede Deuteronomy in the canon and those that follow it, as well as the relationship of prophets like Hosea, Isaiah, and Jeremiah to its teachings. Early scholars, for example, assumed Deuteronomy was the final scroll in the Torah. Then scholars refocused their attention on its literary location as the inaugural tradition in the Deuteronomistic History (Deut., Josh., Judg., 1–2 Sam., 1–2 Kgs.), a theory launched by Martin Noth in 1943 (Noth 2001).

The section on the *Reception History of Deuteronomy* includes chapters like "Deuteronomy and Islam" by John Kaltner and "Latin American Liberation Theology as a Response to Deuteronomy" by Mercedes Garcia Bachmann. To better understand Deuteronomy itself, attention continues to be paid to early interpretations of Deuteronomy in the Dead Sea Scrolls of Judaism, the New Testament of Christianity, and the Qur'an of Islam. There is also increasing interest in studying how contemporary Jewish, Christian, and Muslim spiritualties interpret Deuteronomy and apply the interpretations to both their teachings and lifestyles.

Finally, the goal of this *Oxford Handbook of Deuteronomy* is not to be comprehensive but to be stimulating. When I begin working with graduate students on their dissertations, I ask them to meet me in the library stacks where their first book will be shelved. Then, while separating the volumes to make a space for their book, I tell them: "The goal of your dissertation is to get an invitation to join the conversation, not an attempt to stop the conversation. You want to learn from your predecessors and listen to the scholars already at the table." This handbook is an invitation to its readers to join the conversation on Deuteronomy. It is a first word, not the last.

Bibliography

Benjamin, D. C. "Deuteronomy." In *The Jerome Biblical Commentary* (3rd fully rev. ed.), edited by John J. Collins, Barbara Reid OP, Donald Senior C.P., and Gina Hens-Piazza, pp. 336–360. London: Bloomsbury T & T Clark, 2021.

Benjamin, D. C. *Deuteronomy and City Life: Form Criticism of Texts with the Word CITY in Deut 4:41-26:19*. Lanham: University Press of America, 1983.

Benjamin, D. C. "The Impact of Sargon & Enheduanna on Land Rights in Deuteronomy." *Biblical Theology Bulletin* 49, no. 1 (2019): 22–31.

Benjamin, D. C. "Israel's God: Mother and Midwife." *Biblical Theology Bulletin* 19, no. 4 (1989): 115–120.

Benjamin, D. C. "The Land Rights of Women in Deuteronomy in Memory of John J. Pilch (1937-2016)." *Biblical Theology Bulletin* 47, no. 2 (2017): 67–79.

Benjamin, D. C. *The Old Testament Story: An Introduction*. Fortress, 2004.

Benjamin, D. C. *The Social World of Deuteronomy: A New Feminist Commentary*. Eugene: Wipf & Stock, 2015.

Benjamin, D. C. *Stones & Stories: An introduction to Archaeology & the Bible*. Fortress Press, 2010.

Benjamin, D. C. "Stories of Adam and Eve." In *Problems of Old Testament Theology: Essays in Honor of Rolf Knierim*, edited by H. T. C. Sun, pp. 38–58. Grand Rapids: W. B. Eerdmans, 1997.

Benjamin, D. C. "The Stories of Two Women: Rahab and Jael." *The Bible Today* 51, no. 4 (2013): 213–218.

Benjamin, D. C., and V. H. Matthews. "Mourners and the Psalms." In *Worship and the Hebrew Bible: Essays in Honour of John T. Willis*, edited by M. P. Graham, R. R. Marrs, and S. L. McKenzie, pp. 56–77. Sheffield: Sheffield Academic, 1999.

Coogan, M. D., and Mark S. Smith. *Stories from Ancient Canaan* (2nd ed.). Louisville: Westminster-John Knox, 2012.

Jacobs, S. "Terms of Endearment? The Desirable Female Captive Her Illicit Acquisition." In *Exodus and Deuteronomy*, edited by A. Brenner and Gale A. Yee, pp. 237–257. Minneapolis: Fortress Press, 2012.

Matthews, V. H., and D. C. Benjamin, eds. *Old Testament Parallels: Laws and Stories from the Ancient Near East*. Mahwah: Paulist Press, 2023.

Matthews, V. H., and D. C. Benjamin. *Social World of Ancient Israel, 1250-587 BCE*. Peabody: Hendrickson, 1993.

Noth, M. *The Deuteronomistic History* (2nd ed.). UNKNO, 2002.

Wells, B. "The Cultic Versus the Forensic: Judahite and Mesopotamian Judicial Procedures in the First Millennium B.C.E." *Journal of the American Oriental Society* 29 (2008).

ated.

SECTION I

LITERARY DEVELOPMENT OF DEUTERONOMY

CHAPTER 1

THE LITERARY HISTORY OF DEUTERONOMY

ANSELM C. HAGEDORN

INTRODUCTION

THE final book of the Pentateuch presents itself as a series of farewell speeches delivered by Moses in the plains of Moab on the last day of his life. The addressees are a new generation of Israelites who are prepared for entry into the land. The book, then, marks a pause (McConville 2002, 18) on Israel's path towards the Promised Land and its main focus appears to be the realisation (*Vergegenwärtigung*) of the promise and law of Yahweh (Perlitt 2013, 25). In contrast to previous stipulations delivered to the people of Israel at Mt. Sinai, "Deuteronomy indicates the end of the era of divine legislation" (Bultmann 2001, 135). As Deut. 1:5 makes clear, everything that follows should be read as a Mosaic interpretation of previously promulgated stipulations (Otto 2012, 319–21). The result of such reinterpretation is *tôrāh*, a term used frequently within the book to describe its literary character (Deut. 1:15; 4:8.44; 17:18–19; 27:3.8.26; 28:58.61; 29:20.28; 30:10; 31:9.11.12.24.26; 32:46). This *tôrāh* is a rich blend of legal stipulations, social and political guidelines, religious teaching, and catechism that is to be handed down from one generation to another (Miller 2004). As Dennis T. Olson has observed on the present form of Deuteronomy, the book is "intended to function as a . . . document necessitated by the reality of human death and the need to pass the faith on to another generation" (Olson 1994, 6).

The distinct language employed by Deuteronomy as well as several self-referential statements within the book and the command to write down, make Deuteronomy—together with P (and possibly the Covenant Code)—a clearly discernible literary strata within the Pentateuch (Kratz 2011, 34). There is no doubt that Deuteronomy can be read as an independent book and the transition from Numbers to Deuteronomy emphasises the book's independence. In Num. 36:13, Yahweh's speaking to Moses is concluded, while Moses speech to the Israelites only begins in Deut. 1:1.[1] Despite such distinctiveness, the figure of Moses, the references to the patriarchs (Deut. 1:8; 6:10; 9:5.27; 29:13; 30:20; 34:4), the frequent mentioning of the generation of the fathers, and several allusions to earlier events in the Exodus-Sinai narrative point to a connection of the book to the Pentateuchal narrative, prompting the question whether Deuteronomy ever was either an independent document or the overture of a so-called Deuteronomistic History (DtrH). It is simply not possible to reconcile the "canonical entity Torah (Pentateuch) . . . with Noth's hypothesis of DtrH since both entities claim Deuteronomy as an integral part of the literary corpus" (Kratz 2011, 40). For the current enterprise, we will not treat the question of the existence or extent of a DtrH in detail but it will become apparent that the assumption of a DtrH beginning with Deut. 1 proves to be a hindrance to an analysis of Deuteronomy within the Pentateuch. Such scepticism, however, does not negate the fact that much of Samuel–Kings is shaped and significantly influenced by Deuteronomistic theology.[2]

In the following, we will trace the literary development of the Book of Deuteronomy from its earliest stages by paying close attention to the setting of the book in its larger context as the book's development cannot be understood without it. We will locate the origins of Deuteronomy in the idea of centralisation (Deut. 12) and related laws and move from these laws to further expansions of the core (Deut. 12–26) before looking at those texts that frame the legal material. Here, attention will be paid to the shift in theological ideas that lead to Deuteronomy becoming the closure of the emerging entity called Pentateuch.

DEUTERONOMY 12 AND THE CORE OF THE BOOK

Scholars are in agreement that the core of the book of Deuteronomy can be found in those laws in Deut. 12–26 that are addressed to a second person singular and that revise earlier laws of the Covenant Code in light of cultic centralisation. The law that instigates this legal innovation is placed prominently at the beginning of the collection (Deut. 12:13–14*.15–18.21) and corrects the altar law at the beginning of the Covenant Code (Exod. 24:24–26).[3] Once we strip away all the later additions, we arrive at the following core of Deut. 12 (Veijola 2004, 266–71; Rüterswörden 2011, 21–57; Otto 2016, 1147–67):

> (Deut. 12:13) Take heed that you do not offer your burnt offerings at every place that you see; (14) but at the place which the Lord will choose in one of your tribes, there you shall offer your burnt offerings, and there you shall do all that I am commanding you [. . .] (17) You may not eat within your towns the tithe of your grain or of your wine or of your oil, or the firstlings of your herd or of your flock, or any of your votive offerings which you vow, or your freewill offerings, or the offering that you present; (18) but you shall eat them before the Lord your God in the place which the Lord your God will choose, you and your son and your daughter, your manservant and your maidservant, and the Levite who is within your towns; and you shall rejoice before the Lord your God in all that you undertake [. . .] (21) If the place which the Lord your God will choose to put his name there is too far from you, then you may kill any of your herd or of your flock [. . .] and you may eat within your towns as much as you desire.
>
> (RSV)

Despite several attempts to provide ancient Near Eastern analogies for the concept of cultic centralisation, we have to accept that these analogies "represent the religious-historical prerequisites of the idea of centralization but cannot be regarded as direct parallels" (Kratz 2013, 277). The centralisation of the cult not only transforms the cultic sphere; it is—at the same time—the driving force of a significant reshaping of earlier material, especially from the book of the Covenant. The relationship between Deuteronomy and the Covenant Code is probably best classified as a "modernizing interpretation" (i.e., a revision rather than a recycling of the legal material), since not all laws from Exod. 20–23 are taken over by Deuteronomy and the existence of both collections in the Pentateuch suggests that this revision did not invalidate the older law.[4]

> Therefore what belongs to Ur-Deuteronomy and what does not is not decided either by reconstructed pre-Deuteronomistic collections in Deut. 12–26 or by the supposed external evidence from Hittite and Assyrian treaty texts, which can always have had an influence everywhere, but by these three criteria: the change of number, the relationship to the Book of the Covenant, and the law of centralization of the cult.
>
> (Kratz 2005, 118)

These criteria attempt to reconstruct any history of literary origin of Deuteronomy by using the evidence before us (i.e., the biblical book and the larger literary context).[5] This methodological approach avoids interpretation of the literary history of Deuteronomy by using analogies from ancient Near Eastern sources that cannot serve as "objective" criteria (Levinson/Stackert 2012).

Using these criteria, we arrive at a core of Deuteronomy that reshapes older law in light of the envisaged centralisation of cultic activity.[6] Issues that were normally connected to local sanctuaries such as tithe (Deut. 14:22–29; 15:19–23) and asylum (Deut. 19:1–13) are now restructured and legal procedure is almost removed from the sacred sphere when the central sanctuary (and its priest) only serve sources of counsel for cases difficult to decide (Deut. 17:8–13). Instead, the authors of Deuteronomy envisage a professional judiciary when judges and officials are introduced (Deut. 16:18–20). The traditional institution of kingship is missing. This may reflect a certain scepticism towards the monarchy or a time of writing when there was no king. The later Deuteronomistic addition of the law of the king (Deut. 17:14–20), which introduces a monarch who is more a scribe than a ruler, probably reflects Persian times.[7]

The earliest legal core, or *Urdeuteronomium*, would then encompass Deut. 12:13–14*.15–18.21; 14:22.23a.24a.25–26; 15:19–23; 16:16–17; 16:18;. 17:8–9aαb.10a; 19:2a.3b–7.11–12.15–17a.18bα.21b; 21:1–4.6–7.8b. Here, we see that the beginning of Deuteronomy is void of any polemics against foreign gods or practices of apostasy. Whether this program of reform (Hagedorn 2019) was ever related to a political entity such as the Judean state can be debated, but there are some indications that it is "a comprehensive attempt to define an ethnic culture in terms of a law that is claimed to be ancestral" (Collins 2017, 39).[8] Though the text never names the place that Yahweh will choose, later texts in the so-called DtrH always assume that the Davidic Temple in Jerusalem is the only legitimate sanctuary.[9] The reason for the place's anonymity in Deuteronomy is a literary one: according to Num. 25:1, Moses promulgates the laws of Deut. 12–26 in Shittim (i.e., outside the land and thus Israel does not yet know any places in the Promised Land) and this fiction is maintained when later stages transplant the promulgation of the law to the plains of Moab. Furthermore, the existence of at least two further temples at Elephantine and on Mt. Gerizim show that the stipulation is just the expression of one theological strand in early Judaism and not necessarily reflecting historical realities.[10]

The sacred landscape of Israel changes with Deut. 12. From now on it is made clear that Yahweh, the God of Israel who has travelled with Israel through history and the wilderness, will choose a permanent dwelling for himself. There is a striking parallel here to Apollo who chooses Delphi from amongst all the sites in Greece (Hagedorn 2005). This motion results into a secularisation of the local shrines and altars.

> In draining the local sphere of all cultic content, the authors of Deuteronomy do not leave it as a profane religious void. Instead, they reconceptualize it in secular terms and give it positive new content. The local sphere continues to have a fundamentally religious structure. One continues to receive divine blessing in the local sphere, although it is now mediated. The compensation for the loss of direct access to the divine, with the eradication of the local altars, does not only take place at the cultic center with the repeated emphasis on the "joy" available there to the pilgrim.
>
> (Levinson 1997, 49)

This change results in the introduction of a strong notion of centre and periphery in Deuteronomy. All the local shrines which have previously been centres themselves are no longer at the centre of religious life. The believer has from now on to embark on a religious journey, if he wants to come into direct contact with the divine. The society has to be mobile and texts like Deut. 18:6-8 may also hint at the fact that there has been a certain migration towards the central sanctuary, when it is imagined that Levites, now unemployed after the centralisation, move to the central sanctuary and provide for it.

The assumption that the core of Deuteronomy reworks the Covenant Code (Wellhausen 1899, 201-2; Levinson 1997) sets Deuteronomy in relation to earlier legal material that is now integrated into the Pentateuchal narrative.[11] Since "we have no reason to believe that the covenant law book and the Deuteronomic law were thought to be so mutually contradictory that they could not coexist in one and the same legal corpus" (Blenkinsopp 1992, 210), the question of the relationship between the two legal codes can probably be best described as a revision (Driver 1901, xix)—a process that allows the older laws of the Covenant Code to exist next to the legal innovation (Otto 2012, 234-39).[12] Here, Hindy Najman has introduced the category of "Mosaic discourse" (i.e., a preservation of earlier traditions in the light of "authentic exposition") (Najman 2003, 19-29). This coexistence, then, would serve "as a license to continue the creative hermeneutical endeavor in the future" (Najman 2003, 25). Scholars who advocate that later law codes are intended to supersede earlier material (Stackert 2007) are faced with the problem that the older legal material remains as part of the larger setting.

The theory of an independent Deuteronomic core in Deut. 12–26, a bedrock argument of M. Noth's influential study (Noth 1957), overlooks that the legal passages of Deuteronomy, too, seem to allude to the literary setting of the book, when they, for example, refer to the place that Yahweh will choose (Deut. 12:5.11.14.18.26; 14:23-25; 15:20; 16:2.6f.11.15f.; 17:8.10.15; 18:6; 26:2) or mention the giving of the land in the near future (Deut. 12:9; 13:12; 15:4.7; 16:5.18.20; 17:2.14; 18:9; 19:1f.8.10.14; 20:13.16; 21:1; 24:4; 25:15.19; 26:1f). Since not all of these occurrences can be attributed to later editorial activity as—for example—Deut. 12:14 demonstrates (Veijola 2004, 266-71), we have to assume that Deut. 12-26 was from the beginning composed for its current narrative setting (Kratz 2000, 100-20; Kratz 2005, 123-26).

These considerations prompt the question how the earliest part of Deuteronomy is embedded into the larger literary context.[13] The beginning in Deut. 12:13 is not a proper beginning at all as the admonition "Take care not to sacrifice your burnt offerings in any place you like" triggers the necessary question who is speaking to whom. Yahweh cannot be the speaker as he is only referred to in the third person, making it impossible to describe Deuteronomy as a divine speech. Since the beginning of the last century, scholars have accepted the possibility that Deut. 6:4–5 once formed an older overture (Preuss 1982, 100).[14] As such, the unity of the cultic place would then correspond to the unity of the deity. Furthermore, a beginning with Deut. 6:4–5 would have the advantage that we now have an addressee for the stipulations beginning in 12:13. In other words, the laws of the Deuteronomic core address an Israel that is united under the creed of the preamble in Deut. 6:4. The unity of Yahweh stated in the Shema—and then later manifested in the one central place of worship—is later transformed into an exclusive relationship between God and his people, when the Deuteronomic core is reshaped in light of the first commandment. Here, the Decalogue replaces Deut. 6:4–5 as a new introduction: from now on, all the legal stipulations that follow should be read as an explication of the exclusive monotheism advocated in the Decalogue. On a linguistic level this is done by setting the *'lhym 'ḥrym* (first in Exod. 20:3 and Deut. 5:7 [Decalogue!]) in opposition to *yhwh 'ḥd*. Deut. 6:4–5 also provides a clue to the end of *Urdeuteronomium*. Here, Deut. 26:16 could serve as a closing verse, which would then, together with the Shema, form a frame around the earliest laws concerning centralisation.

> (16) The Lord your God commands you this day to observe these laws and rules; observe them faithfully with all your heart and soul.

Though it has often been observed that Deut. 26:16 is connected to Deut. 11:32–12:1 so that "these laws and rules" refer to the legal material in 12–26 (Mayes 1979, 338; Lundbom 2013, 734),[15] the setting indicated by "this day" poses the question whether it only refers to the promulgation of Deuteronomic law or to the wider context within a larger narrative of Exodus–Deuteronomy.

If we regard Deut. 6:4 as the beginning of an older work, one presupposes a speaker who addresses Israel. Furthermore, the future tense employed in the centralisation formula points ahead to the narratives that will follow in Joshua–Kings. The speaker can only be Moses, who is, however, never introduced properly in Deuteronomy and never mentioned by name in the legal core.[16] This implies that he is known to the reader of the Hexateuchal narrative so that one has to look outside Deuteronomy for a connecting thread, unless one wants to argue that Moses is so famous that he literally needs no introduction. The obvious place would be his first appearance in Exod. 2:10 as the beginning of a larger narrative context that centres around Moses and ends with his death in Deut. 34.[17] In other words, the death of Moses (Deut. 34:4–6) has been part of an earlier narrative strand before Deuteronomy was introduced. It has long been observed that the death of Moses has little to do with the giving of the law and thus cannot really be part of *Urdeuteronomium*. "As Moses can die without the law, but the law cannot have found its way into the context before the death of Moses, the death of Moses is older than the law" (Kratz 2005, 125). Moses dies in Shittim in Moab and is buried nearby as, from this earlier narrative context, too, he is aware that he will never cross into the Promised Land. His death is now delayed because of the insertion of the legal material and the reinterpretation of the Covenant Code by the oldest edition of Deuteronomy. Here, the place of proclamation becomes important. In Num. 25:1a Israel settles in Shittim and remains there until Josh. 2:1; 3:1 (Kratz 2020). Deuteronomy 6:4

is connected to Num. 25:1 via the beginning of the internal framework in Deut. 5:1 ("Moses summoned all the Israelites and said to them..."). The closure of the Deuteronomic core in Deut. 26:1–16 is then connected via Deut. 34:1 to Deut. 34:5–6 and to the following narrative in Josh. 2:1; 3:1. As a result, it is unlikely that Deuteronomy was ever an independent document and it was certainly never composed as the opening text of a DtrH.

The Expansion of the Original Core

To make sense of the order of the material in Deut. 12–26 is a major crux of biblical interpretation. The often-proposed structure of Deut. 12–26 according to the laws of the decalogue (so already M. Luther in his 1523–1525 lectures on Deuteronomy and again proposed by Kaufman 1978; Braulik 1991; Finsterbusch 2011) is attractive but unable to provide more than a rough outline. Also, we have to take into account that the Decalogue was unknown to the earliest compilers of Deuteronomy. Instead it is more fruitful to correlate the structure of Deut. 12–26 with the structure and redaction of Exod. 20:24–23:17 (Otto 2016).

The individual legal stipulation in Deut. 21:1–9* that concludes the original kernel serves as the hinge that connects the core with further legal additions that now treat individual offences (Deut. 21:15–23a). As in the earlier stage the Covenant Code is again revised when in the stipulations regarding family law Exod. 22:15–16 is expanded (Deut. 22:1–23:1). Here, aspects of brotherly ethics are combined with matters of sexuality. The various legal stipulations that deal with the problem of idolatry are all later additions as they already vary the law of centralisation and seem to operate with a clear demarcation of 'Israel' from the outside. Here, the step from a community to a religious fellowship has already been taken.

As with all ancient Near Eastern law codes, Deuteronomy too prompts the question whether this legal vision of a centralised cult and the necessary reforms connected to it could have been implemented. One cannot help to notice that many of the stipulations put forward have a certain utopian character looking more like an ideal vision for Israel than a "constitution" that can be put into practice. Within the narrative context, however, the authors of Deuteronomy regard their work as an exposition of earlier legal material, given to Israel before the entry of the land. This vision, most clearly articulated in Deut. 1:5, seems to presuppose that Israel will implement the statues and ordinances given after the entry into the land.

Moving beyond the Core

The legal core is embedded into a frame that is younger than the laws; the reason for this assumption is simply that Deut. 12–26 can be understood and in fact can exist without the framing chapters, but these, in turn, cannot do so without the laws as the frame draws its intention and meaning from the legal material. The frame of the legal core (Deut. 12–26) is characterised by a certain redundancy when Moses over and over announces the proclamation of the law and stresses the importance of obedience to the law. Even a cursory reading notes the various repetitions, the change in number (*Numeruswechsel*) and several superscriptions, making it very difficult, indeed, to assume a composition by one author.

Generally, scholars distinguish between a more paraenetic internal frame (Deut. 5–11 and 27–30) and a more historical external frame (Deut. 1–3, 4 and 31–34). Here, the internal frame with its paraenetic focus is the older one. Additionally, it is clear that the legal core can function without the frame but the frame of Deuteronomy always presupposes Deut. 12–26. "By using the stylistic device of a speech of Moses delivered in the plains of Moab, Deuteronomy is able to recapitulate the previous narrative as reported in Genesis–Numbers and to point at the same time to the continuation of the narrative in Joshua (–Kings)" (Kratz 2011, 41).[18] The question, however, is how these references to the previous narrative can be explained. In other words, what is the relationship of the frame of Deuteronomy to the other books of the Pentateuch?

Deuteronomy 1–3 has been described as being "one of the most taxing problems in the Pentateuch" (MacDonald 2011, 83) and it has become increasingly clear that the chapters serve the purpose to integrate Deuteronomy into a narrative context from Exodus–Joshua (Kratz 2000; Gertz 2006).[19] Deuteronomy 1–3 is shaped as a series of Mosaic retrospectives that centre around the topic of the delay of the conquest of the Promised Land. The reader notices that every story narrated in the Deut. 1–3 has a parallel in the Tetrateuch and a continuation in the book of Joshua. The chapters presuppose "the present context in Pentateuch and Former Prophets and not simply some general knowledge of the tradition" (Kratz 2012, 36). As such, Deut. 1–3 is no longer a well-structured repetition of previous material at the beginning of a larger literary work like the DtrH, but instead a multilayered composition that is influenced by and in turn influences the book of Numbers.[20] As one of the youngest parts of Deuteronomy, chapters 1–3 are responsible for creating the "book" of Deuteronomy, which will allow both, Deuteronomy itself and later readers to quote from it as "the Book/Torah of Moses."[21] Furthermore, by continuing the narrative of Exodus–Numbers the chapters bridge the distance between Sinai and Moab and thus connect the two places where the law was revealed.

Probably the clearest indication of a setting of Deuteronomy within the Pentateuch can be found in the inner frame (Deut. 5–11 and 27–30) that links the book to the Sinai pericope. Here, the Decalogue provides an important literary clue. In the context of the Pentateuchal narrative God reveals the Ten Commandments at Mt. Sinai (Exod. 20) and Moses seems to repeat them in a modified form forty years later in the plains of Moab (Deut. 5). Though there has been an extensive debate about the two versions, we can pass over the details here (Markl 2013) and will follow the broad consensus of scholarship that regards Exod. 20 as the older text (Köckert 2004, 176–78). While the Decalogue in Exodus seems to interrupt the non-P Sinai pericope this is not the case in Deuteronomy where it is explicitly introduced as a quotation of earlier material (Deut. 5:2–5):

(2) The LORD our God made a covenant with us at Horeb.
(3) It was not with our fathers that the LORD made this covenant, but with us, the living, every one of us who is here today.
(4) Face to face the LORD spoke to you on the mountain out of the fire.
(5) I stood between the LORD and you at that time to convey the LORD'S words to you, for you were afraid of the fire and not go up the mountain – saying:

Whether the laws of Deut. 12–26 are actually structured according to the stipulations in the Decalogue (Kaufmann 1978; Braulik 1991; Finsterbusch 2011) can be debated but seems unlikely in light of the "biography" of the Decalogue itself and the literary history of Deut. 12–26 (Rüterswörden 2005). Additionally, the Sabbath, so prominent in the Decalogue, has no correspondence in the legal material of Deuteronomy. The quotation in Deut. 5 presupposes that the Decalogue in Exodus is already connected to Mt. Sinai and it is highly unlikely that it ever had another literary place than in the context of Sinai in Exodus. A further look at the literary context of the Sinai pericope reveals that the Decalogue was created as an overture to the Covenant Code and the following laws should be understood as a concretisation of the statement in Exod. 20 (Köckert 2004, 176). This hermeneutical function is taken a step further in Deuteronomy. Here, the Ten Commandments not only appear as the sum of the whole Torah but also as the only words directly spoken by Yahweh to the people. Everything else are just words of Moses. Accordingly, Yahweh himself writes the Decalogue, and the Decalogue alone on two stone tablets (Deut. 4:13; 5:22), which are placed in the Ark of the Covenant (10:2.5) while the law is simply placed "beside the Ark of the Covenant of the LORD your God" and will "remain there as a witness against you" (31:26). In the frame of Deuteronomy, Deut. 5 transfers the communication of the law to Sinai in Exodus and in doing so, assimilates the story to Exod. 20–23. As a result, Deut. 5 becomes a new edition of the scene in Exodus and the continuation of the narrative simply becomes a repetition of the law revealed at Mt. Sinai. Now—in parallel to the composition in Exodus—the Decalogue in Deuteronomy precedes the proclamation of the revised Covenant Code in Deut. 6–26 (Kratz 2005, 127). As already noted above, this literary reshaping of the *Urdeuteronomium* in light of the Sinai pericope and the Decalogue transforms the original intention of the Deuteronomic law when the unity of Yahweh is now interpreted in the sense of exclusiveness and uniqueness. It is this guiding principle of exclusiveness that shapes integration of further aspects of the Exodus narrative. Here, the absorption of earlier material from Exodus is not a linear process as Deuteronomistic theology has also influenced the material in Exodus (Achenbach 2004).[22]

Like Deut. 1–3, the concluding chapters Deut. 31–34 want to situate the book in the larger "historical" setting; here especially Deut. 31–32 seem to point towards the continuation of the "narrative" in the book of Joshua and a text like Deut. 32 serves as a powerful tool to reinforce identity (Schmidtkunz 2020). Differently, Deut. 33–34 seems to be focused on creating a definitive caesura (i.e., the five books of the Torah). In doing so, the narrative bridge to the later historical books is severed in favour of a "biography" of Moses running from Exodus–Deuteronomy. At the same time, Deuteronomy now becomes an individual entity (i.e., an archive of Moses's activities on his last day) (Rütersworden 2007; Braulik and Lohfink 2021, 361). Undoubtedly, Deuteronomy can be read as an individual book. The book's setting as Moses's last day ending with his death and the colophon to the book of Numbers clearly favour such a reading. The rich reception history of the book during the Second Temple period is a witness to the importance of Deuteronomy. In the texts from the Dead Sea (Qumran, Naḥal Ḥever, Wadi Murabbaʿat, and Masada), thirty-four copies of Deuteronomy were found with 5Q1 being the oldest one (Lange 2009, 83–106). Additional passages from Deuteronomy are preserved in 4Q364–367 (Lange 2009, 37–42), which may be classified as a "variant literary edition" of the Pentateuch (Ulrich 2000, 57). The "biblical" character of the manuscripts is also supported by their compositional techniques (Kratz 2016). As such, the book rivals Isaiah and Psalms in the number of copies, while in the New Testament these three books are amongst the most frequently cited ones. As far as the textual history is concerned, the Qumran evidence shows that the text of Deuteronomy was not yet fixed (Crawford 2008). Furthermore, Deuteronomy is frequently interpreted in Second Temple literature (Pearce 2013) with the Temple Scroll being the most extensive rewriting.[23]

Conclusion

The literary beginnings of the Book of Deuteronomy can be found in those passages that revise the earlier legal material from the Covenant Code in light of the (exclusive) centralisation of the cult. This is a new idea and yet without any analogy in the ancient world. The focus of the one place of worship for the one god provides the basis for all further additions and innovations. Like P, the language of D is quite characteristic (Braulik/Lohfink 2021) but despite this distinctiveness, it is difficult to argue for an independent Deuteronomy since even the core (*Urdeuteronomium*) is already linked to the larger literary context and connected to the figure of Moses as the speaker. A major revision of the legal core (Deut. 12-26) is done in light of the first commandment, when the exclusiveness of Yahweh and the polemics against foreign gods are introduced. In the course of the long literary history of Deuteronomy, the original document of reform is transformed into four farewell speeches of Moses on his last day, which focus on the reinterpretation (see Deut. 1:5) of the laws given at Mt. Sinai. The intention of this "testament" of Moses is to equip Israel with everything needed *before* the one nation under god enters the Promised Land. As such, Deuteronomy now marks a distinct caesura as it separates the period of Moses from the continuation of the narrative (see Deut. 34) and at the same time creates a literary entity called Pentateuch.

Notes

1. Despite such separation, there is connection as well, when *'lh hmṣwt* echoes *'lh hdbrym* and *b'rbt mw'b* links Num. 36:13 to Num. 22:1 and Deut. 34:1; Josh. 13:32. Maybe Numbers wants to be understood as "text" with Deuteronomy as "commentary" (Kratz 2012, 35). Like Lev. 27:34, Num. 36:13 separates the Torah into individual scrolls (Reinhard Achenbach, *Die Vollendung der Tora: Studien zur Redaktionsgeschichte des Numeribuches im Kontext von Hexateuch und Pentateuch* [BZAR 3] [Wiesbaden: Harrassowitz, 2003], 601).
2. If one regards Joshua as the closing of an older Hexateuchal narrative, Judges seems to be a special case as the book appears to serve as the link between said narrative and the later description of Israel's History found in Samuel-Kings (Sarah Schulz, *Die Anhänge zum Richterbuch: Eine kompositionsgeschichtliche Untersuchung von Ri 17-21* [BZAW 477] [Berlin: De Gruyter 2016], 231-40) and the overview in Uwe Becker, "The Place of the Book of Judges in the So-Called Deuteronomistic History: Some Remarks on Recent Research," in *Book Seams in the Hexateuch I: The Literary Transitions between the Books of Genesis/Exodus and Joshua/Judges*, ed. by Christoph Berner and Harald Samuel, 439-51 [FAT 120] [Tübingen: Mohr Siebeck, 2018]).
3. Whether Deut. 12, in turn, is corrected by Lev. 17 is debated. While earlier scholarship generally assumed that Lev. 17 depends on Deut. 12 (Alfred Cholewiński, *Heiligkeitsgesetz und Deuteronomium: Eine vergleichende Studie*. Analecta Biblica 66 [Rome: Biblical Institute, 1976], 145-76) more recent investigations, however, argue that "the evidence of verbal and conceptual borrowings from Deut. 12 in Lev. 17 is too scant to establish the former as the key source of inspiration for H's centralizing mandate" (Julia Rhyder, *Centralizing the Cult: The Holiness Legislation in Leviticus 17-27* [FAT 134] [Tübingen: Mohr Siebeck,

2019], 258) following Christophe Nihan, *From Priestly Torah to Pentateuch: A Study in the Composition of the Book of Leviticus* [FAT II/25] [Tübingen: Mohr Siebeck, 2007], 302–430).

4. On the problem, see Eckart Otto, "The Pre-exilic Deuteronomy as a Revision of the Covenant Code," in *Kontinuum und Proprium. Studien zur Sozial- und Rechtsgeschichte des Alten Orients und des Alten Testaments* (Orientalia Biblica et Christiana 8) (Wiesbaden: Harrassowitz, 1996), 112–22.
5. See Reinhard G. Kratz, "Der literarische Ort des Deuteronomiums," in *Liebe und Gebot: Studien zum Deuteronomium*, ed. Reinhard G. Kratz and Hermann Spieckermann, 101–20 (FRLANT 109) (Göttingen: Vandenhoeck & Ruprecht, 2000).
6. The relationship of Deuteronomy to P and H is beyond the scope of this article. See Christophe Nihan, "The Holiness Code between D and P: Some Comments on the Function and Significance of Leviticus 17–26," in the "Composition of the Torah," in *Das Deuteronomium zwischen Pentateuch und Deuteronomistischem Geschichtswerk*, ed. Eckart Otto and Reinhard Achenbach, 81–122 (FRLANT 206) (Göttingen: Vandenhoeck & Ruprecht, 2004); and David P. Wright, "Source Dependence and the Development of the Pentateuch," in *The Formation of the Pentateuch: Bridging the Academic Cultures of Europe, Israel, and North America*, ed. Jan C. Gertz, Bernard M. Levinson, Dalit Rom-Shiloni, and Konrad Schmid, 651–82 (FAT 111) (Tübingen: Mohr Siebeck, 2016).
7. See Anselm C. Hagedorn, *Between Moses and Plato: Individual and Society in Deuteronomy and Ancient Greek Law* (FRLANT 204) (Göttingen: Vandenhoeck & Ruprecht, 2004), 141–43 and Reinhard Achenbach, "Das sogenannte Königsgesetz in Deuteronomium 17,14–20, " *ZAR* 15 (2009): 216–33; for a critical view of such proposals, see Ernest Nicholson, *Deuteronomy and the Judaean Diaspora* (Oxford: Oxford University Press 2014), 101–34 and Nili Wazana, "The Law of the King (Deuteronomy 17:14–20) in the Light of Empire and Destruction," in *The Fall and Rise of Jerusalem and the Rise of Torah*, ed. Peter Dubovský, Dominik Markl, and Pierre Sonnet, 169–94 (FAT 107) (Tübingen: Mohr Siebeck, 2016) who opts for a Babylonian setting.
8. We will not enter into the debate about the date or possible Northern provenance of Deuteronomy (Cynthia Edeburg and Reinhard Müller, "A Northern Provenance of Deuteronomy? A Critical Review," *HeBAI* 4 [2015]: 148–61) here and simply note that the aspect of cultic centralisation is difficult to imagine in the pre-exilic period (Ernest W. Nicholson, *Deuteronomy and the Judean Diaspora* [Oxford: Oxford University Press, 2014]) and that a historical location on the basis of 2 Kings 22–23 only leads to a circular argument (Gutsav Hölscher, "Komposition und Ursprung des Deuteronomiums," *ZAW* 40 [1922]: 161–251).
9. Eckart Otto, "Born out of Ruins: The Catastrophe of Jerusalem as *Accoucheur* to the Pentateuch in the Book of Deuteronomy," in *The Fall and Rise of Jerusalem and the Rise of Torah*, ed. Peter Dubovský, Dominik Markl, and Pierre Sonnet, 156–68 (FAT 107) (Tübingen: Mohr Siebeck, 2016), argued that the formula "was already related to Jerusalem as the elected place of a divine 'dwelling.'"
10. See Reinhard Gregor Kratz, "The Second Temple of Jeb and of Jerusalem," in *Judah and the Judeans in the Persian Period*, ed. Oded Lipschits and Manfred Oeming, 247–26 (Winona Lake: Eisenbrauns 2006), and Bob Becking, "Do the Earliest Samaritan Inscriptions Already Indicate a Parting of the Ways?" in *Ezra, Nehemiah, and the Construction of Early Jewish Identity* (FAT 80) (Tübingen: Mohr Siebeck, 2011), 109–17.

11. While it is very likely that the impersonal, casuistic *mišpāṭîm* originally formed an independent collection, the phrasing of the altar law in Exod. 20:23-26 suggests that it is part of the larger narrative context (i.e., Yahweh's command to Moses to mediate the divine laws to the Israelites). It seems that the altar law of the Covenant Code is already the result of a process that R. Albertz and others—following Max Weber (Max Weber, *Die Wirtschaftsethik der Weltreligionen: Das antike Judentum. Schriften und Reden 1911-1920*, ed. Eckart Otto and Julia Offermann [(MWG I/21] [Tübingen: Mohr Siebeck, 2005], 344-46)—have described as "theologizing the law" (Rainer Albertz, "Die Theologisierung des Rechts im Alten Israel," in *Geschichte und Theologie: Studien zur Exegese des Alten Testaments und zur Religionsgeschichte Israels* [BZAW 326] [Berlin: W de Gruyter, 2003], 187-207 and Konrad Schmid, "Divine Legislation in the Pentateuch in its Late Judean and Neo Babylonian Context," in *The Fall of Jerusalem and the Rise of Torah*, ed. Peter Dubrovsky, Dominik Markl, and Jean-Pierre Sonnet, 129-53 [FAT 107] [Tübingen: Mohr Siebeck, 2016]).
12. Kevin Mattison, *Rewriting and Revision as Amendment in the Laws of Deuteronomy* (FAT II/100) (Tübingen: Mohr Siebeck, 2018), on the basis of a detailed analysis of the linguistic processes at work, has proposed that the laws of Deuteronomy should be seen as an amendment to the Covenant Code and were designed to change the way how the earlier collection would be understood by its readers.
13. Here E. Otto has proposed an alternative model. Following earlier proposals by scholars like M. Weinfeld and H. U. Steymans, Otto regards Deut. 13 and Deut. 28 as the kernel of the book. This Judean loyalty oath to Yahweh is modelled on Neo-Assyrian succession treaties (Eckart Otto, "Treueid und Gesetz: Die Ursprünge des Deuteronomiums im Horizont neuassyrischen Vertragsrechts," *ZAR* 2 [1996]: 1-52) and only later transformed into a lawbook. Though there are significant problems with such an assumption of a Neo-Assyrian *Vorlage* (Christoph Koch, *Vertrag, Treueid und Bund: Studien zur Rezeption des altorientalischen Vertragsrechts im Deuteronomium und zur Ausbildung der Bundestheologie im Alten Testament* [BZAW 383] [Berlin: De Gruyter, 2008]; Juha Pakkala,"The Date of the Oldest Edition of Deuteronomy," *ZAW* 121 [2009]: 388-40) the theory has recently been revived (Jacob Lauinger, "Literary Connections and Social Contexts: Approaches to Deuteronomy in Light of the Assyrian *adê*-Tradition," *HeBAI* 8 [2019]: 87-100; Hans Ulrich Steymans, "Deuteronomy 13 in Comparison with Hittite, Aramaic and Assyrian Treaties," *HeBAI* 8 [2019]: 101-32).
14. Nathan MacDonald, "The Date of the Shema (Deuteronomy 6:4-5)," *JBL* 136 (2017): 765-82 has recently challenged the consensus, arguing that Deut. 6:4-5 is rather a restatement of the first commandment than an old beginning of Deuteronomy. He can do so because he follows E. Otto's proposal that the *Urdeuteronomium* has no narrative setting and is not connected to Moses.
15. The Septuagint seems to stress this when it renders πάντα τὰ δικαιώματα ταῦτα καὶ κρίματα as in Deut. 4:6; 7:12. It appears that the authors of the Septuagint deliberately want to connect Deut. 26:17-19 to the frame of Deuteronomy (Eckart Otto, *Deuteronomium 12-34. Zweiter Teilband: 23,16-43,12.* [HThKAT] [Freiburg i.Br.: Herder, 2017], 1876).
16. Moses is mentioned several times in the book of Deuteronomy (1:1.3.5; 4:41.44.45.46; 5:1; 27:1.9.11; 29:1; 31:1.7.9.14.16.22.24.30; 32:44.48; 33:1; 34:5.7-10.12) but always in a way that presupposes knowledge of his person and office by the reader.
17. A note on the death of a main character seems to be a stock feature of Biblical narrative (see Gen. 23:2 [Sarah]; 25:8 [Abraham]; 35:29 [Isaac]). Especially the note on the death of

Miriam in Num. 21:1aβb offers a striking parallel to Moses's death in Num. 25:1a; Deut. 34:5–6.

18. Here we have to note that references to the Patriarchal narratives are scarce in Deuteronomy and do not seem to go beyond the mentioning of Abraham, Isaac, and Jacob (Deut. 1:8; 6:10; 9:5.27; 29:13; 30:20; 34:4). Nevertheless, it has been proposed that the "circumcision of the heart" mentioned in Deut. 10:16; 30:6 is a continuation of the covenant in Gen. 17 (Ernst Ehrenreich, *Wähle das Leben! Deuteronomium 30 als hermeneutischer Schlüssel zur Tora* [BZAR 14] [Wiesbaden: Harrassowitz, 2010], 156–88) and Raik Heckl, *Moses Vermächtnis: Kohärenz, literarische Intention und Funktion von Dtn 1–3* (ABG 9) (Leipzig: Evangelische Verlagsanstalt, 2004), 451–52 following Eduard Nielsen, *Deuteronomium* (HAT I/6) (Tübingen: Mohr Siebeck, 1995), 36 has proposed that some additions to Deut. 2:9–25 seem to refer to Gen. 14, and David M. Carr, *The Formation of the Hebrew Bible: A New Reconstruction* (Oxford: Oxford University Press, 2011), 257–59 has proposed that several later passages of the Abraham narrative are shaped in light of Deut. 7 and related texts.

19. Nathan MacDonald has used the topics of Edom and Seir (Nathan MacDonald, "Edom and Seir in the Narratives and Itineraries of Numbers 20–21 and Deuteronomy 1–3," in *Deuteronomium—Tora für eine neue Generation*, ed. Georg Fischer, Dominik Markl, and Simone Paganini, 83–103 (BZAR 17) (Wiesbaden Ł: Harrassowitz, 2011) as well as the wilderness motif (Nathan MacDonald, "Deuteronomy and Numbers: Common Narratives Concerning the Wilderness and Transjordan," *JAJ* 3 (2012): 141–65) to evaluate the complex relationship between Deut. 1–3 and Numbers arguing that the "narrative overlap and juxtaposition of the two books means that readers of the Pentateuch must operate with some understanding of their interrelationship" (165).

20. Jan Christian Gertz, "Kompositorische Funktion und literarhistorischer Ort von Deuteronomium 1–3," in *Die deuteronomistischen Geschichtswerke: Redaktions- und religionsgeschichtliche Perspektiven zur "Deuteronomismus"-Diskussion in Tora und Vorderen Propheten*, ed. Markus Witte, Konrad Schmid, Doris Prechel, and Jan Christian Gertz, 103–23 (BZAW 365) (Berlin: W. de Gruyter, 2006), notes that the events reported in Deut. 1–3 connect seamlessly to the preceding narrative context and should be seen as a rewriting of Num. 11–32, while Eckart Otto, *Deuteronomium 1–11. Erster Teilband: 1,1–4,43* (HThKAT) (Freiburg i.Br.: Herder, 2012), 296–97 regards the chapters as an introduction that connects the independent Deuteronomistic Deuteronomy with the Deuteronomic edition of Joshua.

21. Reinhard Gregor Kratz, "The Headings of the Book of Deuteronomy," in *Deuteronomy in the Pentateuch, Hexateuch, and the Deuteronomistic History*, ed. Konrad Schmid and Raymond F. Pearson (FAT II/56) (Tübingen: Mohr Siebeck, 2012), 36 has further observed that the introductory chapters of Deuteronomy should be called "a *relecture* or *rewriting*, with the peculiarity, however, that the text is situated within the narration it reproduces and interprets and thus itself becomes part of this narration."

22. Following a proposal by Erhard Blum and Hendrik Stoppel, *Von Angesicht zu Angesicht: Ouvertüre am Horeb. Deuteronomium 5 und 9–10 und die Textgestalt ihrer Folie* (AThANT 109) (Zurich: Theologischer Verlag, 2018) has argued that Deut. 5, 9–10 mainly refer to the following DtrH, when Deut. 9–10 are closely connected to the reforms of Josiah as described in 2 Kings.

23. The nature of the relation between Deuteronomy and Temple Scroll is debated; see Reinhard Gregor Kratz, "Law and Narrative in Deuteronomy and the Temple Scroll," in *The Reception*

of Biblical War Legislation in Narrative Contexts (BZAW 460) (Berlin: De Gruyter, 2015), 109–22; Reinhard Gregor Kratz, "Sources, Fragments, and Additions: Biblical Criticism and the Dead Sea Scrolls," in *The Dead Sea Scrolls and the Study of the Humanities: Method, Theory, Meaning. Proceedings of the Eighth Meeting of the International Organization for Qumran Studies* (STDJ 125) (Leiden: Brill, 2018), 1–27; Bernard M. Levinson, *A More Perfect Torah: At the Intersection of Philology and Hermeneutics in Deuteronomy and the Temple Scroll* (CrStHB 1) (Winona Lake: Eisenbrauns, 2013); Eckart Otto, "Temple Scroll and Pentateuch: A Priestly Debate about the Interpretation of Torah," in *The Qumran Legal Texts between the Hebrew Bible and Its Interpretation* (CBET 61) (Leuven: Peeters, 2011), 59–74; Simone Paganini, *"Nicht darfst du zu diesen Wörtern etwas hinzufügen." Die Rezeption des Deuteronomiums in der Tempelrolle: Sprache, Autoren, Hermeneutik* (BZAR 11) (Wiesbaden: Harrassowitz, 2009).

BIBLIOGRAPHY

Achenbach, Reinhard. "Grundlinien redaktioneller Arbeit in der Sinai Perikope." In *Das Deuteronomium zwischen Pentateuch und Deuteronomistischen Geschichtswerk*. Edited by Eckart Otto and Reinhard Achenbach, pp. 56–80. FRLANT 206. Göttingen: Vandenhoeck & Ruprecht, 2004.

Blenkinsopp, Joseph. *The Pentateuch: An Introduction to the First Five Books of the Bible*. ABRL. New York: Doubleday, 1992.

Braulik, Georg. *Die Deuteronomischen Gesetze und der Dekalog: Studien zum Aufbau von Deuteronomium 12–26*. SBS 145. Stuttgart: Katholisches Bibelwerk, 1991.

Braulik, Georg, and Norbert Lohfink. *Sprache und literarische Gestalt des Buches Deuteronomium: Beobachtungen und Studien*. ÖBS 53. Berlin: Peter Lang, 2021.

Bultmann, Christoph. "Deuteronomy." In *The Oxford Bible Commentary*. Edited by John Barton and John Muddiman, pp. 135–58. Oxford: Oxford University Press, 2001.

Collins, John J. *The Invention of Judaism: Torah and Jewish Identity from Deuteronomy to Paul*. Taubman Lectures in Jewish Studies 7. Oakland: University of California Press, 2017.

Crawford, Sidnie White. *Rewriting Scriptures in Second Temple Times*. Studies in the Dead Sea Scrolls and Related Literature. Grand Rapids: Eerdmans, 2008.

Driver, S. R. *A Critical and Exegetical Commentary on Deuteronomy* (ICC) Edinburgh: T&T Clark, 1901.

Finsterbusch, Karin. "Die Dekalog-Ausrichtung des deuteronomischen Gesetzes: ein neuer Ansatz." In *Deuteronomium—Tora für eine neue Generation*. Edited by Georg Fischer, Dominik Markl, and Simone Paganini, pp. 123–46. BZAR 17. Wiesbaden: Harrassowitz, 2011.

Gertz, Jan Chrstian. "Kompositorische Funktion und literarhistorischer Ort von Deuteronomium 1–3." In *Die deuteronomistischen Geschichtswerke: Redaktions- und religionsgeschichtliche Perspektiven zur "Deuteronomismus"-Diskussion in Tora und Vorderen Propheten*. Edited by Markus Witte, Konrad Schmid, Doris Prechel, and Jan Christian Gertz, pp. 103–23. BZAW 365. Berlin: W. de Gruyter, 2006.

Hagedorn, Anselm C. "Deuteronomy and the Deuteronomic Reform." In *The Oxford Handbook of Biblical Law*. Edited by Pamela Barmash, pp. 199–216. Oxford: Oxford University Press, 2019.

Hagedorn, Anselm C. "Placing (a) God: Central Place Theory in Deuteronomy 12 and at Delphi." In *Temple and Worship in Biblical Israel and the Ancient Near East. Proceedings* of the Oxford Old Testament Seminar. Edited by John Day, pp. 188–211. JSOTSup 422. London: T&T Clark, 2005.

Kaufman, Stephen. "The Structure of the Deuteronomic Law." *Maarav* 1 (1978): 105–58.

Köckert, Matthias. *Leben in Gottes Gegenwart: Studien zum Verständnis des Gesetzes Alten Testament*. FAT 43. Tübingen: Mohr Siebeck, 2004.

Kratz, Reinhard Gregor. "Der literarische Ort des Deuteronomiums." In *Liebe und Gebot: Studien zum Deuteronomium*. Edited by Reinhard G. Kratz and Hermann Spieckermann, pp. 101–20. FRLANT 190. Göttingen: Vandenhoeck & Ruprecht, 2000.

Kratz, Reinhard Gregor. *The Composition of the Narrative Books of the Old Testament*. London: T&T Clark, 2005.

Kratz, Reinhard Gregor. "The Pentateuch in Current Research: Consensus and Debate." In *The Pentateuch: International Perspectives on Current Research*. Edited by Thomas B. Dozeman, Konrad Schmid, and Baruch J. Schwartz, pp. 31–61. FAT 78. Tübingen: Mohr Siebeck, 2011.

Kratz, Reinhard Gregor. "The Headings of the Book of Deuteronomy." In *Deuteronomy in the Pentateuch, Hexateuch, and the Deuteronomistic History*. Edited by Konrad Schmid and Raymond F. Pearson, pp. 31–46. FAT II/56. Tübingen: Mohr Siebeck, 2012.

Kratz, Reinhard Gregor. "'The Peg in the Wall:' Cultic Centralization Revisited." *Law and Religion in the Eastern Mediterranean. From Antiquity to Early Islam*. Edited by Anselm C. Hagedorn and Reinhard G. Kratz, pp. 251–85. Oxford: Oxford University Press, 2013.

Kratz, Reinhard Gregor. "Reworked Pentateuch and Pentateuchal Theory." In *The Formation of the Pentateuch: Bridging the Academic Cultures of Europe, Israel, and North America*. Edited by Jan C. Gertz, Bernard M. Levinson, Dalit Rom-Shiloni, and Konrad Schmid, pp. 501–24. FAT 111. Tübingen: Mohr Siebeck, 2016.

Kratz, Reinhard Gregor. "Schittim: Eine narrative Verbindung zwischen Numeri und Josua." In *Eigensinn und Entstehung der Hebräischen Bibel. Erhard Blum zum siebzigsten Geburtstag*. Edited by Joachim J. Krause, Wolfgang Oswald and Kristin Weingart, pp. 181–210. FAT 136. Tübingen: Mohr Siebeck, 2020.

Lange, Armin. *Handbuch der Textfunde vom Toten Meer Band 1: Die Handschriften biblischer Bücher von Qumran und den anderen Fundorten*. Tübingen: Mohr Siebeck, 2009.

Levinson, Bernard M. *Deuteronomy and the Hermeneutics of Legal Innovation*. Oxford: Oxford University Press, 1997.

Levinson, Bernard M., and Jeffrey Stackert. "Between the Covenant Code and Esarhaddon's Succession Treaty: Deuteronomy 13 and the Composition of Deuteronomy." *JAJ* 3 (2012): 123–40.

Lundbom, Jack R. *Deuteronomy: A Commentary*. Grand Rapids: Eerdmans, 2013.

Markl, Dominik. "The Ten Words Revealed and Revised: The Origins of Law and Legal Hermeneutics in the Pentateuch." In *The Decalogue and Its Cultural Influence*. Edited by Dominik Markl, pp. 13–27. Hebrew Bible Monographs 58. Sheffield: Phoenix, 2013.

Mayes, A. D. H. *Deuteronomy* (NCeB) Grand Rapids: Eerdmans, 1979.

McConville, J. Gordon. *Deuteronomy* (Apollos Old Testament Commentary) Downers Grove: Inter Varsity, 2002.

MacDonald, Nathan. "Edom and Seir in the Narratives and Itineraries of Numbers 20–21 and Deuteronomy 1–3." In *Deuteronomium—Tora für eine neue Generation*. Edited by Georg Fischer, Dominik Markl, and Simone Paganini, pp. 83–103. BZAR 17. Wiesbaden: Harrassowitz, 2011.

Miller, Patrick D. "Constitution or Instruction? The Purpose of Deuteronomy." In *The Way of the Lord: Essays in Old Testament Theology*, pp. 253–68. FAT 39. Tübingen: Mohr Siebeck, 2004.

Najman, Hindy. *Seconding Sinai: The Development of Mosaic Discourse in Second Temple Judaism*. JSJ Sup. 77. Leiden: Brill, 2003.

Noth, Martin. *Überlieferungsgeschichtliche Studien: Die sammelnden und bearbeitenden Geschichtswerke im Alten Testament*. 2nd ed. Tübingen: Max Niemeyer, 1957.

Olson, Dennis T. *Deuteronomy and the Death of Moses: A Theological Reading*. Overtures to Biblical Theology. Minneapolis: Fortress, 1994.

Otto, Eckart. *Deuteronomium 1–11. Erster Teilband: 1,1–4,43*. HThKAT. Freiburg i.Br.: Herder, 2012.

Otto, Eckart. *Deuteronomium 12–34. Erster Teilband: 12,1–23,15*. HThKAT. Freiburg i.Br.: Herder, 2016.

Pearce, Sarah J. K. *The Words of Moses: Studies in the Reception of Deuteronomy in the Second Temple Period*. TSAJ 152. Tübingen: Mohr Siebeck, 2013.

Perlitt, Lothar. *Deuteronomium 1. Teilband: Deuteronomium 1–6**. BKAT V/1. Neukirchen-Vluyn: Neukichener, 2013.

Preuss, Horst-Dietrich. *Deuteronomium*. EdF 164. Darmstadt: Wissenschaftliche Buchgesellschaft, 1982.

Rüterswörden, Udo. "Die Dekalogstruktur des Deuteronomiums—Fragen an eine alte Annahme." In *Die Zehn Worte: Der Dekalog als Testfall der Pentateuchkritik*. Edited by Christian Frevel, Michael Konkel, and Johannes Schnocks, pp. 109–21. QD 212. Freiburg i.Br.: Herder, 2005.

Rüterswörden, Udo. *Deuteronomium*. BKAT V/3.1. Neukirchen-Vluyn: Neukirchener, 2011.

Rüterswörden, Udo. "Moses' Last Day." In *Moses in Biblical and Extra-Biblical Traditions*. Edited by Axel Graupner and Michael Wolter, pp. 51–59. BZAW 372. Berlin: W. de Gruyter, 2007.

Stackert, Jeffrey. *Rewriting the Torah: Literary Revision in Deuteronomy and the Holiness Code*. FAT 52. Tübingen: Mohr Siebeck, 2007.

Schmidtkunz, Petra. *Das Moselied des Deuteronomiums. Untersuchungen zu Text und Theologie von Dtn 32,1–43*. FAT II.124. Tübingen: Mohr Siebeck, 2020.

Ulrich, Eugene C. "The Qumran Scrolls and the Biblical Text." In *The Dead Sea Scrolls: Fifty Years after Their Discovery. Proceedings of the Jerusalem Congress, July 20–25, 1997*. Edited by Lawrence H. Schiffman, Emanuel Tov, and James C. VanderKam, pp. 51–59. Jerusalem: Israel Exploration Society, 2000.

Veijola, Timo. *Das fünfte Buch Mose—Deuteronomium: Kapitel 1,1–16,17*. ATD 8,1. Göttingen: Vandenhoeck & Ruprecht, 2004.

Wellhausen, Julius. *Die Composition des Hexateuchs und der historischen Bücher des Alten Testaments*. 3rd ed. Berlin: W. de Gruyter, 1899.

CHAPTER 2

NEAR EASTERN PRACTICE OF LAW IN DEUTERONOMY

STEPHEN C. RUSSELL

Who Began the Conversation?

Introduction

ALTHOUGH Deuteronomy presents its collection of laws as a legal and religious charter on which the new nation of Israel was to be founded (e.g., Deut 4:1; 5:1; 12:1; 26:16), scholars have questioned the nature of the legal material in the book.[1] Was the Deuteronomic Code authoritative for judges and courts in the late Iron Age, or did it only acquire authoritative status in a later period or within a certain sphere?[2] To what extent was it innovative?[3] How does it relate to other legal material in the Hebrew Bible?[4] Was it written as law or as moral advice in the tradition of wisdom literature?[5] Does its scholastic character—its relationship to the scribal tradition of ordering knowledge in structured lists—indicate that it was removed from direct experience and implementation of ancient law?[6] The debate over the nature of the legal material in Deuteronomy is complicated by the fact that there is very little direct evidence for legal practice in ancient Israel and Judah.[7] No Iron Age trial records or transcripts have been recovered in the extensive archaeological excavations in Israel.[8] Is there indirect evidence that might aid the legal historian interested in Deuteronomy?

In this chapter, I show how documentary evidence for legal practice in other Near Eastern societies—contracts, court records, treaties, letters—provides indirect evidence relevant to understanding the nature of the legal material in Deuteronomy.[9] B. Wells has been an articulate proponent of using such evidence in interpreting biblical law while also acknowledging the inherent limitations of this approach.[10] In part one of this chapter, I summarize and extend his approach in relation to the book of Deuteronomy. I provide examples of what Wells calls similar legal issues, similar legal reasoning, and similar legal remedies shared by Deuteronomy and records of Near Eastern legal practice. The net effect of the data I analyze in the first part of this chapter is to affirm a connection between the Deuteronomic Code and everyday legal practice in the larger world within which Deuteronomy first developed.

In the second part of this chapter, I highlight the gap between the Deuteronomic Code and its historical legal context. As B. Landsberger, M. T. Roth, and others have observed, ancient trial records do not cite the law codes, and recorded legal judgments often imposed penalties that were less harsh than those stipulated in the law codes.[11] I consider the laws regarding fugitives as an example of the gap between literary portrayal and historical reality. Some scholars understand Deuteronomy's fugitive laws as reflecting a more humanitarian impulse than traditional Near Eastern legal practice. I argue instead that these laws reflect the gap between Israel's and Judah's marginal political status on the fringes of the Assyrian and Babylonian empires and Deuteronomy's vision of Israel as independent of foreign powers who might dictate the return of fugitives. The data I treat in the second part urge caution in positing a simplistic connection between Deuteronomy and Iron Age legal practice.

What Is the Status of the Conversation?

The Connection between Deuteronomy and Legal Practice

B. Wells has traced similar legal issues, similar legal reasoning, and similar legal remedies shared by biblical legal material and a wide variety of texts documenting legal practice in the ancient Near East.[12] He focuses on the Covenant Code (Exod 20:22–23:33; 34:11–26) and the Deuteronomic Code (Deut 11:31–25:19), on the one hand, and cuneiform evidence for Near Eastern legal practice from the fourteenth through fourth centuries BCE, on the other. In this section, I summarize and extend his approach to Deuteronomy. Together, these parallels suggest that the scribes who produced Deuteronomy were either directly familiar with legal practice or else utilized textual traditions in turn directly rooted in legal practice.

Similar Legal Issues

As an example of a similar legal issue, consider limits on the right of household heads to appoint legal heirs as they saw fit (Deut 21:15–17). In the background to this casuistic law are three broad principles of inheritance law as it operated throughout the Near East. First, following the death of a male household head, his legally sanctioned heirs held the totality of his assets and debts in common.[13] These joint heirs subsequently divided the inheritance between them.[14] Second, the first-born heir was often entitled to an extra share of the inheritance.[15] Third, a household head could supplement these general principles of customary inheritance law with specific instructions.[16] For example, a household head could demote an heir, assign an extra share to a biologically younger heir, or assign an extra share to an adopted heir.[17]

Against this background, this casuistic law considers the case of a male household head who has two legally sanctioned marital relationships and who "hates" one wife and "loves" the other. Wells argues that "hate" here carries a legal connotation and refers to the husband's demotion of his wife arbitrarily, without grounds.[18] In this situation, Deuteronomy limits the freedom of the father to disenfranchise his eldest legal heir arbitrarily. The law addresses the issue of limits on the freedom of the head of household to dictate how property should be divided after his death.

The legal issue being addressed here can be compared to the legal issue being addressed in SAA 14 442 (= TIM 11 15), an adoption contract from the Neo-Assyrian period.[19] The tablet provides some relevant background information to its main transaction by noting that Abdi-Kurra's daughter had a son, Ahu-iddina, from her *ḫarīmūtu*.[20] The note indicates that Abdi-Kurra had legal and financial responsibility for Ahu-iddina. The tablet records Abdi-Kurra's sale of Ahu-iddina to Puṭi-athiš to be his son, for ten shekels. The contract contains a stipulation that warrants comparison to the legal issue addressed in Deuteronomy (Deut 21:15–17). According to line 9 of the reverse side of the tablet, "Even though the sons of Puṭi-athiš be 10 (in number), Ahu-iddina shall be his eldest son, the heir of Puṭi-athiš."[21] When the contract was made, Puṭi-athiš evidently had no heirs, which is why he was willing to pay to adopt Ahu-iddina. The contract envisions the possibility that biological children may be born to him in the future and that he may come to prefer them over his previously adopted heir. This contractual stipulation seeks to protect Ahu-iddina from having his inheritance rights as the adopted firstborn of Puṭi-athiš displaced. Although this case of adoption is different from the case of children through multiple wives envisioned in Deuteronomy, both texts seek to address the same legal issue: limits on the right of the head of household to distribute his inheritance at will.

Similar Legal Reasoning

More telling than similar legal issues, which arise in part from the general economic and social structure of Near Eastern life, are instances of similar legal reasoning. The Deuteronomic Code presents its casuistic laws using modes of inference and presumption known from documentary evidence for Near Eastern legal practice. As an example of similar legal reasoning, Wells cites murder by an unknown assailant in Deuteronomy (Deut 21:1–9) and in five Akkadian legal texts from Ugarit (RS 17.146; 17.230; 18.115; 20.22; *Ugaritica* V no. 27).[22] The documents reckon with legal responsibility in the absence of witnesses. Wells summarizes the parallel nicely, "in all five [Akkadian documents] the issue is resolved by having the leaders of the city where the body was found be responsible for absolving themselves and their community of the crime, just as Deut 21:1–9 states that the elders of the closest city must do."[23]

As another example, he notes the parallel between the requirement for two witnesses (Deut 17:6; 19:15) and the calling of additional witnesses in some fifty Neo-Babylonian trial records.[24] According to Wells, the Neo-Babylonian courts "demonstrate the same reluctance as the texts in Deuteronomy to rely on a sole accuser."[25] Both sets of analogs reflect similar legal reasoning about their respective issues.

To these examples, I would add the legal reasoning by which courts made inferences about a woman's guilt from her silence. Deuteronomy distinguishes between consensual illegal sex, in which both the man and the woman were to be found guilty, and nonconsensual illegal sex, where legal responsibility was borne by the man alone (Deut 22:23–27).[26] This casuistic law uses the method of evidentiary presumption.

Evidentiary presumption was a form of legal reasoning in which known data related to a legal case were used to make inferences about unknown data by shifting the burden of proof. In turn, the court inferred innocence or guilt from the previously unknown—but now inferred—data. As envisioned within this Deuteronomic law, certain facts were known to the court: the identity of the woman, the identity of the man, the fact that the sex act was illegal because the woman was betrothed to someone else, and the location of the crime. But the court did not know whether the woman was a willing participant or whether she participated against her will. The law instructs the court to reason from the known to the unknown using evidentiary presumption. If the crime took place in the city, the court must assume that some witness would have heard if the woman had cried for help. The court is to equate her silence with consent and impugn her with a guilt equivalent to the man's. If, however, the crime took place in the country, the court must assume that she cried out, but no one heard her, that is, that she did not consent. In this case, the court may not punish her. Thus, a known fact, namely the location of the crime, was to be used to make an inference about an unknown fact, namely whether she cried out or remained silent. From this now inferred fact the court was to make an inference about her consent to participate in the crime. Consent or lack of consent, in turn, implied guilt or innocence.

Here, I wish to focus on one link in this chain of legal reasoning: the court inferred from the woman's silence that she consented to the illegal sex act. This represents a kind of ancient equivalent to the modern legal concept of the reasonable person standard.[27] In modern English and American legal systems, the behavior of an actual individual in real circumstances can be compared to the expected behavior of a fictional reasonable person under similar circumstances. This fictional reasonable person embodies society's norms and allows the court to make inferences about guilt or innocence. Although this Deuteronomic law does not explicitly invoke a reasonable person, it rests on assumptions about how such a person might behave. Within the patriarchal logic of this casuistic law, a reasonable woman who had not consented to this illegal sex act would have expressed her objection by an audible cry loud enough to be overheard at some distance. Here, the standards of what constitutes a reasonable person are used to measure the behavior of an actual person in real circumstances.

Evidentiary presumption was applied to a completely different crime in the so-called Nippur Homicide Trial, the Sumerian record of which is found in multiple manuscripts from the early second millennium BCE.[28] This record presents a legal debate about the guilt or innocence of Nin-Dada in a case involving the murder of her husband. Certain facts were known to the court as recounted at the start of the document: the identity of Nin-Dada, the identity of her husband the victim, the identity of the three men who physically carried out the homicide, the fact they told her about the crime afterward, and the fact that she remained silent about it—"Nin-Dada, daughter of Lu-Ninurta did not open her mouth, she covered it with a cloth."[29] The court debated Nin-Dada's legal responsibility by, as M. T. Roth observes, "probing . . . what the modern English and American legal systems call 'the rational person', that hypothetical person who sets the standard for how an individual could or should respond to a given set of circumstances."[30] Two members of the assembly argued in her defense. The logic of their defense seems to rely on an appeal for mercy considering the imagined inherent weakness of women.[31] The majority did not accept this defense. But in condemning her, they did not argue that she physically participated in the killing. Rather, they presented an imagined scenario in which a woman failed to value her husband, knew—Akkadian *idû*, with a double entendre perhaps intended—his enemy, was made aware that the enemy had murdered her husband, but did not report him to the authorities. Failure to report the murder makes her an accomplice, they argued. Here, the court implicitly held Nin-Dada to the rational person standard. A woman who embodied the societal norms expected by Nippur's patriarchal court would certainly value her husband, she would not know his enemy, and she would report her husband's murderer to the authorities. Nin-Dada was found guilty by this standard, and the court sentenced the three murderers and Nin-Dada to death. The process of legal reasoning here, in which the court made inferences from a woman's silence based on what it expected a rational woman to do in similar circumstances, parallels that in Deuteronomy (Deut 22:23–27).

Similar Legal Remedies

Finally, there are strikingly specific analogs between the legal remedies presented in Deuteronomy and documentary evidence of legal remedies in other Near Eastern texts. As an example of a similar legal remedy, Wells cites talion punishment of a false accuser. To be sure, talion was a broad principle of ancient justice. But the application of this principle in this specific context is notable. According to Deuteronomy (Deut 19:16–21), someone who makes a false accusation against another should be subjected to the same legal remedy that would have applied had the accusation proven true.[32] Wells compares this legal remedy to that imposed on a false accuser in a Neo-Babylonian trial record form the time of Nabonidus (Nbn 13).[33] Belilitu had brought a case against Nabu-aḫḫe-iddin saying that she had sold him a slave for thirty-five shekels but had not received payment. When Nabu-aḫḫe-iddin produced documentary evidence of payment, the court made Belilitu pay Nabu-aḫḫe-iddin the precise amount she had claimed from him. The rhetoric of the text emphasizes the talion nature of this legal remedy: the judges ruled against Belilitu for "thirty-five shekels of silver, as much as her claim was."[34]

In another article, Wells notes analogous legal remedies in cases involving men who discover that their wives had been guilty of illegal sex while betrothed (Deut 22:20–21) and in an Old Babylonian tablet published by D. I. Owen and R. Westbrook (FLP 1340).[35] The legal penalty for such a crime in Deuteronomy (Deut 22:20–21) is the death of the bride. The language of the text emphasizes the bride's connection to her father: "the girl shall be brought out to the entrance of her father's house, and the men of her town shall stone her so that she dies; for she did an outrageous thing in Israel, committing fornication in her father's house." As Wells reconstructs the legal scenario behind FLP 1340, a groom had sued his bride's father alleging illegal sex during the period of inchoate marriage and seeking financial compensation. The father of the bride refused, and the groom responded by invoking the death penalty in language that emphasized the bride's connection to her father: "I will not marry your daughter. Bind her and throw her into the river."[36] Wells shows that a range of legal remedies—what he calls full measures and partial measures—were available to grooms whose brides had been found guilty either of illegal sex while being betrothed or of preconsummation sex with deception. Both Deut 22:20–21 and FLP 1340 point to the maximum legal remedy in this situation being the death of the bride with the legal remedy being phrased in such a way as to highlight the bride's father, with whom the contract of betrothal had been established.

To these examples of similar legal remedies, I would add the punishment of cultic crimes in order to deter future crime in Deut 13:12; 17:13 and SAA 10 369.[37] Legal remedies in the Neo-Assyrian period served multiple functions, including compensating victims and punishing offenders, as K. Radner has noted.[38] Deuteronomy and Neo-Assyrian legal texts also occasionally highlight an additional function. At least in some situations, legal remedies were conceptualized as a deterrent to future crime.[39] Deuteronomy draws attention to this function of legal remedies with distinctive language: the people "will hear and be afraid" and will not commit the crime again.[40] With this language the death penalty is presented as deterring the worship of gods other than Yahweh (Deut 13:12) and disregard for priests (Deut 17:13). A legal remedy conceptualized as a deterrent to future cultic crimes is also found in SAA 10 369, a Neo-Assyrian letter from Mar-Issar to Esarhaddon. Mar-Issar reported that the governor of Dur-Šarruku had overstepped his authority by requisitioning silver, sheep, and oxen from the temples of the gods Šimalu'a and Humhum and distributing them to his retinue. Whatever his personal interests may have been, Mar-Issar framed his accusation in apparently objective terms—no other governor of Dur-Šarruku had acted in this way, nor had royal officials in other towns. The letter reaches its rhetorical climax with an appeal for punishment that would act as a deterrent: "Let the king, my lord, send a trusty bodyguard to investigate (the matter); the man who put the governor up to this should be punished. [Let] (the others) [kn]ow and be frightened off, [or el]se [the govern]ors will dissip[ate] a[ll the treasures o]f the temples" (r.10–r.17).[41] Like Deuteronomy (Deut 13:12; 17:13), the letter imagines news of punishment for a cultic crime reaching those who might be tempted to commit a similar crime and inducing fear in them. The texts conceptualize their respective legal remedies as deterrents to future cultic crimes.

What Is Trending in the Conversation?

The Gap between Deuteronomy and Legal Practice

The evidence discussed earlier should not lead the legal historian to equate Deuteronomy with Near Eastern legal practice. Indeed, other evidence points to the gap between Deuteronomy as a literary work and the historical legal context that produced it.[42] Consider, for example, the treatment of fugitives in Deuteronomy (Deut 23:16–17) and in Near Eastern treaties.[43] According to this Deuteronomic law, Israelites should not return fugitives to their masters. Some details of the law are obscure. Are the fugitives and the masters from whom they flee Israelites or foreigners? Is refuge sought across international borders or within some narrower jurisdiction? In my estimation, the section of the law that permits the fugitive to "reside with you, in your midst, in a place he chooses, in one of your towns [lit. gates]" suggests that the law envisions fugitives from outside the towns affiliated with Israel who seek refuge among the Israelites. I therefore take the law to be dealing with non-Israelites who have fled to Israel from elsewhere. As such, the law deals with international relations.[44] Some scholars regard this law as breaking with Near Eastern tradition by recognizing fugitives as possessing inherent dignity. These scholars see in Deuteronomy the seeds of a humanitarian revolution, something like a precursor to the modern concept of human rights.[45] But the regulations regarding six-year and lifelong slavery (Deut 15:12–18) make me hesitant to see an egalitarian impulse behind Deut 23:16-17. Instead, I see this Deuteronomic law as breaking with its ancient context in a different way.

In my view, this Deuteronomic law, dealing with international relations, is best interpreted in light of Near Eastern treaties. International relations are presented in our sources as personal relationships between kings, often phrased in the language of the household. Within this larger rhetorical context, treaties were written as contracts between kings. They might include general statements of loyalty and affection as well as more specific contractual stipulations. They often contained a stipulation about fugitive extradition. Consider for example an eighth-century Aramaic treaty from Sefire (Sefire III). Although Sefire III is fragmentary, the following requirement is clearly preserved:

> Now if a fugitive flees from me, one of my officials, or one of my brothers, or one of my courtiers, or one of the people who are under my control, and they go to Aleppo, you must not gi[ve th]em food or say to them, "Stay quietly in your place"; and you must not incite them against me. You must placate(?) them and return them to me. And if they [do] not [dwell] in your land, placate(?) (them) there, until I come and placate(?) them. But if you incite them against me and give them food and say to them, "Stay where [yo]u are and do not (re)turn to his region," you shall have been unfaithful to this treaty.[46]

This stipulation in Sefire III echoes a well-established tradition of fugitive extradition in Near Eastern international relations.[47] Stipulations about fugitives are regularly found in treaties imposed by a sovereign on a vassal—for example, in the treaty of Muršili II with Niqmepa of Ugarit (CTH 66 §§12–13)—or in reciprocal treaties between kings who regarded themselves as peers—for example, in the agreement between Pillia and Idrimi (AT 36–43). The related clauses in these treaties guaranteed that there was no realm where a servant of the king could escape a legally established relationship with him.[48] Crucial to my argument here is the observation that ancient suzerains were not required to extradite fugitives to their vassals.[49] Rather, this requirement was imposed by suzerains on vassals or was mutually agreed upon by peers. The requirement to extradite fugitives is thus a marker of international political status.

How does this observation shape my interpretation of the law about fugitives in Deuteronomy? A scholarly consensus regards Deuteronomy as first taking shape in the Neo-Assyrian period and being updated in the Neo-Babylonian and Persian periods.[50] That some core of Deuteronomy emerged in a Neo-Assyrian milieu is suggested by a number of lines of evidence, including the language and themes Deuteronomy shares with Neo-Assyrian loyalty oaths,[51] the language and themes it shares with the narrative of the discovery of the book of the law in the time of Josiah (2 Kgs 22–23),[52] and the independence of some material in the book (Deut 12–18), from literary framing devices that better suit an exilic context.[53] No treaty between an Assyrian king and an Israelite or a Judahite king has been preserved, but the Bible records vassal–suzerain relationships between Menahem and Pul/Tiglath-Pileser III (2 Kgs 15:19); Ahaz and Tiglath-Pileser III (2 Kgs 16:7, 10); and Hoshea and Shalmaneser V of Assyria (2 Kgs 17:3). Both the Bible (2 Kgs 18:14–16) and the earliest account of Sennacherib's third military campaign (RINAP 3 4) agree that Hezekiah of Judah acted in such a way as to invite an Assyrian attack, implying an existing relationship between Judah and Assyria, though not necessarily a formal treaty.[54] Although Israel and Judah enjoyed varying degrees of independence from Assyria in the Neo-Assyrian period, they never became independent or wielded power like Assyria and Babylon.[55]

In my view, then, Deuteronomy 23:16–17 breaks with its historical legal context by presenting a charter for the new nation Israel that envisions it as being free from a legal stipulation that was customarily imposed by a suzerain on a vassal.[56] Israel and Judah were relatively small powers on the fringes of the Assyrian and Babylonian empires. But Deuteronomy envisions Israel on a grander scale, as politically and legally independent from foreign powers.

A second line of evidence points to the gap between Deuteronomy and legal practice. There are known discrepancies between Near Eastern law codes and Near Eastern legal practice. I highlight but two such discrepancies here. First, in a letter to the judges of Sippar, Samsu-Iluna set a legal standard that contradicted the law code of his father Hammurabi.[57] The judges had previously sought Samsu-iluna's advice on two legal issues, including how to deal with *nadîtum* priests who had no dowry and who posed a drain on the state's finances. Whereas CH §180 is premised on such priests being permitted to enter the cloister, Samsu-Iluna ruled that only those who were financially supported by their families could be admitted to the cloister. If we did not have the accidental preservation of Samsu-iluna's letter, we might have incorrectly inferred legal practice from CH §180.

Second, cuneiform records of legal decisions indicate that imposed penalties were at times less severe than the maximum penalties permitted by the cuneiform law codes. For example, consider the penalty for adultery in CH §129 and in a Sumerian record of divorce from the Old Babylonian period published by J. van Dijk (IM 28051).[58] As S. Greengus reconstructs the legal situation described in IM 28051, a woman caught in the act of adultery was subjected to mutilation and public shaming, but not death.[59] According to CH §129, death was the maximum penalty allowed in such a case, though the law envisions the possibility of a lesser penalty. Lesser penalties for legal cases were available as legal remedies even when they are not explicitly mentioned in the law codes. Records of legal judgments with penalties less than those stipulated in the law codes suggest that the law codes are best understood as providing guidance on the maximum permissible penalty rather than stipulating penalties that had to be enforced in every legal situation.[60] If we did not have the accidental preservation of trial records, we might have misjudged the nature of legal remedies in the law codes.

SUMMARY

What are the implications of documentary evidence for Near Eastern legal practice for understanding the nature of the Deuteronomic Code? The evidence is indirect. Nor does it allow definitive answers to the questions outlined at the start of this chapter. But the evidence outlined here corroborates aspects of the interpretation of the Deuteronomic Code that have been advanced based on an internal analysis of the Code itself. The data examined here suggest that the scribes who produced Deuteronomy were either directly and intimately familiar with legal practice—including the real legal issues encountered by the courts, the process of legal reasoning used by the courts, and the forms of legal remedies imposed by the courts—or else that they utilized textual traditions that had at some point been crafted by scribes directly familiar with legal practice. These data, in other words, corroborate the view that the Deuteronomic Code reflects, however imperfectly, legal practice in the Southern Levant in the Neo-Assyrian period. Indeed, the Deuteronomic Code does not contain anything so outlandish as to have been laughable to judges holding court in ancient Israel and Judah. There are no tells that give Deuteronomy away as a work of pure fiction concocted from a scribe's imagination. Rather, by and large, Deuteronomy presents legal practice in a systematic way, probing its underlying principles.[61]

At the same time, the data examined here also suggest that the Deuteronomic Code was not merely descriptive of legal practice. For example, in the law about fugitives the Deuteronomic Code presents a vision of the international status of the new nation Israel that did not precisely match its real political history. As a literary work, Deuteronomy embodied a political and religious vision of Israel, including its legal system.

NOTES

1. Comprehensive introductions to biblical law include R. Westbrook and B. Wells, *Everyday Law in Biblical Israel: An Introduction* (Louisville: Westminster John Knox Press, 2009); P. Barmash, *The Oxford Handbook of Biblical Law* (Oxford: Oxford University Press, 2019).

2. For example, see the differing approaches in M. Greenberg, "Some Postulates of Biblical Criminal Law," in *Yehezkel Kaufmann Jubilee Volume: Studies in Bible and Jewish Religion Dedicated to Yehezkel Kaufmann on the Occasion of his 70th birthday*, ed. M. Haran (Jerusalem: Magnes Press, 1960), 5–28; M. Lefebvre, *Collections, Codes and Torah: The Re-Characterization of Israel's Written Law*, LHB/OTS 451 (New York: T & T Clark, 2006); J. J. Collins, "The Transformation of the Torah in Second Temple Judaism," *JSJ* 43 (2012): 455–474. On authoritative textual traditions more broadly, see Hindy Najman, *Seconding Sinai: The Development of Mosaic Discourse in Second Temple Judaism*, JSJSup 77 (Leiden: Brill, 2003).

3. B. M. Levinson, for example, argues that Deuteronomy subverts the older Covenant Code. See B. M. Levinson, *Deuteronomy and the Hermeneutics of Legal Innovation* (Oxford: Oxford University Press, 1997). E. Otto, on the other hand, sees Deuteronomy as updating the Covenant Code to suit new circumstances. See E. Otto, "The Pre-Exilic Deuteronomy as a Revision of the Covenant Code," in *Kontinuum und Proprium: Studien zur Sozial- und Rechtsgeschichte des Alten Orients und des Alten Testaments* (Orientalia biblica et christiana 8; Wiesbaden: Harrassowitz, 1996), 112–122.

4. For example, J. Stackert shows how the Holiness Code revised the Covenant Code and Deuteronomy. See J. Stackert, *Rewriting the Torah: Literary Revision in Deuteronomy and the Holiness Legislation*, FAT 2/52 (Tübingen: Mohr Siebeck, 2007).

5. For example, J. Blenkinsopp writes, "in Deuteronomy the legal and sapiential traditions flow together" (*Wisdom and Law in the Old Testament: The Ordering of Life in Israel and Early Judaism* [rev. ed.; New York: Oxford University Press, 1995], 118). D. M. Carr notes the similarities between Proverbs and Deuteronomy and sees law and wisdom as having similar pedagogical aims. See D. M. Carr, *The Formation of the Hebrew Bible: A New Reconstruction* (New York: Oxford University Press, 2011), 413–423. See also A. Fitzpatrick-McKinley, *The Transformation of Torah from Scribal Advice to*

Law, JSOTSup 287 (Sheffield: Sheffield Academic Press, 1999); C. Halberstam, "Law in Biblical Israel," in *The Cambridge Companion to Judaism and Law*, ed. Christine Hayes (New York: Cambridge University Press, 2017), 19–47, here 46–47. B. S. Jackson questions the application of modern legal concepts to biblical law and proposes "wisdom-laws" as a more useful category for understanding biblical law. See B. S. Jackson, *Studies in the Semiotics of Biblical Law*, JSOTSup 314 (Sheffield: Sheffield Academic Press, 2000). D. Daube regards Deuteronomy as standing midway between wisdom and legislation (*Law and Legislation in the Bible: David Daube's Gifford Lectures*, vol. 2, edited and compiled by C. M. Carmichael [West Conshohocken: Templeton Press, 2010], 26–55).

6. For example, see the arguments about the nature of Hammurabi's Law Code in J. Bottero, "The 'Code' of Hammurabi," in *Mesopotamia: Writing, Reasoning, and the Gods*, trans. Zainab Bahrani and Marc van de Mieroop (Chicago: University of Chicago Press, 1992), 156–184. Westbrook accepts the scholastic nature of the law codes, but regards them as describing ancient law. See R. Westbrook, "Cuneiform Law Codes and the Origins of Legislation," *ZA* 79 (1989): 201–222. Westbrook writes, "the Ancient Near Eastern Law Codes derive from a tradition of compiling series of legal precedents in the same manner as omens, medical prognoses, and other scientific treatises. The purpose of these series was to act as reference works for the royal judges in deciding difficult cases" ("Biblical and Cuneiform Law Codes," in *Law from the Tigris to the Tiber: The Writings of Raymond Westbrook*, ed. B. Wells and F. R. Magdalene, 2 vols. [Winona Lake: Eisenbrauns, 2009], 1:3–20, here 14).

7. On the lack of source material for legal practice in Iron Age Israel and Judah, compare the comments of Halberstam, "Law in Biblical Israel," 19. Even biblical narrative may not accurately describe legal practice in ancient Israel and Judah, but they may be intended to interrogate the law. See P. Barmash, "The Narrative Quandary: Cases of Law in Literature," *VT* 54 (2004): 1–16.

8. And yet Deuteronomy 24:1, 3 assume a world in which legal documents existed.

9. This approach is by no means new. Until recently, however, comparisons were more commonly made to other collections of ancient law, to law codes, rather than to documentary evidence for legal practice. Over half a century ago, Moshe Greenberg lamented the fact that scholarly treatments of biblical law have too often "been characterized by theorizing which ignores the realities of early law and society as we know them at first hand from the written records of the ancient Near East" ("Postulates," 5). But his treatment focuses on comparisons to the law codes.

10. B. Wells, "What Is Biblical Law? A Look at Pentateuchal Rules and Near Eastern Practice," *CBQ* 70 (2008): 223–243.

11. B. Landsberger, "Die babylonischen Termini für Gesetz und Recht," in *Symbolae adiura Orientis Antiqui Pertinentes Paulo Koschaker Dedicatae*, ed. T. Folkers et al., Studia et documenta ad jura Orientis antiqui pertinentia 2 (Leiden: Brill, 1939), 219–234, here 221–222; M. T. Roth, "The Law Collection of King Hammurabi: Toward an Understanding of Codification and Text," in *La codification des lois dans l'Antiquité: actes du Colloque de Strasbourg 27–29 novembre 1997*, ed. E. Lévy (Paris: De Boccard, 2000), 9–31.

12. Wells, "What Is Biblical Law?" 223–243.

13. R. Westbrook, "Introduction: The Character of Ancient Near Eastern Law," in *A History of Ancient Near Eastern Law*, ed. R. Westbrook, HdO 72, 2 vols. (Leiden: Brill, 2003), 1:1–90, here 56–62.

14. A. M. Kitz, "Undivided Inheritance and Lot Casting in the Book of Joshua," *JBL* 119 (2000): 601–618.
15. Westbrook, "Introduction," 57–58.
16. For example, see A. C. Hagedorn, *Between Moses and Plato: Individual and Society in Deuteronomy and Ancient Greek Law*, FRLANT 204 (Göttingen: Vandenhoeck & Ruprecht, 2004), 200–211.
17. Westbrook, "Introduction," 58–60.
18. B. Wells, "The Hated Wife in Deuteronomic Law," *VT* 60 (2010): 131–146.
19. R. Mattila, *Legal Transactions of the Royal Court of Nineveh, Part II: Assurbanipal Through Sin-šarru-iškun*, SAA 14 (Helsinki: University of Helsinki, 2002). For examples of legal disputes of inherited property, see AT 7; AO 5429; CT 47, 63. Some of these are discussed in D. Charpin, *Writing, Law, and Kingship in Old Babylonian Mesopotamia*, trans. J. M. Todd (Chicago: University of Chicago Press, 2010), 62–65.
20. The CAD defines *ḫarīmūtu* as the state of being a prostitute. J. A. Assante has argued that "the harimtu is a single woman without patriarchal status, either because she grew up without it or because she left, or was coerced to leave, her father's house" (What Makes a "Prostitute" a Prostitute? Modern Definitions and Ancient Meanings," *Historiae* 4 [2007], 126). See also J. A. Assante, "The kar.kid/ḫarimtu, Prostitute or Single Woman? A Reconsideration of the Evidence," *UF* 30 (1998): 5–96.
21. Translation from R. Mattila in SAA 14.
22. Wells, "What Is Biblical Law?" 236–238. Wells cites A. Jirku, "Drei Fälle von Haftpflicht im altorientalischen Palastina-Syrien und Deuteronomium cap. 21," *ZAW* 79 (1967): 359–360; P.-E. Dion, "Deuteronome 21,1–9: Miroir du deveioppemem legal et religieux d'Israel," *SR* 11 (1982): 13–22, here 16–19; R. Westbrook, "Lex Talionis and Exodus 21,22–25," *RB* 93 (1986): 52–69, here 62–65. On the collective responsibility of the town in such cases, compare D. J. Wiseman, "Murder in Mesopotamia," *Iraq* 36 (1974): 249–260, here 259; P. Barmash, "Blood Feud and State Control: Differing Legal Institutions for the Remedy of Homicide during the Second and First Millennia B.C.E." *JNES* 63 (2004): 183–199, here 186–188.
23. Wells, "What Is Biblical Law?" 237.
24. B. Wells, *The Law of Testimony in the Pentateuchal Codes*, Beihefte zur Zeitschrift für altorientalische und biblische Rechtsgeschichte 4 (Wiesbaden: Harrassowitz, 2004), 108–126.
25. Wells, "What Is Biblical Law?" 238 n46.
26. On Deuteronomy 22:22–29, see C. Pressler, *The View of Women Found in the Deuteronomic Family Laws*, BZAW 216 (Berlin: Walter de Gruyter, 1993), 21–43; C. B. Anderson, *Women, Ideology, and Violence: Critical Theory and the Construction of Gender in the Book of Covenant and the Deuteronomic Law*, JSOTSup 392 (London: T&T Clark, 2005), 88; D. L. Ellens, *Women in the Sex Texts of Leviticus and Deuteronomy: A Comparative Conceptual Analysis*, LHB/OTS 458 (London: T.&.T. Clark, 2008), 215–219; C. Edenburg, "Ideology and Social Context of the Deuteronomic Women's Sex Laws (Deuteronomy 22:13–29)," *JBL* 128 (2009): 43–60; T. M. Lemos, *Marriage Gifts and Social Change in Ancient Palestine: 1200 BCE to 200 CE* (Cambridge: Cambridge University Press, 2010), 37–41; R. S. Kawashima, "Could a Woman Say 'No' in Biblical Israel?" *AJS Review* 35 (2011): 15–20.
27. Compare M. T. Roth's discussion of the Nippur Murder Trial in "Gender and Law: A Case Study from Ancient Mesopotamia," in *Gender and Law in the Hebrew Bible and*

the Ancient Near East, ed. V. H. Matthews, B. M. Levinson, and T. S. Frymer-Kensky, JSOTSup 262 (Sheffield: Sheffield Academic Press, 1998), 173–184, here 177–178.

28. On the tablets and the legal logic of the trial, see T. Jacobsen, "An Ancient Mesopotamian Trial for Homicide," in *Studia biblica et orientalia: Edita a Pontificio Instituto Biblico. 3 Oriens Antiquus*, AnBib 12 (Rome: Pontifical Biblical Institute, 1959), 130–150; M. T. Roth, "The Slave and the Scoundrel," *JAOS* 103 (1983): 279–282; Roth, "Gender and Law," 173–184; P. Barmash, *Homicide in the Biblical World* (Cambridge: Cambridge University Press, 2005), 151–152, 205–206. As noted by Roth, manuscripts include (a) CBS 7178 published in Edward Chiera, *Old Babylonian Contracts*, PBS 8.2 [Philadelphia: The University Museum, 1922]), no. 173; (b) 2N-T 54, mentioned in the catalog of tablets in D. E. McCown, R. C. Haines, and D. P. Hansen, *Nippur I, Temple of Enlil, Scribal Quarter, and Soundings: Excavations of the Joint Expedition to Nippur of the University Museum of Philadelphia and the Oriental Institute of the University of Chicago*, OIP 78 (Chicago: University of Chicago, 1967), 75; (c) a joint tablet consisting of manuscripts 3N-T 273 + 3N-T 340 + 3N-T 403, all equal to UM 55-21-436; (d) 3N-T 426 ("Gender and Law," 175).

29. The translation is that of Roth, who notes that "covered it with a cloth" is "Probably an idiom suggesting a refusal to speak, or, more metaphorically, a covering up of the deed" ("Gender and Law," 176).

30. Roth, "Gender and Law," 177–178.

31. Roth, "Gender and Law," 178.

32. On the law referring to the person bringing the charge to the court and not just to false testimony in general, see I. L. Seeligmann, "Zur Terminologie fur das Gerichtsverfahren im Wortsehatz des biblischen Hebraisch," in *Hebrdische Wortforschung: Festschrift zum 80, Ceburtstag von Walter Baumgartner*, ed. B. Hartmann et al., VTSup 16 (Leiden: Brill, 1967), 251–278, here 262–263; Wells, "What Is Biblical Law?" 240.

33. J.N. Strassmaier, *Inschriften von Nabonidus, König von Babylon* (Leipzig: Pfeiffer, 1889), no. 13.

34. Translation taken from Wells, "What Is Biblical Law," 240.

35. B. Wells, "Sex, Lies, and Virginal Rape: The Slandered Bride and False Accusation in Deuteronomy," *JBL* 124 (2005): 41–72, here 65–69. D. I. Owen and R. Westbrook, "Tie Her Up and Throw Her into the River! An Old Babylonian Inchoate Marriage on the Rocks," *ZA* 82 (1992): 202–207. W. H. Halo had compared Deut 22:13–21 to the legal situation in BE 6/2 58. See W. H. Hallo, "The Slandered Bride," in *Studies Presented to A. Leo Openheim; June 7, 1964*, ed. R. D. Briggs and J. A. Brinkman (Chicago: University of Chicago Press, 1964), 95–105.

36. Translation from Wells, "Sex, Lies, and Virginal Rape," 65.

37. S. Parpola, *Letters from Assyrian and Babylonian Scholars*, SAA 10 (Helsinki: University of Helsinki, 1993), no. 369. As another example of an analogous legal remedy, consider the execution of a manslayer as the ultimate available remedy for homicide in Deut 19:4–6 and ADD 321, which dates from the Neo-Assyrian period. See the discussion of ADD 321 in M. T. Roth, "Homicide in the Neo-Assyrian Period," in *Language, Literature, and History: Philological and Historical Studies Presented to Erica Reiner*, ed. F. Rochberg-Halton, American Oriental Series 67 (New Haven: American Oriental Society, 1987), 351–365, here 357–358.

38. See K. Radner, "The Reciprocal relationship between Judge and Society in the Neo-Assyrian Period," *Maarav* 12 (2005): 41–68, here 48.

39. Radner, "Reciprocal Relationship," 48.
40. Compare the language used to describe the believed deterring effect of punishments for other crimes in Deut 19:20; 21:21.
41. Translation from S. Parpola in SAA 10.
42. On the Utopian character of Deuteronomy, see D. C. Benjamin, "How Does Deuteronomy Repurpose Mountains & High Places?" in *Lexham Geographic Commentary on the Pentateuch*, ed. B. J. Beitzel (Bellingham: Lexham Press, forthcoming).
43. See S. Greengus, *Laws in the Bible and in Early Rabbinic Collections: The Legacy of the Ancient Near East* (Eugene: Cascade Books, 2011), 116–121.
44. See R. Westbrook, "Slave and Master in Ancient Near Eastern Law," *Chicago-Kent Law Review* 70, no. 4 (1995): 1631–1676, here 1673.
45. For example, see C. S. Ehrlich, *The Philistines in Transition: A History from ca. 1000–730 BCE*, Studies in the History and Culture of the Ancient Near East 10 (Leiden: Brill, 1996), 49; D. A. Knight, *Law, Power, and Justice in Ancient Israel* (Louisville: Westminster John Knox Press, 2011), 219–222; W. S. Morrow, *An Introduction to Biblical Law* (Grand Rapids: Eerdmans, 2017), 246. D. Y. Tsai argues that underpinning the laws relating to slaves in Deuteronomy are two legal concepts, namely that all agents are persons and that all legal subjects are free, dignified, and self-determining. See D. Y. Tsai, *Human Rights in Deuteronomy: With Special Focus on Slave Laws*, BZAW 464 (Berlin: Walter de Gruyter, 2014). Tsai writes, "Deut 23:16–17 shows that the land promise includes freedom and human dignity for anyone who enters into this land. It is an asylum not only for the Hebrew slaves who escaped from Egypt, but also for any other non-Hebrew slave fugitives. Deut 23:16–17 challenges the entire community to recognize that YHWH is the real Master of the Land" (*Human Rights*, 67).
46. Translation from J. Fitzmeyer in COS 2.82.
47. On fugitives and extradition in the ancient Near East, see D. Elgavish, "Extradition of Fugitives in International Relations in the Ancient Near East," *Jewish Law Association Studies* 14 (2004): 33–57; J. M. Sasson, "Extradition in the Mari Archives," *Wiener Zeitschrift für die Kunde des Morgenlandes* 97 (2007): 453–473; G. Galvin, *Egypt as a Place of Refuge* (FAT 2/51; Tübingen: Mohr Siebeck, 2011), 2–5.
48. Insight into how the status of such international fugitives might become full-blown diplomatic incidents in the Neo-Assyrian period comes from SAA 5 52.
49. R. Westbrook, "International Law," in *Amarna Diplomacy: The Beginning of International Relations*, ed. R. Cohen and R. Westbrook (Baltimore: Johns Hopkins University Press, 2000), 36n18 as cited in Elgavish, "Extradition," 40.
50. T. Römer has provided a lucid introduction to the scholarly discussion of these issues in T. Römer, *The So-Called Deuteronomistic History: A Sociological, Historical and Literary Introduction* (London: T&T Clark, 2005), 56–65, 73–80. A. Hagerdorn's chapter in this handbook also summarizes the evidence and debate nicely. On method in dating Deuteronomy, see especially N. MacDonald, "Issues in the Dating of Deuteronomy: A Response to Juha Pakkala," *ZAW* 122 (2010): 431–435.
51. See, for example, M. Weinfeld, *Deuteronomy and the Deuteronomic School* (Oxford: Clarendon Press, 1972), 116–129, 146–157; E. Otto, "Die Ursprünge Der Bundestheologie Im Alten Testament Und Im Alten Orient," *Zeitschrift für Altorientalische und Biblische Rechtsgeschichte/Journal for Ancient Near Eastern and Biblical Law* 4 (1998): 1–84, here 41–43; B. M. Levinson, "Esarhaddon's Succession Treaty as the Source for the Canon Formula in Deuteronomy 13:1," *JAOS* 130 (2010): 337–347. Note the cautions

sounded by C. L. Crouch in *Israel and the Assyrians: Deuteronomy, the Succession Treaty of Esarhaddon, and the Nature of Subversion*, ANEM 8 (Atlanta: SBL Press, 2014). See also C. L. Crouch's contribution to this handbook.

52. See, for example, L. B. Paton, "The Case for the Post-Exilic Origin of Deuteronomy," *JBL* 47 (1928): 322–357, here 325–326; Levinson, *Deuteronomy*, 9–10. On the possibility of an earlier Holiness stratum in the narrative of the discovery of the Book of the Law in the time of Josiah, see L. A. S. Monroe, *Josiah's Reform and the Dynamics of Defilement: Israelite Rites of Violence and the Making of a Biblical Text* (New York: Oxford University Press, 2018).

53. For example, G. Braulik differentiated between an exilic edition of Deuteronomy that used the Decalogue as its structuring principle and an inherited edition of the book where that structuring principle is less clear. See G. Braulik, *Die deuteronomischen Gesetze und der Dekalog: Studien zum Aufbau von Deuteronomium 12–26* (SBS 145; Stuttgart: Katholisches Bibelwerk, 1991). Compare D. Markl's contribution to this handbook. On the shaping of the exilic edition of Deuteronomy, see T. Römer, "Le Deutéronome à la quête des origines," in *Le Pentateuque: Débats et recherches* (ed. P. Haudebert; Lectio Divina 151; Paris: Éditions du cerf, 1992), 65–98.

54. S. C. Russell, *The King and the Land: A Geography of Royal Power in the Biblical World* (New York: Oxford University Press, 2016), 100–102.

55. On Deuteronomy in the context of Neo-Assyrian imperial ideology, see S. Marzouk, "The Neo-Assyrian Empire through a Postcolonial Lens," in *The Oxford Handbook of Postcolonial Biblical Criticism*, ed. R. S. Sugirtharajah (New York: Oxford, forthcoming).

56. M. R. Glanville argues for a different kind of gap between the fugitive law and legal practice, "Deuteronomy 23:16–17 would probably have been difficult to enforce in judicial procedure, as responsibility rests with a whole community; thus the stipulation is probably best described as divine imperative rather than substantive law" (*Adopting the Stranger as Kindred in Deuteronomy*, AIL 33 [Atlanta: SBL Press, 2018], 79).

57. C. Janssen, "Samsu-iluna and the Hungry *nadîtums*," *Northern Akkad Project Reports* 5 (1991): 3–40; S. Lafont, "Ancient Near Eastern Laws: Continuity and Pluralism," in *Theory and Method in Biblical and Cuneiform Law: Revision, Interpolation and Development*, ed. B. M. Levinson, JSOTSup 181 (Sheffield: Sheffield Academic Press, 1991), 91–118, here 97–98.

58. J. van Dijk, "Textes divers du Musee de Baghdad 3," *Sumer* 15 (1959): 12–14; J. van Dijk, "Neusumerische Gerichtsurkunden in Bagdad," *ZA* 55 (1962): 70–77.

59. S. Greengus, "A Textbook Case of Adultery in Ancient Mesopotamia," *HUCA* 40/41 (1969): 33–44.

60. R. Westbrook writes, "The basic system of retribution for offenses that would be regarded as crimes in modern legal systems was a dual right that accrued to the victim (or his family): 1) revenge against the culprit (or his family), or 2) the acceptance of a payment by way of ransom in lieu of revenge. This right was a legal right, regulated by the courts who intervened to fix not only the appropriate level of revenge but also, in less serious cases, the appropriate ransom. In the latter case, revenge was only available if the ransom was not duly paid" ("Slave and Master," 1638). On a variety of legal remedies available for a particular crime, see S. E. Loewenstamm, "The Law of Adultery and the Law of Murder in Biblical and Mesopotamian Law," *Bet Miqra* 13 (1962): 55–59 (in Hebrew); B. S. Jackson, "Reflections on Biblical Criminal Law," *JJS* 24 (1973): 8–38; R. Westbrook, "Adultery in Ancient Near Eastern Law," *RB* 97 (1990): 542–580; Wells, "Sex, Lies, and Virginal Rape," 63–64.

61. On the arrangement of the laws, see B. M. Levinson, "M. Carmichael's Approach to the Laws of Deuteronomy," *HTR* 83 (1990): 227–257; A. Rofé, *Deuteronomy: Issues and Interpretation* (London: T&T Clark, 2002), 55–77. See also G. Braulik, "The Sequence of Laws in Deuteronomy 12–26 and in the Decalogue," in *A Song of Power and the Power of Song: Essays on the Book of Deuteronomy*, ed. D. L. Christensen; trans. L. M. Maloney (Winona Lake: Eisenbrauns, 1993), 313–335. Braulik shows that at the transitions between legal topics in the book there is often overlap.

Bibliography

Barmash, P., ed. *The Oxford Handbook of Biblical Law*. New York: Oxford University Press, 2019.

Greenberg, M. "Some Postulates of Biblical Criminal Law." In *Yehezkel Kaufmann Jubilee Volume: Studies in Bible and Jewish Religion Dedicated to Yehezkel Kaufmann on the Occasion of His 70th Birthday*, edited by M. Haran, 5–28. Jerusalem: Magnes Press, 1960.

Levinson, B. M. *Deuteronomy and the Hermeneutics of Legal Innovation*. New York: Oxford University Press, 1997.

Lévy, E., ed. *La codification des lois dans l'Antiquité: Actes du Colloque de Strasbourg 27–29 novembre 1997*. Paris: De Boccard, 2000.

Rofé, A. *Deuteronomy: Issues and Interpretation*. London: T&T Clarke, 2002.

Römer, T. *The So-Called Deuteronomistic History: A Sociological, Historical and Literary Introduction*. London: T&T Clark, 2005.

Stackert, J. *Rewriting the Torah: Literary Revision in Deuteronomy and the Holiness Legislation*. Forschungen zum Alten Testament 2/52. Tübingen: Mohr Siebeck, 2007.

Tsai, D. Y. *Human Rights in Deuteronomy: With Special Focus on Slave Laws*. BZAW 464. Berlin: Walter de Gruyter, 2014.

Weinfeld, M. *Deuteronomy and the Deuteronomic School*. Oxford: Clarendon Press, 1972.

Wells, B. "What Is Biblical Law? A Look at Pentateuchal Rules and Near Eastern Practice." *Catholic Biblical Quarterly* 70 (2008): 223–243.

Westbrook, R. "Biblical and Cuneiform Law Codes." In *Law from the Tigris to the Tiber: The Writings of Raymond Westbrook*, edited by B. Wells and F. R. Magdalene, vol. 1, pp. 3–20. Winona Lake, IN: Eisenbrauns, 2009.

CHAPTER 3

DEUTERONOMY—CODE OR COVENANT?

ANNE K. KNAFL

Who Began the Conversation?

The question posed by "Code or Covenant?" is essentially a question of genre: What is the literary genre of Deuteronomy? The question assumes two possible answers, that is, is the genre of Deuteronomy more akin to that of a legal code or a political covenant? Even more specifically, was Deuteronomy intended to serve as a legal code for the people of ancient Israel in a manner similar to other legal codes from the ancient world, such as the Code of Hammurabi, and the earlier, biblical legal tradition in the Covenant Code (Exod 20:22–23:19)?[1] Or was Deuteronomy intended to serve as a binding covenant, establishing the loyalty of the Israelite people to their national deity, YHWH, thereby simultaneously mimicking and supplanting loyalty covenants imposed on Israel, and its neighbors, by the Assyrian Empire?

As with most things in biblical studies, the situation is much more complicated than the either/or choice posed by the title. This is not to disparage the way the question is framed. In many ways, this is the appropriate question to ask when analyzing the genre of Deuteronomy since the question reflects the history of scholarship on this book, as well as recent trends. It is also critical that biblical scholars consider genre as part of any literary analysis of a biblical text. I will present here the relevant evidence and methods and survey the historical and current scholarship and debates.

To what does "genre" refer? The *Oxford English Dictionary* defines genre as "a type of literary work characterized by a particular form, style, or purpose."[2] We are focused on a literary genre since Deuteronomy is a literary work, in that it is a creative, written document. In addition, we are specifically interested in historical, literary genres and genres that date to the first millennium BCE, to which the composition of the core, unified text that became Deuteronomy may be reasonably dated. At the same time, we can compare Deuteronomy to literary genres that developed much earlier, such as Hittite treaties or the Code of Hammurabi, but whose form and content were still known in the first millennium BCE. The broader comparison of literary texts across time and place is instructive, but, as our topic has been framed by the question of code versus covenant, ours is an historical endeavor.

The determination of genre is dependent upon establishing the scope of the literary unit that is under consideration. The boundaries of what has come to us as "the book of Deuteronomy" are a relatively late imposition upon the text and should not be an a priori assumption for the determination of the literary unit. At first glance, Deuteronomy does appear to be a logical, unified unit. Deuteronomy opens with a disjunctive phrase: "These are the words that Moses spoke to all Israel beyond the Jordan—in the wilderness, on the plain opposite Suph, between Paran and Tophel, Laban, Hazeroth, and Di-zahab" (1:1). This starts a new scene, distinguishing it from what precedes and connecting it to what follows. Deuteronomy closes by describing the death of Moses, a logical narrative break (34:1–12).

But, as readers have recognized for millennia, the intervening material is far from unified. While the narrative is introduced as Moses's farewell speech, his speech is interrupted by disjointed narratives, repetitions, shifts in literary style, and insertions of nonnarrative material, such as legal material and poetry. Simultaneously, there are multiple links to the material that precedes and follows through explicit narrative reference, linguistic allusion, and stylistic repetition. This, of course, explains the scholarly arguments that see the final form of Deuteronomy as the result of a compositional history that occurred in stages and as part of a larger composition, particularly the Pentateuch (Gen-Deut) and the Deuteronomistic History (Deut-Kgs). I presume the general scholarly consensus that Deuteronomy is made up primarily, but not exclusively, of a narrative unit that is distinct from Genesis-Numbers and Joshua-Kings and that can be reasonably analyzed as possessing a specific genre. At the same time, I will presume that sections of Deuteronomy are simultaneously part of larger literary units that encompass both the Pentateuch and the Deuteronomic History, to which it is connected through the interweaving of the various narrative traditions.

In his "Covenant Forms in Israelite Tradition" (1954), Mendenhall argues for the influence of Hittite political treaties on the biblical covenant forms. The extant Hittite treaties date from 1450 to 1200 BCE and are of two types: "suzerainty treaties" between the Hittite king and a vassal ruler; and "parity treaties" between the Hittite king and another equally powerful ruler. For Mendenhall, the content and structure of the Hittite suzerainty treaties are preserved in the covenants in Exodus, Deuteronomy, and Joshua. His primary point of comparison is the structural elements shared between Hittite suzerainty treaties and biblical covenants.

The standard structure of the Hittite treaties recovered by archaeologists is as follows: (1) preamble; (2) historical prologue; (3) stipulations; (4) provision for deposit in the temple and periodic public reading; (5) list of gods as witnesses; and (6) blessings and curses. To this, Mendenhall added (7) a formal oath of allegiance; (8) a ritual to commemorate the oath; and (9) procedures of dealing with rebellion. He argued that the Hittite treaties serve as the historical antecedent for the structure of the biblical covenant traditions, particularly the Decalogue (Deut 5:7–21) and the Covenant Code (Exod 20:22–23:33), reflecting their antiquity. The Deuteronomic covenant, in his model, was a revival of the treaty preserved in the Decalogue, merged with the Covenant between YHWH and Abraham (Gen 12:1–9; 17:1–27) and the reality of the monarchy. Mendenhall's comparison with Hittite treaties was groundbreaking. Soon after, his argument was mostly abandoned for a comparison with the Succession Treaties of Esarhaddon (EST)—negotiated in 672 BCE and recovered by archaeologists in 1956.

Two schools emerged in the following decade, with a minority of scholars favoring the Hittite treaties as the primary influence on biblical covenant forms. McCarthy (1963) argues for an unbroken Near Eastern treaty tradition, which originates with the Hittites and is continued in Aramaic and Akkadian treaties. Deuteronomy is the closest biblical manifestation of this treaty tradition. His prioritization of Hittite treaties recently has gained renewed support from scholars like Berman (2011), Taggar-Cohen (2011), Kitchen and Lawrence (2012), Steymans (2019), and Morrow (2023). Wiseman (1958) published the first edition of the succession treaties. He proposes a clear link between the treaty form of the second millennium and the treaty form of the first millennium. Soon after, Frankena (1965) argued for the structural and linguistic similarities between the treaties of Esarhaddon, Deuteronomy, and the Aramaic treaty of Sefire. Weinfeld (1972) lays out a systematic argument that neo-Assyrian, not the Hittite treaties, served as the model for biblical covenants. He shows that Deuteronomy contains all the structural elements of these neo-Assyrian treaties, as opposed to the Covenant Code or the Covenant at Shechem (Josh 24:1–28).

What Is the Status of the Conversation?

Comparisons between neo-Assyrian treaties and Deuteronomy have since focused primarily on EST. For example, *the sky over your heads will be like bronze and the earth under your feet like iron* in Deuteronomy (28:23) parallels *the earth will turn to iron where nothing can grow, and the heavens to bronze without rain or dew for your fields* in EST (§ 63–64). The strongest parallels appear between EST §10//13:1–18 and EST §39–43//28:1–68. The blessings and curses in Deuteronomy (27:11–28:68) also parallel the order and content of the curses in EST, although EST does not include blessings. Likewise, the traditions on apostasy in Deuteronomy (12:29–13:18) have been compared to the loyalty oath in EST (§39–43) by Otto (1999) as well as Levinson and Stackert (2012).

Scholars like Frankena and Weinfeld have noted overlapping language between Deuteronomy and EST, such as the command of subjects to "love" their sovereign and the description of loyalty in both documents as "to go after/follow," "to fear," and "to listen to the voice of" their sovereign. While Deuteronomy contains antecedents for each section, they do not appear in systematic order, as they do in the Hittite treaties. In addition, each of these structural elements is attested in later genres, to varying degrees, such as law collections and the neo-Assyrian treaties. Finally, Hittite treaties describe the sovereign having feelings of affection for the vassal, as in Deuteronomy, but absent in neo-Assyrian treaties.

Weinfeld lays out the strongest argument to date linking the structure and content of Deuteronomy to those of the Assyrian vassal treaties of the ninth–seventh centuries BCE, particularly EST. At the same time, he concedes that there was strong evidence that Deuteronomy was stylistically related to Near Eastern law codes:

> The most important deviation of Deuteronomy from the treaty form is that its central part is dedicated to civil, cultic, and criminal law. While we may regard this section as functionally equivalent to the stipulatory section of a treaty, it is very different in substance, and this difference stems from the fact that the object of the treaty is to assure the partner's loyalty—as reflected in the section which we called the stipulation allegiance [4:1–23; 6:4–7:26; 10:12–22]—and not to impose upon him a system of laws as does the book of Deuteronomy. The convergence of treaty and law-code forms is one of the crucial problems not only in understanding the pattern of the deuteronomic covenant but also in comprehending the covenant between God and Israel as presented in Exodus.
>
> (Weinfeld 1992, 148)

Weinfeld goes on to assert that, despite clear affinities between Deuteronomy and a law code, Deuteronomy's innovation was to conform an inherited tradition to the vassal treaty tradition. His argument became the consensus among biblical scholars, but the tension he identifies between code and covenant has never been fully resolved.

The past decades have seen a renewed interest in challenging the presumption that Deuteronomy can be primarily defined as an Israelite response to the vassal treaty form in general and EST specifically. Historically, scholarship has focused on identifying Deuteronomy's place within the treaty tradition of the Near East. At the same time, scholars have always acknowledged the central role that the Deuteronomic Code plays in the composition as a whole and the connection between these laws and those in the Covenant Code. Van Seters (2003) argues that the Deuteronomic Code precedes the Covenant Code. In contrast, as Levinson (1997) explains, most scholars assume the Deuteronomic Code reworks earlier laws like those in the Covenant Code in drafting its laws like the centralization of the cult. The importance of this legal innovation begs the question, "Does Deuteronomy intend for the Deuteronomic Code to be implemented?" If these laws were intended to be implemented in Judah, then is Deuteronomy best understood to be a legal code?

Frankena and Weinfeld argue for Deuteronomy's general dependence on the neo-Assyrian treaty tradition, of which EST is the most complete example. More recently, a group of scholars, in particular Otto (1999) and Levinson (2010), have argued that Deuteronomy draws directly from and purposefully reworks the language of EST. Other scholars have challenged arguments of direct literary dependence of Deuteronomy upon EST, arguing that ancient Israelite scribes would not have had access to or the ability to read Akkadian treaties. Morrow (2001) and Ramos (2016), for example, argue that scribes in Judah would have had contact with this tradition only through Aramaic equivalents to neo-Assyrian treaties, such as the Sefire treaties of the eighth century BCE.

The core, and largest section, of Deuteronomy is the Deuteronomic Code. Scholars have long observed a striking overlap, and at times near repetition, in language and content between the Deuteronomic Code and the Covenant Code. These parallels include the sabbatical year of remission (Exod 21:2–11//Deut 15:1–18); cities of refuge (Exod 21:12–14//Deut 19:1–13); and pilgrimage festivals (Exod 23:14–19//Deut 16:1–17). Lundbom provides a comprehensive list of parallels (2013, 26–27). In addition, both the Covenant Code (Exod 20:1–17) and the Deuteronomic Code (5:1–21) have a Decalogue. At the same time, the laws in Deuteronomy vary significantly from those in the Covenant Code. When Deuteronomy does treat the same topic, the specifics differ. The most prominent changes relate to Deuteronomy's imposition of a centralized cult, whereas the Covenant Code presumes multiple, local cult sites. Deuteronomy does not deal with damages or civil suits, which is a preoccupation of the Covenant Code. Instead, it is preoccupied with humanitarian concerns, which are largely absent in the Covenant Code.

Deuteronomy was influenced by Near Eastern law codes, both directly and indirectly. Wright (2009) argues that the Covenant Code is a direct reinterpretation of the Laws of Hammurabi, which are then reinterpreted by Deuteronomy. Otto 1999 has shown the influence of the Middle Assyrian Laws (MAL A) on the laws of Deuteronomy (21:15–25:10). There exists, then, strong evidence that Deuteronomy draws on multiple sources—including legal traditions—that were reworked for a new context. This central focus of the laws in Deuteronomy suggests it is primarily a law collection. The traditional scholarly presumption was that the laws of the Pentateuch were the law of the land. But this presumption is difficult to maintain since the collections contradict each other, are incomplete, and are heavily ideological. Current scholarship instead focuses on the extent that individual laws could reflect legal practice and the authority that these law collections carried at and after their composition. Wells (2015), for instance, argues in favor of a real-life connection between biblical law codes and legal practice in ancient Israel and Judah. He shows overlap between content, legal reasoning, and remedies in the Covenant Code and Deuteronomic Code with documents of legal proceedings from Mesopotamia and Syria. In his mind, biblical law collections do not function as "legislation per se but symbolizing ideals that were to guide behavior and social life" (Wells, 2019, 212). Stackert argues that laws are an integral part of the narrative of the D Source, which he distinguishes from the Book of Deuteronomy, a later scribal creation. The centrality of these laws does not make the D Source a legal text. It is a literary text that incorporates laws and is characterized by allegory and etiology (Stackert, 2022, 15–51).

What Is Trending in the Conversation?

There is no exact structural or generic match for Deuteronomy within Near Eastern compositions. That said, Deuteronomy shares aspects in common with the EST and Hittite and Sefire treaties, on the one hand, and the Mesopotamian legal collections and the Covenant Code, on the other. At the same time, the law collections of the Hebrew Bible are distinctive from other collections of law in the Near East, particularly for their extensive narrative contexts and interweaving of secular and religious themes. In addition, the unifying genre of Deuteronomy is narrative exhortation, specifically Moses's farewell speech to the people, containing a collection of laws and instructions for the future.

Appropriation and reinterpretation of earlier compositions and forms is also a defining characteristic of Deuteronomy. Biblical scholars agree that Deuteronomy draws on existing texts, or the traditions they represent, to create the text before us. They disagree over why and how Deuteronomy uses these texts, which texts were primary sources, the process of composition, and purpose of the final product. In addition, there is agreement that the final product is distinct from its predecessors.

> Unlike the treaty, Deuteronomy is not a legal document but an oration. The structure of the speech follows a legal pattern, but its style is that of a sermon. The author of Deuteronomy had in mind the covenantal pattern in the form in which it had been lying before him in the tradition and in the manner in which it was generally formulated in his time. Nevertheless, he presented the materials in a style that is free from rigid adherence to formality.
>
> (Weinfeld 1992, 157)

Is, then, Deuteronomy a covenant or a code? How dependent is the determination of genre on the reception of the text? For whom was the text written and what did they understand it to be? The clearest and most consistent formal markers in Deuteronomy are those of exhortation. Is wisdom literature the source of exhortation genre? Is the exhortation a reflection of the wisdom tradition, particularly that from Egypt? In this model, Deuteronomy is a type of didactic wisdom imparted by Moses likely intended for the future leader of Israel. Or is the exhortation better understood as a succession ceremony inspired by vassal treaties? Should we not place too heavy an emphasis on the hortatory framework? Is it simply meant as a literary convention to package a covenant or law collection?

The variegated nature of the content of Deuteronomy means that we are in fact dealing with multiple, overlapping genres. Therefore, we should distinguish between genres that have been incorporated into the larger unit from what, if any, is the overarching genre of Deuteronomy. In some instances, the text explicitly identifies embedded compositions, as with the shift from narrative to poetry with the Song of Moses (31:30–32:47), which is introduced as "the words of this song" and with "this blessing." In other instances, a shift in genre is unexpressed, such as when exhortation in the second person shifts to third-person casuistic law (21:15–25:10).

In his essay, Bergsma defines *covenant* as "a sacred relationship of obligation established by means of an oath. The oath could be expressed in words, rituals, or both" (2019). The Hebrew Bible includes multiple types of covenants, both between humans like Jacob and Laban, and between a human—like Adam, Noah, Moses, or David—and their deity. YHWH promises that "the days are surely coming, . . . when I will make a new covenant with the house of Israel and the house of Judah" (Jer 31:31). The instructions on monarchs Deut (17:14–18) refer to Deuteronomy as a "second law"—an extension of the covenant at Horeb. A title in Deuteronomy states: "These are the words of the covenant that the Lord commanded Moses to make with the Israelites in the land of Moab, in addition to the covenant that he had made with them at Horeb" (29:1 [28:69]).

Thus, Deuteronomy self-identifies as an extension of both the covenant and laws of Horeb. The exact nature of that extension is a topic of debate, given the legal traditions contained in the Covenant Code and the Priestly laws in Leviticus and Numbers. There is general agreement that Deuteronomy purposefully reworks narratives and laws from Genesis-Exodus-Leviticus-Numbers, but the process, purpose, and date of that reworking are fiercely debated. Some scholars like Baden (2012) and Levinson and Stackert (2012) argue that the Deuteronomic Code supplants the Covenant Code, since the laws are contradictory at places and thus could not complement each other. Others like Otto and Wells argue that the Deuteronomic Code—as "a second law"—supplements earlier legal traditions. They argue that the differences between Deuteronomy and its biblical source material represent an active history of interpretation with ancient Israel focused on adapting but not supplanting earlier traditions. However, Benjamin (2019) identifies in Deuteronomy a rich interaction with Akkadian and Egyptian texts, through which Israelite scribes parallel existing genres while creating something new.

Crouch (2014) argues that even if Esarhaddon imposed a vassal treaty on Judah, knowledge of the structure and contents of that treaty would not have been known to the fathers of the households of Judah. Miller (2008) argues that Assyrian parallels in Deuteronomy are drawn from traditions from Sam'al (1200–609 BCE), not EST. Darby (2014) studies the Judean pillar figurines which appear in excavations of sites occupied during Assyria's control of Syria-Palestine. She argues that the small ceramic statues of the torso of a naked woman holding her breasts are not connected with efforts to challenge Assyria's control of Judah. The works of Miller, Crouch, and Darby question the assumption that Deuteronomy is apologetic by arguing that the audiences are not familiar with the structure of the Assyrian legal traditions establishing Judah's status as a colony of Assyria, but rather that Judah interacted with and benefited from its position in the Assyrian Empire (Darby 2014, 367–397). Patron states like Assyria and client states like Judah were part of a single imperial culture which benefited both. As one of many small client states during the peace enforced in Syria-Palestine between Assyria's conquest of Israel (722 BCE) and its defeat by Babylon at Carchemish (605 BCE), Judah participated in and contributed to the extensive cultural community of the Assyrian Empire.

Deuteronomy shares close parallels between wisdom material like Proverbs, Qoheleth, Psalms, and Job in the Hebrew Bible, as well as with Ben Sira and Wisdom of Solomon in later Jewish wisdom literature. Deuteronomy also parallels the wisdom traditions from Egypt like the Instruction of Amenemope and similar teaching traditions from Babylon. Following the inaugural studies of Weinfeld, Daube and Carmichael (2010) and Lundbom (2010) have studied wisdom genres in Deuteronomy. Wisdom characteristics appear in Deuteronomy in the form of the admonition not to add or subtract from divine command; not to remove landmarks or falsifying weights; not to make reckless vows; the importance of justice and impartiality in judgment; humane treatment of the disadvantaged; fear of the divine; and characterizing proscriptions as divine abomination. From this vantage point, Deuteronomy conforms to wisdom genres, as a didactic exhortation from a wise, divinely inspired leader to his people for the good of future generations. If one accepts, like Fitzpatrick-McKinley (1999) that Near Eastern law collections were intellectual compositions written by and for scribes, Deuteronomy is a wisdom genre which evolves into a legal genre.

For Claassens (2010) Near Eastern and biblical codes are not law codes in a strict sense since they do not attempt to be comprehensive or offer a complete statement of legal principles. Roth and Lévy (2000), Westbrook (2009), and Wells (2008) have all proposed that Near Eastern law codes were never meant to be implemented, at least not explicitly, since they are not cited as precedents in legal decisions, which often deviate from what was prescribed by the written laws. Cuneiform collections of laws can be viewed as part of a larger intellectual, scribal tradition in Mesopotamia that composed scientific or academic treatises that classify knowledge and were meant for study and instruction. Biblical laws, for instance, include detailed laws regarding a goring ox, but no laws governing marriage. Even those topics that are thoroughly covered are lacking instructions for practical application. In other words, the law codes are systematic but not comprehensive. In this sense, Near Eastern legal texts are better thought of as "collections," in that they contain a sample of laws that reflect aspects of society. Biblical law collections, in addition, incorporate religious ideology with civil law, further complicating their application by a court. Deuteronomy shares the qualities of other Near Eastern collections of laws, while at the same time exhibiting distinctive qualities. It is presented as an extended exhortation by Moses to the people, and it identifies itself as a second version of the law given at Horeb. In this way, the Deuteronomic Code, and its narrative framework, makes explicit its place within an interpretive legal tradition.

Making a distinction between "covenant" and "code" is further complicated by the fact that Near Eastern law collections and treaties shared similar structures, such as historical prologue, stipulations, curses, and blessings. In addition, both genres are typically associated with a royal figure and the imposition of divinely sanctioned rules on a group, though treaties seek to regulate a political alliance, or sovereignty, over a foreign group, whereas legal collections seek to establish justice within a native population. Must Deuteronomy conform to a single, preexisting genre? Can it not be both/and instead of either/or? David Wright (2020) argues that the Covenant Code is distinctive in the ancient Near East for its fusion of treaty and law. Deuteronomy then is an inheritor of this hybrid genre. Levinson argues, in contrast to Mendenhall's foundational work, that law, covenant, and religion were always intertwined in the Pentateuch. "The innovation of the biblical authors was to present that covenantal relationship in a new cultural form—as a national treaty between god and people" (Levinson, 2020, 42).

A final complication is the issue of allusion versus intertextuality: Is Deuteronomy's resemblance to Near Eastern genres coincidental or intentional? Does Deuteronomy draw on genres, broadly known in the Near East, or was a specific genre or even a specific composition purposefully adopted? The preceding discussion suggests that Deuteronomy should not be aligned with a single, literary genre. It belongs instead to the practice of inner-biblical interpretation, which is characterized by interpolation, borrowing, reinterpretation, appropriation, and allusion.

Notes

1. Biblical quotations throughout this chapter are from the New Revised Standard Version, unless otherwise indicated.
2. Oxford English Dictionary, s.v. "genre (n.)," July 2023, https://doi.org/10.1093/OED/2380920642.

Bibliography

Baden, Joel S. *The Composition of the Pentateuch: Renewing the Documentary Hypothesis*. New Haven: Yale University Press, 2012.

Beckman, Gary M., and Harry A. Hoffner. *Hittite Diplomatic Texts*. 2nd ed. Atlanta: Scholars Press, 1999.

Benjamin, Don C. *The Social World of Deuteronomy: A New Feminist Commentary*. Eugene: Cascade Books, 2015.

Berman, Joshua. "CTH 133 and the Hittite Provenance of Deuteronomy 13." *Journal of Biblical Literature* 130, no. 1 (2011): 25–44. https://doi.org/10.2307/41304185.

Crouch, Carly L. *Israel and the Assyrians: Deuteronomy, the Succession Treaty of Esarhaddon, and the Nature of Subversion*. Society of Biblical Literature Ancient Near East Monographs 8. Atlanta: SBL Press, 2014.

Daube, David, and Calum M. Carmichael. *Law and Wisdom in the Bible. David Daube's Gifford Lectures* 2. West Conshohocken: Templeton Press, 2010.

Fitzpatrick-McKinley, Anne. *The Transformation of Torah from Scribal Advice to Law*. Sheffield: Sheffield Academic Press, 1999.

Frankena, R. "The Vassal-Treaties of Esarhaddon and the Dating of Deuteronomy." *Oudtestamentische Studiën* 14 (1965): 122–154. https://doi.org/10.1163/9789004497092_006.

Kitchen, Kenneth A., and Paul Lawrence. *Treaty, Law and Covenant in the Ancient Near East*. Wiesbaden: Harrassowitz Verlag, 2012.

Levinson, Bernard M. *Deuteronomy and the Hermeneutics of Legal Innovation*. New York: Oxford University Press, 1997.

Levinson, Bernard M. "Revisiting the 'And' in Law and Covenant in the Hebrew Bible: What the Evidence from Tell Tayinat Suggests About the Relationship Between Law and Religion in the Ancient Near East." *Maarav* 24, nos. 1–2 (2020): 27–43.

Levinson, Bernard M., and Jeffrey Stackert. "Between the Covenant Code and Esarhaddon's Succession Treaty: Deuteronomy 13 and the Composition of Deuteronomy." *Journal of Ancient Judaism* 3, no. 2 (2012): 123-140. DOI: 10.13109/jaju.2012.3.2.123.

Lundbom, Jack R. *Deuteronomy: A Commentary*. Grand Rapids: William B. Eerdmans Publishing Company, 2013.

McCarthy, Dennis J. *Treaty and Covenant: A Study in Form in the Ancient Oriental Documents and in the Old Testament*. Analecta Biblica 21. Rome: Pontifical Biblical Institute, 1963.

Morrow, William. "The Sefire Treaty Stipulations and the Mesopotamian Treaty Tradition." In *The World of the Aramaeans III*, 83-99. Sheffield: Sheffield Academic Press, 2001.

Morrow, William. "The Laws in the Covenant Code and Deuteronomy as Dienstanweisungen." *Scandinavian Journal of the Old Testament* 37, no. 1 (January 2023): 128-147. DOI: 10.1080/09018328.2023.2222044.

Otto, Eckart. *Das Deuteronomium: politische Theologie und Rechtsreform in Juda und Assyrien*. Beihefte zur Zeitschrift für die alttestamentliche Wissenschaft 284. Berlin: De Gruyter, 1999.

Ramos, Melissa. "A Northwest Semitic Curse Formula: The Sefire Treaty and Deuteronomy 28." *Zeitschrift Für Die Alttestamentliche Wissenschaft* 128, no. 2 (2016): 205-220. DOI: 10.1515/zaw-2016-0015.

Roth, Martha T., and Edmond. Lévy. "The Law Collection of King Hammurabi: Toward an Understanding of Codification and Rext." In *La codification des lois dans l'Antiquité: Actes du Colloque de Strasbourg 27-29 Novembre 1997*, 9-31. Travaux du Centre de Reserche sur le Proche-Orient at la Grèce antiques 16. Paris: De Boccard, 2000.

Stackert, Jeffrey. *Deuteronomy and the Pentateuch*. New Haven: Yale University Press, 2022.

Steymans, Hans Ulrich. "Deuteronomy 13 in Comparison with Hittite, Aramaic and Assyrian Treaties." *Hebrew Bible and Ancient Israel* 8, no. 2 (2019): 101-132. DOI: 10.1628/hebai-2019-0011.

Taggar-Cohen, Ada. "Biblical Covenant and Hittite Išḫiul Reexamined." *Vetus Testamentum* 61, no. 3 (2011): 461-488. DOI: 10.1163/156853311X571464.

Van Seters, John. *A Law Book for the Diaspora: Revision in the Study of the Covenant Code*. Oxford: Oxford University Press, 2003.

Weinfeld, Moshe. *Deuteronomy and the Deuteronomic School*. Winona Lake: Eisenbrauns, 1992. First published 1972.

Wells, Bruce. "The Interpretation of Legal Traditions in Ancient Israel." *Hebrew Bible and Ancient Israel* 4, no. 3 (September 2015): 234-266. DOI: 10.1628/219222715X14507102280775.

Wells, Bruce. "The Purpose of the Covenant and Deuteronomic Codes and the Insights of Eckart Otto." *Zeitschrift Für Altorientalische Und Biblische Rechtsgeschichte* 25, no. 1 (2019): 207-210. DOI: 10.13173/zeitaltobiblrech.25.2019.0207.

Wells, Bruce. "What Is Biblical Law?: A Look at Pentateuchal Rules and Near Eastern Practice." *Catholic Biblical Quarterly* 70, no. 2 (April 2008): 223-243. https://www.jstor.org/stable/43726256.

Westbrook, Raymond. *Law from the Tigris to the Tiber: The Writings of Raymond Westbrook*. Winona Lake: Eisenbrauns, 2009.

Wiseman, D. J. "The Vassal-Treaties of Esarhaddon." *Iraq* 20, no. 1 (1958): i-99. DOI: 10.2307/4199630.

Wright, David P. *Inventing God's Law: How the Covenant Code of the Bible Used and Revised the Laws of Hammurabi*. Oxford: Oxford University Press, 2009.

Wright, David P. "The Adaption and Fusion of Near Eastern Treaty and Law in Legal Narrative of the Hebrew Bible." *Maarav* 24, no. 1-2 (January 2020): 85-136. DOI: 10.1086/MAR202024108.

CHAPTER 4

THE DECALOGUE IN DEUTERONOMY

DOMINIK MARKL

The Quest for the Decalogue's Origin

Long after critical scholarship began to question the attribution of the Pentateuch's authorship to Moses, the Decalogue was one of the last strongholds to which scholars retreated to maintain the dignity of its Mosaic origin (see, e.g., the report in Matthes 1904, 17–20). An example of this idealistic conception of an original Mosaic *Urdekalog* is found in *Geschichte des Volkes Israel bis Christus* by Heinrich Ewald (1845, 148–159). According to Ewald, the differences between the Decalogue's versions in Exodus 20 and Deuteronomy 5 allow for the elimination of the secondary expansions found mainly in the theological motivations of the commandments (Ewald 1845, 149). While the received versions have encouraged diverse traditions for counting the Commandments, the original Decalogue must have been marked by a clear structure of exactly ten commandments, evenly distributed on the two tablets (149–153; cf., similarly, Peters 1886). This view may well have been influenced by the iconic representation of the Mosaic tablets, especially since the Reformation (e.g., Mochizuki 2006). The introductory words, "I am Yhwh, your God," which also mark the conclusion of the supposedly ancient commandments in Leviticus 18 and 19, are evidence of the deepest prophetic sentiment of Moses: his voice disappears behind the divine utterance (Ewald 1845, 154–155).

Similar scholarly attitudes are seen behind the version of the Decalogue preserved in the Shapira Manuscripts (the available copies are edited in Dershowitz 2021, esp. 160f., 171f.) that Moses Wilhelm Shapira may have acquired in 1878 (Dershowitz 2021, 2). The version of the Ten Commandments preserved in this text contains neither explanatory additions nor doublets: it renders only one prohibition of false swearing and one of coveting; at the end, it adds "thou shalt not hate thy brother in thine heart" (Lev. 19:17). The commandments are perfectly structured into ten, each marked by the conclusory formula "I am Elohim your God," which authenticates this Decalogue as Mosaic according to Ewald's criteria. The formula constructs an Elohistic version of the Decalogue, mechanically replacing the tetragrammaton with "Elohim" (cf. comparable formulations in the Elohistic Psalter: Ps. 43:4,

45:8, etc.). This reflects the idea of an attribution of the Decalogue to an Elohistic source, which Julius Wellhausen (1876, 557, 564f.) proposed. Through an idiosyncratic conflation of nineteenth-century views on the Decalogue, the Shapira Manuscripts' Decalogue tried to convince contemporary scholars that it was an authentic, ancient, or even Mosaic, version of this text (on this case of forgery, see Hendel/Richelle 2021).

Whereas Wellhausen considered the Decalogue to be part of the Elohistic source (in his *Prolegomena*, it is an "ingredient" of the "Jehovist"; 1883, 8, 13), which still allowed for the assumption of its relatively ancient pre-exilic and pre-Deuteronomic origin, he also dismantled arguments for its attribution to Moses, deconstructing the Decalogue's inscription on the tablets in the ark as a late theological dignification of an ancient idol (1883, 416f.). The form-critical analysis of the Decalogue was advanced by Sigmund Mowinckel and Albrecht Alt, both students of Hermann Gunkel (on the historical context, see Otto 1996, 285–288). Mowinckel located the original *Sitz im Leben* of a decalogic series of commandments in the cultic sphere as *leges sacrae* that were originally pronounced at the entry to the temple and involved in the covenant renewal ceremonies at the new year festival (Mowinckel 1927, 154). The Decalogues that were narratively integrated into the Sinai covenant, however, are seen as the culmination of the development of the decalogic series and dated to the late pre-exilic period, integrated by a Deuteronomic redactor into the book of Deuteronomy around 600 BCE and by a redaction related to P into E around 500–450 BCE (Mowinckel 1927, 112; 1937, 233; cf. Hjelde 2006, 206–209).

Alt, in contrast, proposed the basic form-critical distinction between casuistic and apodictic law (1967 [1934]). Although, in his view, the Israelites adopted casuistic law from Canaanite tradition, the Decalogue's commandments, examples of apodictic law, are genuinely Israelite and ultimately go back to the period of the desert wanderings (Alt 1967, 117–132); part of his argument is the comparison of the Ten Commandments with the curses in Deuteronomy 27:15–26 (121). Alt thus opposed the late dating of the Decalogue based on the assumption that it depended on the ethical demands of the prophets (on the diverse opinions at the time, see Köhler 1929). Alt's work deeply influenced attempts at reconstructing the Decalogue's original form in subsequent decades (cf. the reports Stamm 1961; 1967; Zenger 1968).

Interest in the form-critical quest for the *Urdekalog*'s *Sitz im Leben* shifted to its *Sitz in der Literatur* with a monograph by Frank-Lothar Hossfeld (1982; see Otto 1996, 288–290), which departed from a detailed discussion of the differences between the Decalogues of Exodus 20 and Deuteronomy 5 and arrived at the conclusion that the Decalogue originated from an early Deuteronomistic author and a redactor, while its counterpart in Exodus 20 was integrated into the Sinai pericope when the Pentateuch was compiled (Otto 1996, 283f.). Hossfeld's thesis, however, did not remain undisputed (see Hossfeld 1989; Graupner 2001), and more recent work has advocated for complex redactional processes that involved mutual, bidirectional influences of both versions (see the synthesis in Otto 2012, 688f.). Research on the redactional formation of the Decalogue is thus firmly situated within theory on the compositional history of the Pentateuch (e.g., Blum 2011).

In a recent proposal, Wolfgang Oswald (2020) has addressed the question of the Decalogue's *Sitz im Leben* from a new angle. Comparing the Decalogue to early Greek citizen oaths, Oswald proposes that, notwithstanding its formulation as a series of directive (and not commissive) speech acts, "these words" that are supposed to be recited (Deut. 6:6–7) may have served as a sort of Judean citizen oath in the Babylonian and/or Persian era

(Oswald 2020, 127; for the assumption of an oath practice, see also Weinfeld 1991, 266, with reference to m. Tamid 5:1). Similarly, the Decalogue has been described as a sort of "credo" (Rom-Shiloni 2019, 150) and a "catechism" for Judaism in the Persian period (Römer 2006, 61–64). During the Pentateuch's compositional history, the two versions of the Decalogue were placed before its first and its last law collection—the Book of the Covenant (Exod. 21–23) and the Deuteronomic laws (Deut. 12–26) respectively—which lends the Decalogue a highly significant role for the legal hermeneutics of the Pentateuch. It is comparable to a document of constitutional law (Hossfeld 2004, 60–62; Veijola 2004, 131; Markl 2007; 2013).

Notwithstanding the manifold repetitions and variations in the history of theories of the Decalogue's origin, there has been a clear development in the centuries of historical critical investigation: the once prevalent discussion on its Mosaic or pre-monarchic origin has nearly vanished from critical inquiry (an exception: Coogan 2014, 46–49), while the discussion on the Decalogue's development as a scribal product in the formative period of the Pentateuch continues to be vibrant.

A Portable Monument to the Covenant

While the content of the stone tablets is difficult to determine in the book of Exodus (esp. 24:12; 31:18; 34:4, 28f.), which led to manifold speculations in the history of research, the Decalogue's literary contextualization in Deuteronomy 5 does not leave any doubt that Yhwh spoke precisely "these words" and wrote them on "two stone tablets" (v.22) that carry the "Ten Words" (4:13, 10:4). Deuteronomy emphasizes the immediate connection of these words with the covenant that Yhwh had made with Israel at Horeb (5:2–3), which is also reflected in the expression "tablets of the covenant" (9:9, 11, 15).

The Decalogue's authority is underlined in its oral and written transmission. The divine voice had spoken these words directly at Horeb, as a theophany spoken "from the midst of fire" (emphasized no less than ten times in 4:12, 15, 33, 36; 5:4, 22, 24, 26; 9:10; 10:4). "Fire" is a metaphor for the divine nature explicated by the title "zealous El" (4:24), and Israel's survival of the immediate encounter with these divine, fiery words is presented as a miracle (4:33; 5:24–26), an existential encounter never to be forgotten (4:10–14). Moses quotes the Ten Words at Moab, which are explicitly marked by the addition of the interrupting phrase "as Yhwh your God commanded you" (5:12, 16; cf. v.15). The direct address "you" identifies this phrase as the voice of Moses (Greenstein 2011, 2; Braulik 2008, 174). Within the framework of the Pentateuch, these formulations are most naturally seen as references to the first proclamation of the Decalogue at Sinai in Exodus 20 (Lohfink 1990, 206–208; Artus 2018, 285; on comparable references, see Skweres 1979) and not to the following laws of Deuteronomy (as proposed by Braulik 2008, 174–182).

The Decalogue is thus pronounced by the double authority of the quoted divine command and the quoting voice of Moses, partaking in the literary technique of layering voices to construct authority typical of Deuteronomy (Polzin 1980, 25–72; 1981). Similarly, the Decalogue is a product of both divine and Mosaic writing. It was written, and rewritten, in stone by God himself at Horeb (5:22; 9:10; 10:2, 4; cf. Sonnet 1997, 42–51, 59–71). In addition, it is part of the book of the Torah written down by Moses (31:9). As the tablets of stone are enshrined in the wooden ark (10:1–5), they are also embedded within the Torah scroll written by Moses. As this book of the Torah is shown to readers in the hands of future Levitical priests and the eventually the chosen king of the land (17:18f.), the Decalogue partakes in Deuteronomy's construction of a textual *mise en abyme* in a most complex way (cf. Sonnet 1997, 78–80).

The Decalogue's presentation as a text both proclaimed and quoted, both written and rewritten repeatedly, within the narrated world of Deuteronomy, relates to a hermeneutical conundrum: the tension between the text's canonical form, which consists precisely in "these words" to which God did "not add" anything (5:22; cf. the canon formula Deut. 4:2; 13:1; Levinson 1997, 152), and the evident differences between Exodus 20 and Deuteronomy 5. This tension makes the Ten Words a paradigmatic case of legal development in the course of a tradition. This tension, deliberately inscribed in the redacted forms of the Pentateuch, is mirrored in the pluriformity of the Decalogue's textual tradition (see esp. Himbaza 2004) and brought to a head by the additions to both Decalogues in the Samaritan Pentateuch (Markl 2020a, 451f.).

Imagined as written into tablets of stone "by the finger of God" (9:10), the Decalogue has a monumental character in its narrated world. Its monumentality, however, goes beyond its imagined materiality. In a promising venture of recent Decalogue research, Timothy Hogue (2019) has explored this feature of the Sinai Decalogue. Most importantly, he notes that the "I am" formula that introduces the Decalogue is a typical opening of Northwest Semitic monumental inscriptions: Zakkur, Mesha, and several other kings introduce themselves in this style (86–89). Yhwh thus rhetorically takes the place of a king in the Decalogue, which is comparable to "ancient Near Eastern royal textual monumentality" that "centred on affording an imagined encounter with the king and his ideology for the purpose of molding the monument's users into ideal subjects" (84).

While such exploration of the Decalogue's textual monumentality is illuminating, its imagined materiality creates a paradox. Although the erection of stele and textual monuments is found in the context of covenant ceremonies (Exod. 24:4; Deut. 27:1–8; cf. McCarthy 1978, 194–199), the Decalogue tablets were never supposed to be erected as monuments, or exposed to the sight of any readers (Sonnet 2002, 515). They are not even involved in a foundational reading ritual. To the contrary, as soon as Moses receives the tablets, he is supposed to put them in the ark prepared for this purpose (Deut. 10:1–5). Although monumental inscriptions are essentially a "word bound to a place" (cf. Assmann 1993, 240), the Decalogue is meant to be transported. While landscape monuments are supposed to be seen, since an "object becomes monumental through its interaction with its socio-spatial context" (Cleath 2021, 331f.), the Decalogue tablets are hidden away in the ark right from the beginning. In this sense, it is difficult to compare the Decalogue tablets with a stele such as Codex Hammurabi (as suggested in Schniedewind 2019, 157). Although it is significant that the tablets of stone are created after God's victory over Egypt "at a conspicuous landmark—Mount Sinai" (Hogue 2019, 96), they were not, in difference to their royal counterparts, supposed to be erected at this landmark. Contrastingly, Sinaitic masonry was to accompany the people on their journey to the promised land.

Imagined as a hidden and traveling monument, the Decalogue may be compared with Esarhaddon's Succession Treaty (EST). These treaty tablets have monumental features but were produced to be transported to regional capitals and exposed in sanctuaries (Harrison/Osborne 2012). In contrast to the Decalogue tablets, which were imagined as a unique divine master copy, the copies of EST were products of textual mass production, distributed across the Assyrian empire (Lauinger 2015). The most important point of comparison with the Decalogue tablets may be that the EST is conceived as a sacred textual monument to be held within the sacred space of the sanctuary, entailing a claim to political loyalty. It is interesting to compare the Decalogue tablets with other ancient Near Eastern texts such as the "tablets of destinies" (Schniedewind 2004, 24, 129), foundation deposits placed in protecting containers (Sonnet 2002, 514f.), or the Akkadian expression *ṭuppu dannatu*, "fixed/valid document," with its legal implications (Dohmen 1987, 135–136; Otto 2012, 754; Gertz 2016, 189). The wider one casts the net of comparison, however, the more the Decalogue tablets appear to be a text sui generis.

The tablets of the Ten Words are a transportable and hidden monument, destined to be carried by the Levites (Deut. 10:8; 31:9, 25), and finally to arrive in the Holy of Holies in Jerusalem's temple (1 Kgs. 8:9). While the ark and the tablets disappeared from historical reality (Jer. 3:16), they never disappeared from narrative imagination (Day 2005). The Decalogue's hiddenness in the ark and in the temple's inner sanctum may be a metaphor for the interiorization of "these words" upon the hearts of the Israelites (Deut. 6:6). The tablets' disappearance in sacred darkness, however, rendered them even more attractive for re-imagined externalization: they became the symbolic epitome of the divine will in Christianity and a symbol of Judaism (Sarfatti 1990). The Decalogue tablets may thus be seen as a paradigmatic "portable monument" (Rigney 2004, esp. 383) in the center of migratory texts that became pivotal to Jewish and Christian identities (cf. Markl 2021c).

The Ten Commandments and the "Statutes and Ordinances" (Deut 6–11; 12–26)

Deuteronomy 5 presents, as Norbert Lohfink aptly put it, "*the* foundational narrative of Deuteronomy" that defines the people of Israel as constituted by the events at Horeb (Lohfink 2003, 264). The chapter is placed at a structural turning point of the book, at the beginning of Moses's second and central discourse (Deuteronomy 5–26). After God had revealed the "ten words" at Horeb, the people feared for their lives and requested Moses's mediation (5:22–27). God approved of the request and sent the people to their tents (v.28f.), saying to Moses "stand here by me, and I will tell you all the commandments, the statutes and the ordinances, that you shall teach them, so that they may do them in the land that I am giving them to possess" (v.31). This act of teaching is exactly what Moses fulfills in Deuteronomy 6–26, as the two introductions in 6:1 and 12:1 show: "And this is the commandment, the statutes and the ordinances that Yhwh your God charged me to teach you to observe in the land that you are about to cross into and occupy" (6:1). This first introduction is followed by a second, slightly shorter one in 12:1: "These are the statutes and ordinances that you must observe in the land." The "statutes and ordinances" seem to signify the law collection in Deuteronomy 12–25/26, while "the commandment," the only additional element in 6:1, may refer to the principal commandment of the Decalogue, epitomized in the prohibition of other gods, a topic that is recurring in Deuteronomy 6–11, as Norbert Lohfink has shown in his monograph *Das Hauptgebot* (1963).

The relationship between the Decalogue and the laws was already addressed by Philo of Alexandria, who viewed the Ten Commandments as "headings" (κηφάλαια) or "principles" (ἀρχαί) of the other laws (de Vos 2020, 198). While Philo and a stream of traditional interpretation thought of this connection in thematic terms (on Luther, e.g., see Kreuzer 2000), several modern scholars tried to see the Decalogue as the structuring principle of the laws of Deuteronomy. This view was exposed by Friedrich Wilhelm Schultz (1859) in his commentary on Deuteronomy, in an article by Stephen A. Kaufman (1979) and, most elaborately, in monographs by Georg Braulik (1991) and Dennis T. Olson (1994). Schultz considered the system a work of Moses, who made the Decalogue a key for the law and the laws an interpretation of the Decalogue (1859, i). His theory differed from its successors especially in that it included the exhortations of Deuteronomy 6–11 on the prohibition of other gods, while Kaufman and his followers concentrated on the laws in Deuteronomy 12–25/26. Taking up Schultz's proposal after more than a century, Kaufman argued against what had become the predominant view, namely, that the laws of Deuteronomy lacked any order and considered their Decalogic structure "a unified masterpiece of jurisprudential literature created by a single author" (147). Braulik (1991, 117), in contrast, attributed this structure to a "Decalogue redaction" of the law collection. Schultz's theory was further refined by Kaufman, the latter's proposal, for its part, by Braulik. Olson basically presented a compromise between Kaufman and Braulik. Table 4.1 gives an overview of how these four authors attributed diverse sections of Moses's second discourse to single commandments of the Decalogue (all verse indications follow standard editions of the Hebrew Bible rather than English translations).

Some of the connections between the Ten Commandments and the Deuteronomic laws are quite obvious, especially when they are based on keywords such as in the case of venerating "other gods" (Deut. 5:7; 13:1–18), murder (רצח, Deut. 5:17; 19:3, 4, 6) or stealing (גנב, 5:19; 24:7). Thematically, the Sabbath commandment relates to sacred times discussed in Deuteronomy 15:1–16:17, supported by the motif of the "seventh" day or year (5:14; 15:12; 16:8). The commandment to honor one's parents is seen in thematic relationship to the offices regulated in 16:18–18:22 via the theme of authority. But there are other cases in which more complex hermeneutical operations are required to establish some connection

Table 4.1. Correlations between the Decalogue and the Laws of Deuteronomy

	Schultz 1859	Kaufman 1979	Braulik 1991	Olson 1994
5:6–10 (other gods)	6:1–11:32	12:1–28	12:2–13:19	12:2–13:19
5:11 (name)	12:1–14:29	13:1–14:27	14:1–21	14:1–21
5:12–15 (Shabbat)	15:1–16:17	14:28–16:17	14:22–16:17	14:22–16:17
5:16 (parents)	16:18–18:22	16:18–18:22	16:18–18:22	16:18–18:22
5:17 (murder)	19:1–21:9	19:1–22:8	19:1–21:23	19:1–22:8
5:18 (adultery)	21:10–21	22:9–23:19	22:13–23:15	22:9–23:19
5:19 (stealing)	22:1–29	23:20–24:7	23:16–24:7	23:20–24:7
5:20 (false witness)	23:1–25:19	24:8–25:4	24:8–25:4	24:8–25:4
5:21a (coveting 1)		25:5–16	25:5–12	25:5–12
5:21b (coveting 2)			25:13–16	25:13–26:15

between the Decalogue and the law collection, such as the prohibition of abusing the divine name and the dietary laws in 14:1–21. Moreover, the correspondences between the "purgation laws" (בערת-laws) and the Ten Commandments (Lohfink 2003, 280–281) do not correspond with the Decalogic structure of the law collection. The difficulty that the laws of Deuteronomy 19–25 contain a great variety of matters in a complex order that can hardly be pressed into the scheme of the Decalogue's commandments led Eckart Otto to propose a simplified structural analogy (cf. Otto 2005, 101), as shown in Table 4.2.

Yet another variant of the theory of the Decalogue orientation of the laws of Deuteronomy was proposed by Karin Finsterbusch (2011). Others have rejected outright the theory of any Decalogic arrangement of the laws (e.g., Rofé 2002 [1988], 59, n.21, contra Kaufman; Crüsemann 1996 [1992], 204–207, and Rüterswörden 2005, contra Braulik). Whether or not one finds a strict structural analogy between the Decalogue and the laws of Deuteronomy convincing is not necessarily decisive for the interpretation of either text. Undeniably, the Decalogue and the laws of Deuteronomy display a comparable dynamics from religious to social issues. This thematic dynamic includes, however, as Schultz had rightly observed, Moses's teachings on the principal commandment in Deuteronomy 6–11. The Decalogue thus provides an epitomized synthesis of the flow of normative thought that is elaborately unfolded in Deuteronomy 6–26. The overall layout of Moses's Second Discourse in Deuteronomy 5–26 invites reflection on the hermeneutical relationship between the Ten Commandments and the following "statutes and ordinances," but such reflection might be better advised to focus on thematic dynamics rather than strictly defined structural blocks.

An important difference between the Decalogue and the "statutes and ordinances" concerns their relationship to the Promised Land. While the latter are to be implemented "in the land" (12:1; Lohfink 1991), the Decalogue is free of any such restriction. The Ten Commandments situate themselves after the liberation from Egypt (5:6) and the commandment to honor one's parents involves the prospect of long life in the land (5:16). Conversely, however, this hope may entail an indirect etiology of the eventual loss of the land. An exilic setting, moreover, elucidates the Decalogue's character as a constitutional document of divine rather than royal normativity, a "countermodel" to ancient Near Eastern royal legislation (Otto 2008, 535–537). The Ten Words are divine norms that are supposed to govern Israel's life—in the world of the Pentateuch's narrative—already before the entry into the land, and also in situations of exile and diaspora. The specific importance of the Decalogue for exile is also highlighted at the end of Moses' first discourse in Deuteronomy 4:1–40.

Table 4.2. Eckart Otto's correlations between the Decalogue and the Laws of Deuteronomy

5:6–10 (other gods)	12:1–31
5:11 (name)	13:1–15:23
5:12–15 (Shabbat)	16:1–17:1
5:16 (parents)	17:2–18:22
5:17–21 (social laws)	19:1–25:16

The Subversion of the Decalogue to Monotheism (Deut 4)

As the preceding section has shown, the exposition of the Decalogue in Deuteronomy 5 lays out the setting for the Second Discourse of Moses in Deuteronomy 5–26. At a later, probably one of the latest, redactional stages of the composition of Deuteronomy, the Decalogue received another prominent role in the book, at the rhetorical culmination of Moses's First Discourse (1:6–4:40) in 4:1–40. Deuteronomy 1:6–3:29 prepares the ground by recapitulating the story of Israel's journey from Horeb to Moab. Moses thereby explains that since the generation of the Horeb revelation was condemned to die in the wilderness because of their disobedience in Qadesh-Barnea, he is now addressing the next generation who are supposed to "listen" (4:1). By the following culmination of the discourse (4:1–40), Moses constitutes Israel's general assembly in preparation for the making of the covenant (Braulik/Lohfink 2022, 195) that is realized in the next major discourses in Deuteronomy 5–30 (Markl 2012, 116–118). The Decalogue features in three prominent ways in 4:1–40. First, Moses reminds Israel of the foundational assembly at Horeb where Yhwh revealed the Ten Words and appointed Moses as teacher for Israel (4:9–14). Second, the scene of the Horeb theophany without any "form" (תמונה, v.12) provides the starting point for an elaborate exposition of the prohibition of idolatry (4:15–31; Holter 2003). Third, the revelation at Horeb, where Israel was granted the dignity to survive the direct encounter with the divine voice (4:33, 36; cf. 5:23–26), is one of the decisive motivations for Israel to now "understand" (ידע) that Yhwh "is the God" and that "there is no other" (אין עוד; 4:35, 39).

This ultimate claim of the nonexistence of other gods can be called, notwithstanding the modern origin of the term, a "monotheistic" profession (with Schaper 2019, 38–51, in response to MacDonald 2003). While the Decalogue's insistence on monolatry in the phrase "there shall be no other gods for you against my face" (5:7) and the prohibition of images (5:8) seems to presuppose that other gods *do* exist, Deuteronomy 4:32–39 aims at clarifying once and for all that Yhwh is the only God, and nothing else deserves this attribution. This theological climax is prepared in two ways. First, the elaborate unfolding of the prohibition of representing anything as divine (4:15–18) is followed by the prohibition of recognizing even the celestial bodies as divine, even though they are universally seen as such by "all the peoples" (4:19). This dethronement of prime Mesopotamian deities such as Shamash, Sîn, and Ishtar prepares the ground for the ultimate profession of monotheism. Second, in a sort of prophetic excursion to the future, Moses deeply connects the issue of idolatry with Israel's future exile (4:25–31). Idolatry is both the reason for exile (4:25–27) and the realm where the worship of such lifeless idols is painfully experienced (4:28), where Israel will be converted (שוב) to seek and find Yhwh (4:29–31). It is against this background of "spiritual conversion" that Israel is supposed to reflect and arrive at the theological insight of monotheism (4:32–39). The development of the Mosaic discourse thus implies an etiology of the emergence of monotheism as grounded in the cultural trauma of exile (Markl 2020b, 15–19). The late exilic or postexilic date of these ideas is confirmed by its close parallels in Deutero-Isaiah, where the divine voice proclaims to the Persian King Cyrus that "I am Yhwh, and there is no other [אין עוד]! Besides me, there is no god!" (Isa. 45:5).

The subversive monotheistic reinterpretation of the Decalogue's First Commandment in Deuteronomy 4 means a theological revolution that provides a new hermeneutical lens for reading the rest of the book of Deuteronomy in its redacted form (Braulik 1994, 115). The opening discourse of Deuteronomy 4 thus prepares readers to understand texts such as the First Commandment and the Shema Yisrael (Deut. 6:4) in a monotheistic sense, a reading that became a defining trait of emerging Judaism (Eshel, Eshel, and Lange 2010, 44–54). Moreover, the monotheism proclaimed in Deuteronomy 4 is not only of theological importance, it also has sincere implications for the hermeneutics of divine law. Since Yhwh is the only God, his norms cannot be relativized by any divine opponent, which means an ultimate and unsurpassable authorization of divine law (Markl 2021b). It is "*his* statutes and *his* commandments" (4:40), the commandments of the only God (4:39) that Moses claims to be conveying in Deuteronomy.

The Tablets Broken and Renewed: Symbolism in Historiography

The breaking of the Decalogue's prohibition that "you shall not make for yourself an idol in the form of anything" (5:8: לא תעשה לך פסל כל תמונה) is anticipated by Moses's prophetic statement: "you will make an idol in the form of anything" (4:24: ועשיתם פסל תמונה כל). This will lead to Israel's dispersion "among the peoples" (4:27). Thus the late redaction of the book of Deuteronomy makes it clear that the Decalogue is deeply related to the wide scope of Deuteronomistic historiography. Indeed, the "Decalogue's prohibition of other gods and images" is the first criterion for the Deuteronomists' "account of Israel's subsequent history" (Albertz 2003, 288). Moreover, the prominence of the motif of divine persecution of guilt "to the third and the fourth generation" may well have gained prominence in etiologies of the destruction of Jerusalem and the duration of the Babylonian Exile (Markl 2020c). The prominence of the issue of the "other gods" (אלהים אחרים) is visible within Deuteronomy, as it is unfolded in Moses's exhortations (6:14; 7:4; 8:19; 11:16, 28), in the law collection (13:3, 7, 14; 18:20), in the curses (28:14, 36, 64), and the Moab Covenant discourse (29:25; 30:17; significantly, Deuteronomy 4 does not use this expression: Braulik 1994, 116f.) The issue culminates, however, when Yhwh himself announces that "I will surely hide my face on account of all the evil they have done by turning to other gods" (31:18). Yhwh's certain knowledge of Israel's breaking of the covenant in the future is the reason why Moses is supposed to teach the Song so that it will bear witness against Israel in the future (31:20–21).

In this wider horizon of the principal commandment's prime importance as an anticipated etiology of future catastrophes (to be unfolded in narrative, especially, in 2 Kgs. 17–25), the symbolic value of the breaking and renewal of the tablets deserves consideration. The paradigmatic character of the Golden Calf in relation to Israel's future idolatry is made clear via the motifs of the people's "stiff neck" (9:6; 31:27) and the phrase "you have been rebellious against Yhwh" (9:7; 31:27; Zipor 1996; Sonnet 1997, 168). The Golden Calf serves as a symbolic counterpart to the tablets because Israel's sin provokes the destruction of both the tablets (9:17) and the calf (v.21). The tablets' breaking and renewal are symbolic of the breaking and restoration of the covenant (Weinfeld 1990, 28–29; Gertz 2016, 196; Stoppel 2018, 403f.). Since the tablets, destined to arrive in the Holy of Holies (1 Kgs. 8:1–9), are intimately related to Jerusalem's temple, their breaking may also metaphorically anticipate the temple's destruction (Otto 2016, 164f.). Moreover, their renewal may hint at its restoration. Just as this set of tablets is supposed to be "like the first" (כראשנים; Deut. 10:1, 3), Judah will be, according to Jeremiah, rebuilt, and offerings brought to the temple "like at first" (כבראשנה; Jer. 33:7, 11; cf. Weyringer 2021, 218). While the Golden Calf and its destruction foreshadows Jeroboam's golden calves and the ultimate demise of the cult in the North (1 Kgs. 12–2 Kgs. 17), the destruction and renewal of the tablets may foreshadow the temporary annihilation but eventual rebirth of worship in Jerusalem.

In the long history of its reception, the Decalogue became an icon of ethical discourse, often isolated from its literary contexts (Markl 2021a). Within Deuteronomy, in contrast, the Decalogue is tightly interwoven with the project of Deuteronomy in a wider literary landscape. At the outset of divine revelation of the commandments at Mount Horeb, the Decalogue plays a pivotal role in the hermeneutics of divine law in the Pentateuch as a whole. The late redactional addition of Deuteronomy 4:1–40 subversively converted the Decalogue's outlook to monotheism. The Ten Words, themselves revealed in the liminal space of Horeb, serve Deuteronomistic historiography in explaining disaster. While Moses offers some daring glimpses of hope into a postexilic future (Deut. 4:31; 30:1–10), the Decalogue anticipates a future far beyond it (5:9–10). Although Jerusalem's desolation may last for "three and four generations," the divine voice from Horeb promises prosperity—after the Exile—"to the thousandth generation of those who love me and keep my commandments."

Bibliography

Albertz, Rainer. *Israel in Exile: The History and Literature of the Sixth Century B.C.E.* Trans. David Green. StBibLit 3. Atlanta: SBL, 2003.

Alt, Albrecht. "The Origins of Israelite Law." In *Essays on Old Testament History and Religion*, translated by R. A. Wilson, pp. 101–117. Garden City: Doubleday, 1967.

Artus, Olivier. "Unity and Function of Deuteronomy 5:6-21." *Indian Theological Studies* 55 (2018): 279–290.

Assmann, Jan. "Altorientalische Fluchinschriften und das Problem performativer Schriftlichkeit." In *Schrift*, edited by Hans Ulrich Gumbrecht and K. Ludwig Pfeiffer, pp. 233–255. Materialität der Zeichen A 12. Munich: Fink, 1993.

Blum, Erhard. "The Decalogue and the Composition History of the Pentateuch." In *The Pentateuch: International Perspectives on Current Research*, edited by T. B. Dozeman, K. Schmid, and B. J. Schwartz, pp. 289–301. Tübingen: Mohr Siebeck, 2011.

Braulik, Georg. "Der unterbrochene Dekalog. Zu Deuteronomium 5,12 und 16 und ihrer Bedeutung für den deuteronomistischen Gesetzeskodex." *ZAW* 120 (2008): 169–183.

Braulik, Georg. "Deuteronomy and the Birth of Monotheism." In *The Theology of Deuteronomy*, translated by Ulrika Lindblad, pp. 99–130. BIBAL Collected Essays 2. North Richland Hills: Bibal Press, 1994.

Braulik, Georg. *Die deuteronomischen Gesetze und der Dekalog: Studien zum Aufbau von Deuteronomium 12–26*. SBS 145. Stuttgart: Katholisches Bibelwerk, 1991.

Braulik, Georg, and Norbert Lohfink. *Die Rhetorik der Moserede in Deuteronomium 1–4*. ÖBS 55. Frankfurt: Peter Lang, 2022.

Cleath, Lisa J. "Divine Enthronement in a Conquered Land: Constructing a Landscape Monument in Josh 8:30–35." *HeBAI* 10 (2021): 331–348.

Coogan, Michael D. *The Ten Commandments: A Short History of an Ancient Text*. New Haven: Yale University Press, 2014.

Crüsemann, Frank. *The Torah: Theology and Social History of Old Testament Law*. Trans. A. W. Mahnke. Edinburgh: T&T, 1996.

Day, John. "Whatever Happened to the Ark of the Covenant?" In *Temple and Worship in Biblical Israel*, edited by John Day, pp. 250–270. LHB 422. London: T & T Clark, 2005.

Dershowitz, Idan. *The Valediction of Moses: A Proto-Biblical Book*. FAT 145. Tübingen: Mohr Siebeck, 2021.

Dohmen, Christoph. *Das Bilderverbot. Seine Entstehung und seine Entwicklung im Alten Testament*. BBB 62. Frankfurt am Main: Athenäum, 1987.

Ewald, Heinrich. *Geschichte des Volkes Israel bis Christus*. Zweiter Band. Göttingen: Dieterich, 1845.

Eshel, Esther, Hanan Eshel, and Armin Lange. "'Hear, O Israel' in Gold: An Ancient Amulet from Halbturn in Austria." *Journal of Ancient Judaism* 1 (2010): 43–64.

Finsterbusch, Karin. "Die Dekalog-Ausrichtung des deuteronomischen Gesetzes. Ein neuer Ansatz." In *Deuteronomium–Tora für eine neue Generation*, edited by G. Fischer, D. Markl, and S. Paganini, pp. 123–146. BZAR 17. Wiesbaden: Harrassowitz, 2011.

Gertz, Jan Christian. "Mose zerbricht die Tafeln des Bundes am Sinai. Literarhistorisch ausgereizt, aber praxeologisch unterschätzt?" *Metatexte: Erzählungen von schrifttragenden Artefakten in der alttestamentlichen und mittelalterlichen Literatur*, edited by Friedrich-Emanuel Focken and Michael R. Ott, pp. 178–201. Materiale Textkulturen 15. Berlin: de Gruyter, 2016.

Graupner, Axel. "Zum Verhältnis der beiden Dekalogfassungen Ex 20 und Dtn 5. Ein Gespräch mit Frank-Lothar Hossfeld." *ZAW* 99 (2001): 308–329.

Hendel, Ronald S., and Matthieu Richelle. "The Shapira Scrolls: The Case for Forgery." *BAR* 47, no. 4 (2021): 39–46.

Greenstein, Edward L. "The Rhetoric of the Ten Commandments." In *The Decalogue in Jewish and Christian Tradition*, edited by Y. Hoffman and H. Graf Reventlow, pp. 1–12. LHB OTS 509. New York: T&T Clark, 2011.

Harrison, Timothy P., and James F. Osborne. "Building XVI and the Neo-Assyrian Sacred Precinct at Tell Tayinat." *Journal of Cuneiform Studies* 64 (2012): 125–143.

Hjelde, Sigurd. *Sigmund Mowinckel und seine Zeit: Leben und Werk eines norwegischen Alttestamentlers*. FAT 50. Tübingen: Mohr Siebeck, 2006.

Himbaza, Innocent. *Le Décalogue et l'histoire du texte: Etudes des formes textuelles du Décalogue et leurs implications dans l'histoire du texte de l'Ancien Testament*. OBO 207. Fribourg: Academic Press, 2004.

Hogue, Timothy. "The Monumentality of the Sinaitic Decalogue: Reading Exodus 20 in Light of Northwest Semitic Monument-Making Practices." *JBL* 138 (2019): 79–99.

Holter, Knut. *Deuteronomy 4 and the Second Commandment*. StBL 60. New York: Peter Lang, 2003.

Hossfeld, Frank-Lothar. *Der Dekalog: Seine späten Fassungen, die originale Komposition und seine Vorstufen*. OBO 45. Freiburg: Universitätsverlag, 1982.

Hossfeld, Frank-Lothar. "Der Stand der Dekalogforschung." In *Recht und Ethik im Alten Testament: Beiträge des Symposiums „Das Alte Testament und die Kultur der Moderne" anlässlich des 100. Geburtstags Gerhard von Rads (1901–1971) Heidelberg, 18.–21. Oktober 2001*, edited by B. M. Levinson and E. Otto, pp. 57–65. ATM 13. Münster: Lit-Verlag, 2004.

Hossfeld, Frank-Lothar. "Zum synoptischen Vergleich der Dekalogfassungen. Eine Fortführung des begonnenen Gesprächs." In *Vom Sinai zum Horeb: Stationen alttestamentlicher Glaubensgeschichte*, edited by Frank-Lothar Hossfeld, pp. 73–117. Festschrift E. Zenger. Würzburg: Echter, 1989.

Kaufman, Stephen A. "The Structure of the Deuteronomic Law." *Maarav* 1, no. 2 (1979): 105–158.

Köhler, Ludwig. "Der Dekalog." *Theologische Rundschau* 1 (1929): 161–184.

Kreuzer, Siegfried. "Summa totius legis et sapientiae populi Israel. . . . Die Deuteronomium-Vorlesung Luthers in ihrer Bedeutung für sein Dekalogverständnis und seine Katechismen." *KuD* 46 (2000): 302–317.

Lauinger, Jacob. "Neo-Assyrian Scribes, 'Esarhaddon's Succession Treaty,' and the Dynamics of Textual Mass Production." In *Texts and Contexts: The Circulation and Transmission of Cuneiform Texts in Social Space*, edited by P. Delnero and J. Lauinger, pp. 285–314. Berlin: de Gruyter, 2015.

Levinson, Bernard M. *Deuteronomy and the Hermeneutics of Legal Innovation*. New York: Oxford University Press, 1997.

Lohfink, Norbert. *Das Hauptgebot: Eine Untersuchung literarischer Einleitungsfragen zu Dtn 5–11*. AnBib 20. Rome: Pontifical Biblical Institute, 1963.

Lohfink, Norbert. "Dtn 12,1 und Gen 15,18: Das dem Samen Abrahams geschenkte Land als der Geltungsbereich der deuteronomischen Gesetze." In *Studien zum Deuteronomium und zur deuteronomistischen Literatur II*, pp. 257–285. SBAB 12. Stuttgart: Katholisches Bibelwerk, 1991.

Lohfink, Norbert. "Reading Deuteronomy 5 as Narrative." In *A God So Near: Essays on Old Testament Theology in Honor of Patrick D. Miller*, edited by B. A. Strawn and N. R. Bowen, pp. 261–281. Winona Lake: Eisenbrauns, 2003.

Lohfink, Norbert. "Zur Dekalogfassung von Dt 5." In *Studien zum Deuteronomium und zur deuteronomistischen Literatur I*, pp. 193–209. SBAB 8. Stuttgart: Katholisches Bibelwerk, 1990.

MacDonald, Nathan. *Deuteronomy and the Meaning of "Monotheism."* FAT II, 1. Tübingen: Mohr Siebeck, 2003.

Markl, Dominik. "The Ambivalence of Authority in Deuteronomy: Reaction, Revision, Rewriting, Reception." *Cristianesimo nella storia* 41 (2020a): 427–461.

Markl, Dominik. "The Babylonian Exile as the Birth Trauma of Monotheism." *Biblica* 101 (2020b): 1–25.

Markl, Dominik. "The Decalogue: An Icon of Ethical Discourse." In *Cambridge Companion to the Hebrew Bible and Ethics*, edited by Carly Crouch, pp. 9–22. Cambridge: Cambridge University Press, 2021a.

Markl, Dominik. *Der Dekalog als Verfassung des Gottesvolkes: Die Brennpunkte einer Rechtshermeneutik des Pentateuch in Exodus 19–24 und Deuteronomium 5*. HBS 49. Freiburg im Breisgau: Herder, 2007.

Markl, Dominik. "Divine Law and the Emergence of Monotheism in Deuteronomy." In *Israel and the Cosmological Empires of the Ancient Orient. Symbols of Order in Eric Voegelin's Order and History, Vol. 1*, edited by I. Carbajosa and N. Scotti Muth, pp. 193–222. Eric Voegelin Studies. Supplements 1. Leiden: Brill: Fink, 2021b.

Markl, Dominik. *Gottes Volk im Deuteronomium*. BZAR 18. Wiesbaden: Harrassowitz, 2012.

Markl, Dominik. "Media, Migration, and the Emergence of Scriptural Authority." *Zeitschrift für Theologie und Philosophie* 143 (2021c): 261–283.

Markl, Dominik. "Die Soziologie des babylonischen Exils und die göttliche Vergeltung 'bis zur dritten und vierten Generation.'" *ThPh* 95 (2020c): 481–507.

Markl, Dominik. "The Ten Words Revealed and Revised: The Origins of Law and Legal Hermeneutics in the Pentateuch." In *The Decalogue and Its Cultural Influence*, edited by Dominik Markl, pp. 13–27. HBM 58. Sheffield: Phoenix Press, 2013.

Matthes, J. C. "Der Dekalog." *ZAW* 24 (1904): 17–41.

McCarthy, Dennis J. *Treaty and Covenant: Study in Form in the Ancient Oriental Documents and in the Old Testament*. AnBib 21a. Rome: Biblical Institute Press, 1978.

Mochizuki, Mia M. "At Home with the Ten Commandments: Domestic Text Paintings in 17th Century Amsterdam." In *In His Milieu: Essays on Netherlandish Art in Memory of John Michael Montias*, edited by A. Golahny, M. M. Mochizuki and L. Vergara, pp. 287–300. Amsterdam: Amsterdam University Press, 2006.

Mowinckel, Sigmund. *Le Décalogue*. EHPhR 16. Paris: Alcan, 1927.

Mowinckel, Sigmund. "Zur Geschichte der Dekaloge." *ZAW* 55 (1937): 218–235.

Olson, Dennis T. *Deuteronomy and the Death of Moses: A Theological Reading*. Overtures to Biblical Theology. Minneapolis, MN: Fortress, 1994.

Oswald, Wolfgang. "Die politische Funktion des Dekalogs." In *Eigensinn und Entstehung der Hebräischen Bibel*, edited by Joachim J. Krause, Wolfgang Oswald, and Kristin Weingart, pp. 111–127. FAT 136. Tübingen: Mohr Siebeck, 2020.

Otto, Eckart. "Alte und Neue Perspektiven in der Dekalogforschung." In *Kontinuum und Proprium: Studien zur Sozial- und Rechtsgeschichte des Alten Orients und des Alten Testaments*, pp. 285–292. Orientalia Biblica et Christiana 8. Wiesbaden: Harrassowitz, 1996.

Otto, Eckart. "Born out of Ruins. The Catastrophe of Jerusalem as Accoucher of the Pentateuch in the Book of Deuteronomy." In *The Fall of Jerusalem and the Rise of the Torah*, edited by P. Dubovský, D. Markl, and J.-P. Sonnet, pp. 155–168. FAT 107. Tübingen: Mohr Siebeck, 2016.

Otto, Eckart. "Der Dekalog in den deuteronomistischen Redaktionen des Deuteronomiums." In *Die Zehn Worte: Der Dekalog als Testfall der Pentateuchkritik*, edited by C. Frevel et al., pp. 95–108. QD 212. Freiburg im Breisgau: Herder, 2005.

Otto, Eckart. "Der Dekalog im Horizont des Alten Orients." In *Altorientalische und biblische Rechtsgeschichte: Gesammelte Studien*, pp. 531–538. BZAR 8. Wiesbaden: Harrassowitz, 2008.

Otto, Eckart. *Deuteronomium 4,44–11,32*. HThKAT. Freiburg im Breisgau: Herder 2012.

Peters, J. P. "The Ten Words." *JBL* 6 (1886): 140–144.

Polzin, Robert. *Moses and the Deuteronomist: A Literary Study of the Deuteronomic History. Part One: Deuteronomy, Joshua, Judges*. New York: Seabury, 1980.

Polzin, Robert. "Reporting Speech in the Book of Deuteronomy: Toward a Compositional Analysis of the Deuteronomic History." In *Traditions in Transformation: Turning Points in Biblical Faith*, edited by B. Halpern and J. D. Levenson, pp. 193–211. FS F. M. Cross. Winona Lake: Eisenbrauns, 1981.

Rigney, Ann. "Portable Monuments: Literature, Cultural Memory, and the Case of Jeanie Deans." *Poetics Today* 25 (2004): 361–396.

Rofé, Alexander. "The Arrangement of the Laws in Deuteronomy." In *Deuteronomy: Issues and Interpretation*, pp. 55–77. London: T&T Clark, 2002.

Rom-Shiloni, Dalit. "The Decalogue." In *The Oxford Handbook of Biblical Law*, edited by Pamela Barmash, pp. 135–155. New York: Oxford University Press, 2019.

Römer, Thomas. "Les deux décalogues et la Loi de Moïse." In *Mémoires d'Écriture. Hommage à Pierre Gilbert*, edited by Philippe Abadie, pp. 47–67. Brussels: Lessius, 2006.

Rütersworden, Udo. "Die Dekalogstruktur des Deuteronomiums—Fragen an eine alte Annahme." In *Die Zehn Worte: Der Dekalog als Testfall der Pentateuchkritik*. Edited by C. Frevel et al., pp. 109–121. QD 212. Freiburg im Breisgau: Herder, 2005.

Sarfatti, Gad B. "The Tablets of the Law as a Symbol of Judaism." In *The Ten Commandments in History and Tradition*, edited by B.-Z. Segal and G. Levi, pp. 383–418. Publications of the Perry Foundation for Biblical Research. Jerusalem: Magnes, 1990.

Schaper, Joachim. *Media and Monotheism: Presence, Representation, and Abstraction in Ancient Judah*. ORA 33. Tübingen: Mohr Siebeck, 2019.

Schniedewind, William M. *How the Bible Became a Book: The Textualization of Ancient Israel*. Cambridge: Cambridge University Press, 2004.

Schniedewind, William M. *The Finger of the Scribe: How Scribes Learned to Write the Bible*. New York: Oxford University Press, 2019.

Schultz, Friedrich Wilhelm. *Das Deuteronomium*. Berlin: Schlawitz, 1859.

Skweres, Dieter Eduard. *Die Rückverweise im Buch Deuteronomium*. AnBib 79. Rome: Biblical Institute Press, 1979.

Sonnet, Jean-Pierre. *The Book within the Book: Writing in Deuteronomy*. Biblical Interpretation Series 14. Leiden: Brill, 1997.

Sonnet, Jean-Pierre. "'Lorsque Moïse eut achevé d'écrire' (Dt 31,24): Une 'théorie narrative' de l'écriture dans le Pentateuque." *RSR* 90 (2002): 509–524.

Stamm, Johann Jakob. "Dreisig Jahre Dekalogforschung." *Theologische Rundschau* 27 (1961): 189–239, 281–305.

Stamm, Johann Jakob. *The Ten Commandments in Recent Research*. Trans. and Ed. M. E. Andrew. SBT Second Series 2. London: SCM Press, 1967.

Stoppel, Henrik. *Von Angesicht zu Angesicht: Ouvertüre am Horeb: Deuteronomium 5 und 9-10 und die Textgestalt ihrer Folie*. Abhandlungen zur Theologie des Alten und Neuen Testaments 109. Zürich: TVZ, Theologischer Verlag Zürich, 2018.

Veijola, Timo. *Das 5. Buch Mose. Deuteronomium 1:1–16, 17* (ATD 8,1), Göttingen: Vandenhoeck & Ruprecht, 2004.

Vos, Cornelis de. "Summarising the Jewish Law in Antiquity: Examples from Aristeas, Philo, and the New Testament." In *The Challenge of the Mosaic Torah in Judaism, Christianity, and Islam*, edited by Antti Laato, pp. 191–204. Studies on the Children of Abraham 7. Leiden: Brill, 2020.

Weinfeld, Moshe. *Deuteronomy 1–11*. AncB 5. New York: Doubleday, 1991.

Weinfeld, Moshe. "The Uniqueness of the Decalogue and Its Place in Jewish Tradition." In *The Ten Commandments in History and Tradition*, edited by B.-Z. Segal and G. Levi, pp. 1–44. Jerusalem: Magnes, 1991.

Wellhausen, Julius. "Die Composition des Hexateuchs." *Jahrbücher für Deutsche Theologie* 21 (1876): 531–602.

Wellhausen, Julius. *Prolegomena zur Geschichte Israels*. Berlin: Reimer, 1883.

Weyringer, Simon. *An der Schwelle zum Land der Verheißung: Rhetorik und Pragmatik in Dtn 9,1–10,11*. Beihefte zur Zeitschrift für Altorientalische und Biblische Rechtsgeschichte 26. Wiesbaden: Harrassowitz, 2021.

Zenger, Erich. "Eine Wende in der Dekalogforschung?". *Theologische Revue* 6 (1968): 189–198.

Zipor, Moshe A. "The Deuteronomic Account of the Golden Calf and its Reverberation in Other Parts of the Book of Deuteronomy." *ZAW* 108 (1996): 20–33.

CHAPTER 5

BLESSINGS AND CURSES IN DEUTERONOMY

LAURA QUICK

The law code of the book of Deuteronomy is capped with a series of blessings and curses that either promise reward or threaten harm upon the individuals subject to the Deuteronomic laws. While this might seem surprising from a theological point of view, blessings and curses were an integral part of the legal, political, and religious life of the ancient Near East. In this culture, blessings and curses were essentially instruments of social control (Andersen 1998). So, for example, in ancient Near Eastern treaty texts, blessings and curses function as divine encouragement to enforce the stipulations of the treaty. This is precisely how the blessings and curses function in the book of Deuteronomy, and as we shall go on to see, the book of Deuteronomy has significant commonalities with the ancient Near Eastern treaty genre.

Though the pronouncement of blessings and curses may be accompanied by symbolic gestures or sign acts, the thought world behind them attributes power to speech alone: blessings and curses are essentially performative utterances which are believed to have an efficacious effect (Austin 1962, 6–11). According to Philip Ravenhill, communal witnessing is essential in order to activate the power of the utterance (1976, 37). We might note the ceremonial pronouncements of blessings and curses in Deuteronomy 27, where the entire Israelite community is said to be present. Thus, efficacious utterances such as blessings and curses are constrained by societal and cultural rules in order to be effective, and by exploring these utterances, we gain access to practices of religious ritual and worship.

To "bless" someone imparts favor, whether specified or otherwise, upon the subject. The reverse of this, the curse, solicits injury of some kind. Blessings and curses are usually future oriented. They can be conditional or unconditional and accordingly, the latter work well as encouragement to keep commandments and behave in the correct way:

> If you will only obey the LORD your God, by diligently observing all his commandments that I am commanding you today, the LORD your God will set you high above all the nations of the earth; all these blessings shall come upon you. (28:1–2)[1]

> But if you will not obey the LORD your God by diligently observing all his commandments and decrees, which I am commanding you today, then all these curses shall come upon you. (28:15)

The semantic field of blessing in the Hebrew Bible is typically denoted by the verb *brk* and its derived forms. In Deuteronomy 29, the nominal plural form *běrākôt*, "blessings," are said come upon the Israelites if they keep the Deuteronomic commandments (29:2). The passive participle form, *bārûk*, "blessed," describes this status. Thus, the Israelites will be "blessed" in the city and in the field (28:3). Their offspring, produce, and cattle will be "blessed" (28:4), as will their bread (28:5). The basic items of sustenance and survival in daily life will find favor—should the Israelites be sure to keep the commandments set out in the law code of the book of Deuteronomy. Indeed, longevity of life is explicitly said to be the result of all these blessings (30:16). The concern of the blessings for the routine aspects of mundane life demonstrates the degree to which the practice of blessing and cursing was a part of everyday life.

The curses of Deuteronomy are more vivid in imagery. Indeed, cursing has a rich and varied vocabulary in the Hebrew Bible. Three primary lexemes denote the semantic field of cursing. The verb *'lh* has the meaning of "to pronounce a conditional curse" (Scharbert 1977, 261). Its derived noun *'ālâ* is used in conjunction with the technical term *běrît*, "treaty, covenant," (29:20). Thus a *běrît* refers to a bond between individuals or groups of individuals that is sanctioned and ratified by curses. Curses are thus an integral part of the covenant relationship between Israel and God which is set out in the book of Deuteronomy. The verb *qll* in the Piel and Pual stems also denotes the activity of cursing. In Deuteronomy the verb and its derived noun *qělālâ* are used to describe the activities of the seer Balaam, who had been hired to pronounce curses against the Israelites (Deut 23:4, 6; Num 22). The noun also describes the concrete manifestation of the curses brought upon the Israelites for failing to keep the commandments of the law (29:26). From the verb *'rr*, "to curse," derives the passive participle *'ārûr*, and the *'ārûr* formula is typical of a number of the curses in Deuteronomy. This formula provides a nominal sentence, beginning with the predicate *'ārûr* followed by a subject, and often expanded with a condition explaining the reason for the curse, for example:

> Cursed (*'ārûr*) be anyone who moves a neighbour's boundary marker (27:17).

Since no agent is specified in these curses, debate has raged concerning the role of God in bringing them about. According to Westermann, God is always the agent behind blessings but never in curses (1978, 23). However, there are a number of biblical examples of *'ārûr* where God is specified to be the agent behind the action (Jos 6:26; 1 Kgs 16:34; 1 Sam 26:19; Jer 11:3; Mal 1:14). Certainly, in the curses from the ancient Near Eastern treaty texts, gods and goddesses are correlated with specific curses, usually related to their particular domain or sphere of influence. It is therefore likely that God is the implied agent of the action of the *'ārûr* curses, even when this is not stated explicitly (Aitken 2007, 20–21).

Deuteronomy also develops a number of curses which describe much more precisely how the individual subject to the curse will be afflicted. These curses utilize standard formula as well as content in order to describe vividly the various calamities that will befall the Israelites. Many of the threats are ecological, threatening pestilence, disease, or a general lack of productivity (27–28). The use of culturally relevant terminology and metaphor provides a window into ancient social values, highlighting the importance of agrarian concerns, as well as bodily health and wellness.

Early scholarship on efficacious words in the Hebrew Bible tended to focus on the theological implications of the concept of blessing (Plassmann 1910; Pedersen 1926). However, since it has been recognized that the curses of Deuteronomy might be connected to a wider ancient Near Eastern literary tradition—with implications for the dating and context of the book—the curses have become the main focus of scholarly inquiry. Indeed, scholarship has been quick to note the parallels that exist between the curses of the book of Deuteronomy with ancient Near Eastern treaty texts. The treaty was a characteristic feature of international relations in both the second and first millenniums BCE, first of all among the Hittite Empire, and then again in the eighth and seventh centuries BCE, as the Neo-Assyrians began to incorporate other states into their empire as they expanded westward. Like the book of Deuteronomy, these treaty texts also threaten future help or harm in the form of blessings and curses to any individual subject to the terms of the treaty. These texts show significant commonalities to the book of Deuteronomy, both structurally and, more strikingly, in the content of their curses. Placing the biblical blessings and curses within the larger context of this ancient Near Eastern material provides new insights into the background and function of the blessings and curses in Deuteronomy.

Who Began the Conversation?

In 1954, George Mendenhall published an article that documented his discovery of parallels between the covenants of the Hebrew Bible with Hittite vassal treaties. The dual decision that governed Mendenhall's analysis was (1) the dating of the Decalogue to the time of Moses on the basis of the state treaties of the contemporaneous Hittite Empire (1450–1200 BCE), which (2) he believed obtained only in the latter part of the second millennium (1954, 53–56). However, this form was not confined only to treaties and instructions of the second millennium. Treaties in both Aramaic and Akkadian dating from the eighth to the seventh centuries BCE clearly show that similar treaty forms were prevalent in the first millennium. In particular, a Neo-Assyrian treaty written in Akkadian in the seventh century BCE, "The Succession Treaties of Esarhaddon" (EST), has been suggested by some scholars to provide direct parallels with the book of Deuteronomy. Esarhaddon was the third king of the Sargonid Dynasty of the Neo-Assyrian Empire, and the Succession Treaties are the formal record of a treaty concerning the royal succession of Esarhaddon's chosen heir, his son Assurbanipal, in Assyria, written in 672 BCE. The treaty was enforced by oath upon eight vassal city-lords from bordering states in Iran, though the heading of the treaty unequivocally establishes its intended purpose as a pact not just with these specific recipients, but with a much vaster aggregate comprising all of the people over whom Assyria ruled—which would presumably also include Judah.

Scholars were quick to point out affinities between Esarhaddon's Treaties with the curses of the book of Deuteronomy, culminating in the two detailed studies of Moshe Weinfeld (1965) and Rintje Frankena (1965). Both sketched affinities between the curses of Deuteronomy and the Succession Treaties, with slightly different emphases. Weinfeld convincingly showed that the seemingly arbitrary sequence of the curses threatening leprosy and blindness (28:27–35) derived from Esarhaddon's Succession Treaties. The sequence of curses in this unit moves from skin ailments (28:27) to blindness (28:28–29), violated wife (28:30a), displaced progeny (28:32), foreign military occupation (28:33), and finally again, this time in inverted order, blindness (28:34) and skin ailments (28:35). While in the context of the Hebrew Bible this particular sequence of curses appears to be random, Weinfeld showed that the paired motifs "leprosy" and "blindness," as well as the topical sequence of the other curses in that unit, are attested in EST (§§ 39–42), where the logic of the order follows the hierarchy of the Neo-Assyrian pantheon (1965; 1972: 119–121). Thus, Weinfeld concluded that

> [t]he peculiar association of the curses of leprosy and judicial blindness in Dt 28,27–29 cannot, therefore, be satisfactorily explained unless we assume that the pairing of these two concepts—which is comprehensible only in the light of Mesopotamian religion—was literally transcribed from a Mesopotamian treaty copy to the book of Deuteronomy. (1965, 422)

Frankena's hypothesis concerning the relation of Deuteronomy to EST was also one of literal transcription, supplementing this analysis by explaining how the parallels could have come about. Noting that Manasseh was listed as a vassal in Assyrian sources, Frankena proposed that a copy of EST must have been sent to Jerusalem (1965, 151). The book of Deuteronomy was the expression of the Josianic reform, and the transposition of this, the vassal treaties, had tied Judah to Assyria as vassal state. The historical background of these reforms was the increasing threat of imperial domination: the Northern Kingdom of Israel had fallen under Neo-Assyria only a century before (722 BCE; 2 Kgs 17), and continuing Assyrian incursions in the Levant had seen Judah significantly reduced (2 Kgs 18:13). Hezekiah had made a pact with Assyria to preserve Judah's autonomy (2 Kgs 18:13–18). Josiah's reforms—the restriction of all sacrificial worship to Jerusalem and the removal of foreign elements from the cult—made a bid for Judah's cultural, political, and religious autonomy. Josiah could introduce his reform only because following the death of Assurbanipal the empire of Assyria was politically in decline: Josiah thus extended his reforms into the former Kingdom of Israel and hence into territory directly under Assyrian control (2 Kgs 23:15–20). While the book of Deuteronomy had long been associated with Josiah's reforms, Frankena linked this literary production to a copy of EST putatively available in Jerusalem: Josiah's covenant with the Israelite God was considered a substitution for the former treaty with the king of Assyria, expressing vassalship to God instead of vassalship to the Assyrian king, and reappropriating the curses of the Assyrian treaty for his new composition in an act of literary subversion (1965, 153). Taken together, the studies of Weinfeld and Frankena thus provided not only a wealth of parallels but also a plausible suggestion concerning the means by which these had come about.

Even so, the historical reconstructions of Weinfeld and Frankena were not met with universal acceptance. In 1963 Dennis McCarthy had published his own study concerning the relationship of the biblical concept of covenant to the ancient Near Eastern treaty form. In this study, McCarthy had stressed the general continuity of this form through the centuries. This conclusion governed McCarthy's response to the Weinfeld-Frankena model in his 1978 revision of this earlier study. While in the earlier study he had interpreted elements of Deuteronomy in analogy to Mesopotamian literature, due to the unity which he perceived in the ancient Near Eastern treaty form over the millennia he did not recognize any *specific* treaty to be the primary source of these elements: rather these were characteristic of a common tradition. Thus, he asked:

> What, then, do the parallels say about the text as such? Do they show that Dt. 28, rather than simply belonging to a common ancient near eastern tradition, actually derived from a

> *Vorlage*, an Assyrian treaty? Frankena insists on the parallels between the texts that we have listed. They are striking enough, but he must admit that the variation in the sequence of the curses is odd if they are directly connected. (1978, 178)

Thus, while McCarthy did indeed regard the Mesopotamian treaty tradition to be important for understanding the book of Deuteronomy, he rejected EST as *the* model for Deuteronomic composition. Thereafter the scholarship tended to fall between these positions, either stressing with Frankena and Weinfeld the Deuteronomic reuse of EST, or with McCarthy the more general nature of the affinities. However, in contemporary scholarship a new solution to McCarthy's concerns about the variation in the sequence of curses between EST and Deuteronomy has been proposed by Bernard Levinson, with a model that is far more sensitive to the subtleties of textual reproduction in ancient Israel and Judah.

What Is the Status of the Conversation?

In 1998 Levinson published an exploration into the parallel material found in key passages of the instructions on cultic and legal institutions in Deuteronomy (12, 16–17) and in the Covenant Code (Exod 20–23). Here Levinson argued that the writers of Deuteronomy meant to replace older law with their own legislation of cultic centralization, the replacement of local altars and shrines with the central sanctuary in the seventh century BCE. However, Deuteronomy's authors disguised their legal innovations by claiming continuity with the older tradition: they appropriated idioms and axioms from prior legislation but gave this a new context and meaning that often transformed—even reversed—its previous significance, by means of a so-called hermeneutic of legal innovation. Thus, the creative impulse behind much of biblical literature is in fact *re*creative: intertextual and interactive, a process of radical interpretative activity.

Moving from Deuteronomy's reuse of the Covenant Code to the problem of Deuteronomy and EST, Levinson interpreted these issues according to his understanding of this "hermeneutics of literary innovation." In so doing, Levinson provides an account of the Deuteronomic authors' interaction with this prior tradition that goes beyond the Weinfeld-Frankena model of literal transcription or translation. One of the more difficult chapters of the book of Deuteronomy (13:1–18) commands religiously sanctioned violence requiring the execution of various religious functionaries prophets or oneiromancers—; one's own spouse, son, or daughter; even an entire city; in the case of incitement to apostasy. Compounding the problem of the interpretation of these unpalatable injunctions, the majority of the ancient versions offer variant readings which ensure that any such killing should conform to the laws of due process, and providing an ostensibly more logical list of the family members addressed by the law—and scholarly consensus has long advocated that the Hebrew Masoretic Text (MT) should be restored in light of these versions. But Levinson found context to support the MT in EST.

For example, the MT is correct against the Greek translation (13:7 LXX) in referring only to "your mother's son" and not the father's, the author having redeployed the conspiracy topos of EST §10 along with its requirement of summary execution. Specific clusters of its language are reused, including both its detailed list of the immediate members of the addressee's family (so "brother," "son," "daughter") and the alternative religious officials who serve as divine spokesmen ("prophet," "ecstatic," "oneiromancer"). From this template, the Deuteronomic authors created two consecutive legal paragraphs, the first envisioning incitement to disloyalty against God as coming from "a prophet or oneiromancer" and the second, as arising from the immediate family of the addressee ("brother," "son," "daughter," adding "wife" and "friend"). According to Levinson, beyond merely copying his source text in any linear or literalistic way, the Deuteronomic author has actually *reordered* the source. In the treaty, the addresses are arranged in a single continuum: (A) royal family, (B) addressee's family, (C) divine spokesmen. In Deuteronomy, this has been divided into two separate laws, moving from the sphere of public religion (C) into the sphere of the addressee's private life (B). (In this context, there is of course no reference to threats to the sovereign from within his own family.) The citation in Deuteronomy is thus chiastic, reversing the order of the original composition (Levinson 2001). In this way, Levinson is able to confirm the originality of problematic passages from the MT of Deuteronomy through his creative understanding of textual reuse in ancient Israel, highlighting the more subtle examples of the reuse of EST within Deuteronomy, and so widening the possibilities of this reuse to include nuanced examples of allusion and chiasmus. The variation in the order of the curses apparently shared between Deuteronomy 28 and EST can be accounted for in this way.

These conclusions were bolstered in 2009, when an additional copy of EST was recovered from the archaeological record (Lauinger 2012). In contrast to the original manuscripts, the treaty partners of the new manuscript recovered from Tell Tayinat are the anonymous lords and other officials of the province of Kullania. The Tell Tayinat exemplar therefore brings this famous treaty geographically closer to the biblical world than ever before. While some scholars have argued against the idea that a copy of the Neo-Assyrian text had ever been sent to Judah in the first place (Zehnder 2011), that a copy of EST may have been sent to Judah is more plausible than ever. This provides a conceivable vector for the transmission of the curses of EST to Deuteronomy. However, we still need to think carefully about the *means* of this transmission. A number of scholars have been wary to posit a direct literary relationship between EST and the book of Deuteronomy due to their reticence to attribute the kind of Akkadian literacy that this would require for the Hebrew scribes who wrote the biblical text (Morrow 2005). Further, Carly Crouch has recently renewed McCarthy's argument that the allusions between the curses in Deuteronomy and EST are general rather than specific, concluding that the curses in Deuteronomy must be characteristic of a general tradition of cursing rather than of a specific textual witness such as EST. In this context, Crouch has considered other traditions of cursing recovered from the ancient Levant (Crouch 2014). Crouch's study thus sets the stage for a reconsideration of the curses in Deuteronomy 28 that is sensitive to *native* Northwest Semitic literary traditions, as well as to the larger Neo-Assyrian literary context.

WHAT IS TRENDING IN THE CONVERSATION?

Indeed, the past few decades have brought to light additional inscriptions that also provide paralleled phenomena to the curses in Deuteronomy (28:1–46). Unlike EST, these

Table 5.1. Sefire Treaties (KAI 222 A1:22–23)	
And should seven mares nurse a colt, may it not be sa[ted.	wašabaʿ sūsyāh yuhayniqān ʿīl waʾal yiś[baʿ
And should seven] cows nurse a calf may it not be sated. And should seven ewes nurse a lamb, [may it not be sa]ted.	wašabaʿ] šawrāh yuhayniqān ʿigl waʾal yiśbaʿ wašabaʿ šaʾān yuhayniqān ʾimmēr waʾ[al yiśbaʿ

inscriptions are written in Old Aramaic, a Northwest Semitic language utilized in Syria during the first millennium BCE. Thus, these inscriptions are both geographically and linguistically closer to the biblical world than the Mesopotamian texts that scholars have previously associated with Deuteronomy. The particular curse formula common to the Old Aramaic inscriptions and the book of Deuteronomy can be described as *curses of futility*, with a characteristic syntactical form and commonalities in both vocabulary and intent.

Curses of futility have a protasis that defines an action of some kind, followed by an apodosis in which this action is frustrated. We might typify this curse as a threat of *maximum effort*, but *minimal gain*. Several characteristic examples can be found in the Sefire treaties, three treaties written in Old Aramaic and discovered near present-day Aleppo. The inscriptions are the first and only treaties that have been found in Aramaic, a Northwest Semitic language closely related to Hebrew (see Table 5.1; for the text see Donner and Röllig 2002).

Many biblical texts and Old Aramaic inscriptions utilize this literary form, with a total of forty-three discrete examples of the futility curse across all biblical books, found especially in Deuteronomy and in pre-exilic prophetic texts.[2] Meanwhile, across the corpus of Old Aramaic inscriptions, there are nineteen occurrences of the futility curse, stemming from three separate inscriptions datable within the range of the ninth to the eighth centuries BCE, and with a geographic distribution across the Trans- and Cisjordan: from the Tell Fakhariyah bilingual inscription (x6); the Sefire treaties (x11); and the recently discovered stele from Bukān (x2). The syntactical and lexical regularity of the futility curses demonstrates that it was a standard literary form which was utilized by Northwest Semitic scribes in the first millennium BCE (Ramos 2016). This is important for understanding the book of Deuteronomy, showing that curses of Deuteronomy cannot be understood according to Mesopotamian conceptions alone, despite the previous scholarly ferment in this direction. Rather, Deuteronomy (28:1-46) *mediates* between the traditions of the East and West, featuring characteristic examples of the Northwest Semitic futility curse type, as well as curses more common to Akkadian, East Semitic texts such as EST.

The traditional formulation of the Deuteronomy//EST hypothesis is concerned with Deuteronomy 28:26-35 in comparison with EST §§ 39-42 (see Table 5.2; for the text, see Parpola and Watanabe 1988). This has parallels with Deuteronomy 28:26-29 (see Table 5.3). It appears that the text of EST provides correspondences with these verses from Deuteronomy, with both texts reflecting curses threatening the attack of carrion, skin disease, and blindness, the latter including the terminological overlap of movement "in darkness", although Deuteronomy (28:26) is out of sequence). Indeed, the text in Deuteronomy seems to

Table 5.2. EST §§ 39–41

May Ninurta, the foremost among the gods, fell you with his fierce arrow; may he fill the plain with your blood and feed your flesh to the eagle and the vulture.	ninurta ašarēd ilānī ina šiltāḫīšu šamri lišamqitkunu dāmīkunu limalli ṣēru šīrkunu arû zību lišākil
May Sin, the brightness of heaven and earth, clothe you with leprosy and forbid you from entering into the presence of the gods or king. Roam the desert like the wild-ass and the gazelle!	sîn nannar šamê u erṣeti saḫaršubbû liḫallipkunu ina pānē ili u šarri erēbkunu aji iqbi kī serrēme ṣabīti ṣēru rupdā
May Šamaš, the light of heaven and earth, not judge you justly. May he remove your eyesight. Walk about in darkness!	šamaš nūr šamāmī u qaqqari dīn kitti mīšari aji idīnkunu niṭil īnīkunu lēšīma ina ekleti itallakā

Table 5.3. Deut 28:26–29

Your corpses shall be food for every bird of the air and animal of the earth, and there shall be no one to frighten them away.	wĕhāyĕṯāh niḇlāṯĕḵā lĕmaʾăḵāl lĕkol ʿôp haššāmayim ûlĕḇehĕmaṯ hāʾāreṣ wĕʾên maḥărîd
The Lord will afflict you with the boils of Egypt, with ulcers, scurvy, and itch, of which you cannot be healed.	yakkĕkāh ʾăḏōnāy bišĕḥîn miṣrayim ûḇoʿōpālîm ûḇagārāḇ ûḇeḥāres ʾăšer lōʾ ṯûkal lĕhērāpēʾ
The Lord will afflict you with madness, blindness, and confusion of mind.	yakkĕkah ʾăḏonay bĕšiggāʿôn ûḇĕ ʿiwwārōn ûḇĕṯimhôn lēḇāḇ
You shall grope about at noon as blind people grope in darkness, but you shall be unable to find your way; and you shall be continually abused and robbed, without anyone to help.	wĕhāyîṯā mĕmaššēš baṣṣohŏrayim kaʾăšer yĕmaššēš hāʿiwwēr bāʾăpēlāh wĕlōʾ ṯaṣlîaḥ ʾeṯ dĕrāḵĕḵā wĕhāyîṯā ʾaḵ ʿāšûq wĕḡāzûl kol hayyāmîm wĕʾên môšîaʿ

build upon and amplify the Akkadian, adding additional clauses that stress the perpetuity of the curse, so "you cannot be healed . . . without anyone to help."

Yet immediately following, we find curses that cohere more with the tradition of the futility curse, the curse of maximum effort but minimal gain, which I have suggested was traditional to Northwest Semitic literary compositions. At the same time, EST still provide the conceptual framework for these curses (see Tables 5.4 and 5.5).

Here Deuteronomy develops the idea world of the parallel curse in EST—so unfaithful wives and houses in which the owner cannot reside—but couches these motifs in the characteristic syntactic form of the futility curse, significantly expanding upon the Akkadian original by adding further clauses that develop traditional Northwest Semitic motifs concerning frustrated vineyards and livestock (Smoak 2008). Then the text (28:32) more faithfully reflects the Akkadian, abandoning the syntax of the futility curse and stressing along with EST that the root cause of the curse—which in both seems to envision deportation—will be at the hand of an enemy nation, so in Hebrew "another people" and in the Akkadian a "strange enemy."

Table 5.4. EST §42

May Venus, the brightest of the stars, before your eyes make your wives lie in the lap of your enemy; may your sons not take possession of your house, but a strange enemy divide your goods.	delebat nabât kakkabāni ina niṭil īnīkunu ḫīrātīkunu ina sūn nakirīkunu lišanīl mārīkunu aji ibēlū bītkun nakiru aḫû liza''iza mimmûkun

Table 5.5. Deut 28:30–32

You shall become engaged to a woman, but another man shall lie with her. You shall build a house, but not live in it. You shall plant a vineyard, but not enjoy its fruit.	ʾiššāh tĕʾārēś wĕʾîš ʾaḥēr yišgālennāh bayit tibneh wĕlōʾ tēšēb bô kerem tiṭṭaʿ wĕlōʾ tĕḥallĕlennû
Your ox shall be butchered before your eyes, but you shall not eat of it. Your donkey shall be stolen in front of you and shall not be restored to you. Your sheep shall be given to your enemies, without anyone to help you.	šôrĕkā ṭābûaḥ lĕʿênêkā wĕlōʾ tōʾkal mimmennû ḥămōrĕkā gāzûl millĕpānêkā wĕlōʾ yāšûb lāk ṣōʾnĕkā nĕtunôt lĕʾōyĕbêkā wĕʾên lĕkā môšîaʿ
Your sons and daughters shall be given to another people, while you look on; you will strain your eyes looking for them all day but be powerless to do anything.	bānêkā ûbĕnōtêkā nĕtunîm lĕʿam ʾaḥēr wĕʿênêkā rōʾôt wĕkālôt ʾălêhem kol hayyôm wĕʾên lĕʾēl yādekā

Immediately following this statement, the text shifts again, employing further curses in the guise of the futility form (see Table 5.6). The motifs in this section of text are characteristic of the scriptural and inscriptional Northwest Semitic texts found in Old Aramaic and in the Hebrew Bible, utilizing a similar repertoire of language and stock images of vineyards and olive groves, all couched in the syntax of a maximum effort but a minimal gain. Once again, in this portion of Deuteronomy, the orientation of the text has shifted

Table 5.6. Deut 28:38–41

You shall carry much seed into the field but shall gather little in, for the locust shall consume it.	zeraʿ rab tôṣīʾ haśśādeh ûmĕʿaṭ teʾĕsōp kî yaḥsĕlennû hāʾarbeh
You shall plant vineyards and dress them, but you shall neither drink the wine nor gather the grapes, for the worm shall eat them.	kĕrāmîm tiṭṭaʿ wĕʿābādtā wĕyayin lōʾ tišteh wĕlōʾ teʾĕgōr kî tōkĕlennû hatōlāʿat
You shall have olive trees throughout all your territory, but you shall not anoint yourself with the oil, for your olives shall drop off.	zêtîm yihyû lĕkā bĕkol gĕbûlekā wĕšemen lōʾ tāsûk kî yiššal zêtekā
You shall have sons and daughters, but they shall not remain yours, for they shall go into captivity.	bānîm ûbānôt tôlîd wĕlōʾ yihyû lāk kî yēlĕkû baššebî

back to Northwest Semitic ideas and metaphors. Deuteronomy marries curses from the East Semitic world with native Northwest Semitic traditions, opposing the traditions against each other in a playful exchange (Quick 2017, 137–158).

The recognition of the importance of the Levantine literary tradition has implications for understanding the literary composition and social-cultural background of the blessings and curses in the book of Deuteronomy. In particular, ritual performance could provide a useful perspective with which to think through the connections between these traditions. Both the biblical and inscriptional texts seem to demonstrate a large body of rites and rituals that would have come along with the formalization of a treaty or covenant and its correlated blessings and curses. Very often some sort of sign must mark the spot of the treaty agreement. This seems to have been essential to both cosmic and terrestrial covenants. The rainbow in the Noahic covenant (Gen 9:13), or the tablets of stone in the Mosaic covenant (Exod 24:4), can be understood in this way. In Deuteronomy, this is taken further still: "You shall put these words of mine in your heart and soul, and you shall bind them as a sign on your hand and fix them as an emblem on your forehead. Teach them to your children, talking about them when you are at home and when you are away, when you lie down and when you rise. Write them on the doorposts of your house and on your gates" (11:18–20; cf. 6:9–8). In Joshua (Josh 24:26–27), a large stone acts as witness to "all the words of the Lord that he spoke to us." A standing stone is also utilized in the ratification of the covenant between two human actors, so Jacob and Laban (Gen 31:51–54); while it is a tamarisk tree that marks the spot of the agreement between Abraham and Abimelech (Gen 21:33).

Livestock is also exchanged in this covenant with Abimelech (21:30), while a meal is shared between Abimelech and Isaac when they swear their oath (Gen 26:30). A sacrifice or ritual slaughter seems to have been inherent to many of the biblical covenants. Indeed, that the cutting up of an animal in sacrifice also informed the biblical terminology "to cut" a covenant has been suggested (Day 2003). In particular, note the Abrahamic covenant:

> Then he said to him, "I am the Lord who brought you from Ur of the Chaldeans, to give you this land to possess." But he said, "O Lord God, how am I to know that I shall possess it?" He said to him, "Bring me a heifer three years old, a female goat three years old, a ram three years old, a turtledove, and a young pigeon." He brought him all these and cut them in two, laying each half over against the other; but he did not cut the birds in two. And when birds of prey came down on the carcasses, Abram drove them away [. . .] When the sun had gone down and it was dark, a smoking fire pot and a flaming torch passed between these pieces. On that day the Lord made a covenant with Abram. (Gen 15:7–17)

Here animals are cut in two, before a flaming torch passes between the two parts of the animals in a symbolic procession. A comparable situation is found in Jeremiah:

> And those who transgressed my covenant and did not keep the terms of the covenant that they made before me, I will make like the calf when they cut it in two and passed between its parts: the officials of Judah, the officials of Jerusalem, the eunuchs, the priests, and all the people of the land who passed between the parts of the calf shall be handed over to their enemies and to those who seek their lives. Their corpses shall become food for the birds of the air and the wild animals of the earth. (Jer 34:18–20)

Table 5.7. Sefire Treaties (KAI 222 A1:37–40)

Just as this wax is burned by fire, so may Mati[el be burned by fi]re!	waʾayk zī tiqqad ša ʿawtaʾ zaʾ biʾēš kēn yiqqad ma[tiʿʾ]l biʾē]š
Just as (this) bow and these arrows are broken, so may Inurta and Hadad break [the bow of Matiel],	waʾayk zī tušbar qištaʾ wahiṣṣayyaʾ ʾillēn kēn yišbar ʾinurta wahadad [qišt matiʿʾel] waqišt rabbawh
and the bow of his nobles! And just as the man of wax is blinded, so may Mati[el] be blinded!	waʾayk zī yuʿar gubr šaʿawtaʾ kēn yuʿar matiʿʾe[l
[Just as] this calf is cut in two, so may Matiel be cut in two, and may his nobles be cut in two!	waʾayk zī] yugzar ʿiglaʾ zināh kēn yugzar matiʿʾel wayugzarūn rabbawh

Here God chastises the men who violated his covenant, recalling when they had passed between the two halves of a sacrificed calf, and threatening that he will make these men like that calf. The logic of this passage seems to recall the simile curses found in the Neo-Assyrian and Aramaic treaty texts (see Table 5.7).

Just as certain items are broken, cut, or burnt, so will the treaty partner be broken, cut, or burnt, should he not keep the terms of the agreement. These curses are not just speech acts: the text is explicit that an accompanying rite is meant to posit the association between the broken object and the cursed individual.

Clearly the ritual context of treaty formation in ancient Israel and Judah involved a complex body of rites and actions, encompassing at the very least signs, sacrifice, the recitation and writing of blessing and curses, and perhaps a ritual procession between the two halves of an animal as implied in Genesis and explicit in Jeremiah. All these elements are present in Deuteronomy (27:1–26). This text requires "all the people" to pass between two symbolic extremes in a procession, although here the entities are geographical, between Mount Ebal and Mount Gerizim, rather than between the parts of various sacrificed livestock. Half of the tribes are to ascend Mount Ebal and half Mount Gerizim. Three standing stones are erected to mark the spot of the covenant, and two different types of sacrifice are to be offered, a burnt offering and a sacrifice of well-being. These stones constitute an "altar" upon which the sacrifice is performed, and hence are functionally the same as a place of religious worship. A meal is shared, and the Deuteronomic laws are written upon the three standing stones, clearly meant for visual display since the requirement is that the text is crafted "very clearly." This ritual process is then capped by the recitation of blessings and curses by the Levites (Deut 27:12–15). Finally, additional curses are pronounced on any member of the community who breaks the law. That this pronouncement was recited orally is indicated by the requirement of those present to respond "Amen".

The ceremony, then, is enacted ritually, recited orally, and written upon display stones. Blessings and curses are performative actions, and it is by speaking but also by writing that the power of a curse can be activated: writing can itself be a performative action (Austin 1962, 6–11). In this way, the blessings and curses of Deuteronomy must be understood in the continuum of orality and literacy, both recited and written in the ritual process. While a spoken blessing or curse was a finite event, limited to the speech act, in writing a blessing or curse down its power became unlimited, preserved forever, highlighting the perceived authority of Deuteronomy's law code.

If the ritual aspect of these treaty texts is emphasized, then the need for a formal written translation of EST may very well be negated. Just as Ezra had intermediaries to help the people "understand the law" (Neh 8:7), could this practice of Targum have also played a role in any aural ceremony? Certainly, this is the logic that underlines the treaty formalized between Jacob and Laban, and the "mound of witness" that acts as the sign of their covenant, named in Aramaic by Laban, and in Hebrew by Jacob (Gen 31:47). This may well account for the problem of Akkadian literacy in Judah. As the peoples of Israel and Judah increasingly interacted with and were subjugated by the Neo-Assyrians, the ritual world of their treaty formulation opened up to include East Semitic practices and idioms—and these idioms, translated into Aramaic or Hebrew and shared orally in ritual performance, found their way into the curses of Deuteronomy. In this way, it could be said that the curses of Deuteronomy parallel those of the Aramaic epigraphs and the Neo-Assyrian treaty texts due to the *reality* of the ritual world of the scribes, rather than because of any particular *written* tradition at their disposal.

The book of Deuteronomy cannot be understood apart from the Northwest Semitic tradition of the futility curse. Exploring this tradition enables us to better comprehend the sophisticated literary interplay developed in the book of Deuteronomy, which playfully oscillates between cursing traditions from the West and East Semitic worlds. As well as helping us to understand the compositional process that belies the book of Deuteronomy, this recognition increases our understanding of the ritual context of treaty formation and the pronouncement of blessings and curses in the ancient Near East. Indeed, ritual has a theoretical capacity to account for the transmission of these curse and blessing traditions cross-culturally. Highlighting this ritual context underscores the perceived efficacy of the blessings and curses of Deuteronomy, and thus the authority of Deuteronomy's law code. By exploring the background of the blessings and curses of Deuteronomy, we gain access to practices of ritual and worship in Israel and Judah, as well as the social values that informed these texts. Blessings and curses are therefore an important window into the ancient society which shaped and gave rise to the Hebrew Bible.

NOTES

1. All English Bible translations are from the *New Revised Standard Version*.
2. Lev 26:26; Deut 28:30 (x3), 31 (x3), 38, 39, 40, 41; Isa 5:10 (x2); Jer 11:11; Hos 2:9 (x2); 4:10 (x2); 5:6; 8:7; 9:12, 16; Amos 4:8; 5:11 (x2); 8:12; Micah 3:4; 6:14 (x2), 15 (x3); Zeph 1:13 (x2); Hag 1:6 (x4); Zech 7:13; Mal 1:4; Ps 127:1; Job 31:8; and Prov 1:28 (x2).

BIBLIOGRAPHY

Aitken, James K. 2007. *The Semantics of Blessing and Cursing in Ancient Hebrew* (ANES 23). Leuven: Peeters.
Anderson, Jeff S. 1998. "The Social Function of Curses in the Hebrew Bible." *ZAW* 110: 223–227.
Austin, J. L. 1962. *How to Do Things with Words*. Oxford: Oxford University Press.

Crouch, Carly L. 2014. *Israel & the Assyrians: Deuteronomy, the Succession Treaty of Esarhaddon, & the Nature of Subversion* (ANEM 8). Atlanta: Society of Biblical Literature.

Day, John. 2003. "Why Does God 'Establish' Rather Than 'Cut' Covenants in the Priestly Source?" In *Covenant as Context: Essays in Honour of E.W. Nicholson*, edited by Andrew D. H. Mayes and R. B. Salters, 91–106. Oxford: Oxford University Press.

Donner, Herbert, and Wolfgang Röllig. 2002. *Kanaanäische und aramäische Inschriften 1*. Wiesbaden: Harrassowitz.

Frankena, Rintje. 1965. "The Vassal-Treaties of Esarhaddon and the Dating of Deuteronomy." *OudSt* 14: 122–154.

Lauinger, Jacob. 2012. "Esarhaddon's Succession Treaty at Tell Tayinat: Text and Commentary." *JCS* 64: 87–123.

Levinson, Bernard M. 1998. *Deuteronomy and the Hermeneutics of Legal Innovation*. Oxford: Oxford University Press.

Levinson, Bernard M. 2001. "Textual Criticism, Assyriology, and the History of the Interpretation of Deuteronomy 13:7a as a Test Case in Method." *JBL* 120: 211–243.

McCarthy, Dennis J. 1963. *Treaty and Covenant: A Study in Form in the Ancient Oriental Documents and in the Old Testament* (Analecta Biblica 21). Rome: Pontifical Biblical Institute).

McCarthy, Dennis J. 1978. *Treaty and Covenant: A Study in Form in the Ancient Oriental Documents and in the Old Testament* (rev. 2nd ed.; Analecta Biblica, 21A). Rome: Biblical Institute.

Mendenhall, George E. 1954. "Covenant Forms in Israelite Tradition." *BA* 17: 49–76.

Morrow, William S. 2005. "Cuneiform Literacy and Deuteronomic Composition." *BibOr* 62: 204–213.

Parpola, Simo, and Kazuko Watanabe. 1988. *Neo-Assyrian Treaties and Loyalty Oaths* (SAA 2). Helsinki: Helsinki University Press.

Pedersen, Johannes. 1926. *Israel: Its Life and Culture*. Vol. 1. Oxford: Oxford University Press.

Plassmann, Thomas. 1910. *The Significance of beraka: A Semasiological Study of the Semitic Stem b-r-k*. Paris: Imprimerie Nationale.

Quick, Laura. 2017. *Deuteronomy 28 and the Aramaic Curse Tradition* (OTRM). Oxford: Oxford University Press.

Ramos, Melissa. 2016. "A Northwest Semitic Curse Formula: The Sefire Treaty and Deuteronomy 28." *ZAW* 128: 205–220.

Ravenhill, Philip L. 1976. "Religious Utterances and the Theory of Speech Acts." In *Language in Religious Practice*, edited by William J. Samarin, 26–39. Rowley: Newbury House.

Scharbert, J. 1977. "ʾālâ." *TDOT* 1: 261–266.

Smoak, Jeremy D. 2008. "Building Houses and Planting Vineyards: The Inner-Biblical Discourse on an Ancient Israelite Wartime Curse." *JBL* 127: 19–35.

Weinfeld, Moshe. 1965. "Traces of Assyrian Treaty Formulae in Deuteronomy." *Biblica* 46: 417–427.

Weinfeld, Moshe. 1972. *Deuteronomy and the Deuteronomic School*. Oxford: Clarendon.

Westermann, Claus. 1978. *Blessing in the Bible and the Life of the Church*. Minneapolis: Fortress.

Zehnder, Markus. 2011. "Fluch und Segen im Buch Deuteronomium. Beobachtungen und Fragen." In *Deuteronomium—Tora für eine neue Generation*, edited by G. Fischer, D. Markl, and S. Paganini, 193–212. Wiesbaden: Harrassowitz.

SECTION II
LITERARY MOTIFS IN DEUTERONOMY

CHAPTER 6

MONOTHEISM AND DEUTERONOMY

MATTHEW LYNCH

THE study of monotheism in the Old Testament continues to animate biblical scholars, but from very different perspectives. On the one hand, scholars interested in the history of Israelite religion want to know when and under what conditions monotheism took shape. For these scholars, Deuteronomy is an important datum. Its theology influences the Deuteronomistic History (Josh–2 Kgs), and books like Hosea and Jeremiah. If Deuteronomy is firmly monotheistic, then we can say with greater confidence that the Old Testament is, in large measure, a monotheistic collection. Of course, some argue that because Deuteronomy has a complex redactional history that stretches well beyond the exile, we cannot make pronouncements about pan-monotheism based on Deuteronomy's final form.

On the other hand, scholars ask what monotheism might mean in Deuteronomy. The question of meaning can be asked apart from any concern with historical development. But Deuteronomy poses many challenges, since it seems to speak with many voices on the question of divine supremacy. Moreover, the nature of claims that YHWH is one, or that there are no other gods, or even that "there is no other god" are not necessarily as straightforward as they might appear.[1] To that end a study of monotheism in Deuteronomy is seen to require sensitivity to Deuteronomy's rhetoric and to the interplay of various claims about Israel's God.

After walking through key moments in the study of monotheism in Deuteronomy, I will consider the question of how to best speak of monotheism, and whether the term is ill-suited to Deuteronomy. We then turn our attention to the key texts relating to possible monotheism in Deuteronomy before considering how Deuteronomy's pieces fit together. Finally, we will consider the relationship between monotheism and other Old Testament texts.

WHO BEGAN THE CONVERSATION?

The word *monotheism* can be traced in the English-speaking world to Henry More, a Cambridge Platonist (1614–1687). For the Cambridge Platonists, reason was the "candle of the Lord," the light to guide the intellectual pursuit of the Christian religion.[2] In addition to Christianity, they sought to understand the rational grounds of religion and morality and to organize both in rigorously philosophical terms—a religion-organizing endeavor which included categorizing religions according to the number of deities thought to exist. To this endeavor biblical scholars in the eighteenth and nineteenth centuries added a series of religious entailments that followed "logically" from the claim that there is one God. These included an aversion to magic and ceremony, prohibition on images, and an emphasis on ethical living, as if they all follow obviously from monotheistic claims. The operative assumption in this highly philosophical exercise was Christianity's superiority as a monotheistic religion, with all its attendant qualities.[3] Added to the world-organizing endeavors of the Cambridge Platonists were the historical-developmentalist concerns of the *Religionsgeschichtliche Schule*, for whom religion needed to be considered in all of its complex development and influences.[4]

What Is the Status of the Conversation?

The dominance of the evolutionary paradigm for understanding monotheism and Israel's distinctiveness reflects aspects of the Platonists' project and the developmentalist concerns of the *Religionsgeschichtliche Schule*.[5] In the late nineteenth century, Julius Wellhausen (1844–1918) famously maintained that "the prophets have notoriously no father," incorporating the idea that prophetic *ethical* monotheism broke rank with the primitive polytheism of early Israel, but preceded priestly law and more abstract monotheistic developments during the exile.[6] For Wellhausen, Deuteronomy occupied a middle ground. It was only in the reforms of Josiah (640–609 BCE), a ruler of Judah, that a "strict monotheism" took shape through the elimination of popular paganism.[7]

Abraham Kuenen (1828–1891) argued that "ethical monotheism" took root in the time of Elijah and Elisha (ninth century BCE) and found expression through the time of Jeremiah and Deuteronomy (seventh century BCE). For Kuenen, ethical monotheism referred to the "excellence" of Israel's spiritual life, which enabled it to worship one spiritual being.[8] Deuteronomy was seen to bear the prophetic spirit and spiritual vision.[9]

For Samuel R. Driver (1846–1914) Deuteronomy furthered the implicit monotheism of the prophets, but taught it in a more concerted way. Monotheism also took institutional form through Deuteronomy's centralization of worship and concomitant destruction of other cult sites, which he considered "corollar(ies) of the monotheistic idea."[10] Thus, for Wellhausen, Keunen, and Driver, Deuteronomy represents a strict form of monotheism that advances the ideals of the prophets, but in institutional form.

Later, William F. Albright (1891–1971) argued that, in contrast to its Canaanite neighbors, early Israel was essentially monotheistic. Albright criticized the rigid Hegelianism of Wellhausen, Auguste Comte (1798–1857), and others, who posited stages of development from "fetishism, polytheism, [and] monotheism."[11] While Albright also shared their evolutionary assumptions, he recognized the complex ways that religion and cultures develop. Countercurrents and later refinements meant that monotheism did not develop in a linear fashion.[12] For instance, while monotheism briefly emerged in Egypt during the reign of Akhenaten, paganism was still too widespread for such monotheism to stick.

Albright contends that in Israel monotheism originated in the Mosaic era and was later taught and disseminated by the prophets. It reached its "climactic expression in Deutero-Isaiah and Job, who represented a height beyond which pure ethical monotheism has never risen."[13] Regarding Mosaic monotheism, Albright argued that: (1) For Moses, YHWH was the only God[14]; (2) YHWH was not restricted to one place; (3) YHWH was described in human form to become knowable but was not able to be seen; (4) Mosaic religion was aniconic; (5) Egyptian influences may have shaped Moses and early Israelite monotheism.[15]

While not a philosophical monotheist in the mode of Philo, Paul, or Augustine, Albright argued that Moses nonetheless taught "the existence of only one God, the creator of everything, the source of justice, who is equally powerful in Egypt, in the desert, and in Canaan, who has no sexuality and no mythology, who is human in form but cannot be seen by human eye and cannot be represented in any form."[16] While Albright's critique of developmentalist assumptions is well taken, his use of the term *monotheism* was vague and its applicability to the "Mosaic" period unsubstantiated.[17]

Like Albright, Yehezkel Kaufmann (1889–1963) situates the emergence of monotheism in early Israel. He argued that the standard scholarly assumption that monotheism represents the triumph of the universalist thought of the prophets over the idolatrous nationalism of Yahwism is "wholly in error."[18] The strong prohibitions against idolatry and multiple worship sites in Deuteronomy and Judges do not reflect widespread polytheism but, instead, efforts to concretize (through strong rhetoric) an already present idea. Monolatry—the worship of one deity without denying the existence of other deities—and a single cult followed monotheism, and not the other way around.[19] This idea is reminiscent of Driver's idea that the "ethical monotheism" of the prophets preceded the monotheizing centralization of the cult (12:1–32). Moreover, Deutero-Isaiah is not the creator of "universalist monotheism." Antecedents already existed in earlier periods (Hab 2:18–20).[20] One of Kaufmann's most helpful refinements, where Albright fell short, was in his definition of monotheism. He suggests that monotheism "is not an arithmetical diminution of the number of gods, but a new religious category that is involved, the category of a God above nature, whose will is supreme, who is not subject to compulsion and fate, who is free of the bonds of myth and magic."[21] While one might argue that myth and magic are not necessarily incompatible with all biblical conceptions of monotheism, Kaufmann helpfully recognizes that monotheism is best understood in terms of the categorical distinctiveness of YHWH. While I argue that monotheism need not carry all the entailments Kaufmann touts in his work, this remains an important contribution of his work.[22]

Like others, Gerhard von Rad (1901–1971) saw the seeds of monotheism's development in Israel's early literature. But its full development into "explicit monotheism" occurs in Second Isaiah. Unlike Kaufmann, however, von Rad sees monotheism as a religious development borne out of Israel's struggle with other nations. As Israel confronted the Canaanite deities, the Assyrian political threat, and ultimately Babylon, monotheism took shape. Monotheism's strongest exponents were the prophets, who were "freer" than those who had gone before, able to stand on their own.[23] Deuteronomy finds surprisingly little place in von Rad's thinking about monotheism. Israel's prohibition on worshipping with images, as for example in Deuteronomy, reflected their "more spiritual conception of God."[24] God was not manifest in created things, but by his word (8:3).[25] However, for von Rad, it is the prophets, and especially Second Isaiah, where we see monotheism's fullest expression.[26]

WHAT IS TRENDING IN THE CONVERSATION?

More recent scholarship on monotheism has given more attention to the significance of Deuteronomy, albeit with very different emphases. Some continue to emphasize Deuteronomy's significance in the history of Israelite religion. Georg Braulik speaks of a "monotheistic breakthrough" in Deuteronomy.[27] Braulik argues that the monolatrous teachings in the parenetic and legal portions of Deuteronomy gave way during the exile to monotheism.[28] He discerns at least six stages of theological development in Deuteronomy. These culminate in the postexilic claim that only YHWH is divine (4:35b).[29] This postexilic monotheism precedes Deutero-Isaiah (Isa 40:1–55:13). Hans Rechenmacher makes a similar argument, though he dates Deuteronomy's monotheistic breakthrough to the exile.[30]

Joachim Schaper also considers Deuteronomy to be the site of the monotheistic breakthrough in ancient Israel, but his argument is materialist. Throughout the sixth and seventh centuries BCE, we witness in the development of writing and emergence of money. The emphasis on the written word and suppression of images (4:1–48) reflects a "*liberation* of religious thought" that created an environment for a ban on images—the kinds of abstract conceptions of YHWH that monotheism requires. Schaper assumes that developments in writing and money were accompanied by traceable shifts in religious consciousness, which may not necessarily be the case.[31]

Others have resisted the abstracting tendencies of some history-of-religions approaches in favor of greater attention to Deuteronomy's specific rhetorical and theological claims. J. Gordon McConville, R. W. L. Moberly, and Nathan MacDonald have argued that monotheistic statements need to be understood in relational terms. For McConville "The discussion whether Deuteronomy is monotheistic in the strict sense is arid. The book always thinks of God's oneness in . . . the context of his relationship with Israel."[32]

Moberly suggests that studies of monotheism tend toward conceptual reductionism without concern for the specific factors that led the biblical authors to monotheism. Abstracting monotheism from its relational context between God and Israel ignores the way YHWH's uniqueness was conceptualized, namely, in terms of YHWH's unique acts for Israel and his unique demands upon Israel. Moberly insists that scholars need to attend carefully to "what is, and is not, meant by [YHWH's one-ness] in its various contexts."[33]

MacDonald, following Moberly, argued that the Enlightenment classification of religions along polytheistic and monotheistic lines distorted perceptions of Israelite religion, for it introduced categories and dichotomies alien to ancient cultures. It also failed to deal with the relational dynamics presupposed by God's "oneness" in Deuteronomy.[34] Scholarly debates about monotheism have focused so exclusively on religious development that treatments of so-called monotheistic texts become tone-deaf to Deuteronomy's rhetorical concerns.

The turn toward rhetoric and the relational context of monotheism has significant implications for a study of Deuteronomy.[35] Overly theoretical conceptions of monotheism obscure Deuteronomy's claims about YHWH's character, actions toward Israel, and demands for loyalty. If one assumes that the monotheism of Deutero-Isaiah, is the summit toward which religion is moving, then one also misses Deuteronomy's insistence that Israel could very easily slide back into idolatry and worship other gods. Sensitivity to the rhetoric of Deuteronomy highlights the qualities of texts typically deemed "monotheistic."[36]

MacDonald may go too far when he claims that Deuteronomy never offers a "doctrine of God" that can be deemed monotheism.[37] I contend that a reframed conception of monotheism can illuminate Deuteronomy's specific concerns. But his point stands that a history-of-religions approach to monotheism often obscures the specific rhetorical context and concerns that give rise to monotheizing language. For MacDonald, even texts which seem so unambiguously monotheistic are intimately related to demands on Israel to remain loyal to YHWH (4:35+39). Israel did not "intellectualize" its understanding of YHWH in any way analogous to the way the term "monotheism" has tended to function since the Enlightenment. To that end, MacDonald helpfully problematizes the very use of the term "monotheism." Therefore, we need to attend to (a) the meaning and usefulness of "monotheism" as a category and (b) Deuteronomy's rhetorical aims. Scholars have also drawn attention to the importance of understanding monotheistic rhetoric in Isaiah (Isa 40:1–55:13).[38]

Recent scholarly literature has paid some attention to the meaning of monotheism and its applicability to the Bible. Some argue for a numerical definition. For them, monotheism refers to the belief that only one deity exists.[39] It reflects "the proposition that for the category or set called deity, there is only one member."[40] Such scholars tend to proceed with the assumption that monotheism requires an explicit declaration that YHWH is the only deity and/or that other deities do not exist. This seems straightforward until we observe the prevalence of 'elohim (and 'elim) in late biblical and later Jewish texts. Even in obviously late texts like the *Songs of the Sabbath Sacrifice*, the heavens are duly populated "divinities" and "holy ones" and YHWH is called the "God of gods."[41] Such texts highlight a phenomenon also extant in the earlier biblical material. Terms for "deity" are applied to greater or lesser beings.[42] The more obvious point is that the major monotheistic religions today all hold to some belief that divine beings of many sorts exist. If the term "monotheism" carries any heuristic usefulness for characterizing Judaism, Christianity, and Islam, then the criterion of a depopulated heaven—except God—will not suffice.

Despite its unproductive uses in the past, however, a modified and nuanced understanding of monotheism can yield new insights into the Bible. Most terms used to analyze ancient texts run the risk of anachronism. Those who prefer terms like "henotheism" or "monolatry" often fail to account for the ways that the Bible considers YHWH to be categorically different, and not just the only God Israel was to worship.[43] Other terms like "incomparability" are certainly appropriate, but do not necessarily account for the exclusive demands of YHWH upon Israel. The question, then, is how to properly qualify and deploy a term like "monotheism" such that it illuminates the Bible. I suggest that applying a category like monotheism to Deuteronomy allows us to observe a rhetorical tendency that we might otherwise miss, namely, the assertion of YHWH's categorical supremacy and exclusive demands in their varying forms. To this extent monotheism provides an opportunity to see Deuteronomy's theological claims moving in concert, even if by means of varied expression.

Rhetoric "involves the expression of YHWH's categorical supremacy."[44] Framed this way, YHWH is not just a bigger and better version of other deities but YHWH is of a wholly different being.[45] This definition allows for the Bible to set the terms by which that supremacy is expressed without trying to squeeze texts to make claims about the number of deities in the heavens that they might not want to make. For instance, some express YHWH's supremacy in relation to his unique acts performed for Israel, without reference to other deities. Others express YHWH's supremacy in relation to his exclusive political claims. Still others will attend to the inactivity of the so-called *other gods*. Focusing on rhetoric avoids unnecessary theological speculation about the beliefs of biblical writers, which may not be accessible to us. Rhetoric focuses on the persuasive purposes of traditions, with due consideration of their theological *implications*. This rhetorical emphasis is especially fitting for a study of Deuteronomy, which scholars have long recognized to be homiletic and didactic in tone.[46]

Sensitivity to Deuteronomy's didactic concerns has significant implications for our study of monotheism. To begin, monotheism recognizes that some texts admit other divine beings into their sphere yet distinguish YHWH in absolute terms. Such texts often serve to *warn* Israel of the dangers posed by turning from YHWH, or they emphasize the fact that other deities *praise* YHWH. Others deny other deities a place in the rhetorical picture. Those texts often serve to *extol* YHWH's supreme qualities (Figure 6.1).

We would be mistaken to rank texts in terms of nascent versus pure monotheism, as Wellhausen and others have done. One would hardly say that the presence of Seraphim (Isa 6:1–13) compromises YHWH's distinctiveness. On the contrary, they augment it. Similarly, the presence of "other " in the *Songs of the Sabbath Sacrifice* only augments YHWH's categorical supremacy.[47] The presence of other deities simply cannot be used as a blunt criterion for determining the degree to which a text considers YHWH categorically supreme. Speaking of later Jewish texts involving a divine retinue, Larry W. Hurtado writes: "The description of the heavenly hosts as a gigantic hierarchy of many ranks . . . is quite easily understood as an attempt to defend the power and significance of Israel's God. The point of these descriptions is to say, 'Do you see how great our God is, who has such a vast and powerful retinue to do nothing but serve him?' "[48]

My argument is not that *all* biblical texts view other deities with the same degree of comfort, but that *many* biblical texts give varied witness to YHWH's categorical supremacy. This will help us understand texts like the Song of Moses (32:1–52), which seems to both deny (32:39) and admit (32: 8, 27) other gods into the rhetorical picture. "No other god" rhetoric emphasizes YHWH's categorical distinctiveness, while the references to other gods, seemingly in the same breath, underscore the retinue of subservient beings at YHWH's disposal.

Moreover, some texts are so underdetermined that they could fit comfortably within or outside monotheism. The most obvious example is the commandment: "You shall have no other gods before me" (5:7). Most would agree that in its first iteration, this commandment assumed the existence of other gods. How comparatively great or trivial they are is unclear. Moreover, the rhetorical aim of the text is clearly not to deny the existence of other deities. Indeed, the reality of other competing deities makes the call to loyalty even more powerful. As Patrick D. Miller notes, "The First Commandment is a tacit acknowledgement that there are always claims of an ultimate sort confronting us."[49] However, the pairing of "I am YHWH your God . . . you shall not have other gods before me" (5:6–7) and "You shall not make for yourself an idol" (5:8) was not lost on later interpreters. The prohibition on images provides an opportunity to recast the prohibition of other gods as a prohibition on other

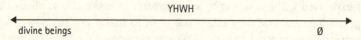

FIGURE 6.1. YHWH and other divine beings.

"idols" in YHWH's presence. One potential interpretation here is that the other gods are *mere* idols. Still other texts presuppose something of a parity between YHWH and other deities (Gen 31:53; Judg 11:24).

Furthermore, monotheistic *rhetoric* should not be equated with monotheistic *belief*. Scholars often assume that the presence of monotheistic rhetoric expresses an underlying belief. While monotheistic rhetoric may indeed reflect shifts in beliefs, this need not follow. Sometimes monotheism is an unintended implication of a text, but not necessarily the author's belief or aim. For instance, "There is none like you among the gods (Ps 86:8)." Yet the same poem exclaims: "You alone are God" (Ps 86:10). The monotheistic rhetoric of first verse, however, does not undermine the claims of the second.

Monotheistic Rhetoric in Deuteronomy

Understanding Deuteronomy's monotheistic rhetoric calls for more careful exegetical work as the following traditions emphasizing YHWH's uniqueness, oneness, supremacy, or relationship to other gods demonstrate.

Deuteronomy 1:1–3:29

The opening chapters of Deuteronomy (1:1–3:29) exhibit little interest in contrasting YHWH with other gods or in asserting YHWH's sole divinity. Given the rest of Deuteronomy's manifest anxiety over the influence of other gods in the outer frame and the Covenant Code, one might expect more (5:7; 6:14; 7:4; 8:19; 11:16, 28; 13:3, 7, 14; 17:3; 18:20; 28:14, 36, 64; 29:25; 30:17; 31:18, 20). These chapters also appear unconcerned about the destruction of altars, high places, or idols in the Trans-Jordan. If the events in the Trans-Jordan presage those in the land, the text's relative silence on the question of other gods or cultic paraphernalia is even more striking. Instead, Moses's renarration of the trans-Jordanian events focuses on high walls and giants, against whom YHWH revealed his power. Not until the prayer of Moses before ascending Pisgah: "Sovereign YHWH, you have begun to show to your servant your greatness and your strong hand. For what god is there in heaven or on earth who can do the deeds and mighty works you do?" (3:24).

Here YHWH's incomparabile "deeds and mighty works" refer to the military actions against Sihon and Og in Heshbon and Bashan (2:24–3:21). Moses's prayer (3:24–25) appeals to the incomplete conquest as a basis for letting him enter the land. YHWH had only *begun* to reveal a "greatness" and "strong hand." Although the prayer admits other gods (3:24) into the rhetorical picture through its comparative statement, it intimates that there is yet more to be seen of YHWH's supremacy in Deuteronomy.

The following tradition (4:1–40) begins and ends with a call to Torah obedience (4:2–5, 40). Israel will find life and know YHWH's presence by keeping the law of Moses. The two outer sections (1–8; 32–40) underscore the need for Torah obedience. The middle section (9–31) rationalizes the *Bilderverbot* in terms of Israel's experience at Horeb. This tradition sets YHWH's sole divinity in sharp relief. YHWH is "the God in heaven above and on the earth beneath; there is no other" (4:32–40). According to Georg Braulik, this claim is "unmistakably monotheistic," though the point of the passage is Torah keeping (4:40).[50]

The tradition employs two word pairs: "heaven and earth" (4:18–19, 26, 39) and "see and hear" (4:6–7, 12, 15, 28, 36, 33) to emphasize the means by which YHWH is to be known. The first pair relates to the fact that Israel is not to make an image or form of any heavenly or earthly bodies. The prohibition on earthly or heavenly images parallels the fact that YHWH is *the* God (האלהים) in heaven and on earth (4:39). YHWH's supremacy cannot be presenced through images or heavenly bodies.[51] Instead, YHWH is revealed through a Torah- keeping people (4: 7–8, 29–31). Hence, YHWH "cannot be perceived by the nations apart from Israel's obedience, and calling on YHWH's name (4:6–8)."[52] Israel is thus akin to YHWH's idol.

The second word pair highlights the fact that Israel knows YHWH through the words they *heard* from the mountain and through Moses *and* through the fire they *saw* on the mountain. The fire and smoke remind the people to keep the commandments, and especially to avoid idolatry (4:23–24). The rationale for not making any "form" of heavenly or earthly beings is that the people saw no "form" of YHWH at Horeb (4:12, 15, 16, 23, 25). Avoidance of images is rooted here in the hiddenness of YHWH's body, and not YHWH's invisibility. The presence of YHWH was not without visual effect, as evident in the fire and thick cloud. These merely shrouded whatever visual form YHWH might have. YHWH's presence was meant to be known indirectly among the nations through a Torah-keeping people, which Deuteronomy considers a point of real difference from other gods (4: 6–8, 20). The prohibition on images drives Israel to "know" YHWH through past deeds and Torah revelation at Horeb (4:9, 35, 39).

A series of positive theological claims conclude the instructions on keeping the commands (4:24–39). These claims follow an historical retrospective (4:1–23). They are unique from others in the chapter in that they predicate YHWH, and each begins with a "for YHWH is" clause (Table 6.1).

The first claim grounds the warning against idolatry by recalling the Decalogue. A commandment (5:8–10) then forbids graven images and warns that YHWH is jealous and visits iniquity to the third and fourth generations. It foregrounds the danger of making idols and the transgenerational effect of doing so. This has obvious implications for a people in exile. Making idols would lead Israel into exile, where they would end up serving "the work of human hands, wood and stone, which neither see nor hear nor eat nor smell" (4:28). The phrase "gods of wood and stone" is uniquely Deuteronomistic (28:36, 64; 29:16; 2 Kgs 19:18; Isa 37:19; Ezek 20:32 omits the reference to deities).

Table 6.1. Descriptions of YHWH

No.	Text	YHWH is...
1	4:24	a consuming fire, a jealous God.
2	4:31	a merciful God will neither abandon you nor destroy you; he will not forget the covenant with your ancestors that he swore to them.
3	4:35	the God (אלהים), there is no other besides him.
4	4:39	the God (אלהים) in heaven above and on the earth beneath; there is no other.

The second theological claim provides a basis for Israel to return to YHWH even when suffering the covenant curses (4:29–30). YHWH's mercy preserves the people who call upon him in their distress and servitude to idols. This latter point recalls that Israel is *gens unique* because YHWH is so near when they call. In sum, the first two theological claims relate to YHWH's intolerance for idols and mercy that extends beyond his intolerance (4:7). They also recall the formative Horeb experience, where Israel broke the second command and yet experienced YHWH's mercy (Exod 32–34).

The second pair of statements concludes two literary panels (4:32–35; 36–39) and culminates with a final exhortation to keep the commands.[53] The first panel emphasizes the unique encounter at Horeb, where Israel heard YHWH's voice and survived (4: 33). This episode parallels Moses's experience, where Moses saw a limited-yet-powerful display of YHWH's glory and lived (Exod 33:20; 34:5–8). Israel heard YHWH's voice "speaking out of a fire . . . and lived" (4:33). This event is so unique that nothing comparable has happened since creation itself. This renders both YHWH and Israel unique. Moreover, Deuteronomy insists that no other god has taken one nation from another with deeds like YHWH's (4:34). The exodus theme is then evident in the summarizing statement (4:35), which uses the "so that you might know" statement that recurs throughout the plagues' narrative (7:17; 8:10, 22; 9:14, 29). The people would come to know that "YHWH is *the* God, there is no other besides him." Taken on its own, the statement may seem like an abstract claim about how many deities exist. But that would blunt the phrase's rhetorical force. In context, the tradition underscores YHWH's mono-agency (4:35). He *alone* brought Israel from Egypt, performed unprecedented signs and wonders, and spoke powerfully from Horeb.

Deuteronomy links "heaven and earth" and "no other." YHWH spoke from "heaven" and the people saw his fire on "earth" at Horeb (4:36). YHWH's revelation at Horeb—"there is none besides me"—is something Israel must "take to heart" so that they prosper in the land. The rhetorical thrust of the second two theological statements is epistemological. Israel was to "know" and "take to heart" the events of the exodus and Horeb so that they did not break the covenant and compromise their hold on the land. As David A. Lambert points out, this kind of "knowing" (*ידע*) is more akin to "experiencing" than anything conveyed by the English "knowing."[54] We might also add that "knowing" involved the embodiment of covenant loyalty. Moses wants the second wilderness generation to re-experience YHWH's mighty deeds in Egypt and the awe-inspiring events at Sinai such that they serve YHWH loyally. The content of that experience is of one divine actor performing all awe-inspiring deeds alone and on behalf of Israel. The phrase "there is no other" (4:35, 39) is thus likely a way of saying "there is no other performing such great deeds" and "there is no other giving such commands with displays of power like these" (4:35, 39). These professions of faith impact an interpretation of *Elohim* as the only deity. Rather than abstract claims about YHWH being the only deity, they refer here to YHWH's monoagency and unique demands. YHWH is the only deity acting on Israel's behalf, and hence the one who lays claim to Israel's loyalty.

Deuteronomy (4:1–40) alternates between (a) admitting other gods into its rhetorical frame for purposes of comparison and (b) emphasizing YHWH's sole agency. On the one hand, it compares YHWH to the deities of other nations, who are *not* near when they call (4:7; 20:10–20). Then it states that other gods were assigned to the nations (4:19), and then asks whether other gods delivered one nation from another (4:34). These texts underscore YHWH's distinctiveness through comparison. On the other hand, the tradition seems just as ready to pull the rug out from under these so-called deities. For instance, it warns that while Israel will serve other gods in exile, they are only wood and stone and cannot see, hear, or smell (28:36, 64). These human-made deities lack agency.

For some, the tradition exercises a controlling function such that references to other gods denote only lifeless human creations (4:28). But that blunts the force of the comparisons, which highlight the threats to YHWH-focused loyalty. Others see the tradition as the end of a long redactional process and assign other texts here to earlier stages in a development toward the monotheistic breakthrough (4:35, 39).[55] Such interpretations ignore the text's rhetoric. If the statements about no other gods (4:35, 39) relate to YHWH as the exclusive deity acting on Israel's behalf, then the idea of a monotheistic breakthrough needs revision.

The significance of the Shema (6:4–5) for a discussion of monotheism is debated. Many reflect the view of Driver, who called this profession of faith "a great declaration of Monotheism."[56] Yet not all are convinced. Daniel I. Block suggests that the Shema should not be taken out of context and interpreted as a "great monotheistic confession." He suggests instead that we are to understand it instead as a "cry of allegiance," a call for covenant loyalty.[57] Some, however, would dispute both claims, suggesting that the Decalogue and the Shema do not epitomize the covenant between YHWH and Israel or Deuteronomy's theology. MacDonald argued that the Shema was a very late addition to Deuteronomy, and thus could not have formed a "bedrock" monotheistic assertion in Deuteronomy[58]

Debates about the pertinence of the Shema for a discussion of monotheism hinge on a range of redactional, translational, and contextual issues. There are several possible ways to translate the brief phrase שמע ישראל יהוה אלהינו יהוה אחד (6:4bc). 1. Hear, O Israel, YHWH our God, YHWH is one. 2. Hear, O Israel, YHWH our God is one YHWH. 3. Hear, O Israel, YHWH is our God; YHWH is one. 4. Hear, O Israel, YHWH is our God; YHWH is One/Unique. 5. Hear, O Israel, YHWH is our God; YHWH alone.[59] Translators generally agree that this brief phrase (6:4bc) consists of two clauses without verbs, but they disagree on their translation and interpretation. The reading: "YHWH our God" (יהוה אלהינו) appears twenty times in Deuteronomy and can be read as the subject or object of a clause which assumes a missing verb.

The phrase "YHWH alone" (יהוה אחד) draws an even wider range of opinions. "YHWH is one" and "YHW is One/Unique" treat אחד as a predicate adjective. They have in their favor the fact that other options exist for the adverbial rendering like "YHWH alone" (יהוה לבדו).[60] For instance, the Israelites "put away the foreign gods and Astartes" (1 Sam 7:4) and served YHWH alone (YHWH לבדו instead of אחד). Similarly, Isaiah (Isa 2:11, 17) states that one day the proud would be humiliated, idols forsaken, and "YHWH alone will be exalted" (ונשגב יהוה לבדו). Moreover, the Septuagint—followed by the NT—and the Nash Papyrus favor the reading: "YHWH is one."[61]

Block, however, observes, examples of "one" (אחת) functioning as an adverbial equivalent—"YHWH alone"—do exist.[62] The Song of Solomon (Song 6:9a) reads, "My dove, my flawless one, is *one*; to her mother she is *one*." This text focuses less on numerical oneness, and instead on uniqueness to her lover and mother. She draws unparalleled attention from her lover and mother.[63] This reading favors either a predicate adjective rendering "unique"—"YHWH is One/Unique"—or an adverbial rendering "alone"—"YHWH alone." Miller is critical of this reading, pointing out that אחת does not necessarily mean "unique" or "without peer" since the mother could have other daughters who are similarly "one and flawless."[64]

The issue of translation cannot be solved on grammatical grounds alone. Contextual considerations come into play, and here debate continues. "YHWH is one" may indicate YHWH's sole divine existence. However, this is an odd way of making such a claim. Also, this line of interpretation runs aground later in the chapter, where other deities re-emerge in the rhetorical picture. Note the impassioned plea not to follow "other gods," which appears in both Deuteronomy (6:14-15; 7:4; 8:19; 11:16, 28) and Jewish daily prayers. Whether these gods exist or not does not seem to concern the writer. Instead, the concern lies with Israel's commitment to YHWH and the exclusivity of that relationship.[65] The warning (6:14-15) to avoid other gods echoes the warning attached to commandments that YHWH your God is a "jealous God" (5:9). This profession of faith likely expands "YHWH is our God, YHWH alone" (6:4bc), a point made convincingly in Karin Finsterbusch's study of the Shema.[66] Here, Deuteronomy is being read as a call to forsake all other gods for YHWH. "Love" (אהב*) here is "loyalty."[67]

Another interpretation of "one" emphasizes the unity of YHWH—"YHWH our God is one YHWH." YHWH is not to be worshipped at multiple cult sites or in a way that might lead to local "versions" of YHWH. The Kuntillet Ajrud inscription, which mentions "YHWH of Samaria" and "YHWH of Teman," tends to feature in such discussions. There is however, little evidence that Deuteronomy is concerned with YHWH's unity, as such. Moreover, the statements "YHWH of Samaria" and "YHWH of Teman" are possibly the same deity recognized in two locations.[68]

Others suggest that YHWH's oneness relates to his consistent character. Building on Miller's insight that the Shema reflects the prologue and first commandments, Janzen suggests that the claim "YHWH is one" refers to "the moral and spiritual integrity of God as manifest in loyalty to Israel."[69] He is "one" in his loyalty toward Israel just as Israel is called to be "one" toward him. "One" here means undivided in one's loyalties, as we see in Jeremiah: "I will give them one (אחד) heart and one (אחד) way, that they may fear me forever . . . and I will plant them in this land, in faithfulness and with all my heart and with all my soul" (Jer 32:38–41).[70]

The roles of Deuteronomy (6:4–5) reverse here in Jeremiah. The people have "one" heart and way, and YHWH remains loyal with his whole heart and soul. Janzen's proposal has two weaknesses. The term "one" in the Jeremiah text modifies "heart" and "way" and does not function like the predicate in Deuteronomy (6:4). "Oneness" as such is never linked to YHWH's own oneness. Also, Deuteronomy focuses solely on the call for Israel's loyalty to YHWH without the kind of reciprocal emphasis of Jeremiah. The reciprocal love of YHWH comes later (7:7–8, 13; 10:12, 18–19).

Contextual clues suggest that "Hear, O Israel: YHWH is our God, YHWH alone" (6:4) grounds the call for unreserved loyalty: "You shall love YHWH your God with all your heart, and with all your soul, and with all your might" (6:5). The command to love is "commensurate" with the revelation that YHWH is "our God" and that, as such, YHWH is "one."[71] YHWH was to be and remain "our God" alone. The command to forsake other deities (6:14–15) thus links "YHWH alone" to "love" (6:4–5).[72] "One" means that "YHWH is unique for Israel, and to receive Israel's wholehearted love."[73] The nations may go their way (6:14–15), but not Israel. Deuteronomy calls for "uncompromising covenant love."[74]

A question remains about the relevance of "Hear, O Israel: YHWH is our God, YHWH alone" (6:4) for our discussion of monotheism. If YHWH's "oneness" relates to YHWH's exclusivity for Israel, does the term "one" bear any relevance for a discussion of YHWH's uniqueness? Moberly suggests that using terms like "monotheism" runs the risk of overintellectualizing Deuteronomy's otherwise persuasive appeal for loyalty to YHWH. "It may have a place, faute de mieux" he suggests, "but it needs at the very least to be a matter of 'handle with care.'"[75] I It is also important to recognize the ways that Deuteronomy grounds the call for loyalty in the uniqueness of YHWH. He is not a deity of the same order as the deities of the nations. YHWH demands utter loyalty only after revealing his utter uniqueness (5:6, 26). While YHWH's "oneness" may relate to an uncompromising devotion, the one to whom Israel is devoted is not just another deity. There is an unrivalled quality to YHWH that warrants Israel's allegiance (7:9).

Deuteronomy warns the people to avoid intermarriage and destroying Canaanite cultic places (7:1–26). Avoiding intermarriage would prevent Israel from "serving other gods" (7:4). Instead of intermarriage, Israelites were to "break," "smash," "cut down," and "burn" their images and altars. This dense set of verses shows the ease with which Deuteronomy moves between talk of other gods and destroying their altars and images. Deuteronomy shows little interest in exploring the ontology of images—whether they manifest the real presence of a deity—and instead focuses on persuading the people to view intermarriage and Canaanite worship as a threat.

More relevant to our discussion of YHWH's sole divinity is: "For YHWH your God, he is the God of gods and Lord of lords, the great God, the mighty and awesome one, who does not show partiality and accepts no bribes" (10:17). These superlatives for YHWH are unprecedented in the Bible. t. h This speech (10:12–22) focuses on the need for Israel to show loyalty to YHWH through loving the foreigner because of YHWH's character and deeds in the past. The pairing of "God of gods" and "Lord of lords" also occurs in a hymn that celebrates YHWH's covenant loyalty (Ps 136:2–3). The phrase "the great God, mighty and awesome" occurs in Nehemiah's prayer (7:21, Neh 8:6, 9:32; Ps 95:3).[76] These may have been common phrases used here in Deuteronomy to highlight the unmatched quality of YHWH's justice and authority.[77] The rhetorical power of this verse depends on the contrast with both deities and human rulers and YHWH's execution of that judicial power on behalf of the vulnerable (16:14–16). It is not by mistake that the string of divine epithets precedes the introduction of the theme of justice (10:18), which reappears (16:18–20) and constitutes a chief concern in Deuteronomy. Unlike earlier claims about YHWH's supremacy discussed in Deuteronomy, which focused on YHWH's unmatched deeds, this text foregrounds his judicial impartiality. Moreover, by contrasting YHWH's impartiality with divine *and* human rulers, Deuteronomy's claim goes beyond a solely *divine* construal of monotheism. Isaiah (Isa 26:13–14) also contrasts allegiance to YHWH with subservience to other אדנים.

YHWH's justice is categorically superior to divine or human power that might vie for Israel's loyalty. In the Neo-Assyrian context in which Deuteronomy may have developed, this claim carries significant force.[78] But it is also specific. It is a *judicial* conception of YHWH's supremacy that carries a persuasive force. It precedes a call for Israel to show "love" for outsiders (16:19), who were at risk of judicial negligence.

Our last case study comes from the Song of Moses (32:1–52). Noticeably absent in our discussion is any reflection on the contributions of the Deuteronomic Code (12:1–26:26) to a discussion of monotheism. Except for references to the threat of "other gods" (13:3, 7, 14; 17:3; 18:18, 20), these chapters do not add anything to our discussion that the outer literary frame does not already contain. While scholars traditionally linked the call for cult centralization to monotheism, nothing in the text commends this, except for the emphasis on the uniqueness of Israel's worship vis-à-vis the nations (12:31).

The Song of Moses constitutes the last portion of divine instruction in Deuteronomy. The introduction (31:16–21) tells us that the poem was a witness against the people when they strayed after "foreign gods of the land" (31:16) they were about to enter. As Brent Strawn and others have observed, the poem's introduction portrays Deuteronomy as a witness against the people (31:26), such that the poem is a "poetic version of (the book of) Torah."[79] It summarizes Deuteronomy's major themes. Its claims about YHWH's supremacy, the status of other gods, and other matters pertaining to YHWH's relationship with Israel are like a prism through which the different rays of Deuteronomy refract. The threefold mention of foreign deities (31:16, 18, 20) sets the parameters for the poem's witness against Israel for its persistent infidelity. The people will surely fall for other gods when Moses dies. To that extent the poem provides an important study in how Deuteronomy intends its readers to hold together Deuteronomy's varied claims about YHWH's supremacy. To begin, we observe the array of claims about YHWH and other deities that impinge on our discussion (see Table 6.2).

Listing these theological claims immediately highlights the oddity of "When the Most High apportioned the nations, when he divided humankind, he fixed the boundaries of the peoples according to the number of the deities; YHWH's own portion was his people, Jacob his allotted share" (32:8–9). The "sons of god(s)" (בני אלים) are hardly of the same order as the "foreign god" (32:12 אל נכר), the "not God" (32:17 לא אלה), or the "no god" (32:21 לא־אל). Moreover, if we are to understand Resheph and Qeteb (32:24) as attacking demons or powers, they are certainly not equivalent to the "sons of gods" who govern the nations. Mashing all these divine beings together into one pantheon against which Israel is to choose YHWH misses the force of the rhetoric. The "other gods" were to be avoided and dismissed as non-gods. The "sons of god(s)," by contrast, were part of a divine assembly that YHWH had apportioned for the nations (4:19; 29:25). The fact that these are called the "sons of god(s)" may reflect the idea that these beings belong to a different class than the "other gods." There is ample evidence that somec traditions conceive of a divine assembly

Table 6.2. Deuteronomy 32 on Divine Supremacy and Other Gods

Text	Theological Claim
32:8–9	Nations fixed according to the number of the sons of (the) god(s)[80]
32:12	YHWH guided Israel alone, with no foreign god
32:16–18, 21	Israel forsakes YHWH and vexes him with "strange (gods)" and "abominations," and sacrificed to "shades," "gods they did not know (before)," "no-god," and "vapors"
32:24	demons(?) Resheph and Qeteb attack[81]
32:37	Taunt: "Where are their gods?"
32:31	"Our God is not like their gods" (in LXX)[82]
32:39	YHWH alone deals death and life, wounds and heals. States that "there is no god beside me."
32:43	The gods' 4QDeut^q and/or sons of god,[83] are summoned to praise YHWH.

over which YHWH presides.[84] While other traditions seem to find mention of the "sons of god(s)" problematic, the earliest versions of the Song of Moses show no such anxiety (Ps 29:1; 96:7).

If so, how do we reconcile "When the Most High apportioned the nations, when he divided humankind, he fixed the boundaries of the peoples according to the number of the gods" (32:8) and "Praise, O heavens, his people, worship him, all you gods!" (32:43) with the other texts in the same chapter that seem to repudiate or dismiss other gods? For Michael Heiser, the other gods *are* the sons of God who "judge unjustly and show partiality to the wicked" (Ps 82:2).[85] It is doubtful, however, that this psalm is to be understood in historical terms, or at least that it forms the backdrop for the negative images of "the gods of the nations".[86]

A rhetorical approach sees the Song of Moses making two simultaneous moves. On the one hand, the deities of the nations are not for Israel. Going after other gods not apportioned to Israel (29:25) is prohibited, even though they are ostensibly there to be followed. On the other hand, insofar as those deities are powerless to help Israel, they are ridiculed as "strange (gods)," "abominations," "shades," and "vapors" (32:16–21). The sequence of derisions set these deities apart as "off limits," but also highlights that they are as nothing—not even worthy of the name "god" (32:21; אל). This latter approach underscores the utter folly of following other gods who cannot provide shelter and protection like Israel's "rock" (32:31). They have no substance. Unlike the "rock" of Israel, they are vapor.

The deities, however, re-emerge to worship YHWH (32:43), this time underscoring the utter praiseworthiness of YHWH.[87] This latter part of the poem returns to the rhetorical mode where the "sons of god(s)" reflect YHWH's stature as supreme (32:8–9).[88] The other gods are insubstantial, highlighting YHWH's unmatched authority and rightful possession of the title "God" (אל), *and* the deities are the chorus that worship him, highlighting YHWH's utter praiseworthiness (Ps 86:8, 10). Both moves stand in service of the claim that YHWH is categorically supreme. While one might isolate specific verses to support a polytheistic perspective, a contextual approach to the poem commends a monotheistic interpretation.[89]

Conclusion

Our study of Deuteronomy highlights several important points about the study of monotheism in Deuteronomy. First, the term "monotheism" can carry unwanted baggage that intellectualizes Israelite religion and obscures the specific claims of Deuteronomy. A modified approach focuses on monotheizing rhetoric, by which Deuteronomy asserts YHWH's uniqueness in varying ways. The term "monotheizing," however, preserves the text's own emphasis on the fact that YHWH is not just the deity who makes demands on Israel, but is unmatched in every way and thus worthy of Israel's devotion. Second, attentiveness to supposed monotheistic texts brings into focus a range of ways of speaking about other deities. In some cases, texts seem to presuppose their existence. In other cases, they are reduced to nothing. Yet here again, a rhetorical approach emphasizes the fact that YHWH is supreme and worthy of Israel's exclusive worship. Moreover, some texts that emphasize YHWH as "the only God" are making claims about YHWH's sole agency, justice, and demands of Israel. YHWH is indeed "the only" in specific senses, namely, through his sole deliverance of the people from Egypt and in the creation of a Torah-keeping people. Those two events, perhaps more than any other, are the terms by which Deuteronomy considers YHWH categorically supreme. Moreover, Israel's knowledge of YHWH's sole divinity is not for pure doctrinal purposes. "Knowing" YHWH's sole divinity is meant to be enacted through Torah-keeping. For other texts, YHWH's "supreme lordship" relates to his judicial impartiality and grounds a call for Israel to practice justice (10:17–18). Finally, rather than using Deuteronomy to trace developments in a belief that YHWH is the only God, this study focused on the complementary range of assertions about YHWH's supremacy in Deuteronomy. The Old Testament bears witness to an even fuller range of monotheizing modes, not all of which are genetically related or traceable in historical terms. Wide swathes of the Old Testament recognize the fact that YHWH is supreme, but the terms by which they do so differ widely, even within Deuteronomy.[90]

Notes

1. Translations are from the New Revised Standard Version (1989) with the substitution of "YHWH" for "the LORD" throughout.
2. G. A. Rogers, "The Other-Worldly Philosophers and the Real World: The Cambridge Platonists, Theology and Politics," in *The Cambridge Platonists in Philosophical Context: Politics, Metaphysics and Religion*, ed. G. A. Rogers, J-M. Vienne, and Yves Charles Zarka, International Archives of the History of Ideas 150 (London: Springer Science & Business Media, 2013), 3–16 [5]. Tod E. Jones, ed., *The Cambridge Platonists: A Brief Introduction* (New York: University Press of America, 2005), 3.
3. Nathan MacDonald, *Deuteronomy and the Meaning of "Monotheism,"* 2nd ed.; FAT II/1 (Tübingen: Mohr Siebeck, 2012), 5–52.
4. Ernst Troeltsch, "The Dogmatics of the 'Religionsgeschichtliche Schule,'" *AJT* 17, no. 1 (1913): 1–21.
5. Peter Schäfer, *Two Gods in Heaven: Jewish Concepts of God in Antiquity* (Princeton: Princeton University Press, 2020), 2.
6. Julius Wellhausen, *Prolegomena to the History of Israel, With a Reprint of the Article "Israel" from the Encyclopedia Britannica*, trans. J. S. Black and A. Menzies (Cambridge: Cambridge University Press, 2013), 398.
7. Wellhausen, *Prolegomena*, 36.
8. Abraham Kuenen, *The Prophets and Prophecy in Ancient Israel: An Historical and Critical Enquiry*, trans. Adam Milroy (London: Longmans, Green and Co., 1877), 590.
9. Kuenen, *Prophets*, 555.
10. Samuel R. Driver, *Deuteronomy*, 3rd ed.; ICC (Edinburgh: T&T Clark, 1902), xxviii–xxix.
11. William F. Albright, *From the Stone Age to Christianity* (Garden City: Doubleday, 1957), 88–89.
12. Albright, *Stone Age*, 170, 182.
13. Albright, *Stone Age*, 122.
14. See the critique by MacDonald, *Deuteronomy*, 33.
15. Albright, *Stone Age*, 260–270.
16. Albright, *Stone Age*, 272.
17. MacDonald, *Deuteronomy*, 33.

18. Yehezkel Kaufmann, *History of the Religion of Israel: Volume IV: From the Babylonian Captivity to the End of Prophecy*, trans. C. W. Efroymson (Jerusalem: Hebrew University, 1977), 13–15.
19. Kaufmann, *History*, 147–148.
20. Kaufmann, *History*, 81.
21. Kaufmann, *History*, 226–227.
22. Benjamin D. Sommer, "Yehezkel Kaufmann and Recent Scholarship: Toward a Richer Discourse on Monotheism," in *Yehezkel Kaufman and the Reinvention of Jewish Biblical Scholarship*, ed. Job Y. Jindo, Benjamin D. Sommer, and Thomas Staubli; OBO 283 (Göttingen: Vandenhoeck & Ruprecht, 2017), 204–239.
23. Gerhard Von Rad, *Old Testament Theology: The Theology of Israel's Historical Traditions: Volume 1*, trans. D. M. G. Stalker (Louisville: Westminster John Knox Press, 2001), 177, 212. For a critique of von Rad's depiction of the free-thinking prophet, see Robert Wilson, *Prophecy and Society in Ancient Israel* (Philadelphia: Fortress Press, 1980).
24. Gerhard Von Rad, "The Origin of Mosaic Monotheism," in *God at Work in Israel*, trans. J. H. Marks (Nashville: Abingdon Press, 1980), 128–138 [131].
25. Von Rad, "The Origin," 132.
26. Von Rad, "The Origin," 136–137.
27. Alexander Rofé, "The Monotheistic Argumentation in Deuteronomy IV 32-40: Contents, Composition, and Text," *VT* XXV/4 (1985): 434–445; cf. Braulik, "Deuteronomy," 122–123.
28. Braulik, "Deuteronomy," 100.
29. Braulik, "Deuteronomy," 121–123.
30. Hans Rechenmacher, *"Außer mir gibt es keinen Gott!": Eine sprach- und literaturwissenschaftliche Studie zur Ausschließlichkeitsformel*; ATSAT 49 (St. Ottilien: EOS Verlag, 1997).
31. Joachim Schaper, *Media and Monotheism: Presence, Representation, and Abstraction in Ancient Judah*, ORA 33 (Tübingen: Mohr Siebeck, 2019), esp. 224–239.
32. J. Gordon McConville, *Grace in the End: A Study in Deuteronomic Theology* (Grand Rapids: Zondervan, 1993), 124. Nathan MacDonald, *Deuteronomy and the Meaning of "Monotheism,"* 2nd ed., Forschungen zum Alten Testament II/1 (Tübingen: Mohr Siebeck, 2012). R. W. L. Moberly, "How Appropriate Is 'Monotheism' as a Category for Biblical Interpretation?" in *Early Jewish and Christian Monotheism*, ed. L. T. Stuckenbruck and W. E. Spronston North; JSNTSup 263 (London: Sheffield Academic Press, 2004), 216–234.
33. Moberly, "How Appropriate Is 'Monotheism,'" 233.
34. MacDonald, *Deuteronomy*, 218.
35. Mark S. Smith, *The Origins of Biblical Monotheism: Israel's Polytheistic Background and the Ugaritic Texts* (New York: Oxford University Press, 2001), 154.
36. MacDonald, *Deuteronomy*, 218.
37. MacDonald, *Deuteronomy*, 209.
38. Mark S. Smith, "The Polemic of Biblical Monotheism: Outsider Context and Insider Referentiality in Second Isaiah," in *Religious Polemics in Context: Papers Presented to the Second International Conference of the Leider Institute for the Study of Religions (LISOR) held at Leiden, 27-28 April 2000*, ed. T. L. Hettema and A. Van der Kooij (Assen: Van Gorcum, 2004), 201–234. Matthew J. Lynch, "Mapping Monotheism: Modes of Monotheistic Rhetoric in the Hebrew Bible," *Vetus Testamentum* 64 (2014): 47–68.
39. Sommer, "Yehezkel Kaufmann," 206–207.
40. Peter Machinist, "Once More: Monotheism in Biblical Israel," *JISMOR* 1 (2005): 25–39 [26].

41. Michael S. Heiser, "Monotheism and the Language of Divine Plurality in the Hebrew Bible and the Dead Sea Scrolls," *TynBul* 65, no. 1 (2014): 85–100.
42. Joel S. Burnett, "אֱלוֹהִים 'Elohim," *TWQT* 1:178– 190; John J. Collins, "Powers in Heaven: God, Gods, and Angels in the Dead Sea Scrolls," in *Religion in the Dead Sea Scrolls*, ed. J. J. Collins and R. A. Kugler (Grand Rapids: Eerdmans, 2000), 9–28; Mark S. Smith, *God in Translation: Deities in Cross-Cultural Discourse in the Biblical World* (Tübingen: Mohr Siebeck, 2008), 11–15; Michael S. Heiser, "Does Divine Plurality in the Hebrew Bible Demonstrate an Evolution from Polytheism to Monotheism in Israelite Religion?," *JESOT* 1, no. 1 (2012): 1–24 [5].
43. Peter Machinist, "The Question of Distinctiveness in Ancient Israel: An Essay," in *Ah, Assyria... Studies in Assyrian History and Ancient Near Eastern Historiography Presented to Hayim Tadmor*, ed. Mordechai Cogan and Israel Ephal (Jerusalem: Magnes Press, 1991), 192–212.
44. Lynch, "Mapping Monotheism," 50.
45. Lynch, "Mapping Monotheism," 47–68 and *Monotheism and Institutions in the Book of Chronicles: Temple, Priesthood, and Kingship in Post-Exilic Perspective*; FAT II/64 (Tübingen: Mohr Siebeck, 2014), 35–48.
46. Gerhard von Rad, "The Form-Critical Problem of the Hexateuch," in *The Problem of the Hexateuch and Other Essays*, trans. E. A. Trueman Dicken (Edinburgh: Oliver & Boyd, 1966), 1–78; August Klostermann, *Der Pentateuch: Beiträge zu seinem Verständnis und siner Entstehungsgeschichte* (Leipzig: Deichert, 1907), 154; Douglas W. Kennard, *Biblical Covenantlism*, vol. 1 (Eugene: Wipf & Stock, 2015), 163–166.
47. 4QShirShabbd frg. 1 col. 1. 30–46. Reinhard G. Kratz, "Deity and Divine in the Hebrew Bible and in the Dead Sea Scrolls," in *Sibyls, Scriptures, and Scrolls*, ed. Joel Baden, Hindy Najman, and Eibert J. C. Tigchelaar; JSJSup 175 (Leiden: Brill, 2017), 636–643.
48. Larry W. Hurtado, *One God, One Lord: Early Christian Devotion and Ancient Jewish Monotheism* (Philadelphia: Fortress Press, 1988), 25; H. Bietenhard, *Die himmlische Welt im Urchristentum und Spätjudentum*; WUNT 2 (J. C. B. Mohr [Paul Siebeck], 1951), 101–142. Lynch, "Mapping Monotheism," 56.
49. Patrick D. Miller, *The Ten Commandments: Interpretation: Resources for the Use of Scripture in the Church* (Louisville: Westminster John Knox Press, 2009), 26–27.
50. Georg Braulik, "Deuteronomy and the Birth of Monotheism," 121; Georg Braulik, "Literarkritik und archäologische Stratigraphie: Zu S. Mittmanns Analyse von Deuteronomium 4, 1–40," *Biblica* 59, no. 3 (1978): 351–383.
51. MacDonald, *Deuteronomy*, 197.
52. MacDonald, *Deuteronomy*, 207.
53. MacDonald, *Deuteronomy*, 189–202.
54. David A. Lambert, "Refreshing Philology: James Barr, Supersessionism, and the State of Biblical Words," *BI* 24 (2016): 332–356 [340–341].
55. Braulik, "Deuteronomy," 122–123.
56. Driver, *Deuteronomy*, 90.
57. Daniel I. Block, "How Many Is God? An Investigation into the Meaning of Deuteronomy 6:4–5," *Journal of the Evangelical Theological Society* 47, no. 2 (2004): 193–212 [211].
58. Nathan MacDonald, "The Date of the Shema (Deuteronomy 6:4–5)," *JBL* 136, no. 4 (2017): 765–782. MacDonald's study challenges and modifies Timo Veijola's, "Hore Israel! Der Sinn und Hintergrund von Deuteronomium VI 4–9," *VT* 42 (1992): 528–541; and Veijola, "Das Bekenntnis Israels: Beobachtungen zur Geschichte und Theologie von Dtn 6,4–9," *ThZ* 48 (1992): 369–381.

59. Block, "How Many Is God?" 196; MacDonald, *Deuteronomy*, 64. For other options, see MacDonald, *Deuteronomy*, 68-70.
60. Block, "How Many Is God?" 197.
61. Block, "How Many Is God?" 198. The Nash Papyrus adds אוה after דחא.
62. Block, "How Many Is God?" 199; Moshe Weinfeld, *Deuteronomy 1-11*; AB 5 (New York: Doubleday, 1991), 338.
63. MacDonald, *Deuteronomy*, 74.
64. Patrick D. Miller, A Review of Nathan MacDonald, *Deuteronomy and the Meaning of 'Monotheism, Biblical Interpretation* (2004): 303-305 [304].
65. McConville, *Deuteronomy*, 141.
66. Karin Finsterbusch, "Bezüge zwischen Aussagen von Dtn 6,4-9 und 6,10-25," ZAW 114 (2002): 433-437 (cited in Block, "How Many Is God?" 205).
67. William L. Moran, "The Ancient Near Eastern Background of the Love of God in Deuteronomy," *CBQ* 25, no. 1 (1963): 77-87; Patrick D. Miller, *Deuteronomy: A Bible Commentary for Teaching and Preaching* (Interpretation; Louisville: WJK Press, 1990), 101-102; Abraham Malamat, "You Shall Love Your Neighbor As Yourself: A Case of Misinterpretation?" in *Die Hebräische Bibel und ihre zwei fache Nachgeschichte, Festschrift für Rolf Rendtorff zum 65. Geburtstag*, ed. E. Blum, C. Macholz, and E. W. Stegemann (Neukirchen-Vluyn: Neukirchener, 1990), 111-115.
68. MacDonald, *Deuteronomy*, 71.
69. J. Gerald Janzen, "Yahweh Our God, Yahweh Is One," *Encounter* 48 (1987): 53-60 [57-58].
70. Janzen's translation, from "Yahweh Our God," 57.
71. R. W. L. Moberly, *Old Testament Theology: Reading the Hebrew Bible as Christian Scripture* (Grand Rapids: Baker Academic, 2013), 20.
72. Finsterbusch, "Bezüge," 434.
73. MacDonald, *Deuteronomy*, 74.
74. Block, "How Many Is God?" 212.
75. Moberly, *Old Testament Theology*, 35.
76. For a study of the early history of the Shema's reception and its growing importance for discussions of monotheism, see E. Eshel, H. Eshel, and A. Lange, "'Hear, O Israel' in Gold: An Ancient Amulet from Halbturn in Austria," *Journal of Ancient Judaism* 1 (2010): 43-64; Dominik Markl, "The Ambivalence of Authority in Deuteronomy: Reaction, Revision, Rewriting, Reception," *Cristianesimo nella storia* 41 (forthcoming 2020). Special thanks to Dominik Markl for pointing me toward these resources; cf. Deut 7:21, Neh 8:6 and Ps 95:3.
77. McConville, *Deuteronomy*, 200-201.
78. Eckart Otto, *Das Deuteronomium: Politische Theologie und Rechtsreform in Juda und Assyrien* (Berlin: Walter de Gruyter, 2015); C. L. Crouch, *Israel and the Assyrians: Deuteronomy, the Succession Treaty of Esarhaddon, and the Nature of Subversion*; SBLANEM 8 (Atlanta: SBL Press, 2014).
79. Brent A. Strawn, *The Old Testament is Dying: A Diagnosis and Recommended Treatment* (Grand Rapids: Baker Academic, 2017), 206; MacDonald, *Deuteronomy*, 145-147.
80. Following 4QDeutj and LXX (Theodotian, Symmachus, Aquila follow the MT with בני ישראל). For a discussion of text-critical issues in 32:8-9, see Emanuel Tov, *Textual Criticism of the Hebrew Bible*, 2nd ed. (Minneapolis: Fortress Press, 1992), 269.
81. Nicholas Wyatt, "Qeteb קטב," *DDD*, 673-674; P. Xella, "Resheph רשף," *DDD*, 700-703; Paul Sanders, *The Provenance of Deuteronomy Thirty-Two*; OS/OTS 37 (Leiden: Brill, 1996), 195-196.

82. The LXX's οἱ θεοὶ αὐτῶν may be correcting the apparently confusing צורם ("their rock") in the proto-MT.
83. LXX has both υἱοὶ θεοῦ and ἄγγελοι θεοῦ in parallel lines and may preserve an original with אלהים and the בני אלים.
84. Ellen White, *Yahweh's Council: Its Structure and Membership*; FAT 2/65 (Tübingen: Mohr Siebeck, 2014), 34–42; Michael S. Heiser, *The Unseen Realm: Recovering the Supernatural Worldview of the Bible* (Bellingham: Lexham Press, 2015).
85. Heiser, *The Unseen Realm*, especially his fourth chapter.
86. Brent A. Strawn, "The Poetics of Psalm 82: Three Critical Notes along with a Plea for the Poetic," *RB* 121 (2014): 21–46.
87. MacDonald, *Deuteronomy*, 94, notes the ambiguity.
88. Lynch, "Mapping Monotheism."
89. Sommer, "Kaufmann," 219–220.
90. Lynch, "Mapping Monotheism," 66–68.

Bibliography

Albright, William F. *From the Stone Age to Christianity*. Garden City: Doubleday, 1957.
Bauckham, Richard. *Jesus and the God of Israel: God Crucified and Other Studies on the New Testament's Christology of Divine Identity*. Grand Rapids: Eerdmans, 2008.
Bietenhard, H. *Die himmlische Welt im Urchristentum und Spätjudentum*. Wissenschaftliche Untersuchungen zum Neuen Testament 2. Tübingen: J. C. B. Mohr [Paul Siebeck], 1951.
Block, Daniel I. "How Many Is God? An Investigation into the Meaning of Deuteronomy 6:4–5." *JETS* 47, no. 2 (2004): 193–212.
Braulik, Georg. "Deuteronomy and the Birth of Monotheism." In *The Theology of Deuteronomy*, edited by Georg Braulik, 87–130. N. Richland Hills: BIBAL Press, 1994.
Braulik, Georg. "Literarkritik und archäologische Stratigraphie: Zu S. Mittmanns Analyse von Deuteronomium 4,1–40." *Biblica* 59, no. 3 (1978): 351–383.
Collins, John J. "Powers in Heaven: God, Gods, and Angels in the Dead Sea Scrolls." In *Religion in the Dead Sea Scrolls*, edited by John J. Collins and R. A. Kugler, 9–28. Grand Rapids: Eerdmans, 2000.
Crouch, C. L. *Israel and the Assyrians: Deuteronomy, the Succession Treaty of Esarhaddon, and the Nature of Subversion*. Society of Biblical Literature Ancient Near Eastern Manuscripts 8. Atlanta: SBL Press, 2014.
Driver, Samuel R. *A Critical and Exegetical Commentary on Deuteronomy*. International Critical Commentary. Edinburgh: T&T Clark, 1902.
Finsterbusch, Karin. "Bezüge zwischen Aussagen von Dtn 6,4–9 und 6,10–25." *Zeitschrift für die Alttestamentliche Wissenschaft* 114 (2002): 433–437.
Heiser, Michael S. "Does Divine Plurality in the Hebrew Bible Demonstrate an Evolution from Polytheism to Monotheism in Israelite Religion?" *Journal for the Evangelical Study of the Old Testament* 1, no. 1 (2012): 1–24.
Heiser, Michael S. "Monotheism and the Language of Divine Plurality in the Hebrew Bible and the Dead Sea Scrolls." *Tyndale Bulletin* 65, no. 1 (2014): 85–100.
Heiser, Michael S. *The Unseen Realm: Recovering the Supernatural Worldview of the Bible*. Bellingham: Lexham Press, 2015.

Hurtado, Larry W. *One God, One Lord: Early Christian Devotion and Ancient Jewish Monotheism*. Philadelphia: Fortress Press, 1988.

Jones, Tod E., ed. *The Cambridge Platonists: A Brief Introduction*. New York: University Press of America, 2005.

Kaufmann, Yehezkel. *History of the Religion of Israel: Volume IV: From the Babylonian Captivity to the End of Prophecy*. Translated by C. W. Efroymson. Jerusalem: Hebrew University, 1977.

Kennard, Douglas W. *Biblical Covenantlism, vol. 1*. Eugene: Wipf & Stock, 2015.

Klostermann, August. *Der Pentateuch: Beiträge zu seinem Verständnis und seiner Entstehungsgeschichte*. Leipzig: Deichert, 1907.

Kratz, Reinhard G. "Deity and Divine in the Hebrew Bible and in the Dead Sea Scrolls." In *Sibyls, Scriptures, and Scrolls*, edited by Joel Baden, Hindy Najman, and Eibert J. C. Tigchelaar, 636–643. Supplements to the Journal for the Study of Judaism 175. Leiden: Brill, 2017.

Kuenen, Abraham. *The Prophets and Prophecy in Ancient Israel: An Historical and Critical Enquiry*. Translated by Adam Milroy. London: Longmans, Green and Co., 1877.

Lambert, David A. "Refreshing Philology: James Barr, Supersessionism, and the State of Biblical Words." *Biblical Interpretation* 24 (2016): 332–356.

Lynch, Matthew J. "Mapping Monotheism: Modes of Monotheistic Rhetoric in the Hebrew Bible." *Vetus Testamentum* 64 (2014): 47–68.

Lynch, Matthew J. *Monotheism and Institutions in the Book of Chronicles: Temple, Priesthood, and Kingship in Post-Exilic Perspective*. Forschungen zum Alten Testament II/64. Tübingen: Mohr Siebeck, 2014.

MacDonald, Nathan. "The Date of the Shema (Deuteronomy 6:4–5)." *Journal of Biblical Literature* 136, no. 4 (2017): 765–782.

MacDonald, Nathan. *Deuteronomy and the Meaning of "Monotheism."* 2nd edition. Forschungen zum Alten Testament II/1. Tübingen: Mohr Siebeck, 2012.

Machinist, Peter. "Once More: Monotheism in Biblical Israel." *Journal of the Interdisciplinary Study of Monotheistic Religions* 1 (2005): 25–39.

Machinist, Peter. "The Question of Distinctiveness in Ancient Israel: An Essay." In *Ah, Assyria . . . Studies in Assyrian History and Ancient Near Eastern Historiography Presented to Hayim Tadmor*, edited by Mordechai Cogan and Israel Ephal, 192–212. Jerusalem: Magnes Press, 1991.

Malamat, Abraham. "'You Shall Love Your Neighbor As Yourself: A Case of Misinterpretation?" In *Die Hebräische Bibel und ihre zweifache Nachgeschichte, Festschrift für Rolf Rendtorff zum 65. Geburtstag*, edited by E. Blum, C. Macholz, and E. W. Stegemann, 111–115. Neukirchen-Vluyn: Neukirchener, 1990.

McConville, J. Gordon. *Grace in the End: A Study in Deuteronomic Theology*. Grand Rapids: Zondervan, 1993.

Miller, Patrick D. *Deuteronomy: A Bible Commentary for Teaching and Preaching*. Interpretation. Louisville: WJK Press, 1990.

Miller, Patrick D. *The Ten Commandments: Interpretation: Resources for the Use of Scripture in the Church*. Louisville: Westminster John Knox Press, 2009.

Moberly, R. W. L. "How Appropriate Is 'Monotheism' as a Category for Biblical Interpretation?" In *Early Jewish and Christian Monotheism*, edited by L. T. Stuckenbruck and W. E. Spronston North, 216–234. Journal for the Study of the New Testament: Supplement Series 263. London: Sheffield Academic Press, 2004.

Moberly, R. W. L. *Old Testament Theology: Reading the Hebrew Bible as Christian Scripture*. Grand Rapids: Baker Academic, 2013.

Moran, William L. "The Ancient Near Eastern Background of the Love of God in Deuteronomy." *The Catholic Biblical Quarterly* 25, no. 1 (1963): 77–87.

Otto, Eckart. *Das Deuteronomium: Politische Theologie und Rechtsreform in Juda und Assyrien.* Berlin: Walter de Gruyter, 2015.

Rechenmacher, Hans. *"Außer mir gibt es keinen Gott!": Eine sprach- und literarturwissenschaftliche Studie zur Ausschließlichkeitsformel.* Arbeiten zu Text und Sprache im Alten Testament 49. St. Ottilien: EOS Verlag, 1997.

Rogers, G. A. "The Other-Worldly Philosophers and the Real World: The Cambridge Platonists, Theology and Politics." In *The Cambridge Platonists in Philosophical Context: Politics, Metaphysics and Religion*, edited by G. A. Rogers, J-M. Vienne, and Yves Charles Zarka, 3–16. International Archives of the History of Ideas 150. London: Springer Science & Business Media, 2013.

Sanders, Paul. *The Provenance of Deuteronomy Thirty-Two.* Oudtestamentische Studiën 37. Leiden: Brill, 1996.

Schäfer, Peter. *Two Gods in Heaven: Jewish Concepts of God in Antiquity.* Princeton: Princeton University Press, 2020.

Schaper, Joachim. *Media and Monotheism: Presence, Representation, and Abstraction in Ancient Judah.* Orientalische Religionen in der Antike 33. Tübingen: Mohr Siebeck, 2019.

Smith, Mark S. *God in Translation: Deities in Cross-Cultural Discourse in the Biblical World.* Tübingen: Mohr Siebeck, 2008.

Smith, Mark S. *The Origins of Biblical Monotheism: Israel's Polytheistic Background and the Ugaritic Texts.* New York: Oxford University Press, 2001.

Smith, Mark S. "The Polemic of Biblical Monotheism: Outsider Context and Insider Referentiality in Second Isaiah." In *Religious Polemics in Context: Papers Presented to the Second International Conference of the Leider Institute for the Study of Religions (LISOR) held at Leiden, 27-28 April 2000*, edited by T. L. Hettema and A. Van der Kooij, 201–234. Assen: Van Gorcum, 2004.

Sommer, Benjamin. *The Bodies of God and the World of Ancient Israel.* New York: Cambridge University Press, 2009.

Sommer, Benjamin. "Yehezkel Kaufmann and Recent Scholarship: Toward a Richer Discourse on Monotheism." In *Yehezkel Kaufman and the Reinvention of Jewish Biblical Scholarship*, edited by Job Y. Jindo, Benjamin D. Sommer, and Thomas Staubli, 204–239. Orbis biblicus et orientalis 283. Göttingen: Vandenhoeck & Ruprecht, 2017.

Strawn, Brent A. *The Old Testament Is Dying: A Diagnosis and Recommended Treatment.* Grand Rapids: Baker Academic, 2017.

Strawn, Brent A. "The Poetics of Psalm 82: Three Critical Notes along with a Plea for the Poetic." *Revue Biblique* 121 (2014): 21–46.

Tov, Emanuel. *Textual Criticism of the Hebrew Bible.* 2nd ed. Minneapolis: Fortress Press, 1992.

Troeltsch, Ernst. "The Dogmatics of the 'Religionsgeschichtliche Schule.'" *The American Journal of Theology* 17, no. 1 (1913): 1–21.

Veijola, Timo. "Das Bekenntnis Israels: Beobachtungen zur Geschichte und Theologie von Dtn 6,4–9." *Theologische Zeitschrift* 48 (1992): 369–381.

Veijola, Timo. "Hore Israel! Der Sinn und Hintergrund von Deuteronomium VI 4–9." *Vetus Testamentum* 42 (1992): 528–541.

Von Rad, Gerhard. "The Form-Critical Problem of the Hexateuch." In *The Problem of the Hexateuch and Other Essays*, translated by E. A. Trueman Dicken, 1–78. Edinburgh: Oliver & Boyd, 1966.

Von Rad, Gerhard. *Old Testament Theology: The Theology of Israel's Historical Traditions: Volume 1.* Translated by D. M. G. Stalker. Louisville: Westminster John Knox Press, 2001.

Von Rad, Gerhard. "The Origin of Mosaic Monotheism." In *God at Work in Israel*, translated by J. H. Marks, 128–138. Nashville: Abingdon Press, 1980.

Weinfeld, Moshe. *Deuteronomy 1–11*. Anchor Bible 5. New York: Doubleday, 1991.

Wellhausen, Julias. *Prolegomena to the History of Israel, with a Reprint of the Article "Israel" from the Encyclopedia Britannica*. Translated by J. S. Black and A. Menzies. Cambridge: Cambridge University Press, 2013.

White, Ellen. *Yahweh's Council: Its Structure and Membership*. Forschungen zum Alten Testament 2/65. Tübingen: Mohr Siebeck, 2014.

Wilson, Robert. *Prophecy and Society in Ancient Israel*. Philadelphia: Fortress Press, 1980.

CHAPTER 7

SPACE THEORY AND THE *MAQOM* (SANCTUARY) IN DEUTERONOMY

MICHAELA GEIGER

Who Began the Conversation?

The issue of "Space Theory and the *Maqom* (Sanctuary) in Deuteronomy" is based on the assumption that space is socially constructed and that the social is spatial (Löw 2018, xiv–xvi). The discourse on "spatiality" in the Old Testament has developed around the Society of Biblical Literature (SBL) conferences since 2000: The International Meetings have regularly offered sessions on "Place, Space, and Identity in the Ancient Mediterranean World," and at the Annual Meetings, the sessions are called "Space, Place, and Lived Experience in Antiquity." Results have been published continuously as "Constructions of Space I–V" (2008–2013).

Henri Lefebvre and Edward Soja

The discussion is dominated by the reception of the spatial theory of Marxist sociologist Henri Lefebvre. In the United States, his work "Production de l'espace" (Lefebvre 1974, French; Lefebvre 1991, English) was introduced first and foremost through the interpretation of geographer Edward Soja, since his initial interpretation of Lefebvre had already been published in English (Soja 1989).

Lefebvre viewed space as the result of processes of social production which can be captured analytically as the interaction among three dimensions: The first dimension describes space as *perceived space* ("l'espace perçu"), as physically experienced space that is created and reproduced through spatial practice. The second dimension, the *conceived space* ("l'espace conçu"), is the cognitive grasp of spaces in the form of models and plans. From this conceptual perspective, Lefebvre distinguished the dimension of subjective images and symbolic meanings, *lived space* ("l'espace vécu") or "spaces of representation." This third dimension can subvert the dominant social spatial practice or order, as it is connected to the hidden, subterranean side of social life and art.

Edward Soja took up Lefebvre's triad, suggesting the terms "Firstspace," "Secondspace," and "Thirdspace," and primarily expanded the concept of Thirdspace in particular (Soja 1996). Contrary to the physically experienced space (Firstspace) and the spatial mores determined by the prevailing power relations (Secondspace), Soja conceptualized Thirdspace as a space of resistance, as "space of all-inclusive simultaneities, perils as well as possibilities: the space of radical openness" (Soja 1989, 68), thus adopting the perspective of the marginalized.

With regard to the *maqom*, two theological publications are particularly relevant. The first monograph, *Daughter Zion, Mother Zion* by Christl M. Maier, deals with the spatial representation of Zion as personification, city, and temple area in Old Testament texts: "the personification allows one to think of Zion as a space and as a woman that represents the inhabitants of this space" (Maier 2008, 2). Based on Henri Lefebvre's theory of space, Maier traced the changes the spatial conception of Zion undergoes in prophetic texts, psalms, and lamentations from the pre-exilic to the exilic and postexilic periods. In her treatment of *perceived space*, Maier analyzed the material shape of Zion as a topographical framework for the bodily experience of space.

Maier saw Lefebvre's second dimension, *conceived space*, as a spatial order shaped ideologically and related in particular to the theology of Zion, which understood Mt. Zion as the throne of YHWH as the place of mediation between YHWH's presence above the ark in the temple and his throne in heaven. The destruction of the temple results in the collapse of the Zion ideology. It is expressed in Lamentations or in the rape images of Zion (Ezek. 16, 23), which Maier interpreted "as a polemical counterimage of *conceived space*" (Maier 2008, 123). Only the late and postexilic texts of Isaiah 40–66 sketch a new vision of Zion as a protective mother and place of pilgrimage (Isa. 54:1–3; 66:7–14), which, however, always carries the reminder of vulnerability.

Maier examined the concrete experiences of space in the biblical Zion texts as examples of Lefebvre's third dimension of *lived space*. On the one hand, she uncovered a spatial practice that includes the praise of YHWH, rituals, and processions (Ps. 46, 48). On the other hand, the spatial experience in Lamentations mirrors the destruction of Jerusalem and the traumatizing of a population determined not to give up this city. The Zion texts in Isaiah 40–66 foreshadow this spatial experience and at the same time transform it adding new images such as the beloved wife and queen (Isa. 54:1–17). Maier showed how the drastic change of the exile is inscribed in the Zion texts. The personified space of Zion proves to be so adaptable that it can absorb and transform experienced horrors and renewed hopes.

Mark K. George in *Israel's Tabernacle as Social Space* (George 2009) focused on the spatial conception of the sanctuary in Exodus 25–31 + 35–40. He emphasized a different element of *perceived space* than Maier—not the topography, but the "spatial practice" is at the core of his investigation. George underscored the actions required to build the tent sanctuary and thus interpreted the sanctuary as a social space, as the product of a space-creating practice. This practice hinges on the conception of space conceived in the texts—therefore, George spoke of "conceptual space" instead of *conceived space*. The priestly conception of space is not interpreted in the sense of a graded holiness but as a social space—based on the three concepts of community membership, descent, and hereditary succession. Access to the sanctuary is determined by membership in the community, the family of the Aaronides, and the hereditary office of the high priest. The increasing limitation of access corresponds with increasing sanctity and decreasing frequency of the rituals associated with these spaces. The third spatial dimension, *lived space*, George interpreted as "symbolic space" that captures how social space acquires social meaning. With the sanctuary texts in Exodus, the priestly scribes succeeded, according to George, in constructing a space for the people of Israel to survive in exile, which enabled Israel to continually recreate its social space and thus its social identity.

Historically, the Deuteronomic conception of the sanctuary has developed alongside and in conflict with the conception of Zion, whereas it precedes the conception in Exodus.

Deuteronomy puts forth a specific concept of the sanctuary that differs from Zion and particularly from the desert sanctuary. The appearance of the sanctuary is of no significance. Quite in contrast to the detailed descriptions of materials and ornaments in Exodus 29–31; 35–40 or Isaiah 54:11–17, there is no description of the *maqom* in Deuteronomy. Readers do not learn where the *maqom* is located, which buildings and grounds belong to it, or how they are designed or decorated. In particular, the Deuteronomic *maqom* is constituted by actions: by God's actions (choosing and letting dwell his name there) and by Israel's corresponding actions (going there, eating, and rejoicing before YHWH). This Deuteronomistic construction of the sanctuary historically precedes the conception of the tabernacle in Exodus 25–31; 35–40. Both conceptualize the sanctuary within a normative text. Accordingly, on the textual level only the Secondspace (i.e., the space of conception and planning) is present. In what way this relates to the spatial practice at the sanctuary, the two sanctuaries, respectively, is discussed below. Since the Deuteronomic conception focuses on actions, the spatial theory of the German sociologist Martina Löw is particularly important here (cf. Geiger 2010c and Geiger 2013a).

Martina Löw: *The Sociology of Space*

As an introduction to her conception of space, Löw intriguingly dwelled on a text about the *maqom*: a biographical description by the Israeli composer Josef Tal of how he perceived the Wailing Wall:

> During the British mandate, before the outbreak of the Second World War, I was already able to go to see the Wailing Wall in the heart of the Arab Old City guided by two senior government officials. We went through a dense network of narrow, winding alleyways, and all of a sudden, we were standing in front of a sheer wall of huge stone blocks. High above there was a slender strip of blue sky between the confined walls of the alleyway. The narrowness made the stone blocks rise all the larger and mightier above the diminutive person. Faced with that, it was only possible to pray to the Almighty, hovering inaccessibly above the immeasurable stone. After the Six-Day War in 1967 the tangle of alleyways in front of the Wailing Wall was cleared. Today, the approach to the Wall is via a large, expansive tract that provides space for thousands of visitors for prayer as well as for religious celebrations. Naturally, these are the same stone blocks as before but their denomination has been changed by the new surroundings. The broad space that has freed them from the constricted alleyways sends their wailing echo in the breadth instead of in the height, thus giving the prayer a different sense. I will beware of blasphemously comparing the Wailing Wall with a museum object—these stones speak a language too full of life for that. But space and matter act together in the formation of meaning.
>
> (Tal 1987, 87, as cited by Löw 2018, 129f)

Löw cited Tal's description, "because it contains a before and after structure and is thus especially vivid in documenting the temporal course from one constitution of space to the next" (Löw 2018, 129). Space includes alleys and ashlars, "products of present and above all of past material and symbolic action" (Kreckel 1992, 77, cited by Löw 2018, 130). Beyond Löw, Tal's quote makes clear that the conception of the sanctuary (or its remains) carries implications for the relationship with God. After 1967, the relationship with God changes along with the architecture. At present, the square has become even larger, and visible from afar, it is dominated by subdivisions, excavations, and the staircase to the Temple Mount.

In line with Josef Tal, Löw defined space as a "relational arrangement of living beings and social goods" (Löw 2018, 131). With this definition, she overcomes the understanding of space as a "container" in which people live and act. Rather, space only comes into being through people arranging something (i.e., through space-creating actions such as erecting, building, or positioning). Space, matter, and people cannot be separated from each other. Löw referred to this process as *spacing*. However, a spatial arrangement only becomes a space when it is linked to a spatial conception. Löw called this process of perception *operation of synthesis* (Löw 2018, 134).

Both processes are determined by social conventions. People reproduce common spatial arrangements through their actions, and they comprehend arrangements as spaces that are familiar to them. Spaces can become institutions if they give rise to habitual behavior patterns. Such patterns are practiced through repetitiveness, through repeated action. "Institutionalized spaces are accordingly those in which the arrangement has effect beyond one's own action and results in conventional operations of synthesis and spacing" (Löw 2018, 139 [original in italics]).

Löw's concept of space certainly bears resemblances to Lefebvre's triad. Mark George interprets *perceived space* in the sense of *spacing*, while his understanding of *conceived space* comes very close to Löw's *operation of synthesis*. Lefebvre's third dimension can also be understood as an *operation of synthesis* if no spatial-theoretical distinction is made between "ideological conception of space" and "resistant conception of space of the marginalized."

What Is the Status of the Conversation?

The spatial conceptualization of Deuteronomy emerged along with its literary-historical development between the seventh and the fourth/third century BCE (Otto 2012, 231). It spans the destruction and reconstruction of the Jerusalem sanctuary and—as a different voice corresponding to the further development of the Zion tradition (Maier 2008)—contributes significantly to the theological processing of this catastrophe.

In the final version, the spatial conception of Deuteronomy is based on spatial concepts such as earth/land ('eretz 197x), Egypt (50x), path (48x), or house (45x), which are each associated with formulas. Each term stands for a spatial concept that is composed of spacing and operations of synthesis, and all concepts together form the composite Deuteronomic spatial conception (Geiger 2010c). This overarching concept is narratively subdivided into the spatial concepts of Israel's past in Egypt and on the way through the desert (Egypt, Mt. Horeb), the spatial concepts of the present within the narrated time beyond Jordan (desert,

Moab) and the future in the Promised Land (house, gate, place). While *maqom* in the frame narrative refers in particular to the setting ("place") of the Deuteronomic narrative (Deut. 1:31; 9:7; 11:5; 26:9; 29:6) or refers to an unspecific place (Deut. 1:33; 11:24; 12:2; 13:3; 21:9; 23:17), in Deuteronomy 12–26, the *maqom* is legally conceived as the center of the Promised Land. These chapters comprise the oldest part of the book, and the *maqom* is central to its space conception.

The *Maqom*

In Deuteronomy 12–26, the *maqom* is characterized by the centralization formula. It is introduced in its long form in Deuteronomy 12:5 and used a total of twenty times in Deuteronomy 12–26 (Deut. 12:5, 11, 14, 18, 21, 26; 14:23, 24, 25; 15:20; 16:2, 6, 7, 11, 15, 16; 17:8, 10; 18:6; 26:2), as well as once in Deuteronomy 31:11. Braulik showed that the formula is presented in "groupings of seven" (Braulik 1997, 75; Lohfink 1991, 162), which expresses "fullness, even completeness" (Braulik 1997, 77f) and emphasizes the importance of the *maqom*.

Many researchers assume that the short form with the elements *maqom* and "election" and a designation of YHWH as subject (Deut. 12:14, 18, 26; 14:25; 15:20; 16:7, 15, 16; 17:8, 10; 18:6; 31:11) derives from Exodus 20:24 and thus predates the long form (Reuter 1993, 136f; Rüterswörden 2011, 43). With Lohfink and Otto (Lohfink 1991; Otto 2016, 1159) it seems more arguable that the long form, as attested in Deuteronomy 12:14 and 14:23, can be found as early as in the pre-exilic Deuteronomy. The formula states that *some* place in the future will be chosen by YHWH and thereby become the place to which the fourteen centralization commands are oriented (for the count, see Lohfink 1991, 151). The *maqom* becomes significant through YHWH's space-creating action and through the corresponding actions of the Israelites. The long form of the centralization formula contains two statements about the space-creating action of YHWH accompanying the election: positing the divine name: *lasum sh^{e}mo sham* (Deut. 12:5, 12, 21; 14:24) and having the divine name dwell there: *l^{e}shakken sh^{e}mo sham* (Deut. 12:5–11; 14:23; 16:2, 6, 11; 26:2). With *sym*, the connection between *maqom* and the divine presence is established, and with *shkhn* pi., it is provided with a permanent perspective. Richter interpreted the construction on the basis of the Akkadian expression *šuma šakānu* (Richter 2002; Rüterswörden 2011, 43–46), meanwhile Otto provided a more differentiated view (Otto 2016, 1176). As to how the divine presence is to be imagined, the term *shem* offers a broad range of interpretations. If the long form is dated pre-exilic, it implies the full presence of God, in line with Exodus 20:24. Otto stated: "just as the name and the bearer of the name are considered identical in the entire Ancient Near East, the Deuteronomic Name Theology promises the presence of YHWH himself at the place chosen by him" (Otto 2016, 1175). In exilic or postexilic times, the centralization formula can be interpreted in the sense of a reduced presence. "In selecting *šēm*, a term was found which was suitable for expressing both the presence of God at the cult site and the distinction between God's being in heaven and his representation on Mount Zion" (Mettinger 1982, 132; von Rad 1947). The scope for interpretation inherent in the term *shem* thus offered the theological possibility of protecting YHWH himself from the destruction of his dwelling place.

YHWH's establishing of the *maqom* in pre-exilic Deuteronomy corresponds to Israel's spacing, which responds to the synthesis of YHWH's presence in that place (cf. Geiger 2010b). Israel's actions at the *maqom* are explicitly characterized fourteen times with the formula *lifnei YHWH* ("before YHWH," Deut. 12:7, 12, 18 [2x]; 14:23, 26; 15:20; 16:11; 18:7; 19:17; 26:5, 10 [2x], 13). In addition, Deuteronomy 16:16 (2x) and 31:11 deal with the "appearance before YHWH" (*yera'e* [nif.] *'et-p^enei* YHWH). This supports the assumption that the full presence of YHWH was originally implied, as Wilson summed it up: "Activities qualified by the expression are intended to take place in the immediate vicinity of the Deity. They therefore provide evidence for a belief in his localized presence at the 'chosen place'" (Wilson 1995, 158f).

Beginning with the centralization command in Deuteronomy 12 (8x *maqom* and once in the plural form for the places to be destroyed in Deut. 12:2), fourteen commandments focus the attention on the *maqom* and prescribe the space-generating actions of the Israelites with regard to the *maqom*.

The *Maqom* and the Gates

All fourteen centralization commands adopt the *maqom* as vantage point and, from there, bring the gates into view: "the Levite who is in your gates" (Deut. 12:12) is to be included in the celebrations at the *maqom*. In other commandments, the Levite is supplemented by "the stranger, the widow, and the orphan who are in your gates" (Deut. 14:29; 16:14, etc.). The sacrificial celebrations are thus meant to transcend the social space "house" and address the people in the social space "gate" as a community of solidarity. Furthermore, the phrase "in your gates" makes it clear that not every gate community is to celebrate for itself at the central sanctuary; rather, a central perspective is adopted on all gates. The phrase "your gates" connects the individual gate communities into the *one* community of Israel that gathers in the *one* place in the presence of their *one* God for celebration. The gate communities are subjects of the celebration, so Eckart Otto concluded, "The *š^eārîm* open towards the central sanctuary, the *māqôm*, which God has chosen, and receive their salvation and potential of life from there" (Otto 1995, 376). As a result of centralizing all sacrifices to the *maqom*, Deuteronomy 12:15f, 20–25 must profane the slaughter of animals and allow it "in all your gates."

The centralization commands include the *operation of synthesis* that the social spaces *gate* and *maqom* can only be conceived together: At the *maqom*, the residents of the gates experience themselves as a community that integrates Levites, strangers, widows, and orphans, and all gates form the community of all Israel at the *maqom*.

The connection between the spatial concepts of gate and *maqom* is established through movements by means of which the Israelites orient themselves toward the *maqom*. They are to seek the central place (Deut. 12:5; 17:9), come (Deut. 12:5; 17:9; 18:6; 26:3; 31:11) and go there (Deut. 14:25; 26:2), appear there (Deut. 16:16; 31:11), set out (Deut. 17:8), and ascend the *maqom* (Deut. 17:8). Israel's paths are always directed toward the *maqom*, never away from it except Deuteronomy 16:7 (Geiger 2010a, 53). Walking these ways regularly, the centrality of the *maqom* is inscribed into minds.

Three functions are associated with *maqom*: The offering of various types of sacrifices and offerings (Deut. 12:6, 11, 17, 26; 14:23; 15:19; 16:2, 4, 6, 10, 13, 16; 18:3, 4; 26:2, 10), resolving legal disputes (Deut. 17:8–13), and the reading of the Torah (Deut. 31:9–13).

The *Maqom* as the Place of Sacrifice

The most important space-creating act associated with the *maqom* is the offering of sacrifices. For this purpose, Deuteronomy only rarely speaks of the altar of YHWH (Deut. 12:27; 16:21; 26:4), which at the same time is the only structure at the *maqom*. All kinds of sacrifices are offered (Deut. 12:5), the tithe (Deut. 14:22–29), the first fruits (Deut. 15:19–23), and the three annual feasts are to be celebrated there (Deut. 16:1–17). Associated with the sacrifices are other actions that characterize the *maqom*: eating (Deut. 12:6, 18, 27; 14:23, 26; 15:20; 16:3, 7), rejoicing (Deut. 12:6, 12, 18, 26; 16:11; 26:11), and celebrating (Deut. 16:15)—and thereby salvage the goods they have earned as YHWH's blessing (Deut. 12:7; 16:10, 17).

Contrary to Exodus 12, the Deuteronomic Passover shall not be celebrated at home but at the *maqom*. The celebration of Passover (Deut. 16:1–8), though, is different. The liturgy commemorates that Israel only came to the Promised Land through the Exodus from Egypt. To this end, circumstances of the Exodus such as eating unleavened bread (Deut. 16:3, 4, 8; Exod. 12:15, 19, 20, 39), haste (Deut. 16:3; Exod. 12:11, 34), and the Passover meal on the last night in Egypt (Deut. 16:1, 4, 6; Exod. 12:8–10) are reenacted (Braulik 1988, 103). Part of the concept of the *maqom*, therefore, is the reminder that Israel's relationship with YHWH was not established through life in the land but first and foremost through the Exodus (Deut. 5:6). Passover orients Israel toward "YHWH, your deity" (Deut. 16:1, 2, 8) and thus redirects the relationship with YHWH to its origins, which predate land ownership and the possibility of offering sacrifices at the *maqom*. Celebrating Passover makes Israel understand: YHWH's relationship with Israel began before the *maqom* and may continue even beyond the *maqom*. While the other sacrificial celebrations reinforce the meaning of *maqom*, Passover, in contrast, represents a deconstruction of the meaning of *maqom* and, by extension, of the Promised Land. The return "to your tents" (Deut. 16:7) at the end of the celebration underscores this.

Offering sacrifices at the *maqom* is an activity of all adult Israelites—free women receive the right to lead the sacrificial ritual as well (Braulik 2001, 84f). Deuteronomy apparently assumes the existence of priests at the *maqom*, but mentions them only in Deuteronomy 18:1–8; 26:2, 3. Their task is to support the actions of the people. They shape the *maqom* (*spacing*) by their actions according to their understanding of the sacrifices and annual festivals (*operation of synthesis*). They practice intertwining *operations of spacing* and *synthesis* through regular repetition (Löw 2018, 136, 141).

Maqom and the Administration of Justice

The second function of the *maqom* is the administration of justice. This is clearly subordinate to the first function, as it is proclaimed only after the commands to offer sacrifices (Deut. 17:8–13). In principle, the administration of justice is to take place in the gates (Deut. 17:8; 21:20; 22:16, 24; 25:7); however, for particularly difficult disputes like "problems between two parties or claims" involving killing and bodily harm, or such "between one kind of legal right and another" (Crüsemann 1996, 97), the court at the *maqom* is supposed to have jurisdiction. This consists of Levitical priests (17:9) and at least one other judge (Deut. 17:9, 12 sg.; 19:17–18; Tigay 1996, 164). At the *maqom*, the judgment is pronounced (Deut.

17:9–10), which qualifies as Torah (17:11; cf. 4:44; 27:3, 8; 31:11–12). "The conclusion we must draw from this is absolutely clear: The decisions of the court have the same significance and the same rank as the things that Moses himself said—which means Deuteronomy itself" (Crüsemann 1996, 97 [original in italics]). The *maqom*'s function as a place of judgment provides guidance on the appropriate interpretation of the Torah in legal matters.

Maqom and Torah

The third function of the *maqom* concerns the entire Torah. Every seven years, at the Feast of Tabernacles, all Israel is to come to the *maqom* (Deut. 31:10–13) to hear and learn "this Torah" (Deut. 31:11). There is a cognitive goal of learning "The Israelites are to take such intensive note of these texts that they stick in the memory, if not word for word, then nevertheless according to sense and content" (Finsterbusch 2005, 290). Furthermore, the Israelites shall learn how to practice the appropriate attitude, namely, "to meet YHWH with reverence" and to be mindful to "realize all the words of this Torah" (Deut. 31:12f). The ceremonial procedures significantly modify the space concept of the *maqom*. It is complemented by a two-fold operation of synthesis, which is set up in the frame narrative.

In Deuteronomy 31:10–13, the depiction of the assembly is reminiscent of Deuteronomy's setting in Moab (Deut. 1:5; 28:69; 34:1), where Moses delivers the Deuteronomic addresses. The key terms recurring in Deuteronomy 29:9f and 31:10–13; characterize the assembly at the *maqom* as a reenactment of the Deuteronomic day of assembly. All Israel gathers (Deut. 1:1; 29:1)—men (Deut. 29:9; 31:12), women (Deut. 29:10; 31:12), children (Deut. 29:10; 31:12), and strangers (Deut. 29:10; 31:12)—to hear the words spoken by Moses in Moab and written down by his own hand (Deut. 31:9). The assembly at *maqom*, like the assembly in Moab, takes place "before YHWH" (Deut. 29:9; 31:11).

Additionally, a second operation of synthesis is evoked. The listeners at the *maqom* and the readers of Deuteronomy are drawn into a suite of spaces, leading to the original place of the proclamation of the commandments on Mt. Horeb (Deut. 4:10–14; 5:2–31; 9:7–10:11). According to the Deuteronomic narrative, Israel stood there "before YHWH" for the first time (Deut. 4:10; 9:18, 25), and it is there that YHWH spoke to the Israelites face to face (Deut. 5:4). This is at least true of the Decalogue. After its proclamation, the elders ask Moses to listen to the other words of YHWH and then report them to the people (Deut. 5:27). According to the narrative logic of Deuteronomy, this is fulfilled during the speeches of Moses in Moab (Deut. 1:6; 5:1–5). The assembly at the *maqom* thus reenacts the assembly in Moab, which, in turn, transfers the addressees back to Mt. Horeb. "The assembling of the people for the proclamation of the written Torah will echo the 'assembling' (see *haqhel* Deut. 4:10), (*qᵉhalkhem*, Deut. 5:22), and 'the day of the assembly' (*yom haqqahal* Deut. 9:10; 10:4; 18:16)—in short, the Mt. Horeb assembly" (Sonnet 1997, 143). This spatial synthesis brings about a temporal synthesis that spans generations. According to Deuteronomy (Deut. 1:35–49; 2:14f), the generation of those standing at Mt. Horeb perished in the desert, except Moses, Joshua, and Caleb. At the Moab gathering, the next generation is introduced to the original events at Mt. Horeb, and the assembly at the *maqom* (Deut. 31:9–13) has each new generation including its infants addressed by "this Torah."

The Spatial Concept of the *Maqom*

The spatial concept of the *maqom* is constituted by the corresponding actions of YHWH and Israel. It is, in particular, the repetitive character of the feasts and sacrificial ceremonies that contributes to the institutionalization of the *maqom* (Löw 2018, 139). In this sense, the intended conduct of Israel "there you shall eat before YHWH, your deity, and rejoice" (Deut. 12:7) can be understood as "conventional operations of synthesis and spacing" (Löw 2018, 139) which give relative permanence to the concept of the *maqom*. This also applies to reading the Torah, which is combined with further acts of synthesizing. The non-specific notion of a place that YHWH will choose in the future of the narrated time makes it possible to develop a new, self-contained concept of this place. The lack of concrete descriptions of the *maqom* helps to avoid connotations that would be associated with "Jerusalem," "the temple," or "the mountain" on the side of the readers—since they would interfere with the Deuteronomic concept. Furthermore, the openness of the formula "the place that YHWH will choose" forms the basis for its reception at the time of exile.

The centralization command is one of the requirements that cannot be fulfilled in exile. Beyond the disrupted routine of sanctuary visits, with the destruction of the Jerusalem Temple, the very presence of YHWH is at stake. The Deuteronomic spatial synthesis offers two possibilities for overcoming this crisis. The first possibility is the formula of establishing or having the name dwell there, which introduces a distinction between divine presence and its realization at the *maqom*. The loss of the *maqom* now only ends the attainability of the divine presence at that place. The second possibility is the deep dimension of YHWH's presence. The actions performed at the *maqom* before the deity (*lifnei YHWH*) become translucent for God's original presence at Mt. Horeb, the mountain "burning in fire" (Deut. 4:11). Returning to the Horeb covenant (Deut. 4:13; 5:2f) "with all your heart and *nefesh*" (Deut. 30:3) is tied in with the hope of the exiles to return to the Promised Land.

What Is Trending in the Conversation?

In terms of compliance with the centralization command, the question to which *maqom* refers is decisive. This is interpreted differently in the Masoretic text (MT) and in the Samaritan Pentateuch (SP). The MT assumes, particularly through the ensuing Deuteronomistic History (DTH), the identification of the *maqom* with Jerusalem. The SP, though, identifies the *maqom* with Mt. Gerizim. The relationship between Samari[t]ans and Judeans during the Persian period, which has been reassessed recently, strongly impacts the spatial concept of the *maqom*.

The Centralization Formula in MT and SP

The MT and the SP attest to different versions of the election formula. Whereas in the MT the election is formulated in the imperfect tense in all twenty-one references: "the place that YHWH will choose" (*yivḥara* 3.sg.m. impf. qal of *baḥar*), the SP form is always in the perfect tense: "the place that YHWH has chosen" (*baḥar* 3.sg.m. perf. qal). The SP form assumes that YHWH has already chosen Mt. Gerizim, respectively Shechem, as a place of worship (Exod. 20:21^{Sam}). This could be supported by the mention of the altars built by Abraham (Gen. 12:6f) and Jacob (Gen. 33:18–20) in Shechem. For a long time, scholars have assumed that the SP makes an ideological textual change here in order to legitimize the sanctuary on Gerizim (Tov 2012, 87f). In the meantime, there are some text-critical studies that assess this differently. Schenker points to independent Coptic and Old Latin textual witnesses of the Septuagint (LXX) that also attest to the past tense "has chosen," so he assumes an original LXX reading that supports SP (Schenker 2008, 339–351). This view has been endorsed by many (Schorch 2011, 32; Otto 2016, 1132f; Nihan 2016, 255; Hensel 2016, 178).

This difference does not play a major role for the spatial conception of the *maqom*. It is foundational that YHWH's election of the *maqom* precedes the space-creating actions of the Israelites at the *maqom*. Whether YHWH had chosen the *maqom* already *before* entering the land as he chose Israel (*baḥar* perf. Deut. 7:6; 14:2), or whether he will choose the *maqom* only upon entering the land—this only assumes importance along with the fact that Israel is given the position of reaction in a space-creating fashion. In the time of the implied readers, the *maqom* was believed to have been chosen by YHWH, and maybe even rejected (2 Kgs. 23:27), and the commands regarding the *maqom* were to be put into practice. Therefore, it is not surprising that the allegedly SP past tense is also attested elsewhere in MT (Neh. 1:9; 1 Kgs. 11:13, 32, 36; 2 Kgs. 23:27; 2 Chr. 6:6; 7:12, 16; Zech. 3:2) and in some Qumran manuscripts (Schorch 2011, 33f).

Maqom and Jerusalem in DTH

Whereas the SP comprises only the Pentateuch, the MT of the Tanakh gradually suggests the identification of the *maqom* with Jerusalem. The Pentateuch contains allusions to the Temple of Jerusalem, in particular, the narratives in Genesis 14; 22 and the sanctuary texts in Exodus 25–31; 35–40—but Jerusalem is not mentioned explicitly. Nor do we find any clear identification of the *maqom* in Deuteronomy. It perfectly suits the Deuteronomic setting of space and time that the election of the *maqom* is announced for the future. "The avoidance of explicit references to Jerusalem reflects the Mosaic presentation." This reveals the biblical writers' ability "to speak in subtle ways about realities which are in the future from the perspective of the literary plot" (MacDonald 2010, 433). Deuteronomy presupposes that implied readers from Judaea equate the *maqom* with Jerusalem.

DTH identifies the *maqom* more and more with Jerusalem (Thelle 2012, 41–52). The name "Jerusalem" is mentioned only in Joshua 10:1, as the seat of a foreign king. In the context of DTH, Jerusalem initially remains in Jebusite hands (Josh. 15:63; compare Judg. 1:8, 21) until David conquers Jerusalem (2 Sam. 5). In this account, however, no reference is made to the Deuteronomistic centralization formula. This is alluded to again only in Solomon's prayer for the dedication of the Temple (1 Kgs. 8), where *maqom* is explicitly mentioned seven times. 1 Kgs. 8:29 quotes the formula explicitly: "this place of which you said, 'My Name shall be there'" (*shem* in 1 Kgs. 8:17–20, 29, 33, 35, 41–43 [2x], 44, 48). However, the phrase "to make his name *dwell* there" from Deuteronomy (Deut. 12:5, 12:11; 14:23; 16:2, 6, 11; 26:2) is not explicitly cited. More strikingly, the spatial conception of the *maqom* is changed. The *maqom* is not associated with the space-creating acts of eating and rejoicing; rather, the *maqom* is the place toward which supplication (*tᵉhinna*) and prayer (*yitpallu*) are addressed (1 Kgs. 8:30), and praise on occasion (1 Kgs. 8:35). This does not take place "before YHWH" (*lifnei YHWH*). YHWH is explicitly separated from the *maqom*: "But will God really dwell on earth? The heavens, even the highest heaven, cannot contain you. How much less this temple I have built!" (1 Kgs. 8:27). The place where YHWH is enthroned (*yashav* 1 Kgs. 8:13, 27, 30, 39, 43, 49—not *shakhan*) is located in heaven (1 Kgs. 8:30, 32, 34, 36, 39, 43, 45, 49). In 1 Kings 8, *maqom* is the place of praying to the name of God, who himself is in heaven. A reflection of this spatial conception has also entered into Deuteronomy 26:15.

The *maqom* "temple" is built by spacing operations of individuals: Solomon gives the commission, Hiram of Tyre is responsible for its construction (1 Kgs. 7:13–47) and Solomon for its furnishing (1 Kgs. 7:48–51). Unlike Deuteronomy, the dimensions and furnishings are precisely described (1 Kgs. 7:13–51). The spatial conception of this temple includes specific furnishings (Exod. 25–31; 35–40). The dedication then involves space-creating actions on the side of elders, men, priests, Levites, and congregation (1 Kgs. 8:1–5). In Solomon's prayer for the dedication of the Temple (1 Kgs. 8:13, 20, 21, 43, 44, 48), he refers to himself as the builder of the "house."

Whereas *maqom* in 1 Kings 8 refers to the temple, the "election phrase" (Thelle 2012, 27) refers to the city in 1 Kings 8:16 in a negative sense (since the Exodus *no* city has been chosen), but in 1 Kings 8:44, 48 positively "the city I have chosen" (perfect tense). 1 Kings 11 finally integrates the name Jerusalem into the election formula "Jerusalem, which I have chosen" (*bahar* perfect 1 Kgs. 11:13), supplemented in 1 Kings 11:32 by the reference to the tribes "out of all the tribes of Israel" (1 Kgs. 11:13; Deut. 12:5: singular). Finally, 1 Kings 11:36 adds the name formula: "in Jerusalem, the city which I have chosen for me, to establish my name there" (*lasum shᵉmo sham* literally in 3.p.sg. Deut. 12:5; 1 Kgs. 14:21; 2 Kgs. 21:7). The Deuteronomic spatial conception of *maqom* is more precisely applied to the city than to the temple, but the *spacing* operations of the Israelites play no role—nor does the centralization of the sanctuary (Thelle 2012, 45). Before the destruction of Jerusalem and the Temple, the formula of election is recalled. YHWH rejects the chosen city and the "house of which I have said: There shall my name be" (2 Kgs. 23:27).

The historical books establish a connection to the centralization formula and the spatial conception of the *maqom*, but at the same time, the differences are unmistakable—opening up avenues of interpretation (cf. Thelle 2012; Hensel 2019a, 25–30).

Maqom and Mt. Gerizim

The openness of the Deuteronomic formulation allows for a different identification of *maqom*. SP consistently associates the election formula with Mt. Gerizim near Shechem. This is backed up by the insertion of a (new) tenth commandment in the Decalogue (Exod. 20:17; Deut. 5:18) which inculcates the sole worship of YHWH on Mt. Gerizim through a combination of quotations (Exod. 13:11a; Deut. 11:29a; 27:2b–3a, 4a, 5–7; 11:30; Dexinger 1977, 112f). Since the Samaritans recognize only the Pentateuch as sacred scripture, the identification with Mt. Gerizim is understandable. For Mt. Gerizim is, unlike Jerusalem, mentioned in Deuteronomy (Deut. 11:29). The opposing Mt. Gerizim and Mt. Ebal are appointed to watch over the observance of the commandments: The blessing for keeping the commandments is placed on Mt. Gerizim, the curse in case of transgression on Mt. Ebal (Deut. 27:11, 13). This is accomplished ritually by six tribes of Israel on each.

Blessing and curse are preceded, immediately after the crossing of the River Jordan, by the building of an altar (Deut. 27:1–8; Josh. 8:30–35). MT and LXX locate the building of the altar on Mt. Ebal (Deut. 27:4; Josh. 8:30), while SP reads "Mount Gerizim" (one word: *harg^erizim*). It is supported by the Vetus Latina (VLB). This reading is probably to be preferred since the VLB "has no Orthodox Jewish claims to process" (Fabry 1985, 94; cf. Tov 2012, 88 n. 140). Tov also points to a fragment from Masada that supports SP (with reference to Talmon 1999, 138–147) and furthermore to LXX Papyrus Giessen 19, which also attests the reading *argarizim* (Kartveit 2009, 300–305; Tov 1971, 355–383). Opposing views (Nielsen 1995, 244; Sonnet 1997, 86–91; and Anbar 1985), maintain the MT reading. No sanctuary tradition is attested for Mt. Ebal, while on Mt. Gerizim a sanctuary has been archaeologically attested since the middle of the fifth century, existing parallel to the Jerusalem Temple. The original location of the altar building on Mt. Gerizim "should be viewed as a concession made to the Yahwists residing in Samaria at the time of the redaction of the Torah. This concession clearly presupposes the rebuilding of a sanctuary on Mt. Gerizim, as well as its recognition by Samarian Yahwists as their central cultic site" (Nihan 2007, 214). In contrast, the MT reading "Mt. Ebal" attests to a later, anti-Samaritan correction (Schenker 2010, 106f; Tov 2012, 88 n. 140; Nihan 2007, 213). McCarthy (2007) states: "However, a considerable number of scholars accept that the Smr tradition represents an earlier, possibly non-sectarian text, and that the M textual tradition here and at Josh 8:30 reflects a very early scribal emendation, which would have taken place before G's translation of both books" (122*). This openly criticizes the sanctuary on Mt. Gerizim (Nihan, Torah, 222f). "The dogmatic change is intended to deprive the Samaritan commandment to erect an altar on Mt. Garizim [...] of its legitimacy by the Torah, and at the same time to place the Samaritan place of worship under the curse" (Fischer 2009, 238).

A reference from Deuteronomy 27:2–8 to the conception of *maqom* is clearly evident (Schorch 2011, 26f). The command from Deuteronomy 12 to offer burnt offerings only on *maqom* (Deut. 12:6, 11, 13, 14, 27), could be redeemed by the injunction in Deuteronomy 27:6. This is also true of the injunction to eat at *maqom* and rejoice before YHWH (Deut. 27:7), which is always referred to *maqom* in Deuteronomic law (Deut. 12:7, 12, 18; 14:26; 16:11, 14, 15). Allusions to the altar law (Exod. 20:24f; Nihan 2007, 210f) underscore the possible identification of the chosen place in Deuteronomy 27:5–7 with Mt. Gerizim. Within SP, Mt. Gerizim is explicitly interpreted as the place of the presence of the divine name through the citation of Exodus 20:24[Sam] in Deuteronomy 27:5, 6.

This interpretation can be challenged by the fact that the place of the altar is not called *maqom* and that the election formula is missing in Deuteronomy 27:2–8. This alone would unmistakably identify the place of the altar with the *maqom* of the central sanctuary. Rather, in Deuteronomy 27, the erecting of the altar is introduced as a rite of passage for the day of the River Jordan crossing (*v^ehaya bayyom*; Deut. 27:2, 4: *yarden*; 27:3, 4: *'avar*). Along this line, the instruction in Deuteronomy 27 is also interpreted in the implementation narrative in Joshua 8:30–35.

The interpretations of SP and MT thus design different spatial concepts for the mountain mentioned in Deuteronomy 27:4. On the one hand, Mt. Gerizim (SP) is the chosen place of the presence of the divine name, to which the commandments of sacrifice (Deut. 12) and pilgrimage (Deut. 16) elaborated in the Deuteronomic law are to be referred and which in this way forms the permanent center of YHWH's presence. On the other hand, Mt. Ebal (Deut. 27:4^{MT}) is a transitional place where only once the liturgy is celebrated, which is on the occasion of entering the land (Josh. 8:30). Its continuing significance during life in the land is that it symbolizes and realizes the curse in case of transgression of the commandment. In my opinion, the spatial conception of the MT for Deuteronomy 27:1–8— but not its text-critical variant on Deuteronomy 27:4—is to be preferred.

Maqom as Thirdspace

The way the centralization command is phrased accomplishes two things—in both versions: With the greatest possible openness in identifying the *maqom*, the unconditional adherence to the commandment is stipulated.

Integrating the Deuteronomic commandments into the frame narrative contributes to this effect. In their combination of demands and paraenetic elements, the commandments presuppose that they can be fulfilled immediately. Embedding them into the Deuteronomic narrative changes its genre: "A legal text becomes a fictional text —the legal text becomes literature and is thereby relieved of the purely legal context" (Liss 2004, 30). Thereby, the authority of the commandments over all who see themselves as "Israel"—which also applied to Samarians (Hensel 2019b, 26)—remains unchanged, but its scope alters. On the text level, the commandments apply to the Israel of the fictional narrative. The reading communities—at different times, in Judea and Samaria—had to decide for themselves how to live up to the commandments. This requires a process of interpretation motivated by the difference between the text-internal world on the one hand and the situation of the reading communities on the other. This process of interpretation yields different conclusions in Samaria and in Judea.

Their respective interpretations are mutually exclusive: the one *maqom* cannot be both in Jerusalem and on Mt. Gerizim at the same time. In view of this aporia, Deuteronomy forms a Thirdspace, a space of openness that undermines current, competing spatial practice. On the narrative level of Deuteronomy, both are possible. The *maqom* can be either Jerusalem or Mt. Gerizim. "Precisely because of this vagueness, one can better appreciate how both the Judean and the Samarian communities accepted basically the same five books of Moses as authoritative scripture. Each community could (and did, and does) read the Pentateuch in its own way. Indeed, the imprecise language is itself a sign that the Pentateuch is fundamentally a compromise document" (Knoppers 2013, 196).

Hensel considers the phase of "coexistence," of "continuous contact with each other" as "equal partner[s] in dialogue" (Hensel 2019b, 35) to have lasted up to the late fourth or early third century (Knoppers 2015, 182–184). Relics of this collaborative project can be traced in the "Common Pentateuch" (Hensel 2019b, 35). In this sense, Nihan (2007, 215f) interprets Deuteronomy 27:4–8, 11–13 as an editorial layer aimed at a compromise with the Samarians in order to maintain the Pentateuch as a common document.

> This suggests that for the author of Deut 27:4–8 the altar on Mount Gerizim *was* legitimate, *but only in the sense that the Torah preserves a law authorizing multiple sanctuaries* that coexists with the centralization law of Deuteronomy 12. In this regard, the tension created by the de facto existence of *two* conflicting altar laws inside the Torah, in Exodus 20 and

Deuteronomy 12, was brilliantly used by the Judean redactor who inserted Deut 27:4–8 to legitimate the coexistence of two major sanctuaries in his own time that claimed to be the unique sanctuary prescribed by Deuteronomy 12.

(Nihan 2007, 215f)

What is more, the Deuteronomic conception of the *maqom* opens up a Thirdspace insofar as the competing identifications of the *maqom*, where YHWH has his name dwell, are merely secondary places of the divine presence. Mt. Horeb remains the original and permanent place of YHWH's presence, "the mountain burning with fire" (Deut. 4:11; 5:23; 9:15; Exod. 3:2). Unlike the *maqom*, according to Deuteronomy, Mt. Horeb cannot be visited. The description in Deuteronomy 1:2 shows that the mountain cannot be located. Sinai (Horeb), originally connected with the Mountains of Seir (Deut. 33:2; Judg. 5:4f), is several days' journey away from them. Through this displacement, the path to the presence of YHWH at Mt. Horeb leads back exclusively through the fictional text of the Book of Deuteronomy (cf. Geiger 2013b). In this Thirdspace, the rivalry between Judea and Samaria can be overcome and the common origin be remembered.

Bibliography

Anbar, Moshe. "The Story about the Building of an Altar on Mt. Ebal. The History of Its Composition and the Question of the Centralization of the Cult." In *Das Deuteronomium. Entstehung, Gestalt und Botschaft*. Edited by N. Lohfink, pp. 304–309. BETL 68. Leuven: University Press/Peeters, 1985.

Braulik, Georg. "Durften auch Frauen in Israel opfern? Beobachtungen zur Sinn- und Festgestalt des Opfers im Deuteronomium." In *Studien zum Deuteronomium und seiner Nachgeschichte*, pp. 59–81. SBAB 33. Stuttgart: Katholisches Bibelwerk, 2001.

Braulik, Georg. "Die Funktion von Siebenergruppierungen im Endtext des Deuteronomiums." In *Studien zum Buch Deuteronomium*, pp. 63–79. SBAB 24. Stuttgart: Katholisches Bibelwerk, 1997.

Braulik, Georg. "Leidensgedächtnisfeier und Freudenfest. Volksliturgie' nach dem deuteronomischen Festkalender (Dtn 16,1–17)." In *Studien zur Theologie des Deuteronomiums*, pp. 95–121. SBAB 2. Stuttgart: Katholisches Bibelwerk, 1988.

Constructions of Space I–V. Edited by Claudia V. Camp, Jon L. Berquist, Jorunn Økland, J. Cornelis de Vos, Karen J. Wenell, Mark K. George, Gert T.M. Prinsloo, and Christl M. Maier. LHBOTS. London/New York: T&T Clark, 2008–2013.

Crüsemann, Frank. *The Torah. Theology and Social History of Old Testament Law*. Translated by Allan W. Mahnke. Minneapolis: Fortress Press, 1996.

Dexinger, Ferdinand. "Das Garizimgebot im Dekalog der Samaritaner." In *Studien zum Pentateuch. Walter Kornfeld zum 60. Geburtstag*. Edited by G. Braulik, pp. 111–133. Vienna: Herder, 1977.

Fabry, Heinz-Josef. "Noch ein Dekalog! Die Thora des lebendigen Gottes in ihrer Wirkungsgeschichte. Ein Versuch zu Deuteronomium 27." In *Im Gespräch mit dem dreieinen Gott. Elemente einer Trinitarischen Theologie. Festschrift zum 65. Geburtstag von Wilhelm Breuning*. Edited by H. Heinz and M. Böhnke, pp. 75–96. Düsseldorf: Patmos, 1985.

Finsterbusch, Karin. *Weisung für Israel. Studien zu religiösem Lehren und Lernen im Deuteronomium und seinem Umfeld*. FAT 44. Tübingen: Mohr Siebeck, 2005.

Fischer, Alexander A. *Der Text des Alten Testaments. Neubearbeitung der Einführung in die Biblia Hebraica von Ernst Würthwein*. Stuttgart: Deutsche Bibelgesellschaft, 2009.

Geiger, Michaela. "Der Befreiung Zeit einräumen. Die Zeitkonzeption des dtn Pessachgebots (Dtn 16,1–8)." In *Zeit wahrnehmen. Feministisch-theologische Perspektiven auf das Erste Testament*. Edited by Hedwig Jahnow Projekt, pp. 40–65. SBS 222. Stuttgart: Katholisches Bibelwerk, 2010a.

Geiger, Michaela. "Gott Präsenz einräumen. Die Raumsoziologie Martina Löw's als Schlüssel für die Raumtheologie des Buches Deuteronomium." In *Die Religion des Raumes und die Räumlichkeit der Religion*. Edited by T. Erne and P. Schüz, pp. 104–121. APTLH 63. Göttingen: Vandenhoeck & Ruprecht, 2010b.

Geiger, Michaela. *Gottesräume. Die literarische und theologische Konzeption von Raum im Deuteronomium*. BWANT 183. Stuttgart: Kohlhammer, 2010c.

Geiger, Michaela. "Creating Space through Imagination and Action: Space and the Body in Deuteronomy 6:4–9." In *Constructions of Space IV. Further Developments in Examining Ancient Israel's Social Space*. Edited by M. K. George, pp. 44–60. LHBOTS 569. London/New York: T&T Clark, 2013a.

Geiger, Michaela. "Fiction and Space in Deuteronomy." In *Constructions of Space V. Place, Space and Identity in the Ancient Mediterranean World*. Edited by G. T. M. Prinsloo and C. M. Maier, pp. 26–48. LHBOTS 576. London/New York: T&T Clark, 2013b.

George, Mark K. *Israel's Tabernacle as Social Space*. SBL Ancient Israel and Its Literature 2. Atlanta: SBL, 2009.

Hensel, Benedikt. *Juda und Samaria. Zum Verhältnis zweier nach-exilischer Jahwismen*. FAT 110. Tübingen: Mohr Siebeck, 2016.

Hensel, Benedikt. "Deuteronomium 12,13–19: Zur Lokalisierung des einen Maqom." *BN NF* 182 (2019a): 9–43.

Hensel, Benedikt. "On the Relationship of Juda and Samaria in Post-Exilic Times: A Farewell to the Conflict Paradigm." *JSOT* 44, no. 1 (2019b): 19–42.

Kartveit, Magnar. *The Origin of the Samaritans*. VTSup 128. Leiden: Brill, 2009.

Knoppers, Gary N. *Jews and Samaritans. The Origins and History of Their Early Relations*. Oxford: Oxford University Press, 2013.

Knoppers, Gary N. "The Northern Context of the Law-Code in Deuteronomy." *HeBAI* 4, no. 2 (2015): 162–183.

Kreckel, Reinhard. *Politische Soziologie der sozialen Ungleichheit*. New York: Campus Verlag, 1992.

Lefebvre, Henri. *La production de l'espace*. Paris: Éditions Anthropos, 1974.

Lefebvre, Henri. *The Production of Space*. Translated by Donald Nicholson-Smith. Oxford: Blackwell, 1991.

Liss, Hanna. "Kanon und Fiktion. Zur literarischen Funktion biblischer Rechtstexte." *BN NF* 121 (2004): 7–38.

Lohfink, Norbert. "Zur deuteronomischen Zentralisationsformel." In *Studien zum Deuteronomium und zur deuteronomistischen Literatur II*, pp. 147–177. SBAB 12. Stuttgart: Katholisches Bibelwerk, 1991.

Löw, Martina. *The Sociology of Space. Materiality, Social Structures, and Action*. Translated by Donald Goodwin. London: Palgrave Macmillan, 2018.

MacDonald, Nathan. "Issues in the Dating of Deuteronomy. A Response to Juha Pakkala." *ZAW* 122 (2010): 431–435.

Maier, Christl M. *Daughter Zion, Mother Zion. Gender, Space, and the Sacred in Ancient Israel.* Minneapolis: Fortress Press, 2008.

McCarthy, Carmel. *Biblia Hebraica Quinta (BHQ). Deuteronomy.* Dublin: Deutsche Bibelgesellschaft, 2007.

Mettinger, Tryggve N. D. *The Dethronement of Sabaoth. Studies in the Shem and Kabod Theologies.* CB.OT 18. Lund: CWK Gleerup, 1982.

Nielsen, Eduard. *Deuteronomium.* HAT I/6. Tübingen: Mohr Siebeck, 1995.

Nihan, Christophe. "Cult Centralization and the Torah Traditions in Chronicles." In *The Fall of Jerusalem and the Rise of the Torah.* Edited by P. Dubovský, D. Markl and J.-P. Sonnet, pp. 253–288. Tübingen: Mohr Siebeck, 2016.

Nihan, Christophe. "The Torah between Samaria and Judah: Shechem and Gerizim in Deuteronomy and Joshua." In *The Pentateuch as Torah. New Models for Understanding Its Promulgation and Acceptance.* Edited by G. N. Knoppers and M. Bernard, pp. 187–223. Winona Lake: Eisenbrauns, 2007.

Otto, Eckart. "שער" *ThWAT* VIII: 358–403. Stuttgart: Kohlhammer, 1995.

Otto, Eckart. *Deuteronomium 1–11. Erster Teilband: 1,1–4,43.* HThKAT. Freiburg im Breisgau: Herder Verlag, 2012.

Otto, Eckart. *Deuteronomium 12, 1–23, 15.* HThKAT. Freiburg im Breisgau, Germany: Herder, 2016.

Reuter, Eleonore. *Kultzentralisation. Entstehung und Theologie von Dtn 12.* Frankfurt am Main: Hain Verlag, 1993.

Richter, Sandra L. *The Deuteronomistic History and the Name Theology.* Berlin: De Gruyter, 2002.

Rüterswörden, Udo. *Deuteronomium.* BK.AT V 3,1. Neukirchen-Vluyn: Neukirchener Verlag, 2011.

Soja, Edward W. *Postmodern Geographies. The Reassertion of Space in Critical Social Theory.* London: Verso, 1989.

Soja, Edward W. *Thirdspace. Journeys to Los Angeles and Other Real-and-Imagined Places.* Oxford: Blackwell, 1996.

Schenker, Adrian. "Le Seigneur choisira-t-il le lieu de son nom ou l'a-t-il choisi? L'apport de la Bible grecque ancienne à l'histoire du texte samaritain et massorétique." In *Scripture in Transition. Essays on Septuagint, Hebrew Bible, and Dead Sea Scrolls in Honour of Raija Sollamo.* Edited by A. Voitila and J. Jokiranta, pp. 341–354. JSJSup 126. Leiden: Brill, 2008.

Schenker, Adrian. "Textgeschichtliches zum Samaritanischen Pentateuch und Samareitikon. Zur Textgeschichte des Pentateuchs "im 2. Jh. v.Chr." In *Samaritans: Past and Present. Current Studies.* Edited by M. Mor and F. V. Friedrich, pp. 105–120. SJ 53/StSam 5. Berlin: De Gruyter, 2010.

Schorch, Stefan. "The Samaritan Version of Deuteronomy and the Origin of Deuteronomy." In *Samaria, Samarians, Samaritans. Studies on Bible, History and Linguistics.* Edited by J. Zsengellér, pp. 23–37. Studia Judaica 66/Studia Samaritana 6. Berlin: De Gruyter, 2011.

Sonnet, Jean-Pierre. *The Book within the Book. Writing in Deuteronomy.* BIS 14. Leiden: Brill, 1997.

Tal, Josef. *Der Sohn des Rabbiners. Ein Weg von Berlin nach Jerusalem.* Munich: Deutscher Taschenbuch-Verlag, 1987.

Talmon, Shemaryahu and Yadin, Yigael (Eds.). *Masada VI: The Yigael Yadin Excavations 1963–1965, Final Reports, Hebrew Fragments from Masada.* Jerusalem: IES, 1999.

Thelle, Rannfrid I. *Approaches to the Chosen Place. Accessing A Biblical Concept.* LHBOTS 564. London: T&T Clark, 2012.

Tigay, Jeffrey H. *Deuteronomy. The Traditional Hebrew Text with the New JPS Translation*. JPSTC. Philadelphia: Jewish Publication Society, 1996.

Tov, Emanuel. "Pap. Giessen 13,19,22,26: A Revision of the LXX?" *RB* 78 (1971): 355–383.

Tov, Emanuel. *Textual Criticism of the Hebrew Bible*. 3rd ed. Revised and Expanded. Minneapolis: Fortress Press, 2012.

von Rad, Gerhard. "Die deuteronomische Schem-Theologie und die priesterschriftliche Kabod-Theologie." In *Deuteronomium-Studien*, pp. 25–30. FRLANT 40. Göttingen: Vandenhoeck & Ruprecht, 1947.

Wilson, Ian. *Out of the Midst of the Fire. Divine Presence in Deuteronomy*. SBL Diss. Ser. 151. Cambridge: Society of Biblical Literature, 1995.

CHAPTER 8

ARCHAEOLOGY AND THE *MAQOM* SANCTUARY IN DEUTERONOMY

GARY P. ARBINO

Who Began the Conversation?

This chapter explores the conversation between archaeologists and literary scholars regarding the *maqom* in Deuteronomy. This exchange over the past two hundred years has often been lopsided, with the agenda and goals stemming from biblical and literary interests, even among archaeologists, many of whom have been biblical scholars.

Maqom commonly means "location" or "place" but can denote "chosen place" or "sanctuary" (Vanderhooft 1999). A tithe inscription on a storage jar from the Iron II Temple complex at Tel Miqne uses *maqom* for sanctuary: "for the *mqm*, 30 units of *tebel*" (Gitin 2003, 289–290).

This chapter will employ the dates for archaeological periods in *The New Encyclopedia of Archaeological Excavations in the Holy Land* (Stern 1993, 2008): Late Bronze Age (1550–1200), Iron Age I (1200–1000), Iron Age II (1000–586), Babylonian Period (586–539), and Persian Period (539–332).

Deuteronomy (Deut. 12:2–28) requires Israel to perform certain ritual obligations at the *maqom*, the sacred site where YHWH will choose to put his name. This was to be a single sanctuary in contrast to the plural *maqommim* of the Canaanites "on the mountain heights, on the hills, and under every leafy tree," which were to be abolished along with their altars, *maṣṣēbôt* (standing stones), *'asherim*, and idols (Deut. 7:5). The formula (Deut. 12:5) is repeated in some form at least twenty-one times in Deuteronomy. It consists of the term *maqom* and YHWH's choosing (all twenty-one times) "from all your tribes" (2×), "to put his name there" (9×: six using *shkkn*—"cause to dwell," three using *sm*- "to put or place"). Sandra L. Richter proposes that *shkkn* is a loan word from Akkadian meaning "establishing by inscribing on a monument" (Richter 2012).

Deuteronomy never locates the *maqom*, or physically describes it, or defines its relationship to either the approved local altars (*b'qal hammaqom*) or to the ark, or specifies whether it is to be understood as the permanently sole, serially central, or local main sanctuary unless such is assumed, indicated by the use of the phrase *lephnay YHWH* ("before the face of YHWH" Deut. 12:7, 12, 18) or implied by Deuteronomy (Deut. 31:11).

Kenneth Kitchen assumed that the *maqom* was wherever the tabernacle was (Kitchen 1972, 9–10n); Roland de Vaux that the *maqom* was wherever the ark was (de Vaux 1961, 320–322); Abraham Kuenen that the *maqom* was "by no means the only sanctuary, merely the first or chief one" (Kuenen 1886, 2:7) and Julius Wellhausen that "'the place which Jehovah shall choose,' by which only the capital of Judah can be meant" (Wellhausen 1885, 37). Many understood the pre-monarchial orthodox *maqom* to include successive *maqommim* (Noth 1960) or multiple sanctioned contemporary *maqommim* as late as Josiah (Halpern 1981).

Deuteronomy identifies several cultic activities to be performed only at this sanctuary: some or all sacrifices, vows, tithes, gifts, the celebration of *Pesach*, *Shavuot*, and *Sukkot*, adjudicating difficult legal cases, and periodic reading of Torah. The *maqom* was also the location for covenant renewal and establishing of plastered stelae (*ebanim*) at the feast of *Sukkot*—an activity, with sacrifices and offerings, commanded to occur on Mt. Ebal, near Shechem.

Canonically subsequent passages indicate there was at least one other place designated as *maqom*—Shiloh (Jer. 7:12)—and other sanctuaries, which are usually termed *bamot*, a word not used in Deuteronomy, except once each in a hymn of Moses (Deut. 31:30–32:47) and a blessing of Moses (Deut. 33:1–29). There are *bamot* at Bethel, Mizpah, Gilgal, Ramah, and Zuph. Gibeon has a great *bamah* housing the altar of burnt offerings and wilderness *mishkan* (1 Chr. 21:29). Kiryat Ye'arim, the House of Obed-Edom where the ark was (1 Sam. 6), and Nob, a sanctuary with priests (1 Sam. 21–22), also have *bamot*. At least thirty biblically attested Iron I sanctuaries with *bamot* have been identified (Zwickel 2012, 586–587).

Eventually, following David's unsolicited choice and the subsequent building of a temple by Solomon, Jerusalem "officially became the chosen place by the building and dedication of the temple" in the Bible (Pitkänen 2004, 273). The land in which YHWH was worshipped was also referred to as the *maqom* (Deut. 11:5).

Nonetheless, the Bible is clear that additional sites for sacrifice and the burning of incense to YHWH (1 Kgs. 15:14) continued to be approved throughout most of the Iron Age. These *bamot* "on every high hill, under every leafy tree" (1 Kgs. 14:23)—the same description used for Canaanite *maqommim* (Deut. 12:2–3)—are seen by the editors of the historical books, and some prophets, as illegitimate.

Literary scholars and theologians have long examined the Bible to determine the locations, characteristics, activities, and uniqueness of the *maqom* itself and its relationship to the *bamot*. The implications of these analyses have led to pivotal interpretations regarding the nature and development of the religions of Israel, including monotheism, and the dating and formation of the Bible.

In 1805, based on a careful reading of the Bible and its historical implications, W. M. L. de Wette produced his pioneering work tying Josiah's reform at the Jerusalem Temple in the late seventh century to the writing of Deuteronomy. At this same time, nascent archaeological and historical geography investigations began with the expedition of Napoleon to Egypt (1798–1802), the explorations of Edward Daniel Clarke in Palestine (1801), and the investigations of Claudius James Rich at Babylon (1807), along with the initial decipherment of cuneiform by Georg Friedrich Grotefend (1802) and of hieroglyphics by Jacques-Joseph Champollion (1822).

Important for discussions assuming a late centralization of the *maqom* were and continue to be epigraphic and textual finds. These include the historical texts of the Assyrians and Babylonians which provided extra-biblical context for the late eighth and seventh centuries enabling more nuanced discussions of the possible political motivations for Josiah's reform. The publication of treaties from both Neo-Assyrian in the late nineteenth century and Hittite in the mid-twentieth century provided literary backgrounds to the discussions regarding the date of Deuteronomy based on proposed similarities to these forms. The Elephantine papyri, initially published around 1900, demonstrated more than one legitimate Temple of YHWH existed after the exile. Stanley Arthur Cook and Rene Dussaud began identifying connections between cultic and ritual texts from nascent excavations in the Levant, especially Ugarit (Cook 1908; Dussaud 1937).

Over the course of the nineteenth–twentieth centuries, biblical interests influenced the archaeology of the Near East, Egypt, and Levant. Concerning the *maqom*, the literary assumption was that it was an Iron Age temple located at Jerusalem, on the site of Herod's later temple as identified by historical geographer Edward Robinson (Robinson 1865). The nature of the Temple itself was understood primarily from the biblical descriptions, informed by classical and emerging Egyptian, Syrian, and Mesopotamian religious architecture and inscriptions.

Following de Wette and later Wellhausen, by 1900 most biblical scholars held that Deuteronomy with its cultic regulations was the product of Josiah's reform. In the twentieth century, two main schools emerged from this consensus. The first holds to the late seventh century dating. The second argues for late eighth century northern prophetic or priestly origins, promulgated under Hezekiah's reform—either mostly written or drafted in the north and transferred to the south following the Assyrian conquest, where it was completed and formed the foundation for Josiah's reform (von Rad 1953). Minority views continued—those proposing a post-exilic date (Pedersen 1926); those maintaining a Late Bronze-Iron IIA dating (Welch 1924, Kline 1963); and some holding to a long process that started with Moses and finally completed as late as Josiah (Tigay 1996). A central issue is whether Deuteronomy created the *maqom* or the *maqom* created Deuteronomy.

Throughout its short history as a discipline, Near Eastern archaeology has been somewhat divided regarding its involvement in conversations with the Bible—some practitioners based their research on biblical literary agendas while others denounced that methodology. Rather than a dialogue partner with biblical scholars, archaeology has often been more of a reference partner in a set of interrelated dialogues concerning literary interpretations and implications. Significant to these has been the textually based discussion of whether the *maqom* was envisioned by Deuteronomy to be the sole sanctuary, a central sanctuary, a main sanctuary, or a particular sanctuary for certain activities, and whether this designation was intended as serial, permanent, or otherwise temporal. Though largely a literary question of orthodoxy and biblical intent, appeal has been made to archaeological evidence to support an answer. Archaeology remains poorly equipped to arbitrate divine, and perhaps even authorial, intentions; even as it may be able to demonstrate human approval and sanctioning.

By 1993, more than three hundred sites had produced cultic materials from the Bronze, Iron, and Persian periods. These excavations in the Levant, almost all during the twentieth century, provided data for the discussions regarding Deuteronomy and its instructions for the *maqom*. Three overlapping discussions emerged:

1. the Jerusalem Temple, its dating, nature, architecture, activities, and contexts;
2. *maqommim* and *bamot* and their relation to the *maqom* in Deuteronomy and implications for Israelite religious and cultic understandings; and
3. the later reform movements centralizing worship at the Jerusalem Temple as described in Kings and Chronicles and perhaps generated by Amos, Hosea, and other prophets.

What Is the Status of the Conversation? (1805–1980)

Several attempts were made to dig at the Temple Mount during the nineteenth century. Little was produced, owing largely to the sacred status of the Haram al Sharif in Islam. The Temple Mount has remained off limits to archaeological investigation, and temple architecture from the Iron Age to Persian Period, if it exists, is unlikely to be uncovered. Thus, the key site for archaeological study of the *maqom* was and is largely unavailable for investigation.

Jerusalem Temple

During the twentieth century, numerous studies were published which utilized excavated materials to illustrate the textual description of the Jerusalem Temple (Davey 1980). These usually engaged in comparing architecture. Early suggestions making connections with Syrian *bit-hilani* style palaces (Galling 1937, 411) were later corrected in light of initial reports of the Iron Age Syrian sanctuaries at Tell Ta'ayinat (1935–1938) and Ain Dara (1956–1964).

During the twentieth century, as the number of excavations in the Levant grew and the diversity of architecture proposed to be sanctuaries broadened, clarifying sanctuary architecture in excavated materials became necessary. By 1971, G. R. H. Wright had created a typology of six Levantine temple types (Wright 1971).

1. The *Long Room*, symmetrical or Syrian-style temple consists of one to three rooms along the long axis of a rectangle, with the entrance at one end allowing for direct access to all chambers. A Bronze Age subset of the Long Room style is the *migdal* or Tower style which has two projecting towers on the front side.
2. The *Broad Room*-style temple has an entrance on the wide side of a rectangular single room and the focus opposite the entrance, similar to the later North Syrian *bit hilani* architectural style.
3. The *Bent Axis or* asymmetrical-style sanctuary has an indirect access between the entrance and the main hall.

4. The *Centralized Square*-style sanctuary consists of a series of concentric squares.
5. The *Courtyard*-style sanctuary is surrounded by side rooms.
6. The *High Place*-style sanctuary is a platform (*bamah*) at an open-air site.

The Jerusalem Temple has been usually understood to be a Long Room temple with three sections: an *ulam* (antechamber), an *hekal* (main chamber), and a *debir* (inner chamber). Two columns flank the entrance to the *ulam* and clerestory windows along the top of its walls allow light into the *hekal*'s interior. A covered walkway encases the main building. The dimensions given in the Bible indicate that the Jerusalem Temple would have been larger than almost all Levantine temples excavated (Shapira 2018). Only a handful of tripartite Iron Age temples have been excavated, notably Tell Afis, Tell Ta'ayinat, and 'Ain Dara.

Temples, as religious, cultural, and economic centers, were sponsored and maintained by, and at times physically connected to, the royal palace. Royal patronage and maintenance of local sanctuaries of the royal cult was a regular feature of centralized control throughout the ancient world. Using available comparative data and the Bible, George Aaron Barton proposed that the Jerusalem Temple was initially a tenth-century foreign-inspired royal chapel for the kings of Judah, and only during the Assyrian and Babylonian crises did it become a national symbol (Barton 1906). Although his proposal supports a late reform dating for *maqom* centralization in Deuteronomy, it has little evidence from archaeology.

While the Temple Mount remained inaccessible, the environs of Jerusalem received considerable archaeological attention. More than seventy-five digs and surveys took place between 1900 and 1980 (Geva 1993). Most unearthed materials from the Hellenistic and later periods. Following early work in and near the City of David (1913–1928), significant Iron Age excavations were led by Kathleen Kenyon (1961–1967) and Yigal Shiloh (1978–1984). The results continue to engender much debate concerning the nature of the Late Bronze and Iron Age I–IIA city, especially in light of more recent interpretations and additional excavations and surveys.

Maqommim and *Bamot*

In addition to the excavations in Jerusalem, archaeologists unearthed other *maqommim* and *bamot*. Physical descriptions of *bamot* are found in the Bible and seen in excavations (Barrick 1992; Fried 2002).

1. Courtyard or *Open bamot* are located either inside villages or as free-standing sites often enclosed by a *temenos* wall or adjoining rooms.
2. *Single-Room bamot* are small, public sanctuaries; some are clearly stand-alone shrines while others may actually be rooms in private dwellings.

These sanctuaries often have raised platforms or benches, standing stones (*maṣṣabot*), altars and stands for incense or sacrifices, and cultic vessels, including *'asherim* and figurines—the same items Deuteronomy lists for the Canaanite *maqommim*. These *bamot* were, according to the biblical texts, often orthodox and sanctioned prior to the Jerusalem Temple, and then sanctioned, but not necessarily orthodox, following its construction.

Prior to World War II, initial excavations also took place at four sites specifically associated with pre-monarchy Israelite sanctuaries in the Bible: Bethel (1927, 1934), Shiloh (1915, 1926–1932), Mizpah (1926–1935), and Shechem (1913–1914, 1926–1927).

The excavations at Bethel, Shiloh, and Mizpah produced little relevant to Israelite sanctuaries. Shechem, however, showed a sequence of Bronze Age temples that continued into the early Iron Age I (Stager 1999). This trend of multiple phases of often superimposed sanctuaries became an important concept for understanding the *maqom*.

Throughout the eastern Levant, twentieth-century excavations produced numerous exemplars of long-duration sacred spaces and multiphase Bronze Age sanctuaries. Some, including Aleppo, Tel Afis, and Pella span the Middle Bronze through Iron II, while other long-span sites like Alalakh, Emar, Mumbaqat, Kamid el-Loz, Ugarit, Tell Kazel, Tell el-Hayyat, Tell Abu al-Kharaz, and Tall Safut were either destroyed or abandoned following the end of the Late Bronze Age. Some were rebuilt in the Iron Age while others were not.

In the southwestern Levant, a complex picture developed, generally understood as a major shift from Late Bronze Canaanite culture with one or more temples in every city to Iron I culture with smaller, but still ubiquitous sanctuaries, which continued, with some modification, in Iron II culture. Key sites for this transition were Tel Qasile, Beth Shean, Hazor, Megiddo, and Lachish.

At Hazor, numerous Bronze Age sanctuaries ended during the Late Bronze/Iron I transition, but were later replaced in the meager settlement of the eleventh century by smaller "cult corners" or "ruin cults" near previous sacred spaces. Yet the Iron Age residents deliberately did not rebuild on the area occupied by the Late Bronze palace, thought by some to be a temple, on the acropolis (Area A). Some have argued that this is in keeping with the prescriptions in Deuteronomy, but since other sacred areas (H, F, C) were rebuilt at Hazor, the argument requires more nuance. Megiddo's two-thousand-year succession of cult sites—broad room sanctuaries like the Great Temple and Temple 4050; megaron sanctuaries like temples 5269, 5192, and 4040; symmetrical tower sanctuaries like Temple 2048; and open-air sanctuaries like the Round Altar 4017, *Bamah* 4009, and Stelae Temple—was phased out during the Iron I. During the same period, elsewhere in the city, new sanctuaries like Building 2072 (Harrison 2004, 18), and Colonnaded Building M/00/44 with underground corbelled Chamber F begin to appear. More recent investigations have unearthed a sanctuary in Area Q near the south gate. It contained three octagonal short *maṣṣabot* standing in front of a podium along with several broken basalt stelae on the pavement. Assaf Kleiman now concludes that it was dismantled prior to its destruction in the mid-tenth century and then used as a ruin cult sanctuary such as those at Hazor (Kleiman et al. 2017). During Iron II, other sanctuaries like Room 2081, Room 340, Building 1A and Room 10 remained operational but appear to have been decommissioned—possibly in the eighth century—rather than destroyed.

Lachish, too, had a number of Bronze Age sanctuaries decommissioned by the early Iron I period. During the tenth century, following a long period of site abandonment, similar to Hazor's, a small sanctuary (Room 49) was in use in the new settlement. Unrelated to previous sanctuaries, it had benches along the walls, and contained a four-horn limestone altar, several incense burners, ceramics, and what may have been a basalt *maṣṣabah*. Some meters away, along a connecting wall, another area with what may be a *maṣṣabah* and wooden ʿasherah (Locus 81) may also be a sanctuary, but that is debated (Zevit 2001, 217–218). The Assyrian relief of Lachish's conquest in 701 BCE depicts soldiers carrying away a large incense burner, which suggests public worship at the site in the Iron IIB. During the Persian period, a small solar shrine was built on the acropolis by Judeans returning from exile.

Sanctuaries (*bamot*), such as those at Hazor, Megiddo, and Lachish, as well as those found at Ai, Ta'anach, and other sites supported biblical accounts that during the Iron I and IIA, prior to the Jerusalem Temple, numerous small sanctuaries, distinct from earlier Canaanite sanctuaries, were acceptable in early Israel. Thus, for those holding to early text dating, the instructions of Deuteronomy were seen to have a temporal dimension, at least in their implementation.

Yet, local sanctuaries like those at Megiddo, Tel Michal, Ta'anach, Kuntillet 'Ajrud, and possibly Lachish also continued into the Iron II. Kuntillet 'Ajrud has important inscriptional materials, even though it may not be a sanctuary (Strawn and LeMon 2018). Dan, Beersheba, and Arad, in particular, were also influential in conversations about Deuteronomy's *maqom*.

Noted in the Bible as one of the northern kingdom's two sanctuaries, excavations at Tel Dan began in 1963 and have unearthed two major sanctuaries from the Iron Age: a large sanctuary enclosed by a *temenos* wall (Area T) and several gate sanctuaries (Area A). The large sanctuary is notable for its 19m^2 ashlar *bamah* and a huge four-horned altar, reconstructed from one stone horn similar to ones found at Megiddo and Beer Sheba. Founded in the Iron IIA/B and reaching its zenith in the mid-eighth century, the sanctuary was probably destroyed in the second half of the eighth century by Tiglath-pileser III. It was rebuilt in the early seventh century and continued into the Roman period. Unlike other sites, Tel Dan did have an active sanctuary throughout the Assyrian period, notably in one of its gates. Sanctuaries in gateways, likely the *bamot hasse'arim* (2 Kgs. 23:8), are known throughout the Levant. Examples include Hazor (Areas K and P), Bethsaida, Khirbat al Mudayna, Khirbet Qeiyafa, Tall al-'Umayri, and, perhaps, Lachish.

Excavations at Beersheba produced the horns and stones of a large finely carved four-horned altar for sacrifice. No sanctuary related to the altar has been uncovered. The stones of the altar were found in secondary use in a late eighth-century wall and thus the altar was likely in use in during the ninth/eighth centuries. Because the altar was dismantled and its stones reused in a later wall that was destroyed by Sennacherib in 701 BCE, Yohanan Aharoni concluded that it was part of a sanctuary which Hezekiah's reform ended (Aharoni 1974). Small Iron IIB cultic caches were recovered in at least three locations (Buildings 25, 430; Street 844), as well as a krater (Building 76) inscribed with the letters *q-d-š* (*consecrated*) similar to finds at Arad, Hazor, Tel Miqne, Beth-Shemesh, possibly Beit-Mirsim, and Tall al-'Umayri.

Perhaps the most significant and debated discovery of the twentieth century regarding the *maqom* was at the southern Judean fortress at Arad. There a sanctuary was unearthed, complete with a large undressed-stone altar for sacrifice in a courtyard, and a smaller, raised room (*debir*) containing a *maṣṣabah* and two limestone incense altars—one with traces of cannabis (Arie et al. 2020). Mind-altering substance residue has also been found in ritual chalices in Philistia (Gadot et al. 2014). It is unclear whether this was a courtyard or long room temple. Unlike Beersheba, the Bible does not mention this sanctuary.

Aharoni and Ze'ev Herzog concluded that the sanctuary at Arad was deliberately buried prior to the destruction of the fortress, yet debate ensued. Aharoni saw two decommissioning phases at Arad, late eighth and late seventh centuries, in support of Hezekiah's and Josiah's reforms (Aharoni 1968). Amihai Mazar agreed with Aharoni both that the initial sanctuary was founded in the tenth century and that there were two decommissioning events (A. Mazar 1990). Herzog held the sanctuary was founded in the ninth century, and then the entire sanctuary was decommissioned during Hezekiah's reform (Herzog 2002).

While most agreed that the site was destroyed by Assyria in 701 BCE, other interpretations of the sanctuary at Arad have been offered. Some, like Christoph Uehlinger, have more recently argued that the dismantling was to protect it for a later reuse which never occurred (Uehlinger 2005). Nadav Na'aman claimed that the sanctuary was simply abandoned after the fortress was taken by the Assyrians (Na'aman 2002). David Ussishkin contended that the sanctuary was initially founded after 701 BCE and was destroyed by the Babylonians after 586 BCE (Ussishkin 1988). Ernst Axel Knauf proposed that Manasseh dismantled the sanctuary, and the Edomites destroyed it (Knauf 2005).

Two issues are to the point. First, regardless of when it was founded and when it ceased, Arad showed that an additional sanctuary in Judah was functioning at a government outpost at the same time as the Jerusalem Temple. This is regardless of whether it was simply an Iron II border or fortress sanctuary. Arad proved that contemporaneous sanctuaries (*maqommim* and *bamot*) were officially sanctioned. Beersheba and Lachish may provide additional examples.

The second issue relates to the date and intent of the dismantling and burial of the sanctuary at Arad. While the majority of archaeologists affirmed some sort of decommissioning, the reason may be less certain. The respect shown to the Arad sanctuary is different from the treatment given to the altar at Beersheba, and if a sanctuary existed at Lachish, it remained active until destroyed by the Assyrians in 701 BCE. Most concurred with a late eighth-century date for Arad's decommissioning, but a seventh-century date could not be ruled out. Archaeological dating methods in the twentieth century were usually not precise enough to pinpoint dates within a fifty-year period, yet specificity has been key for those debating Deuteronomy and understanding the *maqom*.

Materials illustrating *bamot* and *maqommim* spoke to the issues of the intent, interpretations, and dating of Deuteronomy and were utilized in a variety of literary, theological, and historical reconstructions. While these data provided insight, they were unable to resolve any of the key issues. Yet, a consensus emerged that assumed, based on the ubiquity of Late Bronze Age sanctuaries; the ubiquity of the Iron Age cult corners, shrines, and household ritual *realia*; and the presence of a sanctuary at Arad, and possibly at Beersheba and Lachish, that ancient Israel and Judah had sanctuaries in every village (Faust 2010). This comported with the generally comparative and evolutionary view of religion held by the History of Religions School (Smith 1990). Centralization, in this view, was naturally a late development. Literarily, there was broad, but not universal, agreement for a late-date theory of the formation of Deuteronomy (Wenham 1999, 116–119).

Reform

The twentieth century saw a nuancing of the literary discussions based on the consensus presupposition of a late Iron Age Deuteronomy. These focused on the circumstantial impetus for Deuteronomy and which king was responsible for centralization, if any reform happened at all.

Archaeological evidence for such decommissioning is actually quite scarce. Determining what a decommissioned sanctuary would look like in the archaeological remains was a problem faced but rarely discussed. Buildings and artifacts of Arad (eighth and seventh centuries) and Beersheba (eighth century) became the focal points for most discussions. The similar decommissioning of the sanctuaries at Megiddo (eighth century) was usually omitted, perhaps due to both the lack of biblical fit and the ongoing debates concerning Megiddo.

The paucity of evidence, beyond literary reconstructions, aided a shift in the conversation. Theodor Oestriecher argued that Josiah's reform was a politically motivated response to Assyrian weakness and Babylonian aggression (Oestriecher 1923). This aided the discussion to shift from a purely cultic focus. In 1973, W. Eugene Claburn examined the economic elements of Josiah's reign (Claburn 1973). By the 1980s, reconstructions of the reforms focused nonliterary evidence on the historical and political situation of the late Iron Age. Studies of Assyrian imperial policy in the eighth and seventh centuries influenced investigations of centralization under Hezekiah and Josiah. Archaeology provided increasing materials, especially texts, from Assyria and Babylon and widespread evidence for destructions during their incursions in the west. In Judah, the *LMLK* (*for the king*) jar stamps showed economic centralization, but for which king? Early studies of seals and onomastics were seen to confirm a shift toward a YHWH alone ideology during the Iron IIB-C, yet these were meager and debated evidence (Avigad 1986).

What Is Trending in the Conversation? (1980–Present)

By 1980, there was general consensus regarding the archaeological evidence concerning Deuteronomy's *maqom*. Yet even in 1995, William G. Dever lamented that "there is no real dialogue as yet on 'archaeology and the cult'" (Dever 1995, 40).

As surveys and salvage projects in the southern Levant supplemented excavations, the field of archaeology experienced significant development enhanced by subdisciplines like onomastics and epigraphy. Expanding use and availability of new scientific tools added diverse data streams and research possibilities (Sapir and Libi 2018). Computer-aided research became widespread. Alongside a growing comparative database of excavations and their materials, new theoretical models developed, including whether or how to use the Bible to interpret *realia*. Reevaluations of earlier excavations in light of later work, always a part of the process, were fueled by a much-debated proposal for revising the chronological framework, especially for Iron Age I-IIB (Finkelstein 1996). An unintended consequence of these recent developments, especially among nonspecialists, has been confusion concerning archaeological conclusions and results.

Jerusalem Temple

The Temple Mount has remained off limits for archaeological investigation, but a wealth of comparative data continues to be published. A project sifting dump materials from a construction project on the site has yielded some First Temple period finds. About 15 percent of the diagnostic pottery pieces can be dated to the First Temple Period—three seals (only one inscribed—with animals), about thirty bullae (one engraved with "Son of Immer," from the seventh–sixth century) and numerous First Temple figurine fragments which the excavators have linked to Josiah's reform in the late seventh century (Barkay and Dvira 2016).

Several studies of Levantine sanctuaries have been produced as well as numerous archaeologically informed examinations of the literary descriptions of the Jerusalem Temple (Hundley 2013). Jens Kamlah concludes that the description of the Jerusalem Temple in the Bible (1 Kgs. 6:1–8:13) and excavations of Iron Age Levantine sanctuaries elsewhere indicate the description in the Bible is supportive but not architecturally accurate (Kamlah 2012, 521). Victor Avigdor Hurowitz argued that the closest architectural parallel to the Jerusalem Temple remains the ninth-century sanctuary at Tell Tayinat excavated in 1999 (Temple XVI), even as others, especially the tenth-century sanctuary at Ain Dara, have several similarities (Hurowitz 2012). Tayinat Temple XVI also contained an Assyrian *ade* loyalty oath (a so-called "Vassal Treaty of Essarhaddon") inscribed on a tablet and housed in the holy of holies, reminiscent of the ark containing a covenant document (Deut. 31:24–27). Additional studies have been published detailing archeological connections to specific decorative and architectural motifs (Garfinkel and Mumcuoglu 2019).

A few additional sanctuaries around the region excavated since 1980 have provided a wealth of information. A major Iron II temple complex at Philistine Ekron has shed light on priestly practices concerning offerings and tithes and has shown that a functioning regional sanctuary operated alongside smaller public sanctuaries. A sanctuary at Khirbet Ataruz illustrates yet another sacred site operating in ostensibly Israelite territory alongside the Jerusalem Temple, during the Iron IIA. Ataruz was taken over by Moabites in the Iron IIB.

While literary similarities of the Jerusalem Temple show a strong connection to architectural styles of the Iron II period, the specific dating is debated. Early studies assumed a tenth-century founding date, but that has been questioned, especially since the call to minimize that century as a part of Finkelstein's low chronology combined with a relative paucity of Iron IIA remains from Jerusalem (Finkelstein 2003, 2005).

The mid-twentieth-century excavations of Kenyon (Steiner 2001) and Shiloh (de Groot and Berrick-Greenberg 2012) were reevaluated and published with differing results, particularly regarding the LB-Iron IIA periods. Added to these have been the continuation of Benjamin Mazar's work on the Ophel by Eilat Mazar (E. Mazar 2015), and her own work at the City of David (E. Mazar 2009), the work at the Gihon Spring and areas on the east slope by Ronny Reich and Eli Shukron (Reich and Shukron 2021), the Givati Parking Lot excavations which have only minimally reached early Iron Age levels, and a number of surveys and smaller excavations in the Jerusalem environs. These investigations have produced minimal agreed-upon results and numerous detailed and nuanced debates arguing both against (Ussishkin 2003) and for (Cahill 2003) Iron IIA significant settlement in the City of David environs.

Archaeologists have also investigated the regions around Jerusalem in the Iron I-IIB period. Mounting evidence indicates both an Iron IIA centralizing tendency of settlement (Faust 2021) and apparent expansion: west into the Shephelah foothills, illustrated by Khirbet Qeiyafa, and south into the Negev as indicated by Khirbet Summeily. Although strongly debated, many scholars now see some form of regional tenth-century political expansion. A study of bone seals indicates this was centered in Jerusalem which was administratively significant with monumental architecture and international connections in the tenth and ninth centuries (Keel 2012). Nonetheless, excavations and surveys around Jerusalem supplemented by recent radiocarbon studies have produced a still inconclusive picture of the city and its reach. Perhaps it is best to affirm A. Mazar's "glass half full" picture of a Jerusalem that quite possibly served as an Iron IIA administrative center with some monumental architecture, including a temple that compares reasonably with other Iron Age examples from throughout the region (A. Mazar 2006).

Bamot

Since 1980, excavations and reevaluations have continued at the key sites for the LB-Iron I transition, such as Megiddo, Hazor, and Lachish, while adding new southern sites like Beth Shemesh, Azekah, and Tel Burna. In spite of numerous subsequent excavations, Late Bronze Age small-scale or household sanctuaries have not been unearthed, with a single exception coming from Tell es-Safi/Gath. Two Iron I open air sanctuaries figure prominently in discussions—the Manasseh Bull Site and Mt. Ebal. Additionally, Khirbet Qeiyafa's cultic remains are important for Iron IIA discussions.

Exploration on Mt. Ebal, overlooking Shechem, revealed a structure understood by most, but certainly not all, as a large open-air altar and *bamah* (Zertal 1987). Because its pottery dates to the early Iron I, and its faunal remains are consistent with sacrifices, this Iron I edifice could be the Mt. Ebal *maqom* noted in Deuteronomy (Hawkins 2012). Shechem thus continued as a site for sanctuaries, although the exact spot changed. This may also be noted in the Persian period with the erection of a temple to YHWH on Mt. Gerizim overlooking Shechem from the south (Magen 2008), allowing some to claim a post-exilic date for at least Deuteronomy 27. In 1924, Adam Cleghorn Welch (1924, 174–185) raised the question: If Deuteronomy calls for a single *maqom* in Jerusalem, why would that same Deuteronomy call for an altar and *massebot* to be built on Mt. Ebal? Sandra Richter concluded that only an LB/Iron I date for the chapter is actually warranted (Richter 2017).

In addition to Mt. Ebal, several small, mostly underpublished, open-air sites in the western hills overlooking the Jordan Valley have been promoted as Iron I Israelite sanctuaries (Zertal 2021). These *gilgalim* enclosures (stone circles) include El-Unuq, Bedhat esh-Sha'ab, Masua, Yafit, Sha'ab Rumani, and el-Burnat, as well as Manoah's Altar at Zorah (Hanauer 1885), and a possible four horned stone altar near Shiloh; they have received minimal acceptance as *bamot*.

The Bull Site of Manasseh excavated in 1978 and 1981 is a hill-top stone enclosure (23m x 21m) used during the twelfth century. Ritual items found include a small *maṣṣabah*, fragments of a cult stand, and a small bronze figurine of a Zebu bull. The site is clearly a *bamah* of the Iron I, but little else is certain.

The excavated repertoire in Iron Age II Israel and Judah has grown to include sanctuaries at Khirbet Qeiyafa, Tel Rehov, Tel Mazar, and Tel Moza. While still generally fewer and smaller than those in the surrounding polities (Tel Miqne, Tell es-Safi, Khirbat Ataruz, Khirbat al-Mudayna, and Horvat Qitmit), it is increasingly clear that Israelite sanctuaries were not limited to a single *maqom*.

Discussions about the relationship between *bamot* sanctuaries and the *maqom* envisioned by Deuteronomy have been largely supplanted by broader conversations about Israelite religions (Hess 2007). Initially understood as *bamot*, the accumulating material from Iron Age local and household ritual activity complicated interpretations of Deuteronomy. While already noted in the nineteenth century, scholars of the twentieth century increasingly distinguished household sanctuaries from public sanctuaries (McCown 1950), and attempted to distinguish orthodox from heterodox sanctuaries.

The volume of excavated materials by the 1980s led to focused efforts to categorize the *realia* in terms of their ritual use. John S. Holladay, Jr. developed what became a pioneering work categorizing sites and artifacts. He used a broad comparative metric. If something would be religious in sanctuaries elsewhere, they should be assumed so in Israel and Judah, even in domestic contexts. He then examined thirteen essential Iron Age cultic assemblages from the Levant, determining that multiple different levels of corporate religious expression operated simultaneously. These were establishment sanctuaries, distinct from both local, nonconformist shrines which attempted to remedy perceived deficiencies of establishment sanctuaries, and domestic ritual activities (Holladay 1987, 269–275). Scholars continue to debate nomenclature and identification of excavated sites, citing differences between *bamot*, cult corners, room shrines, gate shrines, cult complexes, sanctuaries, and temples. A. Mazar has recently noted that "[i]t appears, therefore, that the heterogeneity of cult places in Iron Age Israel precludes any formal typological classification" (A. Mazar 2015. 30).

The catalogue of cultic items includes altars, *maṣṣabot*, platforms and benches, inscriptions, Egyptian, zoomorphic, horse and rider and pillar figurines, ceramic pomegranates, astragali, rattles, incense burners, and metal utensils as well as elite ceramics like kernoi, cup and saucer vessels, zoomorphic vessels, votive vessels, and chalices. Whether late Iron Age pillar figurines of Judah represent Astarte or Asherah or were used in Assyrian-inspired domestic healing rituals (Darby 2018) remains much discussed. Common domestic ceramics found in abundance would indicate community meals, as would the remains of sacrificed animals. Although caches have been unearthed, many figurines and chalices are found alone or in small numbers with more mundane objects and contexts, indicating small-scale industrial or household ritual activity. Recently, household shrines excavated in both Israel at Tel Rehov and Judah at Tel Halif have received significant study.

The study of household sanctuaries has blossomed since 1980, adding a more nuanced aspect to the understanding of the *realia* (Albertz et al. 2014). Three features are important to note when considering what constitutes a domestic *bamah* or *maqom*: (1) household sanctuaries were common, although not in every house, and appear undisturbed by reform activities; (2) Iron II household, and local, sanctuaries in Judah not served by priests should be interpreted using comparative methods (Daviau 2001); and (3) women as household ritual leaders has permitted archaeology a more intimate and foundational lens through which to view the data, allowing *realia* to be both ritual and functional (C. Meyers 2005).

Reforms

Conversations regarding proposed reconstructions of reforms and their impact on Judah and the Bible continue in creative and detailed nuance along the same basic lines as previously. While looking for archaeological evidence of cultic centralization, most scholars continue to study wider historical reconstructions. The issue of royal and cult centralization itself in the ancient world, even as part of an Iron IIA highland political consolidation at a single capital, has been examined (Kratz and Spieckermann 2010).

Discussions concerning centralization also continue to revolve around views of dating the redactional layers of Deuteronomy and then comparing those conclusions to archaeological data. Recent conversations regarding centralization can be grouped as follows:

1. Centralization, even with little archaeological evidence, took place either under Hezekiah (Moulis 2019) or Josiah (Uehlinger 2005; Čapek 2019).
2. Centralization took place as part of the governmental response to the impending invasions of Judah by Assyria (Borowski 1995) or by Babylon (Koch 2019).
3. Centralization either did not happen at all or was simply a natural consequence of social evolution (Pakkala 2010).

There is little archaeological evidence for decommissioning local sanctuaries in favor of a sole sanctuary. Sites in Israel and Judah disrupted or destroyed by Tiglath-Pileser III (734–732 BCE) or Sennacherib (701 BCE) have made analysis of possible evidence for centralization by Hezekiah more difficult, while the near total destruction wrought by Babylon may mask such efforts by Josiah.

Although the Bible suggests that Manasseh rebuilt the sanctuaries which Hezekiah had closed (2 Kgs. 21:3), there is not the expected increase in local sanctuaries in the archaeological record of the seventh century. This is the time of the Judean pillar figurines, yet very few incense burners from Judah or Israel have been excavated. This situation is even more puzzling when compared to the multiple sanctuaries functioning during the same period in Philistia, Edom, Moab, and Ammon.

Debates regarding Beersheba and Arad have become more clarified. Ze'ev Herzog and Lily Singer-Avitz (Herzog and Singer-Avitz 2016) reexamined earlier interpretations of the horned altar at Beersheba and dated it to 800–820 BCE. While the original location and context of the altar, however, remains unknown, animal sacrifices were offered at Beersheba in the eighth century but were stopped prior to the destruction of the administrative center in 701 BCE.

Arad and Beersheba are within a few miles of each other. These two administratively focused sites had large, sacrificial altars which were constructed very differently from one another. These sites were dismantled in different ways as well, both most likely in the late eighth century, prior to the invasion of 701 BCE (Herzog 2002). Beersheba's altar was dismantled, its stones reused in walls and the repair of the glacis. Arad's incense altars and *maṣṣabah* were buried on site, and after removing its metal stove the altar was buried (Herzog 2010). Whether these constitute proof of centralization or were done simply to protect sanctuaries during the invasion by Assyria is unclear. Neither sanctuary was rebuilt.

Two additional excavations have focused attention on centralization. A proposed gate sanctuary at Lachish is understood to have been decommissioned and desecrated prior to 701 BCE (Ganor and Kreimerman 2019). If true, this would add evidence for centralization by Hezekiah. That interpretation, however, has been challenged. Additionally, the depiction of a large cult stand being carried off in 701 BCE by Assyrian soldiers would indicate another contemporary and functioning sanctuary at the site.

A sanctuary has also been discovered at Tel Moza, about 7km from ancient Jerusalem (Kisilevitz 2015). Although excavation is ongoing, what seems clear is that a small tenth-century sanctuary (Temple 8528) was replaced by a larger Syrian style Temple (4601) with a fronting courtyard and altar of unhewn stones during the late tenth or early ninth century. The finds include ashes and bones near the altar along with four figurines, an incense burner, a pomegranate pendant, and, perhaps, an offering table. The courtyard exhibits four phases spanning the late tenth to early sixth centuries. In the late eighth century, there was a deliberate covering over of the sacred broken objects which may be related to Hezekiah's reform, but would have been short-lived. No destruction layer from the last phase has been published. Its relationship to numerous granaries and the current identification of Tel Moza as a royal estate has led to various interpretations, but that another local temple functioned so close to the Jerusalem Temple is all but certain.

All in all, the physical evidence for cultic centralization by either Hezekiah or Josiah is rather meager, and what is available can be variously interpreted.

Other Trends

As more sites and texts are unearthed, more detail is added to the conversations. Just as Tel Miqne, Tell es-Safi, Tel Moza, Khirbat Ataruz, Khirbat al-Mudayna, Khirbet Qeiyafa, Tel Rehov, Tel Halif, Givati, and Tel Lachish have recently produced results that moved the conversation into new areas of discussion, future excavations will do the same. More refined use of current scientific methods and their increasing availability, along with new scientific analyses, will move the conversation in both unheralded directions and resolution of current debates. New and reenvisioned theoretical models and methods such as the trend toward the "New Biblical Archaeology" (Levy 2010) as well as more nuanced interpretations of texts will continue to impact discussions.

Conversations specifically regarding the *maqom* of Deuteronomy, its intent and its contexts, seem to remain largely a literary endeavor. Recent studies tend to nuance interpretations of the *maqom* in Deuteronomy centered on the consensus late dating. Increasingly, however, there has been a move toward an earlier date for Deuteronomy, informed by archaeological data.

Although much debated, investigations, excavations, and surveys in and around Jerusalem and Judah will likely continue to illustrate the viability of a tenth-century city with its Temple as a political capital for the region. Because no work will be done on the Temple Mount, literary portrayals of the Iron Age Jerusalem Temple will remain predominant. Nonetheless, biblical descriptions of the Temple continue to find correspondences to art and architecture from the Iron Age, even as some aspects—the enormous size given for the Jerusalem Temple, for example—continue to cast doubt on the historical accuracy of the texts. Comparative examinations of other Near Eastern texts which indicate that some parts of the temple literature in the Bible arguably originates from the time of the building itself (Galil 2012).

Investigations surrounding *bamot* likely will show a more nuanced classification of micro-religions in ancient Israel (Hutton 2010) along with a more localized holistic view of the religious landscape (Koch 2020). The sanctuaries at Tel Moza, Arad, and perhaps other sites in Judah during the Iron Age II, although not as common as in surrounding regions, may well nuance understanding of Deuteronomy's *maqom* in terms of a distinction between elite and nonelite populations. For the Iron I, the paucity of temples, as distinct from Late Bronze Age *maqommim*, likely encourages studies into more local and domestic expressions as well as early Israelite sanctuaries at sites like Shiloh and Kiryat Ye'arim.

Studies of materials from the late Iron II devoted to reform and centralization show no signs of slowing down. Increasingly, while glyptics, onomastics, and sanctuary architecture will continue to receive attention, it is the larger geopolitical, economic, and cultural innovations, evidenced through such investigations as the dating the *LMLK* jar stamps and refinement of ceramic chronology, as well as survey work, especially around Jerusalem, that is strongly trending. Several nuances to the basic outlines have been offered recently, and new ones likely will continue to be put forth. The trending view of the archaeological evidence is to see Hezekiah's reform as far more likely, and more substantially represented in the archaeological material than Josiah's reform. Yet even Hezekiah's reform garners only minimal hard evidence for centralizing worship at the Jerusalem Temple, regardless of what type of local activity is being considered.

The ongoing research shift toward the more local and holistic indicates that there may be less focus on the *maqom* in Deuteronomy as the main locus of worship in both Israelite history and the interpretation of the biblical literature.

The increased awareness from the archaeological data that there likely was an Iron IIA tenth-century polity centered on Jerusalem and its temple may point to an earlier date for the traditions, and possibly writings, dealing with the *maqom* concept. Read in harmony with other biblical passages and the Iron I archaeological data, these traditions show a diverse early landscape able to support a tent-housed ark shrine (*maqom*), numerous other smaller orthodox sanctuaries (*bamot*), and domestic ritual activities. This is unlike the Bronze Age Canaanite system of multiple large sanctuaries (the *maqommim* of Deuteronomy 12).

That even the literary biblical Solomon did not require the removal of *bamot*—archaeologically including Moza, Ataruz, and later Arad—indicates that these early traditions were allowed to continue even as traditional concepts were reinterpreted to codify the primacy of the new singular and central *maqom*. In the Iron II, the *maqom* was permanently established in a building in Jerusalem and focused on its elite population. Only at times of pilgrimage festivals and other significant activities did this singular *maqom* interface with the lives of the wider population who continued to worship in their traditional ways. As the kingdom progressed, the central sanctuary allowed the elite to exercise some control over the local sanctuaries, populations, and economies.

Although Deuteronomy never specifically connects the ark, Jerusalem, or the king with the *maqom*, its traditions and text open themselves to an interpretation wherein the Jerusalem Temple was to be the only royal temple housing the ark in Israel, in the city that YHWH chose through David's selection. Later prophetic voices called for an even more singular understanding.

When the situation warranted, the Crown was able to promote this interpretation of the earlier tradition in a more forceful way and attempt to exploit it for both political and economic gain as well as for national security. While excavation may show the secular results of such moves, the religious motives are difficult to establish archaeologically. This use of *maqom* ideology in the Iron IIB does not necessarily mean that the materials and/or traditions of Deuteronomy are late, perhaps, rather, reinterpreted.

Bibliography

Aharoni, Yohanan. "Arad: Its Inscriptions and Temple." *Biblical Archaeologist* 31 (1968): 2–32.

Aharoni, Yohanan. "The Horned Altar at Beer-sheba." *Biblical Archaeologist* 37 (1974): 2–3.

Albertz, Ranier, Beth Alpert Nakhai, Saul M. Olyan, and Rüdiger Schmitt, eds. *Family and Household Religion: Toward a Synthesis of Old Testament Studies, Archaeology, Epigraphy, and Cultural Studies*. Winona Lake: Eisenbrauns, 2014.

Arie, Eran, Baruch Rosen, and Dvory Namdar. "Cannabis and Frankincense at the Judahite Shrine at Arad." *Tel Aviv* 47, no. 1 (2020): 5–28.

Arnold, Bill T. "Deuteronomy 12 and the Law of the Central Sanctuary *noch einmal*." *Vetus Testamentum* 64, no. 2 (2014): 236–248.

Avigad, Nahman. *Hebrew Bullae from the Time of Jeremiah. Remnants of a Burnt Archive*. Eretz-Israel. Jerusalem: Israel Exploration Society, 1986.

Barkay, Gabriel, and Zachi Dvira. "Relics in Rubble: The Temple Mount Sifting Project." *Biblical Archaeology Review* 42, no. 6 (2016): 44–55, 64.

Barrick, W. Boyd. "High Place." In *The Anchor Yale Bible Dictionary*, Vol. 3, edited by David Noel Freedman, 196–200. New York: Doubleday, 1992.

Barton, George A. "Temple of Solomon." In *The Jewish Encyclopedia*, Vol. 12, edited by Isidore Singer, 98–101. New York: Funk & Wagnalls, 1906.

Bloch-Smith, Elizabeth. "Massebot Standing for YHWH: The Fall of a Yhwistic Cult Symbol." In *Worship, Women, and War: Essays in Honor of Susan Niditch*, edited by John J. Collins, Tracy M. Lemos, and Saul M. Olyan, 99–116. Brown Judaic Studies 357. Providence: Brown University Press, 2015.

Borowski, Oded. "Hezekiah's Reforms and the Revolt against Assyria." *Biblical Archaeologist* 58 (1995): 148–155.

Cahill, Jane. "Jerusalem at the Time of the United Monarchy. The Archaeological Evidence." In *Jerusalem in Bible and Archaeology: The First Temple Period*, edited by Andrew G. Vaughn and Ann E. Killebrew, 13–80. Society of Biblical Literature. Symposium Series 18. Leiden: SBL Press, 2003.

Čapek, Filip. "King Josiah between Eclipse and Rebirth: Judah of the Seventh Century BCE in History and Literature." In *The Last Century in the History of Judah: The Seventh Century BCE in Archaeological, Historical, and Biblical Perspectives*, edited by Filip Čapek and Oded Lipschits, 45–62. Ancient Israel and Its Literature 37. Atlanta: SBL Press, 2019.

Claburn, W. Eugene. "The Fiscal Basis of Josiah's Reforms." *Journal of Biblical Literature* 92, no. 1 (1973): 11–22.

Cook, Stanley A. *The Religion of Ancient Palestine in the Second Millennium B.C.: In the Light of Archaeology and the Inscriptions*. London: A. Constable & Company Limited, 1908.

Darby, Erin M. "Judean Pillar Figurines (JPFs)." In *Archaeology and History of Eighth-Century Judah*, edited by Zev I. Farber and Jacob L. Wright, 401–414. Ancient Near East Monographs 23. Atlanta: SBL Press, 2018.

Davey, Christopher. J. "Temples of the Levant and the Buildings of Solomon." *Tyndale Bulletin* 31 (1980): 107–146.

Daviau, P. M. Michele. "Family Religion: Evidence for the Paraphernalia of the Domestic Cult." In *The World of the Arameans II*. Edited by P. M. Michele Daviau, John W. Wevers, and Michael Weigl, Journal for the Study of the Old Testament Supplement Series 325. London: A&C Black, 2001.

De Groot, Alon and Hannah Bernick-Greenberg. *Excavations at the City of David 1978–1985 Directed by Yigal Shiloh, Volume VIIA: Area E: Stratigraphy and Architecture.* Qedem 53. Jerusalem: Institute of Archaeology, Hebrew University of Jerusalem, 2012.

De Groot, Alon and Hannah Bernick-Greenberg. *Excavations at the City of David 1978–1985 Directed by Yigal Shiloh, Volume VIIA: Area E: The Finds.* Qedem 54. Jerusalem: Institute of Archaeology, Hebrew University of Jerusalem, 2012.

De Vaux, Roland. *Ancient Israel.* 2 vols. New York: McGraw Hill, 1961.

Dever, William. G. "'Will the Real Israel Please Stand Up?' Part II: Archaeology and the Religions of Ancient Israel." *Bulletin of the American Schools of Oriental Research* 298 (1995): 37–58.

Dussaud, René. *Les découvertes de Ras Shamra (Ugarit) et l'Ancien Testament.* Paris: Librairie Orientaliste Paul Geuthner, 1937.

Faust, Aviram. "The Archaeology of the Israelite Cult: Questioning the Consensus." *Bulletin of the American Schools of Oriental Research* 360 (2010): 23–35.

Faust, Aviram. "The 'United Monarchy' on the Ground: The Disruptive Character of the Iron Age I–II Transition and the Nature of Political Transformations." *Jerusalem Journal of Archaeology* 1 (2021): 15–67.

Faust, Aviram, Yosef Garfinkel, and Madeleine Mumcuoglu. "State Formation Processes in the Tenth Century BCE Levant." *Jerusalem Journal of Archaeology* 1 (2010): 1–14.

Finkelstein, Israel. "The Archaeology of the United Monarchy. An Alternative View." *Levant* 28 (1996): 177–187.

Finkelstein, Israel. "The Rise of Jerusalem and Judah: The Missing Link." In *Jerusalem in Bible and Archaeology: The First Temple Period*, edited by Andrew G. Vaughn and Ann E. Killebrew, 81–102. Society of Biblical Literature. Symposium Series 18. Atlanta: SBL, 2003. First published in *Levant* 33 (2001): 105–115.

Finkelstein, Israel. "A Low Chronology Update: Archaeology, History and Bible." In *The Bible and Radiocarbon Dating: Archaeology, Text and Science*, edited by Thomas E. Levy and Thomas Highham. London: Equinox, 2005.

Fried, Lisbeth S. "The High Places (*Bāmôt*) and the Reforms of Hezekiah and Josiah: An Archaeological Investigation." *Journal of the American Oriental Society* 122, no. 3 (2002): 437–465.

Gadot, Yuval, Israel Finkelstein, Mark Iserlis, and Aren M. Maier. "Tracking Down Cult: Production, Function, and Content of Chalices in Iron Age Philistia." *Tel Aviv* 44 (2014): 55–76.

Galil, Gershon. "Solomon's Temple: Fiction or Reality?" In *The Ancient Near East in the 12th–tenth Centuries BC: Culture and History*, edited by Gershon Galil, Ayelet Gilboa, Aren M. Maeir, and Dan'el Kahn, 137–148. Alter Orient und Altes Testament 392. Munster: Ugarit-Verlag, 2012.

Galling, Kurt. *Biblisches Reallexicon.* Handbuch zum Alten Testament 1. Tübingen: Mohr, 1937.

Ganor, Saar, and Igor Kreimerman. "An Eighth-Century B.C.E. Gate Shrine at Tel Lachish." *Bulletin of the American Schools of Oriental Research* 381 (2019): 211–236.

Garfinkel, Yosef, and Madeleine Mumcuoglu. "The Temple of Solomon in Iron Age Context." *Religions* 10 (2019): 1–17.

Geva, Hillel. "History of Archaeological Research in Jerusalem." In *The New Encyclopedia of Archaeological Excavations in the Holy Land*, Vol. 2, edited by Ephraim Stern, 801–804. Jerusalem: Israel Exploration Society and Carta, 1993.

Gitin, Seymour. "Israelite and Philistine Cult and the Archaeological Record in Iron Age II: The 'Smoking' Gun Phenomenon." In *Symbiosis, Symbolism and the Power of the Past: Canaan, Ancient Israel and Their Neighbors from the Late Bronze Age through Roman Palaestina*, edited by William G. Dever and Seymour Gitin, 279–295. Winona Lake: Eisenbrauns, 2003.

Gitin, Seymour, ed. *The Ancient Pottery of Israel and Its Neighbors from the Iron Age through the Hellenistic Period*. 2 vols. Jerusalem: Israel Exploration Society, 2015.

Halpern, Baruch. "The Centralization Formula in Deuteronomy." *Vetus Testamentum* 31, no. 1 (1981): 20–38.

Hanauer, James E. "The Rock Altar of Zorah." *Palestine Exploration Quarterly* 17, no. 3 (1885): 183–184.

Harrison, Timothy P. "Chapter Three: The Architecture." In *Megiddo 3. Final Report on the Stratum VI Excavations*, edited by Timothy P. Harrison, 15–22. Oriental Institute Publications, Vol. 127. Chicago: University of Chicago Press, 2004.

Hawkins, Ralph K. *The Iron Age Structure on Mt. Ebal: Excavation and Interpretation*. Bulletin for Biblical Research Supplement 6. Winona Lake: Eisenbrauns, 2012.

Herzog, Ze'ev. "The Fortress Mound at Tel Arad: An Interim Report." Tel Aviv 29 (2002): 3–109.

Herzog, Ze'ev. "Perspectives on Southern Israel's Cult Centralization: Arad and Beer-Sheba." In *One God—One Cult—One Nation: Archaeological and Biblical Perspectives*, edited by Reinhard G. Kratz, and Hermann Spieckermann, 169–199. Beihefte zur Zeitschrift für die Alttestamentliche Wissenschaft 405. Berlin: De Gruyter, 2010.

Herzog, Ze'ev, and Lily Singer-Avitz, eds. *Beer-Sheba III. The Early Iron IIA Enclosed Settlement and the Late Iron IIA-Iron IIB Cities. Vol. III: Artifacts, Ecofacts and Concluding Studies*. Tel Aviv University. Winona Lake: Eisenbrauns, 2016.

Hess, Richard S. *Israelite Religions: An Archaeological and Biblical Survey*. Grand Rapids: Baker Academic, 2007.

Holladay, John S. Jr. "Religion in Israel and Judah Under the Monarchy: An Explicitly Archaeological Approach." In *Ancient Israelite Religion: Essays in Honor of Frank Moore Cross*, edited by Paul D. Miller, Jr., Paul D. Hanson, and S. Dean McBride, 249–299. Philadelphia: Fortress Press, 1987.

Hundley, Michael B. *Gods in Dwellings: Temples and Divine Presence in the Ancient Near East*. Writing from the Ancient World Supplements 3. Atlanta: Society of Biblical Literature, 2013.

Hurowitz, Victor A. "YHWH's Exalted House Revisited: New Comparative Light on the Biblical Image of Solomon's Temple." In *The Ancient Near East in the 12th–tenth Centuries BC: Culture and History*, edited by Gershon Galil, Ayelet Gilboa, Aren M. Maeir, and Dan'el Kahn, 229–240. Alter Orient und Altes Testament 392. Munster: Ugarit-Verlag, 2012.

Hutton, Jeremy. "Southern, Northern, and Transjordanian Perspectives." In *Religious Diversity in Ancient Israel and Judah*, edited by Francesca Stavrakopoulou and John Barton, 149–174. London: T & T Clark, 2010.

Kamlah, Jens. "Temples of the Levant—Comparative Aspects." In *Temple Building and Temple Cult: Architecture and Cultic Paraphernalia of Temples in the Levant (2.-1. Mill. B.C.E)*, edited by Jens Kamlah, 507–536. Abhandlugen des Deutschen Palästina-Vereins 41. Weisbaden: Harrassowitz, 2012.

Keel, Othmar. "Paraphernalia of Jerusalem Sanctuaries and Their Relation to Deities Worshipped Therein during the Iron Age IIA-C." In *Temple Building and Temple Cult: Architecture and Cultic Paraphernalia of Temples in the Levant (2.-1. Mill. B.C.E.)*, edited by Jens Kamla, 317–342. Abhandlugen des Deutschen Palästina-Vereins 41. Weisbaden: Harrassowitz, 2012.

Kisilevitz, Shua. "The Iron IIA Judahite Temple at Tel Moza." *Tel Aviv* 42 (2015): 147–164.

Kitchen, Kenneth A. "On the Old Testament and Its Context: Part 6." *Theological Students Fellowship Bulletin* 64 (1972): 2–13.

Kleiman, Assaf, Margaret E. Cohen, Erin Hall, Robert S. Homsher, and Israel Finkelstein. "Cult Activity at Megiddo in the Iron Age: New Evidence and a Long-Term Perspective." *Zeitschrift des Palästina-Vereins* 133, no. 1 (2017): 24–52.

Kline, Meredeth G. *Treaty of the Great King: The Covenant Structure of Deuteronomy: Studies and Commentary*. Grand Rapids: Eerdmans, 1963.

Knauf, Ernst Axel. "The Glorious Days of Manasseh." In *Good Kings and Bad Kings*, edited by L. L. Grabbe, 164–188. Library of Hebrew Bible/Old Testament Studies, European Seminar in Historical Methodology 5, JSOTS 393. London: T & T Clark, 2005.

Koch, Ido. "Pictorial Novelties in Context: Assyrian Iconography in Judah." In *The Last Century in the History of Judah: The Seventh Century BCE in Archaeological, Historical, and Biblical Perspectives*, edited by Filip Čapek, and Oded Lipschits, 153–165. Ancient Israel and Its Literature 37. Atlanta: SBL Press, 2019.

Koch, Ido. "Southern Levantine Temples during the Iron Age II: Towards a Multivocal Narrative." *Judaïsme Ancien—Ancient Judaism* 8 (2020): 325–344.

Kratz, Reinhard G., and Hermann Spieckermann, eds. *One God—One Cult—One Nation: Archaeological and Biblical Perspectives*. Beihefte zur Zeitschrift für die Alttestamentliche Wissenschaft 405. Berlin: De Gruyter, 2010.

Kuenen, Abraham. *An Historico-critical Inquiry into the Origin and Composition of the Hexateuch*. Princeton: Princeton University Press, 1886.

Levy, Thomas E. *Historical Biblical Archaeology and the Future: The New Pragmatism*. London: Equinox, 2010.

Magen, Yitzhak. *Mount Gerizim Excavations, Volume II: A Temple City*. Judah & Samaria Publications 8. Translated by Edward Levitt and Carl Ebert. Jerusalem: Staff Office of Archaeology – Civil Administration of Judea and Samaria, Israel Antiquities Authority, 2008.

Mazar, Amihai. *Archaeology of the Land of the Bible: 10,000–586 B.C.* New York: Doubleday, 1990.

Mazar, Amihai. "Jerusalem in the Tenth Century B.C.E.: The Glass Half Full." In *Essays on Ancient Israel in Its Near Eastern Context: A Tribute to Nadav Na'aman*, edited by Yaira Amit, Ehud Ben Zvi, Israel Finkelstein, and Oded Lipschits, 255–272. Winona Lake: Eisenbrauns, 2006.

Mazar, Amihai. "Religious Practices and Cult Objects during the Iron Age IIA at Tel Rehov and their Implications Regarding Religion in Northern Israel." *Hebrew Bible and Ancient Israel* 4 (2015): 25–55.

Mazar, Eilat. *The Palace of King David. Excavations at the Summit of the City of David. Preliminary Report of Seasons 2005-2007*. Jerusalem: Shoham Academic Research and Publication, 2009.

Mazar, Eilat. *The Ophel Excavations to the South of the Temple Mount 2009-2013. Final Reports, Volume I*. Jerusalem: Shoham Academic Research and Publication, 2015.

McCown, Chester C. "Hebrew High Places and Cult Remains." *JBL* 69, no. 3 (1950): 205–219.

Meyers, Carol L. *Households and Holiness: The Religious Culture of Israelite Women*. Minneapolis: Fortress Press, 2005.

Moulis, David R. "Hezekiah's Cultic Reforms according to the Archaeological Evidence." In *The Last Century in the History of Judah: The Seventh Century BCE in Archaeological,*

Historical, and Biblical Perspectives, edited by Filip Čapek, and Oded Lipschits, 167–180. Ancient Israel and Its Literature 37. Atlanta: SBL Press, 2019.

Na'aman, Nadav. "The Abandonment of Cult Places in the Kingdoms of Israel and Judah as Acts of Cult Reform." *Ugarit-Forschungen* 34: 585–602, 2002.

Noth, Martin. *A History of Israel*. 2nd ed. New York: Harper & Row, 1960.

Oestreicher, Theodor. *Das Deuteronomische Grundgesetz. Beiträge zur Förderung christlicher Theologie*, 27. Bd. 4. Heft. Gütersloh: C. Bertelsmann Verlag, 1923.

Pakkala, Juha. "Why the Cult Reforms in Judah Probably Did Not Happen." In *One God—One Cult—One Nation: Archaeological and Biblical Perspectives*, edited by Reinhard G. Kratz and Hermann Spieckermann, 201–235. Beihefte zur Zeitschrift für die Alttestamentliche Wissenschaft 405. Berlin: De Gruyter, 2010.

Pedersen, Johannes. *Israel: Its Life and Culture*. 2 vols. London: Oxford University Press, 1926.

Pitkänen, Pekka. *Central Sanctuary and Centralization of Worship in Ancient Israel: From the Settlement to the Building of Solomon's Temple*. Piscataway: Gorgias Press, 2004.

Reich, Ronny, and Eli Shukron. *Excavations in the City of David, Jerusalem (1995–2010)*. Winona Lake: Eisenbrauns, 2021.

Richter, Sandra L. "Placing the Name, Pushing the Paradigm: A Decade with the Deuteronomistic Name Formula." In *Deuteronomy in the Pentateuch, Hexateuch, and the Deuteronomistic History*, edited by Konrad Schmid and Raymond F. Person, 64–78 *Forschungen zum Alten Testament*. 2. Reihe, 56. Tübingen: Mohr Siebeck, 2012.

Richter, Sandra, L. "The Archaeology of Mount Ebal and Mount Gerizim and Why it Matters." In *Sepher Torath Mosheh: Studies in the Composition and Interpretation of Deuteronomy*, edited by Daniel I. Block and Richard L. Schultz, 304–337. Peabody: Hendrickson, 2017.

Robinson, Edward. *Physical Geography of the Holy Land*. Boston: Crocker & Brewster, 1865.

Sapir, Yair, with Shani Libi. "Appendix: Survey of Scientific Methods in Archaeology." In *Archaeology and History of Eighth-Century Judah*, edited by Zev I. Farber and Jacob L. Wright, 529–553. Atlanta: Society of Biblical Literature, 2018.

Shapira, D. "The Moza Temple and Solomon's Temple." *Bibliotheca Orientalis* 75 (2018): 1–2, 25–47.

Smith. Mark S. *The Early History of God: Yahweh and Other Deities in Ancient Israel*. New York: Harper & Row, 1990.

Stager, Lawrence E. "The Fortress-Temple at Shechem and the 'House of El, Lord of the Covenant." In *Realia Dei: Essays in Archaeology and Biblical Interpretation in Honor of Edward F. Campbell, Jr., at His Retirement*, edited by Prescott H. Williams and Theodore Hiebert, 228–249. Atlanta: Scholars Press, 1999.

Steiner, Margreet L. *Excavations by Kathleen M. Kenyon in Jerusalem 1961–1967, III. The Settlement in the Bronze and Iron Ages*. Copenhagen International Seminar 9. Sheffield: Sheffield University Press, 2001.

Stern, Ephraim, ed. *The New Encyclopedia of Archaeological Excavations in the Holy Land*. 5 vols. New York: Simon & Schuster, 2008. First published 1993.

Strawn, Brent A., and Joel M. LeMon. "Religion in Eighth-Century Judah: The Case of Kuntillet 'Ajrud (and Beyond)." In *Archaeology and History of Eighth-Century Judah*, edited by Zev I. Farber and Jacob L. Wright, 379–400. Ancient Near East Monographs 23. Atlanta: SBL Press, 2018.

Tigay, Jeffrey. *Deuteronomy*. The JPS Torah Commentary. Philadelphia: The Jewish Publication Society, 1996.

Uehlinger, Christoph. "Was there a Cult Reform under King Josiah? The Case for a Well-Grounded Minimum." In *Good Kings and Bad Kings: The Kingdom of Judah in the Seventh Century BCE*, edited by Lester L. Grabbe, 279–316. Library of Hebrew Bible/Old Testament Studies 393. European Seminar in Historical Methodology 5. London: T&T Clark International, 2005.

Ussishkin, David. "The Date of the Judean Shrine at Arad." *Israel Exploration Journal* 38 (1988): 142–157, pl. 24.

Ussishkin, David. "Solomon's Jerusalem: The Text and Facts on the Ground." In *Jerusalem in Bible and Archaeology: The First Temple Period*, edited by Andrew G. Vaughn and Ann E. Killebrew, 103–116. Society of Biblical Literature. Symposium Series 18. Leiden: SBL, 2003.

Vanderhooft, David. "Dwelling Beneath the Sacred Place: A Proposal for Reading 2 Samuel 7:10." *Journal of Biblical Literature* 118, no. 4 (1999): 625–633.

von Rad, Gerhard. *Studies in Deuteronomy*. London: SCM Press, 1953.

Welch, Adam C. *The Code of Deuteronomy: A New Theory of Its Origin*. London: James Clarke, 1924.

Wellhausen, Julius. *Prolegomena to the History of Israel: With a Reprint of the Article "Israel" from the Encyclopaedia Britannica*. London: A & C Black, 1885.

Wenham, Gordon J. "Pondering the Pentateuch: The Search for a New Paradigm." In *The Face of Old Testament Studies: A Survey of Contemporary Approaches*, edited by David W. Baker and Bill T. Arnold, 116–144. Grand Rapids: Baker Books, 1999.

Wright, G. R. H. "Pre-Israelite Temples in the Land of Canaan." *Palestine Exploration Quarterly* 103, no. 1 (1971): 17–32.

Zevit, Ziony. *The Religions of Ancient Israel: A Synthesis of Parallactic Approaches*. New York: Continuum, 2001.

Zertal, Adam. "An Early Iron Age Cultic Site on Mount Ebal: Excavation Seasons 1982–1987: Preliminary Report." *Tel Aviv* 14, no. 2 (1987): 105–165.

Zertal, Adam. *The Footsteps of God: The Discovery of Israelite Gilgal Sites Dating to the Iron Age*. Israel: Lipkin Tours, 2021.

Zwickel, Wolfgang. "Cult in the Iron Age I-IIA in the Land of Israel." In *The Ancient Near East in the 12th–10th Centuries BCE: Culture and History*, edited by Gershon Galil, Ayelet Gilboa, Aren M. Maeir, and Dan'el Kahn, 581–594. Münster: Ugarit-Verlag, 2012.

CHAPTER 9

LOVE AND HATE IN DEUTERONOMY

FRANCOISE MIRGUET

INTRODUCTION

DEUTERONOMY uses the roots אהב and שנא, commonly translated by "love" and "hate," in both an interpersonal context and the description of the covenant between the Israelites and their deity.[1] Scholarship has mainly focused on the uses of love and hate in covenants and treaties, in the Hebrew Bible and in the Near East more broadly; in this literary context, the terms express the covenantal partners' duties. Comparison between Deuteronomy and these Near Eastern treaties contributes to shedding light on how the ancient Israelites imagined their relation to their deity. A more recent debate has questioned whether the root אהב maintains a primary emotional meaning in the Hebrew Bible. Drawing upon the cultural and historical study of emotions, as well as the specific perception of emotion and self in the Hebrew Bible, this chapter underscores the contrast between contemporary Western concepts of love and hate, which tend to be understood as private and internal feelings, and the biblical uses of אהב and שנא, which rather describe visible practices, performed in a social and often public context.

LOVE AND HATE IN COVENANTAL CONTEXT

Scholarship on אהב and שנא, especially during the twentieth century, has mainly focused on their use as technical terms in covenants and treaties. In this section, I briefly review אהב and שנא between human rulers in the Hebrew Bible, to then examine the use of the same vocabulary in Deuteronomy for the covenant between YHWH and Israel. Comparison with treaties from across the Near East helps contextualize these lexical uses.

The Hebrew Bible uses the verbs אהב and שנא, in human interactions, with the respective meanings of abiding by the terms of a treaty and breaking those terms. Jonathan, for example, "chooses" (בחר, 1 Sam 20:30) David, shifting his loyalty from his father to his friend.

Jonathan and David make a covenant (ברית) with each other (18:3; 20:8, 16; 23:18) and ratify it by oaths (נשבע, 20:3, 17, 42). One of the terms of the treaty is peace (שלום, 20:42), which is to be maintained between the two men's descendants (20:14–15, 42). Their covenant is accompanied by several statements of their love (אהב)—especially Jonathan's love for David (1 Sam 18:1, 3; 20:17; 2 Sam 1:26). Jonathan's love for David is compared to the love for his own life: Jonathan "loved him [David] as his own life [כנפשו]" (1 Sam 18:1, 3; see also 20:17).[2] Self-love in a modern sense is unlikely; rather, Jonathan commits not to spare his own life in ensuring David's survival (20:33)—a clause also present in Near Eastern treaties. The narrative context makes clear that the bond between Jonathan and David exceeds a military alliance; however, their love cannot be separated from political allegiance (Sakenfeld 1983). On a more strictly political level, Hiram of Tyre is described as a "lover" of David (1 Kgs 5:15), clearly an "ally." Upon David's death, Hiram sends an emissary to congratulate his successor, Solomon; the two conclude an alliance (ברית) and live in peace (שלום) with each other (1 Kgs 5:26). The two narratives thus depict prominent leaders who engage in a covenant, assuring peace between them and their descendants. The root אהב functions as a technical term referring to respect for the treaty's terms.

Conversely, Genesis uses שנא in the opposite sense of failing to abide by the terms of a treaty. Although Abraham and Abimelech have concluded a covenant (ברית, Gen 21:27, 32), Abimelech sends away Abraham's son, Isaac, seeking refuge from famine (Gen 26:16). Later, Abimelech engages contact again, which leads Isaac to wonder: "Why have you come to me? You hate [שנאתם] me and have sent me away from you" (26:27). "Hate" indicates a breach in the respect of the treaty (Botta 2013:117–118). Just as אהב functions as a technical term for the respect of the covenant, שנא denotes its transgression.

Deuteronomy describes the covenant between YHWH and Israel with the same vocabulary. The relationship is imagined as a covenant (ברית), initiated by YHWH. Its terms are not mutually agreed upon; rather, YHWH "declared *his* covenant" (4:13). The deity is the unique subject who "makes the covenant" (4:23; 5:2, 3; 9:9; 28:69; 29:11, 13), "keeps" it (7:9, 12), and "lets it stand" (8:18). The covenant is based on YHWH's "choice" of Israel. Like Jonathan's "choice" of David, YHWH has chosen Israel (בחר, 4:37), among all people of the earth (7:6; 10:15; 14:2), to be his people, his possession (סגלה, 7:6; 14:2; 26:18). Like treaties between human beings, the covenant is sealed by oaths, which only YHWH swears (נשבע, 4:31; 7:12; 8:12; 29:12). Israel is passive in the conclusion of the covenant. Its obligation is to keep (שמר, 29:8) the covenant, not transgress (עבר, 17:2), abandon (עזב, 29:24), or break it (הפר, 31:16, 20). The covenant is not mutual because only one partner, the deity, decides its terms.

Love (אהב) is a central concept in this covenant. It is used with both partners, YHWH and Israel, as subjects, although with slightly different meanings. The root אהב is first used as the label that designates the relationship that YHWH had for Israel's ancestors and has for the contemporary people of Israel—addressed as "you." Love is closely connected to a choice: "Because he loved your ancestors, he chose [ויבחר] his offspring/descendants after him" (4:37; 10:15). This choice is not motivated by Israel's size but is presented as a commitment to protection and deliverance (7:7–8). Divine love will continue if Israel respects the commandments (7:12–13); it is accompanied by blessings, human and animal fertility, good harvests, and health (7:13–15).

The verb אהב also refers to Israel's part in the covenant. Just as YHWH's love is understood as an exclusive preference for Israel over all other people, Israel's love of YHWH is intimately associated with the recognition of YHWH's unicity (6:4–5): to love YHWH is primarily a commitment to serve him alone (Weinfeld 1991; Spieckermann 2000; Janowski 2015). Deuteronomy further describes Israel's love primarily as a set of actions and practices: fear YHWH (10:12), walk in his ways (10:12; 11:22; 19:9; 30:16), serve him (10:12; 11:13), keep his commandments (10:13; 11:1, 13, 22; 19:9; 30:16), listen to his voice (30:20). Love is not depicted as a private feeling but as a public set of practices. Deuteronomy never explicitly describes Israel as loving YHWH (Erbele-Küster 2018; Ackerman 2002). There is less interest in describing the Israelites' bond to their deity than in stressing the duties implied by the covenant.

The image of conjugal love between YHWH and Israel is absent in Deuteronomy. Hosea may have developed this theme based on Deuteronomy (Vang 2011; Schmid 2018: 103; contra Zobel 1992). Although both YHWH and Israel are mutual subjects and objects of אהב, there is no mention of their "loving each other." Indeed, biblical texts do not depict love as a reciprocal feeling that grows with the relationship. Further, divine love and human love are asymmetrical. YHWH's love is about choice, protection, and patronage (Vanderhooft 2018), while Israel's is about obedience and exclusive service. Divine love and human love converge in the law concerning the stranger or resident alien (גר) but remain asymmetrical. YHWH is described as "loving [אהב] the stranger, giving him food and clothing" (10:18). The next verse continues: "And you will love the stranger, because you were strangers in the land of Egypt" (10:19). Along with justice for the widow and orphan, love for the stranger contributes to the depiction of YHWH as caring for vulnerable members of society. Love of the stranger is also part of the requirements of the covenant. Finally, although Deuteronomy does not explicitly teach neighborly love (Lev 19:18), the command to love strangers is sometimes interpreted as a more demanding obligation, considering strangers' status in society (Zehnder 2017).

In a covenantal context, hate (שנא) functions as the opposite of love (אהב), in its two meanings of divine patronage and human obedience. YHWH's hatred is imagined twice. Moses accuses the Israelites of doubting the report of the spies who inspected the land of Canaan; according to him, they assumed that "it is because of YHWH's hatred for us that he brought us out of the land of Egypt, to give us into the hand of the Amorite to destroy us" (1:27). Moses interprets the Israelites' unwillingness to enter the land as a lack of trust in YHWH's love, misinterpreted by them as hate or malevolence. In a prayer, Moses implores YHWH to spare the Israelites. The Egyptians should not think that it was "out of hate" that YHWH delivered Israel, only to let them die in the wilderness (9:28). What the Egyptians would think of YHWH's feelings would not matter much; more dangerous for Israel would be their inferring that YHWH has rescinded his covenant and left his people without support and protection. Here too, context indicates that שנא depicts actions rather than feelings. On the human side, hating (שנא) YHWH (5:9; 7:10; 32:41) similarly functions as the opposite of love. It refers primarily to those who make and worship idols (5:8–9) and thus fail to exclusively serve the deity of Israel. "Hate" does not refer to internal feelings, but rather public acts that violate the terms of the covenant.

The use of the vocabulary of "love" and "hate" in political treaties is well attested throughout the Near East, a case that has first been argued by Assyriologist William L. Moran (Moran 1963). These treaties, from the eighteenth to the seventh centuries BCE, written in

Akkadian, Hittite, and Aramaic, use the vocabulary of love to designate loyalty among kings and between sovereigns and vassals. Other common phrases and formulas—such as "oath," "to cut a pact," "to enter a covenant," and a list of blessings and curses—confirm the close connection that these treaties have with each other (Weinfeld 1973).

Hittite treaties, in the Late Bronze Age (1550–1200 BCE), between the kings of Hatti and the vassal princes who depended on them, require only the vassal to love his sovereign. For example, a treaty between Hatti and Ugarit commands vassal Niqmepa to defend the king of Hatti and hold him dear: "As yourself, Niqmepa, your person, your wife, your [son]s and your country are dear to you, (in the same way) the bod[y of the king], the person of the king, the sons of the king and the land of Ḫatti shall be forever dear to you" (CTH 66 obv. 2–12, quoted by Devecchi 2012, 639–640). Reference to "yourself" probably does not imply self-love, but rather, like in the narrative about Jonathan and David (1 Sam 18:1, 3; 20:17), a commitment to protect life: just as the vassal looks after his own life and safeguards his family, he similarly commits to defend the sovereign's life. In return, the sovereign will protect the vassal and deal with him as with a friend (McCarthy 1978).

In the El Amarna letters (1350–1334 BCE), alliances between rulers are phrased as brotherhood and love (*râmu/ra'āmu*). Vassals declare their love for the sovereign (EA 53:40–44); vassals also often invoke the sovereign's love for his servant as an argument for receiving protection (EA 121:60–64; 123:22–28): "Say to Nimmureya, Great King, the king of Egypt, {my} brother my son-in-law, who loves me, and whom I lov{e}" (EA 19:1–8). Like in Deuteronomy, the love that existed in previous generations may be reminded: "My father loved you, and you in turn loved my father" (EA 17:21–29; also 27:37–40); "As far back as the time of your ancestors, they always showed love to my ancestors" (EA 19:9–16). Like in biblical texts, love is at times situated in the heart: "The gods love us in their hearts very, very much" (EA 24, §8, 78; EA 29:55–60). In another context, doing something "with all one's heart" (EA 29:28–54) is interpreted as doing it "without duplicity, keeping his part of the agreement perfectly" (Moran 1992, 98, note 19). Mention of the "heart" does not suggest an internal drive; it rather indicates that this love has a sole recipient.

In the Neo-Assyrian treaties of Esarhaddon (680–669 BCE), vassals are commanded: "(You swear) that you will love Ashurbanipal, the crown-prince, son of Esarhaddon, king of Assyria, your lord as (you do) yourselves [*ki-i nap-šat-ku-nu*]" (IV: 266–268; Wiseman 1958; Mathys 1986, 26). The last words are likely to mean "as your life" and indicate that the vassal should be ready to die for his sovereign, like in the Hittite treaty (IV: 230–231; Mathys 1986, 26). Vassals also take the following oath: "The king of Assyria, our lord, we will love" (quoted by Moran 1963, 80). While the sovereign demands love and loyalty from his vassals, he does not seem to express his own love (Weinfeld 1972, 69). The vassal is required to swear that he will report any insurrection, because he is "wholeheartedly [*lìb-ba-ku-nu*] with him" (II: 152), which probably means "loyally" or "unreservedly" (Wiseman 1958, 83), as in the El Amarna letters. In another text, the vassal takes the oath, "Ashurbanipal, king of Assyrian our lord, we love [. . .] and another king and another lord for . . . we shall never seek" (Letter 1105, 32–35; Waterman 1930–1936, 267). This declaration of love, like Deuteronomy, is a commitment to exclusive loyalty.

Near Eastern treaties help contextualize Deuteronomy's covenantal language. They shed particular light to commands to love YHWH with "all of your heart [לבבך/כם] and all of your life [נפשך/כם]" (6:5; 13:4; 30:6) and "all of your force [מאדך]" (6:5). The heart, in Biblical Hebrew, is often understood as an organ of thought, will, and decision, as well as of social relations and communication (Müller 2014; Janowski 2015; Erbele-Küster 2018). It is sometimes associated with the inner life; love "in the heart" is then seen as an internalization of obedience (Rütersworden 2006; Levenson 2016). By contrast with these associations, love "with all of one's heart," in the El Amarna letters and the treaties of Esarhaddon, indicates exclusive loyalty and renunciation of other alliances. Reference to the life/self, in Hittite treaties and the Esarhaddon's treaties, suggests the commitment not to spare one's own life in the defense of one's sovereign. Some treaties also add that the vassal should help with all of his "force," that is, his full military resources (Weinfeld 1991). Accordingly, the love command, in Deuteronomy, seems better understood as requiring exclusive devotion and obedience. References to the heart, life, and force may not be about inner parts or aspects of the self; rather, they are more likely to describe *how* this devotion is to be executed—exclusively toward YHWH, at the cost of one's life, and with one's full resources. Two other passages command to *serve* (עבד) YHWH with "all of your heart and all of your life" (10:12; 11:13); they confirm that the phrase indicates full and undivided allegiance.[3] For Lambert, too, לבב/לב does not indicate interiority. The term rather functions as a rhetorical way to designate the separation or borderline of an individual with others, especially in the encounter with a superior power. The individual may resist (e.g., Pharaoh's hard heart) or surrender (e.g., the ideal Israelite in 6:5) to this power (Lambert 2016b).

Hate often functions, in Near Eastern treaties, as the opposite of love, as it does in Deuteronomy. Riley has collected examples of hate (*zêru*) where it functions as "a metaphor for unsound covenant ties" (Riley 2014, 176). Declarations of hate exist between kings and former allies (RS 18.54A, quoted by Riley 2014) and serve to denounce acts betraying the loyalty that treaty partners have sworn to each other. Vassals at times fear that their sovereign may hate them, because of his discontinued protection or slander by others (EA 286:18–20; ARMT 1.2; quoted by Riley 2014). As in Moses's prayer (9:28), evoking hate calls for a renewed commitment to love—to support and defend. Equally, a sovereign can also label his vassals' acts of insurrection as hate (Inscription B of Samsu-iluna, lines 39–49; quoted by Riley 2014). In addition, the root שנא, in a treaty between a sovereign and his vassal reported in the Sefire inscriptions (eighth century BCE), designates those who have not concluded an alliance (I:B:26 and II:B:14) or who are pushing the vassal to break the treaty (II:B:14; quoted in Branson 2007, 7). In all these examples, hate designates a set of actions that undermine loyalty to an existing treaty (Riley 2014, 185) or oppose such an alliance.

Moran has interpreted commands to "love YHWH," particularly in Deuteronomy, in light of these political treaties (Moran 1963). Such love can be commanded and implies concrete actions of service and loyalty. Other kinds of relationships, such as between father and son and between teacher and pupil, express the bond between YHWH and Israel (1:31; 8:5; 14:1; 32:19–20). They are similarly covenantal as they imply loyalty and obedience (McCarthy 1965, 1978, 160–161; McKay 1972). The root אהב retains its political and hierarchical aspects in both interpersonal relationships (Ackerman 2002) and the relation with the deity (Weinfeld 1972, 85). For Konrad Schmid, the adoption of love terminology in Deuteronomy may be a subversive reaction to the Neo-Assyrian Empire: commands to love YHWH express an alternative allegiance while employing the vocabulary conventionally used in Neo-Assyrian treaties (Schmid 2018, 99; contra Crouch 2014).

Are Love and Hate To Be Understood as Emotions?

While most scholars agree that אהב, especially in Deuteronomy, implies actions (Moran 1963; Mathys 1986; Tigay 1996; Levenson 2016, 19; Erbele-Küster 2018; Gertz 2018), there is debate about a possible, perhaps even primary, affective meaning of the root. Jacqueline Lapsley argues that the political use of אהב is imported from the familial context, where the root finds its original setting; the emotional connotations that the terms have in the kinship realm are transferred to their political and covenantal uses (Lapsley 2003; Levenson 2016). In the same vein, Bill T. Arnold has argued that the political or covenantal meaning of אהב is "a natural hyponymous correlative of the larger lexical domain." It is "narrowly focused on behavior" but is in no way devoid of an emotional dimension (Arnold 2011, 556). Prioritizing an emotional meaning, however, risks projecting the lexical field of contemporary Western love onto the Hebrew Bible and other Near Eastern texts (Lambert 2016b; Vanderhooft 2018). The multiple uses of אהב and שנא in the Hebrew Bible reveal the gap between ancient perceptions and the current understanding of emotion.

The root אהב has a broad range of meanings in the Hebrew Bible. Subjects can be either divine or human; in general, women are rarely the subject of love (only in Gen 25:28; Ruth 4:15; 1 Sam 18:20, 28; as well as multiple occurrences in Song of Songs). Objects can be human (male or female) or divine beings; they can also be material items or conceptual ideas—such as food (Gen 27:4), righteousness (Ps 45:8), and divine commandments (Ps 119:47–48). The verb אהב is often associated with actions. With a human subject, אהב can be paired, for example, with help (עזר, 2 Chron 19:2) and not forsaking (אל־תעזב, Prov 4:6). With a divine subject, אהב is accompanied, for example, with giving food and clothing (10:18), preserving someone's life and rescuing (שמר נפשות and הציל, Ps 97:10). In yet other contexts, the root can express sexual attraction and the acts that follow (2 Sam 13:1, 4, 15), including sexual intercourse (as a verb, e.g., Hos 3:1; as a singular noun, Prov 5:19; as a plural noun, Prov 7:18). Terms based on אהב thus broadly take place within descriptions of what individuals *do*. Love is not a private feeling; rather, love designates a set of practices that are clearly perceptible to others (e.g., Gen 37:3–4; 1 Sam 18:28; Ps 119:159).

The root שנא, too, has a wide extension in the Hebrew Bible. Subjects and objects of the verb can be either divine or human; objects can also be material or conceptual—for example, unjust gain (Exod 18:21), abomination (12:31), robbery, and inequity (Isa 61:8). When the verb depicts human interactions, subjects of שנא are always male, while its objects can be either male or female. The root שנא is also used to designate enemies, "those who hate us" (e.g., Exod 1:10). Like אהב, שנא is often accompanied by actions, such as writing a bill of divorce (Deut 24:3) and destroying (הצמית, Ps 69:5). As Botta writes, the meaning of שנא, in the Hebrew Bible, "is active and dynamic and only occasionally describes an internal and/or passive feeling" (Botta 2013, 116). In particular, hate is frequently associated with rejection and physical distancing (Lipiński 2004; Botta 2013): sending away (של, Gen 26:27; Deut 24:3; Mal 2:16), driving out (גרש, Judg 11:7; Hos 9:15), abandoning (עזב, Isa 60:15), rejecting (מאס, Amos 5:21), and staying far away (רחק, Prov 19:7).

Like love, hate can be seen (Gen 29:31) and even heard (Gen 29:33) by others. Some laws in Deuteronomy are particularly clear on the observable character of hate. There is first the law about a murderer who killed "without knowledge" and "who did not hate [לֹא־שֹׂנֵא]" him [the victim] yesterday or the day before" (4:42; 19:4, 6; Josh 20:5). The passages indicate that the murderer's hate, or absence of which, can be observed by others: if hate were a private, internal feeling, it would be difficult to use it as a criterion to assess murder. Similarly, the provisions made about the inheritance of a husband who has two wives, "one loved [אֲהוּבָה] and one hated" (21:15–17), suggest that "love" and "hate" represent practices that others can witness, perhaps as obvious as standing marriage and divorce (Morrow 2017).

Love is not expressed in the Hebrew Bible by the metaphor of a liquid in a container, as in modern Western languages. Images for love and hate are in fact rare in the Hebrew Bible, except for the comparison of love with a force and a flame (Song 8:6–7). It is noteworthy that neither the force nor the flame is situated inside the human being (Müller 2014; Wagner 2018). This paucity of images might be explained by the fact that what אהב and שנא describe is readily visible, unlike in the modern, Western conception, where love and hate happen inside and may be hidden. Emotions do not seem to find their origin *inside* the human being (Wagner 2018, 87); rather, they seem to occur in the space *between* two beings (Lambert 2016b).

Various studies have explored the power dynamics implied by the roots אהב and שנא. The subject of אהב is generally the party who is hierarchically superior, an observation also made about the language of love (*ki áĝ*) in Sumerian (Jaques 2006, 134). In general, in the Hebrew Bible, men love women; parents love their children; superiors love subordinates; YHWH loves human beings (Ackerman 2002; van Wolde 2008; Vanderhooft 2018). Only a woman in a higher position can love a man (1 Sam 18:20, 28). In both interpersonal and political context, love vocabulary is generally one-sided (Ackerman 2002). As Ronit Nikolsky has shown, אהב, in the Hebrew Bible, functions on different continuums: it can be sexual or not; it can be irresistible or practiced at will; it can conform to social norms or be transgressive of these norms; similarly, it can indicate reverence or romantic feelings, like in Song of Songs (Nikolsky 2019). Despite its various uses, אהב describes social interactions that generally presuppose a hierarchical organization. Uses of שנא similarly reflect relationships of power. In the context of a heterosexual relationship, the man is always the one who hates the woman (Gen 29:31, 33; Deut 21:15–17; 22:13, 16; 24:3; Judg 14:16; 15:2; 2 Sam 13:15; Prov 30:23). Other passages show that those socially higher tend to be the subjects of שנא: elders hate a younger man (Gen 37:4, 5, 8; Judg 11:7); a king hates a prophet (1 Kgs 22:8; 2 Chr 18:7), with a similar observation about the Sumerian *ḫul gig*, hate (Jaques 2006, 150–153). In cases where an individual loves or hates someone who is hierarchically superior or socially more powerful—a slave's "love" for his master (Exod 21:5; Deut 15:16), the command to love YHWH, the people's love or hate for a leader (1 Sam 18:16; 2 Sam 19:7)—context clearly indicates allegiance and service, or their absence.

The language of אהב and שנא, in the Hebrew Bible, is associated with preference and rejection. First, it is notable that the verb אהב is used five times in connection with the verb בחר, "to choose" (Deut 4:37; 10:15; Is 41:8; Ps 47:5; 78:68). The verb שנא is also used once in parallel with "not choosing" (לֹא בחר, Prov 1:29). Preference is also implied in narrative and legal contexts (Vanderhooft 2018). When a man is the subject of אהב, with a woman as an object, he generally has access to other females, but shows a preference for the one he loves (Gen 29:18, 20, 30; Deut 21:15–17; Judg 16:4; 1 Sam 1:5; 2 Chr 11:21; Est 2:17; Hos 3:1). When the root is used in parental relationships, it tends to indicate a mother's or father's preference for a particular child over another or others (Gen 22:2; 25:28; 37:3, 4; 44:20). Often, this preference implies that the son will be the designated heir. This meaning of love as designation of a preferred heir is also found in Akkadian (*râmu*), Egyptian (*mry*), and Aramaic (*rḥm*) (Szubin and Porten 1983). When the deity is the subject of אהב with a human being as object, the verb expresses divine selection and favor (2 Sam 12:24; Isa 41:8; 48:14). Contexts suggest a public designation. In parallel, שנא often designates the relationship to the individual who is not preferred (Gen 29:31, 33; Deut 21:15–17). In all these passages, love and hate thus connote a public designation or rejection.

A few occurrences of אהב take place after sexual intercourse (Gen 24:67; 29:30, 32), with a similar use of שנא (Deut 22:13, 16; 24:3; 2 Sam 13:15). For Lambert, אהב provides "an indication that the relationship has taken hold"; it thus depicts a "relational status, the outcome of [. . .] physical joining, a matter that is located not quite within the individual psyche but outside or beyond it" (Lambert 2016b, 352). In turn, hate indicates rejection and rupture of the relationship. In a relational context, hate indicates "unsound covenant ties" (Riley 2014, 176) or even the breach of the covenant (Branson 2007, 8).

The vocabulary of אהב and שנא functions like labels, as terms describe the state of a relationship and publicize it in the social realm. Terms can at times be considered performative, as they establish or terminate this relationship; אהב and שנא not only *describe* the status of a relationship but also *make* or *unmake* it. This performative aspect is particularly clear in the law about the slave who, after six years of service, is set free in the seventh year but chooses to stay in his master's household: "If the slave declares, 'I love [אהבתי] my master, my wife, and my children; I will not go out free'" (Exod 21:5). The verb אהב is at the core of the declaration by which the slave indicates that, rather than abandoning his wife and children, he will continue serving his master for the rest of his life. What is at stake is not what the slave internally feels; it is rather a formal and performative statement that he is waiving his right to freedom (Hillers 1995). "Love" confirms and institutes the relationship, here involving more than two people, but two families. The parallel law in Deuteronomy uses the verb אהב not in the slave's statement, but rather in the explanation of his declared choice not to leave ("because he loves you and your household," 15:16); love still clearly establishes the relationship between slave and master.

In a parallel way, a husband's "hate" (שנא) for his wife, in Deuteronomy's laws about marriage, functions less as an internally experienced feeling than as a public expression of his rejection. For Westbrook, שנא indicates a case of divorce where the wife has committed no misconduct (Westbrook 1986). In 22:13–19, a husband comes to hate his wife after sexual intercourse; he falsely accuses her of not being a virgin, a charge to which her father and mother respond with a proof of her virginity. In 24:1-4, two different cases of divorce are considered: a first husband finds "some indecency [ערות דבר]" in his wife and divorces her, while her potential second husband divorces her this time because "he hated her [ושנאה]," thus with no apparent reason (Westbrook 1986). The term שנא does not describe private feelings but establishes the separation.

The Aramaic papyri of Elephantine present similar uses of hate, performative and public. Several texts describe the termination of a marriage by depicting one of the spouses, man or woman, standing up in an assembly and stating, "I hate [שנאתי] my spouse" (*TAD* B2.6:22–29; B3.3:7–10; 8:21–28; quoted in Botta 2013; Morrow 2017; contra Porten and Szubin 1995). The verb שנא is sometimes read as a wish to break the marriage, thus as a preliminary stage before the marriage's dissolution (Westbrook 1986; Nutkowicz 2007). The performative character of the declaration, however, suggests that it does enact the former spouses' separation. Indeed, for Botta, the language of שנא, in the Elephantine documents, "signifies the metaphor of 'rejection', 'break of covenant', and 'physical separation'"; this use thus functions as a statement of divorce (Botta 2013, 108). Similar uses are found in Sumerian (Jaques 2006, 156–158).

The right to label a relationship and make a declaration on its status is regulated by social norms. In contrast with the Elephantine documents, in the Hebrew Bible the male has, in general, this right over his female partner (van Wolde 2008; Lambert 2016b). A slave who has served six years, although hierarchically inferior, is still entitled to declare his "love"— his decision to serve for life—because the law provides him with this possibility at that given time.

Love and hate, in the Hebrew Bible, are usually not reciprocal (van Wolde 2008; Lambert 2016b). The language of אהב and שנא does not describe feelings that individuals would develop in relative synchrony as their relationship grows. Rather, love and hate are declared by the individual whom the law or custom entitles to do so, often in a public setting. The meaning of love, like many other ancient Hebrew terms, may have transformed during the redaction of biblical texts, possibly toward greater emphasis on interiority (Rüterswörden 2006), as perhaps Song of Songs illustrates. This interesting hypothesis deserves more research.

Finally, it has also been suggested that the emotional value of אהב in Deuteronomy would be reinforced by the parallel use of דבק and חשק (Vang 2011, 188; Levenson 2016, 40–42; Gropp 2018). This argument, however, first requires establishing the so-called emotional meaning of the two terms. In fact, the two verbs, mainly used in contexts that are not interpersonal, depict a visible, if not tangible, reality. The verb דבק renders contact: connecting or overtaking (Gen 31:23; Judg 18:22), clinging or sticking (28:21, 60), and retaining (Num 36:7, 9). The verb חשק is about binding or attaching (Exod 38:28; Isa 38:17). In interhuman contexts, the two verbs occur in the story of Shechem and Dinah (Gen 34:3, 8); חשק is also used in the law concerning the beautiful captive with whom sexual intercourse and marriage can only occur after a month of mourning (21:11). The verbs render a contact or attachment that does not follow an established script and thus requires a special arrangement or procedure toward formalization. The connection or bond seems to be mentioned in both cases precisely because it does not easily lead to an institutionalized relationship, which is otherwise the usual focus in narratives and laws.

When depicting the attachment to the divine, the verb דבק stresses a connection that overcomes challenges and implies hard choices—not following Baal Peor (4:3–4), trusting YHWH to dispossess large nations (11:22–23), ignoring false prophets (13:2–5), choosing life not death (30:19–20). Far from connoting emotion, דבק renders a bond that resists trials and necessitates exclusive choices. As for the verb חשק, it has a divine subject twice in Deuteronomy (7:7; 10:15) and, each time, underlines an unexpected choice. YHWH, although in possession of all the heaven and earth (10:14–15), chose Israel, the least numerous of all peoples (7:7). Just as in the human context underlined earlier, the verb connotes a situation for which no established script is available. When חשק depicts the divine bond to Israel, it does not imply YHWH's emotional involvement, but rather the unparalleled character of such attachment. The two verbs דבק and חשק, therefore, offer weak support for an understanding of אהב as an internally felt emotion. They both focus on the visible—if not tactile—aspect of a bond that is not obvious, whether it defies established scenarios or overcomes challenges.

In conclusion, uses of אהב and שנא—in general but also in a familial context—are very different from an emotion in the narrow, Western contemporary sense. Both אהב and שנא tend to be associated with actions. Biblical love and hate can be seen and heard; they are not internal or private feelings, experienced in the hidden depths of the self. In that sense, metaphors for love and hate are rare and are not situated *inside* the human being. Rather, uses of love and hate are hierarchical, even in a familial context, and thus organize relationships in the social realm. Often connoting preference or rejection, the terms function as labels that establish or terminate relationships, sometimes with a clear performative sense. Far from being a reciprocal and intimate feeling, this act of labeling is practiced only by the individual allowed by law or custom, generally in a public setting. Maintaining a primary affective meaning for אהב and שנא is therefore difficult, as it projects (and universalizes) a category—affect or emotion—that is hard to find as such in the Hebrew Bible.

Are Emotions Universal?

The debate about the affective meaning of אהב (and שנא) extends beyond these two terms. It pertains to other biblical Hebrew terms usually understood as emotions and, more fundamentally, to the universal nature of emotion. From an evolutionary perspective, emotions are adaptations that human ancestors and other animals developed in order to respond to the challenges of their environment. Culture, however, also shapes emotions. Lisa Feldman Barrett has developed a neuroscientific model that accounts for the cultural construction of emotions: when we feel an emotion, our brain makes sense of what happens in our bodies on the basis of our neurological patterns but also past experiences and the concepts that are available in our culture. Emotions are predictions or interpretations made by the brain. They are in no way universal, but variation is the norm (Barrett 2017). A set of physical symptoms can be linked to several emotions, while an emotion can be accompanied by diverse bodily manifestations. Likewise, multiple regions in the brain participate in singular emotional events, while a single region may be involved in a range of activities, including emotions, sensations, cognition, and decision-making. On a neurological level, emotions do not have strict contours; these delineations are rather culturally constructed.

The understanding of emotion is paralleled by research conducted in other disciplines. Anthropologists have demonstrated that cultures and social groups categorize, name, and experience emotions in various ways; human groups also differ in their emotional rules, as different emotions can be promoted or discouraged (Lutz and Abu-Lughod 1990). More broadly, cultures vary in their perceptions of the human self, in the amount of attention that they devote to emotions and even in their understanding of what emotions are (Rosaldo 1984). Linguists have shown that emotions are conceptualized differently across languages; affective metaphors, for example, are based on various perceptions of emotions (Wierzbicka 1999; Kövecses 1990). Historians, too, have established that emotions change over time, in the way they are perceived and experienced (Plamper 2012; Matt and Stearns 2014). No universal concept of emotion can be assumed; likewise, individual emotional experiences are variously constructed across history, languages, and cultures.

In biblical Hebrew, no general term designates an emotion or a feeling; there is also no generic verb "to feel" (Wagner 2006). Ancient Hebrew terms that are usually translated by emotional terms in modern languages tend to have a broad lexical extension in the Hebrew Bible. The root ירא, for example, expresses fear and terror, often in combination with bodily sensations (shaking, boiling, or melting of inner organs); the root also expresses reverence and obedience (Arnold 2011). As a noun, יראה designates a form of knowledge or wisdom; it is less a spontaneous experience than a practice that can be learned (Lasater 2017). Similarly, the noun שמחה, usually translated by "joy," implies specific movements and actions, including dance and sexual intercourse. In the same way, grief tends to be expressed by bodily reactions and ritual practices (Anderson 1991). Biblical Hebrew terms generally translated as emotions, therefore, exceed what speakers of modern, Western languages refer to as an affective meaning. They are more capacious and refer, in an integrative way, to other aspects of experience, such as actions, sensations and bodily symptoms, social and hierarchical standing, and ritual practices (Mirguet 2016, 2019; Lasater 2017).

Biblical texts generally do not emphasize the internal, mental, or private aspects of experiences. In contrast with modern cultures, where selfhood tends to be located in the inner depths and is thus relatively hidden, the Hebrew Bible privileges the description of what human beings do and say (Di Vito 1999). Biblical texts usually show little interest in what characters internally feel. The focus tends to be on what transpires among characters, how their relationships evolve in the public realm, and how social status is negotiated and publicized. David A. Lambert has warned against an interiorizing reading of Biblical Hebrew vocabulary (Lambert 2016a, 2016b). Such a reading, he argues, projects a modern notion of the self onto the biblical lexicon, often imposing a sharp division between mind and body onto ancient texts.

Conclusion

With both divine and human subjects, אהב and שנא, in Deuteronomy and in the Hebrew Bible more generally, illustrate an understanding of human experience that is quite different from the contemporary Western conception. Far from focusing on the internal and private aspects of experiences, biblical texts tend to show more interest in how people relate to each other, how they negotiate their social status, and how these relations are publicly enacted. The roots אהב and שנא usually depict practices that are easily perceptible by others. Often, they refer to a public act of designation or rejection, thus establishing a relational status *between* humans, not a feeling *inside* them (Lambert 2016b). The terms function as labels, sometimes with a performative value, as their uses establish or end relationships. In treaties, the language of love and hate, in the Hebrew Bible and in other Near Eastern texts, takes on the meaning of either obeying the terms of the treaty or terminating it. Deuteronomy uses the same vocabulary to depict the covenant that YHWH establishes with the Israelites: the deity is imagined as a sovereign who chooses and protects his people; in return, the Israelites are required to "love" their God—to show YHWH exclusive loyalty. Love as an internal drive would be anachronistic here; the attention of the biblical text is focused rather on the relationship in its public and overt dimensions. In particular, the command to love YHWH with "all of your heart, and with all of your life, and with all of your force" (6:5), when read in the light of ancient treaties, suggests an allegiance that is exclusive and with no sparing of either resources or life.

Notes

The final version of this chapter was submitted in August 2000. Works published after this date have not been integrated.

1. The roots אהב and שנא occur twenty-three times in Deuteronomy. The words are used in various contexts, with different subjects and objects. The root אהב, used as a verb or noun, can have a divine subject, with "you" (7:8, 13; 23:6), "your ancestors" (4:37; 10:15), or the resident alien [10:18] (גר) as objects. The verb can also have a human subject, as the addressee of the text is expected and commanded multiple times to love the deity (5:10; 6:5; 7:9; 10:12; 11:1, 13, 22; 13:4; 19:9; 30:6, 16, 20) and, in one occurrence, the resident alien (10:19). The addressee of the text ("you") is once the object of אהב, in a declaration uttered by the male slave (15:16). Finally, a "husband" can be the subject of אהב, with one of his wives as object (21:15, 16). As שנא, the verb or noun may be used with a divine subject, with Israel (1:27; 9:28), abomination (12:31), and the stone pillar (16:22) as objects. The verb can also be used with human subjects—a murderer (4:42; 19:4, 6, 11), those who hate Israel (7:15; 30:7; 33:11), and the husband for his/one of his wives (21:15, 16, 17; 22:13, 16; 24:3). Finally, the verb שנא is also used for those who "hate" God (5:9; 7:10; 32:41).
2. All translations from the Hebrew Bible are my own.
3. Leviticus 19:17 commands, "You shall not hate your brother in your heart [בלבבך]," and tends to be understood as referring to internal or hidden hate, as opposed to the open reproach expressed in the second half of the verse, "You will surely reprove your neighbor and you will not carry sin instead of him" (Kugel 1987). Rather than interpreting the verse as opposing an internal and an open attitude, I would read it as contrasting an inimical attitude for no particular reason (שנא, as in Deut 22:13 and 24:3, as argued by Westbrook 1986) with one caused by the neighbor's sin (חטא): the first kind of hostility is prohibited; the second should lead to rebuke.

Bibliography

Ackerman, Susan. "The Personal Is Political: Covenantal and Affectionate Love (*ʾāhēb, ʾahăbâ*) in the Hebrew Bible." *Vetus Testamentum* 52, no. 4 (2002): 437–458.

Anderson, Gary A. *A Time to Mourn, a Time to Dance: The Expression of Grief and Joy in Israelite Religion.* University Park: Pennsylvania State University Press, 1991.

Arnold, Bill T. "The Love-Fear Antinomy in Deuteronomy 5–11." *Vetus Testamentum* 61, no. 4 (2011): 551–569.

Barrett, Lisa Feldman. *How Emotions Are Made: The Secret Life of the Brain.* Boston: Houghton Mifflin, 2017.

Botta, Alejandro F. "Hated by the Gods and by Your Spouse: Legal Use of שנא in Elephantine and Its Ancient Near Eastern Context." In *Law and Religion in the Eastern Mediterranean: From Antiquity to Early Islam,* edited by Anselm C. Hagedorn and Reinhard G. Kratz, 105–128. Oxford: Oxford University Press, 2013.

Branson, Robert D. "The Polyvalent שנא: An Emotional, Performative, and Covenantal Term." *Biblical Research* 51 (2007): 5–15.

Crouch, Carly. *Israel and the Assyrians: Deuteronomy, the Succession Treaty of Esarhaddon, and the Nature of Subversion.* Atlanta: SBL Press, 2014.

Devecchi, Elena. "Treaties and Edicts in the Hittite World." In *Organization, Representation, and Symbols of Power in the Ancient Near East,* edited by Gernot Wilhelm, 637–645. Winona Lake: Eisenbrauns, 2012.

Di Vito, Robert A. "Old Testament Anthropology and the Construction of Personal Identity." *Catholic Biblical Quarterly* 61 (1999): 217–238.

Erbele-Küster, Dorothea. "Gebotene Liebe: Zur Ethik einer Handlungsemotion im Deuteronomium." In *Ahavah: Die Liebe Gottes im alten Testament*, edited by Manfred Oeming, 143–156. Leipzig: Evangelische Verlagsanstalt, 2018.

Gertz, Jan Christian. "Die Liebe Gottes im Deuteronomium." In *Ahavah: Die Liebe Gottes im alten Testament*, edited by Manfred Oeming, 157–170. Leipzig: Evangelische Verlagsanstalt, 2018.

Gropp, David. "Viele Formen der Liebe: Verwandte Begriffe zu Ahavah." In *Ahavah: Die Liebe Gottes im alten Testament*, edited by Manfred Oeming, 57–75. Leipzig: Evangelische Verlagsanstalt, 2018.

Hillers, Delbert R. "Some Performative Utterances in the Bible." In *Pomegranates and Golden Bells: Studies in Biblical, Jewish, and Near Eastern Ritual, Law, and Literature in Honor of Jacob Milgrom*, edited by David P. Wright et al., 757–766. Winona Lake: Eisenbrauns, 1995.

Janowski, Bernd. "Das Herz—ein Beziehungsorgan. Zum Personverständnis des Alten Testaments." In *Dimensionen der Leiblichkeit: Theologische Zugänge*, edited by Bernd Janowski and Christoph Schwöbel, 1–45. Neukirchen-Vluyn: Neukirchener Theologie, 2015.

Jaques, Margaret. *Le vocabulaire des sentiments dans les textes sumériens: Recherche sur le lexique sumérien et akkadien*. Münster: Ugarit-Verlag, 2006.

Kövecses, Zoltán. *Emotion Concepts*. New York: Springer-Verlag, 1990.

Kugel, James L. "On Hidden Hatred and Open Reproach: Early Exegesis of Leviticus 19:17." *Harvard Theological Review* 80, no. 1 (1987): 43–61.

Lambert, David A. *How Repentance Became Biblical: Judaism, Christianity, and the Interpretation of Scripture*. New York: Oxford University Press, 2016a.

Lambert, David A. "Refreshing Philology: James Barr, Supersessionism, and the State of Biblical Words." *Biblical Interpretation* 24, no. 3 (2016b): 332–356.

Lapsley, Jacqueline E. "Feeling Our Way: Love for God in Deuteronomy." *Catholic Biblical Quarterly* 65 (2003): 350–369.

Lasater, Phillip M. "'The Emotions' in Biblical Anthropology? A Genealogy and Case Study with ארי." *Harvard Theological Review* 110, no. 4 (2017): 520–540.

Levenson, Jon D. *The Love of God: Divine Gift, Human Gratitude, and Mutual Faithfulness in Judaism*. Princeton: Princeton University Press, 2016.

Lipiński, Edward. "שנא śānēʾ." In *Theological Dictionary of the Old Testament*, edited by G. Johannes Botterweck, Helmer Ringgren, and Heinz-Josef Fabry, 164–174. Translated by Douglas W. Scott. Volume XIV. Grand Rapids: Eerdmans, 2004.

Lutz, Catherine A., and Lila Abu-Lughod, eds. *Language and the Politics of Emotion*. Cambridge: Cambridge University Press, 1990.

Mathys, Hans-Peter. *Liebe deinen Nächsten wie dich selbst: Untersuchungen zum alttestamentlichen Gebot der Nächstenliebe (Lev 19, 18)*. Freiburg: Universitätsverlag, 1986.

Matt, Susan J., and Peter N. Stearns, eds. *Doing Emotions History*. Urbana: University of Illinois Press, 2014.

McCarthy, Dennis J. "Notes on the Love of God in Deuteronomy and the Father-Son Relationship between Yahweh and Israel." *Catholic Biblical Quarterly* 27, no. 2 (1965): 144–147.

McCarthy, Dennis J. *Treaty and Covenant: A Study in Form in the Ancient Oriental Documents and in the Old Testament*. Rome: Biblical Institute Press, 1978.

McKay, John W. "Man's Love for God in Deuteronomy and the Father/Teacher—Son/Pupil Relationship." *Vetus Testamentum* 22, no. 4 (1972): 426–435.

Mirguet, Françoise. "What Is an 'Emotion' in the Hebrew Bible? An Experience That Exceeds Most Contemporary Concepts." *Biblical Interpretation* 24, no. 4–5 (2016): 442–465.

Mirguet, Françoise. "The Study of Emotions in Early Jewish Texts: Review and Perspectives." *Journal for the Study of Judaism* 50, no. 4–5 (2019): 1–47.

Moran, William L. "The Ancient Near Eastern Background of the Love of God in Deuteronomy." *Catholic Biblical Quarterly* 25, no. 1 (1963): 77–87.

Moran, William L., ed. *The Amarna Letters*. Baltimore: Johns Hopkins University Press, 1992.

Morrow, Amanda R. "I Hate My Spouse: The Performative Act of Divorce in Elephantine Aramaic." *Journal of Northwest Semitic Languages* 43, no. 2 (2017): 7–25.

Müller, Katrin. "Lieben ist nich gleich lieben: Zur kognitiven Konzeption von Liebe im Hebräischen." In *Göttliche Körper—göttliche Gefühle: Was leisten anthropomorphe und anthropopathische Götterkonzepte im Alten Orient und im Alten Testament?*, edited by Andreas Wagner, 219–237. Fribourg: Academic Press, 2014.

Nikolsky, Ronit. "'To Love' (אהב) in the Bible: A Cognitive- Evolutionary Approach." In *Language, Cognition, and Biblical Exegesis: Interpreting Minds*, edited by Ronit Nikolsky et al., 70–87. London: Bloomsbury, 2019.

Nutkowicz, Hélène. "Concerning the Verb *śnʾ* in Judaeo-Aramaic Contracts from Elephantine." *Journal of Semitic Studies* 52, no. 2 (2007): 211–225.

Oeming, Manfred, ed. *Ahavah: Die Liebe Gottes im alten Testament*. Leipzig: Evangelische Verlagsanstalt, 2018.

Plamper, Jan. *Geschichte und Gefühl: Grundlagen der Emotionsgeschichte*. München: Siedler, 2012.

Porten, Bezalel, and Henri Zvi Szubin. "The Status of the Handmaiden Tamet: A New Interpretation of Kraeling 2 (*TAD* B3.3)." *Israel Law Review* 29 (1995): 43–64.

Riley, Andrew J. "*Zêru*, 'to Hate' as a Metaphor for Covenant Instability." In *Windows to the Ancient World of the Hebrew Bible: Essays in Honor of Samuel Greengus*, edited by Bill T. Arnold, Nancy L. Erickson, and John H. Walton, 175–185. Winona Lake: Eisenbrauns, 2014.

Rosaldo, Michelle Z. "Toward an Anthropology of Self and Feeling." In *Culture Theory: Essays on Mind, Self, and Emotion*, edited by Robert A. LeVine and Richard A. Shweder, 137–157. Cambridge: Cambridge University Press, 1984.

Rüterswörden, Udo. "Die Liebe zu Gott im Deuteronomium." In *Die deuteronomistischen Geschichtswerke: Redaktions- und religionsgeschichtliche Perspektiven zur "Deuteronomismus"—Diskussion in Tora und Vorderen Propheten*, edited by Jan Christian Gertz et al., 229–238. BZAW 365; Berlin: De Gruyter, 2006.

Sakenfeld, Katharine Doob. "Loyalty and Love: The Language of Human Interconnections in the Hebrew Bible." *Michigan Quarterly Review* 22 (1983): 190–204.

Schmid, Konrad. "Von der Liebe zu Gott zur Liebe Gottes zu Israel: Die theologiegeschichtliche Genese der Erwählungsvorstellung." In *Ahavah: Die Liebe Gottes im alten Testament*, edited by Manfred Oeming, 93–105. Leipzig: Evangelische Verlagsanstalt, 2018.

Spieckermann, Hermann. "Mit der Liebe im Wort: Ein Beitrag zur Theologie des Deuteronomiums." In *Liebe und Gebot: Studien zum Deuteronomium*, edited by Reinhard G. Kratz and Hermann Spieckermann, 190–205. FRLANT 190; Göttingen: Vandenhoeck & Ruprecht, 2000.

Szubin, Henri Z., and Bezalel Porten. "Testamentary Succession at Elephantine." *Bulletin of the American Schools of Oriental Research* 252 (1983): 35–46.

Tigay, Jeffrey H. *Deuteronomy* דברים The JPS Torah Commentary. Philadelphia: Jewish Publication Society, 1996.

Vanderhooft, David S. "'AHĂBĀH: Philological Observations on *'ahēb*/*'ahăbāh* in the Hebrew Bible." In *Ahavah: Die Liebe Gottes im alten Testament*, edited by Manfred Oeming, 41–54. Leipzig: Evangelische Verlagsanstalt, 2018.

Vang, Carsten. "God's Love according to Hosea and Deuteronomy: A Prophetic Reworking of a Deuteronomic Concept?" *Tyndale Bulletin* 62, no. 2 (2011): 173–194.

Wagner, Andreas. *Emotionen, Gefühle und Sprache im Alten Testament: Vier Studien*. KUSATU 7. Waltrop: Hartmut Spenner, 2006;

Wagner, Andreas. "Liebe Gottes und der Götter: Einige Beobachtungen aus Vergleich Jahwes mit den Göttern Ugarits." In *Ahavah: Die Liebe Gottes im alten Testament*, edited by Manfred Oeming, 77–92. Leipzig: Evangelische Verlagsanstalt, 2018.

Waterman, Leroy. *Royal Correspondence of the Assyrian Empire*. Ann Arbor: University of Michigan Press, 1930–1936.

Weinfeld, Moshe. *Deuteronomy and the Deuteronomic School*. Oxford: Oxford University Press, 1972.

Weinfeld, Moshe. "Covenant Terminology in the Ancient Near East and Its Influence on the West." *Journal of the American Oriental Society* 93, no. 2 (1973): 190–199.

Weinfeld, Moshe. *Deuteronomy 1–11*. AB 5; New York: Doubleday, 1991.

Westbrook, Raymond. "The Prohibition on Restoration of Marriage in Deuteronomy 24:1–4." In *Studies in Bible*, edited by Sara Japhet, 387–405. Scripta Hierosolymitana 31; Jerusalem: Magnes Press, 1986.

Wierzbicka, Anna. *Emotions across Languages and Cultures: Diversity and Universals*. Cambridge: Cambridge University Press, 1999.

Wiseman, D. J. "The Vassal-Treaties of Esarhaddon." *Iraq* 20, no. 1 (1958): I–II and 1–99.

van Wolde, Ellen. "Sentiments as Culturally Constructed Emotions: Anger and Love in the Hebrew Bible." *Biblical Interpretation* 16 (2008): 1–24.

Zehnder, Markus. "Literary and Other Observations on Passages Dealing with Foreigners in the Book of Deuteronomy: The Command to Love the *Gēr* Read in Context." In *Sepher Torath Mosheh: Studies in the Composition and Interpretation of Deuteronomy*, edited by Daniel I. Block and Richard L. Schultz, 192–231. Peabody: Hendrickson, 2017.

Zobel, Konstantin. *Prophetie und Deuteronomium: Die Rezeption prophetischer Theologie durch das Deuteronomium*. BZAW 199; Berlin: De Gruyter, 1992.

CHAPTER 10

WAR IN DEUTERONOMY

PEKKA PITKÄNEN

Who Began the Conversation?

War is a pervasive motif in Deuteronomy, with some thirty-six passages referring to or alluding to war (Table 10.1). The literary setting of Deuteronomy is on the plains of Moab after an exodus from Egypt and a journey through the wilderness of Sinai and Southern Transjordan by the Israelites under the leadership of Moses. He charges the Israelites to cross the river Jordan and wage war on the peoples in the land to demonstrate their faithfulness to YHWH and the commandments (3:21–22; 6:18–19; 7; 9:1–6; 11:22–25; 31:3–8). Deuteronomy reminds its audience how YHWH waged war on the Egyptians during the crossing of the Sea of Reeds (11:4) and how the inhabitants of the land defeated the Israelites at Kadesh-Barnea due to their lack of faith (1:19–43). The description of the journey from Kadesh Barnea to the Plains of Moab describes wars with the kings Sihon and Og (2–3:11). The Israelites, however, are forbidden to make war against the Edomites, Ammonites, and Moabites, because YHWH granted them their lands. Like the Israelites, they took possession of these lands by waging war on its indigenous peoples (2:1–22).

According to the legal code of Deuteronomy, the Israelites are to destroy the religious infrastructure of the indigenous peoples (12:2–3) as well as their towns. Towns outside the territory of Israel, however, may be spared if they surrender peacefully when the Israelites declare war against them (20:10–18). Israelite towns who worship "other gods" must be destroyed (13:12–18). Specific laws describe how to wage war; who is exempt from going to war (20:1–9); purity while in camp (23:9–14); and the use of the trees of a city under siege (20:1–9).

In addition, Deuteronomy portrays war in a more distant future, where the Israelites may be conquered by their enemies and lose their land if they are not faithful to YHWH (4:25–27; 8:19–20; 12:29–31; 28:7, 25, 32–33, 36–37, 41, 48–57, 63–64, 68; 29:22–23, 28; 32:21–35).

After Assyria conquered Israel and Babylon conquered Judah, the peoples of Israel and Judah lacked the independence and the ability to wage war, save for the century-long interlude with the Maccabean revolt (167–160 BCE) and the Hasmoneans (160–30 BCE). The wars between Judea and Rome (66–73; 132–135) resulted in the destruction of the second

Table 10.1. Passages Referring or Alluding to War in Deuteronomy

1:4	Defeat of Sihon
1:6–8	Exhortation to take the land of Canaan (note the extent of territory described RE: Euphrates and Transjordan)
1:19–43	Episode of the spies at Kadesh-Barnea and resultant defeat by the Amorites
2:1–23, 37	Departure from Kadesh-Barnea toward the plains of Moab: refraining from war against the Edomites, Moabites, and Ammonites; historical notes in relation to the Edomites, Moabites, Ammonites, and Philistines as background to their hold of the land in addition to divine legitimation with the Edomites, Moabites, and Ammonites
2:24–3:11; 4:46–49; 29:7	Events after departure from Kadesh-Barnea toward the plains of Moab: defeat of the kings of Sihon and Og
3:12–17; 29:8	Division of conquered land to Reuben, Gad, and Manasseh, with some description of conquest by Manasseh
3:18–20	Order to Transjordanians to participate in the conquest of Cisjordan
3:21–22	Moses's exhortation to Joshua in relation to the conquest of Cisjordan
4:25–27	Potential conquest of the Israelites by others if the Israelites do not stay faithful to YHWH (allusion to war)
6:18–19	Exhortation to faithfulness so that Israel would expel (*lahadop*) nations (allusion to war)
7	Exhortation to destroy nations of the land (*herem*; clear allusion to war at the minimum)
8:19–20	Warning that Israel would be destroyed (*to'bedun*) if it does not follow YHWH (allusion to war)
9:1–6	YHWH's faithfulness in wars against the indigenous peoples (reference to war)
11:4	YHWH's destruction of the Egyptians at the Sea of Reeds (allusion to war)
11:22–25	Exhortation to faithfulness so that Israel would prevail over nations (allusion to war)
12:2–3	Destruction of the religious infrastructure of the indigenous peoples (allusion to war)
12:29–31	Exhortation to follow YHWH with a reference to nations that YHWH will have cut off (*kerat*) (allusion to war)
13:12–18	War against and destruction of an apostate Israelite town
19:1	Reference to nations being destroyed as an introduction to legislation on the towns of refuge (allusion/reference to war)
20:1–9	Exemptions from war
20:10–18	Treatment of towns in war depending on where they are located
20:19–20	Felling of trees when besieging of city
23:9–14	Purity in a war camp

(continued)

Table 10.1. Continued

25:17-19	Injunction against Amalekites (allusion to war and genocide [see later on genocide])
28:7	Victory over enemies as a blessing for following YHWH
28:25, 48	Defeat by enemies as a curse for not following YHWH
28:32, 41	Fall of descendants under the power of foreigners as a curse for not following YHWH (potential/likely allusion to war)
28:33, 49-57	Exploitation by foreigners as a curse for not following YHWH (allusions to war)
28:36-37, 63-64; 29:28	Removal from land as a curse for not following YHWH (likely allusion to war)
28:68	Removal to Egypt as slaves (possible allusion to war)
29:22-23	Afflictions on the land (likely allusion to war)
30:18; 31:3-8, 13; 32:47	Soon-to-be taking of the land (involves war)
32:21-35	YHWH's wrath on Israel in the Song of Moses (allusions to war)
32:40-43	YHWH's revenge on enemies in the Song of Moses (likely allusions to war)
33:7, 11, 17, 20, 22	YHWH's help of Judah, Levi, Joseph, Gad, and Dan in the Song of Moses (allusions to war)
33:27, 29	YHWH's help of Israel in the Song of Moses (allusions to war)

temple and further dispersions of the Jews. Jewish Christians did not participate in the wars against Rome.

The early Christianity that was essentially nonviolent eventually became associated with Rome at the time of Constantine (272–337) and then the official and only legitimate religion at the time of Theodosius (347–395). Christianity was accordingly linked with secular power and its coercive aspects, including war. Augustine (354–430) developed a theory of a just war in the context of the newly Christian state of Rome. The Church could identify outsiders who were a threat, and the state might wage war against them.

As Diarmaid MacCulloch describes in *A History of Christianity* (2009, 381–382), the Spanish efforts toward a Reconquista of Moorish Spain related to a defense and expansion of European Christian states against Islamic caliphates. In the eleventh century, calls for a reconquest of the Holy Land started to emerge. However, as George Strack suggests in "The Sermon of Urban II in Clermont and the Tradition of Papal Oratory" (2012), Urban II (1042–1099), who initiated the first crusade, does not seem to have cited Deuteronomy directly in his famous sermon. He may though have referred to the Exodus and Conquest as a prefiguration of his crusade. In the next three hundred years, except for fighting against Muslims, medieval Christianity could also turn against those deemed as heretics and deviants, with Jews included in groups that could be persecuted, and the crusaders sacked Constantinople, the center of Eastern Christianity, in 1204 in the fourth crusade.

Reformation Christian interpreters, while breaking away from Rome, did keep a link with civil authorities. In his *Institutio Christianae Religionis* (1536), John Calvin (1509–1564) elaborated the duties of the kings and states with regard to war (IV.20.11–12). In his *Mosis libri quinque cum commentariis. Genesis seorsum, reliqui quatuor in formam harmoniae digesti* (1563), he saw the destruction of the Canaanites attested in Deuteronomy in accordance to God's sovereignty (7:2, 16). The wars of religion in sixteenth-, seventeeth-, and eighteenth-century Europe mixed religion and politics.

Christians in the North American colonies could look to the Exodus narrative as liberation from persecution in Europe and then also see their wars against Native Americans as inspired by the war motif in Deuteronomy and Joshua. While it is true that there were also efforts toward Native Americans that could be seen as positive and periods of at least relatively peaceful coexistence, ultimately hostility prevailed and the continent was taken over by the European colonizers, with many of the indigenous peoples of the Americas destroyed.

The understanding of the biblical war motif evolved during the Enlightenment when scholars began to question the Mosaic authorship of Deuteronomy. W. M. L. de Wette (1780–1849) pioneered research on Deuteronomy. Linking what he understood as Deuteronomy's call to centralize the worship of YHWH (12:2–28) with the annals of Josiah (2 Kgs 22–23), he redated Deuteronomy from the time of Moses (late second millennium BCE) to the reign of Josiah (640–609 BCE).

Julius Wellhausen (1844–1918) then proposed that Deuteronomy was a midpoint in a trajectory of four originally independent traditions (JEDP) included in the Pentateuch today. Wellhausen dated the P Source to the postexilic period (after 539 BCE). Whereas for Wellhausen the sources reflected the time of their composition, Hermann Gunkel (1862–1932) suggested oral traditions behind sources, allowing for the possibility of earlier traditions even when the final forms of the books might be late.

In contrast to earlier views that Deuteronomy was part of a Hexateuch (Genesis-Joshua), Martin Noth (1902–1968) in his *Überlieferungsgeschichtliche Studien* (I, 1943:27–40) proposed a Deuteronomistic History (Deuteronomy-2 Kings) composed during the exile and later connected to Genesis-Numbers. While Noth agreed with the overall dating of Deuteronomy in the time of Josiah, he considered it to reflect earlier traditions, including those relating to war. Noth's idea of a Deuteronomistic History became a consensus, however, that has been challenged recently, with some scholars preferring the concept of a Hexateuch.

The rediscovery of the Near East by the West in the nineteenth century brought with it the development of archaeology. At first, archaeology in the "Holy Land" was very much driven by the concerns of those interested in understanding the Bible and demonstrating that it was historically reliable. Eventually, it became its own separate discipline, largely independent from biblical studies, and this was reflected by a preference to label the discipline as "Syro-Palestinian Archaeology" rather than "Biblical Archaeology."

Many biblical scholars still wish to understand the Bible based on relevant archaeological discoveries, and many archaeologists also explicitly attempt to bring out how their discipline can contribute to understanding the world of the Bible and the Bible itself. Once archaeological data from the world of the Bible started to accumulate from the late nineteenth century onward, problems about how it might relate to the Bible started to arise. While events from the period reflected in the book of Judges on (ca. 1200 BCE) were generally seen as actual historical, events earlier than that became suspect. The role that war played in the origins of early Israel became a matter of debate. Scholars proposed three major paradigms. Two involved war, one did not.

William F. Albright (1891–1971) and John Bright (1908–1995) proposed a Conquest Paradigm, which assumed that the Israelites waged war on the peoples of Canaan beginning in ca. 1250 BCE, not 1400 BCE, as previously calculations had concluded. This paradigm was accompanied by a serious conversation about the war motif in Deuteronomy. Eventually, the paradigm was abandoned due to the lack of positive archaeological evidence for an Israelite conquest at sites such as Ai (Josh 7–8), Jericho (Josh 2, 6), Gibeon (Josh 9), and Arad (Josh 12:14; Num 21:1–3).

Subsequently, Albrecht Alt (1883–1956) and Noth proposed an Immigration Paradigm, which assumed the Israelites were nomads who immigrated into unoccupied areas of Canaan. This paradigm did not involve war.

George E. Mendenhall (1916–2016) and Norman K. Gottwald proposed a Peasant Revolt Paradigm, which suggested that the Israelites were Canaanites who revolted against the existing socioeconomic structures and withdrew to the highlands to form a new society. While the Peasant Revolt Paradigm was eventually rejected due to lack of supporting evidence, the idea of an indigenous origin of the early Israelites was generally retained. In other words, scholarship today as described by R. K. Hawkins in *How Israel Became a People* (2013:29–48) tends to think that Israel was a development indigenous to Canaan.

A pioneering work on war in the Hebrew Bible is *Holy War in Ancient Israel* (1958) by Gerhard von Rad (1901–1971). For von Rad, the institution of holy war (*herem*), used by an amphictyony or coalition of tribes to defend their villages and sanctuary, evolved in the premonarchical period. He noted how warriors were mustered and commissioned, how sacrifices were offered before battles, and how YHWH was with the Israelites in war and could strike terror in their enemies. Von Rad did not, however, consider the conquest traditions in the book of Joshua as historical. He went on to trace the evolution of holy war in the time of the monarchy and in the prophets.

For von Rad, Deuteronomy "conceives of the holy wars as predominantly wars of religion, in which Israel turns offensively against the Canaanite cult which is irreconcilable with the faith of YHWH" (von Rad 1958, 118). The concept of *herem* that is notable in relation to war in Deuteronomy also experiences a shift in meaning where instead of simply devoting plunder to YHWH, it is now linked with exterminating the Canaanites to prevent them from leading the Israelites into idolatry. The offensive nature of Deuteronomy that includes strong rhetoric against "the nations," in contrast to the defensive nature of war in the amphictyonic period, can be linked with the new rise of the militia in Judah after the Assyrian conquests in the late eighth century BCE.

What Is the Status of the Conversation?

While later scholarship, reviewed by Charles Trimm in "Recent Research on Warfare in the Old Testament" (2011), challenged most aspects of what von Rad wrote, such issues as holy war, the cultic nature of war, the nature of *herem*, and reading Deuteronomy against its setting in the history of Israel continue to be studied. How to understand Deuteronomy's call for the Israelites to massacre men, women, and children in war in terms of reading the biblical texts today also remains an ethical challenge for many scholars, even if some like Carly L. Crouch in *War and Ethics in the Ancient Near East*

(2009) have expressly sought to analyze war from the perspective of the ancient world only, without making moral judgments of the ancients. Moreover, it should be noted that scholarship has highlighted that war in Deuteronomy and the texts of the Old Testament more widely is comparable to war elsewhere in the ancient Near East. As a case in point, the concept of *herem* studied by E. Stern in *The Biblical Herem: A Window on Israel's Religious Experience* (1991) has parallels with other Near Eastern societies, with the Mesha stele providing the closest similarity.

Susan Niditch in *War in the Hebrew Bible: A Study in the Ethics of Violence* (1993) did ground-breaking work in analyzing *herem* and other theological aspects of war in ancient Israel. For Niditch, there is a diversity of war ideologies in the Hebrew Bible. *Herem* can be seen as YHWH's portion and as a sacrifice and then at a later stage in Deuteronomy as YHWH's justice in "rooting out what they believe to be impure, sinful forces damaging to the solid and pure relationship between Israel and God" (Niditch 1993, 56). In addition, she examines issues that relate to bardic traditions of war, tricksters, expediency, and YHWH's role in war, most of which fall outside the scope of Deuteronomy.

In "Dispossessing Nations: Population Growth, Scarcity, and Genocide in Ancient Israel and Twentieth-Century Rwanda" (2016), T. M. Lemos has studied the Rwanda genocide (1994) to better understand why passages in Deuteronomy (20:16–18) might call for the Israelites to wage *herem* war against the Canaanites.

For Lemos, scarcity linked to population growth can provide an underlying reason for genocide, a concept that Lemos draws in based on a wider interaction with genocide studies. In ancient Israel, there was population growth since the beginning of Iron Age I, with population peaking in the eighth century BCE. The trends in demographics in the late eighth and seventh centuries correlate with the time of the writing of Deuteronomy. Coupled with a time of Assyrian oppression, the increase in population led to lessening of available resources, also creating social stratification and a variety of tensions and intergroup competition. Deuteronomy then projected competition for resources into an idealized time of Moses, including with the utilization of the concept of *herem* that is otherwise attested in the inscription on the Mesha Stele Lemos leaves open the question of whether any of the imagined violence was actually carried out at the time when Deuteronomy was produced.

In *Ancient Israel at War 853–586 B.C.* (2007), Brad E. Kelle presents a digest of the major military conflicts that Israel and Judah had in the period of neo-Assyrian and then Babylonian dominance over the Levant. Kelle notes how before the battle of Qarqar (853 BCE) no clear Assyrian, Babylonian, or Egyptian texts exist that would give detailed evidence on Israel and Judah in relation to their presumed existence. After 853 a large amount of textual and archeological sources exists, including some from ancient Israel itself, but nevertheless even they require careful consideration as only a small amount of "straightforward, particularly first-hand material" that pertains to Israel and Judah exists" (Kelle 2007, 8).

Kelle also points out how the usefulness of the biblical materials is disputed. All this said, a reasonable chronology for the period covered in his book can be constructed, in line with many other treatises on the period. For Kelle, while the wars of the ninth to the sixth centuries were marked by a co-optation of aspects of worship in Israel and Judah by the royal establishment or influence by foreign elements, there were other groups within the kingdoms that were often outside the centers of power that could use religious traditions for challenging social and political developments that took place. For example, it may be that some of the social legislation in Genesis-Deuteronomy was generated in response to consolidation of land by the monarchy, cash cropping, and exploitation of peasantry. Such legislation, presented as coming directly from YHWH, would command that the poor, defenseless, and others vulnerable in society be treated fairly and would picture YHWH as being tied to those groups most closely. In "Postwar Rituals of Return and Reintegration" (2014), Kelle studies the postwar rituals of return and reintegration that utilizes psychological theory with some connection to the book of Deuteronomy as well.

The treatments highlighted here as examples of recent scholarship indicate how the continuing discussions have built on previous endeavors, with some new considerations also drawn in, such as those arising from genocide studies and psychology.

What Is Trending in the Conversation?

In order to help resolve some of the dilemmas that relate to war in Deuteronomy, one can draw in recent social scientific approaches. A particularly promising new avenue is provided by the recent development of settler colonial studies. Against past studies that relate to the formation of ancient Israel, in some ways it expands on the Immigration Paradigm proposed by Alt and Noth, but it also takes more seriously the role of war like the Conquest Paradigm of Albright and the Peasant Revolt Paradigm of Mendenhall and Gottwald. In addition, it considers assimilation as part of identity formation in ancient Israel, tying with considerations of indigenous origins of the Israelites.

I want to make three preliminary clarifications. First, settler colonial studies that I am using to better understand the war motif in Deuteronomy have also been used by Francesco Amoruso, Ilan Pappe, and Sophie Richter-Devroe, "Introduction: Knowledge, Power, and the 'Settler Colonial Turn'" (2019) and others to analyze and critique the policies of the modern state of Israel toward Palestinians. My study here is not part of that conversation. Second, some Near Eastern scholars limit their parallels to cultures that are chronologically or geographically adjacent to ancient Israel like Assyria, Syria, or Egypt. As Howard Eilberg-Schwartz in *The Savage in Judaism: An Anthropology of Israelite Religion and Ancient Judaism* (1990, 87–102) has explained, other scholars who employ social scientific criticism, however, use paradigms drawn from a wider range of cultures regardless of their chronological or geographical relationship to ancient Israel. Therefore, although the settler colonial approach was developed to assess developments in Western European cultures during the nineteenth and twentieth centuries, it can also be useful in developing a better understanding and appreciation of the war motif in Deuteronomy. Third, I consider Deuteronomy to be part of a Hexateuch, not part of a Deuteronomistic History.

From a social scientific perspective, war can be seen in the context of group violence. While there is little agreement in the social sciences as to what violence is, Siniša Malešević in the *Wiley Blackwell Encyclopedia of Social Theory* (2017) defines violence as "a process through which one, intentionally or unintentionally, inflicts by coercion some behavioural change or through which physical, mental, or emotional damage, injury, or death results."

As groups are constituted of individuals, violence between groups also involves individual actions. For example, a duel on a battlefield would, as such, directly involve actions between individuals (1 Sam 17:1–58). The focus here, however, is the bigger context of human groups and their violent interactions. Not all violent interactions between groups, however, should be defined as war. Clearly an armed conflict like World War II (1939–1945) is a war. In contrast, that may not be the case with skirmishes between two hunter-gathering societies 12,000 BP),[1] or a fight between two rival street gangs. While there is no full agreement on the issue, for Malešević and C. Olsson in the *Sage Handbook of Political Sociology* (2018: 717), war is "a simultaneously institutionalized, collective, organized and political form of violent conflict, which pits more or less complex and bureaucratized organizations against each other, but also in the sense that it involves practices that have been organized and hence ordered for particular ends."

Recent scholars have pointed out how violence is essential for the constitution and operation of societies. Malešević in *The Sociology of War and Violence* (2010) also points out how the development of increasing societal complexity has brought with it an increase in organized violence. For Malešević two vital concepts that relate to the constitution and operation of societies are "centrifugal ideologization" and "cumulative bureaucratization of coercion." The former relates to the ideological power that those who control societies can exert on their respective populations and the latter to the ability of societies to administratively control their members.

An important corollary to ideological control can be drawn based on the concept of "hegemony" that dates to the early twentieth century. For Antonio Gramsci (1891–1937), the idea of hegemony is based on cultural continuity and dominance that operates with the consent of the masses. Bruce Routledge in *Archaeology and State Theory: Subjects and Objects of Power* (2014) finds that such hegemonies dominate the ancient world. According to Routledge, elites who hold power in societies need to operate based on common culture so as to make their actions palatable to the masses. Centrifugal ideologization in convincing a population, for example, that war is an essential aspect of national life, whether that is the case or not, must find a way to utilize existing cultural resources for hegemonic purposes.

For Benjamin Foster, *The Age of Agade: Inventing Empire in Ancient Mesopotamia* (2016), organized violence that included centrifugal ideologization was already an essential component of agrarian societies that dominated the Near East at the time of ancient Israel. Therefore, war can be expected to have been part of the experience of ancient Israel as well.

Divine war can naturally be seen from the perspective of "centrifugal ideologization" and "hegemony." Considering the pervasiveness of belief in the divine in the Near East, it would seem natural if those in power would use the divine as legitimation for war. For K. Lawson Younger, Jr. in *Ancient Conquest Accounts: A Study in Ancient Near Eastern and Biblical History Writing* (1990), the idea of centrifugal ideologization is well in line with the specific forms of rhetoric that are typical of Near East war, suggesting that the texts can be taken as propagandistic and yet not necessarily completely fictional. Similarly, again considering the predominance of the cult in the Near East, integrating cultic aspects in war was useful for achieving the consent of the masses and through that also troops in the field, together with coercive measures used for controlling such troops.

An issue with ancient Israel in general and Deuteronomy in particular is to detect how cult and the divine are integrated in the rhetoric that accompanies war. In Deuteronomy, clearly the parenesis in the context of the implied audience emphasizes YHWH's role as the source and condition of Israel's well-being. YHWH led the Israelites out of Egypt and helped them to conquer peoples opposing them. Accordingly, the Israelites can also trust that YHWH will lead them into the new land. Similarly, in the new land, the Israelites are equally to be faithful to YHWH to ensure continued success. If the Israelites, however, do not follow YHWH, great calamities will ensue, just as was already the case in the wilderness, highlighted in the episode of the spies (1:22–46).

While Deuteronomy mostly seeks to persuade, there are some coercive aspects included. Above all, the threat of divine punishment that is inextricably tied with the rhetoric of persuasion can be linked with coercion, by means of persuasion by fear.

There is also provision in Deuteronomy for actual coercive methods. In the context of war, these are mostly limited to the law of the apostate city (13:12–18). At an individual level, however, such issues as penalties for idolatry (13:1–11; 17:1–5), the appointment of judges (16:18; 17:6–12; 19:15–21), legislation about the towns of refuge (19:1–13), and the treatment of a recalcitrant son (21:18–21) can be seen from the perspective of coercion. One needs to keep in mind, however, the question of to what extent the laws in Deuteronomy, as with legal materials in the Near East more widely, should be seen as practical or merely theoretical. Altogether, that Deuteronomy mostly seems to persuade, combined with a description of only rudimentary bureaucratic institutions, could be seen in a context where much appeal is made to persuasion due to a lack of such institutions. And, in such a context, even if the laws were meant to be followed, one may ask to what extent they could be implemented in practice, including when conducting war.

The "Settler Colonial Paradigm" offers a strategy for interpreting its description of the birth of the ancient Israelite society in the context of migration and colonialism in the Near East during 1300–900 BCE. Patrick Manning in *Migration in World History* (2005) stressed the importance of migration in human history. Current migration studies incorporate considerations of historical sources, archaeology, linguistics, and genetics, cutting across the whole of human history across time and space, including prehistoric times. These studies suggest that human migration was extensive and a vital component in the spread of humankind and in the formation of the foundations of today's world, in contrast to a number of approaches in the second part of the twentieth century that tended to minimize the role of migration in human history, as discussed in Peter Bellwood, *First Migrants: Ancient Migration in Global Perspective* (2013).

Migration and colonialism are closely related. According to Jürgen Osterhammel in *Colonialism: A Theoretical Overview* (2005), a "colony" is a new political organization built on precolonial conditions, created by invasion, conquest, or settlement colonization. The invaders are dependent on a geographically remote imperial center or "mother country," which claims exclusive rights of possession of the colony. Colonialism, for Osterhammel, is a relationship of domination between an indigenous majority and a minority of foreign invaders. The fundamental decisions affecting the lives of the colonized people are made and implemented by the colonial rulers in pursuit of interests that are often defined by the mother country. Rejecting cultural compromises with the population that is colonized, the colonizers are convinced of their own superiority and of their ordained mandate to rule.

Michael Dietler in *Archaeologies of Colonialism: Consumption, Entanglement, and Violence in Ancient Mediterranean France* (2010, 18), however, defines "colonization" as an expansionary act of imposing political sovereignty over foreign territory and people—the projects and practices of control marshalled in interactions between societies linked in asymmetrical relations of power and the processes of social and cultural transformation resulting from those practices. It is the "interactions between societies linked in asymmetrical relations of power and the processes of social and cultural transformation resulting from those practices" that would fit with the context of colonizing migration. The idea of "imposing political sovereignty over foreign territory and people" also fits.

One can also note that war and colonialism are interlinked. If one society wins over another in war, this will often result in the former ruling over the latter. Conversely, a war to liberate a society from the rule of another can result in a colonial relationship being discontinued. It is, of course, possible that a war will result in a draw, in which case a status quo will prevail. Guerrilla attacks that may not be classifiable as full-scale war may, for example, also end a colonial relationship. The occurrences of YHWH in Judges delivering the Israelites to the power of the surrounding nations are examples of the Israelites falling under an alien colonial regime from which a judge liberates them, with the events narrated in terms of overall cycles of apostasy, oppression, repentance, and deliverance.

For Lorenzo Veracini in *Settler Colonialism: A Theoretical Overview* (2012, 3), "settler colonialism" is essentially a phenomenon that accompanies "autonomous collectives that claim both a special sovereign charge and a regenerative capacity." Settlers consist of people who move into a new land and establish a new society of their own liking there.

The Hexateuch indicates that Abraham, Israel's forefather, migrated into the land of Canaan from Mesopotamia, and that his descendants subsequently migrated to Egypt to protect themselves from a famine. The Israelites became a nation in Egypt but were enslaved. They were later liberated and left Egypt under the leadership of Moses. They then crossed a wilderness and arrived at the edge of Canaan, where Moses died, and it was left to his successor Joshua to lead the Israelites into the land of Canaan in order to conquer it and settle it. In settler colonial terms, the Israelites, especially toward the end of the Hexateuch, become an autonomous collective that claims both a special sovereign charge and a regenerative capacity. Also, they vie for land to claim for themselves under their sovereign charge where they are to establish a new society.

At the edge of the so-called Promised Land, Deuteronomy focuses on its conquest and life in the new land. The Holiness Code (Lev 17–26) also focuses on life in the land. The indigenous peoples or "indigenous others" can be killed (7:1–26), driven away (9:1–4; cf. Ex 23:20–30), or assimilated (Josh 2: 1-24; 6:22-25). Overall the idea is that the settler body polity is "cleansed" of its indigenous and exogenous others. As Patrick Wolfe in "Structure and Event: Settler Colonialism, Time and the Question of Genocide" (2008) explains, "structural genocide" occurs where an existing indigenous society is destroyed, and a new society takes its place.

In 1948, the United Nations defined "genocide" as "any of the following acts committed with intent to destroy, in whole or in part, a national, ethnic, racial or religious group, as such:

(a) Killing members of the group;(b) Causing serious bodily or mental harm to members of the group;(c) Deliberately inflicting on the group conditions of life calculated to bring about its physical destruction in whole or in part;(d) Imposing measures intended to prevent births within the group;(e) Forcibly transferring children of the group to another group."

Raphael Lemkin (1900–1959), whose work *Axis Rule in Occupied Europe: Laws of Occupation, Analysis of Government, Proposals for Redress* (1944, 79) during World War II in relation to the Nazi occupation of Europe was foundational for developing an understanding of the notion, coined the word "genocide" as meaning "the destruction of a nation or an ethnic group."

> Genocide does not necessarily mean the immediate destruction of a nation, except when accomplished by mass killings of all members of a nation. It is intended rather to signify a coordinated plan of different actions aiming at the destruction of essential foundations of the life of national groups, with the aim of annihilating the groups themselves. The objectives of such a plan would be disintegration of the political and social institutions of culture, language, national feelings, religion, and the economic existence of national groups, and the destruction of the personal security, liberty, health, dignity, and even the lives of individuals belonging to such groups. Genocide is directed against the national group as an entity, and the actions involved are directed against individuals, not in their individual capacity, but as members of the national group.... Genocide has two phases: one, destruction of the national pattern of the oppressed group; the other, the imposition of the national pattern of the oppressor. This imposition, in turn, may be made upon the oppressed population, which is allowed to remain, or upon the territory alone, after removal of the population and the colonization of the area by the oppressor's own nationals. (Lemkin 1944, 79)

The definition has clear links with settler colonialism, especially in hindsight of the recent development of settler colonial studies by scholars like Damien Short in *Redefining Genocide: Settler Colonialism, Social Death and Ecocide* (2016). The more restrictive definition by the United Nations is more directly focused on physical and perhaps mental harm caused to individuals as part of a specific group, without really considering the wider context of the group.

Overall, genocide and colonialism relate to group violence with varying levels and intensity to that violence. In terms of intensity, again, modern technologies enable more effective killing, probably culminating to date in the gas chambers of the Nazi regime, and one may ask to what extent genocide could have occurred in the ancient world. In this, one may, however, keep in mind that, as John Docker in *The Origins of Violence: Religion, History and Genocide* (2008) has demonstrated, even chimpanzees have been shown to employ genocidal means against other chimpanzee groups. Therefore, the possibility of genocide in the ancient world should not be excluded. Also, importantly, as Martin Shaw in *What Is Genocide?* (2015) shows, genocide is a conflict between groups, and few genocides if any can be seen as one-sided.

Returning to considerations of settler colonialism directly, one may note that indigenous others are normally considered as a threat to the settler collective as their continuing existence constitutes a threat and challenge to the very existence and legitimacy of the settler collective (7:1–26), whereas exogenous others are generally seen as people who can collaborate with the settler collective. In ancient Israel, exogenous others include, at least at a literary level, the mixed multitude (*ereb rab*) that went out of Egypt (Exod 12:38) and Caleb (Josh 14:6). And the Israelites legislate for a foreigner (*ger*) in several places in the Pentateuch. Thus, people from outside the main settler collective would then have been taken into the settler collective, whether initially as indigenous or exogenous others. There can also be abject others, those permanently excluded from the settler polity, having lost their indigenous or exogenous status. In ancient Israel, these include people who have been subject to the punishment of being cut off (*kerat*) from the people (Lev 7:20–27; 17:4–14; 18:29) and the Ammonites and Moabites who according to Deuteronomy (23:1–7) cannot be uplifted into the Israelite community, even when an Edomite and Egyptian can be included in the third generation. These processes in a basic tripartite setting of a settler society consisting of the settler collective and indigenous and exogenous others would go on for centuries in Israel after the initial invasion reflected in Joshua and would result in transforming the Late Bronze societies as attested in the Amarna letters into later Iron Age Israel.

As Patrick Wolfe in "Settler Colonialism and the Elimination of the Native" (2006) emphasizes, settler colonialism is a structure rather than an event where an initial invasion gives rise to a prolonged process of eliminating the indigenous population. One may also note that the legal materials in the Hexateuch provide a blueprint for the new Israel, even when it is not certain how much this was a theoretical rather than a practical construct. As Wolfe (2008, 130n71) has pointed out, "settler colonialism has, as observed, two principal aspects—not only the removal of native society, but also its concomitant replacement with settler institutions. This latter, positive aspect involves the establishment and legitimation of civil hegemony." For Wolfe (2008, 103) "eliminatory strategies all reflect the centrality of the land, which is not merely the component of settler society but its basic precondition."

If one then thinks of Deuteronomy's rhetoric, it is preparing for life in a new land in its message to its implied audience. An important function of war is to clear the land from its indigenous inhabitants, and, in modern conceptualized terms, these can be labeled as "colonial wars." A strong legitimation for the conquest and the accompanying colonialism is made based on the "YHWH Alone" motif. The Israelites commitment to YHWH Alone is also a strong unifying principle in holding the Israelite society together, especially in a setting that lacks a centralized administration that could offer bureaucratic structures to the same effect.

The early colonial context is implied in the war law (20:10–18). According to the material, the Israelites are to offer peace to towns they fight against, and if the town capitulates peacefully, it is to serve Israel and pay taxes, and if not, the Israelites are to kill its men after a successful conquest and take the rest, including women, as plunder. However, this is to apply only to towns outside the Promised Land. In the land itself, the Israelites are to kill all indigenous peoples. Clearly here they are to be treated according to the overall settler colonial framework of the Hexateuch. Those outside the land can fall under franchise colonial approaches where it is not necessary for kill all indigenous peoples but simply exploit them for gain. The lands of Edom, Ammon, and Moab do not belong to Israel, based on their familial relationship with the Israelites and accompanying divine promise. Therefore, the Israelites are not to wage war against them (2:1–9, 19).

Furthermore, according to the concepts of centrifugal ideologization and hegemony, the issue here is not whether the posited familial relationship and the related patriarchal narratives more widely are factually true but whether the Israelites believed in them and their implications. In this sense, for example, it is also not necessary to take everything in Deuteronomy literally. The main issue is whether the rhetorical strategy of Deuteronomy was convincing and believable to its audiences.

From a historical perspective, the Late Bronze Age was an era of empires accompanied with international trade and diplomacy which collapsed around 1200 BCE. The collapse of the Mycenaean palatial system caused a migration of Aegean and Anatolian peoples toward the south along the Levantine seacoast. Their migration then contributed to the collapse of Ugarit and the Hittite Empire. In the process, as Assaf Yasur-Landau describes in *The Philistines and Aegean Migration at the End of the Late Bronze Age* (2010), a new Philistine entity in the southwestern coast of the Levant was formed. As K. Lawson Younger, Jr.

describes in *A Political History of the Arameans: From Their Origins to the End of Their Polities* (2016), an Aramean ethnogenesis in the east and subsequent expansion caused the retreat of the Middle Assyrian Empire in the Jazira area in northern Mesopotamia. Meanwhile, Semitic migrants from Egypt sometime after the expulsion of the Hyksos moved into areas in the southern Levantine highlands where Egypt's control was limited. In addition to migration, these processes involved colonial interactions, and the birth and initial development of Israel can be seen in the context of ancient settler colonialism in a continuum that ranges from franchise colonialism to settler colonialism. While there is nothing in the Late Bronze–Early Iron Age I material remains that can at least conclusively be read as indicating an entry of an external group of people into Canaan, interestingly, the presence of Egypt in Canaan in the early New Kingdom period is poorly attested in the material culture, with only the presence of Egyptian-style pottery implying an Egyptian character of the site. As E. F. Morris discusses in *Ancient Egyptian Imperialism* (2018), the Egyptians utilized local buildings, and information about their doings must be based on textual records. Architecturally there are no differences except in some southern coastal sites Also, more widely, in his "The Israelite Conquest of Canaan: A Comparative Review of the Arguments Applicable" (1983), Benedikt S. J. Isserlin (1916–2005) has pointed out that the Norman conquest of England in the eleventh century and the Muslim conquest of the Levant are not easy to attest archaeologically.

Deuteronomy itself suggests that the Israelites utilized local structures (6:10–11), and Joshua speaks of burning and other destruction only in connection with Jericho, Hazor, and Ai (Josh 6:20–24; 8:28; 11:13), with Judges adding Laish (Judg 18:27). In this, Joshua (Josh 11:13) even explicitly states that towns that existed on tells ('al-tillam) were not burnt. Altogether, the Bible is consistent with the initial invasion of the Israelites being undetectable archaeologically.

In regard to the four sites of Jericho, Hazor, Laish, and Ai, evidence of destruction has been found at Hazor and Laish at the end of the Late Bronze Age. Jericho is badly eroded, and the evidence there is equivocal. It seems that Joshua (Josh 6:26) was added when the books from Genesis to Kings in the canon today were first connected into a single literary unit. This leaves Ai, which remains a difficult problem, and the issue must be left open. Altogether, one may highlight here that part of the problem with a conquest model that traces back to Albright is that it reads the biblical materials in a simplistic manner.

An idea of a quick and complete conquest of the land in Joshua is seen to be in contradiction to Judges, which indicates a more gradual process of settlement. However, Joshua, in addition to some exaggerated rhetoric of quick conquests, itself also indicates a long process of conquest that, moreover, was an incomplete one (Josh 13:1–7). That much of the settlement was in new, previously unsettled areas in the highlands is compatible with the idea of settler colonial migration where not every event relating to settlement needs to be directly violent. The colonial setbacks by surrounding nations as described in Judges on their part also show that the process was not always unilinear. The Merneptah stele on its part does support the existence of Israel in the highlands in 1207 BCE.

As to why early Israel was able to expand overall, as the Hexateuch indicates, the priestly elite considered that the land was given to them by YHWH. It would not have been difficult to foster such feeling among ordinary people as well. But a decisive advantage was offered by the ability of the Israelites to act in concert as against individual city-states. Together with a population explosion in the highlands in Iron Age I, this would have given them an overall military advantage that proved to be decisive. The cumulative effect of even small skirmishes would have been enough to cover a large territory during a long enough time frame, such as a century or two. Joshua, even when stripped off from some of its rhetorical embellishments, also indicates that the Israelites were even able to hold their own against indigenous coalitions (Josh 10–11). The same ultimately went with surrounding entities that at times encroached into areas that Israel claimed for itself, as attested in Judges.

All in all, then, one can see how settler colonialism provides a consistent and overarching theme for understanding early Israel that correlates with the Hexateuch and with the book of Judges. In this, Deuteronomy provides an important ideological component for the settler colonial project, and war in Deuteronomy is predominantly part of a colonial enterprise of claiming a land for a new society in the ancient southern Levantine highlands.

Note

1. Before Present (BP) years is a time scale used mainly in archaeology, geology, and other scientific disciplines to specify when events occurred prior to the origin of practical radiocarbon dating in the 1950s.

Further Reading

Hawkins, R. K. 2013. *How Israel Became a People*. Nashville: Abingdon.
Kelle, B. E. 2007. *Ancient Israel at War 853–586 B.C.* Westminster: Osprey.
Lemkin, R. 1944. *Axis Rule in Occupied Europe: Laws of Occupation, Analysis of Government, Proposals for Redress*. Washington: Carnegie Endowment for International Peace.
Malešević, S. 2010. *The Sociology of War and Violence*. Cambridge, UK: Cambridge University Press.
Niditch, S. 1993. *War in the Hebrew Bible: A Study in the Ethics of Violence*. New York: Oxford University Press.
Pitkänen, P. 2010. *Joshua*, Apollos Old Testament Commentary 6. Leicester: IVP.
Pitkänen, P. 2017. *A Commentary on Numbers: Narrative, Ritual and Colonialism*. Routledge Studies in the Biblical World. Abingdon: Routledge.
Pitkänen, P. 2019. *Migration and Colonialism in Late Second Millennium B.C.E. Levant and Its Environs: The Making of a New World*. Studies in the History of the Ancient Near East. London: Routledge.
Rad, G. von. (1958) 1991. *Holy War in Ancient Israel*. Grand Rapids, MI: Eerdmans; German original *Der Heilige Krieg im alten Israel*, Göttingen: Vandenhoek & Ruprecht, 1958.
Stern, E. 1991. *The Biblical ḥerem: A Window on Israel's Religious Experience*. Brown Judaic Studies 211. Atlanta: Scholars Press.
Veracini, L. 2012. *Settler Colonialism: A Theoretical Overview*. Basingstoke: Palgrave Macmillan.
Wolfe, P. 2008. *Structure and Event: Settler Colonialism, Time and the Question of Genocide*. New York: Berghahn Books.

CHAPTER 11

MOSES AND A PROPHET LIKE MOSES IN DEUTERONOMY

STEPHEN L. COOK

Who Began the Conversation?

The role of Moses in Deuteronomy is difficult to minimize. Moses's words, Deuteronomy insists, make up the book's contents. From the first line, Deuteronomy identifies itself as revelations uttered by Moses on the plain opposite the promised land proper on the eve of the settlement. Deuteronomy's overall framework establishes the initial claim, which only grows in significance as it unfolds. In Deuteronomy, we encounter Moses as Israel's primal covenant mediator (5:5, 27; 18:16), its suffering deliverer (1:37; 3:26; 4:21; 9:9, 18, 25; 10:10), the greatest of all its prophets (34:10–12), and the founder of a crucial ongoing Mosaic prophetic role (18:15–19). These understandings of Moses as the founding covenant mediator predate Deuteronomy and extend their influence long after its appearance.[1]

Moses as Conveyer of YHWH's Very Word

Deuteronomy as a seventh-century BCE literary composition stems from six hundred years after Moses's day, so his estimable role there compels investigation. What does Deuteronomy assume and pronounce in making Moses central? How does grappling with Moses's significance thrust us into the heart and soul of Deuteronomy?

The contours of Moses's role in Deuteronomy emerge most sharply in the account of the events at Mount Horeb. As the great mountain of the *tôrâ* shakes and blazes at YHWH's theophany, Moses risks his life for the sake of the people. The Israelites say to Moses, "This great fire will consume us; if we hear the voice of the LORD our God any longer, we shall die. For who is there of all flesh that has heard the voice of the living God speaking out of fire, as we have, and remained alive? Go near, you yourself, and hear all that the LORD our God will say. Then tell us everything that the LORD our God tells you, and we will listen and do it (5:23–27)."[2]

The implication is clear. Any human who hears the divine voice out of the fiery otherness of Mount Horeb will die. Afraid of death, the people ask Moses to stand in their stead as their mediator with YHWH, and Moses stands in the place of death for the people. In the end, Moses will die outside the land. The burden of mediating YHWH's word will lead to the premature death of the greatest prophet Israel ever had (34:10–12).

Already the key significance of the voice of Moses in Deuteronomy emerges. The paradoxical YHWH of Deuteronomy is a deity of fiery, vocal presence and of purposeful absence, of epistemic distance. We may speak of Deuteronomy's God as "numinous," as of a transcendent otherness that is simultaneously tremendous and fascinating.[3] Because Moses obeys YHWH's summons toward the numinous, he becomes YHWH's unassailable representative. Drawn into YHWH's fascinating otherness, he comes to reflect the divine passions and intentions. Because this is so, the *tôrâ* of Deuteronomy, placed on the lips of Moses, stands as an entrance way to YHWH's presence.

No longer is the king the recipient of YHWH's teachings, nor is it he who delivers them to the people. Rather, Moses, who at the time of Josiah's reign and the discovery of the book of the Law (2 Kgs 22:3–20) was an unassailable authority, received the law from YHWH and delivered it directly to the people, without royal intermediation (5:1–5). In this model, the king, in relationship to the law, is on the same plane as all other citizens (17:20).

The significance of Moses in Deuteronomy and related literature correlates directly to a vision of the concrete potency of YHWH's word. The divine word propels history through Moses and Mosaic successors such as Joshua and Samuel.[4] The tenacious endurance of YHWH's word is clear in statements that the words of true prophets never "fall" (1 Sam 3:19; 2 Kgs 10:10). Its extended trajectory is very clear in Kings (2 Kgs 23:16–17), where Josiah learns that a Mosaic prophet had set his deeds in motion centuries earlier (1 Kgs 13:1–2). Jeremiah (Jer 36) drives home the irrepressibility of YHWH's word. A king can ban a Mosaic prophet and burn his scroll but cannot thwart YHWH's word. Christopher R. Seitz points out how Jeremiah (Jer 36:28) recapitulates Deuteronomy (10:1–2) on this point.[5]

Moses and Trajectories of Leadership in Israel

Moses, for Deuteronomy, initiates key patterns, roles, and trajectories of leadership in Israel. S. Dean McBride, Jr. has argued that these new patterns for leadership represent the charter for an ideal constitutional society hoped for by Deuteronomy.[6] Moses's generative role first emerges in a brief account of Moses distributing some of his judicial authority (1:9–18). Moses does not horde power in Deuteronomy but works to distribute control and empower Israel as a people. Here, he appoints many additional leaders beyond himself to administer justice among the people.

Moses's first leadership act in Deuteronomy aims to let go of central authority to empower society's local spheres. Here, Deuteronomy first betrays its suspicion of monarchy and advocacy of Israel's earlier lineage-based polity norms. Note that Deuteronomy (1:13, 15) specifically selects and organizes Israel's future leadership on a tribal basis. Moses states that he had installed "lineage-heads of your tribes" (1:15 author's translation; *rāʾšê šibṭêkem*).

Deuteronomy pursues a *political* agenda critical of centralized rule and a *theological* agenda applying covenantal norms and empowerment to Israel's judiciary. Deuteronomy's source in Exodus (Exod 18 E) stresses awe of YHWH (Exod 18:21) and *tôrâ* instruction (Exod 18:16, 20), both central to Israel's Sinaitic and Mosaic judicial traditions. So, too, Numbers (Num 11 E) makes the numinous (Num 11:18, 24) and YHWH's incalculable *word* (Num 11:23, 27) central in jurisprudence. Deuteronomy (1:17) presupposes the selfsame, numinous YHWH of Moses.

The spirit upon Moses lends him covenantal authorization for his judicial role. This Mosaic spirit stands at the heart of Numbers 11 (see 11:17, 24–25, 29; cf. 34:9; 2 Kgs 2:9). Here, Numbers 11 joins traditions in Num 12:6–8 (E) and in Micah (Mic 3:8) to present an ideal of a Mosaic spirit and office. YHWH takes some of the spirit that is on Moses and places it on seventy traditional kin-group heads chosen as judges (Num 11:15–30). The same or similar group of seventy elders of old Israel partakes of the Sinai experience with Moses atop Mount Horeb (Exod 24:9–11E). YHWH invites them to an intimate meal, in connection with which they enjoy a tangible audience with YHWH, who ratifies their mediatorial role within Israel (Num 11:16–17, 24–25). Fretheim notes the intimacy with YHWH here, "a deeply personal level of involvement."[7]

Moses's early act of distributing judicial authority using structures of Israel's old tribal polity is matched later in Deuteronomy (16:18–20). The passage begins a widely studied section of Deuteronomy that presents the ideal polity of YHWH's covenant people living in the promised land (16:18–18:22).[8] It reaffirms the principle that Israel's local communities have Mosaic judges insuring covenant justice. In this way, covenant shapes and transforms society at the local level, and society's periphery enjoys its proper share of political and judicial authority. The passage's distinctive idiom again echoes and repristinates early Israel's acephalous, genealogically organized polity.

Moses declares, "In all the communities which the LORD, your God, is giving you, you shall appoint judges and officials throughout your tribes" (16:18 NABR). The language of "communities" (*ša'ar*) and "tribes" (*šēbeṭ*) is *lineage* language. The semantic spectrum of *ša'ar*, like Akkadian *bābu(m)* ("gate"), includes the sense of kin-group or extended family (Akk. *bābtū*). This *genealogical* connotation of *ša'ar* rises to prominence especially in those Deuteronomic texts in which a pronominal suffix is added to the term (12:18; 16:11, 14; Ruth 3:11; 4:10). In many such cases the sense of "clan" or "extended family" fits the context very well.[9]

What Is the Status of the Conversation?

Deuteronomy's Law over the Prophets (18:15–22)

Deuteronomy's new model of governance provides for a continuation of Mosaic intermediation. The "Law over the Prophets" (18:15–22) elaborating this fascinating dimension of Deuteronomy's ideal polity is certainly original to the edition of the scroll during the reign of Josiah (640–609 BCE).[10] Deuteronomy holds up Moses as the gold standard of all prophecy. Now, this ideal will apply to a line of Mosaic successors. YHWH promises Moses that for each new generation, "I [God] will raise up ... a prophet like you from among their [the Israelites'] kindred" (18:18–19 NABR).[11]

Jeremiah expands on Deuteronomy, specifying that Mosaic prophets speak *all* YHWH's words (Jer 1:7, 17; 42:4) and *nothing but YHWH's words* (Jer 23:18, 22; cf. 1 Kgs 22:14). In their Mosaic role, they are YHWH's very mouth (Jer 15:19).[12] YHWH promises, "I will put my words into the mouth of the prophet; the prophet shall tell them all that I command . . . my words which the prophet speaks in my name" (Deut 18:18 NABR).

Jeremiah is such a Mosaic prophet, speaking "the pure word of God."[13] For Deuteronomy and Jeremiah, verbal revelation trumps dreams and visions, which are deemed less plenary, intimate, and immediate. Echoing the brief on Mosaic prophets in Numbers (Num 12:6–8), Jeremiah reads: "Let the prophet who has had a dream tell it for a dream! And let him who receives a word from me, deliver my word accurately! What have straw and wheat in common?" (Jer 23:28 NJB).

Jeremiah here stresses the immediacy with YHWH enjoyed by Mosaic intermediaries. True prophets stand among YHWH's heavenly confidants. Sometimes Jeremiah speaks out in the heavenly council, interceding for his people (Jer 15:1; 18:20). At other times, YHWH's private inner circle empowers Jeremiah as YHWH's messenger to Israel, YHWH's veritable mouth and lips (Jer 15:19; 23:18, 22). Having "stood in the council of the LORD," one departs empowered as YHWH's genuine messenger (Jer 23:18–22; Ps 82:1–8; 1 Kgs 22:19–23).[14]

The intimacy with YHWH of the Mosaic prophet correlates directly with what I described earlier as the willingness of Moses to draw near and hear the voice of the living deity speaking out of Mount Horeb's fire. As Rudolph Otto has taught us, the numinous provokes trembling but proves irresistibly fascinating.[15] It attracts the Mosaic prophet to the point of arousing intense desire. Moses found the bush aflame on Mount Horeb too fascinating to ignore (Exod 3:3 E; Deut 33:16 NJPS, REB, NIV). As YHWH's word comes stealing to him, Elijah, hiding his face as did Moses, ventures forth to hear the whisper of it (1 Kgs 19:13; cf. Job 4:12–16). Jeremiah speaks of YHWH's intense seduction (Jer 20:7 NABR, NJB). YHWH and the Mosaic intermediary develop a complex intimacy over time.

Can such an intimate of YHWH ever be mistaken? Yes, Mosaic prophecy is not sheer concept or abstract reason, but operates within the vicissitudes of actual life. True, a Mosaic prophet delivers YHWH's direct speech—*only YHWH's speech*—with minimal filtering and sugarcoating (1 Kgs 22:14; Jer 23:18, 22).[16] That word is a force unto itself, resisting manipulation (Num 11:26–29; 22:18; Jer 5:14; 6:11; 20:9). Central to Deuteronomy's theology is also the conviction that YHWH's foreknowledge is conditional upon historical contingency and human imperfection (Jer 6:27–29). Thus, even Jeremiah once received YHWH's chastening for uttering "what is worthless" (Jer 15:19). For this, YHWH suspended him as a Mosaic prophet for a time.

Scholars debate where Jeremiah went wrong, but the error likely relates to his painful pendulum swings between identifying totally with YHWH's perspective and sympathizing thoroughly with Israel. Here, he has erred in too quickly sympathizing with Israel. "Do not let them influence you!" YHWH commands (Jer 15:19 NLT).[17]

Huldah's prophecy of Josiah's peaceful death proved inaccurate. Josiah died unexpectedly, before the ink was dry on the first edition of the Deuteronomistic History (DTH) that recorded Huldah's promising word. The Chronicler ends up laboring to apologize for this historical contingency. The king's ignoring of a new oracle must have nullified Huldah's promise. "He did not listen to the words of Necho from the mouth of God" (2 Chr 35:22).

The Centrality of Intermediation and Teaching for Mosaic Prophets

Deuteronomy (5:23–27) reveals the volatile, lethal effect of YHWH's presence, as does the Elohist tradition (E) in Exodus (Exod 19:16–17, 21; 20:18–19). Divine volatility necessitates the Mosaic prophet's intermediation. The eighth-century Mosaic prophets thus correlate intermediation and divine dread. Recapitulating the exodus, Micah describes YHWH as the breach-maker (Mic 2:13; *happōrēṣ*, NJPS, NABR), the one bursting bounds. As in Exodus (Exod 19:22, 24) we see YHWH bursting bounds—breaching such limits as contained Mount Horeb. In Psalms (Ps 106:23) the *breach* is what Moses braves (Ezek 13:5; 22:30). To do so risks being tranced (Num 11:26) or appearing raving mad, as did Hosea (Hos 9:7) and Micah (Mic 1:8; 3:8).

Moses selflessly "stood in the breach" (Ps 106:23) and later Mosaic prophets did, likewise, as attested in Hosea (Hos 9:8–9) and Micah (Mic 7:7). The former passage was quite influential, funding later texts in Jeremiah (Jer 6:17) and Ezekiel (Ezek 3:17; 13:5) that stress the prophetic roles of sentinel and defender. Moses's duty was to stand between YHWH and a sinful people, warning, representing, and protecting the people.[18]

The parade example of Moses stifling YHWH's anger occurs at the golden bull incident, when Moses successfully calms YHWH down (Exod 32:11–14 E; Deut 9:19–20, 25–29). His protective intercessions continue all along the wilderness journeying (Num 11:2; 14:19; 21:7). In Jeremiah (Jer 15:1), YHWH speaks of Moses and Samuel as preeminent intercessors. Jeremiah, too, is distinguished in this regard. He reminds YHWH; "Remember how I stood before you to speak good for them, to turn away your wrath" (Jer 18:20).

The Mosaic prophet is YHWH's ideal intermediary and the ideal *teacher* of covenantal instruction. Representing the people, Moses receives YHWH's teachings (*tôrâ*), finding his mouth brimming with YHWH's words (Jer 15:19). To attend to YHWH's word (*dābār*) is to embrace YHWH's teachings as taught by the prophet. Jeremiah (Jer 6:19) places YHWH's "words" and "teaching" directly in parallel. The Mosaic prophet insists YHWH's people should attend to covenantal teachings, consent to them, and follow through.

The teaching role of the Mosaic prophet comes to the fore particularly in cases where the prophet is a Levite, a genealogical pedigree shared by Moses; Samuel—a Levite by adoption; Hosea—arguably a Levite; Jeremiah; Malachi, and others.[19] For Deuteronomy, Levitical priests properly fill the role of covenant teacher. "They teach Jacob your ordinances, and Israel your law [*tôrâ*]" (33:10). It is their duty to transmit and apply the *tôrâ* teachings given at Mount Horeb (Deut 17:9–12, 18; 24:8; 31:9–13; 2 Kgs 17:27–28; Jer 2:8; 8:8; 18:18; Mic 3:11; Hos 4:6; 8:12; Mal 2:6–7).

There is no evidence, despite the Levitical priestly ideal that Samuel and Jeremiah represent, that Deuteronomy and other Sinai-oriented texts assigned Levites the *exclusive* right to teach the covenant. Counterexamples appear in Exodus (Exod 13:8–9 E), Deuteronomy (11:19), and an Asaphite Psalm (Ps 78:5), where each Israelite generation, parents especially, transmit covenantal instruction to the rising generation. Numbers (Num 24:16 E) describes a foreign seer with privileged "knowledge" (*daʿat*) only available to YHWH's close confidants. Deuteronomy (17:9–12; 19:17–18) gives both Levites and elders of the people seats on a proposed appeals court for interpreting and administering the covenant. A rotation system brings both types of local, tribal leadership into the center for fixed periods. Two eighth-century Mosaic prophets who taught the Sinai covenant, Hosea and Micah, appear to represent a Levite and an elder, respectively.[20]

Deuteronomy (31:9–13) pictures Moses entrusting the *tôrâ* teachings to both Levites and elders, who are to teach them to Israel at the central shrine at least every seventh year. Deuteronomy aims to restore the authority of both these groups of "peripheral intermediaries," groups opposed by society's center as seen in Hosea (Hos 6:9; 9:8) and Micah (Mic 3:11–12; 7:3). Before Hosea, Micah, and Deuteronomy, E showed Moses distributing to Israel's elders some of his duties transmitting and authoritatively applying the *tôrâ* teachings (Exod 18:17–23). The new judges are lineage heads with judicial experience.

What Is Trending in the Conversation?

The Mosaic Paradigm in the Tetrateuch

A story about prophetic conflict in Numbers (Num 12:1–16 E) is perhaps the earliest biblical presentation of the Mosaic prophet. The story begins as a complaint about Moses's marriage to Zipporah, but the actual issue soon emerges as a conflict over prophetic authority. How should Israel deal with situations involving differing channels of intermediation in tension? As Robert R. Wilson articulates the problem, any society with multiple intermediaries must grapple with adjudicating their claims.[21]

Numbers handles the problem of conflicting claims of intermediation within Israel by establishing a hierarchy of prophetic authority. When prophecies are in tension, Mosaic prophecy has priority. It must win out due to the close relationship of Moses and YHWH. Rather than employing vague and parabolic means of intermediation, such as dreams and riddles, Moses directly hears YHWH's perspicuous, verbal revelation.

> "When a prophet of the LORD arises among you,
> I make Myself known to him in a vision,
> I speak with him in a dream.
> Not so with My servant Moses...
> With him I speak mouth to mouth, plainly and not in riddles." (Num 12:6–8 NJPS)

Such revelation is inherently on target since Moses is the personal confidant of YHWH. As Numbers puts it, "With him I speak mouth to mouth" (Num 12:8 NJPS)—or as in Exodus "as one speaks to a friend" (Exod 33:11). Moses does not see YHWH as YHWH is; that is impossible (Exod 33:20). Rather, Moses has special access to YHWH and enjoys an intimate fellowship. YHWH trusts Moses, enjoys his company, and communicates with him as YHWH's confidant, with immediacy and directness (34:10). YHWH declares: "Throughout my house [covenant territory] he is worthy of trust" (Num 12:7 NABR).[22]

In Exodus (Exod 24:9–11 E) atop Mount Horeb the seventy kinship-heads of Israel enjoy a one-time experience of the intimacy that the Mosaic prophet has with YHWH. Though exposed to YHWH's presence, it "did no harm" to the seventy elders (Exod 24:11 NJB). The experience of YHWH's very self is not for their individual benefit. They represent the people below, who all need tangible connection with YHWH's direct presence. "Would that all the

LORD's people were prophets!" Moses will later exclaim (Num 11:29). The Deuteronomic project is leading *all* Israel into connection with YHWH.

Moses affirms that without direct connection with YHWH's actual person, the Deuteronomic covenant-project has no chance of success, as Exodus (Exod 33:14–16) affirms. The Hebrew idiom employing the noun "face" in this text signals the presence of YHWH's very person (Exod 33:14–15). Deuteronomy quotes this idiom (4:37). For Israel to be YHWH's covenant people requires intimacy with YHWH (Gen 32:30 E; Deut 5:4). Moses insists that no avatar could ever substitute for this (Exod 33:2–3). True, YHWH's numinous presence could consume Israel, but Israel must take the risk. Indeed, not the divine presence alone, but the *speaking* divine presence is requisite (Exod 33:19; 34:6).[23] Israel's vocation requires the Deuteronomic soft, articulate divine voice (1 Kgs 19:12 NIV, NLT, TEV).

The Mosaic Paradigm in the Former Prophets

DTH shows Moses' role continuing in a great variety of key figures, including Samuel (1 Sam 12:23), Ahijah (1 Kgs 12:15); Elijah (e.g., 1 Kgs 19:8), Elisha (2 Kgs 2:8, 14), and Huldah, "*the* [Mosaic] prophetess" (2 Kgs 22:14). The case for certain of these figures, such as Elijah and Huldah, is very tight. Others have parallels to Moses but lack explicit evidence of a role of intermediation.

Gideon, in his commissioning, resonates with Moses (Judg 6:16; Exod 3:12). Like Moses, he encounters YHWH intimately (Judg 6:22; Deut 34:10). He is not called to be a prophet, however, nor does he teach or apply covenantal instruction.[24] Joshua specifically succeeds Moses as Israel's leader and has Moses's spirit upon him (34:9). He experiences a commissioning that obviously echoes Moses's own (Josh 5:15). Joshua, however, is not called a "prophet."

The case is much clearer for Samuel, a most significant Mosaic prophet (Ps 99:6; Jer 15:1).[25] YHWH raises Samuel up to enforce the covenant for an era lacking in intermediation (1 Sam 3:1). Parallels with Moses are evident beginning with Samuel's initial commissioning. Just as in Moses's call, YHWH calls Samuel's name twice (1 Sam 3:10 MT; LXX: 3:3, 6, 10). Like Moses, Samuel is quickly drawn into YHWH's confidence. Soon, Samuel is "trustworthy" (*ne'ĕmān*) throughout the land—"from Dan to Beer-sheba" (1 Sam 3:20)—just as Moses was "trustworthy" (*ne'ĕmān*) throughout YHWH's land (Num 12:7 E).

The commissioning narrative establishes that Samuel enjoys the continued presence of YHWH, becoming the central intermediary between YHWH and Israel (1 Sam 3:19–4:1a 3:20). As Chapman aptly puts it, "Samuel is here styled deuteronomistically as a prophet like Moses (3:19–41a)."[26] YHWH speaks directly to Samuel and Samuel speaks for YHWH.

YHWH intends to lead all Israel through Samuel, channeling the divine communication through YHWH's prophet to the people. Remarkably, YHWH's word is the "word of Samuel" (1 Sam 4:1 *dĕbar- šĕmû'ēl*). Samuel, like Moses and Jeremiah, functions essentially as YHWH's mouth (Deut 18:18; Jer 23:18, 22). This being the case, YHWH ensures that his words never "fall to the ground" (1 Sam 3:19). This idiom is later associated with Elijah's wielding of YHWH's word as a Mosaic prophet (2 Kgs 10:10). It expresses the reliability of all Mosaic prophecy (Deut 18:22; Jer 28:9).

Intercession is a major role of Samuel as a Mosaic prophet. His position as Israel's intercessor is prominent (1 Sam 7:4–9; 12:19–25). When asked to cry to YHWH to intervene, he does so on the people's behalf and YHWH answers and acts. As with Moses, the people recognize Samuel's uniquely effective role as their mediator in their covenant with YHWH (1 Sam 7:8; 12:19). Samuel is a reliable go-between, both taking requests to YHWH and delivering answers. As Walter Brueggemann puts it "the claims and assumptions of the covenantal order are shown to be reliable."[27] Jeremiah (Jer 15:1) later speaks of Samuel and Moses in one breath, considering them the epitome of intercessors for Israel. Their effectiveness in defending Israel before YHWH is legendary. As Seitz notes, these prophets' role of continually praying for Israel and *instructing* Israel is mandatory (1 Sam 12:23).[28]

The responsibility of the Mosaic prophet to teach and interpret the covenant is rooted in Moses's example (6:18; 12:28). As Moses says, "The LORD charged me . . . to teach you statues and ordinances for you to observe in the land" (4:5, 4; 5:31; 6:1). Further, according to Exodus (Exod 18:16, 20 E), the responsibility to teach was ongoing. Moses continually taught the people the covenant, "the way they are to go and the things they are to do."

The language of instruction in the "good" (1 Sam 12:23) is a significant part of the "B-source"—a literary strand of 1 Samuel aligned closely with Deuteronomy's covenant theology. Deuteronomy makes the "good and right way" of the covenant a recurring theme (4:40; 5:16, 29; 6:3, 18; 12:25, 28; 22:7; Jer 7:23). To instruct Israel in the "good and right way" means to teach the people the path that eventually brings them covenantal blessings.

Kings describes both Elijah and Elisha as prophets like Moses. The prophetical legends about Elijah specifically portray him as a channel for the irrepressible word of YHWH (1 Kgs 17:16). As the widow of Zarephath puts it, "The word of the LORD in your mouth is truth" (1 Kgs 17:24). Elijah performs actions laden with Mosaic symbolism. Elijah rolls up his mantle and strikes the Jordan River with it, parting the river just as Moses had parted the Red Sea (2 Kgs 2:8). Rather than using vocabulary from the Priestly Source (P) in Exodus (Exod 14:21–22) to describe the crossing of the Sea, the Elijah story echoes the vocabulary of Joshua (Josh 3:17), which is a recapitulation of the crossing. Both Joshua (Josh 3:17) and Kings (2 Kgs 2:8) use "cross over" (*'ābar*) and "dry land" (*ḥārābâ*) twice.

Elijah's experience on Mount Horeb (1 Kgs 19:9–18), which repeats the primal Mount Horeb theophany, represents the text's strongest identification of him as a new Moses. As Wilson puts it, the theophany "confers new status on Elijah and by extension on all future Mosaic prophets. Elijah's authority is the authority of Moses, and the prophet's word is a divine word, fully comparable to the *tôrâ*."[29]

The fasting of forty days and nights (1 Kgs 19:8) also corresponds to Moses's experience (Exod 24:18; 34:28; Deut 9:9, 18, 25). The Hebrew grammar indicates that upon arrival at "the mount of God," Elijah entered "the cave," that is, where Moses had earlier hidden from YHWH's lethal presence at Mount Horeb (Exod 33:21–22).

Just as Moses ascends Mount Horeb after Israel's golden bull incident, Elijah ascends the same mountain after confronting Israel's Ba'al worship. As Wilson astutely observes, the apostasy confronted by Elijah (1 Kgs 19:10, 14) devolved out of a history tracing back precisely to the worship of bull images described in Exodus (Exod 32) and Kings (1 Kgs 12).[30] Both the prophets Moses and Elijah experience theophanies on Mount Horeb followed by a succinct verbal revelation (Exod 34:4–7; 1 Kgs 19:11–12).

The starkest example of the Mosaic prophet as YHWH's stand-in occurs in the story of Elijah atop the fiery mountain (2 Kgs 1:9–17).[31] Sitting atop a symbolic "Mount Horeb," Elijah witnesses numinous fire bursting forth against two army units breaching the mount's perimeter. A third unit is spared only when its captain shows the sort of reverence befitting contact with Mount Horeb's fire (5:25).

Following his experiences on Mount Horeb, Elijah anoints Elisha as the next Mosaic prophet (1 Kgs 19:15–17). Elisha receives his role directly from Elisha at the latter's ascent to heaven (2 Kgs 2). He requests, and is granted, a double share (21:17) of Elijah's spirit (2 Kgs 2:9–10, 15). The language echoes the transfer of the Mosaic spirit in Numbers (Num 11:16–17, 24–26).

Elisha recovers Elijah's mantle as it falls from the sky and uses it to split the Jordan River, repeating Elijah's earlier recapitulation of Moses's miracle (2 Kgs 2:13–14). The mantle had earlier been draped over him as a sign of his succession (1 Kgs 19:19–21). The pattern of a disciple repeating his mentor's splitting and crossing of waters portrays the Elijah-Elisha succession as a mirror of Joshua's taking up Moses's role. Joshua also crossed the Jordan and entered the promised land near Jericho (Josh 3).

Huldah validated and interpreted the *tôrâ* teachings in an act launching Josiah's Deuteronomic reform of Judah (2 Kgs 22:11–23:3). Notably, DTH refers to Huldah with the title "the prophetess," suggesting that she is the premier Mosaic prophet of her day, at the top of a hierarchy of prophets (2 Kgs 22:14).[32] Specific evidence suggests that Kings reflects actual history—evidence including the disconfirmation of Huldah's prophecy of Josiah's peaceful death and references to Huldah's oracle in Jeremiah, some of which are authentic to the prophet (Jer 7:20; 19:3–4; 44:2–6).

The account of Josiah's reform makes him the ideal king (18:9–14). As such, he should consult with the Mosaic prophet of his day on matters of the *tôrâ* teachings (18:15–22). Huldah, then, must be that very prophet. H. G. M. Williamson correctly concludes, "When the ideal Deuteronomic king Josiah needs to consult with the deity about the book he has found and does not do it by consulting wizards or mediums but rather a prophetess, the conclusion seems inevitable that that prophetess is, from the historian's point of view, one in the Mosaic succession."[33] Josiah specifically "heeds" the words of the Mosaic prophet (2 Kgs 22:18, 19) as Deuteronomy requires.

Huldah's position as the final named prophet in DTH creates an *inclusio* with the figure of Deborah, DTH's first named prophet and a woman (Judg 4–5).[34] The way DTH introduces Deborah as a prophetess (Judg 4:4) may intentionally mirror Huldah, in which case the redactors understood Deborah as a Mosaic prophet.[35] If we bracket out Joshua, whom DTH does not term a "prophet," Deborah, not Samuel, is the first known "prophet like Moses."

The Mosaic Paradigm in the Latter Prophets

Turning from the Former to the Latter Prophets, we encounter notable scholarly disagreement in recognizing significant instances of the Mosaic paradigm. Lothar Perlitt found the paradigm entirely lacking.[36] More recently, Cristophe Nihan has argued that Moses found his way into the Latter Prophets only in the Second Temple era.[37] In what follows I contest these assessments. The core elements of *Mosaic* prophecy are amply attested in pre-exilic prophecy, mostly in those prophets oriented on the Sinai covenant.

Hosea makes the earliest reference to Moses as the ideal prophet. The context is a history lesson. Hosea (Hos 12) emphasizes the power of prophecy to channel YHWH's care and liberation. Hosea (Hos 12:13; MT 12:14) declares the prophet Moses superior even to Jacob, the founding ancestor. Jacob was renowned for shepherding animals, but Moses liberated YHWH's human flock. Israel should allow YHWH to shepherd anew, through Hosea, and thus rediscover YHWH's exodus love and salvation. "By a prophet the LORD brought Israel out of Egypt, and by a prophet Israel was tended" (Hos 12:13 NABR).

Hosea is a shepherd-prophet like Moses. As in Deuteronomy (18:9–22), the grammatically singular wording here has a plural, successive sense.[38] "Your real identity is formed through YHWH-sent prophets, who led you out of Egypt and served as faithful pastors" (Hos 12:13 THE MESSAGE). Hosea here draws on Asaphite poetic artistry, where Moses leads Israel as a *shepherd* or *pastor* out of Egypt and through the Red Sea (Ps 77:20). Psalms (Ps 78:52) and Micah (Mic 2:12) use the same shepherding images to illuminate YHWH's liberation of Israel. Hosea, the Asaphites, and Micah cluster together in their linguistic and theological affinities and in their preservation of Moses traditions.[39]

Hosea (Hos 6:4–6) elaborates on Israel's history of encounter with YHWH-sent Mosaic prophets. As Wilson writes, they "deliver God's pure effective words to the people."[40] Hosea (Hos 6:5) seems to read "Through prophets, I communicated them [i.e., my statutes] / As words from my mouth, my statutes went forth . . . " (author's translation). There are other valid emendations, but almost all speak of prophets with direct access to the potent words of YHWH's mouth (18:18).

Wilson persuasively argues that Hosea (Hos 8:1–3; 5:15–6:6) reflects the intermediary functions of a Mosaic prophet.[41] Here, YHWH and Israel carry on a dialog with Hosea as covenant go-between. The prophet's language reflects village-era legal trials held at the threshing floor, in this case a trial over violating a binding commitment. YHWH indicts Israel (Hos 4:6; 6:7; 8:1, 12) for breaking the covenant (*běrît*), specifically its "binding regulations" (*tôrâ*). The wording paralleling *covenant* and *stipulations* reflects an Asaph psalm (Ps 78:10). The dire consequence is that Assyria will swoop as a bird of prey against "the house of the LORD," that is, the whole land viewed as a suzerain's manor (Hos 9:15; Num 12:7).

The people respond with aims of appeasement (Hos 8:2), objecting that they *are* devoted to YHWH (Hos 6:1). YHWH's response, delivered by the prophet, declares YHWH unconvinced (Hos 6:4; 7:14). "In vain [they cry], 'We, Israel, know you!' " (Hos 8:2 NJB). "It is too late" (NLT). The enemy (*'ôyēb*) will pursue (Hos 8:3 *rādap*). Deuteronomy (30:7) echoes the very wording. Israel's betrayal of YHWH's love had cost them. They had lost the "good and right way" (*tôb*), they had lost life from YHWH, for the *good* was paired with *life* (30:15).

Hosea, along with Micah, two of Deuteronomy's precursors, spoke of the "good" (*tôb*). Both Mosaic prophets identified the "good" with the transformed and enriched life deriving from covenant obedience (Mic 6:8; Hos 8:3). Deuteronomy's recurring theme is that covenantal obedience makes life "good"—makes things "go well" (4:40; 5:16, 29; 6:3, 18; 12:25, 28; 22:7). YHWH declares, "I have set before you this day life and good [*tôb*]" (30:15 NABR).

According to Jeremiah (Jer 7:25–26; 25:5; 35:15), YHWH sent a line of prophetic servants beginning with Moses to call Israel back (Hos 6:5).[42] Jeremiah was the prophet like Moses for his generation. Like Moses and Samuel, YHWH directs Jeremiah's life from birth (Jer 1:5; Exod 2; 1 Sam 1). The almond branch of his inaugural vision (Jer 1:11) recalls both Moses's staff—his Levite staff (Num 17:8)—and the burning bush (Exod 25:33).[43] As Jeremiah presents the prophet, he is, in fact, the ultimate bearer of the Mosaic mantle. In later tradition he is the one "who spoke from the mouth of the LORD" (2 Chr 36:12). The recollection fits "You shall serve as my mouth" (Jer 15:19).

Jeremiah (Jer 1) and Deuteronomy (18) share the Mosaic prophet tradition; both have YWHW use unique wording to describe the divine word and the prophet's mouth (see later). So, too, in Jeremiah (Jer 1:7) as in Deuteronomy (18:18) YHWH demands, "You shall speak whatever I command you." William Lee Holladay argues cogently that Jeremiah himself modeled his call account on the Moses paradigm in Deuteronomy (18).[44] If, instead, it was Deuteronomistic editors who styled Jeremiah on Deuteronomy, they operated homogeneously with his own self-conception.[45]

A self-conception as a Mosaic prophet is likely original to Jeremiah (Jer 15:1, 16; 18:20; 20:9; 23:28; 28:15–17; 35:15–16). Mark Leuchter illuminates well how Jeremiah (Jer 28:15–17; 35:15–16) attests to his Mosaic pedigree.[46] The "confession" (Jer 20:7–13) attests to the intimacy of a Mosaic prophet with YHWH, who compels him to speak "in his name" (Jer 20:9), a phrase used four times in Deuteronomy (18:19–22). When Hananiah, a prophet of YHWH, opposed Jeremiah by breaking to pieces Jeremiah's symbolic yoke, Jeremiah accused him of lying (Jer 28:15) and levied a death sentence upon him in accordance with Deuteronomy (18:20). Probably alluding to Deuteronomy's initial discovery (2 Kgs 22:13; 23:2),[47] Jeremiah (Jer 15:16) speaks of YHWH's words, meant for the Mosaic prophet's lips, being "found." Once discovered, they go straight into Jeremiah's mouth (Jer 1:9)—he *eats* them just as the desert generation in Deuteronomy (8:3) *eats* manna. That the eating metaphor is expanded by Ezekiel (Ezek 2:8–3:3) supports its likely authenticity.

Mirroring Moses's precedent in Deuteronomy (18:18), Jeremiah receives YHWH's revelation *hand delivered*. YHWH stretched out a hand, touched Jeremiah's mouth, and inserted YHWH's Word: "Now I have put my words in your mouth" (Jer 1:9).[48] This precise wording occurs only three times in the Bible (18:18; Jer 1:9; 5:14).[49] In one of the occurrences YHWH tells the prophet, "I am putting My words into your mouth as fire" (Jer 5:14 NJPS). The fire metaphor recurs in Jeremiah (Jer 23:29) around 609 BCE, when the prophet describes an extended experience of YHWH's words as an uncontainable burning deep in the bones (Jer 20:9).

As Abraham Joshua Heschel astutely observed, Jeremiah's words about fire here are more than colorful language for the coming physical destruction. Far from dispassionate judgment, such destruction is the outworking of a divine pathos, YHWH's felt wrath, which Jeremiah experienced as his own passion. "The divine word moved in Jeremiah as fire because he lived through the experience of divine wrath." As a new Moses, deeply interconnected with YHWH, Jeremiah felt YHWH's pathos "springing up from within."[50]

Divine wrath, in YHWH's experience, is agonizing pathos. From the perspective of YHWH's people, however, divine wrath is an encounter with the numinous. True to his allegiance with Deuteronomy's language and theology, Jeremiah's images of divine word as fire recall the divine fire atop Mount Horeb, out of which issued YHWH's words (4:12, 15, 33, 36; 5:4, 22, 24, 26; 9:10; 10:4). Long after Moses's overpowering experience at Mount Horeb, the divine word burns irrepressibly in Jeremiah's prophetic preaching. This word provokes dread, burns up oppression, and steers history toward YHWH's goals.

The role of Mosaic prophet reemerges in Malachi, which concludes the biblical prophetic collection—the Nevi'im—in its present form. Malachi, like Moses and Hosea, was both a Levite and a prophetic mediator of the covenant. Intermediation characterizes the book's six interchanges, which typically begin with a statement of YHWH's perspective, turn to quote the audience's objections, and then lay out a response. Malachi's prioritizing of responsibility for *tôrâ* teachings is clear (Mal 2:6–7).

Appendixes in Malachi (Mal 4:1–6) align his overall message with his identity as a prophet in the tradition of Moses and Elijah. "Be mindful of the Teaching of My servant Moses, whom I charged at Horeb," YHWH commands (Mal 4:4 NJPS). The paralleling of Elijah with Moses (1 Kgs 19:8–9; 2 Kgs 2:8) in Malachi (4: 5–6) strongly reflects the Mosaic prophet tradition and promises that Elijah will return as a culminating Mosaic prophet at the eschaton (Mal 4:6)—appearing as "the messenger of the covenant" (Mal 2:7; 3:1), a new Moses who successfully trains the people in YHWH's *tôrâ* teachings.

Notes

1. For Moses's key early role in Israel's covenant life, see Cross (1973, 205–215) and Leuchter (2017, 199–200). As Wilson (1980, 221–222) correctly notes, Deuteronomic theology, with its theme of the Mosaic prophet, "was simply the crystallization of older . . . views." For sample evidence, see Wilson (1980, 156, 223, 233–234, 299).
2. English translations are from the New Revised Standard Version (1989) unless otherwise indicated.
3. R. Otto (1966); Cook (2015).
4. Seitz (1989, 7–8).
5. Seitz (1989, 14n20).
6. McBride (1987, 235–238).
7. Fretheim (1991, 259–260).
8. I concur with Pearce (2013, 3) on the dating of 16:18–18:22, "The most plausible hypothesis is that the laws of [this section] have their origins in the era of Josiah but were reworked by a new generation in the setting of the exile." I elaborate on this later.
9. E. Otto (2006, 380).
10. Here, I take issue with scholars arguing for a postexile dating, such as Römer (2013, 133). The Mosaic paradigm of chapter 18 is already embedded in pre-Josianic texts such as Num 12 (E), the prophetical legends of Elijah and Elisha (Leuchter 2008, 96), and Hosea's oracles (against Atkins, 2013). At Josiah's time, Huldah's role as a Mosaic prophet conforms to Deut 18, as shown by Williamson (2010, 71). Soon afterward, Jeremiah (Jer 23:28) draws on the Mosaic ideal (Num 12:6–7).
11. The syntax expresses a plural, successive sense like the sense of Judg 2:16, 18 in grammatically singular language, as in 1 Sam 2:35b (NLT, NIV). At crucial junctures, Moses will have a representative ("such a prophet" [n. e: "such prophets"]). For discussion, see Driver (1902, 227–229), Hagedorn (2004), Williamson (2010, 71), Nihan (2010, 27n14).
12. As Balaam puts it, "If Balak should give me his house full of silver and gold, I would not be able to go beyond the word of the LORD" (Num 24:13, cf. Num 22:18, both E). Micaiah ben Imlah at first appears an exception to accurate prophecy (1 Kgs 22:15), but, in fact, Micaiah does relay verbatim the deceptive word that YHWH has sent as a judgment.
13. Wilson (1980, 237).
14. Lundbom (2004, 195).
15. Rudolph Otto (1966).
16. Wilson (1980, 210).
17. Also see Lundbom (1999, 750). Heschel (1962, 126–127) thought the problem was the opposite pendulum swing: an excessive amount of sympathy with YHWH's wrath against Israel (Jer 15:15). Doubtless, this was also an issue for this hyperintermediary.

18. Wilson (1980, 229, 241).
19. On the Levites as scribal teachers, see Leuchter (2017, 203). On Samuel's role as both Mosaic prophet and Levite, see Wilson (1980, 180); Leuchter (2013, 151–157). On Hosea as a Levite, see Cook (2004, 247) and Leuchter (2017, 244). On Jeremiah as a Levite, see Leuchter (2008, 265–266n19). On Malachi as a Levite, see Redditt (1994). For arguments that Elijah and Elisha were able to function as priests, see Sweeney (2013).
20. Cook (2004).
21. Wilson (1980, 156).
22. The idiom of "covenant territory" is used later in Hos 8:1; 9:15.
23. Fretheim (1991, 300). Fretheim further writes, "What is now true for Moses will also be true for Israel."
24. Holladay (1986, 27).
25. On the witness in Psalms (Ps 99:6) to Samuel as a Mosaic prophet and on the equation of Samuel and Moses here as pre-Deuteronomistic, see Leuchter (2013, 150). Like Samuel, Moses wore several hats, including Levitical priest, prophet, and political leader.
26. Chapman (2016, 90).
27. Brueggemann (1990, 50).
28. Seitz (1989, 8).
29. Wilson (1980, 199).
30. Wilson (1980, 198n102).
31. Sweeney (2013, 41–43).
32. Wilson (1980, 220, 222).
33. Williamson (2010, 71).
34. Hamori (2015, 150); Butting (2001, 99–100); Fischer (2002, 185); Christensen (1984).
35. Williamson (2010, 69, 72).
36. Perlitt (1971, 3).
37. Nihan (2010, 23).
38. Wilson (1980, 227–228).
39. Hosea's reference to Moses resonates with Psalms (Ps 77:20), Micah (Mic 6:4), and Samuel (1 Sam 12:8 B source). I have argued elsewhere that Hosea strove alongside others such as the Asaphites and Micah to preserve traditions oriented on the Sinai covenant and a village-oriented lifestyle in an era when this lifestyle was outmoded. "They helped form a rear line of a whole phalanx of predecessors" (Cook 2004, 271). Wilson (1980, 227–228) earlier noted how Hosea, like his allies, regarded Moses as a prophet and "accepted the Deuteronomic notion that in each generation Yahweh raised up a Mosaic prophet."
40. Wilson (1980, 229).
41. Wilson (1980, 228–229).
42. Römer (2013, 136–140).
43. Lundbom (1999, 237).
44. Holladay (1986, 30).
45. Wilson (1980, 233); Leuchter (2006); Leuchter (2017, 196).
46. Leuchter (2008, 94–99).
47. Jeremiah (Jer 36:24) contrasts Jehoiakim's and Josiah's treatment of YHWH's scrolls; this is another authentic reference to Deuteronomy's discovery (2 Kgs 22:11).
48. Wilson (1980, 237).
49. For cogent arguments about the probable dating of Jeremiah's texts discussed here, see Lundbom (1999, 399).
50. Heschel (1962, 148).

Bibliography

Atkins, J. D. "Reassessing the Origins of Deuteronomic Prophecy: Early Moses Traditions in Deut 18:15–22." *Bulletin of Biblical Research* 23 (2013): 323–341.

Brueggemann, Walter. *First and Second Samuel*. Int. Louisville: John Knox Press, 1990.

Butting, Klara. *Prophetinnen Gefragt: Die Bedeutung der Prophetinnen im Kanon aus Tora und Prophetie*. Erev-Rav-Hefte Biblisch-feministische Texte 3. Wittingen: Erev-Rav, 2001.

Chapman, Stephen B. *1 Samuel As Christian Scripture: A Theological Commentary*. Grand Rapids: Eerdmans, 2016.

Christensen, D. L. "Huldah and the Men of Anathoth: Women in Leadership in the Deuteronomic History." *SBLSP* 23 (1984): 399–404.

Cook, Stephen L. *Reading Deuteronomy: A Literary and Theological Commentary*. Reading the Old Testament. Macon: Smyth & Helwys, 2015.

Cook, Stephen L. *The Social Roots of Biblical Yahwism*. Society of Biblical Literature Studies in Biblical Literature 8. Leiden: Brill, 2004.

Cross, Frank Moore. "The Priestly Houses of Early Israel." In *Canaanite Myth and Hebrew Epic*, 195–215. Cambridge: Harvard University Press, 1973.

Driver, S. R. *A Critical and Exegetical Commentary on Deuteronomy*. ICC. Edinburgh: T&T Clark, 1902.

Fischer, Irmtraud. *Gotteskünderinnen: Zu einer geschlechterfairen Deutung des Phänomens der Prophetie und der Prophetinnen in der Hebräischen Bibel*. Stuttgart: Kohlhammer, 2002.

Fretheim, Terence E. *Exodus*. Interpretation, a Bible Commentary for Teaching and Preaching. Louisville: John Knox Press, 1991.

Hagedorn, Anselm C. *Between Moses and Plato: Individual and Society in Deuteronomy and Ancient Greek Law*. FRLANT 204. Göttingen: Vandenhoeck & Ruprecht, 2004.

Hamori, Esther J. *Women's Divination in Biblical Literature: Prophecy, Necromancy, and Other Arts of Knowledge*. The Anchor Yale Bible Reference Library. New Haven: Yale University Press, 2015.

Heschel, Abraham Joshua. *The Prophets*. New York: Harper & Row, 1962.

Holladay, William Lee. *Jeremiah 1 A Commentary on the Book of the Prophet Jeremiah Chapters 1–25*, Hermeneia. Philadelphia: Fortress Press, 1986.

Leuchter, Mark. *Josiah's Reform and Jeremiah's Scroll: Historical Calamity and Prophetic Response*. Hebrew Bible Monographs 6. Sheffield: Sheffield Phoenix, 2006.

Leuchter, Mark. *The Levites and the Boundaries of Israelite Identity*. New York: Oxford University Press, 2017.

Leuchter, Mark. *The Polemics of Exile in Jeremiah 26–45*. Cambridge: Cambridge University Press, 2008.

Leuchter, Mark. "Samuel: A Prophet Like Moses or a Priest Like Moses?" In *Israelite Prophecy and the Deuteronomistic History: Portrait, Reality, and the Formation of a History*, edited by M. R. Jacobs and R. E. Person Jr., 147–168. AIL 14. Atlanta: SBL, 2013.

Lundbom, Jack R. *Jeremiah 1–20: A New Translation with Introduction and Commentary*. AYB 21A. New York: Doubleday, 1999.

Lundbom, Jack R. *Jeremiah 21–36: A New Translation with Introduction and Commentary*. AYB 21B. New York: Doubleday, 2004.

McBride, S. Dean Jr. "Polity of the Covenant People: The Book of Deuteronomy." *Int* 41 (1987): 229–244.

Nihan, Christophe. "'Moses and the Prophets': Deuteronomy 18 and the Emergence of the Pentateuch as Torah." *SEA* 75 (2010): 21–55.

Otto, E. "שָׁעַר." *TDOT* 15 (2006): 359–405.

Otto, Rudolf. *The Idea of the Holy: An Inquiry into the Non-Rational Factor in the Idea of the Divine and Its Relation to the Rational.* New York: Oxford University Press, 1966.

Pearce, Sarah J. K. *The Words of Moses: Studies in the Reception of Deuteronomy in the Second Temple Period.* Texte und Studien zum Antiken Judentum, Texts and Studies in Ancient Judaism 152. Tübingen: Mohr Siebeck, 2013.

Perlitt, Lothar. "Mose als Prophet" (1971). In *Deuteronomium-Studien*, 1–19. FAT 8. Tübingen: Mohr Siebeck, 1994.

Redditt, Paul L. "The Book of Malachi in Its Social Setting." *CBQ* 56 (1994): 240–255.

Römer, Thomas C. "Moses, Israel's First Prophet, and the Formation of the Deuteronomistic and Prophetic Libraries." In *Israelite Prophecy and the Deuteronomistic History: Portrait, Reality, and the Formation of a History*, edited by M. R. Jacobs and R. E. Person Jr., 129–145. AIL 14. Atlanta: SBL, 2013.

Seitz, Christopher R. "The Prophet Moses and the Canonical Shape of Jeremiah." *ZAW* 101 (1989): 3–27.

Sweeney, Marvin A. "Prophets and Priests in the Deuteronomistic History: Elijah and Elisha." *Israelite Prophecy and the Deuteronomistic History: Portrait, Reality, and the Formation of a History*, edited by M. R. Jacobs and R. E. Person Jr., 35–49. AIL 14. Atlanta: SBL, 2013.

Williamson, H. G. M. "Prophetesses in the Hebrew Bible." In *Prophecy and the Prophets in Ancient Israel*, edited by John Day, 65–80. Proceedings of the Oxford Old Testament Seminar. New York: T&T Clark, 2010.

Wilson, Robert R. *Prophecy and Society in Ancient Israel.* Philadelphia: Fortress, 1980.

SECTION III
SOCIAL WORLD OF DEUTERONOMY

CHAPTER 12

ISRAEL IN DEUTERONOMY

C. L. CROUCH

The book of Deuteronomy is engaged in an intensive project of Israelite identity formation, provoked initially by an increased exposure to alternative cultural matrices in the southern Levant in the long seventh century BCE and then reinforced by the global scope of Israelite experience in the wake of the destruction of the kingdom of Judah in the early sixth century. Although the construction of a distinctively Israelite religious and cultural identity is not the book's sole concern, it accounts for a number of the book's preoccupations and constitutes one of its most significant contributions to the theology of the Hebrew Bible and associated religious traditions.

This chapter discusses some of the most important features of Israelite identity developed in Deuteronomy's legislative and exhortatory core (chs 12–26), including the distinctively Israelite cultural characteristics of exclusive Yahwism, centralized worship, and a shared mythology of Israel's origins in an exodus from Egypt, as well as examining ways in which this Deuteronomic material seeks to protect the distinctive Israelite identity it constructs.[1] A final section discusses some of the ways that this construction of Israelite identity was adjusted in response to Israel's deportation, displacement, and long-term diaspora.

DEVELOPING A DISTINCTIVE ISRAELITE CULTURE

The deuteronomic legislation is designed to differentiate Israelites from non-Israelites. Many of the distinctive features of Israelite practice that it chooses to highlight are religious in nature, including a commitment to exclusive Yahwism and centralization of worship at a single cult site. Others are more broadly cultural, although the separation between these categories is far from absolute.

Exclusive Yahwism

The Israel that Deuteronomy constructs is exclusively Yahwistic. This is perhaps the single most distinctive feature of Israelite culture and identity as defined by the Deuteronomic project. Israel is distinguished from all other groups by its identification with YHWH and by the fact that it worships YHWH exclusively: whereas non-Israelites may have a chief deity while worshipping multiple deities, Israel is characterized by a highly unusual, monolatrous worship practice. This devoted worship of YHWH is the focus of the opening exhortative Shema ("Hear, O Israel . . .," 6:4), which calls upon Israel to acknowledge its fundamentally Yahwistic character, while texts such as Deut. 13:2–19; 16:21–22; and 17:2–7 reinforce this exclusivity from a legal perspective.

The Shema summons the Israelites to "a confession . . . that will serve to shape their identity and their way in the world" (Miller 1990, 98). Israelites, this credo makes clear, are *necessarily* Yahwistic: according to the Deuteronomic definition, an "Israelite" who is not Yahwistic is not really an Israelite. The Shema also emphasizes that Israelites are *exclusively* Yahwistic: an Israelite who worships any other god in addition to YHWH is not really an Israelite. These two elements of Israelite Yahwism are articulated in the two halves of Deut. 6:4. The first half, "Hear, O Israel, YHWH is our god," establishes that Israel is defined as a people who recognize YHWH as its deity. The second half, "YHWH alone," establishes that it is only YHWH whom the Israelites recognize in this way.

An anthropological perspective on identity formation draws attention to the way that these statements deliberately homogenize Israelite religious culture.[2] Actual religious practice and belief in pre-exilic Judah was diverse and far from exclusively Yahwistic, but the Deuteronomic emphasis on the Israelites' sole worship of YHWH represents a rejection of this diversity in favor of the worship of a single deity at a single cult site.[3]

Many of the Deuteronomic laws are designed to enact this exclusively Yahwistic vision of Israel. One of the most significant such passages is Deut. 13:2–19, which highlights the importance of exclusive Yahwism to Israel's identity by presenting three potential challenges to Israel's distinctively and exclusively Yahwistic character, together with their consequences: exhortations to worship other gods pronounced, in turn, by the diviner (13:2–6), the family member (13:7–12), and the inhabitants of a particular city (13:13–19). In each case, an individual or group pursues the worship of deities other than YHWH and encourages Israelites to do the same. The incompatibility of this worship of other deities with membership in the Deuteronomically defined, exclusively Yahwistic Israelite community means that these people are no longer Israelites. Moreover, because their non-Israelite practices threaten this exclusively Yahwistic Israel, they must be removed from the community (cf. 20:10–16).[4]

Deuteronomy constructs Israelite identity, here and elsewhere, in a way that means it is not solely ascribed—that is, accorded by virtue of birth or other event beyond an individual's control. Rather, it contains a strong element of achieved identity—that is, identity gained by virtue of deliberate action or inaction on the part of the individual.[5] Because the book makes extensive use of kinship language—referring to Israel as a community of "brothers," for example—much attention has been paid to ascriptive elements of Deuteronomic Israelite identity. Yet, there are several passages that indicate Deuteronomy's Israel is not solely of that type. To the contrary: a person whose ascriptive qualities—namely, birth into the Israelite community—predispose him or her to an identification as Israelite can effectively forego that identity by acting like a non-Israelite—most prominently, by failing to enact the primary feature of Israelite identity, namely, exclusive Yahwistic worship (cf. Reeder 2012, 23).[6] An Israelite, in other words, can cease to *be* an Israelite if they fail to *act* like an Israelite.[7]

Centralized Religious Praxis

The centralization of the Yahwistic cult at a single cult site (Deut. 12) is the second most prominent feature of Deuteronomy and is also closely involved in the book's construction of a distinctive Israelite identity. The mandate that Israel worship its deity at a single worship site is distinctive, representing a rejection of the existing diversity of cultic sites and an exception in the broader ancient Near Eastern context. It also underscores the exclusively Yahwistic nature of the Israelite cult by associating that worship with an exclusively Yahwistic cult site, away from non-Yahwistic sites elsewhere. Last but not least, centralizing Israel's worship gathers the Israelites together into a restricted, proximate space and thereby promotes Israelites' interactions only with fellow Israelites.

From an identity perspective, the centralization agenda is notable because one way that a group can facilitate and reinforce shared identity is by promoting the spatial proximity of its members (Cohen 1969, 203–204). The most recognizable of such efforts is the tendency to associate collective identity with a particular piece of territory—and a territorial form of this mechanism is also evident in Deuteronomy's interest in Israelite claims to a Levantine homeland, mostly in the Deuteronomistic material. Yet the centralization legislation goes well beyond the proximity entailed by life in a shared homeland: it legislates a much more immediately intensified proximity among members by focusing Israelite ritual at a single cult site and requiring the Israelites to be present there at regular intervals (cf. 16:1-17). These mandated assemblies promote interaction among Israelites, bringing Israelites together in an explicitly Israelite space where Israelite practice and identity may be reinforced and challenges from outside are minimal.

Origins in Egypt

Another way that Deuteronomy establishes Israel's identity is in its regular appeals to a shared Israelite origin story, the exodus from Egypt.[8] Though the book's various ways of referring to the exodus probably reflect different nuances, the unifying theme of all these statements is the centrality of the event for the community's definition of itself: "Israel was Israel in the strictest sense only from Egypt onward" (Schmid 2010, 145–46). An Israelite, by definition, is someone who shares this story: someone who lays claim to the exodus tradition and the narrative of Israelite origins that it articulates.

Notably, this story presents an in-built danger to Israelite identity, insofar as this story of Israel's origins outside the eventual Levantine homeland implies that that homeland was previously inhabited by non-Israelites. Indeed, the implications of this origin story arise almost immediately in the Deuteronomic introduction, where there is a strong emphasis on avoiding or eradicating the land's non-Israelite inhabitants in order to protect Israelite distinctiveness (Deut. 6–7*). Frequent reminders that Israel came out of Egypt—in the introduction and throughout the text—are another means of counteracting the danger posed by Israel's allochthonous origins: these statements underline Israel's special status as those whom YHWH chose to be associated with YHWH and reiterate that the Israelites who are now in the land are distinct from the land's non-Israelite inhabitants, precisely because they came from elsewhere. If Israel constitutes those whom YHWH brought out from Egypt, Israel is by definition distinct from the autochthonous inhabitants of the land.

Other Forms of Cultural Distinctiveness

While Deuteronomy foregrounds these major features of Israelite identity, it also legislates a variety of other behavior designed to differentiate and protect Israel.

Israel is distinct, for example, in the means by which it communicates with its deity: the prioritization of intuitive prophecy, to the exclusion of all technical forms of divination, sets Israel apart from other ancient Near Eastern divinatory hierarchies (18:9–22). Although many other cultures employed prophets to communicate with their gods, the prophet's status in these cultures was among the least esteemed of the divinatory practitioners. In Deuteronomic Israel, the prophet is preeminent, and the technical practitioners whose skills were so prized by Israel's neighbors are devalued to the point of rejection. The prophet will also be "from among you, from your brothers": here as elsewhere, the Deuteronomic law protects Israelite identity by minimizing interactions with non-Israelites (Cohen 1969, 203; cf. Geertz 1973). This is also another case of homogenization, in which an existing diversity of practices is rejected in favor of a single approach.

A variety of other laws also are designed to differentiate Israel from their neighbors. Thus, Deut. 23:18 prohibits a son or daughter of Israel from becoming either קדש (a male holy person) or קדשה (a female holy person). Although the precise function of the קדשה and the קדש are unclear, they are here opposed on the grounds that this cultic profession is unacceptable for Israelites: "A קדשה (female holy person) will not be *from the daughters of Israel*, nor will a קדש (male holy person) be *from the sons of Israel*." The prohibition is not on general principle; implicitly, non-Israelites are permitted to be קדשים (cultic functionaries of this particular kind).

Similarly, Deut. 23:19 addresses types of offerings permissible for presentation to YHWH, using terminology that suggests that the concern is with ritual specialists whose (Deuteronomically) Yahwistic credentials were suspect. Even more explicitly, Deut. 16:21–22 prohibits objects associated with deities other than YHWH. Here, too, the prohibition is not categorical; it is specifically "near to the altar of Yahweh your god" that the אשרה (Asherah, meaning either the goddess or an object associated with her) is banned. As with other prohibited practices, the problem relates to the possibility of confusion on the part of worshippers with regard to the identity of the deity(ies) they worship. The centrality of exclusive Yahwism to Israelite identity means that objects that are not also exclusively Yahwistic must be rejected.

A large number of passages addressing issues of Israelite identity use the term תועבה, usually translated "abomination." This term is used to signal that something is somehow strange, alien, or unfamiliar, relative to the perspective of the speaker (Gerstenberger 2004, 1431; cf. L'Hour 1964, 503; Crouch 2015). This aspect is overt in Deuteronomic prohibitions that use it regarding the use of images of non-Israelite gods (7:25–26); divinatory practices involving children (12:31; cf. 18:10); a variety of technical divinatory practices (18:9–12); and the worship of deities other than YHWH (13:15, 17:4; cf. 27:15, 32:16).[9] A number of other passages describe a given practice as תועבה, suggesting that they, too, reflect similar concerns about Israelite distinctiveness. These include legislation regarding voluntary offerings (23:19) and transvestitism (22:5), sacrificial offerings (17:1), dishonest weights (25:13–16), and dietary prescriptions (14:3, 21).

The homogenization of Israelite culture through the elimination of diverse subcultures, and specifically through the differentiation of Israelites from non-Israelites, is a major feature of the Deuteronomic identity project. Exclusive Yahwism differentiates Israelites by virtue of the identity of their particular deity as well as by the distinctiveness of worshipping a single deity. This is supported through the physical congregation of Israelites at a single cult site, promoting regular interaction among group members and reinforcing common beliefs and values. A shared story of Israel's origins in an exodus from Egypt unites the group around a shared past. Ritual practices, including the particularities of cultic officials, divinatory experts, and permissible offerings, contribute to Israelite differentiation. Collectively, these features of Israelite identity go some way toward achieving the Deuteronomic identity project.

AVOIDING OUTSIDERS

The Deuteronomic project also seeks to protect Israelite identity by isolating Israelites from non-Israelites wherever possible. In some instances, these protective efforts overlap with the definitional legislation—Deut. 13:2–19, for example, underscores the importance of exclusive Yahwism in conjunction with efforts to physically eliminate potential threats to it. A number of passages, however, are focused simply on minimizing interaction between Israelites and non-Israelites, as a means of minimizing Israelite exposure to the non-Israelite practices. These texts discourage social interaction outside the group and encourage social interaction inside it, creating a self-perpetuating endoculture in which "primary relations . . . are governed by [the group's] specific values, norms, and beliefs" (Cohen 1969, 203). Kinship language is prominent in these passages: these "[e]xploit the strong sentiments and emotions that are associated with primary relationship between members and the elementary family" to focus Israelite attention safely inward, away from external dangers (Cohen 1969, 208–209; cf. Jones 1997, 84, with further references).[10]

Prohibiting Intermarriage

Perhaps the single foremost threat to Israelite identity is the possibility of its dissolution through intermarriage with non-Israelites.[11] Endogamy is correspondingly prioritized, in keeping with identity phenomena observed in other times and places: marriage within a group is widely recognized as a means of reinforcing a mythology of common genetic origins and enforcing cultural commonality (Cohen 1969, 203; Southwood 2012, 62, 67).[12]

Deuteronomy 7:1–4a focuses on intermarriage with the existing inhabitants of the land and makes clear that the danger of such unions is the intimate contact with persons outside the Yahwistic Israelite community that they entail—specifically, the risk that Israelites will be exposed through marriage to non-Israelite, non-Yahwistic practices. The text accordingly adjures Israelites to shun contact, especially intimate contact, with the non-Israelite inhabitants of the land. Notably, the text's focus on cultural distinctiveness belies the ostensibly genetic orientation of the endogamy principle itself.

Differentiating Kingship

The Deuteronomic material also discourages interaction between Israelites and non-Israelites more generally. This takes several forms, including the isolation of the Israelite royal figurehead. The strict limitations on the powers of the Israelite king (17:14–20) have puzzled commentators but reflect Deuteronomic identity concerns arising from the social, political, and economic context of the long seventh century. The focus is on the king's high-risk position as a nexus of Israelite interaction with non-Israelites. Indeed, his very existence is confusable with non-Israelite practice: rhetorically, at least, the Israelite king exists because the people have said "Let me set over myself a king, *like all the nations which surround me*" (17:14 [emphasis added]). Given that a king is nevertheless apparently unavoidable, the text legislates his behavior in a way that secures Israel's insularity and makes the role fundamentally different from its non-Israelite analogues. Most prominently, Israel's king must be chosen by YHWH, Israel's deity (17:15a); he must also be an Israelite (17:15b). The bans on acquisition of horses (17:16a) and numerous wives (17:17) are designed to protect the Israelites' distinctive identity through isolationism. This king does not engage in international political alliances, does not amass a powerful army or an extensive harem, and does not enrich the royal coffers or himself. He is thus unlike any other king known from the ancient Near East: "Though a king might make Israel 'like all the nations' (*kĕkol-haggōyīm*; v. 14), the nature of the kingship would distinguish Israel, in ideal terms, from those other groups" (Mullen 1993, 74; see also discussion in Barrett 2009, 210–17). Although the people wished to be like the nations in having a king, the Deuteronomic law effectively subverts these intentions by delineating a royal role that sets Israel's ruler apart.

Eliminating or Excluding Non-Israelites

Also in an isolationist vein is the elimination of non-Israelites from the territory claimed for Israelite habitation (20:10–18). The identification of the danger in terms of Israel's predecessors in the land (20:17) and in the language of תועבות (20:18) make the identity concerns of this violence explicit. The differentiation between "the cities which are very distant from you" and those which are "here among the cities of these nations" (20:15) also signals that the issue is specifically with the non-Israelites present in the land (not foreigners in general), whose physical proximity constitutes an immediate risk of interaction and, thereby, for the dissolution of Israelite identity.

Less lethal Deuteronomic efforts to defend Israel's cultural borders include the explicit exclusion of various categories of non-Israelites from the Israelite community. These include overtly ethnically based exclusions, as in the exclusions of the Ammonite and Moabite (23:4) and probably in the case of persons of mixed Israelite and non-Israelite heritage (23:3), as well as more general exclusions, as in the case of the eunuch (23:2). Though sometimes opaque, the intention in each of these cases appears to be the minimization or elimination of Israelites' social interactions with non-Israelites.

Disadvantaging Foreigners

The principal means by which the Deuteronomic material distinguishes between Israelites and genuine foreigners—non-Israelite persons originating outside the land, rather than those found within it—is by taking advantage of the economic circumstances in which most foreigners are encountered. Three cases establish distinct protocols for dealing with foreigners: a law dealing with the disposal of carrion (14:21a), a law instructing the remission of Israelite debts (15:1-3), and a law concerning lending at interest (23:20-21). Notably, these texts take an essentially neutral attitude regarding the foreigner: though they consistently favor Israelites, they do so by treating the Israelite rather than the foreigner extraordinarily. Thus, the sale of meat to foreigners (14:21a) is only notable in the context of the injunction against such a sale to a fellow Israelite (or its gift to those in need). The charging of interest (23:20-21) is remarkable only insofar as it is a practice not permitted within Israel. The immutability of debt contracts (15:2-3) is likewise entirely mundane; contracts were assumed to be so, barring a change in rulership and a royal declaration of debt remission. Each of these laws, in other words, is in keeping with normal ancient Near Eastern practice—at least as far as the foreigner is concerned. They are only unusual with regard to the extraordinary treatment they instruct with regard to Israelites.[13]

Exceptions

Although one might expect an absolute Deuteronomic rejection of all non-Israelites' interaction with Israelites, there are some exceptions, collectively facilitated by the Deuteronomic conception of Israelite identity as ultimately achieved rather than simply ascribed. The case of the war captive (21:10-14) is the ultimate example: the passage reiterates that, though theoretically ascribed through birth into the Israelite community, Israelite identity may nevertheless be achieved by individuals to whom the status was not automatically accorded at birth. This conception of Israelite identity is apparent also in passages that present "Israelite-ness" as something that may be lost as a result of failure to act like an Israelite (e.g., 13:2-19). In the case of the war captive, however, it may be gained through positive action.[14] As anthropologists note, ethnic "[i]dentities are ambiguous, and . . . this ambiguity is connected with a negotiable history and a negotiable cultural content" (Eriksen 1993, 73).[15]

The case of the admission of the Edomite to the community (23:8-9), in its turn, reflects the paradoxical potential of a perceived genetic relationship with Israel. The use of familial language draws on a rhetoric of common ancestry, which is typical of articulations of ethnic unity and is in keeping with the rationale used when justifying laws that differentiate between Israelites and non-Israelites (on this, see Cohen 1969, 202; Jones 1997, 84; Keyes 1981, 5-7). Such language appears especially in cases that might be perceived as particularly difficult to implement.

Of all Israelite interactions with non-Israelites, the case of the גר—traditionally "sojourner," more recently "resident alien" or "migrant"—is the least straightforward. The identity of persons named with this term in Deuteronomy has been the source of significant contention—in part because of the apparent inconsistency of a Deuteronomic agenda focused on defining and protecting Israelite identity and a Deuteronomic law code that allows a non-Israelite regular, albeit limited, access to the Israelite community.

The reason for this incongruity is that while Israelite identity is a major Deuteronomic concern, it is not the only one. The Deuteronomic material is also notably attentive to the needs of socially and economically marginal persons—and it is the classification of the גר in this category that, despite his non-Israelite status, complicates the otherwise straightforward rejection and avoidance of non-Israelites. Caught awkwardly between the desire to minimize Israelites' social interaction with outsiders and an interest in protecting marginalized persons, the liminal location of the גר is carefully delineated: he is provided with specific economic rights that must be protected by the Israelite community, even as he is not included as a member of that community. Thus, the גר is included in festivals celebrating agricultural success (16:9–15) but excluded from the celebration of Passover, which is focused on the origins of Israel in the exodus event (16:1–8).

The toleration of the non-Israelite גר on the periphery of Israelite existence is a testament to the perceived strength of Deuteronomic Israelite identity.[16] Throughout the rest of the Deuteronomic text, Israelite identity is decisively formulated, enacted, and protected using a diverse arsenal of identity formation strategies. Foremost among the distinctively Israelite practices advocated by the Deuteronomic material is the establishment of an exclusively Yahwistic religious framework, with Israel defined in terms of an exclusive relationship with a single deity. The differentiation of Israelites from non-Israelites by virtue of their exclusive identification with YHWH is further supported by the many ways in which the Deuteronomic text works to differentiate Israelite practices, whether by reorganising the hierarchy of divinatory techniques or by the modification or elimination of culturally ambiguous officials and practices. Expressions of Israelite kinship are prominent, especially in efforts to motivate difficult legislation, as well as in laws dealing with Israel's (purported) genetic cohesion, including those promoting endogamy and those excluding the Ammonite and the Moabite. References to Israel's origins in Egypt make a claim to Israel's genetic and social cohesion through appeal to a shared Israelite past. Other mechanisms of the Deuteronomic identity project include spatial proximity, achieved especially through centralization, and efforts to isolate Israelites from non-Israelites—via endogamy, limitations on the Israelite king, refusals to incorporate non-Israelites into the community, and differential treatment between Israelites and non-Israelites.

Israel beyond the Land

The material that deals with Israelite identity in the Deuteronomic core is mostly devoid of interest in people or political apparatuses outside the immediate land in which Israel resides. The true foreigner appears only a few times, and where he does he is presumed to be a temporary visitor. This essentially parochial perspective was profoundly altered by Israelite experience in the sixth century, when the kingdom of Judah was destroyed and its literate elites were displaced to Babylonia and elsewhere. A much wider, post-disaster perspective on Israelite identity is assumed by the Deuteronomistic material incorporated in this period, mostly at the beginning and the end of the book.

This is most immediately apparent in the much greater level of attention paid in the Deuteronomistic material to actual outsiders. Non-Israelites are mentioned on nearly fifty occasions, and nearly two thirds of these refer overtly to a wider global population. It is "the peoples under all the heavens" who will fear Israel in Deut. 2:25 and a "distant nation, from the end of the earth" whom YHWH employs to exact punishment on Israel (28:49); thereafter, it is "among all the peoples from the end of the earth to the end of earth" that Israel will be scattered (28:64, cf. 4:27). It is among the nations that Israel has been banished (30:1) and from them that YHWH will ultimately gather Israel up (30:3).

This wider perspective is also reflected in Deuteronomistic injunctions about Israelite behavior. The rationale given for keeping the commandments, for example, concerns Israel's status in the eyes of outsiders: "You must observe [these statutes and ordinances] diligently, for this will show your wisdom and discernment to the peoples, who, when they hear all these statutes, will say, 'Surely this great nation is a wise and discerning people!'" (4:6). Unlike the Deuteronomic texts, which reflect an internal dialogue within the community about its requirements for membership, the Deuteronomistic material introduces a strong outward-facing element: it matters not only that the Israelites can identify their fellow Israelites but that non-Israelites are able to do so as well.

The new, Deuteronomistic introduction in Deut. 1–3 articulates Israel's identity with reference to this global context. Describing Israel's wanderings in the wilderness, these rescript Deuteronomic concerns about contact with non-Israelites for Israelites who are now outside the land. Thus, when the Israelites engage Sihon of Heshbon (2:24–36), he and his people are annihilated in terms echoing the war laws of Deut. 20:10–16. But the account deviates from the Deuteronomic legislation, which instructs complete destruction only in the case of cities that are "near to you"—that is, cities in the land. When it comes to cities that are "far from you"—cities outside the land—the Deuteronomic law is more lenient. When Deut. 2–3 adopts the harsher policy, despite referring to an encounter that occurs outside the land, it is applying the logic of Deut. 20—that those who pose a threat to Israelite identity must be destroyed—in a global context. It is no longer only those who co-inhabit the land who threaten Israel but also those encountered in other lands.

The book's final chapters reflect a similar outlook when they address the temptation to worship gods other than YHWH. In the Deuteronomic texts, the non-Yahwistic deities that Israelites must shun are referred to as "other gods." In the Deuteronomistic material, they are more specifically "the gods of these nations" (29:17), "gods of foreignness" (31:16), "strange things" (31:16), or a "foreign god" (32:12). Such nomenclature suggests that the deities in mind in these passages are gods without a history in the land, unlike those that posed a problem in the Deuteronomic material. As Israelites move among the nations, they must fend off the temptation to worship the deities they encounter there.

The Deuteronomistic passages presuppose an underlying reality in which Israel is no longer present in its Levantine homeland. Non-Israelites are no longer the non-Yahwists living alongside the Israelites in the land, but "all the peoples" "under all the heavens", and the gods whom these non-Israelites worship are accordingly identified as "foreign." Though these later texts are congruent with the Deuteronomic desire to protect a distinctive Israelite identity, the global, diasporic horizon introduced by the Israelites' displacement in the sixth century is clear in their language and logic.

Notes

1. A more detailed discussion of these and related concerns may be found in Crouch (2014b).
2. See Cohen (1969, 204) on homogenization of culture and practice as characteristic of ethnic phenomena.
3. See the essays in Stavrakopoulou and Barton (2010).
4. Observing the role of violence in identity formation, Reeder (2012, 8) describes this as "constructive violence," that is, "violence that intends good."
5. For discussion of ascribed and achieved identity, see Peek (2005); Banks (1996, 117). On religious identity as achieved identity, see Hammond (1988); Warner (1993). Ascribed and achieved identities are rarely absolute, nor are they mutually incompatible; see Eriksen (1993, 57).
6. Israelite identity as both achieved and ascribed has also been noted by Nestor (2010, 200–201).
7. Conversely, the Deuteronomic material also conceives of the possibility of an ascribed non-Israelite achieving Israelite status (21:10–14; 23:8–9).
8. Stories about a people's shared origins is one of the most recognizable features of ethnic groups. Like shared ancestry, whether these shared historical origins are real or imagined is largely beside the point.
9. While some things described with this terminology can be persuasively argued to reflect practices known to have been engaged in by non-Israelites, indications that many practices thus stigmatized were also engaged in by "Israelites" suggests that the use of הבעות language is constructive as well as descriptive in intent: it is used to actively create an "Israelite" identity by advocating the abandonment of certain practices on the grounds that they are "non-Israelite." Compare the constructive capacity of ethnic identity formation as described by Cohen (1969) and Barth (1969); see also Peel (1989) and Keyes (1981), and Southwood's discussion of the language of "foreignness" in Ezra 9–10 (Southwood 2012).
10. Brother language is especially prominent in legislation that provides preferential treatment for Israelites and in cases that might be considered particularly difficult to implement, including the law of the king (17:14–17), the law of the prophet (18:15), the list of those who might be most persuasive in encouraging non-Yahwistic worship (13:7), the law of levirate marriage (25:5–8), and the explanation for the admission of the Edomite into the Israelite community (23:8–9), as well as the laws of debt remission (15:1–11) and manumission (15:12–18), the law concerning usury (23:20–21), and the law mandating the return of lost property (22:1–4). It often seems intended to evoke an extra degree of responsibility or to imply a certain standard of behavior, as in the laws concerning false witness (19:16–19), enslavement (24:7), military exemptions (20:5–9), and fraternal conflicts (25:1–3, 11–12). On the appeal to familial relations to evoke empathy in motivating ethical behaviors in Deuteronomy, see Kazen (2011, 102–109); on its use as affective language, see Williams (2009, 113–32); and Hamilton (1992, 34–40).
11. The imagined nature of genetic cohesion may be readily recognizable as myth but remains necessary: "there is nothing strange or modern in overlooking a gap between the real and the mythical. The latter establishes the necessary moral unity of a group.... The recognition of ancestry pretends, 'imagines' if you like, a genetic origin which may not be

12. Similarly: "Ethnicity defines the group within which one is normally expected to marry" (Hastings 1997, 168).
13. This neutrality contradicts the common claim that Deuteronomy is trying to undermine imperial authority: rather, the author has devised an ingenious means of achieving the Deuteronomic goal of Israelite differentiation without threatening the imperial status quo. See further Crouch (2014a).
14. Whether this was voluntary or forced is another matter; on the realities behind this law, see Washington (1997, 1998) and Thistlethwaite (1993, 64–65).
15. Similarly: "Ethnic identities are neither ascribed nor achieved: they are both" (Eriksen 1993, 57). Hastings (1997, 170), speaking more generally, notes that: "In adopting the ancestors and gods of one's hosts, one's conquerors or even those one has conquered, one is adopting their *mores* and a shared moral community which leaps beyond any genetic bond, without, however, disallowing the latter's symbolic meaning."
16. Perhaps even its perceived inevitability, to borrow a concept from Bourdieu (1977); and Nestor (2010, esp. 216–36).

Bibliography

Banks, Marcus. *Ethnicity: Anthropological Constructions*. London: Routledge, 1996.
Barrett, Robert. *Disloyalty and Destruction: Religion and Politics in Deuteronomy and the Modern World*. LHBOTS 511. London: T&T Clark, 2009.
Barth, Fredrik. "Introduction." Pp. 9–38 in *Ethnic Groups and Boundaries: The Social Organization of Cultural Difference*. Edited by Fredrik Barth. London: George Allen & Unwin, 1969.
Bourdieu, Pierre. "The Economics of Linguistic Exchanges." *Social Science Information* 16 (1977): 645–68.
Cohen, Abner. *Custom and Politics in Urban Africa: A Study of Hausa Migrants in Yoruba Towns*. London: Routledge, 1969.
Crouch, C. L. *Israel and the Assyrians: Deuteronomy, the Succession Treaty of Esarhaddon, and the Nature of Subversion*. ANEM 8. Atlanta Ga.: Society of Biblical Literature, 2014a.
Crouch, C. L. *The Making of Israel: Cultural Diversity in the Southern Levant and the Formation of Ethnic Identity in Deuteronomy*. VT Sup 162. Leiden: Brill, 2014b.
Crouch, C. L. "What Makes a Thing Abominable? Observations on the Language of Boundaries and Identity Formation from a Social Scientific Perspective." *VT* 65 (2015): 516–41.
Eriksen, Thomas H. *Ethnicity and Nationalism: Anthropological Perspectives*. Anthropology, Culture and Society 1. London: Pluto, 1993.
Geertz, Clifford. *The Interpretation of Cultures: Selected Essays*. London: Fontanà, 1973.
Gerstenberger, Erhard. "בעת *t'b* pi. to abhor." Pp. 1428–31 in *Theological Lexicon of the Old Testament*. 3 vols. Edited by Ernst Jenni and Claus Westermann; translated by Mark E. Biddle. Peabody: Hendrickson, 2004.
Hamilton, Jeffries M. *Social Justice and Deuteronomy: The Case of Deuteronomy 15*. SBLDS 136. Atlanta: Scholars, 1992.
Hammond, Phillip E. "Religion and the Persistence of Identity." *Journal for the Scientific Study of Religion* 27 (1988): 1–11.

Hastings, Adrian. *The Construction of Nationhood: Ethnicity, Religion and Nationalism*. Cambridge: Cambridge University Press, 1997.

Jones, Siân. *The Archaeology of Ethnicity: Constructing Identities in the Past and Present*. London: Routledge, 1997.

Kazen, Thomas. *Emotions in Biblical Law: A Cognitive Science Approach to Some Moral and Ritual Issues in Pentateuchal Legal Collections*. Sheffield: Sheffield Phoenix, 2011.

Keyes, Charles F. "The Dialectics of Ethnic Change." Pp. 3–30 in *Ethnic Change*. Edited by Charles F. Keyes. London: University of Washington Press, 1981.

L'Hour, Jean, "Les interdits to'eba dans le Deutéronome." *RB* 71 (1964): 481–503.

Miller, Patrick D. *Deuteronomy*. IBC. Louisville: John Knox, 1990.

Mullen, E. Theodore Jr. *Narrative History and Ethnic Boundaries: The Deuteronomistic History and the Creation of Israelite National Identity*. SBLSymS. Atlanta: Scholars, 1993.

Nestor, Dermot A. *Cognitive Perspectives on Israelite Identity*. LHBOTS 519. London: T&T Clark, 2010.

Peek, Lori. "Becoming Muslim: The Development of a Religious Identity." *Sociology of Religion* 66 (2005): 215–42.

Peel, John D. Y. "The Cultural Work of Yoruba Ethnogenesis." Pp. 198–215 in *History and Ethnicity*. ASA Monographs 27. Edited by Elizabeth Tonkin, Maryon McDonald, and Malcolm Chapman. London: Routledge, 1989.

Reeder, Caryn A. *The Enemy in the Household: Family Violence in Deuteronomy and Beyond*. Grand Rapids: Baker, 2012.

Schmid, Konrad. *Genesis and the Moses Story: Israel's Dual Origins in the Hebrew Bible*. Translated by James Nogalski. Siphrut 3. Winona Lake: Eisenbrauns, 2010.

Southwood, Katherine E. *Ethnicity and the Mixed Marriage Crisis in Ezra 9–10: An Anthropological Approach*. OTM. Oxford: Oxford University Press, 2012.

Stavrakopoulou, Francesca, and John Barton, eds. *Religious Diversity in Ancient Israel and Judah*. London: T&T Clark, 2010.

Thistlethwaite, Susan B. "'You May Enjoy the Spoils of Your Enemies': Rape as Biblical Metaphor for War." *Semeia* 61 (1993): 59–75.

Warner, R. Stephen. "Work in Progress Toward a New Paradigm for the Sociological Study of Religion in the United States." *American Journal of Sociology* 98 (1993): 1044–93.

Washington, Harold C. "'Lest He Die in the Battle and Another Man Take Her': Violence and the Construction of Gender in the Laws of Deuteronomy 20–22." Pp. 185–213 in *Gender and Law in the Hebrew Bible and the Ancient Near East*. Edited by Victor H. Matthews, Bernard M. Levinson, and Tikva Frymer-Kensky. London: T&T Clark, 1998.

Washington, Harold C. "Violence and the Construction of Gender in the Hebrew Bible: A New Historicist Approach." *BibInt* 5 (1997): 324–63.

Williams, Michael J. "Taking Interest in Taking Interest." Pp. 113–32 in *Mishneh Todah: Studies in Deuteronomy and Its Cultural Environment in Honor of Jeffrey H. Tigay*. Edited by Nili S. Fox, David A. Glatt-Gilad, and Michael J. Williams. Winona Lake: Eisenbrauns, 2009.

CHAPTER 13

WOMEN IN DEUTERONOMY

SANDRA JACOBS

What Is the Background?

THE demand for absolute loyalty, together with Deuteronomy's monotheistic imperatives, leaves little room for distinctions of gender in its narration. On leaving the plains of Moab, not only will the promised land yield milk and honey but the trappings of statehood will materialize—with judges and courts, alongside a native-born king, dotted firmly on the imagined horizon. Recasting the Israelites in an urban environment, held in check by a "rhetoric of social solidarity," the vision of shared kinship is developed through the language of brotherhood (Morrow 2017, 246–247). Accordingly, the absence of any named women, other than the cursory reference to Miriam is hardly surprising (Deut 24:8–9). This, albeit brief, recollection of Miriam's punishment is key to Deuteronomy's view of women, whose very presence constituted a potentially destructive threat. While Israel's priests converged on "dirt as matter out of place" (Douglas 2006, 44), Deuteronomy addressed the presence of women similarly as "matter out of place." As such, its legislation maximized the patriarch's permitted sexual relationships, without compromising his membership in "the congregation of the Lord" or his cult.[1] This chapter clarifies how this was achieved, making no presumption about the historicity or statutory force of its laws.

Female Status and the Absence of Individual Rights

In ancient Near Eastern societies, women appear only in relation to their fathers, masters, husbands, brothers, or uncles, rather than as autonomous individuals. As subject to authority of the male head of household, a daughter, and even a wife, served as a disposable asset, who could be given or taken in marriage, or even forced into prostitution (Jacobs 2018, 337–355). In times of dire need, the sale of any family member as a slave could be realized, where the father's house (Hebrew, *beit 'av*, and Akkadian *bit abi*) constituted a recognized social and legal entity. Hence widows, orphans, and aliens—essentially those devoid of membership of a household—were commonly singled out for protection from injustice. This status quo was compounded by the absence of what we today would describe as "human rights," as Robert Kawashima (2011, 6–7) explains:

> Not even the patriarch should be thought of as an autonomous individual. He may have represented the household as its head, but his legal status was still a function of his position relative to this corporate legal entity. In fact, thanks to the principle of patrilineal succession, the household itself constituted but a moment in the larger life of the "lineage" (*toledot*), whence the importance of the family estate or patrimony—"inheritance, possession" (*yerushah, nahalah*) or "holding" (*'ah. uzzah*)—the continuous possession of which linked generation to generation. What we would now call "private property" was not fully at the patriarch's disposal, since his house was beholden both to its past and future: Witness the restrictions placed upon the selling of family property in Leviticus 25.22. Ultimately, the very nation of Israel was an extension of these tribal realities.

This background heavily informs the Pentateuchal laws, especially those geared to protecting the patriarch's property, where "only the household males in general and the patriarch in particular effectively attained full legal status—only they, technically speaking, could be victims" (Kawashima 2011, 9). Women could thus only appear as plaintiffs in the absence of a male head of household, either if widowed (2 Sam 14:1–20) or fatherless and of marriageable age like Mahlah, Noah, Hoglah, Milcah, and Tirzah (Num 27:1–11). By marrying their first cousins, they ensured that their father's land remained within his tribal and familial estate (Num 36:10–12). Their petition to Moses was documented not out of concern for their plight, but because it illustrated the optimum outcome for patrimonial succession, in the absence of direct male heirs. Their status, as "eternal minors," left them entirely at the whim of male power and "at times treated like exchangeable objects, especially in the marital context" (Démaire Lafont 2011, 110).

While protection of the patriarch's land was a priority, controlling sexual access to the female body was as crucial to guarantee paternity and safeguard the continuity of male hereditary succession. Here, Deuteronomy's "ethos of encroachment" meant that "the most profound danger to the social order of D is posed by wanton individuals/groups who reside in the community boundaries but do not conform to its social and cosmic restraints" (Stulman 1990, 631). It is the fear of this transgression which informs Deuteronomy's family laws, as Adele Berlin (2009, 112) explains:

> when we look at the outcomes for a woman who has had sex outside of marriage, we find an amazing polarization. Either the woman is married as quickly as possible (the unbetrothed woman and the betrothed victim of forced sex = non-consensual sex), or she is put to death (the promiscuous young woman, the betrothed woman who had consensual sex, and the adulterous married woman = consensual sex). There is no permanent place in Deuteronomy's world for sexually experienced, never-married women, be they one-time victims of premarital sex or professional prostitutes, for this is an "unstable" status for women, inconsistent with Deuteronomy's ideals.

These dangers did not, however, warrant any restraint on the part of the Israelite male, but rather served to "institute and regulate rape so that men's proprietary sexual access to women is compromised as little as possible. The laws do not interdict sexual violence; rather they stipulate the terms under which a man may commit rape, provided he pays reparation to the offended male party" (Washington 1998, 211). This discussion will focus on the free-born Israelite woman, rather than the female slave—a subject which merits greater attention than is available here.

WHAT IS THE STATUS OF THE CONVERSATION?

Until the late 1980s the subject of women in Deuteronomy was largely ignored, except by scholars penning a running commentary. Gordon McConville's (1984) monograph *Law and Theology in Deuteronomy* is typical, dealing with (1) The Theology of Deuteronomy, (2) The Altar-Law and Centralization of the Cult, (3) The Sacrifices, (4) The Tithe, (5) The Law of Firstlings, (6) The Feasts, and (7) The Priests and Levites. Other than Elizabeth MacDonald's (1931) *The Position of Women as Reflected in Semitic Codes of Law* and Grace Emmerson's (1989) essay "Women in Ancient Israel," it is no surprise that "feminist exegetes took their time in addressing the books of Exodus, Leviticus, Numbers, and Deuteronomy" (Freedman 2017, 62).

This changed dramatically, initially upon the publication of Denise Carmody's valuable overview *Biblical Woman: Contemporary Reflections on Scriptural Texts* (1992), which was followed in quick succession by Carolyn Pressler's trail-blazing monograph *The View of Women Found in Deuteronomic Family Laws* (1993). Here Pressler explained that the dependence and subordination of women within male-led households was essential to preserve the order, integrity, and continuity of the family unit. Although Deuteronomy depicts a hierarchical and patrilineal family structure, whose interests benefit exclusively adult male heads, it still provides a framework protecting for dependent family members, endowing them with a degree of economic security and social legitimacy. At the same time, Athalya Brenner launched her ground-breaking series, *A Feminist Companion to the Bible* (Leiden and Sheffield 1993–2000), with editions on Genesis, Ruth, Song of Songs, and Judges appearing in its first year. The series ran into a second edition and shifted gears to refocus on the predominant first-world orientation of scholarship, with the *Texts@Contexts* series, appearing in 2010. Its *Exodus and Deuteronomy: Texts@Contexts* volume included studies on the female captive (Jacobs 2012, 237–257) and the Decalogue (Brenner 2012, 197–204). Additionally, the essays of J. Cheryl Exum (1995, 248–271) and Alice Bach (1999, xiii–xxvi) provided significant methodological refinements to the study of gender in the Hebrew Bible.

These were soon followed by Harold Bennett's strident critique, *Injustice Made Legal: Deuteronomic Law and the Plight of Widows, Strangers and Orphans in Ancient Israel* (Bennett 2002). Claiming that Deuteronomic law constituted the ongoing denigration of underprivileged groups, suffering financially from the centralization of the sacrificial cult, Bennett asserted that Deuteronomy's agenda would enrich Priesthood and temple officials, through exploitation of the Israelite farming communities. Consequently privileged groups, including members of the Omride dynasty (associated with Baal worship), and a Yahweh-alone group (represented by prophets such as Elijah), displayed no real concern for alleviating the plight of the weak or vulnerable, outside of reinforcing their own powerbases. This afforded a more historically orientated reconstruction than Mark Sneed's earlier assessment: that the triadic concern for the widow, orphan, and stranger, "a seemingly iron-clad case of altruism" (Sneed 1999, 500), functioned as a rhetorical literary device which perpetuated the interests of the ruling elites.

Focusing on *Women, Ideology and Violence: Critical Theory and the Construction of Gender in the Book of the Covenant and the Deuteronomic Law*, Cheryl Anderson further concluded that "such violence is systematized and legitimated in ways that serve to maintain sexist (as well as racist and heterosexual) privilege" (Anderson 2004, 99). Shortly after, Hilary Lipka extended the discussion by exploring the trespass of sexual boundaries, in *Sexual Transgression in the Hebrew Bible* (2006). Lipka noted that while women had no legal autonomy over their own bodies, this did not automatically render them powerless, where limited accounts of female autonomy are attested. Her supplementary "Biblical Lexicon of Sexual Transgressions" adds substantially to Sandie Gravett's (2004, 279–299) earlier synthesis.

Further strides were then taken by Deborah Ellens in *Women in the Sex Texts of Leviticus and Deuteronomy: A Comparative Conceptual Analysis* (2008). Ellens evaluated the underlying construct of the Leviticus sex texts (LST)—which reveal an ontological focus, preoccupied by classifying infractions of the cultic sphere—in contrast to the Deuteronomy sex texts (DST), which represent women explicitly as property. Neither corpus provides protection to women from any predatory male guardians, including their owners, husbands, uncles, or brothers, where their sexual consent was a "non-issue" (Ellens 2008, 313). The enduring legacy of this study is twofold: First, where the account of women's marginalization, focalization, and objectification, is generating new exploration of female agency and personhood. Second, where discussions of "the *mix* of agencies and conscriptions that play out in the text" (Ellens 2008, 318), is informed by the late Judith Wegner's definitions of property and personhood. Wegner, like other Jewish women writing in the late 1980s and 1990s, received a consistently prejudicial and negative reception from her male peers, ill-disguised as veritable differences of opinion. While much of this has changed, unjustifiable criticism of Wegner's scholarship continues to appear (Jacobs 2020, 185–187).

In the following year, Cynthia Edenburg published her compelling treatment, "Ideology and Context of the Women's Sex Laws (Deut. 22:13–29)." By examining ancient Near Eastern legal parallels, Edenburg clarified how Deuteronomy's sequence afforded a definitive account of all potential sexual offences that could be incurred by a free-born Israelite women, and also how the "section as a whole was designed to convey signification beyond that of its constituent parts" (Edenburg 2009, 44–48). Additionally, she proposed that the integrity of the Deuteronomic social structure was dependent on women's exclusive fidelity to their male patrons, modeling the ideal of Israel's exclusive worship of her God (Edenburg 2009, 58).

Caryn Reeder's monograph, *The Enemy in the Household: Family Violence in Deuteronomy and Beyond*, then examined the reception of Deut 13.6–11, 21.18–21, 22.13–21 in 1 Maccabees, Sirach, Philo, Josephus, Mark, Matthew, 1 Corinthians, and early rabbinic sources. Reeder designated the assaults on women in these sources as acts of "constructive violence," whose goal was to preserve and protect the ethnic integrity of the Israelite community (Reeder 2012, 17–167). Not least importantly is Mercedes García Bachmann's indispensable study, *Women at Work in the Deuteronomistic History*, which affords a panoramic view of female roles beyond Deuteronomy's laws.

GENDER DIFFERENTIALS AND FEMALE EXCLUSION

While women are ethnically differentiated, either as Israelite or "foreign," Deuteronomy's directive "you shall not oppress"—so emphatic for protecting the stranger, orphan, and widow—did not extend to any daughter or wife. The physical assault of women was considered an infringement of male property rights, engendering shame and distress for the girl and her family (Jackson 2006, 382–383). This raises the inevitable question: "Are we, women, the addressees?" as Hagith Sivan, *Between Women, Man, and God: A New Interpretation of the Ten Commandments* (Sivan 2004, 220–229) and Athalya Brenner, "The Decalogue: Am I An Addressee?" both ask (Brenner 2012, 197–204).

At first glance, the language of the Ten Commandments suggests the affirmative, since this addresses all Israelites alike: male and female, young and old, freeborn or enslaved. In Hebrew, however, all second- and third-person pronouns are gendered masculine and feminine, as in "I am the Lord your God who brought you [masc. sing.] out of the land of Egypt, the house of bondage. You [masc. sing.] shall have no other gods beside me" (Deut 5:6–7), where the singular form is understood as collective reference to the entire people. This is evident from the instruction that "the seventh day is a sabbath of the Lord your God; you [masc. sing.] shall not do any work—you [masc. sing.], your son or your daughter, your male or female slave, your ox or your ass, or any of your cattle, or the stranger in your settlements, so that your male and female slave may rest as you do" (5:14). Here scholars concur that a wife is subsumed in the masculine singular "you," and that she, too, would be exempt from working on the Sabbath. However, by the tenth commandment the law seamlessly shifts to address the married Israelite male exclusively: "You [masc. sing.] shall not covet your neighbor's wife." This shift is consistent in both versions of the Decalogue, where the following variants are witnessed:

Exodus 20:14 [Eng. 20:17]	Deuteronomy 5:18 [Eng. 5:21]
You shall not covet	You shall not covet
your neighbor's house.	your neighbor's wife
You shall not covet	You shall not crave
your neighbor's wife,	your neighbor's house
	or his field,
or his manservant, or his maidservant,	or his male or female slave,
or his ox, or his ass	or his ox, or his ass,
or anything that is your neighbor's.	or anything that is your neighbor's.

Does this indicate that Deuteronomy elevates women as the most desirable object to covet (as Sivan 2004, 215)? Or is it simply that this is typical of a legal list of household possessions subject to sale or exchange, as William Moran asserts (Moran 1967, 552)? Understandably, Brenner acknowledges, "it is largely agreed that I am by proxy a sub-genre of the m/M 'you,' indirectly implicated albeit never explicitly addressed" (Brenner 2012, 203), and continues:

two decades ago readers seemed blissfully unaware that a "you (m)," not to mention other fine textual points . . . actually and decidedly excludes women from *Standing Again at Sinai* and from receiving the Commandments, thus from participating equally in the foundation myth of Torah reception. That there is a possibility of *Standing Again at Sinai,* according to the pioneer Judith Plaskow (1990) and her successors, is hardly a consolation for me—although I can empathize with the necessity to get there, even at this late stage.

(Brenner 2012, 199)

Such pragmatism is based on the criteria for "admission into the congregation of the Lord" (קהל יהוה, Deut 23:1–9), where Andrew Mayes (1981, 315) elucidates, "The Israel from which such people are excluded is called the "Assembly of the Lord" (קהל יהוה), a phrase older than Deuteronomy (Mic 2:5). It is clearly a cultic term; as a designation for all those eligible for membership it denotes the fully enfranchised male citizens, not only in cultic gatherings in the narrow sense, but also in the military levy." Admittedly this did not negate women's value entirely, since they were clearly required to hear the ceremonial recitation of Israel's covenant oath on two occasions: First, Deut 29:9–11 states: "You stand this day, all of you, before the Lord your God—your tribal heads, your elders and your officials, all the men of Israel, your children, your wives, even the stranger within your camp, from woodchopper to water drawer—to enter into the covenant of the Lord your God, which the Lord your God is concluding with you this day." Second, Deut 31:12 instructs: "Gather the people, the men, women, children, and the strangers in your communities—that they may hear and learn to revere the Lord your God and to observe every word of this teaching." Thus, women are invited to hear and learn Deuteronomy's covenant, in order to instill due reverence and obedience to its teachings. However, both invitations are extended to women at the same time as that of children and strangers—neither of whom were conventionally participants in the cult, let alone "fully enfranchised citizens" (Mayes 1981, 315). All three groups were either dependents or visiting guests, who could not be *ab initio* integral members of "the congregation of the Lord," and certainly no exegete has suggested that children and strangers attained equal status in the official cult or its assemblies, by virtue of their presence at these ceremonials. This is irrespective of the fact that young boys would later gain membership upon maturity.

The women's inclusion here was driven by the practical necessity: to ensure that they were informed of the binding nature of the covenant into which their fathers had entered, and that its instructions were to be obeyed and communicated to their children. This objective was, as Karin Finsterbuch maintains, of utmost importance for the transmission of "the Deuteronomic Torah (Deut 5–26; 28; 32) the foundation for the existence and the identity of the people" (Finsterbuch 2011, 430). It was motivated by the basic reality—that there would be no next generation without women's cooperation, and that the most effective transmission of Deuteronomy's teachings required the input of the children's mothers.

This reasoning is not negated by Amnon Shapira's "Woman's Equal Standing" claim (Shapira 2010, 7–42), which counts women as equal members in five out of the eight covenant ceremonials—twice in Deuteronomy (28–29, 31:11–12), once in Joshua (8:30–35), and at the two public readings of the Torah in Nehemiah (8:2–3; 10:1). Thus, he asserts, "we find women being positioned in the central junctions in the life of the people, enjoying equal status with men, by virtue of their being partners to the national covenant ceremonies" (Shapira 2010, 24). Yet being in close geographical proximity to an event does not automatically confer equality on everyone present at that time and place. And it is by no means evident that women had the same status as the men at the ceremony at Mount Ebal (Josh 8:30–35), even if they did get to hear Joshua's recitation of Moses's commands, where the NJPS (1999) translation of verse 8:35 provides: "There was not a word of all that Moses had commanded that Joshua failed to read in the presence of the entire assembly of Israel, including the women and children and the strangers who accompanied them." Unfortunately, however, this translation of והנשים to mean "including the women" is incorrect—since "including the women" would be written וגם הנשים in Hebrew, where it is accurately rendered "and the women":

There was not a word of all that Moses had commanded	לא היה דבר מכל אשר צוה משה
that Joshua failed to read	אשר לא קרא יהושע
in the presence of the entire assembly of Israel	נגד כל קהל ישראל
and the women	והנשים
and [the] children	והטף
and the stranger who accompanied them.	והגר ההלך בקרבם

Once correctly translated, neither women, children, nor strangers, were equal members of the designated "assembly of Israel." Moreover, the alleged female equity in five ratification ceremonies drops significantly down from five to two (out of eight).

Shapira's accompanying account of the participation of women in the construction of the wilderness tabernacle is also questionable: that women and their donations could be utilized for the benefit of the cult did not render them equal "in the receiving of the Torah and in participation in all public covenantal convocations in the Bible" (Shapira 2010, 25). The historical (albeit considerably later) evidence of wealthy women donors to the early synagogues did not confer the benefits of equal membership upon them, where they would not have been accepted in an all-male quorum for public prayer (Brooten 1982, 64–68 and 139–147). Even by Shapira's own reckoning, women were still excluded from the covenant at Sinai (Exod 19), at the assembly in Shechem (Josh 4:20–24), and in the reading of the newly found Torah scroll (2 Kgs 23). Admittedly this is less blatant than women's relegation in priestly law, in which the requirement of circumcision was explicit. As Isaac Sassoon explains, "in choosing as its rite of entry into the covenant an exclusively male rite, the Priestly Torah intended the covenant itself for men only" (Sassoon 2011, 149).

Similarly, the opportunity for women to donate burnt offerings (12:14), harvest tithes (14:22), present voluntary offerings (16:10), gift first fruits (26:20), and consecrate firstborn males (15:19) did not confer equal status in the cult. Such activities are frequently informed by the account of Hannah (1 Sam 1: 4–28), who was admitted into the House of the Lord to pray and dedicated her firstborn to the temple (Meyers 1994, 93–104). Yet access to the Temple to pray, gift, and donate valuables is not the same as being an integral member of its assembly. What is often forgotten is that Hannah's bequest was only possible because her husband, Elkanah, had at least one son, and thus a legitimate male heir from his other wife, Penina. Hannah would not necessarily have been able to gift her firstborn son (Samuel) to the temple, if this was not the case. Nor is it correct to assume, as Georg Braulik has argued, "if there was no father of the house in a family, then it stands to reason that functions during the sacrifice were taken over by the mother of the family" (Braulik 1999, 922) since this is never allowed in the biblical texts, and it takes no account of the defiling effects of female menstrual impurity, which would have contaminated the sacrifice through the mother's touch.

Even more problematic is the equation of "[the] communion of the meal and the rights enjoyed by women" (Braulik 1999, 934–938). Apart from the absence of actual "rights," women's participation in the sacrificial meal was as much to prepare, cook, and clean up after the men. Here, Nancy Jay's study, "Sacrifice as a Remedy for Being Born Female," provides a more critical account of the development of blood sacrificial religions, in which male lineages appear purged entirely of women (Jay 1985, 291). As was the case with patrilineal ancestor cults, male communities were ordered hierarchically and controlled the killing, distribution, and consumption of the sacrificial animal. Concomitantly, while access to childbearing women (or "reproductive resources") was heavily regulated (Jay 1985, 290), there is no evidence that a woman's consumption of the festive meal "elevates her to the level of her husband as having equal rights within the cult" (Braulik 1999, 937).

In this context it is also crucial to differentiate domestic female participation in the patriarchal household from their agency in the public cult, where Nicole Ruane further notes: "That women never have these prerogatives is a clear indication of their inferior status in the official sacrificial cult(s), showing that they are removed from the highest levels of official sanctity and ritual power and authority. Moreover, the exclusion of women from the priesthood enables the patrilineal group to have exclusive control of the donations made by the congregation" (Ruane 2013, 23). As willing donors to the cult, it is also unclear whether women were "frequently led to prostitute themselves in order to fulfil their vows," as Karel van der Toorn (1989, 193) has suggested (see also Bird 2019). Consequently the invitation to women to hear the public recitation of the law (Deut 29:9–11 and 31:12) did not indicate equal status with men but was due to the recognition of their irreplaceable roles in bearing the future generation of Israelites, and ensuring that its laws and theology were inculcated effectively to them. This is demonstrated by Deuteronomy's representation of women in the following categories, which can be checked in this essay's accompanying appendices:

(a) As passive subjects, whose positions and interests are subordinate to their husbands, fathers, or head of household.
(b) Equal to men in law and narrative.
(c) As recipients of punishments and curses, including those activated by the failure to observe the covenant, and which have been described as "equal opportunity" curses (Pressler 2012, 101).
(d) The two rare occasions in which concern for women is explicit.

In the first (a) category, women appear as passive subjects, where the laws "primarily serve male interests by undergirding patriarchal structures, while offering limited protection to family members" (Pressler 2012, 93). This is apparent in the prohibition of the restoration of marriage (24:1–4), which provided the unconditional and unilateral right for an Israelite man to divorce his wife, and where "the clear implication of the law is that the woman is disposable" (Carmody 1992, 23). In addition, the "levir's duty" (25:5) has little to do with the ongoing welfare of the widow, but rather to establish the deceased's "house," or lineage (25:9), and ensure that his landholdings remained in the locus of his ancestral tribe. Moreover, in those few instances where women are depicted as active participants

(22:22, 22:28; 25:11–12), their involvement was limited to actions that benefitted their husband, father, or preferred male exclusively—as confirmed by the summary of these laws in the accompanying appendices.

In the second (b) category the representation of women equally alongside males occurs primarily in a negative capacity, either to confirm their identical punishment or indicate their immanent death, with the exceptions of Deut 29:11 and 31:12, as noted. Nor is it possible to suggest any humanitarian concern for women in the punishments and curses from the third (c) category where equality for women was attested only to inform their potential future punishment and death, on a par with identical warnings to adult Israelite males. In the fourth (d) category Deut 3:18–19 affirms no more than the prevalent norm that women (like children and livestock) did not go to war. Equally, the exemption of a husband from military service in the first year of his marriage, on account of the "happiness" of his wife (24:5), affords a superficial concern for her, at best. Here the desire to provide optimal conditions for the newly wed bride to conceive would have been paramount, particularly if her husband could soon be facing death on the battlefield. Such fears are effectively reinforced by the conditional curse in which a groom who had paid a bride-price for his wife would live to see another man "enjoy her" (Deut 28:30; although see also 20:7).

This analysis confirms, first, that women in Deuteronomy's laws did not have autonomy over their bodies, where they appear primarily as passive objects, subject to the controls of their father, husband, or master, and where their physical assault was deemed an infringement of male property rights. Second, it confirms that a woman's intrinsic worth was thus limited to her reproductive capacity, sexual availability, and childrearing skills. Third and finally, it confirms that by being identified as a group apart—alongside children and strangers when Deuteronomy's laws were disseminated in public—women were never equal or integral members of "the congregation of the Lord," ranking below men in the public and cultic sphere. Accordingly, Judith Hauptman asks of the early rabbinic sages:

> Is there any evidence that they are uncomfortable with their patriarchal privilege? My answer stated succinctly, is that the rabbis upheld patriarchy as the preordained mode of social organization, as dictated by the Torah. They thus perpetuated women's second-class, subordinate status. They neither achieved equality for women nor even sought it. But of critical importance, they began to introduce numerous, significant, and occasionally bold corrective measures to ameliorate the lot of women. In some cases, they eliminated abusive behaviors that had developed over time. In others, they broke new ground, granting women benefits they never had before, even at men's expense.
>
> (Hauptman 1998, 4)

What Is Trending in the Conversation?

Scholarship on women in Deuteronomy is evolving in various directions, where issues of intersectionality are gaining traction. Dora Mbuwayesango's essay "Canaanite Women and Israelite Women in Deuteronomy: The Intersection of Sexism and Imperialism" examines how the Bible creates and negotiates hybrids—and often conflicting—identities (2009, 45–57). Her study highlights points of rupture within imperializing texts, which are particularly relevant to constructions of masculine agency in the Second Temple period.

With reference to Deuteronomy's laws, to what extent did its scribes select the harshest punishments from the known legal repertoire to impose on women? This is pertinent to Deuteronomy's account of the attractive female captive, where the instruction to "bring her into your house and she shall trim her hair, pare her nails and discard her captive's garb," before lamenting her loss of parents (Deut 21:12–13), appears more in keeping with Spartan marriage ritual (as Jacobs 2012, 251–256). Several exegetes maintain that this constitutes "a fundamental improvement of the status of women" (Otto 1998, 133), presumably because the girl may not be sold for profit if her captor tired of her but must be freely released. In the same vein, Alexander Rofé claims, "this humane ruling reflects a universal concern with limiting the soldiers' unbridled brutality and demonstrates consideration for the feeling of captives" (Rofé 1996, 137). Yet would the status of a homeless (and probably orphaned) female be significantly "improved" had she remained as a female slave? And how exactly could this girl (or woman) provide for herself, once emancipated, even if she had not fallen pregnant by her captor? Nor does this acceptance of wartime rape sit well with Deuteronomy's imperatives to desist from carrying out the surrounding (i.e., non-Israelite) abominations.

Likewise, no concern was extended to a wife who, when defending her husband in a public brawl, had injured the genitals of his opponent. In this case the injunction "you shall cut off her hand, show no pity" (25:12) functioned as "a punishment of the offending organ" (Shemesh 2005, 352), namely that the limb which carried out the crime was intended to be correspondingly injured. Scholarly interpretations of this punishment as a symbolic form of female circumcision, or vaginal shaving, remain unsupported—where both Middle Assyrian Law (MAL A8) and Nuzi case law provide stronger analogues (Jacobs 2010, 271–278). Fresh examination of Deuteronomy's injunction to "show no pity" (25:12) is also needed in relation to the Akkadian imperative, *la uballuṭuši* "they shall not spare her life," from the Middle Assyrian Palace Decrees, which has been associated only with the punishment of blasphemers (Lev 24:10–23; Paul 1990, 346–350), to date.

To what extent did Deuteronomy's attitude inform the denigration of women in later sources (e.g., "I find woman more bitter than death"; Eccl 7:18), alongside the imagined female evils present in Proverbs (2:13, 6:20, 7:24, 26, 21:9, 21:19. 23:27–28, 27:15, 30:15, 31:20, and 31:23)? This disdain, which fueled the intense misogyny in Jewish writings from Ben Sira to the New Testament, evokes the image of women in Hellenistic societies, where the production of dutiful and obedient wives submissive to their husbands was promoted, in stark contrast to dangerous and transgressive females, including wild Bacchics and witches (Goff 2004; see also Schmitz 2020, 411–426). This shared mindset remains insufficiently acknowledged, despite Anselm Hagedorn's (2004) astute insights in *Between Moses and Plato: Individual and Society in Deuteronomy and Ancient Greek Law*.

Deuteronomy's stance, furthermore, perpetuated the elimination of women's voices as Tal Ilan's impressive study, *Silencing the Queen: The Literary Histories of Shelamzion and Other Jewish Women* (2006), demonstrates. Its alignment with the circulation of highly fictionalized dramas is particularly striking, where Ruth, Esther, Susannah, and Judith celebrated stereotypically dutiful (but sexually desirable) heroines, whose actions reinforced national aspirations, often via an approved male: Ruth, as the ancestress of David, with the intervention of Boaz, Esther as the savior of her people at the instigation of Mordechai, Susannah as the conduit for illuminating Daniel's superior wisdom, albeit where Judith's decapitation of Holofernes was undertaken at her own initiative.

For Deuteronomy, with its obsessive preoccupation on the binding nature of the covenant, there was little choice but to acknowledge the presence of women to ensure the continuity of the nation and disseminate its message effectively to the next generation. Far more than "the priority of men and the irrelevance of women" (Brueggemann 2001, 243) was the need to control sexual access to, and the actions of, the female body in the future promised land. And in answer to the question, "Are Women Addressees" in Deuteronomy? Only inasmuch as they support and inculcate its message to their children—but never as members of the "congregation of the Lord" in their own right.

APPENDICES

(a) Women Subordinate to Male Privilege

5:18	Prohibition of coveting a neighbor's wife.
17:17	Prohibition of a king taking excessive wives.
20:7	"Is there anyone who has paid the bride-price for a wife, but who has not yet married her? Let him go back to his home, lest he die in battle and another marry her."
20:14	Women, children, and livestock to be enjoyed as enemy spoils.
21:11–14	Prohibition of the sale of a female captive as a slave.
21:15–17	The protection of a firstborn son's inheritance, where a preferred wife had born a son.
22:13–21	Circumstances in which a man, who takes aversion to his bride, can slander her.
	Conditions for sexual intercourse with a betrothed virgin:
22:23–24	(a) who fails to cry out when raped in a town.
22:25–27	(b) who cries for help when raped in open country.
22:28	(c) who has consensual sexual relations.
23:1	The prohibition of marriage and/or sexual relations with a father's former wife.
24:1–4	The prohibition of the restoration of marriage with a former wife, from which a man's unilateral right to divorce is inferred.
25:5–10	Levirate law, affording a childless widow the option to marry her late husband's brother.
25:11–12	Cutting a woman's palm as punishment for injuring her husband's opponent's genitals.
27:20	"Cursed be he who lies with his father's wife, for he has removed his father's garment."
28:30	The threat that "if you pay the bride-price for a wife, another man shall enjoy her."

(b) Equal Inclusion in Law and Narrative

4:16	Prohibition of making a sculptured image in male or female form.
5:18	Prohibition of craving a neighbour's male or female slave.
7:3	"Do not give your daughters to their sons or take their daughters for your sons."

7:14	"There shall be no sterile male or female among you."
13:13-10a	Instruction to kill anyone who entices illicit worship.
15:12-18	Emancipation of male and female debt slaves.
17:2-3	Stoning of any worshipper of other gods.
21:18-19	Stoning "a wayward and defiant son, who does not heed his father or his mother."
22:5	Prohibition of male and female cross-dressing.
23:18-19	Prohibition of male and female cult prostitution.
29:11	Women (after men and children) as covenantal recipients.
31:12	Women (after men, but before children) as covenantal recipients.
33:8-9	In the critique of Levi "who said of his father and mother, 'I consider them not.'"

(c) Equal Punishments and Curses

2:34 as 3:6	"we doomed every town—men, women, and children—leaving no survivor."
22:22	Capital punishment of male and female adulterers.
24:8-9	"Remember what the Lord your God did to Miriam ... after you left Egypt."
27:16	"Cursed be he who insults his father or mother."
27:19	Curse of anyone subverting "the rights of the stranger, the fatherless, and the widow."
28:32&41	Captivity of sons and daughters
28:53-57	Cannibal consumption of "the flesh of your sons and daughters."
28:68	The threat of male and female enslavement.
32:19	Divine spurning of sons and daughters.
32:25	Death "to youth and maiden alike, the suckling as well as the aged."

(d) Explicit Concern for Women

3:18-19	The exemption of wives, children, and livestock from battle.
24:5	One year's military exemption for a newlywed groom, to ensure his wife's happiness.

Note

1. English translations throughout are from *NJPS Hebrew-English Tanakh: The Traditional Hebrew Text and the New JPS Translation*, 2nd ed. (Philadelphia: The Jewish Publication Society, 1999).

Bibliography

Anderson, Cheryl B. 2004. *Women, Ideology and Violence: Critical Theory and the Construction of Gender in the Book of the Covenant and the Deuteronomic Law*. London: T & T Clark.

Bach, Alice. 1999. "Man's World, Woman's Place: Sexual Politics in the Hebrew Bible." In *Women in the Hebrew Bible: A Reader*, edited by A. Bach, xiii–xxvi. London: Routledge.

Bachmann, Mercedes L. García. 2013. *Women at Work in the Deuteronomistic History*. Atlanta: SBL Press, 2013.

Bennett, Harold. 2002. *Injustice Made Legal: Deuteronomic Law and the Plight of Widows, Strangers and Orphans in Ancient Israel*. Grand Rapids: Eerdmans.

Berlin, Adele. 2009. "Sex and the Single Girl in Deuteronomy 22." In *Mishneh Todah: Studies on Deuteronomy and Its Cultural Environment in Honor of Jeffrey H. Tigay*, edited by N. Sacher Fox, D. A. Glatt-Gilad, and M. J. Williams, 95–112. Winona Lake: Eisenbrauns.

Bird, Phyllis A. 2019. *Harlot or Holy Woman? A Study of Hebrew Qedešah*. University Park: Eisenbrauns.

Braulik, Georg. 1999. "Were Women, Too, Allowed to Offer Sacrifices in Israel? Observations on the Meaning and Festive Form of Sacrifice in Deuteronomy." *Hervormde Teologiese Studies* 55, no. 4: 909–942.

Brenner, Athalya. 2012. "The Decalogue: Am I an Addressee?" In *Exodus and Deuteronomy: Texts@Contexts*, edited by G. A. Yee and A. Brenner, 197–204. Minneapolis: Fortress Press.

Brooten, Bernadette J. 1982. *Women Leaders in the Ancient Synagogue: Inscriptional Evidence and Background Issues*. Atlanta: Scholars Press, 1982.

Brueggemann, Walter. 2001. *Deuteronomy: Abington Old Testament Commentaries*. Nashville: Abingdon Press.

Carmody, Denise L. 1992. *Biblical Woman: Contemporary Reflections on Scriptural Texts*. New York: Crossroad, 1992.

Douglas, Mary. 2006. *Purity and Danger: An Analysis of Concepts of Pollution and Taboo*. London: Routledge.

Edenburg, Cynthia. 2009. "Ideology and Context of the Women's Sex Laws (Deut. 22:13–29)." *Journal of Biblical Literature* 128, no. 1 (2009): 43–60.

Ellens, Deborah L. 2008. *Women in the Sex Texts of Leviticus and Deuteronomy: A Comparative Conceptual Analysis*. New York: T & T Clark.

Emmerson, Grace I. 1989. "Women in Ancient Israel." In *The World of Ancient Israel Sociological, Anthropological, and Political Perspectives: Essays by Members of the Society for Old Testament Study*, edited by R. E. Clements, 371–394. Cambridge: Cambridge University Press.

Exum, J. Cheryl. 1995. "The Ethics of Biblical Violence against Women." In *The Bible in Ethics: The Second Sheffield Colloquim*, edited by J. W. Rogerson, M. Davies, and M. D. Carroll, 248–271. Sheffield: Sheffield Academic Press.

Finsterbusch, Karin. 2011. "Women between Subordination and Independence: Reflections on Gender-Related Legal Texts of the Torah." In *Torah*, edited by J. Økland, 407–435. Atlanta: Society of Biblical Literature.

Freedman, Amelia Devin. 2017. "Image, Status, and Regulation: Feminist Interpretative History of Exodus to Deuteronomy." In *Feminist Interpretation of the Hebrew Bible in Retrospect. Volume I: The Biblical Books*, edited by S. Scholtz, 62–79. Sheffield: Sheffield Phoenix Press.

Goff, Barbara. 2004. *Citizen Bacchae: Women's Ritual Practice in Ancient Greece*. Berkeley: University of California Press.

Gravett, Sandie. 2004. "Reading 'Rape' in the Hebrew Bible: A Consideration of Language." *Journal for the Study of the Old Testament* 28, no. 3: 279–299.

Hagedorn, Anselm C. 2004. *Between Moses and Plato: Individual and Society in Deuteronomy and Ancient Greek Law*. Forschungen zur Religion und Literatur des Alten und Neuen Testaments 204. Göttingen: Vandenhoeck & Ruprecht.

Hauptman, Judith. 1998. *Rereading the Rabbis: A Woman's Voice*. Boulder, CO: Westview Press.

Ilan, Tal. 2006. *Silencing the Queen: The Literary Histories of Shelamzion and Other Jewish Women*. Tübingen: J.C.B. Mohr Siebeck.

Jackson, Bernard S. 2006. "Seduction." In *Wisdom Laws: A Study of the Mishpatim of Exodus 21:1–22:16,"* 367–383. Oxford: Oxford University Press.

Jacobs, Sandra. 2010. "Instrumental Talion in Deuteronomic Law." *Zeitschrift für altorientalische und biblische Rechtsgeschichte* 16: 263–278.

Jacobs, Sandra. 2012. "Terms of Endearment? The ראת-תפי תשא (Desirable Female Captive) and Her Illicit Acquisition." In *Texts@Contexts: Exodus and Deuteronomy*, edited by G. Yee and A. Brenner, 237–257. Minneapolis: Fortress Press.

Jacobs, Sandra. 2018. "'The Disposable Wife' as Property in the Hebrew Bible." In *Gender and Methodology in the Ancient Near East: Approaches from Assyriology and Beyond*, edited by S. Budin, M. Cifarelli, A. Garcia-Ventura, and A. Millet-Albà Barcino, 37–355. Barcelona: Universitat de Barcelona.

Jacobs, Sandra. 2020. Book Review: Tracey Lemos, *Violence and Personhood in Ancient Israel and Comparative Contexts*. Oxford: Oxford University Press, 2017. *Association for Jewish Studies Review* 44, no. 1: 185–187.

Jay, Nancy B. 1985. "Sacrifice as a Remedy for Being Born Female." In *Immaculate and Powerful: The Female in Social Image and Sacred Reality*, edited by C. W. Atkinson, C. H. Buchanan, and M. R. Miles, 283–309. Boston: Crucible Press.

Jay, Nancy B. 1992. *Throughout Your Generations Forever: Sacrifice, Religion, and Paternity*. Chicago: University of Chicago Press.

Kawashima, Robert S. 2011. "Could a Woman Say 'No' in Biblical Israel? On the Genealogy of Legal Status in Biblical Law and Literature." *Association of Jewish Studies Review* 35, no. 1: 1–22.

Lafont, Sophie Démaire. 2011. "The Status of Women in the Legal Texts of the Ancient Near East." In *Torah*, edited by I. Fischer, M. Navarro Puerto, A. Taschl-Erber, and. J. Økland, 109–132. The Bible and Women: An Exegesis of Cultural History 1. Atlanta: SBL.

Lipka, Hilary. 2006. *Sexual Transgression in the Hebrew Bible*. Sheffield: Sheffield Phoenix Press.

MacDonald, Elizabeth M. 1931. *The Position of Women as Reflected in Semitic Codes of Law*. Toronto: Toronto University Press.

Mayes, Andrew D. H. 1981. *The New Century Bible Commentary: Deuteronomy*. London: W.B. Eerdmans and Marshall, Morgan & Scott.

Mbuwayesango, Dora R. 2009. "Canaanite Women and *Israelite* Women in Deuteronomy: The Intersection of Sexism and Imperialism." In *Postcolonial Interventions: Essays in Honor of R. S. Sugirtharajah*, edited by T-S. B. Liew, 45–57. Sheffield: Sheffield Phoenix Press.

McConville, J. Gordon. 1984. *Law and Theology in Deuteronomy*. Sheffield: JSOT Press.

Meyers, Carol L. 1994. "Hannah and Her Sacrifice: Reclaiming Female Agency." In *Feminist Companion to Samuel and Kings*, 93–104. Sheffield: Sheffield Academic Press.

Moran, William. 1967. "The Conclusion of The Decalogue (EX 20,17 = DT 5,21)." *Catholic Biblical Quarterly* 29, no. 4: 543–554.

Morrow, William S. 2017. *An Introduction to Biblical Law*. Grand Rapids: William B. Eerdmans, 2017.

Otto, Eckart. 1998. "False Weights in the Scales of Justice? Different Views of Women from Patriarchal Hierarchy to Religious Equality in the Book of Deuteronomy." In *Gender and Law in the Hebrew Bible and the Ancient Near East*, edited by T. Frymer-Kensky, B. Levinson, and V. Mathews, 128–146. Sheffield: Sheffield Academic Press.

Paul, Shalom M. 1990. "Biblical Analogues to Middle Assyrian Law." In *Religion and Law*, edited by E. B. Firmage, B. G. Weiss, and J. W. Welch, 333–350. Winona Lake: Eisenbrauns.

Plaskow, Judith. 1990. *Standing Again at Sinai: Judaism from a Feminist Perspective*. New York: Harper San Francisco.

Pressler, Carolyn. 1993. *The View of Women Found in Deuteronomic Family Laws*. Berlin: Walter de Gruyter.

Pressler, Carolyn. 2012. "Deuteronomy." In *Women's Bible Commentary: Revised and Updated*, edited by C. A. Newsom, S. H. Ringe, and J. Lapsey, 88–102. Louisville: Westminster John Knox Press.

Reeder, Caryn A. 2012. *The Enemy in the Household: Family Violence in Deuteronomy and Beyond*. Grand Rapids: Baker Academic.

Rofé, Alexander. 1996. "The Laws of Warfare in the Book of Deuteronomy: Their Origins, Intent and Positivity." In *The Pentateuch: A Sheffield Reader*, edited by J. W. Rogerson, 128–149. Sheffield: Sheffield Academic Press, 1996.

Ruane, Nicole J. 2013. *Sacrifice and Gender in Biblical Law*. New York: Cambridge University Press.

Sassoon, Isaac. 2011. *The Status of Women in Jewish Tradition*. Cambridge: Cambridge University Press.

Schmitz, Barbara. 2020. "The Book of Judith and Tyrannicide: How the Book of Judith Takes Up a Greek-Hellenistic Discourse." In *Stones, Tablets, and Scrolls: Periods of the Formation of the Bible*, edited by P. Dubovský and F. Giuntoli, 411–426. Wiesbaden: Mohr Siebeck.

Shapira, Amnon. 2010. "On Woman's Equal Standing in the Bible—A Sketch: A Feminist Re-Reading of the Hebrew Bible: A Typological View." *Hebrew Studies* 51: 7–42.

Shemesh, Yael. 2005. "Punishment of the Offending Organ in Biblical Literature." *Vetus Testamentum* 55: 343–365.

Sivan, Hagith H. 2004. *Between Women, Man, and God: A New Interpretation of the Ten Commandments*. London: T & T Clark International.

Sneed, Mark R. 1999. "Israelite Concern for the Alien, Orphan, and Widow: Altruism or Ideology? *Zeitschrift für die alttestamentliche Wissenschaft* 111, no. 4: 498–507.

Stulman, Louis. 1990. "Encroachment in Deuteronomy: An Analysis of the Social World of the D Code." *Journal of Biblical Literature* 109, no. 4: 613–632.

Stulman, Louis. 1992. "Sex and Familial Crimes in the D Code." *Journal for the Study of Old Testament* 53: 47–63.

Van Der Toorn, Karel. 1989. "Female Prostitution in Payment of Vows in Ancient Israel." *Journal of Biblical Literature* 108, no. 2: 193–205.

Washington, Harold. 1998. "Lest He Die in Battle and Another Man Take Her": Violence and Construction of Gender in the Laws of Deuteronomy 20–22." In *Gender and Law in the Hebrew Bible and the Ancient Near East*, edited by T. Frymer-Kensky, B. Levinson, and V. Mathews, 185–213. Sheffield: Sheffield Academic Press.

Wegner, Judith R. 1988. *Chattel or Person? The Status of Women in the Mishnah*. New York: Oxford University Press.

CHAPTER 14

DEUTERONOMY AND SCRIBES

JOACHIM L. W. SCHAPER

Preliminary Remarks

Given the topic of this chapter, we should first clarify the term "scribes." In the relevant secondary literature, it is often used in a vague manner. The English noun "scribe" is typically employed to render the Hebrew *sôfer* and the cognate terms in other Northwest Semitic languages, the Sumerian *dub-sar* and the Akkadian *tupšarru*. It needs to be kept in mind that the work of scribes went well beyond "passive" work like the copying of texts. In Mesopotamia as well as in Egypt, scribes were members of a prestigious class of officials with a wide range of expertise, ranging from the actual writing techniques, a philological understanding of the language, and a knowledge of traditional literature to an understanding of mathematics and metrology, with some scholar-scribes achieving remarkable philological skill, literary artistry, and hermeneutical refinement and mastering the full range of scientific, literary, cultic, and other knowledge of their time (Cancik-Kirschbaum and Kahl 2018, 59–66, 86–99). Scribes as a professional class emerged very early in both Mesopotamia and Egypt, not long after the rise of the proto-cuneiform notation system and of hieroglyphic writing, respectively, in the late fourth millennium BCE.

It has been surmised that scribes in the kingdoms of Israel and Judah had training that was, in a number of ways, inferior to that of their Mesopotamian colleagues operating in the context of cuneiform cultures—not only because of the higher intellectual demands supposedly posed by learning and practicing cuneiform writing (as opposed to "mere" alphabetic scripts) but also because of the long and unbroken tradition of scribal education in Mesopotamia and Egypt, as opposed to the later origins of Israel and Judah, their writing systems, and their administrative apparatuses. Let us therefore look at the deep roots of the activity of the scribes who contributed to the composition of the book of Deuteronomy and see where their work can be situated in the overall history of scribal activity in Israel and Judah from its beginnings.

With regard to Israel and Judah, we know of the significance of scribes in the process of the emergence of statehood (Sanders 2009; Schniedewind 2019). The importance of scribes and their work to social, economic, and political development was probably even higher in Israel and Judah than it had been and continued to be in Mesopotamia. There seems to have been some continuity between scribal activity at the time of the Egyptian domination of the Levant (which came to an end in the Late Bronze Age) and the scribes that accompanied the rise of the small states forming after the withdrawal of Egypt. That transitional period, from the twelfth to the ninth century BCE, did not see a complete cultural disruption and an utter demise of the knowledge and skills brought to fruition by the Egyptians. There was no discontinuity in the practice of writing as such in the Levant, but the scribes of early Israel and Judah, like those of the other emerging small states neighboring them, adopted not the cuneiform writing of the earlier Egyptian administration of the Levant but an alphabetic system (i.e., the Phoenician alphabet), ultimately derived from Egyptian hieratic writing, which they then developed further into an alphabet yet more suited to their purposes.

The paleo-Hebrew script that emerged in the ninth century BCE probably was the result of a conscious effort on behalf of the nascent Israelite state; Christopher Rollston "contend[ed] that the fledgling Israelite kin[g]dom(s) made a conscious decision to create a national Hebrew script during this time period, thereby formally breaking with the Phoenician *Mutterschrift* that had been used prior to this in Israel": in Rollston's view "[t]he creation of the Old Hebrew script was [. . .] a nationalistic statement, not merely an evolutionary development" (Rollston 2010, 44). While "nationalism" is an anachronistic category in this context, it is quite clear that the features that distinguish the paleo-Hebrew from the Phoenician script are the results of conscious efforts. Whether there was "a conscious decision to create a national Hebrew script," however, is a different matter. It is more likely that the new, distinctively "Israelite" features of the script were the result of a move toward a uniform style once the Israelite scribes were in the process of becoming a distinct category of functionaries (a development that might be compared to the emergence of a distinctive *Kanzleistil* in the formalized written communications of bureaucracies in late medieval/early modern Germany).

The reconstruction of the history of the Phoenician script and its "daughter" scripts shows that, from the early times of the Israelite and Judahite polities onward, its scribes had been experienced and prolific practitioners of administrative and other writing activities (literacy among the general population was a different matter, though).[1] Adopting the Phoenician alphabet and transforming it into a distinctively Hebrew one in the ninth century, they were of crucial importance to their polities.[2]

This development was ultimately dependent on the economic factors that accelerated the need for the use of writing for bureaucratic and administrative purposes in the emerging states of Israel and Judah. The technology of writing was exercised by scholar-scribes who—among other things—formulated, and assisted in imposing, the incipient legal systems for those states. We shall return to this important point in the section "New Perspectives on Deuteronomy, Scribes, and Scribal Culture."

It is in the earliest parts of the book of Deuteronomy that we find some of the most salient vestiges of the efforts of the scribes of the Judahite monarchy to keep up with, adjust to, and make use of the ever-accelerating pace of economic change that inescapably led to a more and more complex society and thus to new political and social challenges.[3]

As far as the actual range of tasks of Israelite and Judahite scribes is concerned, Karel van der Toorn has rightly pointed out—with regard to the production of written texts (as opposed to the *reproduction* of such texts)—that there probably were "six ways in which scribes produced written texts. They might engage in (1) transposition of oral lore;

(2) invention of a new text; (3) compilation of existing lore, either oral or written; (4) expansion of an inherited text; (5) adaptation of an existing text for a new audience; and (6) integration of individual documents into a more comprehensive composition" (van der Toorn 2007, 110). This questions "any distinction in antiquity between the scribe as author and as editor" (Van Seters 2008, 100).

Van der Toorn's view is based on, among other things, analogies he draws between Israelite and Mesopotamian scribes. Comparing what we know of both the work of Mesopotamian scribes, as discussed above, and the ways in which Deuteronomy interacts with earlier Israelite texts and portrays scribal activity, we can see that these analogies make sense, contrary to the views of some scholars in the field. Deuteronomy's scribes were serious "players" in the international context of scribal cultures, which has been demonstrated with regard to the manner in which Deuteronomy's scribes interacted with and transformed earlier texts of national and international origins, like the Covenant Code and the Vassal Treaties of Esarhaddon (see most recently Steymans 2022).

Earlier Research on Deuteronomy and Scribes and the *Status Quaestionis*

When it comes to outlining the history of research into Deuteronomy *as a result of specific scribal activities* (i.e., of activities that are characteristic of the work of scribes, as opposed to other professional groups in the society of ancient Judah), it should be pointed out that research devoted to this aspect of the history of the book of Deuteronomy is a fairly recent phenomenon. It is of course true that generations of scholars have commented on passages in Deuteronomy that betray the strong interest of the authors and redactors of the book in the *practice of writing* and the distinctive characteristics of Deuteronomy *as a book*. But the scribes who produced Deuteronomy often did not receive specific attention *qua* scribes, with the exception of, for example, Weinfeld's magisterial work *Deuteronomy and the Deuteronomic School*, which devotes an entire chapter to the "scribal rôle in the chrystallization of Deuteronomy" (Weinfeld 1972, 158–178) and concentrates on the family of the Shafanids and their work.

However, these features of Deuteronomy, and the significance of "scribal culture" for the history and content of the book, did not really attract much systematic attention until Jean-Pierre Sonnet's groundbreaking study *The Book within the Book* (Sonnet 1997), flanked by a number of works concentrating on scribes, their "schools," and their practices published during the same decade (cf. Jamieson-Drake 1991; Davies 1998). Sonnet analyzes the remarkably artful literary structure of the final form of Deuteronomy as a literary work in which the structure of the book itself and the process of its production are implicitly and explicitly addressed. Therefore, one might call Deuteronomy, in a manner of speaking, a *self-reflexive* piece of literature produced by highly qualified scribes.

In the same year, Bernard M. Levinson published his *Deuteronomy and the Hermeneutics of Legal Innovation*. It is a crucially important book in the history of the exploration of the work of the scribes as exegetes of authoritative texts, especially with regard to the *hermeneutic* skills of those scribes in dealing with those earlier texts—skills that enabled them to propose a radically new model of cult and society, without ever giving the impression of breaking with tradition.

Schaper pointed out that the process Martin Hengel had called *Schriftauslegung und Schriftwerdung* (Hengel 1994) effectively began before the Babylonian Exile and that the scribal exegesis practiced by the Levites in the Second Temple period carried on the exegetical and hermeneutical traditions of the scribes and priests of late pre-exilic and exilic times, laying the groundwork for the Pharisaic concept of scriptural interpretation (Schaper 1999, 2000; specifically Schaper 2000, 307 on the "Levitical-Pharisaic tradition"; on Hengel's thesis, see more below in this section). Schaper (2004) described the presentation of divine writing in the book of Deuteronomy as being indicative of the role of scribes and the prevalence of their professional concerns in the production of the book.

Timo Veijola demonstrated that the book of Deuteronomy displays features otherwise seen as being characteristic of the work of the later *Schriftgelehrten* (Veijola 2000). Like Veijola, Eckart Otto arrived at the conclusion that the scribes who produced Deuteronomy can be seen as the forerunners of the later Jewish scribes (Otto 2005; cf. Heckl 2013).

Karel van der Toorn, in his study on scribal culture (van der Toorn 2007), refers to Deuteronomy as a key example of that culture and its significance for the formation of the Hebrew Bible (for a different approach to the same kind of problem, cf. Carr 2005). His work is especially interesting in that it combines the quest for an understanding of the actual, practical work of scribes in ancient Israel with the attempt to reconstruct the literary history of the Hebrew Bible. Van der Toorn uses the book of Deuteronomy "as an example of the various scribal modes of text production within the legal and narrative traditions of the Bible as a whole" (Van Seters 2008, 101). It is characteristic of van der Toorn's approach that he "asserts that the text was rigidly controlled by using a single master copy that was under the supervision of the Levitical scribes. Although it was subject to revision and expansion over the course of 200 years, these changes were limited to only four major editions subsequent to Josiah's original reform document" (Van Seters 2008, 101, summarizing one of van der Toorn's key theses), a view of the scribes' activity and text production that was criticized by John Van Seters (2008, passim).

Research into the scribal culture that brought forth the book of Deuteronomy needs to be conceptualized in the context of the history of what we might call "scriptural exegesis," in the sense of interpreting authoritative, or indeed "holy," texts for religious (including legal) purposes. Although there had been a perception that such scriptural exegesis began to emerge only in the Hellenistic age, it was demonstrated early on by Martin Hengel that this phenomenon can be traced back at least to the Persian period (Hengel 1994). The beginnings of scriptural exegesis could therefore safely be backdated to the early or middle period of the Achaemenid era. However, the research conducted by Levinson, Sonnet, Veijola, Otto, van der Toorn, Schaper, and others has demonstrated that the roots of such scriptural exegesis reach as far back as the earliest strata of Deuteronomy and the ways in which the scribes who produced them interacted with earlier material and created a coherent, highly complex text. That text was then adapted, by the successors of those earlier scribes, to new social, political, economic, and intellectual requirements in the course of producing a number of new editions across a time span of well over a hundred years.[4]

The question to what extent exactly, and in what ways, the pre-exilic and the later parts of the book of Deuteronomy and the work of the scribes who produced them can be seen as foreshadowing the scribal and exegetical activity of the Jewish scribes in the Persian,

Hellenistic, and Roman periods continued to occupy scholars and led to innovative work being produced. With regard to this historical trajectory, Hengel's groundbreaking research made scholars aware of the significance of scribal traditions in Persian-period Judaism, but the roots are deeper still, as Veijola, Otto, and others then demonstrated. And the exploration of scribal techniques in *later* periods (i.e., in Hellenistic and Roman Judaism) has led scholars to reconsider the relation between earlier and later scribal activities in Jewish history. In a remarkable study, Hindy Najman reconstructed the history of "Mosaic discourse" from Deuteronomy to the late Second temple period (Najman 2003), a discourse that started with the development of Deuteronomy through its several stages. According to her view, Deuteronomy became a paradigm for the unfolding of a discourse that resulted in texts like Jubilees and 11QTemple. The scribes of Deuteronomy effectively provided an exegetical and hermeneutical model for the reinterpretation of scriptural tradition which later generations adopted and adapted. In Najman's view, Philo of Alexandria, too, contributed to the Mosaic Discourse but approached the figure of Moses in a manner distinctly different from that of Jubilees and 11QTemple in a way that was innovative yet did not become part of the Jewish exegetical and hermeneutical mainstream.

The scribal culture that produced Deuteronomy was a cultural phenomenon of the highest order, indeed of world-historical significance. In Deuteronomy, we have the first example of a view of the significance and interpretation of texts that unfolded over the following centuries (Najman 2003; Schaper 2013) and led, among other things, to the rise of Pharisaism (Schaper 1999), which transformed the practices of the Jewish religion and effectively also laid some of the groundwork for the rise of Christianity in that it established exegetical concepts that enabled emergent Christianity to use them in the service of its own interpretation of "holy scriptures."

It is interesting to see that the focus on interpretative strategies and literary artistry in Deuteronomy also led to an increase in interest in the actual *Lebenswelt* and the practical aspects of the work of the scribes. We shall discuss this area of research in the next section.

New Perspectives on Deuteronomy, Scribes, and Scribal Culture

It is important to attend to the insights garnered from current research and the new perspectives emerging from them. As pointed out, earlier research demonstrated that the first traces of a concept of scriptural exegesis can already be found in the earliest sections of the book of Deuteronomy (e.g., Levinson 1997, 23–52), and this crucial area of research into Deuteronomy continues to flourish. But there are other key aspects of Deuteronomy and the scribal culture that produced it that will require more attention in the future. The next section discusses aspects that deserve such attention. First, epigraphic research and biblical exegesis need to be more closely correlated. Second, the theological, social, and political "message" of the scribes should be explored in greater depth. Third, the scribes of Deuteronomy need to be understood as an "informational elite" who fulfilled a very specific function in the context of the cultural evolution of ancient religion. And fourth, the ideologization of writing should be explored in greater depth in the context of that cultural evolution.

Epigraphic Research and Biblical Exegesis

Epigraphic texts in Hebrew cover the whole range of the activities of the society whose scribes produced them. Ostraca, vessels, seals, weights, and a range of different monuments (graves, buildings, and others) carried inscriptions (see Richey 2021). Among the writing implements were pens, incising tools, and chisels; surfaces included leather, parchment, papyrus, pottery, and stone.[5] The epigraphic evidence complements the biblical texts and enables scholars to broaden and deepen their appreciation of the development of the Hebrew alphabet, the scribal culture of Israel and Judah, the history of classical Hebrew literature and the formation of the books of the Hebrew Bible, and the biblical canon as a whole. Epigraphic evidence is particularly helpful with regard to the interpretation of Deuteronomy, since it is the book in the Bible which is the most self-reflexive with regard to processes of writing.

Zhakevich's recent study is helpful in this regard because it is devoted to understanding down-to-earth aspects of the world of the scribes, exploring Hebrew terminology (in the Bible, inscriptions, Ben Sira, and the Dead Sea Scrolls) pertaining to writing on papyrus, stone and plaster, and "skins, scrolls, tablets, ostraca, and uncommon writing surfaces," while "scribal instruments and glyptics" are also discussed (Zhakevich 2020).

From the point of view of biblical studies generally (as opposed to Semitic philology), the exploration of epigraphic material has, on the whole, not been correlated with the biblical evidence, in spite of the fact that the two illuminate each other. That is why the work of scholars like Johannes Renz (see especially Renz 2022) is particularly relevant to the study of biblical texts and will in the future rightly attract greater attention than it has so far.

The Theological, Social, and Political "Message" of the Scribes

Levinson captured the essence of the activity of the scribes/authors behind Deuteronomy when he stated that "[t]he authors of Deuteronomy had a radically new vision of the religious and public polity and sought to implement unprecedented changes in religion and society" (Levinson 1997, 16). So what was the social setting in which Deuteronomy's scribes operated, and what kind of society were they propagating? The scribes who produced the book of Deuteronomy were propagators of a new model of society. Whether we see this model as a liberating new concept—indeed as an attempt at "secularizing" society (Weinfeld 1972)—or as an Orwellian dystopia (Lang 1984), the scribes who were responsible for its production were responding to economic and social changes that have been explained by Weber (2005) and others. As J. Blenkinsopp has pointed out (1995), following and building on Weber, the laws in the book of Deuteronomy reflect the desire to oppress ancestor worship and promote the restructuring of society which was effectively already underway in Judah from the late pre-exilic period onward. From an anthropological perspective, Mary Douglas has drawn attention to the same fact (i.e., the attempt at undermining ancestor worship), admirably summed up as "one god, no ancestors, in a world renewed" (Douglas 2004, 176).

Whence this suppression of the ancient kinship bonds? The successive groups of scribes who produced Deuteronomy were both heavily affected by and active contributors to a momentous process of transformation of Judahite society that started well before the

Babylonian Exile, entailed the cataclysm of the exilic period, and ended with the stabilization of a new system in the Persian period. In the first phase of that transformation, the scribes found themselves caught up in it and reacted to it, supporting Josiah, who effectively acted as a "modernizer." Central to that process of modernization was the need to undermine the old kinship bonds (Blenkinsopp 1995), which paved the way for a new correlation between the monotheistically conceived Yahweh-god and the concept of the human self (Schaper 2018).

While the scribes who produced Deuteronomy were in the service of a greater societal transformation, the society they projected through their writing and redacting was very much inspired by their own experience *as scribes*.

> The text in Deuteronomy is a way of expressing the scribal elite's identity and hope; it is Torah piety, a new form of piety; it is a book religion. The social system envisioned in Deuteronomic didacticism is the vision of a society of scribes who ponder over the word of the Torah and teach their families about it. It is both practical and utopian, but only in the manner that it is a "forward dawning" (an expression from Bloch) of the writers' identity and ideals and a "principle of hope," which they see as the only way of avoiding the same guilt as their forefathers.
> (Berge 2019, 27)

Kåre Berge thinks that "the national entity presented in Deuteronomy is defined first of all through an ideology of a utopian totality of closure and system" (2019, 36). Its characteristic features are "its juridical practice, its laws of social structure, its centralization of the sacrificial cult and its national celebrations." He posits that "[a]ll these features enable the central power to take care of the national myth, the kingdom, which however is reduced to a function of the scribes, and finally, the connection with the Land" (36).

The utopian nature of the evolving vision presented by the book of Deuteronomy in the successive stages of its development indicates not least that the scribes who produced it seem to have lived the lives of professionals who found themselves more and more removed from the day-to-day lives of the average person. It has been argued against the thesis of the "utopian" nature of Deuteronomy that some of the key stipulations in Deuteronomy (e.g., Deut. 15:12–18) were by no means utopian but addressed, in very concrete terms, problems induced by the monetarization and commercialization of economic life in Judah (Steymans 2022, 359). While this observation is perfectly correct, the overall character of Deuteronomy as an all-encompassing reorientation of society and the state may nevertheless be called utopian in the sense that the society it envisaged was a projection with little basis in reality at the time it was proposed.

The literary history of the book of Deuteronomy includes the time of upheaval that was the Babylonian Exile, during which the scribal class, as part of the societal elite, underwent a significant transition. As van der Toorn (2007, 95) says with regard to the Levitical scribes:

> In light of the historical differentiation within the priesthood after the Exile, the forerunners of the Levitical scribes of the Second Temple are to be sought among the priesthood of the First Temple. The "scribes" to whom Jeremiah 8:8 attributes the forerunner of Deuteronomy belonged to the same group as the priests who are said to "hold" or "handle" (Hebrew *tāpaś*) the (written) Torah (Jer 2:8). Jeremiah identifies these scribes with the "sages" (*ḥakāmîm*, Jer 8:8-9). To understand the significance of that term, it is necessary to know that, in Jeremiah, the sages are a professional group alongside the priests and the prophets. The *locus classicus* that mentions the three groups (Jer 18:18) makes it clear that together they constituted the

religious establishment. The sages, then, were scribes who, on account of their access to the written tradition, claimed superior knowledge (compare Jer 9:22-23; note the use of verbs denoting insight [śkl] and knowledge [ydʿ] in verse 23). They were the scholars of the temple.[6]

All this is the expression of a far-ranging reconceptualization of the source of law and justice. In Mesopotamia, the king was seen as the source of law (with assistance from the gods, so to speak) and as being responsible for its implementation. He was a mediator figure between the divine and the human realms. In Judah, by contrast, it was Yahweh who was now, under the impact of the social and political upheaval brought about by the end of the Judahite monarchy, seen as the exclusive source of law and of justice (Otto 1994, 103–104, also cf. Markl 2021). A royal intermediary was no longer necessary. While in the Pentateuch, both in the Priestly Writing and in Deuteronomy, mediation is still—to some degree—required, it is achieved by Moses. Moses is human and mortal, and the mediation of the Law he accomplishes is the kind of mediation accomplished by a *messenger*, not that enacted by a co-originator.

The "excarnation of the law" made the law independent of the king; the Torah now replaced him (Assmann 2006, 66–67). The law could be excarnated because of the status of writing as a societally crucial, high-profile activity, and the perceived quasi-numinous quality of written documents made it possible, and indeed necessary, to conceive of the divine law as being fixed in writing. The scribal class had an obvious interest in making the law's excarnation central to its concept of revelation.

The Scribes as an "Informational Elite": "Deep Correspondences" and Their Expression

The term *Formzusammenhang*, originally introduced by Oswald Spengler in the context of his work of historical-philosophical speculation and recently systematized by scholars working on cultural evolution, denotes the "deep uniformities" between different modes of abstraction.[7]

One crucial deep uniformity in Judahite society during the time period in question is the one between *different types of abstraction* across various segments of society: the increasing importance of writing and the flourishing of literature, the refinement of commodity exchange and value-equivalences, and the suppression of divine images. They all hang together. As shown by Schaper (2019)—without yet using the category of "deep correspondence" to conceptualize the nexus between them—those abstractions, combined, paved the way for another, further abstraction: that of monotheism—which finds one of its first clear biblical expressions in Deuteronomy 4 and in turn contributed to the formation of the concept of the human self/person in the biblical tradition (again, in Deuteronomy; see Schaper 2018). The three different types of abstraction mentioned, and the further abstraction in which it resulted (i.e., monotheism), are all reflected in crucial chapters of the book of Deuteronomy (viz. chapters 4, 5, and 14). The scribes who produced Deuteronomy gave expression to those deep correspondences between the abstractions arising in diverse sectors of society. Those scribes were the "informational elite"[8] of their time, at the forefront of societal change. They put the technological and procedural innovations of their time to good use by producing a blueprint for a new society.

The Ideologization of Writing: God as Scribe—And the Social Reality Reflected in This Concept

In Deuteronomy, as in other key texts of the Hebrew Bible, one of the most fascinating phenomena in the conceptualization of Yahweh is the way in which the deity is portrayed as a scribe. A few studies partly or wholly devoted to this topic have been published (cf. Schaper 2004; Eggleston 2016). It is intriguing to see that, unlike in other ancient cultures, the invention of writing is not attributed to the deity or a human being—rather, its existence is simply taken for granted. And it would indeed have been counterintuitive to ascribe the invention of cultural practices, such as writing, to the deity in the context of a monotheistic belief system, whereas this is much easier where, in a polytheistic culture, a "division of labor" between the gods or a "delegation" of the task to semi-divine or human beings is assumed: in Egypt, the invention of writing was ascribed to Thoth; in Mesopotamia, to Nisaba and then to Nabu; in Greece, to Hermes or Prometheus; and so forth.

In the book of Deuteronomy and elsewhere in the Pentateuch, only Yahweh and Moses are portrayed as engaging in the practice of writing. The first person portrayed as a scribe in the narrative sequence of the Pentateuch is indeed Elohim/Yahweh himself. Within the Pentateuch, writing receives the highest amount of attention in Deuteronomy. These facts about the Pentateuch indicate that writing as a cultural practice was taken even more seriously, and probably was socially and culturally even more significant, in ancient Israel and Judah than it was in, say, Mesopotamia and Egypt. From the point of view of the Pentateuch's authors and redactors, writing received its approbation directly from—and its practice was imposed on select human individuals by—the one, only, and unique deity, the creator of heaven and earth. It should thus come as no surprise that later, in rabbinic Judaism, God was depicted as creating the world according to the "blueprint" provided by the Torah (Midrash Bereshit Rabbah 1.1)! Exodus and Deuteronomy make it abundantly clear that writing is a pursuit ennobled by the deity who effectively is the first scribe in history (Exod. 24:12, Deut. 4:13). Thus writing is a divine activity, and human scribes emulate the deity.

One of the effects of the introduction of written language (and thus the production of written utterances) in a given society is that it becomes autonomous from spoken language: written utterances establish written language as a primary (!) sign system, in the sense that written texts no longer signify signs but things.[9] This invests written texts with a very significant authority: the autonomy of the "written norm," in the great Czech linguist Vachek's terminology, leads to a perceived immediacy between written words and things. The "written norm" is no longer secondary; it is now primary. It is not an overstatement to say that this provides the basis for a fetishization of the written word, indeed, a fetishization of writing and writing systems generally. The Hebrew Bible provides us with fascinating examples of that fetishization. Deuteronomy probably contains the most salient ones: that God is depicted as a scribe writing down the commandments he has previously uttered orally, as well as the self-reflexivity of the "book within the book" (Sonnet 1997), indicates how far such fetishization could go. Other ancient Near Eastern cultures (including Egyptian culture, of course) provide us with other, equally characteristic features of the fetishization of writing. In that sense, writing is deeply ambiguous: while it creates distance, it can also produce (imagined) presence (cf. Schaper 2019).

The correlation between writing and reciting, between the written and the oral is characteristic of Deuteronomy and encourages scholarship further to explore the scribes' interest in memory and mnemonic techniques and their use in the service of religion (for earlier contributions, cf. Lohfink and Fischer 1995, 181–203; Graham 1987).

Conclusion

The scribes of Deuteronomy were members of the crucial informational elite of the Judahite state—its scribal class. They adjusted the traditional authoritative texts and their interpretation to the massive societal changes in the times of Josiah, the Babylonian Exile, and the early Persian period. Throughout those troubled times, the scribal class was able to maintain its coherence, its traditions, and its practices. The scribes thus provided cultural continuity in times of political, social, and economic turmoil and laid the groundwork for the continuation of their hermeneutical and exegetical outlook in the work of the Levites later in the Persian period and of the Pharisees in the Hellenistic and Roman periods.

Notes

1. "Of course, literacy rates in ancient Mesopotamia and Egypt are estimated to be very low, with some studies suggesting that the rate is in the low single digits. Therefore, even if it is plausible to posit higher rates of literacy for those living in ancient Israel than for those living in Mesopotamia or Egypt, this does not lead to the conclusion that the non-elite populace was literate" (Rollston 2010, 137). I should like to take this opportunity to thank my colleague Dr. Nathaniel Greene for reading and commenting upon an earlier version of this essay.
2. On the paleography of the Hebrew script, cf. especially the detailed account in Renz 1995, 95–208.
3. On the increasing complexity of Judahite society to which the Josianic Reform was an answer, cf. Weber 2005, 497–499 (as well as p. 501 on the erosion of the clan system). The function of writing as a "means of communication" in such processes is summarized by J. Goody: "Changes in the means of communication [. . .] alter the range of possibilities open to man, internal as well as external, increasing not his abilities but his capacities and the skills needed to take advantage of these" (Goody 1987, 272).
4. Schniedewind (2019, 166) posits discontinuity between Judahite scribal culture before and after the Babylonian Exile: "The Hebrew Bible was influenced by the education of its scribes and, in particular, by their curriculum. This scribal education was quite conservative. It was passed along from generation to generation with little change. Major social upheavals, however, did profoundly shape innovation and changes. [. . .] The Assyrians put an end to the Israelite states, and the Babylonians took over the Assyrian Empire and finally extinguished the Judean state. The destruction of Jerusalem and Judah resulted in the eclipse of the scribal infrastructure of the Hebrew alphabetic writing. The conditions during the Babylonian and early Persian periods were no longer conducive to the flourishing of Hebrew literature. A new scribal infrastructure would

be built in the Persian period, but it was a new system complete with a different alphabet (borrowed from Aramaic) and presumably a new curriculum. Unlike the transition from the Late Bronze Age to the early Iron Age, the transition from the Iron Age to the Persian period was a break—not merely a waning and waxing." Schniedewind probably overemphasizes the supposed discontinuity. In any case, that discontinuity did not prevent successive generations of scribes from responding to the turmoil of the times by authoring and editing and thus producing a work of remarkable complexity and literary ingenuity whose history of composition spans the time from Josiah to the early Persian period.

5. Inscriptions on leather, parchment, and papyrus normally have not survived, with the exception of a few late examples such as the leather scrolls found in Qumran.

6. Cf. van der Toorn 2007, 95–96: "Another piece of evidence on the temple scribes is the Book of Deuteronomy. As witnessed in their preoccupation with 'the Levitical priests,' the scribes who wrote Deuteronomy had affinities with, and may have belonged to, the Levitical priesthood. A telltale occurrence of 'the Levitical priests' is found in connection with a ruling concerning the king [. . .] [i.e., Deut 17:18–19; J.S.]. [. . .] the copying takes place 'in the presence of' the Levitical priests, because they are the guardians of the original Torah. The latter interpretation is entirely in keeping with the role of the Levites as guardians of the ark (Deut 31:24–26)."

7. Cf. Pahl 2022, 3: "Spengler leads the attention to similarities in the modes of abstraction that can be found in various historical societies or civilizations. He was impressed by the fact that in rather different social arenas—art, the military, technology, government, economy, etc.—structurally analog forms of abstraction can be identified. By means of these deep uniformities, societies can be historically distinguished from each other and also put in relation to one another."

8. The term seems to have been used first in the 1980s, with reference to the emerging "netocracy." On "informatorische Eliten," cf. Löffler 2019, 270–272.

9. Cf. Josef Vachek, "Zum Problem der geschriebenen Sprache," in *A Prague School Reader in Linguistics*, Indiana University Studies in the History and Theory of Linguistics (1964). Repr., Bloomington: Indiana University Press 1966, pp. 441–460, on the historical ("diachronisch") analysis of the relation between spoken and written language: "Da kann man nun sicher nicht leugnen, daß die ersten Schriftäußerungen einer Sprachgemeinschaft von den Sprechäußerungen ausgehen und daß die Schriftnorm eine bloße Transposition der Sprechnorm darstellen will. Dies wurde übrigens schon von Artymovyč anerkannt. Wir möchten zugeben, daß in einer solchen Phase die Schriftnorm als sekundäres Zeichensystem betrachtet werden muß, da jeder von den Bestandteilen dieses Systems ein Zeichen für ein Zeichen darstellt—mit anderen Worten, das ganze sekundäre Zeichensystem spiegelt nicht das System der Dinge wider, sondern nur das primäre Zeichensystem (in diesem Falle die Sprechnorm), und erst von diesem gibt es einen geraden Weg zum System der Dinge. Aber die spezifische Form der Schriftäußerungen erzwingt sich in jeder Sprachgemeinschaft sehr bald jene Autonomie der Schriftnorm, die zuerst von Artymovyč nachdrücklich betont wurde. Und sobald dies geschehen ist, nimmt die Schriftnorm im System der sprachlichen Werte eine neue Stellung ein: aus einem sekundären wird ein primäres Zeichensystem, das heißt von nun an stellen Bestandteile der Schriftnorm nicht Zeichen von Zeichen, sondern Zeichen von Dingen dar. Somit wird die Schriftnorm der Sprechnorm koordiniert. Diese zwei Normen sind natürlich allen Gliedern der Sprachgemeinschaft nicht gleich geläufig" (Vachek 1966, 450).

Bibliography

Assmann, Jan. *Religion and Cultural Memory: Ten Studies*. Translated by R. Livingstone. Stanford: Stanford University Press, 2006.

Berge, Kåre. "Ṣedaqa and the Community of the Scribes in Postexilic Deuteronomy: A Didactical Perspective." In *Ṣedaqa and Torah in postexilic discourse*. Edited by Susanne Gillmayr-Bucher and Maria Häusl, pp. 19–36. London: T&T Clark, 2019.

Blenkinsopp, Joseph. "Deuteronomy and the Politics of Post-Mortem Existence." *VT* 45 (1995): 1–16.

Braulik, Georg. "Das Deuteronomium und die Gedächtniskultur Israels: Redaktionsgeschichtliche Beobachtungen zur Verwendung von lmd." In *Biblische Theologie und gesellschaftlicher Wandel: Für Norbert Lohfink SJ*. Edited by Norbert Lohfink, Sean McEvenue, and Walter Gross, pp. 9–31. Freiburg: Herder, 1993.

Braulik, Georg. *Die Mittel deuteronomischer Rhetorik erhoben aus Deuteronomium 4,1-40*. Analecta Biblica 68. Rome: Biblical Institute Press, 1978.

Cancik-Kirschbaum, Eva, and Jochem Kahl. *Erste Philologien: Archäologie einer Disziplin vom Tigris bis zum Nil*. Tübingen: Mohr Siebeck, 2018.

Carr, David M. *Writing on the Tablet of the Heart: Origins of Scripture and Literature*. Oxford: Oxford University Press, 2005.

Charpin, Dominique. *Lire et écrire à Babylone*. Paris: Presses Universitaires de France, 2008.

Clifford, Richard J. "What the Biblical Scribes Teach Us about Their Writings." *Theological Studies* 79 (2018): 653–667.

Davies, Philip R. *Scribes and Schools: The Canonization of the Hebrew Scriptures*. Library of Ancient Israel. London: SPCK, 1998.

Douglas, Mary. *Jacob's Tears: The Priestly Work of Reconciliation*. Oxford: Oxford University Press, 2004.

Eggleston, Chad L. *"See and Read All These Words": The Concept of the Written in the Book of Jeremiah*. Siphrut 18. University Park: Eisenbrauns, 2016.

Goody, Jack. *The Interface between the Written and the Oral*. Studies in Literacy, Family, Culture and the State. Cambridge: Cambridge University Press, 1987.

Graham, William A. *Beyond the Written Word: Oral Aspects of Scripture in the History of Religion*. Cambridge: Cambridge University Press, 1987.

Heckl, Raik. "Mose als Schreiber: Am Ursprung der jüdischen Hermeneutik des Pentateuchs." *ZAR* 19 (2013): 179–234.

Hengel, Martin. "'Schriftauslegung' und 'Schriftwerdung' in der Zeit des Zweiten Tempels." In *Schriftauslegung im antiken Judentum und im Urchristentum*. WUNT 74. Edited by Martin Hengel and Hermut Löhr, pp. 1–71. Tübingen: Mohr Siebeck, 1994.

Jamieson-Drake, David W. *Scribes and Schools in Monarchic Judah*. JSOTS 66. Sheffield: Sheffield Academic Press, 1991.

Knoppers, Gary N., and Bernard M. Levinson, eds. *The Pentateuch as Torah: New Models for Understanding Its Promulgation and Acceptance*. Winona Lake: Eisenbrauns, 2007.

Lang, Bernard. "George Orwell im gelobten Land." In *Kirche und Visitation: Beiträge zur Erforschung des frühneuzeitlichen Visitationswesens in Europa. Vol. 14: Spätmittelalter und Fruher Neuzeit*. Edited by Ernst W. Zeeden and Peter T. Lang, pp. 21–35. Stuttgart: Klett-Cotta, 1984.

Levinson, Bernard M. *Deuteronomy and the Hermeneutics of Legal Innovation*. New York: Oxford University Press, 1997.

Levinson, Bernard M. "The First Constitution: Rethinking the Origins of Rule of Law and Separation of Powers in Light of Deuteronomy." *Cardozo Law Review* 27 (2006): 1853–1888.

Levinson, Bernard M. "*You Must Not Add Anything to What I Command You*: Paradoxes of Canon and Authorship in Ancient Israel." *Numen* 50 (2003): 1–51.

Löffler, Davor. *Generative Realitäten I: Die Technologische Zivilisation als neue Achsenzeit und Zivilisationsstufe: Eine Anthropologie des 21. Jahrhunderts*. Weilerswist: Velbrück, 2019.

Lohfink, Norbert. "Gab es eine deuteronomistische Bewegung?" In *Jeremia und die "deuteronomistische Bewegung."* BBB 98. Edited by Walter Gross, pp. 313–382. Weinheim: Beltz Athenäum, 1995.

Lohfink, Norbert. "Der Glaube und die nächste Generation: Das Gottesvolk der Bibel als Lerngemeinschaft." In *Das Jüdische am Christentum: Die verlorene Dimension*. 2nd ed., pp. 144–166. Freiburg: Herder, 1989.

Lohfink, Norbert. "Zur Fabel des Deuteronomiums" (1995). Repr., *Studien zum Deuteronomium und zur deuteronomistischen Literatur IV*. Stuttgarter Biblische Aufsatzbände 31, pp. 65–78. Stuttgart: Verlag Katholisches Bibelwerk GmbH, 2000.

Lohfink, Norbert, and Georg Fischer. '"Diese Worte sollst du summen': Dtn $w^e dibbarta bam$—Ein verlorener Schlüssel zur meditativen Kultur in Israel" (1987). Repr., *Studien zum Deuteronomium und zur deuteronomistischen Literatur III*. Stuttgarter Biblische Aufsatzbände 20. Edited by Norbert Lohfink, pp. 181–203. Stuttgart: Verlag Katholisches Bibelwerk GmbH, 1995.

Markl, Dominik. "Divine Law and the Emergence of Monotheism in Deuteronomy." In *Israel and the Cosmological Empires of the Ancient Orient. Symbols of Order in Eric Voegelin's Order and History. Vol. 1*. Eric Voegelin Studies: Supplements 1. Edited by Ignacio Carbajosa and Nicoletta. Scotti Muth, pp. 193–222. Paderborn: Brill/Wilhelm Fink, 2021.

Najman, Hindy. *Seconding Sinai: The Development of Mosaic Discourse in Second Temple Judaism*. JSJS 77. Leiden: Brill, 2003.

Otto, Eckart. *Theologische Ethik des Alten Testaments*. Theologische Wissenschaft 3, 2. Stuttgart: Kohlhammer, 1994.

Otto, Eckart. "Mose, der erste Schriftgelehrte: Deuteronomium 1,5 in der Fabel des Pentateuch." In *L' Écrit et l'Esprit: Études d'histoire du texte et de théologie biblique en hommage à Adrian Schenker*. OBO 214. Edited by Dieter Böhler, Innocent Himbaza, and Philippe Hugo, pp 273–284. Fribourg and Göttingen, 2005.

Pahl, Hanno "Deep Uniformities in Modes of Abstraction: On the Co-Evolution of Money, Writing, and Number Systems." Paper presented at the University of Aarhus, at a workshop of the project "Measuring Value and Accommodating the Gods," June 29, 2022.

Renz, Johannes. *Die althebräischen Inschriften, Teil 2: Zusammenfassende Erörterungen, Paläographie und Glossar*. Darmstadt: Wissenschaftliche Buchgesellschaft, 1995.

Renz, Johannes. "Der Beitrag der althebräischen Epigraphik zur Exegese des Alten Testaments und zur Profan- und Religionsgeschichte Palästinas: Leistung und Grenzen, aufgezeigt am Beispiel der Inschriften des (ausgehenden) 7. Jahrhunderts vor Christus. In *Steine-Bilder-Texte: Historische Evidenz außerbiblischer und biblischer Quellen*. ABG 5. Edited by Christoph Hardmeier, pp. 123–158. Leipzig: Evangelische Verlagsanstalt, 2001.

Renz, Johannes. *Inschrift, Religion und Geschichte: Studien zur Profan- und Theologiegeschichte des antiken Palästina*. BZAW 531. Berlin: de Gruyter, 2022.

Renz, Johannes. *Schrift und Schreibertradition: Eine paläographische Studie zum kulturgeschichtlichen Verhältnis von israelitischem Nordreich und Südreich*. ADPV 23. Wiesbaden: Harrassowitz, 1999.

Richey, Madhad. "The Media and Materiality of Southern Levantine Inscriptions: Production and Reception Contexts." In *Scribes and Scribalism. The Hebrew Bible in Social Perspective* 1. Edited by Mark Leuchter, pp. 29–39. London: T&T Clark, 2021.

Rofé, Alexander. *Deuteronomy: Issues and Interpretation*. Old Testament Studies. London: T & T Clark, 2002.

Rollston, Christopher. *Writing and Literacy in the World of Ancient Israel: Epigraphic Evidence from the Iron Age*. Atlanta: Society of Biblical Literature, 2010.

Sanders, Seth L. *The Invention of Hebrew (Traditions)*. Urbana: University of Illinois Press, 2009.

Schaper, Joachim. "Hebrew Culture at the 'Interface between the Written and the Oral.'" In *Literacy, Orality, and Literary Production in the Southern Levant: Contextualizing Sacred Writing in Early Israel*. Edited by Brian B. Schmidt, pp. 323–340. Atlanta: Society of Biblical Literature, 2015.

Schaper, Joachim. "The Literary History of the Hebrew Bible." In *The New Cambridge History of the Bible*, vol. I: *From the Beginnings to 600*. Edited by Joachim Schaper and J. Carleton Paget, pp. 105–144. Cambridge: Cambridge University Press, 2013.

Schaper, Joachim. *Media and Monotheism: Presence, Representation, and Abstraction in Ancient Judah*. ORA 33. Tübingen: Mohr Siebeck, 2019.

Schaper, Joachim. "The Pharisees." In *The Cambridge History of Judaism*, Vol. III. Edited by William Horbury, W. D. Davies, and John Sturdy, pp. 402–427. Cambridge: Cambridge University Press, 1999.

Schaper, Joachim. *Priester und Leviten im achämenidischen Juda: Studien zur Kult- und Sozialgeschichte Israels in persischer Zeit*. FAT 31. Tübingen: Mohr Siebeck, 2000.

Schaper, Joachim. "Eine Skizze zur Korrelation von Gottesbild und Menschenbild im Buch Deuteronomium: Unter besonderer Beachtung von Personverständnis und Monotheismus im antiken Juda." In *Gott und Mensch im Alten Testament: Zum Verhältnis von Gottes- und Menschenbild*. VWGTh 52. Edited by Jürgen van Oorschot and Andreas Wagner, pp. 123–134. Leipzig: Evangelische Verlangsanstalt, 2018.

Schaper, Joachim. "A Theology of Writing: The Oral and the Written, God as Scribe, and the Book of Deuteronomy." In *Anthropology and Biblical Studies: Avenues of Approach*. Edited by Louise J. Lawrence and Mario I. Aguilar, pp. 97–119. Leiden: Deo, 2004.

Schmidt, Brian B., ed. *Literacy, Orality, and Literary Production in the Southern Levant: Contextualizing Sacred Writing in Early Israel*. Atlanta: Society of Biblical Literature, 2015.

Schniedewind, William M. *The Finger of the Scribe: How Scribes Learned to Write the Bible*, Oxford: Oxford University Press, 2019.

Schniedewind, William M., *How the Bible Became a Book: The Textualization of Ancient Israel*, Cambridge: Cambridge University Press, 2004.

Sonnet, Jean-P. *The Book within the Book: Writing in Deuteronomy*. Biblical Interpretation Series 14. Leiden: Brill, 1997.

Steymans, H. U. "Der historische Ort der Sozialgesetze des Deuteronomiums." In *Congress Volume Aberdeen 2019*. VTS 192. Edited by Grant Macaskill, Christl M. Maier, and Joachim Schaper, pp. 358–415. Leiden: Brill, 2022.

Tov, E., *Scribal Practices and Approaches Reflected in the Texts Found in the Judean Desert*. Studies on the Texts of the Desert of Judah 54. Leiden: Brill, 2004.

Van Seters, John. "The Role of the Scribe in the Making of the Hebrew Bible." *JANER* 8 (2008): 99–129.

van der Toorn, Karel. *Scribal Culture and the Making of the Hebrew Bible*. Cambridge: Harvard University Press, 2007.

Veijola, Timo. "Die Deuteronomisten als Vorgänger der Schriftgelehrten: Ein Beitrag zur Entstehung des Judentums." In *Moses Erben: Studien zum Dekalog, zum Deuteronomismus und zum Schriftgelehrtentum*. Beiträge zur Wissenschaft vom Alten und Neuen Testament 149. Edited by Timo Veijola, pp. 192–240. Stuttgart: Verlag W. Kohlhammer, 2000.

Veijola, Timo. *Das fünfte Buch Mose: Deuteronomium, Kapitel 1,1-16,17*. ATD 8, 1. Göttingen: Vandenhoeck & Ruprecht, 2004.

Weber, Max. *Das antike Judentum* (Gesamtausgabe Abteilung I, vol. 21 [in two parts]: *Schriften und Reden 1911-1920: Die Wirtschaftsethik der Weltreligionen: Das antike Judentum*). Tübingen: Mohr Siebeck, 2005.

Weinfeld, Moshe. *Deuteronomy and the Deuteronomic School*. Oxford: Clarendon Press, 1972.

Zhakevich, Philip. *Scribal Tools in Ancient Israel: A Study of Biblical Hebrew Terms for Writing Materials and Implements*. History, Archaeology, and Culture of the Levant 9. University Park: Eisenbrauns, 2020.

CHAPTER 15

PRIESTS, LEVITES, AND LEVITICAL PRIESTS IN DEUTERONOMY

NATHAN MACDONALD

INTRODUCTION

READERS of the Pentateuch do not encounter the Levites in a sustained way until the book of Numbers,[1] where a sharp distinction is made between the Levites and the priests.[2] Though both groups trace their descent back to Levi, one of the twelve sons of Jacob, the priesthood is restricted to the descendants of Aaron. The priests conduct sacrificial worship and may enter the most holy places in the Tabernacle. The Levites, however, assist Aaron and his sons in their duties and can only access the Tabernacle's court (Num 1–4). Whereas the priests are consecrated for holy service (Lev 8), the Levites are merely dedicated in a manner analogous to a sacrificial offering (Num 8). The different duties of the priesthood and the lower clergy result in gradated rewards. The priests receive the rich rewards of the sacrificial dues, the first fruits and firstlings, whereas the Levites receive only the annual tithe, and even some of that they must pay over to the priests (Num 18). But if any Levites contemplate rebelling against the divinely instituted order, the story of Korah and his followers provides a stark warning that such rebellion will be severely punished (Num 16–17).

Viewed from the clear perspective of the book of Numbers, the presentation in Deuteronomy appears to be seriously confused. The disorder is articulated well by the expression "levitical priests" (17:9, 18; 18:1; 24:8; 27:9), an expression which is unknown to the book of Numbers and appears to muddle what has been kept distinct. Deuteronomy (31:1–29) is inconsistent about who it is that bears the ark. Moses gives the lawbook to the priests so that they might deposit it in the ark that they carry (31:9), but it is the Levites who are charged with this task of porterage (31:25). But the confusion is perhaps most apparent in the legal prescriptions about the priests and Levites in a passage that has become a perennial puzzle for scholarship.

> [1]The levitical priests, the whole tribe of Levi, shall have no allotment or inheritance within Israel. They may eat the sacrifices that are the LORD's portion [2]but they shall have no inheritance among the other members of the community; the LORD is their inheritance, as he promised them.

³This shall be the priests' due from the people, from those offering a sacrifice, whether an ox or a sheep: they shall give to the priest the shoulder, the two jowls, and the stomach. ⁴The first fruits of your grain, your wine, and your oil, as well as the first of the fleece of your sheep, you shall give him. ⁵For the LORD your God has chosen Levi out of all your tribes, to stand and minister in the name of the LORD, him and his sons for all time.

⁶If a Levite leaves any of your towns, from wherever he has been residing in Israel, and comes to the place that the LORD will choose (and he may come whenever he wishes), ⁷then he may minister in the name of the LORD his God, like all his Fellow-Levites who stand to minister there before the LORD. ⁸They shall have equal portions to eat, even though they have income from the sale of family possessions. (18:1–8)[3]

On first appearances, the passage's structure appears to conform to the differentiated picture that we find in Numbers. An opening statement treats the tribe of Levi as a whole and prescribes that it will have no land inheritance among the other tribes of Israel (18:1–2). The priestly dues are then outlined (18:3–5) and then the reader learns about the provision of the Levites. They, too, will be cared for, if they make the journey to the chosen sanctuary (18:6–8). On closer examination, however, any clear distinction between priests and Levites appears to evaporate. The levitical priests are identified as the whole tribe of Levi, and not a small subset of the tribe (18:1). It would appear that the entire tribe enjoys consuming the sacrificial portions (18:1) despite the restriction of these in the book of Leviticus to Aaron and his family (Lev 1–7). The priests are said to stand and serve in YHWH's name (18:5), but a couple of verses later precisely the same is said of the Levites (18:7).

The reader is perplexed not only by the confusion of what were clear terminological distinctions but also by the strange socioeconomic situation Deuteronomy presupposes. The law code of Deuteronomy envisages the Levites finding themselves in straitened circumstances, which is surprising given that they seem relatively well provided for in the book of Numbers with the proceeds of the tithe. They number among Israel's needy—the resident alien, the widow, and the orphan—whom the Israelites are exhorted to treat generously (14:29; 16:11, 14; 26:12–13). They do not possess exclusive rights to the tithe, enjoying it only every third year and, even then, sharing it with other needy groups. These impoverished Levites, however, are never identified as levitical priests.

In the following essay, I will examine how attempts have been made to solve these puzzles by drawing on texts outside of Deuteronomy that are believed to shed light on the pre-Deuteronomic history of the Levites. Having shown the difficulties with these arguments, I will then turn to attempts to resolve the puzzles by examining what Deuteronomy has to say on priests and Levites. I will conclude by re-examining the legal prescriptions about the priests and Levites in Deuteronomy (18:1–8).

SOLUTIONS OUTSIDE OF DEUTERONOMY

Since reading the canonical portrayal of the Levites and priests in Numbers and Deuteronomy seems to present innumerable problems, a different kind of solution would seem to be needed. The decisive steps to resolving this conundrum were taken by Julius Wellhausen. Wellhausen's contribution is to be found in a single chapter of his *Prolegomena* to the *History of Israel* (Wellhausen 1885). The critical insight that animated the *Prolegomena* was that the priestly material in Exodus through Numbers represented the latest stage of Israel's religious development, not the earliest. As a result, Wellhausen insisted that it made no sense to approach Deuteronomy from the perspective of the priestly literature, such as the book of Numbers. Instead, Deuteronomy should be understood in the historical context of Josiah's reign when the book had been discovered in the Jerusalem temple—or perhaps even, written in order to be discovered. The central demand of this discovered lawbook was that sacrificial worship was no longer to be conducted at multiple sanctuaries around Judah but was to be restricted to Jerusalem alone. Wellhausen equated the Levites with the priests of these sanctuaries outside Jerusalem who were effectively made redundant when Josiah enacted the programmatic agenda of Deuteronomy in his seventh-century reform. The Deuteronomic lawgiver had already perceived that without some intervention the agenda of centralizing all cultic worship to Jerusalem and ending the provincial sanctuaries would inevitably result in the impoverishment of the priests who had serviced those local shrines. In anticipation, he legislated that they should have rights to officiate at the altar in Jerusalem alongside the local Jerusalem priesthood, who were descended from David's priest Zadok, and receive from the sacrificial dues (18:6–8). For the Deuteronomic legislator, then, there was to be no distinction between the local priesthood in Jerusalem and the incoming priests from the provinces—or, in his words, between the priests and the Levites. The radical reorganization of the priesthood that had to flow from the programme of centralization was succinctly expressed by the composite term "levitical priests."

In Wellhausen's view this idealistic scheme of Deuteronomy was not fully realized. According to the account of Josiah's reform,

> [Josiah] brought all the priests out of the towns of Judah, and defiled the high places where the priests had made offerings, from Geba to Beer-sheba; he broke down the high places of the gates that were at the entrance of the gate of Joshua the governor of the city, which were on the left at the gate of the city. The priests of the high places, however, did not come up to the altar of the LORD in Jerusalem, but ate unleavened bread among their kindred. (2 Kgs 23:8–9)

In Wellhausen's words, "The sons of Zadok were well enough pleased that all sacrifices should be concentrated within their temple, but they did not see their way to sharing their inheritance with the priesthood of the high places, and the idea was not carried out" (Wellhausen 1885, 124). The priests who had been forced to migrate to Jerusalem were not allowed to participate in the sacrificial cult or receive a share of the sacrificial portions; they had to make do with a meagre handout of unleavened bread. Ultimately, the Levites were to be given a diminished role in the Jerusalem temple as cultic assistants. Ezekiel (Ezek 44:15–31) attributes their demotion to their association with idolatrous worship but in the book of Numbers, composed somewhat later than Ezekiel, the origins of the Levites were projected back into the very beginnings of Israel as a nation and worshipping community.

In the history of the Israelite priesthood, as in so many other areas, Wellhausen's proposals have been the starting point for subsequent scholarly discussion. By identifying the Jerusalem priests with the Zadokite family who claimed descent from the preeminent priest during the reigns of David and Solomon (1 Kgs 2:26–35) and the priests at other sanctuaries as Levites, Wellhausen ensured that a much wider set of textual data was available for reconstructing the pre-Josianic history of the Levites. In this way, an extensive history of the Levites could be told from the historical books of Joshua to 2 Kings and the pre-exilic prophetic writings using references to the Levites *and* references to the priests at sanctuaries other than Jerusalem (Cody 1969; Leuchter 2017; Nurmela 1998).

In North America, Frank Moore Cross's essay on the priestly houses of Israel posited a long-running rivalry between priestly dynasties at Shiloh and Dan who saw Moses as their forebear and a priestly dynasty from Hebron that relocated to Jerusalem and claimed descent from Aaron (Cross 1973). Brief though it was, Cross's essay inspired a number of textual studies that plotted the history of pre-exilic rivalries within the priesthood (Halpern 1976; Olyan 1982). The centralization of the cult in Josiah's reign did nothing to diminish those rivalries in the early Second Temple period, and although the ascendancy of the descendants of Aaron was assured, the marginalized Levites continued to fight for some cultic rights (Hanson 1975).

Cross's Harvard colleague, Lawrence E. Stager, proposed seeing the Levites as landless young men who attached themselves to a patron as cult specialists (Stager 1985). The inspiration for this idea was the story of Micah's Levite (Judg 17–18) and a comparison to an important anthropological study of the priestly groups in the Moroccan Atlas Mountains (Gellner 1969). Stager's brief observation has been developed in a series of sophisticated cross-cultural studies by Jeremy Hutton that helps explain why the Levites were scattered throughout the secular tribes and what their role was in religious ceremonies and promoting community coherence (Hutton 2009, 2011a, 2011b, 2018).

The net result of this North American scholarship inspired by Cross and Stager is to suggest that a rich and complex sociological reality lay behind the references to the Levites in the biblical text and that this, in turn, can inform our understanding of the Levites in Deuteronomy. First, centralization was not a unique moment in the history of the Israelite cult, but just one episode in a long struggle for its control. Second, the impoverishment and landlessness of the Levites and their distribution throughout the Israelite tribes which Deuteronomy presupposes was a result of the Levites' unique function which can be explained by sociological comparison.

Problems with Seeking Solutions outside Deuteronomy

Wellhausen's equation of Deuteronomy's levitical priests with the priests of the high places in Josiah's day has proved highly influential with a number of scholars still holding it today (Leuchter 2007; Schaper 2000, 84–95). In one respect, recent scholarship has brought Deuteronomy's levitical priests closer to the priests of the high places. "The priests of the high places, however, did not come up to the altar of the LORD in Jerusalem, but (*ki 'im*) ate unleavened bread among their kindred" (2 Kgs 23:9). This translation is consistent with Wellhausen's understanding which construes the perfect "they ate unleavened bread" as a frequentative determined by the preceding imperfect "they did not come up" (Nicholson 2014, 19). But other examples of sentences with *ki 'im* seem to suggest instead that the perfect is a condition that must be met before the preceding statement can occur. Thus, a more appropriate translation would be "The priests of the high places, however, did not come up to the altar of the LORD in Jerusalem, until (*ki 'im*) they had eaten unleavened bread among their kindred" (Leuchter 2007). Consistent with the other measures, Josiah's actions (2 Kgs 23:1–27) seek to deal with the impurity resulting from the illicit cults that had flourished in Judah (Monroe 2011). The priests had defiled themselves through worshipping at the high places and as a result of their impurity they need to be removed from the towns (2 Kgs 23:8a).

The reference to unleavened bread would not be a reference to the priestly income but would possibly be related to a ritual of ordination or reconsecration, since a basket of unleavened bread is a component of the ordination ceremony for priests (Exod 29:1–37).[4] Thus, the priests of the high places in Judah could participate in priestly service at the temple in Jerusalem once they had been purified and reconsecrated. Whereas Wellhausen regarded Deuteronomy (18:1–8) as an idealistic legislation that was never realized, the revised understanding of Kings (2 Kgs 23:9) would see the redundant priests redeployed at the Jerusalem temple in accordance with the legislation's intent.

Unfortunately, though, the identification of the Levites and the priests of the high places encounters some insuperable difficulties. First, the Levites are nowhere identified in Deuteronomy as officiants at the high places, nor are the priests at the high places (2 Kgs 23) ever identified as Levites. Secondly, in Josiah's reform all the priests are forcibly removed from the high places and are presumably relocated to Jerusalem (2 Kgs 23: 9), but Deuteronomy envisages Levites serving at the central place on a voluntary basis and assumes that not all Levites exercised their rights (Gunneweg 1965, 118–126; Samuel 2014, 347–352).

If the impoverished Levites of Deuteronomy cannot be equated with the priests of the high places (2 Kgs 23), the consequences are that the numerous references to the priesthoods at various sanctuaries in pre-exilic literature cannot be utilized as evidence for the history of the Levites. We are, instead, reliant on identifying reliable references to the Levites before Josiah. Unfortunately, this proves to be a difficult.

Most references in the Pentateuch, outside of the book of Deuteronomy, are not only associated with the priestly literature, but with a developed stage of it. There are various texts that associate the patriarch Levi and his descendants with violence (Gen 34; 49:5–7; Exod 32:26–29) and these would appear to be etymological texts that already assume the Levites' role as guardians of the cult (Baden 2011). Most interest has circulated around the blessing of the tribe of Levi (Deut 33:8–11) since the blessing of Moses is a poetic text that is regarded as typologically early (Cross and Freedman 1975). It mentions the responsibility of caring for the Urim and Thummim as well as the Levitical role of teaching Torah. The blessing of Levi is difficult to interpret, but we should avoid assuming that a difficult text is necessarily an early one. The references to the covenant and the Levites' teaching function is clear evidence that the text has, at very least, been subject to later editing.

There are no references to the Levites that originate from the pre-exilic period in any of the Latter Prophets. The Former Prophets present a more complex picture. Although all the texts that refer to Levites portray events before Josiah, it is well known that Israel's history has been edited from a variety of perspectives, not least a Deuteronomistic one. There are a number of references to the Levites as bearers of the ark (Josh 3:3; 8:33; 1 Sam 6:15; 2 Sam 15:24; 1 Kgs 8:4), all of which appear to reflect Deuteronomistic, and often also priestly, texts that portray the Levites bearing the Tabernacle and its holy items. There is an isolated reference to the Levites (1 Kgs 12:31) that accuses Jeroboam of installing non-Levites to serve at his cult centres at Dan and Bethel. Such a reference appears to presuppose a legalistic perspective that priests must be Levites (Ueberschaer 2015, 199). There are two remaining sets of references to Levites in the Former Prophets that have drawn considerable interest: the list of Levitical cities (Josh 21) and the appendices to the book of Judges (Judg 17–21).

When Joshua divided up the land of Israel (Josh 13:1–21:45), the tribe of Levi is mentioned alongside the other tribes, but unlike them, it does not receive an inheritance. The portrayal of twelve tribes reflects the developed picture of Israel as a tribal confederacy that reaches this final, canonical state only in the Persian period. Equally late is the oft-repeated aphorism that Levi received no inheritance because YHWH—or, alternately, the offerings or the priesthood—is their inheritance (Josh 13:14, 33; 18:7). The division of the land has long been recognized to have a close relationship with the final parts of the book of Numbers and to have a distinctly priestly cast. In spite of this, the list of Levitical cities (Josh 21:1–34) has been the source of considerable speculation about its origins (Hutton 2011b). Wellhausen regarded the list with considerable skepticism and dated it to the late exilic or Persian period (Wellhausen 1885), but from Albright onward the list has not lacked for those who have discerned elements that can claim considerable historicity (Albright 1945). It is difficult to avoid the impression that the list is highly schematized and idealized, but also that it preserves topographical lists with an archival quality. Yet what kind of archive do they represent? The recognition that several cities occur along tribal boundaries suggests that the list of names may have originated with quite a different purpose in view and was only subsequently repurposed. It is a highly speculative basis upon which to reconstruct a pre-exilic history of the Levites.

The appendices to the book of Judges tell two stories about two individual Levites. The first tells of how a wandering Levite is employed as a priest in the household of Micah the Ephraimite until he is forcibly engaged by the passing Danite tribe as they relocate from lands on the coastal plain to the north of Israel. The narrative ends with a polemical etiology of the cult site at Dan and its priesthood (Judg 17–18). The second describes how a Levite and his concubine are set upon by the inhabitants of Gibeah as they were overnighting there (Judg 19–21). In their present literary context, the two narratives describe Israel's chaotic decline, and they do not seem to have a significant relationship with the stories about Israel's deliverers in the preceding chapters. This observation suggests that the stories have their own independent history. Unfortunately, it is unlikely that the Levite is deeply embedded in either story. This is most apparent in the second, where the characterization of the concubine's man as a "Levite" plays no part in the narrative and appears to be nothing more than a superficial hook to link the story of the Levite and his concubine with the story of Micah's Levite. If Micah's Levite is more deeply embedded in Judges (Judg 17–18), this is true only to a degree. The references to the Levite (Judg 17:7–13) are easily marked out by the repetitive resumption "in those days there was no king in Israel" (Judg 17:6; 18:1). The remaining story tells not of a Levite, but of a priest, and the two references to a Levite (Judg 18:3, 15) are clearly a gloss on the term *naʿar*, "cult servant."[5] As a result, we must conclude that the transformation of this story into a story about a Levite was relatively late and was part of a polemic against the northern sanctuary at Dan. As such, it cannot tell us very much, if anything, about Levites in the pre-exilic period.

Our brief survey has shown that there are no secure references to Levites before Josiah. Whereas certain texts, such as the list of the Levitical cities and the story of Micah's Levite, have played a significant role in textual and sociological reconstructions of the Levites in the time of the Hebrew monarchies, and sometimes even for the premonarchic period, they simply cannot bear the interpretive weight that has been placed upon them. They do not assist in understanding the problem of the Levites and the priests in Deuteronomy. The problem originates in the text of Deuteronomy, and only the text of Deuteronomy can assist us.

Seeking Solutions within Deuteronomy

One of the great attractions of Wellhausen's proposal was that it provide a solution to the major incoherence that seems to lie at the heart of Deuteronomy's presentation of the priests and Levites. The priests would appear to be identical with the Levites, such that they can be identified as "levitical priests," but the Levites are regarded as a group just as impoverished as the widow, the orphan, and the resident alien. If the Levites of Deuteronomy are not the redundant priests of the high places, how is this puzzling feature to be explained?

George Ernest Wright argued that we are not dealing with one group, but two. There are the altar clergy, which Deuteronomy identifies as "levitical priests," and the client Levites, whose religious function was to teach. The altar clergy enjoyed a share of the sacrificial offerings, while the client Levites were dependent upon the liberality of their fellow Israelites. On the basis of their context, the various references to the Levites in Deuteronomy could be related to either one group or the other (Wright 1954). Wright's proposal not only had the apparent advantage of explaining the perplexing material in Deuteronomy, it also suggested that the difference with the priestly code was overstated. By the time the priestly literature was composed a century or so later than Deuteronomy, the "levitical priests" had become priests from the household of Aaron and the client Levites were a lower clergy that assisted them.

The difficulty with Wright's proposal, as John Emerton shows, is that nowhere does Deuteronomy make this distinction between levitical priests and client Levites explicit, and there are texts that seem to assume the altar service is a right of the entire tribe (10:8; 18:5). More problematic still is Wright's interpretation of Deuteronomy (18:1–8). The most natural way to read לא יהיה לכהנים הלוים כל שבט לוי חלק ונחלה עם ישראל (18:1) is to understand "the levitical priests" in apposition with "all the tribes of Levi," and so to translate with something like "The levitical priests, *namely* the whole tribe of Levi, shall have no allotment or inheritance with Israel." Wright uses his understanding of the levitical priests and the Levites elsewhere in Deuteronomy to override the syntax and renders the Hebrew as though it referred to one group and a larger group that included it: "the levitical priests and the whole tribe of Levi." Similarly, Wright has to understand the Levite who relocates to the central sanctuary in order to serve there as an altar priest (18:6–8), despite the fact that elsewhere in Deuteronomy, he interprets mentions of "the Levite" as a reference to his client Levites. The decision appears to be driven by his interpretive framework rather than the textual evidence (Emerton 1962).

Wright's essay and Emerton's response inspired further articles that sought to reinforce Wright's arguments and counter Emerton's objections. Raymond Abba argued that the terms "priest" and "Levite" were not synonymous terms in Deuteronomy, even if certain functions such as the carrying of the ark could be discharged by either group. Interestingly, he observes that this ambiguity about the carrying of the ark is found in both Deuteronomy (10:8) and the appendices to Deuteronomy (31:1–34:12). The overlap between the responsibilities of the two groups can also be seen in the terms that are used. The Levites are said to שרת בשם יהוה, "minister in the name of YHWH," and עמד לפני יהוה, "stand before YHWH" (18:6–8). It has often been claimed that these terms refer to priestly duties, but Abba observes that neither term is used exclusively of altar service. Thus, in his view Deuteronomy (18:6–8) refers to all the Levites, both the altar priests and the remaining Levites (Abba 1977).

Gordon McConville is similarly concerned to eliminate the differences between the priestly literature and Deuteronomy. He examines texts in Deuteronomy (27:9–14; 31:9, 25) where the alternation of priests and Levites is most conspicuous and concludes that there is a certain looseness or terminological inconsistency, such that in Deuteronomy we seem to have an easy movement between levitical priest and Levite (27:1–26). McConville locates the reasons for this ambiguity in a theological concern to avoid any distinction within the tribe of Levi just as there is a concern to avoid distinction between the different Israelite tribes. Thus, like Abba he also regards Deuteronomy (18:6–8) as addressed to all within the tribe of Levi (McConville 1984, 125–153).

Rodney Duke focused simply on Deuteronomy (18:6–8) and argued that the syntax had been incorrectly understood. The legislation about the Levite opens with a protasis, "If a Levite leaves any of your towns ... and comes to the chosen place." Most translations have assumed that the apodosis begins with "then he may minister" (18:7), but Duke makes a compelling case that the apodosis does not begin until the following verse (18:8). The legislation insists that the Levite who comes to the chosen place and ministers there with his fellow Levites may enjoy the rewards that accrue to those who minister there. The text does not prescribe how a Levite (18:6) may function as a priest (18:7), but rather stipulates that a Levite who undertakes (nonpriestly) cultic service receive compensation (Duke 1987).

The course of the scholarly debate reveals a number of important features of the problem with the Levites and priests in Deuteronomy. First, it proves very difficult to provide a reading of the developed form of Deuteronomy that can make sense of its portrayal of the priests and Levites. In some places there appear to be two quite distinct groups—those who function as priests and an impoverished group dependent on the generosity of other Israelites. But in other places, the distinction appears to evaporate. McConville's candid admission that there is a certain terminological looseness and inconsistency is not so much a solution as an admission that it is impossible to provide a satisfactory account of the present form of the text. Second, the terminological problems are not so much a problem of looseness or imprecision. Rather, there is a wealth of terms that are used in distinct ways elsewhere in the Hebrew canon but related to one another in ways that are perplexing considering their usage elsewhere. "Levi," "the Levites," "the sons of Levi," "the tribe of Levi," "levitical priests," and "priests" jostle alongside one another in unexpected ways. Third, the problems are not equally distributed through Deuteronomy but occur in distinct patterns. The regulations dedicated to the provision of the priests and Levites (18:1–8) clearly presents difficulties. But so do the references to the priests and Levites in the framework to the law code (10; 27; 31).

Such features have led several scholars to diachronic solutions, not least in light of the fact that the book of Deuteronomy is held by many to have a particularly complex literary history. Its origins may well begin in the late monarchic period with the law code and its emphasis on centralization (Levinson 1997), but a relatively slim framework was developed especially as Deuteronomy found itself located at the beginning of an extensive history of Israel's life in the land and then at the conclusion of a priestly history of Israel's life outside the land (Otto 2000).

In light of Deuteronomy's development, it is striking that the references to the impoverished Levites are restricted to the law code, and especially to those parts concerned with centralization (12:2–16:17; 26:1–15). The Levite appears either in two different lists. In the household list of those who feast at the chosen sanctuary, the Levite is mentioned last after the male and female servants. "You shall rejoice before YHWH your God, you together with your sons and your daughters, your male and female slaves, and the Levites who reside in your towns" (12:12; cf. 12:18; 14:26–27). In the list of the needy who benefit from the largesse of Israelite households, such as those who share in the triennial tithe, the Levite appears first (14:29; 26:11–13). In the festival legislation (16:1–17) the two lists are combined with the Levite acting as the pivot between the two lists (16:11, 14). In the law code, we also have references to "priests" without any qualification of them as Levitical in any respect (17:12; 18:3; 19:17; 26:3–4). There are also several laws which refer to levitical priests. One critical issue is whether there was an early stage of Deuteronomy's development when Levites and priests were completely distinct from one another, with the priests subsequently being "leviticized" (Achenbach 1999; Dahmen 1996), or whether the earliest stages of Deuteronomy's law code already identified the priests as Levitical (Samuel 2014). In the later stages of Deuteronomy's development, the priests are provided with a Levitical genealogy. They are no longer the "Levites," but "the sons of Levi" (21:5; 31:9). They are also granted a tribal status, "the tribe of Levi" (10:8; 18:1). Consistent with the later stages of the priestly literature, Levitical descent includes both the priests and the Levites, and so the Levites can be said to have ritual responsibilities that may elsewhere be limited only to priests: they carry the ark, they stand before YHWH, they minister to him, and they bless in his name (10:8).

While a diachronic approach to Deuteronomy provides a satisfactory explanation for many of the perplexing features that we have identified in the text, it also generates puzzles of its own. What was the nature of the impoverished Levites? One possibility is that they were named in the household lists because of their association with the cult. An alternative possibility is that they were simply landless individuals who were attached (לוה) to a landowner for whom they worked. A further perplexing puzzle is to explain why an association between impoverished Levites and priests occurred. Did the impoverished Levites already have a cultic association which might explain their presence at the pilgrimage feasts? Or was their association with cult ceremonies, the development in the Persian period of an ideal that the priests were to gain their income from their cultic service alone, and not from their own landholdings? On these issues the text is frustratingly silent, and we can only speculate.

THE INTERPRETATION OF DEUTERONOMY 18:1-8

No text has been more challenging than Deuteronomy's portrayal of priests, Levites and levitical priests (18:1–8). As a conclusion to our examination of this issue, I return to this crucial and puzzling text. It will further illustrate the difficulties with a synchronic approach to the problem, demonstrate the insights that can result from a diachronic approach, and also highlight the uncertainties that remain.

The regulations concerning the Levites and priests is a clearly defined unit of text. It opens with a general principle, "the levitical priests, the entire tribe of Levi, shall have no allotment or inheritance with Israel," which signals the beginning of a new topic after the regulations concerning the king (17:14–20). The following topic is also clearly indicated by the temporal clause, "When you come into the land" (18:9).

The purpose of the regulations is to prescribe the provision for the cultic officials. The general principle (18:1–2) describe this in a negative way: the tribe of Levi is not to receive a tribal allocation within the Promised Land. Two positive regulations follow, one for the priests and one for the Levites. The priests are to receive a share of the sacrifices and the first fruits (18:3–4), while the Levites will receive an unspecified portion of food if they participate in the cultic worship at the chosen sanctuary (18:6–8). This reading understands "They shall have equal portions to eat, even though they have income from the sale of family possessions (18:8)" as the apodosis, rather than "then he may minister in the name of the Lord his God, like all his fellow-Levites who stand to minister there before the Lord. They shall have equal portions to eat, even though they have income from the sale of family possessions" (18:7–8). The instructions concerning the Levites are consistent with the rest of the unit in providing for the material sustenance of a cultic group, rather than setting the conditions for them undertaking cultic ministry (Duke 1987). In its present form the instructions about the provision of cultic officials clearly reflects the settled position of the priestly literature. The Israelite clergy are all members of a single tribal grouping, the tribe of Levi, and fall into two major groups: the priests and the Levites. While the entire tribe is responsible for the proper conduct of the cult—both priests and Levites are said to "stand and minister before YHWH"—their distinct provisions points to their differentiated statuses within the cult.

The consistency of Deuteronomy (18:1–8) with the priestly literature's portrayal of the priests and Levites cannot obscure some of the features that betray a complex editorial history. First, there is the profusion of terms for the cultic officials: "levitical priests" (18:1), "the tribe of Levi" (18:1), "the priests" (18:3), and "the Levites" (18:7). The use of "levitical priests" as a synonym for "the entire tribe of Levi" is particularly problematic and is at odds with the settled position of the priestly literature. Second, "The levitical priests, the whole tribe of Levi, shall have no allotment or inheritance within Israel. They may eat the sacrifices that are the Lord's portion" (18:1) and "but they shall have no inheritance among the other members of the community; the Lord is their inheritance, as he promised them" (18:2) are doublets; one mostly in the plural, the other in the singular. Third, the instructions concerning the priests and the Levites do not form neat parallels. The priests are spoken of in plural (18:3–5), while we have a case concerning an individual Levite (18:6–8). The priestly dues occur in a prescription, but the case of the Levite is presented in a conditional form. As a result, the discussion of the Levite appears to introduce a new theme, rather than a continuation of the existing one, as recognized by the Masoretic division marker (Samuel 2014, 112).

The doublet (18:1–2) is easily dealt with. The second verse depends on the first verse and cannot have existed independently, and the singular would appear to refer to "the tribe of Levi" in the previous verse. The reference to "what YHWH promised him" is similar to "as the LORD your God promised him" (10:9), and both are probably best understood as allusions to Numbers (18:1-7), a late priestly text (Dahmen 1996, 58-66). Rather more problematic are the specific cases of the priests (18:3-5) and the Levite (18:6-8). They do not sit together easily, and we might expect that one or other has been added at some stage in order to assimilate Deuteronomy's regulations with the priestly literature's division of the cultic officials into priests and Levites. The most detailed examinations of this problem in the recent literature have taken divergent approaches. Dahmen regards the rules about the Levite to be secondary, while Samuel sees the regulation for the priests as later (Dahmen 1996, 263-320; Samuel 2014, 108-124).

The disagreement between Dahmen and Samuel illustrates that the issue is finely poised. The two regulations have quite different characters. The priestly regulation reads like a typical tariff text and much of the language is uncharacteristic of Deuteronomy except for the typical Deuteronomic archaism for the so-called Mediterranean triad—"the first fruits of your grain, your wine and your oil" (18:4). It seems likely that the tariff had its origins outside of Deuteronomy before being incorporated into the book. But at what stage was it incorporated? The differences between this tariff and those in the priestly literature suggest it was incorporated at an early stage in the book's development. The Levitical ruling, however, repeatedly echoes Deuteronomic idioms. The Levite comes "from one of your gates" to "the place YHWH will choose" and he does so according to his own wish (12:15, 20, 21). These similarities could show that the verses (18:6-8) were composed as part of the *Urdeuteronomium*, but it is difficult to see how the impoverished Levites found elsewhere in the *Urdeuteronomium* can have had income from the sale of a patrimony. To this observation we may add the fact that the language echoes Deuteronomic idiom, but the use here (18:6-8) is a distinctive application that suggests a later appropriation of Deuteronomic diction for new purposes. Thus, the balance of the evidence suggests then that we view the regulation of the priests as earlier and the regulation of the Levite as a later addition.

One further issue remains to be addressed: were the priests of the tariff regulation (18:3-4) always identified as levitical priests (18:1)? This goes to the heart of another disagreement between Dahmen and Samuel. Were the priests "leviticized" at a later stage in Deuteronomy's textual development or were Deuteronomy's priests always "levitical priests"? One suggestion is to view הלוים (18:1) as a gloss, and while the possibility cannot be excluded, textual evidence is lacking. Another suggestion is that in its original form, the priestly tariff began with "This shall be the priests' due" (18:3). The formula could certainly be the beginning of a new legal ruling parallel with "These will be the ways of the king" (1 Sam 8:11), though similar expressions in Deuteronomy do not introduce laws (15:2; 19:4). The parallel in Samuel (1 Sam 8:11) and the fact that the Deuteronomic examples are not exact parallels possibly tilts the argument toward seeing "This shall be the priests' due" (18:3) as the original beginning of the rule.

In conclusion, Deuteronomy's teaching in the law of the levitical priests is arguably the most complicated text in the book that concerns priests and Levites, but because of this it illustrates well the problems that confront the interpreter. The present form of the text can be read as consistent with the settled position of the priestly literature on the distinction between priests and Levites, but there are too many wrinkles in the portrayal for this to be a satisfactory reading. And yet if we try to explore those wrinkles, we soon encounter the limitations of the evidence our material provides. The origins of the Levites remain something of a mystery as does the reason for their association with the cult.

Notes

1. The exceptions are Exod 6:25; 32:25–28; 38:21; Lev 25:32–33. Exodus 6:25 concludes the genealogy of Moses and Aaron (6:14–25), a text that has long been recognized as intrusive and has affinities with some of the latest parts of the Pentateuch, including texts in Numbers (Achenbach 2003, 110–124). Similarly, the reference to the Levites in the story of the Golden Calf (Exod 32:25–28) has also been judged an addition. Their appearance is unanticipated and the slaughter of just three thousand when the entire people is guilty is unexplained. For a recent examination coming to a different view, see Samuel (2014, 270–294). The mention of the Levites in Exod 38:21 is entirely unanticipated and seems to have in view their work of transportation. It appears rather oddly in a text that is concerned with the fabrication of the Tabernacle (Driver 1911, 392; Samuel 2014, 294–295). The reference to the Levites in the Jubilee legislation (Lev 25:32–33) presupposes the legislation about the levitical cities and is usually judged an interpolation (Nihan 2007, 522n503).
2. I am grateful to Anselm Hagedorn for reading an early draft of this essay and for his incisive suggestions.
3. Unless otherwise noted, English translations are from the New Revised Standard Version (NRSV) 1989.
4. The alternative suggestion that the unleavened bread relates to the celebration of Passover suffers from the lack of any connection between 2 Kgs 23:9 and Exod 29:21–23. Recently, Nicholson has suggested that eating unleavened bread means enjoying the hospitality of their "brother" Israelites (Nicholson 2014, 29–34): "it means nothing more than that these now 'altarless' priests received the support appropriate to their status deriving from their priestly pedigree" (Nicholson 2014, 31). Nicholson's syllogism links unleavened bread to hospitality, and the Levites to showing hospitality, but there is no link between Levites and unleavened bread, for nowhere else is unleavened bread identified as a priestly prerogative.
5. NRSV's translation of *hanna'ar hallevi*, as though it were a typical combination of noun and adjective, "the young Levi," obscures the difficulties.

Bibliography

Abba, R. 1977. "Priests and Levites in Deuteronomy." *Vetus Testamentum* 27: 257–267.

Achenbach, R. 1999. "Levitische Priester und Leviten im Deuternomium: Überlegungen zur sog. 'Levitisierung' des Priestertums." *Zeitschrift für Altorientalische und Biblische Rechtsgeschichte* 5: 285–309.

Achenbach, R. 2003. *Die Vollendung der Tora: Studien zur Redaktionsgeschichte des Numeribuches im Kontext von Hexateuch und Pentateuch*. Wiesbaden: Harrassowitz.

Albright, W. F. 1945. "The List of Levitic Cities." In *Louis Ginsberg Jubilee Volume on the Occasion of his Seventieth Birthday*, 49–73. New York: American Academy for Jewish Research.

Baden, J. S. 2011. "The Violent Origins of the Levites: Text and Tradition." In *"The Lord is Their Inheritance": Levites and Priests in History and Tradition*, edited by J. M. Hutton and M. Leuchter, 103–116. Atlanta: Society of Biblical Literature.

Cody, A. 1969. *A History of Old Testament Priesthood*. Rome: Pontifical Biblical Institute.

Cross, F. M. 1973. "The Priestly Houses of Early Israel." In *Canaanite Myth and Hebrew Epic: Essays in the History of the Religion of Israel*, 195–215. Cambridge: Harvard University Press.

Cross, F. M., and Freedman, D. N. 1975. *Studies in Ancient Yahwistic Poetry*. Missoula: Scholars Press.

Dahmen, U. 1996. *Leviten und Priester im Deuteronomium: Literarkrititische und redaktionsgeschichtliche Studien*. Bodenheim: Philo.

Driver, S. R. 1911. *The Book of Exodus*. Cambridge: Cambridge University Press.

Duke, R. K. 1987. "The Portion of the Levite: Another Reading of Deuteronomy 18:6–8." *Journal of Biblical Literature* 106: 193–201.

Emerton, J. A. 1962. "Priests and Levites in Deuteronomy." *Vetus Testamentum* 12: 129–138.

Gellner, E. 1969. *Saints of the Atlas*. Chicago: University of Chicago Press.

Gunneweg, A. H. J. 1965. *Leviten und Priester: Hauptlinien der Traditionsbildung und Geschichte des israelitisch-jüdischen Kultpersonals*. Göttingen: Vandenhoeck & Ruprecht.

Halpern, B. 1976. "Levitic Participation in the Reform Cult of Jeroboam I." *Journal of Biblical Literature* 95: 31–42.

Hanson, P. D. 1975. *The Dawn of Apocalyptic*. Philadelphia: Fortress Press.

Hutton, J. M. 2009. "The Levitical Diaspora (I): A Sociological Comparison with Morocco's Ahansel." In *Exploring the Longue Durée: Essays in Honor of Lawrence E. Stager*, edited by J. D. Schloen, 223–234. Winona Lake: Eisenbrauns.

Hutton, J. M. 2011a. "All the King's Men: The Families of the Priests in Cross-Cultural Perspective." In *"Seitenblicke": Literarische und historische Studien zu Nebenfiguren im zweiten Samuelbuch*, edited by W. Dietrich, 121–151. Göttingen: Vandenhoeck & Ruprecht.

Hutton, J. M. 2011b. "The Levitical Diaspora (II): Modern Perspectives on the Levitical Cities Lists (A Review of Opinions)." In *Levites and Priests in Biblical History and Tradition*, edited by J. M. Hutton and M. A. Leuchter, 45–81. Atlanta: SBL Press.

Hutton, J. M. 2018. "Levitical Aspirations and Saintly Foundation Stories in Judges 17–18." *Eretz-Israel* 33: 98–108.

Leuchter, M. 2007. "'The Levite in Your Gates': The Deuteronomic Redefinition of Levitical Authority." *Journal of Biblical Literature* 126: 417–436.

Leuchter, M. 2017. *The Levites and the Boundaries of Israelite Identity*. Oxford: Oxford University Press.

Levinson, B. M. 1997. *Deuteronomy and the Hermeneutics of Legal Innovation*. Oxford: Oxford University Press.

McConville, J. G. 1984. *Law and Theology in Deuteronomy*. Sheffield: JSOT Press.

Monroe, L. A. S. 2011. *Josiah's Reform and the Dynamics of Defilement: Israelite Rites of Violence and the Making of a Biblical Text*. Oxford: Oxford University Press.

Nicholson, E. 2014. *Deuteronomy and the Judaean Diaspora*. Oxford: Oxford University Press.

Nihan, C. 2007. *From Priestly Torah to Pentateuch: A Study in the Composition of the Book of Leviticus*. Tübingen: Mohr Siebeck.

Nurmela, R. 1998. *The Levites: Their Emergence as a Second-Class Priesthood*. Atlanta: Scholars Press.

Olyan, S. 1982. "Zadok's Origins and the Tribal Politics of David." *Journal of Biblical Literature* 101: 177–193.

Otto, E. 2000. *Das Deuteronomium im Pentateuch und Hexateuch: Studien zur Literaturgeschichte von Pentateuch und Hexateuch im Lichte des Deuteronomiumrahmens*. Tübingen: Mohr Siebeck.

Samuel, H. 2014. *Von Priestern zum Patriarchen: Levi und die Leviten im Alten Testament.* Berlin: De Gruyter.
Schaper, J. 2000. *Priester und Leviten im achämenidischen Juda: Studien zur Kult- und Sozialgeschichte Israels in persischer Zeit.* Tübingen: Mohr Siebeck.
Stager, L. E. 1985. "The Archaeology of the Family in Ancient Israel." *Bulletin of the American Schools of Oriental Research* 260: 1–35.
Ueberschaer, F. 2015. *Vom Gründungsmythos zur Untergangssymphonie: Eine Text- und Literaturgeschichtliche Untersuchung zu 1Kön 11–14.* Berlin: de Gruyter.
Wellhausen, J. 1885. *Prolegomena to the History of Israel with a Reprint of the Article Israel from the "Encyclopaedia Britannica."* Translated by J. S. Black and A. Menzies. Edinburgh: Adam & Charles Black.
Wright, G. E. 1954. "The Levites in Deuteronomy." *Vetus Testamentum* 4: 325–330.

CHAPTER 16

THE "STRANGER, FATHERLESS, AND WIDOW" IN DEUTERONOMY

MARK R. GLANVILLE

WHO BEGAN THE CONVERSATION?

THE "stranger, fatherless, and widow," (הגר והיתום והאלמנה), is a formula in Deuteronomy that refers to vulnerable people in the community who lack meaningful kinship connection, and thereby the subsistence, protection, and belonging that comes with such connection. Within Deuteronomy this triad appears in feasting texts, laws of judicial procedure, social law, curse ceremony, and covenant texts. The triad occurs with the purpose of both providing for and incorporating these vulnerable people. As such, the formula is a part of Deuteronomy's vocabulary for integration. In the literary development of the Pentateuch, the vulnerable triad appears first in Deuteronomy.

The triad appears in its simple form four times in Deuteronomy (24:19, 20, 21; 27:19). It also appears with some variation: in two cases the triad appears with separation between the people categories (10:18; 24:17). In five references the Levite is listed with the triad, forming a quartet: the Levite, stranger, fatherless, and widow (14:29; 16:11, 14; 26:12, 13). In the Feast of the First Fruits, only the Levite and stranger are listed (26:11).

The lists are shaped in light of the literary or theological context of each occurrence. The Feast of First Fruits (26:1–11) is concerned with displacement (26:5b), a theme which applies particularly to the *gēr*. Due to the Levite's association with the cultus, the Levite alone appears with the household in the Tithe Feast (14:27). The stranger is the only category of vulnerability to appear in various laws of judicial procedure (1:16–17) and covenant ceremony (29:9–14; 31:9–13), due to the particular concern for displaced people in Deuteronomy's framework (1–11, 27–34) which comprises later redactions.

In the past fifty years or so, numerous scholars have analyzed the pregnant ethics in Deuteronomy on behalf of the most vulnerable in the community. Notably, in 1972, Moshe Weinfeld published *Deuteronomy and the Deuteronomic School*, in which he observes the "humanist" character of Deuteronomy, among other things. Weinfeld finds the source of

Deuteronomy's concern for vulnerable people in the wisdom tradition. "Scribes and wise men" produced Deuteronomy, he argues, recasting the wisdom tradition in terms of humanism, didacticism, and the doctrine of reward.

Georg Braulik has probed Deuteronomy's ethics in numerous articles. In "Deuteronomy and Human Rights" (1986),[1] Braulik explores how Deuteronomy embeds the provisions for the most vulnerable in the theology and ethics of the exodus. Not only is the exodus an act of slave emancipation of massive proportions but also with the exodus YHWH is birthing an entirely new community. YHWH not only "brought out" the people from slavery but also "brought in" this people, into the land (6:10–12), in order to live as "a society which is the opposite of the system from which Israel has escaped."[2] Much work has been done on the stranger, fatherless, and widow in Deuteronomy, beyond that of Baulik and Weinfeld, and we summarize the scholarly analysis in the following two sections, in addition to making our own observations.

Stranger, Fatherless, and Widow

Historical Development of the Triad

We may trace the historical development of the literary trope "stranger, fatherless, widow." The doublet "fatherless, widow" appears in many texts from the Near East, especially from Mesopotamia. The oldest extant reference is found in the reform texts of Urukagina: "Urukagina made a covenant with Ningirsu that a man of power must not commit an [injustice] against an orphan or widow."[3]

Another early reference is in the Epic of Aqhat from Ugarit. As Fensham tells the story: "While Daniel the king was waiting for the god of Crafts, Kothar-wa-hasis, to bring a bow for Aqhat, his son, he was busy judging the cause of the widow and orphan."[4] Building upon this established formula, the Covenant Code (Exod 20:22–23:19) associates the stranger with the fatherless-widow doublet. Yet in the Covenant Code the stranger is not included in the list: "You shall not wrong or oppress a stranger, for you were strangers in the land of Egypt. You shall not abuse any widow or fatherless" (Exod 22:21–22; cf. 23:9).[5]

The Deuteronomic Code, authored later than the Covenant Code, both appropriates and develops upon the Covenant Code. Deuteronomy incorporates the stranger at the head of the traditional doublet. In addition, Deuteronomy reverses the order of doublet as it is found in the Covenant Code: "widow, fatherless" is rendered: "fatherless, widow." Thus, the vulnerable triad, "stranger, fatherless, widow," is an innovation of Deuteronomy.[6]

On the one hand, the stranger fits easily with the doublet "fatherless, widow," as all three figures have in common an absence of meaningful kinship connection. On the other hand, there are differences in the vulnerabilities of each category. In a sense, the fatherless and widow are especially vulnerable, for there is no male kinsperson who takes responsibility for such people. Yet the fatherless and widow may nonetheless belong within the clan within which they reside, providing protection that the stranger does not enjoy (Ruth 2:1). Thus, the common claim in scholarship that the triad "stranger, fatherless, and widow" is "the poor par excellence"[7] lacks precision. Furthermore, the fact that the stranger comes first in the triad of the vulnerable is significant, for given the legacy of the doublet—"fatherless and widow"—one would expect otherwise. This is evidence that widespread displacement is a primary social issue in the community before Deuteronomy. Ramírez Kidd has catalogued other class nouns that occur in Near Eastern texts along with the doublet—"fatherless and widow"—observing that the stranger does not appear alongside the "fatherless and widow" outside of the Hebrew Bible. This again highlights the significance of the appearance of the stranger in Deuteronomy.[8] With this transformation of the established doublet—"fatherless and widow"—Deuteronomy articulates its ethics regarding displaced people in terms of an already established literary tradition within Israel and the ancient Near East.

Fatherless, Widow, and Stranger in the Near East

Separated from the protection of male kindred, the fatherless and widow were particularly vulnerable in the world of the Near East. Safeguarding the well-being of the fatherless and the widow was a common policy and the particular responsibility of kings.[9] It is clear that these groups were vulnerable to indebtedness and ultimately to slavery from, among other texts, an edict of release of King Uru-inimgina of Lagash, who is said to have established freedom for debtors, widows, and orphans.[10]

Similarly in Egypt, the divine assembly cared for the orphan and widow, and so the pharaoh was also responsible to care for these, in harmony with the cosmic order.[11] Although such beneficence was an indispensable part of royal ideology, in practice it was common enough for households to co-opt the poor in order to provide cheap labor. Ignatius Gelb states that "Women and children without household and other 'rejects of the society' were an important component of the labour force of large early Mesopotamian households."[12] The temple household could bolster its labour force by taking in the fatherless, the widows and other vulnerable people, sometimes under the guise of charity and sometimes by force.[13] These vulnerable people would then assume semi-free status.

Deuteronomy resists this practice of co-opting the fatherless and the widow as cheap labor. Moreover, Deuteronomy envisages that the fatherless and the widow would become full participants in the familial, ritual, religious, and working life of the household, the village, and, indeed, the nation.

Fatherless

"Fatherless" (יתום, *yātôm*) always appears alongside the widow and/or the stranger in the Pentateuch. The term in the Hebrew Bible refers to a child who is fatherless and may or may not have a mother (Exod 22:24; Ps 109:9). On the one hand, when children lost only their father and not their mother, they shared vulnerability with the widowed mother. They may dwell with the mother on patrimonial land for the duration of the mother's life, and sons may inherit the land.[14] Kristine Garroway states, "Without a male guardian, a child was without legal representation."[15] Yet, according to Deuteronomy, women had legal agency (21:19; 22:15; 24:4; 25:7–9), and so it is probably more accurate to surmise that the fatherless lacked the protection, provision, patrimony, and cultic rights that a paterfamilias would provide. If the mother remarried, the stepfather was not obligated to include the child in his inheritance, and the child could be vulnerable to abuse.[16] On the other hand, if a child had a father but no mother, then the child was not fatherless for he or she was under the authority of the father.[17] Needless to say, the fatherless who had also lost his or her mother was in a perilous situation indeed. In what follows, we will use the English term "fatherless" in translating *yātôm*.

A child could be orphaned involuntarily or voluntarily, on the part of the parents.[18] In the first scenario, the child's parents may have died, orphaning the child. Yet voluntarily abandoning a child was not uncommon in the Near East. A child could be "exposed," a term which refers to the legal relinquishment of an unwanted child.[19] In such a case, another household could adopt the child, taking the child into a new household.[20] This process of legal relinquishment and subsequent adoption is reflected in the Psalter: "If my father and mother forsake [עָזַב] me, YHWH will take me up [אָסַף]" (Ps 27:10).

At one level, abandoning and adopting children was a common way of balancing the diverse and challenging needs of households in Israel and in the Near East. Whereas in normal circumstances an adopted child tended to enjoy the privileges of inheritance, the fortunes of an abandoned orphan who was subsequently adopted depended upon the desire of the adoptee. An abandoned child may even be enslaved.[21]

Widow

"Widow" (אלמנה, *'almānâ*) is, according to Paula S. Hiebert, "A woman without males who are responsible for supporting her."[22] It is evident that the English word *widow* does not accurately translate the Hebrew term. The English term refers to a woman who has lost her husband through death and who has not remarried. Such a person may or may not be an *'almānâ* in the ancient world. When a woman married in ancient Israel, she transferred from the sphere of authority of her natal household to the authority of the household of her husband (Gen 38:24; Num 30:1–11; Ruth 1:9).[23] Thus, upon the death of her husband, the responsibility for a women's sustenance fell upon her sons of a suitable age or upon her father-in-law.[24]

The ongoing authority and responsibility of the father-in-law for a woman who has lost her husband may be observed negatively in the tyrannical authority of Judah over Tamar. Even though Tamar had returned to live within the household of her father, Judah was able nonetheless to decree her execution (Gen 38:24). Thus, the term *'almānâ* describes a woman whose husband has died and who has no sons and no father-in-law to take responsibility for her. Legally, the *'almānâ* was not under the authority of any man (Num 30:9). In what follows, we will use the English term "widow" in translating *'almānâ*.

Evidently, some widows owned land or money which could be used for their subsistence; some were independent and even of some means (Jud 17:1–6; 1 Sam, 25:42; 2 Kgs 8:1–3; Jdt 8:4, 7).[25] However, the vast majority of widows in ancient Israel barely subsisted, if at all (16:11, 14; 21:19–21). In this light, widowhood became a metaphor for destitution in Israel and throughout the Near East (Is 54:4). Regardless of whether an *'almānâ* was impoverished or of some means, with no male patron she was virtually an outsider in the kin grouping of her husband. And, with no male to be outraged at any offense committed against her, the *'almānâ* was vulnerable to oppression (24:17; 27:19). Nonetheless, widowhood seems to have been free from negative stigma in Israel. According to the Holiness Code (Lev 17:1–26:46), a priest may marry a widow but not a divorcee (Lev 21:1–15).[26] A High Priest, however, may *not* marry a widow (Lev 21:14).

Evidently, then, the terms "fatherless" and "widow" refer to a person of a specific status. Notwithstanding, it seems that in Deuteronomy the doublet "fatherless and widow" has a generic quality as a reference to the poor, while the terms "stranger" (גר, gēr) and "Levite" represent figures who are of peculiar social and theological concern for Deuteronomy.

Stranger

The noun "stranger" occurs twenty-two times in Deuteronomy. In an earlier monograph, Christiana van Houten suggested a translation, "resident alien."[27] Although this translation may be appropriate in the Holiness Code, it is inappropriate in Deuteronomy. In Deuteronomy, the stranger is not only resident in a new context but also dependent in that context. Dependency is visible in the stranger's labour within the household and the settlement (5:14; 24:14), in his or her inclusion within the triad of the vulnerable (16:11a, 14), in the reference "your stranger" (5:14; 29:10), in the phrase, "in your midst,"[28] and in the local provision for his or her sustenance (14:28–29; 26:12–15). Thus, a better translation for gēr is "dependent stranger." In what follows, we will use the English term "stranger" in translating gēr.

The stranger has left kinship ties, village, and land, and she or he now dwells within a community within which she or he has no blood relations or patrimony (24:14–15; 26:5). She or he is therefore without the protection and privileges that kin ties and place of birth afford (26:6). The stranger is easily oppressed, as there are no household members to be outraged at any injustice that may be perpetrated against her or him (1:16–17).

There are three contending views in the scholarship for the origin of the stranger: a refugee displaced by the Assyrian invasion of Israel in the seventh century BCE;[29] a foreigner from a kingdom other than either Judah or Israel;[30] and an internally displaced Judahite.[31] The second model represents the current scholarly trend. To be sure, there is evidence that some of the strangers for whom Deuteronomy is concerned were foreigners. The provision that the stranger may consume a carcass that has not been properly slaughtered exempts the stranger from the principle of not eating blood (14:21), which probably signifies that here the stranger stands outside of the community of YHWH (28:43–44). Mark Awabdy, in his recent monograph translates gēr as "immigrant," arguing that the gēr in Deuteronomy is a non-Judahite and non-Israelite who is residing within Israelite settlements.[32]

Deuteronomy, however, does not conceive of identity in exclusively "national" or "ethnic" categories that yield a simple binary distinction: Israel/not-Israel. Indeed, Deuteronomy most often refers to the stranger in relation to the household and to the clan, "within your gates" (16:11, 14). Otherness is often located at this local level. In this vein, the term gēr does not usually signify otherness at the level of the nation. Rather, as Christoph Bultmann argued, gēr in Deuteronomy simply identifies a vulnerable person who is from outside of the core household, whether foreign or Israelite.[33] This figure is simply one who is a dependent "outsider" in relation to the kinship grouping within which he or she resides. This would certainly include "internally displaced people." It may also include those displaced from Israel, at least for redactions of Deuteronomy dating to the seventh century. It would also include people who were non-Judahite/non-Israelite.

What Is the Status of the Conversation?

Social-Historical Reconstruction and Redaction

The appearance of the stranger in the various redaction layers of Deuteronomy offers a social-historical reconstruction in light of historical realities of displacement in ancient Israel. The Deuteronomic redaction, an original version of the Deuteronomic Code (12:2–26:15), is an appropriation of the Covenant Code. The high number of references to the stranger in this original layer projects a society experiencing widespread displacement (14:28–29; 16:9–15; 24:14, 19–22).[34] Sennacherib's invasion of Judah (701 BCE) may be a starting point for Deuteronomy's developing response to displacement.

The displacement seems to be intensified in the periods within which the Deuteronomistic redactions of Deuteronomy emerge, for the stranger is the dominant social issue of Deuteronomistic framing texts (1:16–17; 5:12–15; 29:9–14). These redactions may be composed partially in response to catastrophic levels of displacement following the Neo-Babylonian conquest. Indeed, within Deuteronomistic texts other categories for vulnerability diminish in importance, including the "fatherless and widow" and even the slave. Displacement is equally pressing in texts that seem to be authored later again, the so-called post-Deuteronomistic redactions (10:17–19; 31:9–13).[35] These redactions may respond to displacement in the Persian period, created by socioeconomic stratification and by the return of the *golah* household exiled from Judah by the Babylonians.[36]

The Stranger in the Covenant Code and the Holiness Code

The stranger occurs four times in the Covenant Code. Here, the stranger seems to have a similar social profile as in Deuteronomy (22:20; 23:9 [2x], 12). In the Holiness Code, the noun *gēr* occurs twenty times. Here, the *gēr* seems to assume two distinct social profiles: In a small number of passages, *gēr* refers to a person who is both displaced and dependent within their new context, as with Deuteronomy (Lev 19:9–10, 33, 34; 23:22). In most passages, however, the term *gēr* designates a non-Israelite, meaning outside of the YHWH-group, who is economically independent (Lev 17:8, 10, 12, 13; 20:2; 22:18; 24:16; 25:35–38).

Females as Strangers, Widows, and Fatherless

Vulnerable females may associate with the terms "strangers, widows, and fatherless" in complex and overlapping ways. A widow like Naomi or Ruth may belong to the clan within which she resides, or she may be an "outsider" in relation to a clan within which she seeks to dwell, and thereby also a stranger. By comparison, a female stranger is, by definition, always on the outside of the clan grouping in which she seeks to subsist. A female stranger may or may not be attached to male kindred, who would also be *gēr*. Table 16.1 relates these terms for vulnerable women to their social location.

Although scholars typically characterize the stranger, fatherless, and widow as landless groups, the triad's commonality is more fundamentally located in an absence of protective kinship ties and the resulting lack of means for sustaining themselves.[37] This is displayed

Table 16.1. Terms for Vulnerable Females: *gēr*, *álmānâ*, and *yātôm*

	Protected by male kin	Not protected by male kin
Belongs to the clan	Daughter, woman, wife	אלמנה or, if unmarried, יתום
Does not belong to the clan	גר *(limited protection; shared vulnerability with male kin)*	May be referred to as אלמנה, גר, or, if unmarried, יתום

Source: This table is taken from Glanville, *Adopting*, 99.

especially in the figure of the widow, who evidently was capable of owning land—it is her lack of kin connection that is definitive.

Provision and Protection for the Stranger, Fatherless, and Widow

We turn now to Deuteronomy's response to these vulnerable groups of people. In this section, we stay at the level of protection and provision for these groups—the level at which the scholarship typically moves. In the section that follows we will probe more deeply in order to discern the social transformations that Deuteronomy seeks to nourish for the sake of those who are marginalized.

Social Law

"Do not oppress a needy and destitute hired labourer, whether one of your brothers or your stranger who is in your land and within your gates. You shall give him his wage in his day, before night comes upon him, for he is poor, he is always in dire need of it, so he will not call out against you to YHWH and you will incur guilt" (24:14–15, AT). This law dealing with the stranger as hired labourer contains two parts. First, there is a prohibition against oppressing a hired labourer and, second, a stipulation for prompt payment. We learn here that a stranger commonly lived the highly insecure existence of a day labourer. A motivation clause indicates the efficacy of a curse uttered by a day labourer to YHWH: "So s/he will not call out against you to YHWH and you will incur guilt" (24:14–15). This curse associates with a blessing that may be uttered by a debtor in an earlier stipulation "s/he will bless you" (24:13). In this way, Deuteronomy teaches that YHWH is attentive and responsive to both the curse and blessing that vulnerable people may utter toward those with the power to either protect or injure them.

Judicial Procedure and Pledges

"Do not pervert the justice due to the stranger and the fatherless. Do not take a widow's garment in pledge" (24:17, author's translation). The vulnerable triad appears in broken form across these two stipulations: The first stipulation concerns law of judicial procedure for the stranger and the fatherless. The second stipulation (24:17b) prohibits taking a widow's garment in pledge. The unity of the vulnerable triad trope suggests that both stipulations apply to all three figures: the stranger, fatherless, and widow. As for the second stipulation, an outer garment functioned both as protection from rain during the day and for warmth in the evening.[38] This section (24:6–13) of the Deuteronomic Code stipulates various limitations upon the rights of creditors in the process of taking pledges as security against a debt (Amos 2:8). The present stipulation insists that a widow's garment should not be taken in pledge *in any way whatsoever*. Here Deuteronomy encourages sensitivity to the unique needs of each vulnerable person, prioritizing these needs over one's own economic gain.

Gleaning Law

"Supposing that you reap your harvest in your field and you accidentally leave behind a sheaf in the field, do not return to get it. It shall be for the stranger, the fatherless, and the widow, in order that YHWH your God may bless you in all the work of your hands" (24:19–22, author's translation).

The gleaning stipulations are framed by the "remember Egypt" motive clause, embedding the command within Israel's narrative history (24:18, 22).[39] In Egypt, Israel had first dwelled as a stranger (10:17, 23:7b, 26:5), and then subsequently Israel was enslaved (26:6). The gleaning stipulation demonstrates that "remember Egypt" is not merely a cognitive activity, but it must be embodied in practical action that mirrors the compassionate action of YHWH.

Sabbath Law

"The seventh day is a Sabbath to YHWH your God. Do not do any work, you, your son or daughter, your male or female slave, your ox or your ass or any of your cattle, or your stranger who is within your gates" (5:12–15, author's translation). This Sabbath command includes the stranger, slaves, and even beasts of burden. The word used for *work* (5:14 עבד) evokes a memory of slavery in Egypt (Exod 23:12 תעשה), but it is unusual in Deuteronomy.[40] With this evocative reference to work in Egypt, the Sabbath command curiously contrasts good work and bad work: work that blesses and work that exploits.

Judicial Procedure

Law of judicial procedure is a subgroup of law in Deuteronomy's system of protection and inclusion. Four commands require that vulnerable people are to receive a hearing and a judgment without bias due to their lack of kinship connection and poverty. In ancient Israel, as in the Near East, displaced people lacked influential advocates and were often ignored in legal proceedings.[41]

"Hear cases between your brothers-sisters,[42] and judge justly between a person and his or her brother-sister and his or her stranger" (1:16b, author's translation) provides that officials show no partiality in their judgment at the gates (1:16–17).

"For YHWH your God, he is God of Gods, who is impartial in judgement, who does not accept a bribe, the one who secures justice for the fatherless and the widow, and who loves the stranger, giving him/her food and clothing. So, you are to love the stranger, for you were strangers in the land of Egypt" (10:17–19, author's translation) positions YHWH as the great and impartial judge.

"Do not pervert the justice due to the stranger and the fatherless" (24:7a, author's translation) prohibits denying judicial justice to the stranger and the fatherless and, by extension, the widow (24:7b).

"Cursed be anyone who perverts the justice due to the stranger, fatherless, or widow. And all the people shall say, 'Amen'" (27:9, author's translation) in the Shechem covenant ceremony protects the judicial rights of the vulnerable triad by means of a curse.

Deuteronomy insisted as a matter of the highest priority that vulnerable people should receive a hearing and just judgment in their lawsuits. These laws required elders and judges to be willing and ready to decide cases against their own clans-people, if justice so required.

Third-Year Tithe Law

The third-year tithe of the produce is to be stored up in local towns and settlements for the sustenance of the Levite, stranger, fatherless, and widow (14:28–29). The third-year tithe here is then subsequently pictured in its fulfilment at the conclusion of the law corpus (26:12–15).

In the Near East, the tithe was a temple tax, and temples grew enormously wealthy as a result.[43] The consumption of the third-year tithe by landless populations is not only a reallocation of resources to the periphery; it is also a part of Deuteronomy's theology of cooperate holiness (14:1, 21). By participating in the tithe, these vulnerable groups are marked as holy, as members within the distinctive people of YHWH.

Levirate Law

The Levirate Law (25:5–10) comprises two sections. The first contains the core stipulation that a brother should marry the widow of his deceased brother who has no son (25:5–6), in order to "establish the name" of the deceased man. The phrase "establish the name" occurs three times (25:6–7) and may be a reference to providing progeny for the brother or of maintaining his patrimony, or both.[44]

The second section provides for a scenario where a surviving brother is unwilling to fulfil this obligation to his deceased brother (25:7–10). In this situation, a procedure is to be followed whereby the widow takes a complaint to the elders, who in turn counsel the man. If the man still refuses to marry the widow, a procedure is laid out whereby the widow takes off the brother's sandal and spits in his face (25:9–10). While the spitting is a ritual of humiliation, removing the brother's sandal signifies the woman's legal autonomy from this point forward (Ruth 4:7–8).

The Levirate Law balances the obligations of the household for the continuance of patrimony, alongside tensions within those obligations, with the individual needs of the surviving brother who may incur loss from the marriage.[45] The widow has a degree of agency both as the complainant and also as the primary actor in the ritual of release. In assessing gender and agency in the text, we must, in part, agree with Eyelet Seidler when she states that the widow's voice "represents the party who can no longer make its own voice heard—the deceased husband."[46] And yet in Deuteronomy's household law, women act as legal agents (21:19; 22:15; 24:4; 25:7-9), and thus the widow also represents herself as one who is no longer under the authority of any man.

An Alternative View: Laws That Serve Class Interests

In the past thirty years, some scholars have applied the insights of critical legal theory to Deuteronomy, a method that analyzes the text in terms of the class interests of the elite. Some argue that it was necessary for the scribes to include laws that on the surface stipulated care for vulnerable people, in order to establish both the validity of the law corpus and the just rule of the sponsors of the Deuteronomic Code.

Critical legal theory also argues that it is necessary to placate the nonelite, who are most of the population.[47] Therefore, critical legal theory considers the intention of these laws to be far from benevolent.

Mark Sneed argues that the covenant text "YHWH executes justice for the fatherless and the widow and *loves* the stranger, giving them food and clothing. *Love* the stranger, therefore, for you were strangers in the land of Egypt" (10:17-19, author's translation) legitimizes YHWH's reign as the patron of the vulnerable, while paradoxically reinforcing the status quo.[48]

Harold V. Bennett asserts that the third-year tithe law serves the class interests of the elite and dehumanizes the vulnerable trio. For Bennett, the tithe is only stored up locally for the vulnerable every third year, which would be insufficient for their sustenance.[49]

Yet critical legal theory fails to recognize that Deuteronomy *decentralizes* resources and authority in many ways. For example, the law of the king severely limits his prerogatives (17:14-20). Both the annual tithe and the third-year tithe reallocate resources that traditionally belong to the temple and its clergy to households and to marginalized people (14:22-29; 26:12-15). The law of judicial procedure prohibits the efforts of the elite to tilt legal proceedings to their own advantage.

Critical legal theory also fails to account for the deep societal realignment that Deuteronomy envisages, a realignment made visible when we view these texts through the lens of kinship.

What Is Trending in the Conversation?

Kinship, Responsibility, Identity, and the Nature of Deuteronomy

Skeptical readings of Deuteronomy's response to vulnerability, such as those of Bennett and Sneed, are sharply challenged by considering Deuteronomy through the lens of kinship. Deuteronomy envisages that the stranger, fatherless, and widow should be enfolded as kindred within the household, clan, and nation.

Social anthropologist Janet Carsten reflects upon the imagination and creativity that people invest in extending the boundaries of belonging: "creativity is not only central to kinship conceived in its broadest sense, but . . . for most people kinship constitutes one of the most important arenas for their creative energy.... It is, among other things, an area of life in which people invest their emotions, their creative energy, and their new imaginings."[50]

Frank Moore Cross reflects upon the adoption of outsiders into the kin grouping: "In West Semitic tribal societies we know best, such individuals or groups were grafted onto the genealogies and fictive kinship became kinship of the flesh or blood. In a word, kinship-in-law became kinship-in-flesh."[51]

We will now consider Deuteronomy's response to the stranger, fatherless, and widow, through the lens of adoptive kinship.[52]

Household

The vulnerable trio appears in household lists in Deuteronomy, indicating that they dwell and work within a household (5:14; 14:27; 16:11, 14; 26:11).[53] The household list appears in almost identical form in the calendar for the Feast of Weeks and the Feast of Booths. "And you shall feast before YHWH your God, you and your son and your daughter, your male slave and your female slave, the Levite who is within your towns, the stranger, the fatherless, and the widow who are among you, at the place that YHWH your God will choose, to make YHWH's name dwell there" (16:11, 14, author's translation).

The list moves from those who are at the centre of the household, namely blood relatives, to slaves who are bonded to the household, through to vulnerable people who have no legal connection. Such lists indicate that, for Deuteronomy, the household bore the primary responsibility for enfolding vulnerable people. In many cases, the stranger, fatherless, and widow would have shared a roof with the landed household (Lev 25:35), and in some cases they may have lived in separate dwellings within a settlement or city.[54] Vulnerable people participated in the life of Near Eastern households as inexpensive labour, and so they were vulnerable to exploitation. In this light, Deuteronomy may not be so much *initiating* relationships between the vulnerable and landed households as much as *transforming* relationships that may already be established.

Kinship in the Feastal Calendar (16:1–17)

During the Feast of Weeks (16:9–12) and the Feast of Booths (16:13–15), the household pilgrimages to the chosen place for cultic feasting before YHWH.[55] The whole household is enjoined to feast, and the vulnerable trio is swept up in the invitation. The word "rejoice" (NIV, NRSV), is not only a reference to emotion. For the list of foods to be consumed (14:23b, 26a) and the command to "eat" (7:12, 18; 14:26; cf. 14:24, 29b; 16:9, 10, 13) indicate that rejoice is nothing less than a call to cultic feasting.[56] Therefore, rejoice is better translated as "feast!" These cultic feasts take place "Before YHWH your God" (16:11; 26:11). In this way, the calendar of feasts enfolds the most vulnerable within the very heart of the community and of religious participation.

The goal of Deuteronomy's feasts may be discerned by the absence of motifs common to Near Eastern feasting texts, and by motifs peculiar to Deuteronomy. For example, the customary enumeration of the host's contribution is missing, downplaying the prominence of the human host.[57] Numerous signifiers of status are also absent, such as the host's cup and the seating arrangement. In Deuteronomy's feasts, YHWH is the host, and the most vulnerable in the community are brought into the very center of the community.

The power of Deuteronomy's feasts to transform relationships is clarified by the work of anthropologist Victor Turner on pilgrimage feasts. Victor Turner argues that pilgrimage feasts foster *communitas*, which is a transformative social experience that is "undifferentiated, equalitarian, direct, nonrational."[58] Pilgrimage feasting entails a suspension of cultural scripts and hierarchical structures in a way that has the power to forge new and creative relationships. Significantly for Deuteronomy's feasts, Turner argues that feasts have the potential to form lasting relationships and to permanently reorganize social structures and dynamics.[59]

In addition, across feasting cultures, an unusually large percentage of annual food consumption is consumed at feasts, as well as a large percentage of total wine consumption. So this is not mere charity. It is clear that the inclusion of the vulnerable trio in cultic feasting nourishes a deep mutuality and kinship connection. These feasts nourish the incorporation of vulnerable people into the kinship groupings of the household (16:11, 14) and the clan (5:14; 16:14; 22:24; 24:14–15; 25:7–9; 31:12).

Covenant Texts

In Deuteronomy's framework (1:1–11:32, 27:1–34:12), the categories of the fatherless and the widow fade and the stranger is uniquely prominent. Also, the sphere of the all-Israel grouping is in focus in the framework (29:9–10; 31:12).

"YHWH executes justice for the fatherless and the widow and *loves* the stranger, giving them food and clothing. *Love* the stranger, therefore, for you were strangers in the land of Egypt" (10:18–19, author's translation) is perhaps the best-known passage regarding the stranger in the Hebrew Bible.

A few verses prior is an affirmation of YHWH's love for Israel: "Yet YHWH set YHWH's heart in *love* on your fathers and chose their offspring after them, you above all peoples, as you are this day" (10:15, author's translation). There is a deliberate association here between YHWH's love for ancient Israel, YHWH's love for the stranger, and Israel's love for the stranger.

The term "love," should be understood in at least three senses. First, the term was used in Near Eastern treaty texts to express a covenant commitment between rulers.[60] The use of "love" here, parallel as it is to an expression of YHWH's "love" for Israel, communicates that YHWH also has a covenant commitment to the vulnerable stranger.

Second, the language of Near Eastern covenant treaties is taken from the domain of kinship. Covenant treaties include terms like "love, brotherhood, fatherhood, and loyalty."[61] To enter a covenant is "to enter another bond of blood and also to take the partner into one's own."[62] The use of "love" here, then, suggests that the stranger is to be enfolded within the web of kin and covenant relationships binding Israel to their divine kinsperson.

Third, "love" here even entails emotional connection between YHWH, the stranger, and the Israelite (10:15).[63] The deep emotional attachments that entwine kinsfolk should weave together those who have been displaced with YHWH's people (see Figure 16.1).

The stranger is included within the covenant renewal ceremony in Moab (19:9–14). By virtue of their participation in this ceremony, the stranger is thereby also grafted into

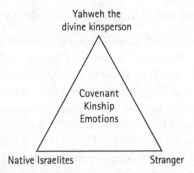

FIGURE 16.1. Triangle of kinship between YHWH, Israelites, and the stranger (10:15–19).

the narrative history of Israel (29:1–8) and into the genealogy of the fathers, along with YHWH's sworn covenant with the fathers. In this way, the Moab covenant ceremony creates associations of adoptive kinship for the stranger within the Israelite grouping.

Deuteronomy's Social Law and Kinship

Deuteronomy's social laws place responsibility upon YHWH's people to provide for vulnerable people in their midst. Yet this observation begs a question that is rarely asked: "According to custom, for whom did an Israelite have responsibility?" Approached negatively, the Israelites had no responsibility to those outside of their near kinship group. The story of Lot in Sodom illustrates the suspicion and even violence that outsiders could attract (Gen 19). As Raymond Westbrook reflects, foreigners "had no legal rights outside of their own country or ethnic group unless they fell under the local ruler's protection."[64] Not only were Israelites suspicious of outsiders, they were often even reluctant to fulfil customary obligations toward their own, as we have observed in the Levirate Law (25:5–10; Num 27, 36; Ruth 4:5–6; Ps 50:20).

Given this cultural reality, what does Deuteronomy's insistence that YHWH's people should take responsibility for the vulnerable trio signify? Perhaps we may shift our conception of social law from mere charity and provision to the solidarity required of kinsfolk. The conception of kinship responsibility is made explicit in the day labourer law. In this law, clans-folk are to be treated as sister-brother, and in the same way also the stranger is to be treated as sister-brother (24:14). As for the gleaning laws, the stipulation that the harvest is to be shared with the vulnerable trio nourishes also a kinship connection. For sharing of possessions is a mark of kinship (Gen 13:8–9; c.f. 20:14; 21:25–30; 34:8–10; Exod 19:5–6; Deut 33:1–29). In sum, the social problems that these laws are addressing are in fact kinship problems: the vulnerable trio lacked a kin group who would take responsibility for them and enfold them. In requiring that YHWH's people take responsibility for the stranger, fatherless, and widow, Deuteronomy is also nurturing a kinship connection for these vulnerable people.

Through feasting texts, covenant texts, and even social law, Deuteronomy is nourishing the incorporation of the stranger, fatherless, and widow as kindred. These vulnerable people are being enfolded within the kinship grouping of a local household, settlement, and all-Israel.

Identity Formation and the Nature of Deuteronomy

Deuteronomy is reconfiguring kinship connections within the community for the sake of the stranger, fatherless, and widow, and this before the face of YHWH. This social reconfiguring is connected to Israel's status as YHWH's people. We might reflect, then, that Deuteronomy is describing the movement of *being/becoming the household of YHWH*.[65] Deuteronomy is ultimately shaping a kinship group that is circumscribed both by its heeding the words of the Torah (31:9-13) and also by its relentless inclusivity for the sake of the most vulnerable. This movement of becoming the household of YHWH is perhaps most clearly visible in the feasting texts, whereby the whole community feasts before YHWH with celebration and thanksgiving. Elsewhere I have offered the term "festive kinship" to describe the character of the inclusive community that Deuteronomy is imagining.[66] Interestingly, in these texts, the stranger is not considered a religious threat. Rather, Deuteronomy envisages that the stranger, fatherless, and widow will be very naturally caught up in the joy, the kinship, and the festivity of the people of YHWH.

Notes

1. Georg Braulik, "Deuteronomy and Human Rights," in *Theology of Deuteronomy: Collected Essays of Georg Braulik, O.S.B.*, trans. U. Lindblad (N. Richland Hills: Bibal, 1994), 131-150; trans. of "Das Deuteronomium und die Menschenrechte" *TESOL Quarterly* 166 (1986): 8-24.
2. Ibid., 136.
3. In S. N. Kramer, *The Sumerians: Their History, Culture and Character* (Chicago: University of Chicago Press, 1963), 319.
4. F. Charles Fensham, "Widow, Orphan, and the Poor in Ancient Near Eastern Legal and Wisdom Literature," *Journal of Near Eastern Studies* 21 (1962): 129-139, at 134.
5. Unless otherwise indicated, English translations are from the NRSV with minor changes: Gēr is translated "stranger," "yātôm" is translated "fatherless," Lord is rendered as "YHWH," and gender-neutral translations are used throughout.
6. The occurrence of the triad in Deuteronomy (14:29; 16:11, 14; 24:19-21) may be assigned to the earliest version of Deuteronomy (12:1-26:15)
7. Emphasis original; Kristine Henriksen Garroway, *Children in the Ancient Near Eastern Household* (Winona Lake: Eisenbrauns, 2014), 92.
8. José E. Ramírez Kidd, *Alterity and Identity in Israel*, BZAW 283 (Berlin: de Gruyter, 1999), 35-40.
9. Fensham, "Widow," 129.
10. J. J. Finkelstein, "Ammiṣaduqa's Edict and the Babylonian 'Law Codes,'" *Journal of Cuneiform Studies* 15 (1961): 91-104, at 103-104. Note the cry of the widow to Elisha: "A creditor has come to take my two children as slaves" (2 Kgs 4:1).
11. Pnina Galpaz-Feller, "The Widow in the Bible and the Ancient Near East," *Zeitschrift für die alttestamentliche Wissenschaft* (2008): 231-253, at 233; and Frank S. Frick, "Widows in the Hebrew Bible: A Transactional Approach," in *A Feminist Companion to Exodus to Deuteronomy*, ed. Athalya Brenner (Sheffield: Sheffield Academic, 2001), 139-151, at 241.
12. Ignace J. Gelb, "Household and Family in Early Mesopotamia," in *State and Temple Economy in the Ancient Near East: Proceedings of the International Conference Organized*

by the Katholieke Universiteit Leuven from the 10th to the 14th of April 1978, ed. E. Lipiński; OLA 5 (Leuven: Dept. Oriëntalistiek, 1979), 1–98, at 26.
13. Ibid., 21, 23.
14. See Laws of Hammurabi §170–171 (Matha T. Roth, *Law Collections from Mesopotamia and Asia Minor*, 2nd ed. [Atlanta: SBL, 1997], 113–114).
15. Garroway, *Children*, 109.
16. See ibid., 108n75.
17. See ibid., 110.
18. Ibid., 93.
19. Cf. Ezek 6:5; Is 49:14–15. See further, M. Coogan, "A Technical Term for Exposure," *Journal of Near Eastern Studies* 27 (1968): 133–135.
20. See further, Garroway, *Children*, 106; Shawn W. Flynn, *Children in Ancient Israel: The Hebrew Bible and Mesopotamia in Comparative Perspective* (Oxford: Oxford University Press, 2018), 105.
21. Garroway, *Children*, 112.
22. Paula S. Hiebert, "'Whence Shall Help Come to Me?': The Biblical Widow," in *Gender and Difference in Ancient Israel*, ed. Peggy L. Day (Minneapolis: Fortress, 1989), 125–141, at 128.
23. Ibid., 129.
24. See especially Middle Assyrian Law §33 (Roth, *Law Collections*, 165).
25. See the discussion in Galpaz-Feller, "Widow," 233 and Frank S. Frick, "Widows in the Hebrew Bible: A Transactional Approach," in *A Feminist Companion to Exodus to Deuteronomy*, ed. Athalya Brenner (Sheffield: Sheffield Academic, 2001), 139–151, at 140, 148. For an alternative view see Hiebert, "Widow," 137.
26. See further, Sarah Shectman, "The Social Status of Priestly and Levite Women," in *Levites and Priests in History and Tradition*, ed. Mark A. Leuchter and Jeremy M. Hutton (Atlanta: SBL, 2011), 83–99, at 88.
27. Christiana van Houton, *The Alien in Israelite Law: A Study of the Changing Legal Status of Strangers in Ancient Israel*, JSOTSup 107 (Sheffield: Sheffield University Press, 1991), 16.
28. Regarding the phrase בקרבך see Mark R. Glanville, *Adopting the Stranger as Kindred in Deuteronomy*, AIL (Atlanta: SBL, 2018), 184–185.
29. For example, Moshe Weinfeld, *Deuteronomy and the Deuteronomic School* (Oxford: Clarendon, 1972), 90–91.
30. For example, Mark A. Awabdy, *Immigrants and Innovative Law: Deuteronomy's Theological and Social Vision for the "Gr,"* FAT II, 67 (Tübingen: Mohr Siebeck, 2014); Ruth Ebach, *Das Fremde und das Eigene: Die Fremdendarstellungen des Deuteronomiums im Kontext israelitischer Identitätskonstruktionen*, BZAW 471 (Berlin: de Gruyter, 2014); Reinhard Achenbach, "gêr – nåkhrî – tôshav – zâr," in *The Foreigner and the Law: Perspectives from the Hebrew Bible and the Ancient Near East*, ed. Reinhard Achenbach, Rainer Albertz, and Jakob Wöhrle; BZABR 16 (Wiesbaden: Harrassowitz, 2011), 29–52; van Houten, *Alien*, 89–90; Kidd, *Alterity*, 46.
31. For example, Christoph Bultmann, *Der Fremde im antiken Juda: Eine Untersuchung zum sozialen Typenbegriff "ger" und seinem Bedeutungswandel in der alttestamentlichen Gesetzgebung*, FRLANT 153 (Gottingen: Vandenhoeck und Ruprecht, 1992).
32. Awabdy, *Immigrants*, 24.
33. Bultmann, *Fremde*," 17.

34. On the literary development of Deuteronomy, see Reinhard Kratz, *The Composition of the Narratives Books of the Old Testament*, trans. J. Bowden (London: T & T Clark, 2005), 114–132.
35. For a discussion of the *gēr* in the various redaction layers of Deuteronomy, see Achenbach, "gēr," 29–52.
36. See further, Rainer Kessler. *The Social History of Ancient Israel: An Introduction* (Minneapolis: Fortress, 2008), 134–136.
37. See further Garroway, *Children*, 92.
38. Philip J. King and Lawrence E. Stager, *Life in Biblical Israel*, LAI (Louisville: Westminster John Knox, 2001), 269.
39. See further Glanville, *Adopting*, 71–74.
40. Also, 15:19; cf. מעשׂה in 14:29; 15:10; 27:15; 31:29; מלאכה in 16:8.
41. See, for example, Genesis 12:10–20; 19:9; 26:6–11; see further Raymond Westbrook, "Slave and Master in Ancient Near Eastern Law," in *Law from the Tigris to the Tiber: The Writings of Raymond Westbrook*, ed. Bruce Wells and Rachel Magdalene, 2 vols. (Winona Lake: Eisenbrauns, 2009), 1:161–216, at 171.
42. "Brother-sisters": both men and women have the right to give testimony at the gate in Deuteronomy (e.g., Deut 21:18–20).
43. See, for example, H. Jagersma, "The Tithes in the Old Testament," in *Remembering All the Way*, ed. A. S. van der Woude; OtSt 21 (Leiden: Brill, 1981), 116–128, at 123.
44. See further, Ayelet Seidler, "The Law of Levirate and Forced Marriage—Widow vs. Levir in Deuteronomy 25.5–20," *Journal of the Study of the Old Testament* 42 (2018): 435–456, at 439–440.
45. Dvora E. Weisberg, *Levirate Marriage and the Family in Ancient Judaism* (Waltham: Brandeis University Press, 2009), 44.
46. Seidler, "Levirate," 447. This comports with other texts in the Hebrew Bible where a widow continues to be known in relation to her deceased husband (Ruth 4:5, 10).
47. See, for example, Mark Sneed, "Israelite Concern for the Alien, Orphan and Widow: Altruism or Ideology?" *Zeitschrift für die alttestamentliche Wissenschaft* 111 (1999): 498–507, 504; Douglas A. Knight, *Law, Power, and Justice in Ancient Israel* (Louisville: Westminster John Knox, 2011), 219–222.
48. Sneed, "Israelite," 502–503.
49. Harold V. Bennett, *Injustice Made Legal: Deuteronomic Law and the Plight of Widows, Strangers, and Orphans in Ancient Israel* (Grand Rapids: Eerdmans, 2002), 120.
50. Janet Carsten, *After Kinship* (Cambridge: Cambridge University Press, 2004), 9.
51. Frank Moore Cross, *From Epic to Canon: History and Literature in Ancient Israel* (Baltimore: John Hopkins University Press, 1998), 7.
52. For an extended discussion kinship in Deuteronomy, see Glanville, *Adopting*.
53. In addition, the phrase "your *gēr*" suggests that the *gēr* works and dwells within a household (5:14; 24:14; 29:10; 31:12; cf. 1:16).
54. Avraham Faust, *The Archaeology of Israelite Society in Iron Age II* (Winona Lake: Eisenbrauns, 2012), 101–102.
55. For a recent study of Deuteronomy's feasting texts, see Peter Altmann, *Festive Meals in Ancient Israel: Deuteronomy's Identity Politics in Their Ancient Near Eastern Context*, BZAW 424 (Berlin: de Gruyter, 2011).
56. See further, Altmann, *Festive*, 205.
57. See Irene Winter, "The King and the Cup: Iconography of the Royal Presentation Scene on the Ur III Seals," in *Insight through Images, Studies in Honour of Edith Porada*, ed. M. Kelly-Buccelati et al. (Malibu: Undena, 1986), 253–268, at 265.

58. Victor Turner, *Dramas, Fields, and Metaphors: Symbolic Action in Human Society* (Ithaca: Cornell University Press, 1974), 47.
59. Ibid., 200–201, 205–206.
60. See further, William L. Moran, "The Ancient Near Eastern Background for the Love of God in Deuteronomy," *Catholic Biblical Quarterly* 25 (1963): 77–87.
61. See further, Frank Moore Cross, *Canaanite Myth and Hebrew Epic: Essays in the History of the Religion of Israel* (Cambridge: Harvard University Press, 1973), 6–7.
62. Gottfried Quell, "διαθήκη," *Theological Dictionary of the New Testament*, 2.106–124, at 114.
63. Jacqueline E. Lapsley, "Feeling our Way: Love for God in Deuteronomy," *Catholic Biblical Quarterly* 65 (2003): 350–369, at 362.
64. Westbrook, "Slave," 171. On a suspicion of outsiders in the pan-Mediterranean area, see David D. Gilmore, "Anthropology of the Mediterranean Area," *Annual Review of Anthropology* 11 (1982): 175–205, at 178–179.
65. See also Altmann, *Festive*, 2–3.
66. Mark R. Glanville, "'Festive Kinship': Solidarity, Responsibility, and Identity Formation in Deuteronomy," *Journal of the Study of the Old Testament* 44 (2019): 133–152, at 52.

Bibliography

Altmann, Peter. *Festive Meals in Ancient Israel: Deuteronomy's Identity Politics in Their Ancient Near Eastern Context*. Beihefte zur Zeitschrift für die alttestamentliche Wissenschaft 424. Berlin: de Gruyter, 2011.

Awabdy, Mark. *Immigrants and Innovative Law: Deuteronomy's Theological and Social Vision for the "Gr."* Forschungen zum Alten Testament. Second Series 67. Tübingen: Mohr Siebeck, 2014.

Bennett, Harold, V. *Injustice Made Legal: Deuteronomic Law and the Plight of Widows, Strangers, and Orphans in Ancient Israel*. Grand Rapids: Eerdmans, 2002.

Braulik, Georg. "Deuteronomy and Human Rights." In *Theology of Deuteronomy: Collected Essays of Georg Braulik, O.S.B.*, 131–150, translated by U. Lindblad. N. Richland Hills: Bibal, 1994. Translation of "Das Deuteronomium und die Menschenrechte." *Theologische Quartalschrift* 166 (1986): 8–24.

Bultmann, Christoph. *Der Fremde im antiken Juda: eine Untersuchung zum sozialen Typenbegriff >ger< und seinem Bedeutungswandel in der alttestamentlichen Gesetzgebung*. Forschungen zur Religion und Literatur des Alten und Neuen Testaments 153. Gottingen: Vandenhoeck und Ruprecht, 1992.

Carsten, Janet. *After Kinship*. Cambridge: Cambridge University Press, 2004.

Coogan, M. "A Technical Term for Exposure." *Journal of Near Eastern Studies* 27 (1968): 133–135.

Cross, Frank Moore. *Canaanite Myth and Hebrew Epic: Essays in the History of the Religion of Israel*. Cambridge: Harvard University Press, 1973.

Cross, Frank Moore. *From Epic to Canon: History and Literature in Ancient Israel*. Baltimore: John Hopkins University Press, 1998.

Ebach, Ruth. *Das Fremde und das Eigene: Die Fremdendarstellungen des Deuteronomiums im Kontext israelitischer Identitätskonstruktionen*. Beihefte zur Zeitschrift für die alttestamentliche Wissenschaft 471. Berlin: de Gruyter, 2014.

Faust, Avraham. *The Archaeology of Israelite Society in Iron Age II*. Winona Lake: Eisenbrauns, 2012.

Fensham, F. Charles. "Widow, Orphan, and the Poor in Ancient Near Eastern Legal and Wisdom Literature." *Journal of Near Eastern Studies* 21 (1962): 129–139.

Finkelstein, Jacob. J. "Ammiṣaduqa's Edict and the Babylonian 'Law Codes'." *Journal of Cuneiform Studies* 15 (1961): 91–104.

Frick, Frank S. "Widows in the Hebrew Bible: A Transactional Approach." In *A Feminist Companion to Exodus to Deuteronomy*, edited by Athalya Brenner, 139–151. Sheffield: Sheffield Academic, 2001.

Galpaz-Feller, Pnina. "The Widow in the Bible and the Ancient Near East." *Zeitschrift für die alttestamentliche Wissenschaft* 120 (2008): 231–253.

Garroway, Kristine Henriksen. *Children in the Ancient Near Eastern Household*. Winona Lake: Eisenbrauns, 2014.

Gelb, Ignace. J. "Household and Family in Early Mesopotamia." In *State and Temple Economy in the Ancient Near East: Proceedings of the International Conference Organized by the Katholieke Universiteit Leuven from the 10th to the 14th of April 1978*, edited by E. Lipiński, 1–98. Orientalia Lovaniensia Analecta 5. Leuven: Dept. Oriëntalistiek, 1979.

Gilmore, David. "Anthropology of the Mediterranean Area." *Annual Review of Anthropology* 11 (1982): 175–205.

Glanville, Mark R. *Adopting the Stranger as Kindred in Deuteronomy*. AIL. Atlanta: SBL, 2018.

Glanville, Mark R. "'Festive Kinship': Solidarity, Responsibility, and Identity Formation in Deuteronomy." *Journal for the Study of the Old Testament* 44 (2019): 133–152.

Hiebert, Paula S. "'Whence Shall Help Come to Me?': The Biblical Widow." In *Gender and Difference in Ancient Israel*, edited by Peggy L. Day, 125–141. Minneapolis: Fortress, 1989.

Jagersma, H. "The Tithes in the Old Testament." In *Remembering All the Way: A Collection of Old Testament Studies Published on the Occasion of the Fortieth Anniversary of the Oudtestamentisch Werkgezelschap in Nederland*, edited by A. S. van der Woude, 116–128. Oudtestamentische Studiën 21. Leiden: Brill, 1981.

Kessler, Rainer. *The Social History of Ancient Israel: An Introduction*. Minneapolis: Fortress, 2008.

Kidd, José E. Ramírez. *Alterity and Identity in Israel*. Beihefte zur Zeitschrift für die alttestamentliche Wissenschaft 283. Berlin: de Gruyter, 1999.

King, Philip J., and Lawrence E. Stager. *Life in Biblical Israel*. Library of Ancient Israel. Louisville: Westminster John Knox, 2001.

Kittel, Gerhard, and Gerhard Friedrich, eds. *Theological Dictionary of the New Testament*. Translated by Geoffrey W. Bromiley. 10 vols. Grand Rapids: Eerdmans, 1964–1976.

Kramer, S. N. *The Sumerians. Their History, Culture and Character*. Chicago: University of Chicago Press, 1963.

Kratz, Reinhard. *The Composition of the Narratives Books of the Old Testament*. Translated by J. Bowden. London: T & T Clark, 2005. Translation of *Die Komposition der erzählenden Bücher des Alten Testaments*. Göttingen: Vandenhoeck & Ruprecht, 2000.

Lapsley, Jacqueline E. "Feeling our Way: Love for God in Deuteronomy." *Catholic Biblical Quaterly* 65 (2003): 350–369.

Moran, William L. "The Ancient Near Eastern Background for the Love of God in Deuteronomy." *Catholic Biblical Quarterly* 25 (1963): 77–87.

Roth, Martha T. *Law Collections from Mesopotamia and Asia Minor*. Writings from the Ancient World. Atlanta: SBL, 1995.

Seidler, Ayelet. "The Law of Levirate and Forced Marriage—Widow vs. Levir in Deuteronomy 25.5–20." *Journal for the Study of the Old Testament* 42 (2018): 435–456.

Shectman, Sarah. "The Social Status of Priestly and Levite Women." In *Levites and Priests in History and Tradition*, edited by Mark A. Leuchter and Jeremy M. Hutton, 83–99. Atlanta: SBL, 2011.

Sneed, Mark. "Israelite Concern for the Alien, Orphan and Widow: Altruism or Ideology?" *Zeitschrift für die alttestamentliche Wissenschaft* 111 (1999): 498–507.

Turner, Victor. *Dramas, Fields, and Metaphors: Symbolic Action in Human Society*. Ithaca: Cornell University Press, 1974.

van Houten, Christiana. *The Alien in Israelite Law: A Study of the Changing Legal Status of Strangers in Ancient Israel*. Journal for the Study of the Old Testament Supplementary Series 107. Sheffield: Sheffield University Press, 1991.

Weinfeld, Moshe. *Deuteronomy and the Deuteronomic School*. Oxford: Clarendon, 1972.

Weisberg, Dvora E. *Levirate Marriage and the Family in Ancient Judaism*. Waltham: Brandeis University Press, 2009.

Westbrook, Raymond. "Slave and Master in Ancient Near Eastern Law." In *Law from the Tigris to the Tiber: The Writings of Raymond Westbrook*, edited by Bruce Wells and Rachel Magdalene, 161–216. 2 vols. Winona Lake: Eisenbrauns, 2009. Repr. of, *Chicago-Kent Law Review* 70 (1995): 1631–1676.

Winter, Irene. "The King and the Cup: Iconography of the Royal Presentation Scene on the Ur III Seals." In *Insight through Images, Studies in Honour of Edith Porada*, edited by M. Kelly-Buccelati, P. Matthiae, and M. Van Loon, 253–268. Bibliotheca Mesopotamia 21. Malibu: Undena, 1986.

CHAPTER 17

DEUTERONOMY AND THE REIGNS OF KINGS HEZEKIAH AND JOSIAH OF JUDAH

MARVIN A. SWEENEY

FOLLOWING the 1805 publication of W. M. L. de Wette's doctoral dissertation on Deuteronomy at the University of Jena, modern critical interpreters have generally recognized that a version of Deuteronomy must be the *Sefer Torah* discovered in the Jerusalem Temple during the reign of King Josiah of Judah (2 Kgs 22).[1] Indeed, King Josiah's subsequent reform program appears to have followed Deuteronomy's stipulations to adhere to YHWH alone, eschew the worship of other gods, recognize only one Temple where the Name of YHWH is to reside, observe the festival of Passover, have the king observe YHWH's Torah, and other provisions required by Deuteronomy. As a result, Josiah is judged to be the ideal king of the House of David, like no other before or after him, who turned to YHWH with all his heart, soul, and might according to all the Torah of Moses.

Scholars are nevertheless divided concerning the provenance of the book. Many interpreters agree that Deuteronomy must have been originally written in relation to Josiah's reign, not only because of its correspondences to the major features of his reform, but also because it gives greater rights to the poor, women, and to Levites, the very groups who would constitute the *'am ha'aretz*, the people of the land, who placed young Josiah on the throne following the assassination of his father, Amon ben Manasseh (640 BCE).[2] Others maintain that Deuteronomy originates in prophetic circles from northern Israel, who sought to reform the northern monarchy and brought their work south to Judah following the destruction of the northern kingdom of Israel during the reign of King Hezekiah ben Ahaz of Judah.[3]

This paper analyzes the arguments offered to support these viewpoints. It rejects the contention that Deuteronomy originated in the north and was brought to Judah during the reign of Hezekiah, and holds instead that Deuteronomy, although dependent in part on northern material, originates in Judah during the mid- to late seventh century BCE as part of an effort to initiate and support the religious and national reforms of King Josiah of Judah.

WHO BEGAN THE CONVERSATION?

Most modern scholars point to the periods of the Renaissance and the Enlightenment as the historical contexts for the emergence of modern, critical scholarship. But the roots of such study extend back to the period of the composition of the Babylonian Talmud, which was formed between the third and sixth centuries CE, and the subsequent period of medieval Jewish biblical interpretation from the onset of Islam on through the Renaissance and the Enlightenment. The Babylonian Talmud discusses the authorship of biblical books in tractate b. Baba Batra 14b–15a, where it maintains that Moses could not have written the account of his own death in Deuteronomy 34. Instead, b. Baba Batra 14b–15a maintains that Joshua wrote this section, bearing in mind accounts in the Torah that YHWH would not permit Moses to enter the promised land of Israel (Num 20:1–13). Subsequent Jewish scholarship during the Middle Ages focused especially on the development of critical, philologically based scholarship that both built on prior work in the Talmud and the Targums and attempted to answer the charges of Muslim scholars that the Jews had lied concerning the interpretation of the Bible to hide their claims that Islam—and not Judaism—was true.[4]

One of the key figures to anticipate later critical scholarship was R. Abraham ibn Ezra (d. 1167 CE), who followed the Babylonian Talmud in raising questions concerning traditional Jewish scholarship. In addition to raising questions concerning Isaiah's authorship of the entire book of Isaiah and Samuel's authorship of the book of Samuel, ibn Ezra pointed to additional evidence that Moses could not have authored the entire Pentateuch. His examples included statements that "the Canaanites were then in the land" (Gen 12:6; 13:7) in the time of Abraham and Sarah, which would have been impossible in Moses's lifetime since the Canaanites were still in the land at the end of Moses's life. For perspective on Deuteronomy, ibn Ezra pointed to "these are the words which Moses spoke to all Israel on the other side of the Jordan" (Deut 1:1), which indicates that the author must have been in the land of Israel, something that would have been impossible for Moses. Ibn Ezra also points to "Moses wrote this Torah, and he gave it to the priests, the sons of Levi, who carry the ark of the covenant of YHWH, and to all the elders of Israel" (Deut 31:9). Although this statement had often been used as a proof text to confirm Moses's authorship of the Pentateuch, ibn Ezra demonstrates that the Hebrew word, *Torah*, does not refer to the entire Pentateuch, but it instead functions as an expression of its philological meaning as a reference to a specific teaching or instruction, in this case, the preceding command that Joshua shall apportion the land of Israel to the people of Israel (Deut 31:7–8).

Other scholars, such as Baruch Spinoza, Richard Simon, and Jean Astruc, raised questions concerning the Mosaic authorship of the Pentateuch during the periods of the Renaissance, the Protestant Reformation, and the Enlightenment, but the Dutch scholar, Wilhelm Martin Leberecht de Wette 1780–1859 CE), is generally considered to be the founder of modern research on Deuteronomy.[5] He argued that the Book of Torah discovered in the Temple purification and renovations undertaken by King Josiah of Judah (640–609 BCE) must have been an early version of the book of Deuteronomy. De Wette observed that Deuteronomy is a book that can stand on its own in relation to the preceding books of the Pentateuch and that it has a very distinctive understanding of Israel's early history and of the laws that it presents when compared to those books. Exodus–Numbers presents its own account of

Moses's life, including the revelation of Torah to Israel at Sinai, his audience with YHWH on Mt. Sinai to write down YHWH's revelation, the episode of the Golden Calf and reformulation of the covenant with YHWH, his leadership of Israel through the wilderness to Moab, immediately prior to Israel's entry into the land, the apportionment of the land to the tribes of Israel, and the appointment of Joshua ben Nun as Moses's successor. Deuteronomy recounts these narratives, often in terms that differ from those of Exodus–Numbers, and the laws that Deuteronomy presents often differ markedly from their predecessors even though Moses is ostensibly simply repeating the earlier laws to remind the people of their obligations to YHWH.

In de Wette's view, Deuteronomy was written after the completion of the Exodus and Numbers narratives and constitutes a separate, independent, and later account of the Mosaic period. Deuteronomy's theologically informed sermons are markedly different from that of Exodus and Numbers. Deuteronomy calls for the worship of YHWH at only one Temple site, which differs from the multiple altars (Exod 20:21–23). Because earlier accounts in Joshua, Judges, Samuel, and Kings presupposed the existence of multiple sanctuaries up until the time of Josiah's reform, de Wette concluded that Deuteronomy, with its strict prohibitions of multiple sanctuaries together with its prohibitions of the worship of other gods, must be the time of Josiah's reform. In his view, Deuteronomy was written specifically to support Josiah's efforts.

De Wette's contention that Deuteronomy was the *Sefer Torah* found in the Temple during King Josiah's reform is "the Archimedean point" of modern biblical scholarship.[6] Most interpreters followed de Wette's lead throughout the nineteenth century and beyond. Wellhausen, for example, accepts de Wette's conclusions as the basis for his own view of Deuteronomy as a discrete source in his foundational four-source theory for the composition of the Pentateuch.[7] But Wellhausen also recognized that the present form of the book of Deuteronomy was not the form that was discovered in Josiah's time; rather, there had to be an Urdeuteronomium (Deut 5–11; 12–26)—an early form of Deuteronomy—that was found in the Temple and motivated Josiah's reforms. Other scholars pursued the question of what must have constituted the earlier forms of Deuteronomy. S. R. Driver carefully distinguished the laws of Deuteronomy from the preceding materials in the JE narratives of the Pentateuch and those of the subsequent P source.[8] But he also pointed to the prophetic character of Deuteronomy in which Moses is portrayed as a prophet and not as a Levite and in which one sees repeated calls to return to YHWH, to eschew other gods and to do justice much as the prophets of Israel and Judah had done. Although Driver saw some affinities with Isaiah and therefore considered the possibility that Deuteronomy could have originated during Hezekiah's reign, in the end he opted for the reign of Josiah or perhaps Manasseh as the sociohistorical setting for the composition of the earliest forms of the book.

Carl Steuernagel experimented with the shifting address forms in Deuteronomy as the basis for his attempts to identify the earliest edition of the book.[9] Deuteronomy shifts repeatedly between second-person masculine singular address forms and second-person masculine plural address forms, and many nineteenth- and twentieth-century scholars saw in this feature a key to unraveling its redactional history. This shift in address forms, however, appears to function as a feature of ancient Israelite and Judean rhetoric in which the speaker simultaneously addresses both the audience as a whole and the individual members of the audience during a public speech. Steuernagel argued that the earliest version of the book could be dated to the time of Hezekiah and that subsequent redactional expansion took place during the reigns of Manasseh and Josiah, although he admitted that he was unable to show clear evidence of this conclusion. Similar attempts to identify an earlier edition of Deuteronomic law were offered by Antti Filemon Puukko, Johannes Hempel, and Theodor Oestreicher, but none of these proposals gained support despite widespread belief that such efforts were warranted.[10]

What Is the Status of the Conversation?

Scholarly understanding of the sociohistorical background of Deuteronomy changed markedly following the work of Adam C. Welch.[11] Welch argued that the earliest form of the code originated in the northern kingdom of Israel in the tenth century BCE and that the original form of the code never called for cultic centralization. Welch's theses were based upon a thoroughgoing examination of the Deuteronomic law code (Deut 12–26). He recognized that the law of cultic centralization (Deut 12:1–7) could not have originated in the northern kingdom of Israel because northern Israel had at least two state sanctuaries, one in Beth El and one in Dan, and not one as Deuteronomy envisions. Although some have later argued that the call for cultic centralization would have been a result of prophetic critique of northern practice, the issue with the cultic establishment in northern Israel was not the need for a single Temple site; rather, it was the contention that the northern sanctuaries actually pursued Canaanite forms of pagan or idol worship as indicated by the presence of the golden calves in Beth and Dan (1 Kgs 12:25–31). Welch maintained that the law of cultic centralization is a postexilic addition to the text and that the original form of Deuteronomy is nowhere else concerned with the issue insofar as any other references to cultic centralization must also be considered later additions to the text.

Welch further pointed to the creedal statement (Deut 26:1–11) made by Israelite farmers when they brought their first fruit offerings to the sanctuary to demonstrate the concern with fertility in the law code and in northern Israel. Insofar as Baal is the Canaanite deity charged with ensuring fertility, he pointed to this statement as evidence that northern Israel was indeed syncretistic and that such a charge was the basis for Hosea's charges in Hosea 2 that Israel had abandoned YHWH in order to pursue Baal or other gods, whom they perceived as the source of their agricultural produce. Welch therefore argued that the creedal statement in Deut 26:1–11 was included in the law code in order to force recognition of YHWH—and not Baal or any other god—as the deity who brought fertility to the fields of northern Israelite farmers. He further argued that the concern with the tithe (Deut 26:1–11) and elsewhere (Deut 12:6, 11, 17; 14:22, 23, 28) must have originated at the northern Israelite sanctuary at Beth El, insofar as Amos 4:4 referred to Beth El and Gilgal as the site for the paying of the tithe as a long-standing practice.

Welch further pointed to the law concerning prophets and dream interpreters (Deut 13:2–6), and he further noted that dream interpretation is not prohibited (Deut 18:9–12). Dream interpretation like the interpretations of Jacob's dream at Beth El (Gen 28) and Joseph's dreams (Gen 37) is a prominent part of the northern Israelite E source of the Pentateuch. Therefore, Welch concluded that the tacit approval of dream interpretation points to Deuteronomy's northern origins. Dream interpretation comes into question with Jeremiah (Jer 23:9–40). He argued that Deuteronomy's concern with the observance of Passover

(Deut 16:1–8) is like that of Samaritan practice and therefore points once again to northern Israelite origins. Finally, the Torah of the King (Deut 17:14–20) calls for the appointment of a righteous king who does not amass wives, horses, and gold to himself and who does not cause the people to cross the sea once again to return to Egypt. Insofar as Solomon was charged with all these wrongdoings, Welch argued that Deuteronomy must originate in the north insofar as northern Israel revolted against the House of David as a result of Solomon's actions. Once again, he pointed to the analogy of Hosea's alleged opposition to kingship (Hos 11) and elsewhere to justify his thesis.

Altogether, Welch maintained that the northern Israelite Deuteronomic law code was brought south to Judah and edited into its present form following the destruction of the northern kingdom of Israel by the Assyrian empire in 722–721 BCE.

A second major voice to argue for the northern origins of Deuteronomy was Albrecht Alt, who pointed to the origins of the book in northern Israelite reform circles which flourished during the eighth century BCE and brought the earlier form of the book south after 722–721 BCE.[12] Alt rejected Welch's view that Deuteronomy originated in the tenth century BCE, but he held that Deuteronomy's calls for fidelity to YHWH alone and its suspicious view of kingship corresponds to the views of the prophets, such as Amos, Isaiah, and Hosea. He cited the critiques of the kings by Amos and Isaiah, who both charge kings with enriching themselves at the expense of Israelite and Judean working-class people (Amos 7; Isa 5), but Hosea gets the bulk of Alt's attention. Alt believed that Hosea is fundamentally opposed to kingship, insofar as he sees kingship as a long-standing institution since the time of Saul that repeatedly prompted the people to abandon YHWH for other gods. Such views were apparent in Hosea's charges that Israel behaves like an adulterous wife by pursuing other gods, and by their association with the sanctuaries at Beth El and Gilgal where syncretism, idolatry, and injustice are promoted and practiced. The example of the Torah of the King (Deut 17:14–20)—with its prohibition of kings who amass wives, horses, and gold to themselves like Solomon—weighed heavily on his mind as he considered northern Israelite resentment against Solomon and the House of David as influences for its distrust of the northern Israelite kings.[13] Hans Walter Wolff lent considerable support to Alt's position by arguing that Hosea found his intellectual home in the Levitical circles of northern Israel that preserved the older tradition of love of YHWH as the foundation of Israel's covenant.[14]

A third major voice arguing for the northern origins of Deuteronomy was that of Gerhard von Rad. Von Rad argued that the prophetic spirit evident in Deuteronomy and its understanding of the need for adherence to YHWH and YHWH's commandments as the foundation of the covenant could be traced backed to the ancient YHWH amphictyony from the time of the Judges and Samuel's prophetic leadership of Israel.[15] In von Rad's view, the ancient YHWH faith remained alive among the free peasantry of northern Israel, which opposed northern Israelite kings for their alliances with foreign nations and their resulting syncretistic views of G-d. He posited that the Levitical priests of the northern Israelite countryside kept this tradition alive, and in the aftermath of the destruction of northern Israel, brought the Deuteronomic tradition south to Jerusalem and Judah, where it ultimately found its way into King Josiah's program of religious reform and national restoration. Von Rad closely examined the literary form of Deuteronomy. He noted that the laws of Deuteronomy share much in common with the laws of the Covenant Code (Exod 20–24), which suggests that although Deuteronomy is presented as revelation from Sinai—or Horeb as the case may be—historically the Deuteronomic law code appears to have rewritten many Covenant Code laws that apparently originated in the northern kingdom of Israel. A further formal observation was that Deuteronomy appears to rely on the forms of ancient Near Eastern treaties between nations, beginning with Hittite forms, but also including the Assyrian forms that have influenced Deuteronomy. But his most important observation was that Deuteronomy presents Moses's speeches to Israel on the last day of his life as four major sermons that are designed to exhort the people to adhere to YHWH alone and to observe YHWH's Torah as the basis for its possession of the land of Israel that YHWH is about to grant them. Insofar as such a form is typical of priestly and Levitical preaching, von Rad concluded that Deuteronomy must originate among the priests and Levites of the northern kingdom of Israel who began to lose support as Assyrian oppression following the Syro-Ephraimite War (734–732 BCE) would have deprived them of their sources of income and their influence in northern Israelite society. Von Rad therefore posited that Deuteronomy originated in the north among priests and Levites in the northern sanctuaries who were dissatisfied with life under the northern monarchs, who envisioned a reform program to address their views of what had gone wrong in northern Israel, and who moved to the south in the aftermath of the destruction of the northern kingdom of Israel (722–721 BCE).

A fourth major voice in this discussion is E. W. Nicholson, who argued that Deuteronomy is the product of northern prophetic circles that fled northern Israel for Judah in the aftermath of the Assyrian destruction and composed the book of Deuteronomy during the reign of King Manasseh ben Hezekiah (687–642 BCE) in an attempt to reform the Judean monarchy and Temple establishment.[16] Nicholson followed the work of Ronald E. Clements, who presented a similar argument for a northern movement that moved south following the Assyrian destruction and then attempted to reform the southern David/Zion tradition of an eternal covenant by infusing it with Mosaic, prophetic foundations that called for adherence to YHWH commandments.[17] Nicholson argued that there was no evidence for the claims of Alt, von Rad, Wolff, and others who had argued that Deuteronomy had originated in Levitical circles because Deuteronomy lacks reference to the Levites as the source of its authority and instead looks to Moses as the ideal, foundational prophet of Israel, who served as YHWH's covenant mediator with Israel and as the model for a succession of northern prophets, such as Samuel, Elijah and Elisha, and Hosea. Indeed, Nicholson maintained that Hosea 12 points to the prophetic character of the movement by referring to the anonymous prophet who led Israel out of Egyptian exile, through the wilderness, and to the land of Israel. In the aftermath of the Assyrian destruction of Israel, elements of this movement made their way to southern Judah where they wrote Deuteronomy during the reign of Manasseh, who is judged in the Deuteronomistic History (2 Kgs 21) as the worst king of the Davidic line. Following Manasseh's death, the representatives of this movement ensured that Deuteronomy would become the basis for King Josiah's program of religious reform and national restoration.

What Is Trending in the Conversation?

As a result of Nicholson's work and that of the scholars noted earlier, the thesis that the Deuteronomic tradition originated in northern Israelite circles, came south during the reign of Hezekiah, and ultimately provided the foundations for Josiah's reforms remained highly influential in the later work of Norbert Lohfink and Moshe Weinfeld.[18] But a number of serious problems with the arguments offered here demand that the thesis be fundamentally rethought. Although Deuteronomy is clearly designed to appeal to the remnants of the northern kingdom of Israel in the aftermath of the Assyrian destruction, it must be judged to be a fundamentally southern composition that draws upon northern tradition in an effort to attract northerners to accept Davidic rule and the centrality of the Jerusalem Temple during the reign of King Josiah of Judah.[19]

The first observation pertains to the sociopolitical context of the northern kingdom of Israel argued by the aforementioned scholars. The arguments of Alt, von Rad, and to a certain extent, Nicholson, presuppose Martin Noth's once influential hypothesis of an Israelite amphictyony, but Noth's thesis has been rejected. Noth posited that premonarchic Israel was organized along the patterns of an ancient Greek amphictyony in which Israel's twelve tribes united in a federation in which each tribe was responsible for the care and maintenance of the central sanctuary to which all of the tribes adhered.[20] The model was based to a certain extent on the descriptions of Solomon's twelve prefectures in which each prefecture was responsible for the support of the monarchy. But Noth and many scholars presumed that the amphictyony and Solomon's administrative structure were based on a model of a united twelve-tribe Israel. The model does not hold. Solomon's administrative structure does not impose any such obligation on his own home tribe of Judah, but instead imposes it upon the tribes of northern Israel that are divided into twelve prefectures. The restructuring converts the northern tribes into vassals ruled by Solomon.[21] Indeed, the model of the amphictyony collapses on closer examination of the narratives concerning the judges of Israel and the early monarchies of Saul and David. Scholars of Judges have consistently pointed out that the book is composed on the basis of six narratives concerning local rulers who delivered their tribes from outside oppressors and that it has been unified by a Deuteronomistic narrative framework that unites these six local traditions as expressions of the actions of all Israel. Examination of the overall framework shows an interest in demonstrating the inadequacy of the northern judges as rulers of their people; whereas the first judge, Othniel of Judah, easily delivers his people, subsequent northern judges, including Ehud of Benjamin, Deborah of Ephraim, Gideon of Manasseh, Jephthah of Gilead in the Trans-Jordan, and Samson of Dan, demonstrate progressively increasing inadequacies that result in the dissolution of the tribal federation when the tribes must declare holy war against Benjamin for its crimes of the rape and murder of the Levite's concubine, from Judah, no less, that demonstrate the need for a king who can effectively rule the tribes. Through the narratives, Ephraim's attempts to bully the Gideon of Manasseh and the Trans-Jordanian Jephthah demonstrate that Ephraim cannot rule effectively and the idealization of Othniel of Judah, the victimization of Judean Levites in the account of Micah's establishment of the Dan sanctuary and the rape of the Levite's concubine, and the association of the Benjaminite rapists and murderers with Saul's city of Gibeah in Benjamin indicate that the ideal king would best be a Judean.[22] Furthermore, although Saul is depicted as the king of all Israel, his conflicts with David of Judah and his failed attempts to force David to accept his authority indicate that Saul's kingdom actually comprised only the ten tribes of northern Israel. Saul failed to incorporate Judah into his kingdom. Israel was not united as a twelve-tribe federation until the reigns of David and Solomon. Even then, the federation was formed based on a union between David's tribe of Judah and the ten northern tribes of Saul in the aftermath of David's defeat of the northern tribes at Gibeon and the appeal to David by the elders of

Israel to serve as their king. Thus, the northern tribes became vassals of David, and subsequently of Solomon, just as they had been vassals of Saul.

The second observation is that Deuteronomy did not originate among Levitical circles in the north. There is little evidence that the tribe of Levi exercised substantial authority in northern Israel. There is literary evidence that the sons of Eli, allegedly descended from Aaron, exercised priestly authority in the north at Shiloh, but with the deaths of Eli and his sons, Hophni and Phineas, during the battle with the Philistines at Aphek, and the subsequent massacre of the priests from the House of Eli at Nob, Abiathar was the only survivor. Once Solomon exiled Abiathar to Anathoth, it is not clear that the House of Eli exercised influence outside of Anathoth until Jeremiah came to Jerusalem from Anathoth. Even then, the superscription of Jeremiah (Jer 1:1–3) identifies Jeremiah as a priest, not as a Levite. The accounts of the so-called first northern monarch, Jeroboam ben Nebat, expelling Levites from the Temples at Beth El and Dan and allowing priests from other households to serve at these shrines indicates the northern practice of designating the firstborn sons of mothers to serve as priests in northern sanctuary. The model for such practice is Samuel of Ephraim who was the firstborn son of Hannah, the wife of Elkanah, who was apprenticed to Eli at Shiloh to be raised as a priest.[23] Even the account of Josiah's reign (2 Kgs 22–23), which indicates that Josiah invited priests of the northern shrines to serve in the Jerusalem Temple, does not designate them as Levites; instead, it refers to them as *komerim*, a term for non-Levitical priests. Nicholson is correct to point to the northern prophets as a potential source for adherence to YHWH like that of Deuteronomy. As the examples of Samuel, Elijah, and Elisha show, these northern prophets engage in priestly activity, but none of them are Levites.

The third observation is that the northern prophet, Hosea, who calls for adherence to YHWH, is hardly a Deuteronomic-influenced prophet who is opposed to Israelite kingship.[24] Hosea does call for adherence to YHWH, but interpreters must be clear as to what adherence to YHWH means. Most interpreters who view Hosea as a Deuteronomic-influenced prophet point to his call to return to YHWH from foreign gods and his opposition to northern Israelite kingship as the institution that promotes the worship of foreign gods. Such a position is influenced by the contention that King Jeroboam ben Nebat promoted idol worship of the golden calves in Israel and that all northern monarchs followed his example, which led ultimately to Israel's destruction (1 Kgs 12). But closer examination of the portrayal of Jeroboam ben Nebat in Kings and the portrayal of Hosea's views in his book demonstrates that such views are unfounded.

Interpreters generally maintain that the northern kingdom of Israel engaged in syncretistic worship of the Canaanite gods based upon the narratives (1 Kgs 12:25–33).[25] The narrative presents an account of Jeroboam's construction of the golden calves at the sanctuaries at Beth El and Dan as well as his statement that "these are your gods who brought you up out of the land of Egypt." Interpreters have taken this presentation at face value to charge Jeroboam with idolatry and concluded that it serves as the basis for Hosea's charges that Israel has pursued other gods.

Such a reading fails to recognize two major factors, first, the polemical character of the narrative and, second, the true character and function of the golden calves. To explain the destruction of the northern kingdom of Israel by the Assyrian empires (722–721 BCE), the narrative, which developed in Judah, charged Jeroboam and all the rest of the northern kings with apostasy. The intention of the narrative was an effort to explain how YHWH, who promised to make Israel a great nation, was unable to protect Israel from the Assyrians. In fact, Israel was destroyed for revolting against its Assyrian suzerain and failing to abide by its treaty obligations as a vassal of Assyria. From Judah's perspective, YHWH was beyond reproach and, therefore, the kings and people of Israel had to be responsible for their own demise. Indeed, the charge of apostasy would convince the people of Judah to continue to adhere to YHWH despite YHWH's failure to protect the northern kingdom.

Interpreters must also consider the true function of the golden calves. Although the narrative portrays them as Israel's gods that demand worship, such a portrayal is a polemic. As portrayals of deities throughout the ancient Near East demonstrate, gods are frequently mounted on thrones or on the backs of animals of various sorts, including bulls, lions, horses, and donkeys as one of the privileges of leadership and symbols of such status. Animal mounts appear for gods such as Hathor/Kadeshah, Hadad, Ishtar, and others.[26] Assur is seated on a winged throne chariot flying through the heavens.[27] In Jerusalem, YHWH is seated invisibly above the Ark of the Covenant, which functions as a throne as indicated by the cherubim mounted atop the Ark, a typical feature of ancient Near Eastern thrones for kings and gods, and the oft-repeated reference to "YHWH, who is enthroned above the cherubim."[28] The golden calves are not gods to be worshipped. They are mounts above which YHWH is invisibly seated in Israel much like YHWH is seated above the cherubim of the Ark of the Covenant in Judah. The difference is not one of deities; rather, it is one of different iconographies for YHWH's throne, even though YHWH is the same G-d. The narrative (1 Kgs 12:25–33) portrays the golden calves as gods in order to explain why YHWH failed to defend northern Israel and to rally Judah to the worship of YHWH and the observance of YHWH's expectations.

The recognition that northern Israel continued to worship YHWH mounted invisibly above the golden calves also calls for reconsideration of Hosea's understanding of Israel. The prophet's charges of Israel's pursuit of other gods and questions concerning Israel's kingship must be placed into context. Hosea is not opposed to kingship in principle; he is concerned specifically with the royal House of Jehu as indicated by the initial narrative of the book where YHWH commands him to give his children with Gomer symbolic names. The first son is named "Jezreel," which refers to the Jezreel Valley, located to the south of the Galil and to the north of the northern Israelite hill country. Jezreel is a prescient name for determining Hosea's concerns with the monarchy because it is the site where Jehu overthrew the House of Omri by assassinating King Jehoram ben Ahab of Israel and his mother, the Phoenician Princess, Jezebel, who married King Ahab ben Omri of Israel and thereby became Queen of Israel. YHWH's and the prophet's dissatisfaction with this dynasty is further emphasized by the symbolic names given to Hosea's other two children, "Lo Ruḥamah" meaning "No Mercy," for the daughter, and " Lo ʾAmmi" meaning "Not My People," for the second son, both of which signaled YHWH's readiness to leave Israel to its fate and allow its punishment. Hosea was opposed to the House of Jehu, including Kings Jehu, Jehoahaz, Jehoash, Jeroboam, and finally Zechariah. The House of Jehu was the most powerful dynasty in northern Israel's history, particularly during the long reign of Jeroboam ben Joash, but it was overthrown (742 BCE) some six months into the reign of Zechariah ben Jeroboam.

Interpreters must also consider the reasons for the demise of the House of Jehu in order to understand the basis for Hosea's dissatisfaction with the dynasty. Jehu overthrew the House of Omri out of dissatisfaction with the failure of its monarchs to protect the nation against the Arameans. King Ahab was killed in battle against Aram at Ramoth Gilead (1 Kgs

22) and his son, King Jehoram, was wounded in battle against the Arameans at the same location. Jehu, a commander in Israel's army, was dissatisfied with the failure of the House of Omri to defeat the Arameans and travelled to Jezreel to assassinate Jehoram and take control of the kingdom. He failed to relieve Israel from Aramean pressure, but eventually the Arameans relented. The reason was that Jehu concluded a treaty with Assyria, which had been trying for years to invade Aram, but had been repulsed repeatedly. But when King Shalmaneser III of Assyria marched against Phoenicia, King Jehu submitted to him and apparently concluded a treaty with the Assyrians. Jehu's submission to Shalmaneser is depicted in the Black Obelisk of Shalmaneser III, which portrays Jehu bowing at the feet of the Assyrian monarch.[29] Most scholars overlook Jehu's submission, but interpreters must also note that Jehu's grandson, Jehoash (Joash) ben Jehoahaz, is also named among the vassals of Shalmaneser's successor, King Adad Nirari III of Assyria.[30]

The benefits of Israel's submission to Assyria are clear. Assyria was positioned along Aram's northern border, and Israel was located to the south of Aram. With Aram caught between Assyria and Israel, Assyria was able to pressure Aram and thereby prevent Aram from threatening Israel any longer. Israel's alliance with Assyria and the resulting end of the Aramean threat explains the long period of peace enjoyed by Israel under the reign of the Jehu dynasty. But at what cost? The submission of Israel to Assyria gave Assyria access to the trade routes controlled by Israel that led down to Egypt, and thereby enabled Assyria to trade with Egypt by means of Israel and prepare for the day when Assyria might invade Egypt, apparently a major strategic goal of Assyrian policy. Hosea objected to trade with Egypt as indicated throughout his book. Egypt had been Israel's oppressor as indicated in the Pentateuchal tradition cited by Hosea (Hos 12), and alliance with Assyria placed Israel into an alliance with Egypt, much as Solomon had been allied with Egypt while imposing state slavery upon his Israelite subjects while he built his palace, the Jerusalem Temple, and the various cities of northern Israel. By contrast, Israel had a close relationship with Aram. Indeed, the Pentateuch indicates that Israel's eponymous ancestor, Jacob, renamed as Israel twice in the Pentateuch, found his brides, Rachel and Leah and their handmaidens, Bilhah and Zilpah, in Aram. Hosea cites this tradition, too (Hos 12). Interpreters must also note that King Zechariah ben Jeroboam from the House of Jehu was assassinated by parties interested in breaking Israel's alliance with Assyria and reestablishing its relationship with Aram. Indeed, the repeated assassinations of Israel's kings during its last years indicate a struggle in the country between pro-Aramean and pro-Assyrian parties. Ultimately, the pro-Aramean faction won and brought Pekah ben Remaliah to the throne, who broke Israel's relationship with Assyria and reestablished Israel's relationship with Aram. The result was the fiasco of the Syro-Ephraimite War in which Assyria destroyed Damascus, subjugated Aram, and stripped Israel of its holdings outside of the Israelite hill country for violating its treaty with Assyria. When Israel revolted again under Hoshea (724 BCE), the Assyrians invaded again and destroyed the northern kingdom.

For Hosea, Israel's alliance with Assyria meant submitting not only to the Assyrian King but to Assyria's gods as well, whereas alliance with Aram meant acknowledging YHWH alone, insofar as Aram was the land of Jacob's wives, Israel's ancestors, and Israel's G-d. Never did Hosea call for the worship of YHWH at only one sanctuary. The issue for him was the pursuit of other gods, which came with Israel's alliance with Assyria. Northern Israelite refugees, including Hosea, fled south in the face of the Assyrian destruction of Samaria. It is possible and even likely that King Hezekiah sought to reestablish Davidic control over the territory and people of the former northern kingdom of Israel when he revolted against Assyria. Modern interpreters will never know if Hezekiah used a form of Deuteronomy as part of his efforts to regain control of the north—or even the extent of his ambitions to do so. There remains no convincing proof that an edition of Deuteronomy played any role in Hezekiah's thinking. So we must return to consideration of Josiah's reform and Deuteronomy's place in it.

Altogether, Deuteronomy supports Josiah's program. It envisions a unified twelve tribes of Israel adhering to YHWH alone and not to any foreign gods. It envisions only one major site for the worship of YHWH, which represents the institutional religious structure of the southern kingdom of Judah with its Temple in Jerusalem, and it also represents the fundamental religious principle of King Josiah's reform with its foci on both YHWH and the Jerusalem Temple alone. It allows for YHWH's presence throughout the land of Israel and beyond by specifying that the one sanctuary is the place for YHWH's holy name, and therefore does not envision YHWH as confined to the one Temple. It allows for the holy slaughter of meat outside of the Temple and throughout the land, which entails worship outside of the one Temple while allowing that Temple to serve as the focal point for Judean/Israelite worship. It adapts northern Israelite tradition to southern perspectives, in particular by revising the older northern Israelite Covenant Code (Exod 20–24) to give greater rights and privileges to the poor, including the widow, orphan, and Levite, the very class that supported King Josiah's ascent to the throne following the assassination of his father, Amon.[31] And it further portrays Moses at Shechem, the ancient assembly point in northern Israel on the border between Ephraim and Manasseh where Joshua gathered the people (Josh 24),[32] Abimelech ben Gideon attempted to start a monarchy (Judg 9), and where northern Israel made its decision to abandon Rehoboam ben Solomon from the House of David and reestablish a northern monarchy under Jeroboam ben Nebat (1 Kgs 12). It calls for the establishment of a judiciary system that is under the control of the high priest of the Temple and not under the control of the monarch as exemplified by David and Solomon, who both heard cases and were known to give rulings that were more interested in serving the interests of the monarch rather than the people, particularly the poor class. It promises that adherence to YHWH and YHWH's Torah will not only bring agricultural plenty, but it will also prevent any invasion of the land like that suffered by Israel and Judah from ever happening again. And it calls upon the king to submit to YHWH's Torah and thereby prevent another monarch like Solomon, whose policies prompted the northern tribes to revolt against the House of David in the first place. Altogether, Deuteronomy supports Josiah's goals of reuniting Israel under Davidic rule; in this regard, it is especially designed to appeal to the surviving northern population to return to the House of David and thus to return to YHWH.

Notes

1. Wilhelm M. L. de Wette, *Dissertatio critic-exegetica qua Deuteronomium a prioribus Pentateuchi Libris diversum, alius cuiusdam recentioris auctioris opus esse monstratur; quam . . . auctoritate amplissimi philosophorum ordinis pro venia legend AD XXVII* (Jena: Universität Jena, 1805); see Thomas B. Dozeman, *The Pentateuch: Introducing*

the Torah (Minneapolis: Fortress, 2017), 33–77, esp. 53–62. For discussion of research on Deuteronomy, see esp. Horst Dietrich Preuss, *Deuteronomium*; ErFor 164 (Darmstadt: Wissenschaftliche Buchgesellschaft, 1982); Ronald E. Clements, *Deuteronomy*; OTG (Sheffield: Sheffield Academic Press, 1989).

2. Marvin A. Sweeney, *King Josiah of Judah: The Lost Messiah of Israel* (Oxford: Oxford University Press, 2001); Richard D. Nelson, *Deuteronomy: A Commentary*; OTL (Louisville: Westminster John Knox, 2002); cf. Mark Leuchter, *Josiah's Reform and Jeremiah's Scroll: Historical Calamity and Prophetic Response* (Sheffield: Sheffield Phoenix Press, 2006).
3. Albrecht Alt, "Die Heimat des Deuteronomiums," in *Kleine Schriften* (Munich: C. B. Beck, 1953) 2:250–275; Gerhard von Rad, *Studies in Deuteronomy*; SBT 9 (London: SCM, 1953), 60–69; Ernest W. Nicholson, *Deuteronomy and Tradition* (Philadelphia: Fortress, 1967), esp. 58–82.
4. Anne-Sylvie Boisliveau, "Qur'ānic Discourse on the Bible," *MIDÉO* 33 (2018): 3–38.
5. Dozeman, *The Pentateuch*, 33–77.
6. Moshe Weinfeld, *Deuteronomy 1–11*; AB 5 (New York: Doubleday, 1991), 16. N.b., De Wette's argument that Deuteronomy was the Book of Torah found in the Temple serves as a fundamental basis for scholarly dating of Deuteronomy.
7. Julius Wellhausen, *Die Composition des Hexateuchs und der historischen Bücher des Alten Testaments* (Berlin: Georg Reimer, 1889), 189–210.
8. Samuel Rolles Driver, *Deuteronomy*; ICC (Edinburgh: T and T Clark, 1895), i–xcv.
9. Carl Steuernagel, *Deuteronomium und Josua*; HKAT I/3 (Göttingen: Vandenhoeck & Ruprecht, 1900), i–xlii.
10. Antti Filemon Puukko, *Das Deuteronomium* (Leipzig: J. C. Hinrichs, 1910); Johannes Hempel, *Die Schichten des Deuteronomiums* (Leipzig: R. Voigtländer, 1914); Theodor Oestreicher, *Das Deuteronomiche Grundgesetz* (Gütersloh: Carl Bertelsmann, 1923).
11. Adam C. Welch, *The Code of Deuteronomy: A New Theory of its Origin* (London: James Clarke, 1924).
12. Alt, "Die Heimat."
13. Cf. Kurt Galling, "Das Königsgesetz im Deuteronomium," *ThLZ* 76 (1951): 133–138.
14. Hans Walter Wolff, *Hosea* (Hermeneia; Philadelphia: Fortress, 1974); Hans Walter Wolff, "Hoseas geistige Heimat," *Gesammelte Studien* (Munich: Chr. Kaiser, 1964), 232–250.
15. Von Rad, *Studies in Deuteronomy*, 60–69; Von Rad, *Deuteronomy: A Commentary*; OTL (Philadelphia: Westminster, 1966), 11–30.
16. Nicholson, *Deuteronomy and Tradition*, 58–106.
17. Ronald E. Clements, "Deuteronomy and the Jerusalem Cult Tradition," *VT* 15 (1965): 300–312.
18. Norbert Lohfink, "Die Bundesurkunde des Königs Josias (Eine Frage an die Deuteronoimiumserforschung)," *Biblica* 44 (1963): 261–288, 461–298; Norbert Lohfink, "The Cult Reform of Josiah of Judah: 2 Kings 22–23 as a Source for the History of Israelite Religion," in *Ancient Israelite Religion*, ed. P. D. Miller et al.; Fs. F. M. Cross, Jr. (Philadelphia: Fortress, 1987), 459–475; Moshe Weinfeld, "The Emergence of the Deuteronomic Movement: The Historical Antecedents," in *Das Deuteronomium*, ed. N. Lohfink (Leuven: Peeters, 1985), 76–98; Moshe Weinfeld, *Deuteronomy and the Deuteronomic School* (Winona Lake: Eisenbrauns, 1992, first published 1972); Moshe Weinfeld, *Deuteronomy 1–11*, 1–84.

19. Sweeney, *King Josiah*, 137–169.
20. Martin Noth, *Das System der Zwölf Stämme Israels* (Darmstadt: Wissenschaftliches Buchgesellschaft 1966, first published 1930).
21. Marvin A. Sweeney, *1 and 2 Kings: A Commentary*; OTL (Louisville: Westminster John Knox, 2007), 95–104.
22. Sweeney, *King Josiah*, 110–134; Sweeney, "Davidic Polemics in the Book of Judges," *VT* 47 (1997): 417–429.
23. Marvin A. Sweeney, "Samuel's Institutional Identity in the Deuteronomistic History," in *Constructs of Prophets in the Former and Latter Prophets and Other Texts*, ed. L. L. Grabbe and M. Nissinen (Atlanta: Society of Biblical Literature, 2011), 165–174; Marvin A. Sweeney, "Prophets and Priests in the Deuteronomistic History," in *Israelite Prophecy and the Deuteronomistic History*, ed. Mignon Jacobs and Raymond F. Person; AIL 14 (Atlanta: Society of Biblical Literature, 2013), 35–49.
24. See my discussion of Hosea in Marvin A. Sweeney, *The Twelve Prophets*; Berit Olam; 2 vols. (Collegeville: Liturgical, 2000), 1:1–144.
25. For discussion of the presentation of Jeroboam ben Nebat in 1–2 Kings, see Marvin A. Sweeney, *Reading the Hebrew Bible after the Shoah: Engaging Holocaust Theology* (Minneapolis: Fortress, 2008), 67–72; Sweeney, *1–2 Kings*, 172–182.
26. James B. Pritchard, *The Ancient Near East in Pictures* (Princeton: Princeton University Press, 1969), 470–473, 486, 500–501, 522, 531, 534.
27. Pritchard, *ANEP*, 536.
28. 1 Sam 4:4; 2 Sam 6:2; Isa 66:1; see *ANEP* 456, 458.
29. *ANEP* 351, 353.
30. Stephanie Page, "A Stele of Adad Nirari III and Nergal Erges from Tell al Rimah," *Iraq* 30 (1968): 139–153.
31. Bernard M. Levinson, *Deuteronomy and the Hermeneutics of Legal Innovation* (Oxford: Oxford University Press, 1997).
32. Edward F. Campbell, "Shechem," *NEAEHL* 4:1345–1354.

Bibliography

Alt, Albrecht. "Die Heimat des Deuteronomiums." *Kleine Schriften* 2 (1953): 250–275.
Campbell, Edward F. "Shechem." In *The New Encyclopedia of Archeological Excavations in the Holy Land* 4, edited by E. Stern et al., 1345–1354. Jerusalem: Israel Exploration Society and Carta, 1993.
Clements, Ronald E. "Deuteronomy and the Jerusalem Cult Tradition." *VT* 15 (1965): 300–312.
Clements, Ronald E. *Deuteronomy*. OTG. Sheffield: Sheffield Academic Press, 1989.
Dozeman, Thomas B. *The Pentateuch: Introducing the Torah*. Minneapolis: Fortress, 2017.
Driver, Samuel Rolles. *Deuteronomy*. ICC. Edinburgh: T and T Clark, 1895.
Galling, Kurt. "Das Königsgesetz im Deuteronomium." *ThLZ* 76 (1951): 133–138.
Hempel, Johannes. *Die Schichten des Deuteronomiums*. Leipzig: R. Voigtländer, 1914.
Leuchter, Mark. *Josiah's Reform and Jeremiah's Scroll: Historical Calamity and Prophetic Response*. Sheffield: Sheffield Phoenix Press, 2006.
Levinson, Bernard M. *Deuteronomy and the Hermeneutics of Legal Innovation*. Oxford: Oxford University Press, 1997.

Lohfink, Norbert. "Die Bundesurkunde des Königs Josias (Eine Frage an die Deuteronomiumserforschung)." *Biblica* 44 (1963): 261–288, 461–498.

Lohfink, Norbert. "The Cult Reform of Josiah of Judah: 2 Kings 22–23 as a Source for the History of Israelite Religion." In *Ancient Israelite Religion*, edited by P. D. Miller et al., 459–475. Fs. F. M. Cross, Jr. Philadelphia: Fortress, 1987.

Nelson, Richard D. *Deuteronomy: A Commentary*. OTL. Louisville: Westminster John Knox, 2002.

Nicholson, Ernest W. *Deuteronomy and Tradition*. Philadelphia: Fortress, 1967.

Noth, Martin. *Das System der Zwölf Stämme Israels*. Darmstadt: Wissenschaftliches Buchgesellschaft 1966, first published 1930.

Oestreicher, Theodor. *Das Deuteronomiche Grundgesetz*. Gütersloh: Carl Bertelsmann, 1923.

Page, Stephanie. "A Stele of Adad Nirari III and Nergal Ergeš from Tell al Rimah." *Iraq* 30 (1968): 139–153.

Preuss, Horst Dietrich. *Deuteronomium*. ErFor 164. Darmstadt: Wissenschaftliche Buchgesellschaft, 1982.

Pritchard, James B. *The Ancient Near East in Pictures*. Princeton: Princeton University Press, 1969.

Puukko, Antti Filemon. *Das Deuteronomium*. Leipzig: J. C. Hinrichs, 1910.

Rad, Gerhard von. *Deuteronomy: A Commentary*. OTL. Philadelphia: Westminster, 1966.

Steuernagel, Carl. *Deuteronomium und Josua*. HKAT I/3. Göttingen: Vandenhoeck & Ruprecht, 1900.

Sweeney, Marvin A. "Davidic Polemics in the Book of Judges." *VT* 47 (1997): 417–429.

Sweeney, Marvin A. *1 and 2 Kings: A Commentary*. OTL. Louisville: Westminster John Knox, 2007.

Sweeney, Marvin A. *King Josiah of Judah: The Lost Messiah of Israel*. Oxford: Oxford University Press, 2001.

Sweeney, Marvin A. "Prophets and Priests in the Deuteronomistic History." In *Israelite Prophecy and the Deuteronomistic History*, edited by M. Jacobs and R. F. Person, 35–49. AIL 14. Atlanta: Society of Biblical Literature, 2013.

Sweeney, Marvin A. *Reading the Hebrew Bible after the Shoah: Engaging Holocaust Theology*. Minneapolis: Fortress, 2008.

Sweeney, Marvin A. "Samuel's Institutional Identity in the Deuteronomistic History." In *Constructs of Prophets in the Former and Latter Prophets and Other Texts*, edited by L. L. Grabbe and M. Nissinen, 165–174. Atlanta: Society of Biblical Literature, 2011.

Sweeney, Marvin A. *The Twelve Prophets*. Berit Olam. 2 vols. Collegeville: Liturgical, 2000.

Von Rad, Gerhard. *Studies in Deuteronomy*. SBT 9. London: SCM, 1953.

Weinfeld, Moshe. *Deuteronomy and the Deuteronomic School*. Winona Lake: Eisenbrauns, 1992, first published 1972.

Weinfeld, Moshe. *Deuteronomy 1–11*. AB 5. New York: Doubleday, 1991.

Weinfeld, Moshe. "The Emergence of the Deuteronomic Movement: The Historical Antecedents." In *Das Deuteronomium*, edited by N. Lohfink, 76–98. Leuven: Peeters, 1985.

Welch, Adam C. *The Code of Deuteronomy: A New Theory of Its Origin*. London: James Clarke, 1924.

Wellhausen, Julius. *Die Composition des Hexateuchs und der historischen Bücher des Alten Testaments*. Berlin: Georg Reimer, 1889.

de Wette, Wilhelm M. L. *Dissertatio critic-exegetica qua Deuteronomium a prioribus Pentateuchi Libris diversum, alius cuiusdam recentioris auctioris opus esse monstratur; quam . . . auctoritate amplissimi philosophorum ordinis pro venia legend AD XXVII.* Jena: Universität Jena, 1805.

Wolff, Hans Walter. *Hosea*. Hermeneia. Philadelphia: Fortress, 1974.

Wolff, Hans Walter. "Hoseas geistige Heimat." In *Gesammelte Studien*, edited by N. Lohfink, 76–98. Munich: Chr. Kaiser, 1964.

CHAPTER 18

THE SOCIO-ECONOMIC WORLD OF DEUTERONOMY

SANDRA LYNN RICHTER

THE provenance of Deuteronomy remains one of the most debated questions of modern biblical scholarship. Broadly recognized as the "constitution and bylaws" of some era of biblical Israel's existence and identified as the "linchpin" of the documentary hypothesis, the *Sitz im Leben* of this book has profound implications. According to Deuteronomy itself, the physical setting from which this compilation of Mosaic speeches emerges is the liminal space between the emigrating tribes' past (the wilderness) and future (the promised land). Here on the plains of Moab, "across the Jordan, in the wilderness, in the Arabah," on the "first day of the eleventh month of the fortieth year" after the tribes' departure from Egypt, Moses offers his final message to the gathered offspring of Abraham, Isaac, and Jacob (1:1–3, 8). This is the day of Moses's death, and the day in which authority will be passed from Moses the sage to Joshua the military champion (31:2; 34:48; 34:7). But the contents of Deuteronomy speak to a future time, "the day that you cross the Jordan" (27:2), and the norms and mores communicated engage a new life in a new territory. If the internal indicators of Deuteronomy are to be taken at face value, they should direct the reader to Israel's early settlement as a tribal coalition in the Central Hill country of Canaan. If not, then an array of contexts emerges as potential candidates. This chapter is an attempt to narrow those potential contexts via an economic read of Deuteronomy.

WHO BEGAN THE CONVERSATION?

Although the complexities of Pentateuchal composition and compilation have been debated since Talmudic times, it was W. M. L. de Wette in his 1805 *Dissertatio critico-exegetica* who first proposed that the provenance of *Urdeuteronomium* could be found in the events recorded in Kings (2 Kgs 22). De Wette argued that Deuteronomy was a seventh-century Judahite document, composed by the Jerusalem elite to facilitate Josiah's federally sponsored reforms via its "centralizing formula" (12:5, 11, 21; 14:23, 24; 16:2, 6, 11; 26:2).[1] Julius Wellhausen (1878) embraced this assessment and via his *Prolegomena zur Geschichte Israels* established the identity of *Urdeuteronomium* (D) as the urban and monarchic product of Josiah's Jerusalem.[2] Variations of this thesis—composed either in the era of Hezekiah, Manasseh, or Josiah—have dominated biblical scholarship since.

A significant alternative to Wellhausen's thesis arose when Heinrich Ewald (1878) highlighted supposed influences upon Deuteronomy from the eighth-century prophets (Hosea in particular), opening up the possibility for older northern source material behind Deuteronomy.[3] Affirming these northern connections, Adam C. Welch (1924) postulated that *Urdeuteronomium* originated as a mechanism for covenant renewal in one of the northern sanctuaries—Shechem, Samaria, or Bethel—and envisioned an early Deuteronomic code from the era of the Judges.[4] Albrecht Alt (1953) identified the authors of this northern code as prophets, proposing that this circle of Yahwists subversively preserved their traditions after the Assyrian conquest (722 BCE), traditions that eventually found their way to Judah "*und dort im Tempel Jahwes deponiert wurde.*"[5] G. von Rad (1953) also affirmed older, northern origins, but championed the country Levites as the conduit to the south.[6] R. E. Clements (1965) embraced the potential of either prophets or Levites as "the heirs of the religious traditions of the Northern Kingdom," but insisted that Deuteronomy itself was composed in Jerusalem "to lead to a reform of the Jerusalem cult tradition."[7] Nicholson (1967) added Deuteronomy's treaty structure, a supposed reflection of the northern amphictyony, to the indicators of northern provenance.[8] Weinfeld (1976) affirmed the northern provenance, but connected the treaty structure to a seventh-century reworking of the text under the Josianic reform and the influence of the vassal treaties of Esarhaddon (672 BCE).[9] A contemporary rehearsal of this early northern provenance for *Urdeuteronomomium* is championed by J. Tigay (1996), who points to Deuteronomy's portrayal of a society "a good deal less advanced than that of seventh century Judah."[10]

In contrast, G. Hölscher and R. H. Kennett[11] proposed that *Urdeuteronomomium* was an exilic composition of utopian imagination and not actual, practicable legislation, "but the pious dream of the later priesthood."[12] Discredited for a time, this exilic theory has made a contemporary "comeback" in the work of Juha Pakkala, who compellingly argues that "[i]t would be necessary to assume some very special circumstances to explain why the monarch, the state, its structure, Judah, Jerusalem and the temple are completely missing in the document when they should all be present during the time of the writing."[13]

What Is the Status of the Conversation?

A newer paradigm pushes the social location of Deuteronomy—and the Pentateuch as a whole—even further into the Persian period. As summarized by Christophe Nihan:

> The Torah is a sophisticated composition that, on the basis of earlier traditions, defines a new legend establishing the origins of "Israel," a legend capable of rivaling other prestigious national traditions inside the Achaemenid Empire, as is apparent for instance, in Deut 4:8: "And what great nation has statutes and ordinances as equitable as this whole law that I am setting before you today?"[14]

In this new paradigm, the Torah redefines the identity of "Israel" via an "inner-Judean compromise" in the complex situation following the state's collapse.[15] Deuteronomy is seen, therefore, as an attempt to synthesize the scribal traditions shared by the Judeans and Samarians in a quest for compromise between the two communities.[16] This theory holds that a "harmonistic version of the Pentateuch" was shared "during the 2nd and 1st centuries BCE and perhaps even in later periods,"[17] and although these communities suffered significant internal conflicts, in reality Yehud and Samaria existed in the Persian period as "coreligionists."[18] Thus, the "imprecise language" of Deuteronomy's centralizing formula and the rotating roles of Mt. Gerizim and Mt. Ebal (11:27; 27:1–8) are an intentional and strategic exercise in compromise.[19] The end goal? A text in which "the Torah would be just as acceptable to Samarians as to Judeans."[20] Thus, as Nihan details, the final form of Deuteronomy is to be located in the second phase of the Persian period, in the "late 5th or early 4th century BCE."[21]

What Is Trending in the Conversation?

As we survey this landscape, the horizon of proposed contexts from which Deuteronomy emerges is bewildering at best—from the Iron Age to the Persian period; north to south to east; rural to urban; prophet to priest to scribe. Each of these reconstructions has sought some external benchmark to help locate *Urdeuteronomium*'s original author(s) and audience(s) in real space and time to better understand Deuteronomy and its purpose(s). The objective of this chapter is to offer a new benchmark. By means of an interdisciplinary reading of Deuteronomy that takes "into account the social world(s) of Deuteronomy,"[22] we will consider how the embedded economic realities of Deuteronomy—assumed, inferred, or commanded—help narrow the horizon. Toward this end, our literary focus will be *Urdeuteronomium* (4:44–27:26), our material focus, the archaeologically reconstructed economies of the southern Levant in the Iron I through the Persian periods.[23]

Economics via Text and Artifact

Economic behavior may be described in three categories: production, consumption, and distribution. Within these categories the mechanisms by which a household, polity, or empire obtains wealth are an essential part of daily life, and therefore have distinct consequences for individuals at every level of society. These mechanisms may be tracked via material remains. Grinding stones, threshing floors, storage silos, faunal remains, and carbonized seeds all have a tale to tell regarding local production and consumption. Wineries, apiaries, and olive oil installations together with their written receipts of exchange speak to distribution and trade. Booty and tribute lists and the final resting place of artifacts serve to identify trade networks. The synthesis of this physical evidence brings the economies of the southern Levant into focus.

Equally so, the mechanisms of production, consumption, and distribution may be tracked via textual remains. Deuteronomy captures a snapshot of the lifeways of the people who inhabit its traditions. The economic and legal structure of household and village, the products of farm and trade, taxation, fines, centers of commerce and highways, and even acceptable means of warfare are all addressed in *Urdeuteronomium*. Here the norms and mores of a society are portrayed—at times forthrightly as an element of narrative or law, at times indirectly via metaphor or backdrop, or at times even mistakenly by means of anachronism. Our task is to compare these two bodies of evidence and through the intersectionality of our data, attempt to identify "benchmarks" that further refine the author(s) and audience(s) of Deuteronomy.

The Economics of *Urdeuteronomium*

As I have detailed elsewhere,[24] *Urdeuteronomium* assumes and describes a populace living on small farms, dependent on the "householder" economics of the *bêt 'āb*, in which production, consumption, and distribution emerge from a mixture of pastoralism and diversified agriculture of crops native to the Central Hill country. Here the short-term agricultural investment of grain is paramount, but the longer-term economic investments of grape and olive cultivation are also present (6:11; 16:9, 13; 20:6; 22:9; 23:24–25; 24:19; 25:21). The domestic beasts named are the mainstays of the Levantine pastoralist—mixed herds of sheep and goats for milk, meat, and wool; the ox for cultivation; and the donkey for labor and transport. References to the slaughter and consumption of the gazelle and wild deer common to the fringe areas of the hill country frequent *Urdeuteronomium* as well (12:15, 22; 14:5; 15:22). Distribution in this society is described in terms of reciprocal exchange in local village settings. The hallmarks of a centralized or empire-driven economy—public works, fortifications (the *ḥômâ* of the biblical text[25]), international trade, ships, and camels, imported luxury items, industrial zones, government officials and trade centers—are absent. The network of rural villages that make up the economy in *Urdeuteronomium* is also the backbone of judicial and notary action. Civil law assumes a robust, rural kinship structure as evinced by the levirate law (25:5–10), the execution of incorrigible young adults (21:18–21; 22:23–24), and the particular economic and legal concern for those located outside the protections of the household—the orphan, widow, *gēr*, and Levite (10:18; 14:19–22, 28–29; 16:11–14). Even the laws of manumission also assume a local, reciprocal economy characterized by the diversified agriculture of the Central Hill country (15:14). Deuteronomy's distinctive phrase "in your gates" communicates the public, communal village space essential to the gathering of the bounded community where the Sabbath, tithe, secular slaughter, and charity toward the marginalized occurred (5:14; 12:12, 15, 17, 18, 21; 14:21, 27, 28, 29; 15:22; 16:5, 11, 14, 18; 24:14; 26:12).[26] And the epicenter of this network is the central cult site "the place that YHWH will choose" (12:5, 11, 14, 18, 21, 26; 14:23, 24, 25; 15:20; 16:2, 6, 7, 15, 16; 17:8; 18:6; 23:16; 26:2),[27] at which taxation, collection, and reciprocal exchange occur. As many have noted, there is no suggestion of any state infrastructure in *Urdeuteronomium*: "[i]t is as though the context of state and temple does not even exist . . . the burden of social support [is placed] entirely on the farmer, while ignoring artisans, merchants, and officials."[28] Deuteronomy seems to know nothing of centralized government or the taxes, corveé, public works, professional army, and tribute that emerge from the same. It is unaware of the "geopolitically and economically strategic" urban centers that controlled the trade routes of the Jezreel Valley, Coastal Highway, and caravan routes active during the Iron II period and beyond.[29] Most telling as regards economic infrastructure is the conspicuous absence of currency and coinage. Although *Urdeuteronomium* interacts with taxation and commerce frequently, these actions are nearly always described in terms of a simple, barter-based, "in-kind" exchange. Silver is known, but primarily in the limited and predictable circumstances of an unstratified society. The references to the "*nešek* of silver"—"Do not charge your brother interest, whether on money or food (23:20 [ET 19])"—and the exchange of silver—"exchange your tithe for silver (14:25)"—show movement toward a stratified and redistributive society, but an integrated, urban economy is clearly not the dominant portrayal of Israel in Deuteronomy.[30]

Obviously, the economic details rehearsed here are not descriptive of Hezekiah or Josiah's Jerusalem. Rather, the hegemony of the Neo-Assyrian Empire will completely transform the economy of Judah, embedding the appurtenances of a wide-scale, redistributive, "command" economy at every level of Israelite society. For those like Adam Welch and Jeffrey Tigay who see in Deuteronomy an early and functioning law code, this profile seems to support their hypothesized early, northern provenance. For those like Hölscher and Pakkala who argue for an exilic provenance, the embedded economic and governmental details of *Urdeuteronomium* must become the idealized memories of a lost age, or perhaps the imagination of exilic scribes and priests intentionally designing a utopian society that would not fall prey to the same temptations that destroyed the Davidic monarchy.[31] The issue here will be how a sixth-century religious official, raised in Jerusalem, living in Babylon might retain such precise detail regarding an economy long past. For those attempting to place Deuteronomy in the Persian period, this political and economic profile would need to reflect the recovering post collapse community of "Beyond the River" in the second phase of the Persian period—an equally challenging pursuit.

Iron I Period (c. 1200–980 BCE)

The Iron I period of the southern Levant is witness to hundreds of small, rural villages appearing in the previously unsettled Central Hill country.[32] The portrait emerging from archaeology offers us a newly sedentary populace organized around households of fifteen to twenty persons, engaged in a mixture of dry farming on terraced hillsides—grain, grapes, and olives—and mixed animal husbandry.[33] In this economy, bovines were for labor while mixed flocks of sheep and goats provided wool, meat, and milk.[34] Long-term cultivation of grapes and olives emerged toward the end of the period. This was a subsistence economy whose strategy was to diversify risk, optimize labor, and preserve essential resources at an "optimal level in order to sustain household requirements."[35]

These "small holders" of the Central Hill country occupied farmsteads and simple villages with minimal permanent architecture. Encircled domestic dwellings safeguarded silos and flocks; low, nondefense walls marked the perimeters of the human habitat; defense construction was very limited.[36] This design dissipates with the end of Iron I when real fortifications appear—facilitated by the taxation and corvée labor of a centralized government. Storage was minimal, and unlike the large, elevated structures of the Iron II, Iron I facilities were small, in-ground, and targeted at sustaining the household.[37] There is little evidence for trade, rather the Iron I highland economy seems to have been a "closed" economy, conservative and self-sufficient. Exchange was chiefly in-kind and nonmonetary with small-scale redistribution occurring by means of cultural institutions such as holy sites. And although interaction with the Canaanite urban centers, trade routes, and port cities occurred, such interaction was limited. "Householding rather than market exchange, was paramount."[38]

Iron IIA (980–840 BCE) and Iron IIB (c. 840–732/701 BCE)

With the Iron IIA, a new economic zone emerges.[39] The dearth of public architecture that characterized the Iron I is transformed.[40] Villages and cities are fortified; public storage facilities and water systems are constructed; and monumental, ashlar architecture abounds in urban sites. Industrial agricultural production centers appear and multiply, and trade networks are secured and expanded as evinced by permanent markets, foreign goods, a shift in settlement pattern, and biblical references to foreign markets.[41] The transformation of Samaria and Jerusalem into political and commercial centers is particularly illustrative. Jerusalem expands dramatically, evincing monumental architecture as early as the tenth century, magnificent private burials by the ninth, and an enormous public water system by the eighth. During this era, Omri rebuilt Samaria replete with magnificent public architecture, daunting fortifications, imported luxury items, and taxation directed toward the support of the king's table.[42] The "Samaria Ostraca" and "Samaria Ivories" further corroborate the progressively centralized and redistributive character of this economy—as well as the international character of its stored assets.[43]

Of particular interest to us is the emerging, currency-based economy of the Iron IIA-B. Whereas "low value" money such as grain or livestock had functioned efficiently in the local, nonmonetized exchange of goods typical to the reciprocal economy of the Iron I, the redistributive economy of the Iron II required a fully fungible medium of exchange— silver. The bagged and bound *Hacksilber* (*ṣror késeph*[44]) of Jehoash's temple repair fund (2 Kgs 12:9–10) testifies to the use of silver domestically.[45] Menahem of Israel's tribute to Tiglath-pileser III (2 Kgs 15:15–20) tells us that bullion was also the currency of international exchange. Moreover, the fact that this northern king could exact one Mesopotamian mina of silver from *every* family in the Northern Kingdom to pay his debt demonstrates that his citizenry *has* silver, and "there must already have been some established fail-safe system for gathering up and forwarding large quantities of wealth reliably to Samaria."[46] The appearance of the permanent market (*ḥûṣôt*), the ostraca from Samaria, Jerusalem, and Arad,[47] and the description of Solomon's kingdom also attests to a centralized and redistributive economy—prefects and charioteers (1 Kgs 4); corveé labor, public buildings, and storage cities (1 Kgs 9:10–23); international commerce facilitated by ships and camels (1 Kgs 9:26–10:11); scores of court employees (e.g., 1 Kgs 4:6; 9:15; 11:28; 12:18); "very much gold" (1 Kgs 10:2); and numerous imported products (1 Kgs 10:28–29). Not only did Solomon make "silver as common as stones in Jerusalem," but he utilized this same silver for the import of cedar from Lebanon, and horses and chariotry from Egypt (1 Kgs 10:27–29).

As the era progresses, we find Hosea paying his bill for Gomer in both "high" and "low value money" (3:2) and castigating the dishonest merchants of Israel for their false scales (12:8). Amos rebukes his countrymen for "selling" the righteous for "silver" (2:6). Elisha prices barley in "shekels" (2 Kgs 7:1) and at one point exhorts a rural widow to "sell" her oil to pay her "debts" (2 Kgs 4:7). Permanent markets are named in Philistia (2 Sam 1:20) and Damascus (1 Kgs 20:35), and *land* is sold for "silver" (1 Kgs 16:24; 21:1–19; Jer 32:9–10). There are fifteen descriptions of tribute paid out to foreign powers by Judah and Israel in Kings (Joash 2 Kgs 12:17–18; Joash of Israel 1 Kgs 20:1–6; Amaziah 2 Kgs 14:13–14; Menahem 2 Kgs 15:19–20; Ahaz 2 Kgs 16:5–10; Hezekiah 2 Kgs 18:13–16 and 19:8–9, Jehoahaz 2 Kgs 23:32–35). Both text and archaeology testify that "early state formation of the Iron Age IIA reached a more comprehensive stage of redistribution in the Iron Age IIB," and this redistribution was being facilitated by means of "high value money"—silver.[48]

Iron IIC (c. 732/701–586 BCE)

The final phase of Israel's economic evolution emerges with the rise of the Neo-Assyrian Empire (745–612 BCE).[49] This is the economy of pre-exilic Israel for which we have the most data.[50] It is also the era in which the composition of Deuteronomy has been most often postulated, and therefore where our external benchmark of the economic profile of the southern Levant offers the most insight.

As Nam details, in this era the integrated, urban economies of the Iron II period are "completely overhauled" such that the region reaches "a pinnacle of redistribution through wide-scale economic specialization."[51] The industrialization of olive oil production at Philistine Ekron,[52] the Iron IIC industrial zone for wine production at Ashkelon,[53] and the widespread economic boom throughout the eastern Mediterranean basin[54] all testify to the economic impact of Assyrian hegemony. Moreover, the profusion of inscribed limestone weights recovered from an array of contexts in seventh-century Judah; the silver hoards at Ekron and Ein Gedi; the ostraca from Samaria, Jerusalem, and Arad; and Ashkelon's "South Street" marketplace demonstrate that goods were being exchanged at every level of Israelite society via an official silver sale-weight system.[55]

Consider Hezekiah's tribute to Sennacherib in 701 BCE. Holladay argues that the bullion necessary for this enormous reparation (900 kg of gold and 24,000 kg of silver) was present in Hezekiah's coffers because of Judah's exploitation of the trade routes between the Arabian caravan network and the Mediterranean port cities of Gaza and Arpad. And whereas many have presumed Judah's economy to be primarily agricultural (perhaps by relating it to the taxation systems articulated in Deuteronomy), Holladay categorically states that "[w]heat, wine, and oil were never major tributary requirements for 'Royal States' during the Neo-Assyrian period." Rather, the tributary system was mostly about *money*.[56] And as Liverani points out, only kingdoms with royal palaces and treasuries outfitted to collect and hoard could deliver bullion for tribute, whereas chiefdoms and "depressed" or obscure regions unassociated with trade networks could not.[57]

In sum, whereas Israel's Iron II period sees the onset of centralized power with the resulting mechanisms of taxation, corvée labor, and redistribution, it is with the Iron IIC period that Israel and Judah are incorporated into a world economy. Catalyzed by the rise of the Neo-Assyrian Empire and a rapidly expanding Phoenician trade network, the result in the southern Levant is massive growth in Mediterranean maritime commerce, foreign sponsorship of local production, industrialization, and export. Another result is "the dissolution of the traditional economic unit of the patrimonial family."[58] Enormous sums are transferred between nations due to taxation, tribute, and trade, and the internationally recognized medium of exchange that expedites this increasingly complex system is silver. This Neo-Assyrian "command economy" is clearly *not* the economy of *Urdeuteronomium*.

Persian Period (539–332 BCE)

With the fall of Jerusalem to the Neo-Babylonian Empire in 586 BCE, Judah and its economy suffer a tremendous blow. Whereas the *pax Assyriaca* had created an economic boom in the southern Levant, a boom largely maintained during Babylonian rule, the destruction of Jerusalem (587–586 BCE) reduced this region to what Avraham Faust identifies as a "post collapse" society.[59] Here war and deportation have led to famine, disease, looting, and flight. Urban centers have been decimated. Jerusalem and its environs appear to be completely uninhabited.[60] Of the fifty late Iron Age rural sites excavated in Judah, only seven show possible continuity into the Persian period.[61] Oded Lipschits reports that the settled area in Judah between the seventh and fifth centuries BCE declined by approximately 70 percent, the number of settlements by 83.5 percent, and the population by more than 70 percent.[62]

But when Cyrus the Great conquers Babylon (539 BCE), the new empire's investment in its western frontier launches the slow process of recovery. In place of decimated infrastructure and a collapsed economy, the imperial administration of Darius I begins to emerge. The result is that almost all of the Persian-period sites in Yehud have at least two major phases of occupation: an early, undeveloped phase reflecting recovery (539–450 BCE), and a later phase reflecting a maturing economic infrastructure (450–332/331 BCE). It is this latter era that has been proposed as the provenance of Deuteronomy in recent years.

Predictably, evidence of recovery is first found along the coast. Acco's impressive administrative and commercial remains and the thirty-seven sites south of the Carmel range showing Phoenician-influenced, Persian period occupation point to the restoration of maritime trade.[63] The Philistine cities of Ashdod, Ashkelon, and especially Gaza see tremendous growth as "way stations" in the Persian trade network. Sites located near these commercial centers and their well-trafficked trade routes flourish.[64] Persian military and administrative installations designed to guard the coastal highway, gather taxes, and manage regional agriculture (e.g., Lachish, Tell Jemmeh, Tel Haror, Beer-sheba, and Tel Seraʿ) expand dramatically as well. Sidon becomes the site of an important Persian administrative center.[65] In the Central Hill country, however, early period Persian occupational debris is nearly nonexistent.[66] Not until the days of Ezra and Nehemiah (450–333 BCE) is there evidence that Yehud had begun to actively function.[67] Twenty Persian satrapies, federally appointed governors, an imperial road and postal system, and numerous fortified installations for the purpose of facilitating a centrally administered trade and tax-collection system becomes the backdrop of Ezra/Nehemiah.[68] With the second phase of the Persian period, as Ezra and Nehemiah report, Jerusalem is refortified and becomes the בירה (*bîrâ*, "capital") of Yehud. But the exploitation of the empire continues to impact economic recovery. Nehemiah speaks of "the king's tax" (המלך למדת, Neh 5:4), and the corruption of the "former governors" (הראשנים והפחות; cf. Neh 5:15; cf. 2:7, 9; 3:7).[69] Louis Jonker, working from Roland Boer's research, argues that Jerusalem eventually "occupied a double economic position, acting as a buffer between the village communes of the rural areas and the allocative regime of the imperial center."[70]

As regards Samaria, it is clear from the papyri, coins, and bullae recovered from the Wadi ed-Daliyeh as well as the "Samaria" and "Nablus" hoards that in the second phase of the Persian period the city was serving as a political and redistributive center for Samaria. The nearly 250 sites catalogued in Samaria with Persian-period pottery (particularly its western reaches) demonstrate the widespread Persian military and economic influence in the province and its connection to burgeoning Mediterranean trade.[71]

Of particular interest to this chapter is that the new Persian imperial system was facilitated by an equally new monetary unit—coinage. First appearing here toward the end of the sixth century, the introduction of coins is a pivotal economic transition in the Near East.[72] In Persia, Darius I's 8.4 gram gold coin—the *daric*—became the standard gold coinage of the realm. The *daric* is named in Ezra 8:27 (*ădarkōnîm* אדרכנים) as one of the precious items Ezra collects in Persia to restore the temple in Jerusalem, and anachronistically when David attempts a similar task for the *first* temple in Jerusalem (1 Chr 29:7).[73] The Hebrew term *darkĕmōnîm* (דרכמנים) also refers to a minted coin, likely the Attic silver "drachma" (6 *obols*; 4.3 grams).[74] This coin is named along with the silver *mina* (Hebrew *māneh* [מנה]) as part of the returning exiles' contributions for the restoration of the temple (Ezra 2:69; Neh 7:70–71). Persian coinage also included the *sigloi*—twenty silver *sigloi* equaled one gold *daric*—which after ca. 450 BCE could be minted by local authorities in the satrapies.[75] The minting of the *daric*, however, required the approval of the central government. Thus, the discovery of this particular coin via literary or material remains is a significant historical marker, and the presence of coinage, especially *gold* coinage, in Chronicles, Ezra, and Nehemiah is a clear indication of their Persian-era provenance.[76]

The use of coins increased rapidly with the return of economic prosperity under the Persian Empire. Coins minted in Sidon, Tyre, Aradus, Byblos, and North Africa appear in Palestine in the fifth century, supplemented by coins from Greek and East Greek cities like Athens, all of which became normative for purchase and payment. An extensive collection of "Philisto-Arabian" coins (450–333 BCE) indicates that mints existed in Gaza, Ashdod, and Ashkelon.[77] The subsatrapies of Samaria and Yehud soon followed suit, and the "Yehud" coin—emanating from a mint in or near Jerusalem—made its first appearance soon after 400 BCE.[78] Coinage from sites along the major trade routes of Syria-Palestine and up and down the Levantine coast reflects a flourishing, redistributive, empire-driven, centralized economy.

In sum, at the beginning of the Persian period the archaeology indicates that (at least most of[79]) Judah is a recovering, post collapse society with a decimated population and radically abridged kinship networks resulting in a dearth of household farms and local infrastructure.[80] With Persian-sponsored Mediterranean trade, economic recovery begins. The logistical support of the Persian military stimulates and protects local growth along the coast, and by the period of Ezra and Nehemiah (450–332/331 BCE) the hill country of "Beyond the River," although still bereft of urban centers, is fully incorporated into the redistributive economy of the Persian Empire. It is clear that by the second phase of the Persian period, produce from the farmsteads and villages of Yehud was being collected, stored, and redistributed as an aspect of imperial rule, which was seen and felt everywhere in "Beyond the River."

Most significant for our discussion is that this new economy is facilitated by coinage, which expedited domestic and international commerce while communicating the ideological and political identity of the empire.[81] And although coinage was not the *only* medium of exchange, the Persian imperial economy rendered minted silver and gold coins ubiquitous in the southern Levant (Ezra 2:69; 8:27; Neh 5:1–9; 7:70–71; 1 Chr 29:7). Yet these realities, centralization, taxation, industrial zones, and trade, and most quantifiable—the coinage that had become the currency of the empire—are completely absent from *Urdeuteronomium*.

Conclusions

As Roger Nam states, scholars have tended to "artificially separate economic matters from other social-scientific categories such as political, religious and sociological concerns," resulting in a lack of biblical scholarship that addresses the intersection of Israelite economic systems and biblical interpretation.[82] In this chapter we have seen that the culturally embedded assumed, inferred, or commanded economic realities of *Urdeuteronomium* have much to teach us regarding the social world of Deuteronomy and therefore its provenance—an important external benchmark.

As we consider the provenance of *Urdeuteronomium*, which of the reconstructed economies of the southern Levant bests reflects the content of Deuteronomy? Whereas references to permanent markets, trade, merchandise, retailer, storehouse, and customer frequent the market exchanges in 1–2 Kings, the economically informed critiques of the seventh- and eighth-century prophets, and the postexilic national history (1 Chr 7:28; 2 Chr 32:30; Neh 3:31–32; 13:20), and these *realia* are well known in the material culture of the southern Levant in the Iron IIB-C and Persian periods, these terms and concepts are conspicuously absent from *Urdeuteronomium*.[83] Whereas international trade and its mechanisms characterized the Neo-Assyrian and Persian hegemony of biblical Israel's existence, ships, camels, luxury imports, and the urban centers and port cities necessary to such exchange are equally absent from *Urdeuteronomium*. The governmental infrastructure essential to taxation in the centralized economies of the Israelite monarchy and the Neo-Assyrian and Persian hegemony—the redistributive medium of currency—is missing as well. In contrast, the measures used for exchange of goods in *Urdeuteronomium* are primarily those of a barter system—there is no šeqel (Lev 19:35–36; 27:3, 4, 7, 16; Amos 8:5) or "weighing out" (nāṭîl) of silver (Zeph 1:11). Deuteronomy (25:13–15) does speak of "a full and just stone" (אֶבֶן i.e., "weight," logically to be associated with the weighing of precious metals), but juxtaposes this with the more primitive form of evaluated exchange a "full and just measure" (אֵיפָה, a dry measure for cereal).[84] And whereas Micah's word for "scales" (מֹאזְנַיִם) frequents the eighth-, seventh-, and sixth-century prophets as well as the Levitical law code (Lev 19:36; Hos 12:8; Amos 8:5; Isa 40:12, 15; Jer 32:10; Ezek 5:1, 45:10), it cannot be found in Deuteronomy. The many references to offerings brought to the central cult site in Deuteronomy are paid *in kind* (12:6–7, 11, 17, 27; 14:22–23; 15:19–21; 18:3–5; 26:1–12). Deuteronomy describes the tithe/tax of the Israelite in terms of the "produce of the ground," which is brought in a "basket" to the holy place to be distributed to the marginalized and the priesthood and "eaten" (26:1–12; cf. 12:17–19; 14:22–29). Thus, whereas the use of precious metal for trade is evident throughout the material culture of eighth- to sixth-century Israel and Judah, is equally evident in the textual witness of the eighth- to sixth-century prophets, and in the Persian period is formalized into coinage used throughout the empire,[85] *Hacksilber* is at best ancillary in *Urdeuteronomium* and coinage is unknown. In other words, the taxation system described in *Urdeuteronomium* is nonmonetary and, at least in part, reciprocal.[86]

Only one exception to this moneyless taxation system is found in Deuteronomy (14:22–26). As I and others have demonstrated, the passage contains a doublet (14:22–23; 24–26).[87] The first (14:22–23) reflects an earlier strata of the law code, whereas the second (14: 24–26) reflects a later expansion designed to resolve evolving circumstances in the community. I have argued that these evolving circumstances are best understood as an emerging redistributive economy in which currency was replacing barter-based exchange. Hence, at one time or in one context, Deuteronomy specified that the citizen's tithe of grain, wine, oil, and firstborn must go to the Tabernacle *in kind* (14: 22–23); and in some different or later scenario the law was expanded, specifying that "if the place is too far" this same tithe might be converted into *Hacksilber* (בַּכֶּסֶף וְצַרְתָּ הַכֶּסֶף בְּיָדְךָ) to relieve the onerous difficulties and expense of transport (14: 24–26). Thus, whereas the monarchic world of Israel is "an economic world with a substantial amount of silver in general circulation, touching every household in the kingdom,"[88] in *Urdeuteronomium* silver for tithe and taxation is found only in this interpolation into Deuteronomy (14:24–26). And the foreign and locally minted coinage characteristic of urban and rural sites throughout the burgeoning, empire-driven Persian economy, is completely absent.

Compare the scenario in *Urdeuteronomium* with Chronicles (1 Chr 29:6–7). Here David is collecting precious items for the adornment of the first temple. Although coinage (and particularly the *daric*) has yet to be invented, the biblical writer reports:

> [6]Then the officers of the ancestral houses, and the officers of the Israelite tribes, the commanders of the thousands and of the hundreds, and the overseers of the royal work, made freewill offerings. [7]They gave for the work of the house of God 5,000 talents, and **10,000 *darics of gold* [אדרכנם]**, and 10,000 talents of silver, and 18,000 talents of bronze, and 100,000 talents of iron. (emphasis mine)

Clearly, the Chronicler was unable to recreate the economy of a world long past without stumbling into anachronism. Rather, predictably, the economy of the historian's own day made its way into his treatment of the past. Historiography teaches us that this sort of anachronism is to be expected when the subject of study lies beyond the author's own experience. In the Chronicler's case, the anachronism involved the Persian coinage of his day. Can we reasonably assert that the Deuteronomist would have been immune to the same impulse?

In conclusion, via an economic lens, the data reviewed here compel us to conclude that the genesis of *Urdeuteronomium* cannot be located in the urban, centralized monarchic era of the Iron IIB, or the complex economic realities of the Neo-Assyrian or Persian Empires. Rather, the intersection of text and artifact directs us toward the Iron I (c. 1200–980 BCE) and Iron IIA (980–840 BCE) periods—a society transitioning from the utilitarian and subsistence realities of the Iron I into the centralized and redistributive norms of the Iron II.[89] For those who find in *Urdeuteronomium* an exilic, utopian work of imagination, we must address the highly unlikely scenario that such a writer could succeed in flawlessly recreating Israel's early economy for later ideological purposes—an economy he had never seen, but one that we can now quantify as an Iron I/early Iron IIA reality. The possibility that a Persian-period historian could accomplish something similar, without once falling victim to the same anachronisms as the Chronicler is even more unlikely. In sum, with the data we now have available to us, the economic profile of *Urdeuteronomium* does indeed offer an external benchmark. And that benchmark, via the *realia* of the archaeologically reconstructed economies of the southern Levant, is pointing us to the early theories of "northern" origins for *Urdeuteronomium*, and the transition period between the Iron I and Iron IIA.

Notes

1. Wilhelm M. L. De Wette, *Dissertatio Critica Exegetica qua Deuteronomium a Prioribus Pentateuchi Libris Diversum, Alius Cuiusdam Recentioris Actoris Opus Esse Monstratur* (Jena: Literis Etzdorfi, 1805).
2. Wellhausen's *Prolegomena zur Geschichte Israels* was initially published under the title *Geschichte Israels*, vol. 1 (Berlin: G. Reimer, 1878), and then republished as a single monograph in 1883. See summaries of the "altar law" and cult centralization in Gordon J. Wenham, "Deuteronomy and the Central Sanctuary," *Tyndale Bulletin* 22 (1971): 103–118 and J. G. McConville, *Law and Theology in Deuteronomy*, JSOTSup 33 (Sheffield: JSOT Press, 1984), 21–38.
3. Heinrich Ewald, *The History of Israel*, vol. 1 (London: Longmans, Green, 1878), 63–132. See Bill T. Arnold's full discussion in "Deuteronomy, Hosea, and the Theory of Northern Origins," in this volume.
4. Adam C. Welch, *The Code of Deuteronomy: A New Theory of Its Origin* (London: J. Clarke & Co., Limited, 1924), 34, 190–220.
5. A. Alt, "Die Heimat des Deuteronomiums," in *Kleine Schriften zure Geschichte des Volkes Israel*, 3 vols. (Munich: Beck, 1953–59), 2:250–275, here 275.
6. G. von Rad, *Studies in Deuteronomy*, SBT 9 (London: SCM, 1953), 66–70.
7. R. E. Clements, "Deuteronomy and the Jerusalem Cult Tradition," *VT* 15 (1965): 300, 312.
8. E. W. Nicholson, *Deuteronomy and Tradition* (Oxford: Blackwell, 1967), 58–69, 80, 94–106; cf. Cynthia Edenburg and Reinhard Müller, "A Northern Provenance for Deuteronomy? A Critical Review," *HBAI* 4 (2015): 148–161.
9. Moshe Weinfeld, "The Loyalty Oath in the Ancient Near East," *UF* 8 (1976): 379–414.
10. Tigay, *Deuteronomy*, JPS Torah Commentary (Philadelphia: Jewish Publication Society, 1996), xix–xxiv, esp. xxi. For others arguing for northern origins, see: I. Provan, B. Halpern, and D. Vanderhooft, "The Editions of Kings in the 7th–6th Centuries B.C.E.," *HUCA* 62 (1991): 179–244; B. Peckham, *The Composition of the Deuteronomistic History*, HSM 35 (Atlanta: Scholars Press, 1985); S. L. McKenzie, *The Chronicler's Use of the Deuteronomistic History* (Atlanta: Scholars Press, 1985); and N. Lohfink, "Culture Shock and Theology: A Discussion of Theology as a Cultural and Sociological Phenomenon Based on the Example of Deuteronomic Law," *BTB* 7 (1977): 12–22.
11. R. H. Kennett, "The Origin of the Aaronite Priesthood," *JTS* 6 (1905): 161–186; R. H. Kennett, "The Date of Deuteronomy," *JTS* 7 (1906): 481–500; R. H. Kennett, *Deuteronomy and the Decalogue* (Cambridge: Cambridge University Press, 1920); G. Hölscher, "Komposition und Ursprung des Deuteronomiums," *ZAW* 40 (1922): 161–255; G. Hölscher, *Geschichte der judischen und israelitischen Religion* (Giessen: De Gruyter, 1922), 130–134; F. Horst,

"Die Kultusreform des Königs Josia," *ZDMG* 77 (1923): 220–238; G. R. Berry, "The Code Found in the Temple," *JBL* 39 (1920): 44–51; G. R. Berry, "The Date of Deuteronomy," *JBL* 59 (1940): 133–139.

12. Welch, *A New Theory of Its Origin*, 42–43. See Nicholson, *Deuteronomy and Tradition*, 4–6 for a synopsis.
13. Juha Pakkala, "The Date of the Oldest Edition of Deuteronomy," *ZAW* 121 (2009): 388–435, here 399. Cf. Norbert Lohfink, *Studien zum Deuteronomium und zur deuteronomistischen Literatur*, vol. 1, SBAB 8 (Stuttgart: Katholisches Bibelwerk, 1990), 305–323; Frank Crüsemann, "Das Bundesbuch: Historischer Ort und institutioneller Hintergrund," in *Congress Volume: Jerusalem 1986*, ed. J. A. Emerton, VTSup 40 (Leiden: Brill, 1988), 27–41; Philip R. Davies, *In Search of "Ancient Israel*," JSOTSup 148 (Sheffield: JSOT Press, 1992), 40–41; cf. Nicholson, *Deuteronomy and Tradition*, 7.
14. Christophe Nihan, "The Torah between Samaria and Judah," in *The Pentateuch as Torah: New Models for Understanding Its Promulgation and Acceptance*, ed. Gary N. Knoppers and Bernard M. Levinson (Winona Lake: Eisenbrauns, 2007), 187–223, here, 188.
15. Nihan, "Torah between Samaria and Judah," 188. Cf. Jean-Louis Ska, *Introduction à la lecture du Pentateuque: Clés pour l'interprétation des cinq premiers livres de la Bible*, Le livre et le rouleau 5 (Brussels: Lessius, 2000), 310–321.
16. Gary Knoppers, *Jews and Samaritans: The Origins and History of Their Early Relations* (New York: Oxford University Press, 2013); cf. Hölscher, "Komposition und Ursprung des Deuteronomiums," 227–230.
17. Jan Dušek, *Aramaic and Hebrew Inscriptions from Mt. Gerizim and Samaria between Antiochus III and Antiochus IV Epiphanes*, CHANE 54 (Leiden: Brill, 2012), 117.
18. Nihan, "Between Samaria and Judah," 191. Knoppers, *Jews and Samaritans*, 9, 108, 115–133, 141–143, 167, 171, 184–188. Knoppers suggests that "normal diplomatic relations" between north and south were standard for the period, citing Neh 6:10–14; 13:28 and Josephus, *Ant.* 11:306–312 ("Revisiting the Samarian Question in the Persian Period," in *Judah and the Judeans in the Persian Period*, ed. M. Oeming and O. Lipschits (Winona Lake: Eisenbrauns, 2006), 273–279.
19. See my discussion of DSS F.154 [DSS F.Deut2] in "The Archaeology of Mount Ebal and Mount Gerizim and Why It Matters," in *Sepher Torath Mosheh: Studies in the Composition and Interpretation of Deuteronomy*, ed. Daniel Block and Richard L. Schultz (Peabody: Hendrickson, 2017), 322–327. Cf. James H. Charlesworth, "What Is a Variant? Announcing a Dead Sea Scrolls Fragment of Deuteronomy," *MAARAV* 16 (2009): 201–212; E. Ulrich, *The Dead Sea Scrolls and the Developmental Composition of the Bible*, VTSup 169 (Leiden: Brill, 2015); E. Ulrich, *The Dead Sea Scrolls and the Developmental Composition of the Bible* (Leiden: Brill, 2017); Eugene Ulrich, Frank Moore Cross, et al., *Qumran Cave 4, IX: Deuteronomy, Joshua, Judges, Kings* (Oxford: Clarendon, 1995), 53–54, plate xv; Knoppers, *Jews and Samaritans*, 211, 189–197.
20. Nihan, "Between Samaria and Judah," 193.
21. Nihan, "Between Samaria and Judah," 214–217. See N. Na'aman, "The Law of the Altar in Deuteronomy and the Cultic Site near Shechem," in *Rethinking the Foundations: Historiography in the Ancient World and in the Bible: Essays in Honour of John Van Seters*, ed. S. L. McKenzie and T. Römer, BZAW 294 (Berlin: de Gruyter, 2000), 141–161.

22. Thomas Römer "The Book of Deuteronomy," in *The History of Israel's Traditions: The Heritage of Martin Noth*, ed. Steven L. McKenzie and M. Patrick Graham, JSOTSup 182 (Sheffield: Sheffield Academic, 1994), 211–212.
23. I am aware that Deuteronomy 27 is typically not included in *Urdeuteronomium*, and 28 often is. For my rationale, see Sandra Richter, "The Place of the Name in Deuteronomy," *VT* 57 (2007): 342–366.
24. Sandra Richter, "The Question of Provenance and the Economics of Deuteronomy," *JSOT* 42, no. 1 (2017): 23–50 and "The Question of Provenance and the Economics of Deuteronomy: The Neo-Babylonian and Persian Periods," *CBQ* 82 (2020): 547–566.
25. See Richter, "Question of Provenance," 45–47; cf. Ze'ev Herzog, *Archaeology of the City: Urban Planning in Ancient Israel and Its Social Implications* (Tel Aviv: Tel Aviv Univ, Institute of Archaeology, 1997), 198–211, figs. 5.6, 5.14.
26. See Richter, "Question of Provenance," 45–47; cf. Daniel A. Frese, "A Land of Gates: Covenant Communities in the Book of Deuteronomy," *VT* 65 (2015): 33–55 (33–35). Lauren Ristvet's study of "inclusive spaces" as loci for civic institutions in the ANE is helpful here. Unlike the tightly controlled space of temple and palace, town squares and plazas were accessible to all members of the community (*Ritual, Performance, and Politics in the Ancient Near East* [New York: Cambridge University Press, 2015], 54–66).
27. Sandra Richter, *The Deuteronomistic History and the Name Theology: lĕšakkēn šĕmô šām in the Bible and the Ancient Near East*, BZAW 318 (Berlin: de Gruyter, 2002).
28. Richard D. Nelson, *Deuteronomy: A Commentary*, OTL (Louisville: Westminster John Knox, 2002), 183.
29. Richter, "Question of Provenance," 38–47. See Avraham Faust, *The Archaeology of Israelite Society in Iron Age II* (Winona Lake: Eisenbrauns, 2012), 68; Daniel M. Master, "Economy and Exchange in the Iron Age Kingdoms of the Southern Levant," *BASOR* 372 (2014): 89–91; Lily Singer-Avitz, "Beersheba—A Gateway Community in Southern Arabian Long-Distance Trade in the Eighth Century B.C.E.," *Tel Aviv* 26 (1999): 3–75; John S. Holladay, Jr., "The Kingdoms of Israel and Judah: Political and Economic Centralization in the Iron IIA-B," in *The Archaeology of Society in the Holy Land*, ed. Thomas E. Levy (London: Leicester University Press, 1998); John S. Holladay, Jr., "Hezekiah's Tribute, Long-Distance Trade, and the Wealth of Nations Ca. 1000–600 BC: A New Perspective," in *Confronting the Past: Archaeological and Historical Essays on Ancient Israel in Honor of William G. Dever*, ed. Seymour Gitin, J. Edward Wright, and J. P. Dessel (Winona Lake: Eisenbrauns, 2006), 327.
30. Richter, "Question of Provenance," 19–22, 40–44.
31. Hölscher, "Komposition und Ursprung," 161–255; cf. Nicholson in his later reflections in *Deuteronomy and the Judaean Diaspora* (Oxford: Oxford University Press, 2014), 1–10; 88–89.
32. Exactly when the transitions between the Iron I and Iron IIA, B, and C periods occur is debated. This chapter assumes Amihai Mazar's "Modified Conventional Chronology," affirming that the Iron IIA launches in c. 980 BCE and endures for approximately 150 years (see Amnon Ben-Tor and Anabel Zarzecki-Peleg, "Iron Age IIA–B: Northern Valleys and Upper Galilee," in *The Ancient Pottery of Israel and Its Neighbors from the Iron Age through the Hellenistic Period*, ed. Seymour Gitin [Jerusalem: Israel Exploration Society, 2015], 135–88 and Amihai Mazar, "From 1200 to 850 B.C.E.: Remarks on Some Selected Archaeological Issues," in *Israel in Transition: From Late Bronze II to Iron IIa (c. 1250–850 B.C.E.)*, ed. Lester L. Grabbe [New York: T&T Clark International, 2008], 86–120).

33. See Richter, "Question of Provenance," 26–29; cf. Elizabeth Bloch-Smith and Beth Alpert Nakhai, "A Landscape Comes to Life: The Iron I Period," *NEA* 62, no. 2 (1999): 62–92; David C. Hopkins, "Life on the Land: The Subsistence Struggles of Early Israel," *BA* 50, no. 3 (1987): 178–191; Baruch Rosen, "Subsistence Economy in Iron Age I," in *From Nomadism to Monarchy: Archaeological and Historical Aspects of Early Israel*, ed. Israel Finkelstein and Nadav Na'aman (Jerusalem: Israel Exploration Society, 1994), 339–351; Shimon Gibson, "Agricultural Terraces and Settlement Expansion in the Highlands of Early Iron Age Palestine: Is There Any Correlation between the Two?" in *Studies in the Archaeology of the Iron Age in Israel and Jordan*, ed. Amihai Mazar, JSOTSup 331 (Sheffield: Sheffield Academic, 2001), 113–146; Caroline Grigson, "Plough and Pasture in the Early Economy of the Southern Levant," in *The Archaeology of Society in the Holy Land*, ed. Thomas E. Levy (Hong Kong: Facts on File, 1995), 245–268; and Faust, *The Archaeology of Israelite Society in Iron Age II*, 7–27, 255.

34. Aharon Sasson, *Animal Husbandry in Ancient Israel: A Zooarchaeological Perspective on Livestock Exploitation, Herd Management and Economic Strategies* (London: Equinox, 2010), 60–61, 119–122; cf. Baruch Rosen, "Subsistence Economy of Stratum II," in *'Izbet Ṣarṭah: An Early Iron Age Site Near Rosh Ha'ayin, Israel*, ed. I. Finkelstein, BAR International Series, 299 (Oxford: BAR, 1986), 156–185.

35. Sasson, *Animal Husbandry*, 60.

36. See Carol Meyers, "The Family in Early Israel," in *Families in Ancient Israel, The Family, Religion, and Culture* (Louisville: Westminster John Knox, 1997), 1–47; Oded Borowski, *Daily Life in Biblical Times*, SBLABS 5 (Atlanta: Society of Biblical Literature, 2003), 13–42; Avraham Faust, "Cities, Villages, and Farmsteads: The Landscape of Leviticus 25.29–31," in *Exploring the Longue Durée: Essays in Honor of Lawrence E. Stager*, ed. J. David Schloen (Winona Lake: Eisenbrauns, 2009), 103–112 (106).

37. Shiloh stands as an important exception evincing large-scale, small-temple storage (Israel Finkelstein, *The Archaeology of Israelite Settlement* [Jerusalem: Israel Exploration Society, 1988], 205–34.

38. Phillip J. King and Lawrence E. Stager, *Life in Biblical Israel* (Louisville: Westminster John Knox, 2001), 191.

39. The transition into the Iron IIC occurs in the north/Israel several decades before it occurs in Judah. See Ayelet Gilboa, "Iron Age IIC: Northern Coast, Carmel Coast, Galilee, and Jezreel Valley," and Seymour Gitin, "Iron Age IIC: Judah," in *The Ancient Pottery of Israel and Its Neighbors from the Iron Age through the Hellenistic Period*, ed. Seymour Gitin (Jerusalem: Israel Exploration Society, 2015), 301–344, 345–363, respectively.

40. See Richter, "Question of Provenance," 29–35.

41. Master, "Economy and Exchange," 1–17 n. 25; cf. Roger S. Nam, *Portrayals of Economic Exchange in the Book of Kings*, BibInt 112 (Leiden: Brill, 2012), 118–122.

42. See Ronald E. Tappy, "Iron Age IIA-B: Samaria," in Gitin, *Ancient Pottery of Israel*, 189–190; Nahman Avigad, "Samaria (City)," *NEAEHL* 4: 1300–1306; and Tappy, "Samaria," *DOTHB* 855. Samaria's corresponding military might is illustrated in Shalmanessar III's account of the Battle of Qarqar (853 BCE); see W. W. Hallo and K. Lawson Younger Jr., *COS* 2.113A:263.

43. See Matthew J. Suriano, "Wine Shipments to Samaria from Royal Vineyards," *TA* 43 (2016): 99–120; Faust, *Archaeology*, 13–26, 255–262; Lawrence Stager, "The Finest Olive Oil in Samaria," *JSS* 28, no. 2 (1983): 241–245; Lawrence Stager, "Shemer's Estate," *BASOR* 277/278 (1990): 93–107; Anson Rainey and R. Steven Notley, *The Sacred Bridge*

(Jerusalem: Carta, 2006), 221–222. Sandra Richter, "Eighth Century Issues: The World of Jeroboam II, the Fall of Samaria, and the Reign of Hezekiah," in *Ancient Israel's History: An Introduction to Issues and Sources*, ed. Bill T. Arnold and Richard S. Hess (Grand Rapids: Baker Academic, 2014), 323–326.

44. *HALOT* s.v. "ררצ" (1058); cf. the Joseph narrative, Gen 42.35.
45. Bullae associated with bundles from Dor, Tell Keisan, Old Babylonian Larsa, and Ashkelon and the standardized weights of these recovered bundles indicate that the collections of *Hacksilber* were not random, but were predetermined quantities bound into bags by string and "locked" with bullae to indicate that these had been "reviewed or prepared in some official manner" (Christine M. Thompson, "Sealed Silver in Iron Age Cisjordan and the 'Invention' of Coinage," *OJA* 22, no. 1 [2003]: 67–107, especially 81). Cf. John S. Holladay, Jr., "How Much Is That In . . . ? Monetization, Money, Royal States, and Empires," in Schloen, *Exploring the Longue Durée*, 207–222 and Izabela Eph'al-Jaruzelska, "Officialdom and Society in the Book of Kings: The Social Relevance of the State," in *The Books of Kings: Sources, Composition, Historiography and Reception*, ed. Baruch Halpern and André Lemaire, VTSup 129 (Boston: Brill 2010), 467–500.
46. Holladay, Jr., "How Much is That In . . . ?" 212.
47. *ḥûṣôt* are found in 1 Sam 1:20; 1 Kgs 20:34; Nah 2:4; Ezek 26.11; Isa 24:11; Jer 5:1; and Lam 4:5. See Daniel Master's discussion, "Economy and Exchange," 14–24; Daniel Master, "Institutions of Trade in 1 and 2 Kings," in Halpern and Lamaire, *The Books of Kings*, 512–513; Daniel Master, "Trade and Politics: Ashkelon's Balancing Act in the Seventh Century B.C.E.," *BASOR* 330 (2003); cf. Leon Levy et al., *Ashkelon 1: Introduction and Overview (1985–2006)* (Winona Lake: Eisenbrauns, 2008), 309–313.
48. Nam, *Portrayals of Economic Exchange*, 88–95, 126, 134–136.
49. Richter, "The Question of Provenance," 35–38.
50. See Joshua T. Walton, "The Regional Economy of the Southern Levant in the 8th–7th Centuries BCE" (PhD diss., Harvard University, 2015).
51. Nam, *Portrayals of Economic Exchange*, 106–110, 117, 127, 186–188, 193.
52. Seymour Gitin, "Tel Miqne-Ekron in the 7th Century B.C.E.: The Impact of Economic Innovation and Foreign Cultural Influences on a Neo-Assyrian Vassal City-State," in *Recent Excavations in Israel: A View to the West: Reports on Kabri, Nami, Miqne-Ekron, Dor, and Ashkelon*, ed. Seymour Gitin (Dubuque: Kendall/Hunt, 1995), 61–79.
53. Master, "Trade and Politics," 47–61; cf. A. Faust and E. Weiss, "Judah, Philistia, and the Mediterranean World: Reconstructing the Economic System of the Seventh Century B.C.E.," *BASOR* 338 (2005): 79–80.
54. Lawson K. Younger, Jr., "The Assyrian Economic Impact on the Southern Levant in the Light of Recent Study," *IEJ* 65, no. 2 (2015): 179–204; F. M. Fales, "On *Pax Assyriaca* in the Eighth-Seventh Centuries BCE and Its Implications," in *Isaiah's Vision of Peace in Biblical and Modern International Relations: Swords into Plowshares*, ed. R. Cohen and R. Westbrook (New York: Palgrave Macmillan, 2008), 17–35.
55. Roger S. Nam, "Power Relations in the Samaria Ostraca," *PEQ* 144, no. 3 (2012): 155–163; Master, "Economy and Exchange," 90–93.
56. Holladay, "Hezekiah's Tribute," 309–331, here 311.
57. Mario Liverani, *Studies on the Annals of Ashurnasirpal II* (Rome: University of Rome, 1992), 155–158.
58. Nam, *Portrayals of Economic Exchange*, 130.
59. Avraham Faust, *Judah in the Neo-Babylonian Period: The Archaeology of Desolation*, ABS 18 (Atlanta: Society of Biblical Literature, 2012), 167–180. Tell en-Naṣbeh and Ramat

Raḥel are exceptions to this larger portrait; see Richter, "Neo-Babylonian and Persian Periods," 550–554.

60. Oded Lipschits, "Demographic Changes in Judah between the Seventh and Fifth Centuries B.C.E.," in *Judah and the Judeans in the Neo-Babylonian Period*, ed. Oded Lipschits and Joseph Blenkinsopp (Winona Lake: Eisenbrauns, 2003), 323–376, here 365. Cf. Ephraim Stern, *Archaeology of the Land of the Bible*, vol. 2, *The Assyrian, Babylonian, and Persian Periods (732–332 B.C.E.)* ABRL (New York: Doubleday, 2001) 309–310.
61. Faust, *Judah in the Neo-Babylonian Period*, 33–72, 244.
62. Lipschits, "Demographic Changes," 332–355, 357–364.
63. Lawrence E. Stager, *Ashkelon Discovered: From Canaanites and Philistines to Romans and Moslems* (Washington, DC: Biblical Archaeology Society, 1991), 23; cf. Stern, *Archaeology of the Land*, 2:370–372, 379–422.
64. Stern, *Archaeology of the Land*, 2:370–438, 581; cf. Rainey and Notley, *Sacred Bridge*, 281; Oded Lipschits, "Achaemenid Imperial Policy, Settlement Processes in Palestine, and the Status of Jerusalem in the Middle of the Fifth Century B.C.E.," in *Judah and the Judeans in the Persian Period*, ed. Oded Lipschits and Manfred Oeming (Winona Lake: Eisenbrauns, 2006), 19–52, here 26–29.
65. John W. Betlyon, "A People Transformed Palestine in the Persian Period," *Near Eastern Archaeology* 68, no. 1 (2005): 6, 23, 31, 51–52.
66. See Richter, "Neo-Babylonian and Persian Periods," 554–557. Cf. Oded Lipschits, "Shedding New Light on the Dark Years of the 'Exilic Period': New Studies, Further Elucidation, and Some Questions Regarding the Archaeology of Judah as an 'Empty Land,'" in *Interpreting Exile: Displacement and Deportation in Biblical and Modern Contexts*, SBL Ancient Israel and Its Literature 10, ed. Brad Kelle, Frank Richard Ames, and Jacob L. Wright (Leiden: Brill, 2011); Oded Lipschits et al., "Palace and Village, Paradise and Oblivion: Unraveling the Riddles of Ramat Raḥel," *Near Eastern Archaeology* 74 (2011): 1–49; Oded Lipschits and David Vanderhooft, "Forty Unpublished *yhwd* Stamp Impressions," in Lipschits, Gadot, and Freud, *Ramat Raḥel III*, 2:409–436. See also Israel Ephʻal, "Changes in Palestine during the Persian Period in Light of Epigraphic Sources," *IEJ* 48, no. 1/2 (1998): 106–119, here 114–115; and Oren Tal, "Pottery from the Persian and Hellenistic Periods," in *Ramat-Raḥel III: Final Publications of Aharoni's Excavations at Ramat-Raḥel (1954, 1959–1962)*, ed. Oded Lipschits, Yuval Gadot, and Liora Freud; 2 vols. (Winona Lake: Eisenbrauns, 2016), 1:266–271, 409–435, 721.
67. See Lisbeth S. Fried, "Exploitation of Depopulated Land in Achaemenid Judah," in *The Economy of Ancient Judah in Its Historical Context*, ed. Marvin Lloyd Miller, Ehud Ben Zvi, and Gary N. Knoppers (Winona Lake: Eisenbrauns, 2015), 149–162; Oded Lipschits, "The Rural Economy of Judah during the Persian Period and the Settlement History of the District System," in Miller, Ben Zvi, and Knoppers, *Economy of Ancient Judah*, 237–264.
68. Ephraim Stern, *Archaeology of the Land of the Bible*, vol. 2, *The Assyrian, Babylonian, and Persian Periods 732–332 B.C.E.)*, ABRL (New York: Doubleday, 2001), 2:576–581; David Vanderhooft, "The Israelite *Mishpaha* in the Priestly Writings, and Changing Valences in Israel's Kinship Terminology," in Schloen, *Exploring the Longue Durée*, 485–496; see also Faust, *Judah in the Neo-Babylonian Period*, 108.
69. Betlyon, "People Transformed," 23, 29, 38; Lipschits, "Achaemenid Imperial Policy," 41; and Lipschits, "Rural Economy of Judah," 237. See also Lipschits, "Demographic Changes," 364–365.
70. Louis Jonker, "Yehud Economy in the Genealogies of Chronicles," in Miller, Ben Zvi, and Knoppers, *Economy of Ancient Judah*, 77–101, here 99; see also Ephʻal, "Changes in

Palestine," 114–115; Charles E. Carter, *The Emergence of Yehud in the Persian Period: A Social and Demographic Study*, JSOTSup 294 (Sheffield: Sheffield Academic, 1999), 216.

71. See N. Avigad, "Samaria [City]," 4:1306; Sandra Richter, "Archaeology of Mt. Ebal and Mt. Gerizim," in Block and Schultz, *Sepher Torath Mosheh*, 304–337; Stern, *Archaeology of the Land*, 2:422–443, 35; Stern, "A Persian-Period Hoard of Bullae from Samaria," in Schloen, *Exploring the Longue Durée*, 421–437; D. Ashkenazi et al., "Metallurgical Investigation on Fourth Century BCE Silver Jewelry of Two Hoards from Samaria," *Scientific Reports* 7 (Jan. 2017), art. number 40659, https://www.nature.com/articles/srep40659.
72. Although definitions of "coinage," "currency," and "money" differ, the fundamental qualities of coinage are broadly recognized as a piece made of metal, measured to a standard weight, and marked with a design or seal; cf. Thompson, "Sealed Silver," 67 n. 2; Betlyon, "Coinage," *ABD* 1078–1080.
73. See Knoppers on this term in 1 Chr 29:7 (Gary N. Knoppers, *I Chronicles 10–29: A New Translation with Introduction and Commentary* [AB 12A; New York: Doubleday, 2004], 946–947). See also H. G. M. Williamson, *Ezra, Nehemiah*, WBC 16 (Nashville: Thomas Nelson, 1985), 28–29, 118–119, as well as his "Eschatology in Chronicles," *TynBul* 28 (1977): 123–126.
74. Although the Attic drachma was typically silver, in Ezra 2:69 and Neh 7:70–71 the *darkĕmōnîm* are identified as gold, leading Blenkinsopp, Williamson, Stern, and others to identify the coins here as *darics* (see Richter "Neo-Babylonian and Persian Periods," 560, n. 73; cf. *HALOT* s.v. אֲדַרְכֹנִים).
75. Betlyon, "Coinage," 1:1079, 1082–1083; and Williamson, *Ezra, Nehemiah*, 38; see also Philip J. King and Lawrence E. Stager, *Life in Biblical Israel*, 199.
76. Only two gold darics have been recovered from archaeological contexts—one from Samaria and one from the TransJordan (Betlyon, "People Transformed," 48); Stern, *Archaeology of the Land*, 2:461–469, 555–575; Rainey and Notley, *Sacred Bridge*, 284–285.
77. Haim Gitler, "Coins of the Fifth and Fourth Centuries B.C.," in *Ashkelon 1*, 373–384; and Haim Gitler and Oren Tal, "Reclassifying Persian-Period Philistian Coins: Some New Identifications," *Israel Numismatic Research* 11 (2016): 11–22.
78. See Ya'akov Meshorer and Shraga Qedar, *The Coinage of Samaria in the Fourth Century BCE* (Jerusalem: Numismatic Fine Arts International, 1991); Gitler and Tal, "Reclassifying Persian-Period Philistian Coins," 11, n. 1, 20–21.
79. See notes 59, 66, and 67.
80. Richter, "Neo-Babylonian and Persian Periods," 557–562.
81. Eph'al, "Changes in Palestine," 48, 117–118.
82. Nam, *Portrayals of Economic Exchange*, 1.
83. Richter, "Question of Provenance," 11–12, 33–34, 38.
84. See Marvin A. Powell, "Weights and Measures," *ABD* VI: 897–908, esp. 905.
85. Richter, "Neo-Babylonian and Persian Periods," 563–565; cf. Israel Eph'al, "Changes in Palestine," 114–115.
86. By the Persian period this tithe has become a tax gathered by the Levites under the supervision of the priests for the Jerusalem temple (Neh 10:38–40).
87. See Richter, "Question of Provenance," 41–44 and Richter, *Deuteronomistic History*, 41–52; 60–63.
88. Master, "Economy and Exchange," 2014.
89. An isolated, village-based economic zone in the Israelite hill country that survived into the Iron IIB also has potential (Richter, "Question of Provenance," 48–50; cf. David Hopkins, "Bare Bones: Putting Flesh on the Economics of Ancient Israel," in *The Origins of the Ancient Israelite States*, ed. Volkmar Fritz and Philip R. Davies; JSOTSup 228 [Sheffield: Sheffield Academic Press, 1996], 121–139).

SECTION IV

INTERTEXTUALITY OF DEUTERONOMY

CHAPTER 19

DEUTERONOMY AND THE PENTATEUCH

RICHARD J. BAUTCH

Who Began the Conversation?

In Historical Perspective

Introduction

THE relationship between Deuteronomy (D)[1] and the Pentateuch developed over several centuries. As a result, one must take a diachronic approach and think in terms of four distinct phases: (a) the early development of Deuteronomy alongside other pre-Pentateuchal texts; (b) the joining of Deuteronomy to non-D materials; (c) the aligning of the D-based collection with Priestly traditions, also known as the formation of the Hexateuch; and (d) the Pentateuchal Redaction. The timeframe for these phases is the seventh–fourth centuries BCE, and this chapter will explore each phase in turn.

Deuteronomy and the Pentateuch in Past Research

For much of the nineteenth and twentieth centuries, studies of Deuteronomy and the Pentateuch drew upon paradigms developed in Europe in the nineteenth century and earlier. The leading paradigm posited documentary sources that were integrated into a common text through redactional processes said to occur in the pre-exilic, exilic, and postexilic periods.[2] Deuteronomy was identified as the D source, and its distinguishing feature was the reiteration of legal material contained in one of the earlier sources. Deuteronomy's precursor was said to be the Covenant Code (Exod 20:22–23:19). Because Deuteronomy rearticulated the Covenant Code so freely, it was clearly not a copy of the existing law; Deuteronomy was likely intended to displace the prior expressions of Israelite law.[3] In this scenario, Deuteronomy as the successor to the Covenant Code was a "second law," as implied by the book's Greek title, *deuteronomion*. It is worth noting that Deuteronomy contains not only a second law but also a retelling of Israelite history as found in documentary sources thought to predate D.

Over the course of the twentieth century, consensus around the documentary model of the Pentateuch unraveled. Scholars questioned the sources said to precede D, or Deuteronomy. Under new light, the evidence for the so-called E source was less compelling and often disputed.[4] In the end it was said that only geographic references in the north of Israel plausibly indicated an E source in that region during monarchic times. The J source, originally thought to be monarchic as well, was subject to revised dating, with some locating J in the exilic or postexilic period.[5] Most importantly, Pentateuchal passages attributed to the J source were reclassified under different authorship, a prime example being the golden calf episode (Exod 32–34). Even before the revising of the J corpus began in earnest, certain scholars were designating the episode more circumspectly while suggesting a greater role for the Deuteronomic writers in its composition.[6] Indeed, J's waning led to the waxing of D, and as the traditional documentary models of the Pentateuch became less serviceable, D along with the Priestly writers (P) became the focus of scholars' attention. Here, I am presuming a documentary-type model of the Pentateuch but in the form of a two-source hypothesis, P and D.

What Is the Status of the Conversation?

The Development of Deuteronomy alongside Other, Pre-Pentateuchal Texts

Urdeuteronomion

At present, the scholarly consensus is that Deuteronomy is a seventh-century composition that also reflects precursor traditions that the Deuteronomists took up exegetically, such as the Covenant Code (Exod 20:22–23:19). There were as well significant redactions of Deuteronomy that took place later in the postexilic period. The point of departure, however, is the seventh century, and this first literary edition of Deuteronomy is associated with the southern kingdom, Judah, and the environs of Jerusalem.[7] *Urdeuteronomion* comprises a core (12–26) along with those writings attached to the core. Scholars do not much debate the outer limits of *Urdeuteronomion*, but for some it is wide (4:44–28:68).[8] There is an abiding interest in the Esarhaddon Succession Treaty (EST) as a marker for dating Deuteronomy to the seventh century, but EST itself did not significantly influence the shape and substance of Deuteronomy.[9]

At the core's center is a mandate for centralized worship—ostensibly in Jerusalem—that would appear to benefit the Temple priests and the king of Judah. The text, however, also serves the interests of rural Levites who are singled out on three occasions (12:12, 18, 19).[10] Scholars who hold that this instruction favors the Levites and gives them leverage with the king would align it with an instruction limiting royal power (17:16–18) and a listing of the Levites' rights and privileges (18:1–8).[11] The theory, however, leaves unanswered key questions about cult centralization, namely why and how it came to be *under royal auspices* around the time of Josiah (r. 640–609 BCE). If a king were seeking to monetize cult worship, why would he centralize the practice? It would be more lucrative to have multiple cult sites producing tithes and taxation.

I read Deuteronomy not as self-contradictory in this regard, but as holding in tension different prerogatives, in this case those of the Levites and the monarchy. Given its parenetic quality, Deuteronomy is often thought to be linear and univocal, but its ability to hold two different viewpoints in tension is evidence of its literary sophistication.[12]

Early Biblical Materials outside Deuteronomy

Originally, Deuteronomy was viewed in isolation from other biblical materials. The point of view, although artificial, allowed us to understand Deuteronomy's trajectory as an Israelite legal tradition independent of the non-D Pentateuchal materials, which developed alongside D in their own manner. Genesis, for example, although in many ways postexilic, contains a significant amount of material that dates from the ninth to the seventh centuries BCE. As with Deuteronomy, the earliest non-D Pentateuchal materials are quite early and unaligned with other elements in the Pentateuch. This is especially true of the patriarchal narratives. Konrad Schmid notes that in Genesis (Gen 12–36), "The texts seem to be multilayered, and even some of the later layers do not seem to presuppose the Deuteronomic centralization of the cult—e.g. Jacob's vow in Bethel to tithe the tenth to the sanctuary of Bethel in Gen 28:22."[13] Schmid adds that some texts in Genesis may emerge from a much older oral history. Thus, when one thinks about Deuteronomy and the Pentateuch, one thinks initially of origins expressed as separate and distinct literary traditions. With such an approach, the conjoining of these traditions and texts, to which we now turn, can be understood as an editorial endeavor.

The Joining of Deuteronomy to Non-D Materials

Diverse Models Pre-exilic and Postexilic

Scholars theorize that it was the desire to spawn a narrative of "biblical" proportions that led historically minded scribes to combine D with materials in the Tetrateuch involving the patriarchs and the exodus from Egypt, among other events. There are different models of the "Israel" narrative. Eckart Otto locates this development in the seventh century, when Assyria cast its shadow over Israel.[14] The empire exercised its power both militarily and rhetorically, with the EST as a reminder of Assyria's control over the lands beyond its border. EST projected the Assyrian leader as a great king.

Israel subverted Assyria's claims to power by issuing its own narrative and asserting itself. The narrative of Israel was a counternarrative featuring Moses as the antitype of the great Assyrian king and depicting the people of Israel as leading actors in the primordial history, the patriarchal and matriarchal sagas, the deliverance after wandering in the wilderness, and the successful settlement of Canaan. According to Otto, the preeminence of Moses was expressed in the events from his birth (Exod 1:22—2:10) through the making of the covenant on the mountain.[15]

Deuteronomy, in contrast, had more limited associations with Moses at this time, and Deuteronomy's role in the grand narrative was originally quite modest (providing the reformulated Covenant Code). As for the final part of the narrative, Joshua's taking the land of Canaan, Otto initially included the Joshua material (our book of Joshua) in what he proposed to be a seventh-century Hexateuch. He subsequently revised his position to argue that this material, and so the Hexateuchal literary structure, was devised later by scribes in the Second Temple period.[16]

In contrast, the model of David M. Carr aligns Joshua with Deuteronomy and the Tetrateuch in a narrative of Israel's origins dated to postexilic times, as families were returning from Babylon to Yehud. Accordingly, the narrative of origins points throughout to Joshua's taking of the land. Joshua's covenant at Shechem (Josh 24:1–28) is the pinnacle of this narrative, which was designed to rival the founding legends of other nations.[17] In the postexilic era, when the legacies of monarchic Israel—Temple, kingship, covenant—were being rearticulated, an overarching narrative of origins was essential. Memories of the halcyon past inspire metaphors that form a society's connective tissue and point it toward the future. More practically, diverse social groups in Yehud could each claim links to "ancient Israel" by means of the grand historical narrative into which they inserted themselves.[18] Indeed, certain postexilic groups formed their identity by selectively interpreting Deuteronomy and the texts with which it came to be associated at this time.[19] The assemblage of texts took the form of a Hexateuch.

Textual Evidence of the Deuteronomic (Non-P) Hexateuch

Because the Hexateuch in question is hypothetical, it can be challenging to identify where the Deuteronomic and non-D materials were fused together. Nonetheless, Deuteronomic editing in the Tetrateuch is at times conspicuous.[20] An example is an Abrahamic treatment of covenant that is devoid of P material (Gen 15:1–21). P rather has provided a later discussion of covenant revolving around the figure of Abraham (Gen 17:1–27). The first tradition, therefore, can be considered pre-Priestly and influenced by Deuteronomy in its beginning, middle, and end. The Deuteronomic theme of inheritance (Gen 15:1–6) aligns nicely with the Hexateuchal narrative of origins. The narrative's conclusion in which Joshua gains the promised land is anticipated (Gen 15:7–21). In fact, a segment of this tradition (Gen 15:18–21) reads like a redactional intervention by Deuteronomic scribes, who in this scenario make the issue of covenant explicit (Gen 15:18) and list the peoples to be displaced from the land (Gen 15:19–20) as a codicil. This literary horizon was explored by Joseph Blenkinsopp at the close of the last century, and Carr has more recently characterized this tradition as a product of the harmonization process involving Deuteronomy and the Tetrateuch during the formation of the non-P Hexateuch.

Another example of Deuteronomic editing in the Tetrateuch arises in a divine speech (Gen 18:17–19). YHWH's statements bridge the story of Abraham hosting three visitors (Gen 18:1–16) and the punishment of Sodom and Gomorrah (Gen 18:20–32). This short unit has long been considered an appendage, and its Deuteronomic character is manifested linguistically. YHWH refers to Abraham as a nation that is both "great and mighty" (Gen 18:18).[21] The only other such reference to Israel occurs in Deuteronomy (26:5), recounting Israel's early history when it was in bondage to Egypt.[22] The conclusion refers to "all the nations of the earth (Gen 18:18)," a distinctive phrase that also punctuates Deuteronomy (28:1). Finally, the tradition evokes a series of instructions about the teaching of Israelite children (Gen 18:19 cf. Deut 6:20–25). One observes here two features of Deuteronomic pedagogy: an imperative for legal instruction and conditionality added to the ancestral promises. As an addition to an Abrahamic text, the tradition (Gen 18:17–19) provides a trace of the Deuteronomic, non-P Hexateuch in the postexilic period.

Similar traces are discernible in, a divine speech that appears to have been added (Gen 22:15–18).[23] After Abraham has shown himself willing to offer Isaac as a sacrifice, YHWH states, "All the nations of the earth shall gain blessing for themselves because you have obeyed my voice." As Carr notes, an unconditional divine blessing is attenuated along Deuteronomic lines with "the addition of obedience as a pre-condition to already given promises."[24] A multiplication formula—"I will make your offspring as numerous as the stars of heaven" (Gen 22:17aα)—is a motif in Deuteronomy (1:10; 4:18; 10:22; 28:62). An echo of the formula reads: "I will make your offspring as numerous as the sand that is on the seashore" (Gen 22:17aβ). Such language has occasioned a range of interpretation, including Carr's view that this promise is focused on the future conquest of the Canaanite people.[25] In such a scenario, the reference to sand alludes to Joshua's conquest, the final act in the narrative of origins.

Virtually all experts consider a final Deuteronomic passage in Genesis (Gen 26:3–5) to be secondary. In this third iteration of the wife-sister story in Genesis (cf. Gen 12:10–20; 20:1–18), YHWH extends to Isaac the promises of land and progeny. The two gifts are linked inextricably: "I will make your offspring as numerous as the stars of heaven, and I will give to your offspring all these lands" (Gen 26:4a). What links them is a clause indicating the motivation: "I will fulfill the oath that I swore to your father Abraham" (Gen 26:3b). Scholars have tended to parallel the gift of the land here with the land-oath tradition in Deuteronomy.[26] Expressed in Deuteronomic language, Abraham's keeping the divine instructions becomes the key to YHWH extending the Abrahamic promises to Isaac and his progeny (Gen 26:4–5).[27]

The Sinai pericope (Exod 19–24) was also subject to editing at this time. There is ample evidence of a Deuteronomic hand reworking the text, in particular the two sections (Exod 20:22; 23:20–33) before and after the long series of casuistic laws. The two sections form a literary frame around the law and provide it with D flavoring. Blenkinsopp notes that YHWH speaking from heaven (Exod 20:22) expresses the "ultimacy of authority" in patently Deuteronomic terms and approaches "the beginnings of the idea of a *unique* divine communication at Sinai/Horeb."[28] He similarly notes that the epilogue to the laws (Exod 23:20–33) "assumes the absolute necessity for a mediating agency by which the Sinai experience would be perpetuated and embodied in fully authorized institutional forms."[29]

These Deuteronomic notions will advance from the embryonic stage evidenced in Exodus (Exod 20:22; 23:20–33) to a more mature expression in other texts. When later scribes undertake the Pentateuchal Redaction (see later), they aim to settle questions about the authority and interpretation of revealed law by designating Mosaic hermeneutical forms and a text that is self-authenticating. Such theories have not yet crystallized here in texts (Exod 20:22; 23:20–33) that Blenkinsopp dates to the early Persian period.[30]

In sum, Deuteronomy came of age during the postexilic period and served as a distinctive and defining element within the larger narrative of origins that encompasses the themes of the patriarchs, Moses, and the exodus, and the entering into the land. In its design the narrative sequence was a Hexateuch, with Deuteronomy in the penultimate position as legal instruction that also provided a rhetorical elegance to the materials that preceded it and followed it. Genesis in particular contains multiple examples of Deuteronomic editing that took place in postexilic fifth century Yehud.

The Formation of the P–Non-P Hexateuch

Expanding the Hexateuch

The next iteration of the Hexateuch came to light through a fourth century amalgamation of the D-infused narrative of origins and certain Priestly materials constituting another, distinct legal tradition.[31] P and non-P materials were combined to make an expansive Hexateuch that would prove to be the forerunner to the Pentateuch. Carr refers to this critical stage in the collection's growth as "the formation of a combined P/non-P Hexateuch."[32] Myriad social factors precipitated this development, chief among them the call to communal cohesion as expressed in Deuteronomy (see n. 3) and elsewhere. Aspirations for community became the impetus for a large-scale integration of D and P, which resulted in an expanded and more inclusive program of teaching and textualization. The formation of this comprehensive document, the combined P/non-P Hexateuch, likely occurred in the early fourth century.

The Compositional Level: How D Influenced the Priestly Corpus

When combining P with the D-based narrative of origins, scribes sought a good fit and harmonization. A standard technique was adding Deuteronomic elements to the preexisting P materials (Lev 11:44–45; 17:3–7, 10–14; 20:24; Num 36:1–13), although interestingly D itself was rarely subject to comparable Priestly edits.[33] Thus, much of the evidence for the P–non-P Hexateuch consists of Deuteronomic elements located outside of Deuteronomy. This D evidence subsists at a level of the text ascertained diachronically and referred to as the Compositional Level. To put this in perspective, the Compositional Level is later than the D-based narrative of origins running from Genesis to Joshua but not as late as the Pentateuchal Redaction.[34]

Numbers 36:1–13—A Deuteronomic Ruling on Inheritance Law in P

In Numbers (Num 36:1–13), Josephite clans in the line of Manasseh seek a ruling from Moses with regard to ancestral land that is associated with and effectively controlled by Mahlah, Tirzah, Hoglah, Milcah, and Noah, the daughters of Zelophehad. When daughters marry outside the line of Manasseh, their land transfers to another tribe, but in the case of the five sisters, the Josephites seek to retain ownership. Moses renders his decision "at the direction of the LORD" (Num 36:5). The daughters may marry whom they please, provided that they marry into a clan of their ancestral tribe. As long as they marry into a clan of their ancestral tribe, the Israelites will "cleave to" ("retain" NRSV) their own ancestral heritage (Num 36:7, 9) and "possess" the heritage (Num 36:8). The verbs "cleave" (דבק, see Deut 4:4; 10:20; 11:22; 13:5; 13:18; 28:21, 60; 30:20) and "possess" (ירש, see Deut 4:21; 15:4; 19:10; 20;16; 21:23; 24:4; 26:1, 25) are reflective of D discourse.[35] The former denotes cleaving to kindred or to YHWH, but it sometimes applies to peoples and their land (Josh 23:12; 1 Kgs 11:2). Scribes fused these two D expressions to express a complex idea, inheritance within a kinship system such as that of the Josephites. The scribes further enhanced the passage's Deuteronomic character with the phrase "commandments and ordinances the LORD commanded" (Num 36:13). The passage may be located within the P–non-P Hexateuch because the D expressions ("cleave," "possess") are blended with P phrases like "at the direction of the Lord" (Num 36:5 על־פי יהוה, 13x in P). With this particular synthesis of sources, this tradition in Numbers (Num 36:1–13) is readily located at the compositional level of the P–non-P Hexateuch.[36]

Leviticus 11:44–45—You Shall Be Holy

Leviticus (Lev 11:1–47) enumerates a series of dietary laws and includes Deuteronomic phrasing such as: "I am the LORD who brought you up from the land of Egypt, to be your God" (Lev 11:45a). The verse is punctuated by the words "You shall be holy, for I am holy (Lev 11:44–45)." The reference to being led out of Egypt is rare in Leviticus. Moreover, "brought you up" (עלה in the form of a *hiphil* participle) is anomalous. This is the only place that P uses the verb in this context.[37] In contrast, both the motif of leaving the land of Egypt and the verb עלה are common in Deuteronomy although D typically indicates deliverance from Egypt with a *hiphil* form of a related verb, [38]יצא. The evidence suggests that Leviticus (Lev 11:44–45) contains Deuteronomic material that scribes integrated into a Priestly instruction during the Compositional Level of the P–non-P Hexateuch.

Throughout the twentieth century, commentators tended to assign this tradition in Leviticus (Lev 11:44–45) to the Holiness Code (H, Lev 17:1–26:46). Jacob Milgrom and Baruch A. Levine, for example, identify the dietary list with the legal instructions linking personal and corporate holiness.[39] Because the code's treatment of holiness per se does not begin until later (Lev 19:2), the commentators must maintain that this tradition *anticipates* the code, a dubious proposition that creates difficulty for their larger analysis of the literary sources. Indeed, their arguments for H rely on the multiple attestations of קדש (Lev 11:44aα, 44aβ, 45bα, 45bβ) serving as an interpretive crux that relativizes the other evidence, such as the Deuteronomic reference to Egypt.

Taking a different approach, Reinhard Achenbach has presented evidence that the tradents responsible for this tradition in Leviticus (Lev 11:44–45) correlated their text with an earlier tradition in Deuteronomy (14:3–21), which also lists clean and unclean animals while incorporating the phraseology "You are a people holy to the LORD your God" (14:2a, 21a).[40]

Achenbach argues that scribes incorporated Deuteronomy into Leviticus, as opposed to freely composing this Leviticus tradition (Lev11:44-45) in anticipation of H (Lev 17:1-26:46). The evidence for this view is persuasive. Both Leviticus and Deuteronomy use קדש strategically to fashion an envelope structure (Lev 11:44aα, 44aβ, 45bα, 45bβ; Deut 14:2a, 21a), with the former more compressed than the latter. If קדש is the interpretive crux of the dietary list in Leviticus (Lev 11:44–45), it points to an editorial reappropriation of the D source. This dietary list is thus an example of the good fit and rich harmonization that characterizes the Compositional Level of the P–non-P Hexateuch.

Leviticus 20:22–26—A Land Flowing with Milk and Honey

The Holiness Code (Lev 17:--26:46) is relatively free of redactional seams and editorial intrusions. After the discourse on holiness was integrated into P, it remained largely intact and unaltered by later scribes. An exception is an exhortation within a series of prohibitions:

> You shall keep all my statutes and all my ordinances, and observe them, so that the land to which I bring you to settle in may not vomit you out. You shall not follow the practices of the nation that I am driving out before you. Because they did all these things, I abhorred them. But I have said to you: You shall inherit their land, and I will give it to you to possess, a land flowing with milk and honey. I am the LORD your God; I have separated you from the peoples. You shall therefore make a distinction between the clean animal and the unclean, and between the unclean bird and the clean; you shall not bring abomination on yourselves by animal or by bird or by anything with which the ground teems, which I have set apart for you to hold unclean. You shall be holy to me; for I the LORD am holy, and I have separated you from the other peoples to be mine (Lev 20:22–26).

The exhortation is among the few texts that postdate the incorporation of H into P and provide evidence of a subsequent rearticulation of H. The later work was done systematically and in light of Deuteronomy. On the basis of the Deuteronomic expression "a land flowing with milk and honey (Lev 20:24)," the exhortation (Lev 20:22–26) may be associated with the combined P/non-P Hexateuch, in the early fourth century. Put differently, this exhortation reflects the Compositional Layer formed when Deuteronomy's territorially oriented narrative of Israel's origins was joined with P.

Elsewhere in Leviticus prohibitions are wide ranging, from child sacrifice (Lev 20:1–5) to incest (Lev 20:14–21). The issue in the exhortation (Lev 20:22–26) is separating clean animals from unclean (Lev 20:25), with the analogy that YHWH has set these people apart from other peoples to be holy.

The exhortation (Lev 20:22–26) contains three P expressions. First, it features the verb בדל, "to set apart" (Lev 20:24b). YHWH, in the first person, has set the addressees apart (הבדלתי) from other peoples (מן־העמים). Second, the motive clause (Lev 20:25) for separating unclean beasts and birds from clean ones is "lest you draw abomination upon yourselves (ולא־תשקצו את־נפשתיכם)." Third, the prohibition concludes "you shall be holy (קדשים) to me" (Lev 20:26).

In light of the lexical evidence, Milgrom suggests that an H tradent appended the prohibition (Lev 20:22–26) to the H corpus based on parallel passages already in Leviticus (Lev 18).[41] Although Milgrom would date such activity earlier than the fourth century, the point is that the prohibition is likely secondary and a redaction. The scribes focused on the Holiness Code but knew other traditions, too, as evidenced by the expression "a land flowing with milk and honey" (Lev 20:24a). This description of the land is never found in P except here, although it occurs twelve times in the Hebrew Bible with eight of those in Deuteronomy (6:3; 11:9; 26:9, 15; 27:3; 31:20) or Jeremiah (Jer 11:5; 32:22). Scholars have regarded "a land flowing with milk and honey (Lev 20:24a)" as an echo of Deuteronomy.[42] The phrase may have been designed to align Leviticus with a broader Hexateuchal *Weltanschauung* grounded in Deuteronomy.[43] Such coordination was standard in the P-non-P Hexateuch.

Interestingly, the exhortation (Lev 20:22–26) contains no Deuteronomic language or ideas other than "a land flowing with milk and honey (Lev 20:24a)." There is no mention of a holy people that would harmonize the passage in Leviticus with, for example, other traditions in Deuteronomy (7:6 or 14:2a, 21a). In Deuteronomy, these three verses are motive clauses that address the people broadly and inclusively as a sacral collective: "You are a people holy to the LORD your God." Rather, "a land flowing with milk and honey" is the extent of the D influence here (Lev 20:22–26), despite the good fit and richer harmonization that would result were there a reference to holy people (Deut 7:6; 14:2, 21a).

Perhaps in the context of Leviticus (Lev 17–26), holiness is a leitmotif unto itself that precludes extensive blending with D materials dealing with holiness.[44] Thus, the exhortation within Leviticus (Lev 20:22–26) suggests that scribes were working with surgical precision to incorporate certain D language, namely, "a land flowing with milk and honey" (Lev 20:24a), while eschewing a D-based reference to the "holy people" or to the people as holy.

Leviticus 17:3–8 and Deuteronomy 12:20–28—The Centralization of Slaughter

There are exceptions to the rule that Deuteronomy was unaffected in the formation of the P–non-P Hexateuch. Scholars increasingly think that Deuteronomy's instruction on secular slaughter (12:20–28) contains a reflex of the H prohibition on slaughter outside the cult (Lev 17:3–8). A variation on this position is that the two legal texts were written in coordination at more or less the same time and place. The new trend in interpreting Deuteronomy's prohibition stands in contrast to what scholars have traditionally held.

The setting of the instruction in Deuteronomy is telling inasmuch as it resonates with the narrative of origins that is foundational to the Hexateuch. At a point in the future, the people have settled the promised land and are living there comfortably (12:20). A diet with meat is available as the situation describes eating sheep or goat that is slaughtered for common consumption, not ritual sacrifice. The instruction offers an exemption for persons who live too far from the central "place where the LORD your God will choose to put his name" (20:21). When preparing their meals, they themselves may slaughter sacrificial animals locally, as opposed to transporting them to the central sanctuary where priests would butcher them. The instruction to those living in the hinterland goes further by allowing them to dispose of the animal's blood by pouring it out on the ground like water (12:23–25). They are not required to bring the blood to the central sanctuary, except in cases of ritual sacrifice when both the blood and the flesh of the animal must be placed on the altar of YHWH (12:27). In such instances, Deuteronomy states that the butchering as well must occur at the cult because the animal in question is being sacrificed.

The instruction on secular slaughter is a subunit within a chapter understood by many to be the most forceful mandate for a centralized cult in Israel (12:2–28). Although there are other texts that envision a single, central site of sacrificial worship, it has long been assumed that Deuteronomy influenced Leviticus (Lev 17:3–8).[45] According to this view, Deuteronomy first instructed settlers of the land to forego a long trip to the central sanctuary if it were simply a matter of slaughtering a sheep or goat in order to make a meal of it, and later the H writers reacted to D's teaching by issuing the opinion that *all* sacrificial animals must *always* be slaughtered at the central sanctuary, regardless of the circumstances.

The engrained view that Leviticus is derivative of Deuteronomy has faced multiple challenges over the years. Baruch J. Schwartz and others have read Leviticus on its own terms and found that the instruction on slaughter has greater affinity with P than with Deuteronomy.[46] Julia Rhyder has shown that an almost genetic relationship exists between the P account of the Yom Kippur rituals (Lev 16:1–34) and the instruction on slaughter (Lev 17:3–8), which evokes a sense of the forbidding wilderness in contrast to the central cult.[47] The field outside the camp (Lev 17:3, 5) where the secular slaughter of animals takes place parallels the desert where Azazel receives the goat that Aaron has designated for the demonic figure (Lev 16:10). Rhyder's analysis also reconsiders the lexical evidence that has been marshalled to argue that Deuteronomy (12:23) influenced Leviticus on blood prohibitions (Lev 17:11). She notes how the texts, despite showing verbal overlap, are conceptually different. Leviticus uniquely states that the blood is a ransom for the people's lives, with "ransom" carrying the sense of compensation for the life of the one offering sacrifice, who otherwise has bloodguilt "on account of the taking of an animal life."[48] H's innovative construal of ritual bloodshed and bloodguilt appears to have its origins not in Deuteronomy but rather in P (for example, Gen 9:1–17).[49]

With the consensus no longer in place, new explanations of the relationship between Leviticus and Deuteronomy are emerging. Rhyder hypothesizes that Deuteronomy first established the concession of secular slaughter (12:15–16) and implied that the meat in question must serve as food and not sacrifice.[50] Subsequently, H reacted to the legislation in Deuteronomy (12:15–16) and issued its own, stricter teaching. The matter was then "clarified" (12:20–28), where "new temporal and spatial limitations to this process are introduced and explained."[51] Rhyder construes Deuteronomy's instruction (12:20–28) as a late, additional text "that knows and responds to the laws of Leviticus 17."[52]

Although Rhyder does not align the debate about secular slaughter with the formation of the P–non-P Hexateuch, the situation she describes approximates that literary context. Rhyder also offers an intriguing possibility that "Lev 17 reflects the strategies by which the central shrine in Jerusalem negotiated with the cultic periphery in the Persian period."[53] Such prospects are doubly revealing. On the one hand, they indicate the type of internal negotiations that took place around issues during the formation of the P–non-P Hexateuch, and, on the other hand, they recall Deuteronomy's propensity to hold two different viewpoints in a creative tension.

Otto hypothesizes that the scribes who are responsible for instructions on slaughter in Leviticus (Lev 17:3–8) and Deuteronomy (12:20–28) belong to the same redactional level of the Pentateuch.[54] The scribes crafted the instruction in Leviticus in reaction to Deuteronomy and then appended an additional instruction (12:20–28) to refine the restrictions on local butchery. Otto's suggestion is consistent with the paradigm of the P–non-P Hexateuch. Furthermore, it makes sense that both of the instructions in Leviticus and Deuteronomy would belong to the Compositional Level. Yet the uncompromisingly rigorous instruction in Leviticus[55] and the instruction in Deuteronomy that considers people's wishes do not come from the same place. Perhaps the two instructions were written near one another, temporally and geographically, by scribes who were in communication but aligned with different schools.

In relatively short time—perhaps less than a century—the Hexateuch that integrated Deuteronomy and P would be structurally modified. The scribes' work took a new direction, leading to the emergence of the first five books as a literary collection with a distinctive theology as well as claims to authority. Scholars describe the process as the Pentateuchal Redaction.

What Is Trending in the Conversation?

The Pentateuchal Redaction

Pentateuch and Torah

Early diachronic studies dated the development of the Pentateuch to the seventh century but more recent studies have dated the development of the Pentateuch to the fourth century, or the late Persian period. The final development is the crafting of the Pentateuch through a textual process known as the Pentateuchal Redaction. To clarify, "Pentateuch" is different from "Torah." Torah refers to revealed religious teaching in ancient Israel. During the Persian period, Torah had different denotations, some of which were earlier and some of which were later. Haggai (Hag 2:11) refers to Torah as an instruction (תורה) that speaks to a certain sacrificial rite. Zechariah (Zech 7:12) refers to it as a form of prophetic revelation (תורה). These sources suggest that at the time of their writing Torah was still a piecemeal teaching and not yet a composite. A change is visible in the literary materials associated with Ezra and Nehemiah, which by the fourth century refer to Torah as a revealed legal tradition associated with Moses and Sinai (Ezra 6:18; 7:26; 10:3; Neh 8:1, 8, 18; 10:35). In fact, standard textbooks routinely taught that Torah expressions such as "the book of the law of Moses" (Neh 8:8) refer to the Pentateuch in its final form, the completed collection of five books. The view still exists that Ezra brought the Pentateuch back from Babylon. The Torah read publicly in Nehemiah (Neh 8:1–12), however, is still in the process of becoming a Pentateuch; the major legal traditions of ancient Israel have not yet crystallized as one, but they soon will.

Addition by Redaction

In this study, each historical stage has involved the joining of two corpora by means of redactional texts that bridge and shape them. This was true with the joining of Deuteronomy to non-D materials and the formation of the P–non-P Hexateuch. Similarly, the Pentateuchal Redaction encompasses a series of redactional texts "that show an awareness of a literary horizon that comprises the entire Pentateuch."[56] Schmid further describes these texts as "passages in the Pentateuch that can be connected to the final composition of the Torah in terms of binding together the Torah complex from Genesis to Deuteronomy in a way that can be conceived literarily and theologically."[57] As an example, he cites "Moses was 120 years old when he died; his sight was unimpaired and his vigor had not abated (34:7)."

Schmid links the notice of Moses's death in Deuteronomy (34:1–12) to Genesis (Gen 6:3), which defines a human lifetime as 120 years. For Schmid, the connection forms an *inclusio* joining the end of the Pentateuch to its beginning. In both Genesis and Deuteronomy, death comes as "the divinely ordained limitation of the human life-span,"[58] caused by fate and not by personal or collective guilt. The theology expressed in Moses's obituary (34:1–12), however, is different from other traditions in Deuteronomy and P. D links Moses's death to the collective guilt of the people (1:36; 3:26) while P assumes that Moses defied YHWH by striking the rock in the desert (Num 20:12). In certain literary contexts, such as that of the P–non-P Hexateuch, scribes would have harmonized D and P,[59] or perhaps juxtaposed them. The absence of D and P traditions in the notice of Moses's death (34:7 indicates that this literary context is different from that of the Hexateuch and aligns rather with the Pentateuchal Redaction. While the *inclusio* formed by Genesis and Deuteronomy is the parade example of the Pentateuchal Redaction, there are other links underscoring how Genesis through Deuteronomy form a collection. While such texts are clustered in the obituary (34:4, 7, 10), scribes have inserted them elsewhere as well (Num 6:24–27).[60]

The Hermeneutical Theory of Deuteronomy

There are also links between two texts *within* Deuteronomy, one of which is typically in its final chapter, that provide evidence of the Pentateuchal Redaction. Otto illustrates this by connecting the attribution of Moses's death to fate rather than to his sin (34:7) with the celebration of Moses for his mighty deeds and terrifying displays of power (34:10–12). Moses's YHWH-like feats require him to be sinless, and beyond human failings. Otto then associates *this* depiction of Moses with the beginning of Deuteronomy: "Deut 1:1–5 defines Deuteronomy as interpretation of the Sinai-*torah* through Moses' scribal erudition."[61] Moses's erudition, along with other qualities, made possible the *Mosaic* interpretation of the law code associated with Sinai, otherwise known as Deuteronomy. The "second law" had been in existence in one form or another since the seventh century, but now it is being framed more explicitly than ever as the miraculous work of Moses. What is more, it is being framed with verses in Deuteronomy's first and final chapters that mutually reflect the theology of the Pentateuchal Redaction.

For Schmid, displaying Moses's deeds as comparable to those of YHWH is not only a "theologizing of Moses," but it also confers authoritative status on the Torah with which Moses is intimately associated: "'Moses' is placed in close connection to YHWH so that the Torah can lay claim to equivalent authority."[62] Related to the authority of the Pentateuch is the thorny issue of its interpretation. To the question of who may interpret the Pentateuch, the key again is Moses. Otto demonstrates how the legacy of Moses's scribal interpretation of the Sinai-torah gives rise at this time to "the hermeneutical theory of Deuteronomy."[63]

The hermeneutical theory of Deuteronomy is built upon the tradition that at Sinai Moses did not simply interpret the Torah, he mediated it as well. For Otto, after Moses's death "the role of mediator of divine revelation was assumed by the written Torah itself.... Moses had to die so that the transcribed Torah could assume Moses' function of mediating the divine will to the generations of addressees of the Torah in the Promised Land."[64] Such is the hermeneutic of the scribes responsible for the Pentateuchal Redaction: the Torah understood as the first five books is both self-mediating and self-interpreting.

Moses is no sorcerer's apprentice, and the Pentateuch is not his broom over which he has cast a magical spell.[65] Rather, the hermeneutic is the scribes' own claim to textual authority over and against other interpreters of the Torah. The Pentateuchal Redaction provoked significant challenges and fueled the postexilic debate over the possible modalities of divine revelation. Certain scribes working in the Jeremiah traditions formed an opposition to the Pentateuchal Redaction. In "Jeremia und die Tora. Ein nachexilischer Diskurs,"[66] Otto juxtaposes the commissioning of Aaron, who is an eloquent speaker because Moses puts words in his mouth (Exod 4:14–17), with Jeremiah (Jer 1:7–9), where YHWH puts words in the mouth of Jeremiah. For Benedetta Rossi, the new covenant initiative in Jeremiah (Jer 31:31–34) is another locus of opposition to the Pentateuchal Redaction; the Jeremiah text challenges the pattern of revelation established in Deuteronomy (34:10) through the figure of Moses, whose status as arch-prophet precludes other programs of Torah interpretation.[67] Such attempts to develop a rival hermeneutic were not successful in the long run. Deuteronomic scribes held in check approaches to Torah other than their own and neutralized opposition to the Pentateuchal Redaction.

Implications

Certain of the late fourth century redactional texts clustered in Deuteronomy (34:1–12) undermine statements elsewhere in the book. The claim that there has been no prophet in Israel since Moses, whom YHWH knew face to face, is inconsistent with Moses's teaching that YHWH will raise up "a prophet like me" (18:15). Similarly, the report that Moses died at age 120 in relatively good health, his sight unimpaired and his vigor unabated (34:7), is inconsistent with another tradition in Deuteronomy (31:2), where the man of 120 years is weakened, "no longer able to get about." These differences are further evidence of Deuteronomy's holding contrasting viewpoints in tension, and they shed light on an editing process that, in the words of Bernard M. Levinson, "intentionally preserves conflicting perspectives on a full range of key issues central to Israelite religion."[68] Levinson concludes: "There is no facile 'air-brushing' away of this interplay of perspectives, which reflects an ongoing ancient debate about fundamental religious assumptions."[69]

The Pentateuchal Redaction also eclipses Joshua, who stands at the climax of the Hexateuch, although Joshua and the narrative of conquering the land are not excised or otherwise removed. Rather, the Pentateuchal Redaction recasts Joshua in the terms developed for Moses at his death. Like Moses, Joshua and subsequent leaders derive authority uniquely from the Torah (Josh 1:7–8; 17a). As Joachim J. Krause explains, "Joshua's authority hinges on that of Moses . . . Moses' authority, in turn, does not exist on its own terms either. It is due to his role as mediator of the will of Yhwh, ascribed to him in a most systematic fashion by the Deuteronomistic redaction which put the original Deuteronomy into the form of a monologue by Moses. Yet, this authority to mediate the will of Yhwh for Israel and her leaders does remain an exclusive prerogative of Moses. It is not transmitted to anyone, including Joshua."[70]

For Krause, Mosaic authority was not indigenous to the "original" Deuteronomy and was the effect of a systematic redaction, although not necessarily the Pentateuchal Redaction. Krause bases the authority of Moses on his mediation of the Torah, a function that Moses can delegate to his successors beginning with Joshua. Joshua neither mediates nor interprets the Torah left by Moses, although he is told to consult it and indeed to study it sedulously "like a biblical scholar."[71] Thus the Joshua model that Krause develops involves the leader in the application of Torah teaching, whereas the Pentateuchal Redaction stipulates a hermeneutic whereby the mediatorial and interpretive functions rest exclusively with the Torah itself. This difference aside, the Joshua model is consistent with and extends from the Pentateuchal Redaction. As a result, Israel's achievements portrayed in Joshua are as much an epilogue to the notice of Moses's death in Deuteronomy (34:1–12) as they are the culmination of the five preceding books.

Conclusion

For several decades, Pentateuchal studies have been shifting tectonically. Amid new initiatives, the contrasting scholarly approaches of the past have yet to be sorted out. The discussion of paradigms, models, and methodologies will continue for the foreseeable future. In the discussion, there are two currents that run alongside and at times intersect with the documentary-type model of the Pentateuch presented in this chapter.

Whereas the model employed here is keyed to a two-source hypothesis (D and P), some scholars continue to advance the long-standing four-source hypothesis, with large swathes of Pentateuchal text assigned to J and E. The Neo-Documentarians locate J and E largely in the Tetrateuch, not Deuteronomy.[72] Another current of note identifies texts as post-Priestly, a temporal designation based upon when the verses in question were joined to the Pentateuch. The post-Priestly approach presupposes a decisive redaction of the Pentateuch by priestly scribes, after which textual materials of disparate origin continued to be layered onto the structure comprising Genesis-Deuteronomy or Genesis-Joshua. Post-Priestly additions tend to be not earlier than the fourth century BCE.[73]

My aim here has been to critique neither the Neo-Documentarians nor the post-Priestly approach. Both are making valuable contributions, in terms of their insights, to the study of Deuteronomy and the Pentateuch. I view them rather as two currents at some distance from one another on an intellectual map. From that perspective, they allow us to see that the *via media*, and thus a way forward, is in fact the type of approach put forth in this chapter. I have made the case for a documentary-type approach to the Pentateuch in the form of a two-source hypothesis, P and D. I have focused on D and the critical role that Deuteronomy has played in the formation of the Pentateuch. In the coming decade, this heuristic framework of Deuteronomy and the Pentateuch will continue to command scholars' attention, as Christophe Nihan indicates:

> In my opinion, one of the most significant achievements of Pentateuchal scholarship in recent decades remains the recognition that the Pentateuch was not merely achieved by the mechanical compilation of discrete sources but that it reflects a sophisticated scribal attempt to partially align Priestly [P] and non-Priestly traditions [such as D] during the Persian (and possibly early Hellenistic) periods. Identifying and reconstructing that process of gradual realignment remains, therefore, one of the most important tasks of Pentateuchal scholarship.[74]

Notes

1. D here refers to the writers largely responsible for the book of Deuteronomy, but not for all the material in its later chapters (27–34), which include portions from P as well as other, non-D sources. The related term "Deuteronomic" refers to the type of writing in Deuteronomy, with the exceptions just noted, and to segments in the Tetrateuch that contain the legal phraseology and other expressions reminiscent of Deuteronomy. Dtr refers to the Deuteronomistic writers who worked on Joshua, Judges, Samuel, and Kings.
2. While the documentary approach is often attributed to Julius Wellhausen, other figures such as Karl Heinrich Graf and Abraham Kuenen were influential in its development. See Julius Wellhausen, *Die Composition des Hexateuchs und der historischen Bücher des Alten Testaments*, 3rd ed. (Berlin: Reimer, 1899); 4th ed. (Berlin: de Gruyter, 1963); Karl Heinrich Graf, "Die s.g. Grundschrift des Pentateuchs," *Archiv für die wissenschaftliche Erforschung des Alten Testaments* 1, no. 4 (1869): 466–477; Abraham Kuenan, *An Historico-Critical Inquiry into the Origin and Composition of the Hexateuch* (London: Macmillan, 1886).

3. In the seventh century, one may ask, how exactly were certain laws from the Covenant Code updated and articulated anew as Deuteronomic statutes? This process involved lexical shifts that are readily observed. For example, in Deuteronomy, אח (brother) often appears with רע (neighbor) and it even comes to describe individuals once considered enemies (ביא), as evidenced by a comparison of Exod 21:35, 22:9, 23:4, and Deut 22:1.
4. See, for example, Erhard Blum, "Zwischen Literarkritik und Stilkritik. Die diachrone Analyse der literarischen Verbindung von Genesis und Exodus—im Gespräch mit Ludwig Schmidt," *ZAW* 124, no. 4 (2012): 492–515.
5. John Van Seters, "Joshua 24 and the Problem of Tradition in the Old Testament," in *In the Shelter of Elyon: Essays on Ancient Palestinian Life and Literature in Honor of G.W. Ahlström*, ed. W. Boyd Barrick and John R. Spencer, JSOTSupp 31 (Sheffield: JSOT Press, 1984), 139–158; more recently, Christoph Levin, "The Yahwist: The Earliest Editor in the Pentateuch," *JBL* 126, no. 2 (2007): 209–230, esp. 212.
6. Joseph Blenkinsopp, *The Pentateuch: An Introduction to the First Five Books of the Bible*, ABRL (New York: Doubleday, 1992), 193–197, esp. 193–194, where Blenkinsopp notes that "the case for a primitive J version of covenant making collapses," while Exodus 32–34 "conform to the pattern of sin, punishment, and forgiveness encountered frequently in Deuteronomy and Dtr."
7. Within this consensus, one finds nuance. For example, David Carr suggests that Deuteronomy is possibly a northern stream of tradition (on these prospects there is a separate chapter in this volume). He offers examples of "independent" materials derived from sources such as "an earlier West Semitic covenant with Yhwh at Shechem." Here his use of the word "independent" may be substituting for "original." Elsewhere Carr points to "originally independent materials" such as the Shechem covenant that may serve as the foundation for Deuteronomy. David M. Carr, *The Formation of the Hebrew Bible: A New Reconstruction* (New York: Oxford University Press, 2011), 313, 346.
8. Some of the material peripheral to Deuteronomy 12–26, scholars would allow, is redactional, but redaction is not critical to their understanding the original Deuteronomy's shape and substance.
9. Donald J. Wiseman, "The Vassal-Treaties of Esarhaddon," *Iraq* 20 (1958): 1–100; and more recently, Bernard M. Levinson, "Esarhaddon's Succession Treaty as the Source for the Canon Formula in Deut 13:1," *JAOS* 130, no. 3 (2010): 337–347. An impact of aligning EST with Deuteronomy was to question the conclusion that only Hittite treaties served as models of the biblical covenant expressed in Deuteronomy.
10. See the historical reconstruction in Stephen L. Cook, *Reading Deuteronomy: A Literary and Theological Commentary* (Macon: Smyth and Helwys, 2015), 9–11. Cook locates Deuteronomy's origins in a scenario of "Rural Israel vs. the Royal Court."
11. In the view of William Schniedewind, leaders from rural Judea were responsible for the original Deuteronomy, including chapters 12 and 17. These Levitical priests formed the Deuteronomic movement that impacted Israelite society. Their seminal work was done between 640, the assassination of King Amnon, and 622, the rise to power of Josiah, who was born of this movement but changed it by reclaiming royal privileges. See his *How the Bible Became a Book: The Textualization of Ancient Israel* (Cambridge: Cambridge University Press, 2004), 106–114.
12. For a discussion of how a tradition of an outlying altar fits into the design of Deuteronomy with its emphasis on cult centralization, see Richard J. Bautch, "The Altar Not Destroyed in Deuteronomy 16:21," *JSOT* 40, no. 3 (2016): 321–336, esp. 334–336. Also, Thomas Römer,

"Cult Centralization in Deuteronomy," in *Das Deuteronomian zwischen Pentateuch und Deuteronomistischem Geschichtswerk*, ed. Eckart Otto and Reinhard Achenbach, FRLANT 206 (Göttingen: Vandenhoeck & Ruprecht, 2004), 168–180, esp. 179.

13. Konrad Schmid, "How to Identify a Persian Period Text in the Pentateuch," in *On Dating Biblical Texts to the Persian Period: Discerning Criteria and Establishing Epochs*, ed. Richard J. Bautch and Mark Lackowski, FAT II 101 (Tübingen: Mohr Siebeck, 2019), 101–118, esp. 106–107.
14. Otto, "Pentateuch," 687.
15. Otto, "Pentateuch," 687.
16. Eckart Otto, "The Integration of the Post-exilic Book of Deuteronomy," in *The Post-Priestly Pentateuch: New Perspectives on its Redactional Development and Theological Profiles*, ed. Federico Giuntoli and Konrad Schmid, FAT 101 (Tübingen: Mohr Siebeck, 2015), 331–341, esp. 339–340.
17. Carr, *Formation of the Hebrew Bible*, 219.
18. Carr, *Formation of the Hebrew Bible*, 219.
19. In Ezra 9–10, one such group appears, initially as a cohort who "trembled for the words of the God of Israel" (Ezra 9:4). The tremblers, in postexilic texts, represent those who adhered strictly to the law (Isa 66: 2, 5). In the words of Bob Becking (*Ezra-Nehemiah*, HCOT [Leuven: Peeters, 2018], 144), "They form the true community that the narrator [of Ezra] aims toward." Subsequently in Ezra 10:1, a large crowd that would include the tremblers forms around Ezra; it is this expanded community (or social group) that Ezra organizes through a covenantal agreement (10:4) to dissolve mixed marriages, a precedent adopted and adapted from Deut 24:1–4.
20. The following examples have been acknowledged in scholarship going back to the middle of the nineteenth century. Alongside these examples, additional passages in the Tetrateuch have been identified as Deuteronomic, with varying degrees of plausibility. The tendency to find aspects of D all throughout the first four books is referred to as pan-Deuteronomism.
21. Biblical citations are from the NRSV.
22. Israel is described as a mighty nation in Deut 9:14.
23. On the redactional character of these verses, see Walter Moberly, "The Earliest Commentary on the Akedah," *VT* 38 (1988): 302–323.
24. David M. Carr, *Reading the Fractures of Genesis: Historical and Literary Approaches* (Louisville: Westminster John Knox, 1996), 158.
25. Carr, *Formation of the Hebrew Bible*, 278.
26. That is, the Deuteronomic land-oath tradition as dated to the fifth century BCE or earlier. With such dating, Gen 26:3 stands as evidence of Deuteronomic influence on the Tetrateuch and the formation of a territorially oriented Hexateuch. A trend in recent research has been to locate passages where the oath to grant land specifies the patriarchs by name at a later point in the Second Temple period, at the time of the Pentateuchal Redaction (see later in the section titled "Implications" the reference to Deut 34:4). The example of Deut 34:4 and related verses (Gen 50:24; Exod 32:12, 33:1; Num 32:11) is identified by Konrad Schmid ("The Late Persian Formation of the Torah: Observations on Deuteronomy 34," in *Judah and the Judeans in the Fourth Century B.C.E.*, ed. Oded Lipschits, Gary N. Knoppers, and Rainer Albertz (Winona Lake: Eisenbrauns, 2007), 237–251, esp. 242). According to Schmid, a key feature is that these decidedly later examples name the patriarchs but do not refer to them appositionally as "fathers"; the verse in

question here, Gen 26:3, does however refer to Abraham as "your father," thus calling into question any dating of the verse to the fourth century or later.
27. Moshe Weinfeld, *Deuteronomy and the Deuteronomic School* (Oxford: Clarendon Press, 1972), 336.
28. Joseph Blenkinsopp, "Deuteronomic Contribution to the Narrative in Genesis-Numbers: A Test Case," in *Those Elusive Deuteronomists: The Phenomenon of Pan-Deuteronomism*, ed. Linda S. Schearing and Steven L. McKenzie, JSOTSup 268 (Sheffield: Sheffield Academic Press, 1999), 84–115, esp. 94.
29. Blenkinsopp, "Deuteronomic Contribution," 95. Blenkinsopp adds that here the Deuteronomic rhetoric contains an appeal to the role and mission of Moses as prophet.
30. Blenkinsopp, "Deuteronomic Contribution," 111–112.
31. Admittedly, it is something of a misnomer to refer to the fifth-century narrative of origins (Gen-Josh) as a "Hexateuch." The six biblical "books" in question did not yet exist. For example, large sections of cultic law would be added later to Exodus and Numbers. Moreover, certain "books" existed only in anticipation, as with Leviticus, a compendium of cultic law and ethical teaching based largely on the concept of holiness.
32. Carr, *Formation of the Hebrew Bible*, 204–225.
33. In a separate literary development, Deuteronomy in this period underwent internal editing by D scribes. Their redactional efforts created strata that signaled new literary editions of Deuteronomy. See, for example, Christoph Levin, "Rereading Deuteronomy in the Persian and Hellenistic Periods: The Ethics of Brotherhood and the Care of the Poor," in *Deuteronomy-Kings as Emerging Authoritative Books: A Conversation*, ed. Diana V. Edelman, ANEM 6 (Atlanta: Society of Biblical Literature, 2014), 49–71.
34. To anticipate a point made later in this chapter, the criteria for assigning texts to the Pentateuchal Redaction have to do with Moses and his role as interpreter and mediator of divine revelation. This role was initially associated with Moses on the basis of his transcribing the laws of Sinai and expanding them into a second law, Deuteronomy. With the advent of the Pentateuchal Redaction, however, the mediatorial role of divine revelation was assumed by the written Torah itself. In the words of Otto ("Deuteronomy as the Legal Completion and Prophetic Finale of the Pentateuch," in *Paradigm Change in Pentateuchal Research*, ed. Matthias Armgardt, Benjamin Kilchör, and Markus Zehnder, BZAR 22 [Wiesbaden: Harrassowitz, 2019], 179–188, esp. 182–183): "The transcribed Torah could assume Moses' function of mediating the divine will." Thus, passages in which Moses himself clearly plays the role of mediator predate the Pentateuchal Redaction and function as a *terminus ad quem* of the P–non-P Hexateuch.
35. Weinfeld, *Deuteronomy and the Deuteronomic School*, 8 n. 2, 313–316.
36. For additional discussion of Numbers 36 (as linked to Numbers 27) as a text of the late Persian period, see Christian Frevel, "The Book of Numbers—Formation, Composition and Interpretation of a Late Part of the Torah. Some Introductory Remarks," in *Torah and the Book of Numbers*, ed. Christian Frevel, Thomas Pola, and Aaron Schart, FAT II 62 (Tübingen: Mohr Siebeck, 2013), 1–37, esp. 26, n. 99.
37. Jacob Milgrom, *Leviticus 1–16: A New Translation with Introduction and Commentary*, AB (New York: Doubleday, 1991), 688.
38. In exodus contexts, Deuteronomy prefers יצא in *hiphil*. "In Dtr and other Deuteronomically authored or edited texts, however, הלע predominates, although יצא also occurs, and there are places where both occur together." See Blenkinsopp, "Deuteronomic Contribution," 96–97.

39. Milgrom, *Leviticus*, 688; Baruch A. Levine, *Leviticus*, JPS Torah Commentary (Philadelphia: JPS, 1989), 72. Regarding the concept of holiness in Leviticus, P absorbed a distinct strand of holiness teaching, the H material, that was joined to it at a point relatively early in the Persian period, before the P tradition was integrated into a larger narrative of Israel's origins. For more on the dating of H relative to P, see Richard J. Bautch, *Glory and Power, Ritual and Relationship: The Mosaic Covenant in the Postexilic Period*, LHBOTS 471 (New York: T&T Clark, 2009), 54–57.
40. That is, the concept of holiness was not unique to the Priestly writings and is also attested in Deuteronomy. See Reinhard Achenbach, "Zur Systematik der Speisegebote in Leviticus 11 und in Deuteronomium 14," *ZABR* (2011): 161–209, esp. 187. Whereas Achenbach argues cogently that Leviticus is dependent on Deuteronomy, Benjamin Kilchör and others maintain the priority of Leviticus. See Kilchör's *Mosetora und Jahwetora: Das Verhältnis von Deuteronomium 12–26 zu Exodus, Levitikus und Numeri*, BZAR 21 (Wiesbaden: Harrassowitz, 2015), 97–108. The literary relationship between these two texts remains a point of discussion.
41. Jacob Milgrom, *Leviticus 17–22: A New Translation with Introduction and Commentary*, AB3A (New Haven: Yale University Press, 2000), 1759, 1767.
42. See H. Holzinger, *Einleitung in den Hexateuch* [Tübingen: JCB Mohr (Paul Siebeck), 1893], 412, 444. More recently, Richard J. Bautch, "'Holy Seed': Ezra 9–10 and the Formation of the Pentateuch," in *The Formation of the Pentateuch: Bridging the Academic Cultures of Israel, Europe, and North America*, ed. J. C. Gertz et al., FAT 111 (Tübingen: Mohr Siebeck, 2016), 521–538.
43. Weinfeld notes that the teaching on clean and unclean animals in Lev 20:25 (and the surrounding verses that provide context) emphasizes the sacral character of the law, while Deuteronomy in general "rests on a distinctively secular foundation" and legislates all law as civil law. He offers a paradigm in which P/H and D are two theological schools, the former theocentric and the latter anthropocentric. *Deuteronomy and the Deuteronomic School*, 187–189.
44. Christophe Nihan argues along these lines in his analysis of Lev 20:22–26; he describes the concept of holiness embedded in the Holiness legislation as "different from the one laid out in D." Specifically, holiness in H does not extend beyond the boundaries of the sanctuary to the entire community. "As a result, H, contrary to D, does posit a difference between the holiness of the priests and the holiness of the rest of the community, which is evident, for instance, in the fact that the consumption of carcasses of dead animals is formally prohibited for the priests [Lev 22:8] because of their elevated holiness but not for the lay members of the community." Christophe Nihan, "The Laws about Clean and Unclean Animals in Leviticus and Deuteronomy and Their Place in the Formation of the Pentateuch," in *The Pentateuch: International Perspectives on Current Research*, ed. Thomas B. Dozeman, Konrad Schmid, and Baruch J. Schwartz, FAT 78 (Tübingen: Mohr Siebeck, 2011), 401–432, esp. 428–429, n. 59.
45. Wellhausen, *Die Composition des Hexateuchs*, 150–151; Kuenen, *A Historico-Critical Inquiry*, 266–267.
46. Baruch J. Schwartz, "The Prohibition Concerning the 'Eating' of Blood in Leviticus 17," in *Priesthood and Cult in Ancient Israel*, ed. Gary A. Anderson and Saul Olyan, JSOTSup 125 (Sheffield: Sheffield Academic Press, 1991), 43.
47. Julia Rhyder, *Centralizing the Cult: The Holiness Legislation in Leviticus 17–26*, FAT 134 (Tübingen: Mohr Siebeck, 2019), 208.

48. Rhyder, *Centralizing the Cult*, 249.
49. Rhyder, *Centralizing the Cult*, 228.
50. Rhyder, *Centralizing the Cult*, 225.
51. Rhyder, *Centralizing the Cult*, 226.
52. Rhyder, *Centralizing the Cult*, 192.
53. Rhyder, *Centralizing the Cult*, 255.
54. Eckart Otto, *Deuteronomium 12-34: 12:1-23:15*, HThKAT (Freiburg: Herder, 2016), 1163-1165.
55. Note how in this ruling one who slaughters a sacrificial animal away from the cult is guilty of bloodshed and liable to banishment.
56. Schmid, "Late Persian Formation," 240. See also Konrad Schmid, *Schriftgelehrte Traditionsliteratur Fallstudien zur innerbiblischen Schriftauslegung im Alten Testament*, FAT 101 (Tübingen: Mohr Siebeck, 2011), 160.
57. Schmid, "Late Persian Formation," 240.
58. Schmid, "Late Persian Formation," 249.
59. Illustrative is the case of 2 Chr 35:13, which describes the roasting of the Passover lamb with fire as well as a boiling of the offerings in pots, caldrons, and pans. It is noteworthy that the lamb is *both* roasted over fire "according to the ordinance" *and* boiled before serving. The P source stipulates roasting (Exod 12:8-9), whereas the D source calls for boiling the lamb (Deut 16:7). In Chronicles, the redundant process of preparation indicates that the Chronicler knew both the D and P legal traditions and sought to harmonize the two, because those two sources had by this point both been included in the version of a narrative of origins that was then current.
60. Raik Heckl has demonstrated that the Pentateuchal Redaction involved the incorporation of explicitly priestly texts such as Num 6:24-27 in order to claim that Aaron and his sons receive from YHWH an authority commensurate with that conferred upon Moses. Thus, the Aaronic blessing comes to support "a view of successive composition of the priestly books of the Pentateuch in their finished form." See his "The Aaronic Blessing (Numbers 6): Its Intention and Place in the Concept of the Pentateuch," in *On Dating Biblical Texts to the Persian Period: Discerning Criteria and Establishing Epochs*, ed. Richard J. Bautch and Mark Laskowski, FAT II 101 (Tübingen: Mohr Siebeck, 2019), 119-138, esp. 136.
61. Otto, "Deuteronomy as Legal Completion," 180.
62. Schmid, "Late Persian Formation," 247.
63. Otto, "Deuteronomy as Legal Completion," 182.
64. Otto, "Deuteronomy as Legal Completion," 183.
65. See Johann Wolfgang von Goethe's poem "Der Zauberlehrling." In the poem, an apprentice sorcerer is tasked with cleaning his master's workshop; to lighten his workload, he casts a magic spell on a broom so that it will carry pails of water for him. Because the apprentice is unskilled, his spell goes awry and the churlish broom brings so much water that it floods the workshop. Chaos ensures until the master reappears and restores order.
66. Eckart Otto, "Jeremia und die Tora. Ein nachexilischer Diskurs," in *Die Tora: Studien zum Pentateuch. Gesammelte Schriften*, ed. Eckart Otto (Wiesbaden: Harrassowitz, 2009), 515-560.
67. See Benedetta Rossi, "Conflicting Patterns of Revelation. Jer 31:33-34 and Its Challenge to the Post-Mosaic Revelation Program," *Bib* 99, no. 2 (2018): 202-225.

68. Bernard M. Levinson, "Introduction to Deuteronomy," in *Engaging Torah: Modern Perspectives on the Hebrew Bible*, ed. Walter Homolka and Aaron Panken (Cincinnati: Hebrew Union College Press, 2018), 61–76, esp. 73–74.
69. Levinson, "Introduction to Deuteronomy," 74.
70. Joachim J. Krause, "Post mortem Mosi: Conceptualizing Leadership in the Book of Joshua," in *Debating Authority, Concepts of Leadership in the Pentateuch and the Former Prophets*, ed. Katharina Pyschny and Sarah Schulz, BZAW 507 (Berlin: De Gruyter, 2018), 193–205, esp. 198–199.
71. Krause, "Post mortem Mosi," 199.
72. Like the classic Documentary Hypothesis, the Neo-Documentarian approach maintains that J and E were written earlier in the monarchic period while Deuteronomy, the second law, was later. Thus, influence and literary dependence travels linearly in one direction following the course of history. As a result, the Deuteronomic editing of materials in Genesis, argued here in the section titled "Textual Evidence of the Deuteronomic (Non-P) Hexateuch," is largely suspect among the Neo-Documentarians. It is more likely, Joel Baden counters, that the D author reworked passages and "amplified the linguistic and stylistic formulations of his predecessors." As a result, the Genesis passages are essentially "Yahwistic" or "Elohistic" and should be referred to as such, rather than "Deuteronomic." See Joel S. Baden, *The Promise to the Patriarchs* (Oxford: Oxford University Press, 2013), 34. Another aspect of the Neo-Documentarians' reconstruction is that the influence of J and E is asserted in Deuteronomy. For example, Jeffrey Stackert holds that D's view of Mosaic prophecy (e.g., Deut 1:9–18; 5:27–28; 13:2–6; 18:15–22) builds upon the presentations of such prophecy in its sources, J and E. In the case of Deut 13:26, Stackert argues that the verses are intentionally modeled upon the E story in Exod 3:9–13, which D is said to allude to and reference implicitly, as opposed to a more direct "lemmatic style of citation." Jeffrey Stackert, "Mosaic Prophecy and the Deuteronomic Source of the Torah," in *Deuteronomy in the Pentateuch, Hexateuch, and the Deuteronomistic History*, ed. Konrad Schmid and Raymond F. Person, Jr., FAT II 56 (Tübingen: Mohr Siebeck, 2012), 47–63, esp. 54–57, n. 30.
73. The current of scholars associated with the post-Priestly category is too widespread to describe in detail, and it includes names that have been cited prominently in this chapter, such as Thomas Römer and Konrad Schmid. Post-Priestly is not a cohort or a school; it is rather an assessment that speaks to the literary and historical character of a given biblical text. Illustrative is Genesis 15, which has been presented here (in the section "Textual Evidence of the Deuteronomic (Non-P) Hexateuch") as evidence that Deuteronomic editing (in Gen 15:18–21) took place early in the Persian period, prior to the formation of the P/non-P Hexateuch. Recently, some scholars have taken a different view of Genesis 15 and designated it as a post-Priestly addition. In this analysis, Genesis 15 is unitary and contains a significant amount of P material (e.g., Gen 15:7, understood as a reference to the P tradition that Abraham entered Canaan from Ur of the Chaldeans). Crucially, the text is said to be later than the fifth century and not pre-Priestly but rather a post-Priestly supplement to the Pentateuch. See, for example, Thomas Römer, "Abraham and the 'Law and the Prophets,'" in *The Reception and Remembrance of Abraham*, ed. Pernille Carstens and Niels Peter Lemche (Piscataway: Georgias, 2011), 94; Konrad Schmid, *Genesis and the Moses Story: Israel's Dual Origins in the Hebrew Bible*, tr. James Nogalski, Siphrut 3 (Winona Lake: Eisenbrauns, 2010), 158–160.
74. Nihan, "Laws about Clean and Unclean Animals," 432.

Bibliography

Achenbach, Reinhard. "Zur Systematik der Speisegebote in Leviticus 11 und in Deuteronomium 14." *Zeitschrift für Altorientalische und Biblische Rechtsgeschichte / Journal for Ancient Near Eastern and Biblical Law* 17 (2011): 161–209.

Albertz, Rainer. "Die erstmalig Konstituierung des Pentateuch durch die spat-deuteronomistiche Redaktionsschict (K^D bzw D)." In *Eigensinn und Entstehung der Hebräische Bibel. Erhard Blum zum siebstigen Geburtstag*, edited by J. J. Krause, W. Oswald, and K. Weingart, 129–145. Forschungen zum Alten Testament 136. Tübingen: Mohr Siebeck, 2020.

Baden, Joel S. *The Promise to the Patriarchs*. Oxford: Oxford University Press, 2013.

Bautch, Richard J. *Glory and Power, Ritual and Relationship: The Mosaic Covenant in the Postexilic Period*. The Library of Hebrew Bible/Old Testament Studies 471. New York: T&T Clark, 2009.

Bautch, Richard J. "'Holy Seed': Ezra 9–10 and the Formation of the Pentateuch." In *The Formation of the Pentateuch: Bridging the Academic Cultures of Israel, Europe, and North America*, edited by J. C. Gertz et al., 521–538. Forschungen zum Alten Testament 111. Tübingen: Mohr Siebeck, 2016.

Bautch, Richard J. "The Altar not Destroyed in Deuteronomy 16:21." *Journal for the Study of the Old Testament* 40, no. 3 (2016): 321–336.

Becking, Bob. *Ezra-Nehemiah*. Historical Commentary on the Old Testament. Leuven: Peeters, 2018.

Blenkinsopp, Joseph. "Deuteronomic Contribution to the Narrative in Genesis-Numbers: A Test Case." In *Those Elusive Deuteronomists: The Phenomenon of Pan-Deuteronomism*, edited by L. S. Schearing and S. L. McKenzie, 84–115. Journal for the Study of the Old Testament Supplement Series 268. Sheffield: Sheffield Academic Press, 1999.

Blenkinsopp, Joseph. *The Pentateuch: An Introduction to the First Five Books of the Bible*. Anchor Bible Reference Library. New York: Doubleday, 1992.

Blum, Erhard. "Zwischen Literarkritik und Stilkritik. Die diachrone Analyse der literarischen Verbindung von Genesis und Exodus—im Gespräch mit Ludwig Schmidt." *Zeitschrift fur die altestamentliche Wissenschaft* 124, no. 4 (2012): 492–515.

Carr, David M. *Reading the Fractures of Genesis: Historical and Literary Approaches*. Louisville: Westminster John Knox, 1996.

Carr, David M. "Strong and Weak Cases and Criteria for Establishing the Post-Priestly Character of Hexateuchal Material." In *The Post-Priestly Pentateuch: New Perspectives on Its Redactional Development and Theological Profiles*, edited by F. Giuntoli and K. Schmid, 19–34. Forschungen zum Alten Testament 101. Tübingen: Mohr Siebeck, 2015.

Carr, David M. *The Formation of the Hebrew Bible: A New Reconstruction*. New York: Oxford University Press, 2011.

Cook, Stephen L. *Reading Deuteronomy: A Literary and Theological Commentary*. Macon: Smyth and Helwys, 2015.

Dozeman, Thomas B. *The Pentateuch: Introducing the Torah*. Minneapolis: Fortress, 2017.

Frevel, Christian. "The Book of Numbers—Formation, Composition and Interpretation of a Late Part of the Torah. Some Introductory Remarks." In *Torah and the Book of Numbers*, edited by C. Frevel, T. Pola, and A. Schart, 1–37. Forschungen zum Alten Testament II 62. Tübingen: Mohr Siebeck, 2013.

Graf, Karl Heinrich "Die s.g. Grundschrift des Pentateuchs." *Archiv für die wissenschaftliche Erforschung des Alten Testaments* 1, no. 4 (1869): 466–477.

Heckl, Raik. "The Aaronic Blessing (Numbers 6): Its Intention and Place in the Concept of the Pentateuch." In *On Dating Biblical Texts to the Persian Period: Discerning Criteria and Establishing Epochs*, edited by R. J. Bautch and M. Laskowski, 119–138. Forschungen zum Alten Testament II 101. Tübingen: Mohr Siebeck, 2019.

Holzinger, Heinrich. *Einleitung in den Hexateuch*. Tübingen: JCB Mohr (Paul Siebeck), 1893.

Kilchör, Benjamin. *Mosetora und Jahwetora: Das Verhältnis von Deuteronomium 12–26 zu Exodus, Levitikus und Numeri*. Beihefte zur Zeitschrift für altorientalische und biblische Rechtsgeschichte 21. Wiesbaden: Harrassowitz, 2015.

Krause, Joachim J. "Post mortem Mosi: Conceptualizing Leadership in the Book of Joshua." In *Debating Authority, Concepts of Leadership in the Pentateuch and the Former Prophets*, edited by K. Pyschny and S. Schulz, 193–205. Beihefte zur Zeitschrift fur die alttestaentliche Wissenschaft 507. Berlin: De Gruyter, 2018.

Kuenan, Abraham. *An Historico-Critical Inquiry into the Origin and Composition of the Hexateuch*. London: Macmillan, 1886.

Levin, Christoph. "The Yahwist: The Earliest Editor in the Pentateuch." *Journal of Biblical Literature* 126, no. 2 (2007): 209–230.

Levine, Baruch A. *Leviticus*. Jewish Publication Society Torah Commentary. Philadelphia: JPS, 1989.

Levinson, Bernard M. "Esarhaddon's Succession Treaty as the Source for the Canon Formula in Deut 13:1." *Journal of the American Oriental Society* 130, no. 3 (2010): 337–347.

Levinson, Bernard M. "Introduction to Deuteronomy." In *Engaging Torah: Modern Perspectives on the Hebrew Bible*, edited by W. Homolka and A. Panken, 61–76. Cincinnati: Hebrew Union College Press, 2018.

Milgrom, Jacob. *Leviticus 1–16: A New Translation with Introduction and Commentary*. Anchor Bible 3. New York: Doubleday, 1991.

Milgrom, Jacob. *Leviticus 17–22: A New Translation with Introduction and Commentary*. Anchor Bible volume 3A New Haven: Yale University Press, 2000.

Nihan, Christophe. "The Laws about Clean and Unclean Animals in Leviticus and Deuteronomy and Their Place in the Formation of the Pentateuch." In *The Pentateuch: International Perspectives on Current Research*, edited by T. B. Dozeman, K. Schmid, and B. J. Schwartz, 401–432. Forschungen zum Alten Testament 78. Tübingen: Mohr Siebeck, 2011.

Otto, Eckart. *Deuteronomium 12–34: 12:1–23:15*. Herders Theologischer Kommentar zum Alten Testament. Freiburg: Herder, 2016.

Otto, Eckart. "Deuteronomy as the Legal Completion and Prophetic Finale of the Pentateuch." In *Paradigm Change in Pentateuchal Research*, edited by M. Armgardt, B. Kilchör, and M. Zehnder, 179–188. Beihefte zur Zeitschrift für altorientalische und biblische Rechtsgeschichte 22. Wiesbaden: Harrassowitz, 2019.

Otto, Eckart. "Jeremia und die Tora. Ein nachexilischer Diskurs." In *Die Tora: Studien zum Pentateuch. Gesammelte Schriften*, edited by E. Otto, 515–560. Wiesbaden: Harrassowitz, 2009.

Otto, Eckart. "The Integration of the Post-exilic Book of Deuteronomy." In *The Post-Priestly Pentateuch: New Perspectives on its Redactional Development and Theological Profiles*, edited by F. Giuntoli and K. Schmid, 331–341. Forschungen zum Alten Testament 101. Tübingen: Mohr Siebeck, 2015.

Rhyder, Julia. *Centralizing the Cult: The Holiness Legislation in Leviticus 17–26*. Forschungen zum Alten Testament 134. Tübingen: Mohr Siebeck, 2019.

Römer, Thomas. "Abraham and the 'Law and the Prophets.'" In *The Reception and Remembrance of Abraham*, edited by P. Carstens and N. P. Lemche, 87–102. Piscataway: Gorgias Press, 2011.

Römer, Thomas. "Cult Centralization in Deuteronomy." In *Das Deuteronomian zwischen Pentateuch und Deuteronomistischem Geschichtswerk*, edited by E. Otto and R. Achenbach, 168–180. Forschungen zur Religion und Literatur des Alten und Neuen Testaments 206. Göttingen: Vandenhoeck & Ruprecht, 2004.

Rossi, Benedetta. "Conflicting Patterns of Revelation. Jer 31:33–34 and Its Challenge to the Post-Mosaic Revelation Program." *Biblica* 99, no. 2 (2018): 202–225.

Schmid, Konrad. *Genesis and the Moses Story: Israel's Dual Origins in the Hebrew Bible*, translated by J. Nogalski. Siphrut: Literature and Theology of the Hebrew Scriptures 3. Winona Lake: Eisenbrauns, 2010.

Schmid, Konrad. "How to Identify a Persian Period Text in the Pentateuch." In *On Dating Biblical Texts to the Persian Period: Discerning Criteria and Establishing Epochs*, edited by R. J. Bautch and M. Lackowski, 101–118. Forschungen zum Alten Testament II 101. Tübingen: Mohr Siebeck, 2019.

Schmid, Konrad. *Schriftgelehrte Traditionsliteratur Fallstudien zur innerbiblischen Schriftauslegung im Alten Testament.* Forschungen zum Alten Testament 101. Tübingen: Mohr Siebeck, 2011.

Schmid, Konrad. "The Late Persian Formation of the Torah: Observations on Deuteronomy 34." In *Judah and the Judeans in the Fourth Century B.C.E.*, edited by O. Lipschits, G. N. Knoppers, and R. Albertz, 237–251. Winona Lake: Eisenbrauns, 2007.

Schwartz, Baruch J. "The Prohibition Concerning the 'Eating' of Blood in Leviticus 17." In *Priesthood and Cult in Ancient Israel*, edited by G. A. Anderson and S. Olyan, 34–66. Journal for the Study of the Old Testament Supplement Series 125. Sheffield: Sheffield Academic Press, 1991.

Schniedewind, William. *How the Bible Became a Book: The Textualization of Ancient Israel.* Cambridge: Cambridge University Press, 2004.

Smith-Christopher, Daniel. *A Biblical Theology of Exile*. Minneapolis: Fortress, 2002.

Stackert, Jeffrey. "Mosaic Prophecy and the Deuteronomic Source of the Torah." In *Deuteronomy in the Pentateuch, Hexateuch, and the Deuteronomistic History*, edited by K. Schmid and R. F. Person, Jr., 47–63. Forschungen zum Alten Testament II 56. Tübingen: Mohr Siebeck, 2012.

Van Seters, John. "Joshua 24 and the Problem of Tradition in the Old Testament." In *In the Shelter of Elyon: Essays on Ancient Palestinian Life and Literature in Honor of G. W. Ahlström*, edited by W. B. Barrick and J. R. Spencer, 139–158. Journal for the Study of the Old Testament Supplement Series 31. Sheffield: Journal for the Study of the Old Testament Supplement Series Press, 1984.

Weinfeld, Moshe. *Deuteronomy and the Deuteronomic School*. Oxford: Clarendon Press, 1972.

Wellhausen, Julius. *Die Composition des Hexateuchs und der historischen Bücher des Alten Testaments*, 3rd ed. Berlin: Reimer, 1899; 4th ed. Berlin: de Gruyter, 1963.

CHAPTER 20

DEUTERONOMY, THE DEUTERONOMISTIC HISTORY, AND THE BOOKS OF JOSHUA THROUGH KINGS

RANNFRID I. LASINE THELLE

DEUTERONOMISTIC HISTORY HYPOTHESIS OF MARTIN NOTH

MARTIN Noth first presented the Deuteronomistic History (DH) hypothesis in *Überliefe rungsgeschichtliche Studien* (1943). In this seminal work, Noth argues that Deuteronomy, Joshua, Judges, Samuel, and Kings were written as a unified work of history by one single author around 560 BCE. Relying on existing sources, the Deuteronomistic historian created this work to present a coherent, unified history from the conquest through the time of the Judges, the time of the monarchy, and the eventual demise of the Northern and Southern Kingdoms. The historian was named "Deuteronomist" (Dtr) by Noth because he believed that this writer combined the law collection of Deuteronomy and other sources to form one ideologically unified work.

Although published in 1943 during World War II in Königsberg, then still a part of Germany, Noth's work did not become widely known until after the publication of the second edition in 1957, and in English as *The Deuteronomistic History* (1981). His approach was that of tradition history, which was interested in tracing the development of concepts and ideas through time. In many ways, Noth preempted the methods of redaction criticism and *Fortschreibung* (updating), which focuses on the growth of texts by editorial additions to an original textual kernel.

Noth's thesis builds on a few established positions. First, he assumes the existence of an *Urdeuteronomium* (proto-Deuteronomy). He takes as a given that "Josiah's law is the same as the basic text of Dt" (Noth 1991, 124; Dt = Deuteronomy in Noth's writings), but that Deuteronomy's limitation of worship to one cult site comes across as disproportionately central in Kings' records of Josiah's actions. Noth goes on to claim that all the law was important to Josiah, even though the biblical record does not specify it. The key point for Noth is that the Deuteronomist incorporated Deuteronomy as the introduction to his history. By doing this, the Deuteronomist gave the law a key role in the conception of history, as a yardstick for judging human conduct. Noth says this at the end of his book, and although he does not highlight the content of the law code of Deuteronomy, it is an underlying assumption throughout.

The dating of some form of Deuteronomy to the seventh century has been fundamental in Pentateuchal scholarship, and thus also to the DH hypothesis. A long tradition identified the law book found in the temple (2 Kgs 22:8) with the Torah (Montgomery and Gehman 1986, 534–544). W. M. L. de Wette's proposal that the book that Hilkiah found was some form of Deuteronomy, constituted a breakthrough in scholarship (Paul 1988). Deuteronomy was not an ancient book written by Moses but a document contemporary with King Josiah. De Wette's claim has been referred to by many as an "Archimedean point" in biblical literature (Weinfeld 1967, 249–250; 1992, 16; Paul 1985; Eißfeldt 1965).

Noth's work built on the results of earlier source criticism, most notably the documentary hypothesis. In further developing the insights of de Wette, Vatke, Reuss, Graf, and others, Julius Wellhausen had formulated the classic documentary hypothesis (Wellhausen 1899, 1905). Observing that "cultic centralization" as expressed in Deuteronomy 12 was not a concern of the prophets in either the prophetic books or in the Former Prophets until late in the monarchic period, Wellhausen dated Deuteronomy to the seventh century and the Priestly law to the sixth century BCE. The idea of "cultic centralization," a term used by Wellhausen, is a centerpiece in this dating scheme that held the main ground of scholarship until recently (Thelle 2012, 4–9).

The identification of Deuteronomy as a separate source then led scholars to distinguish a D-source in other books (e.g., Driver 1903, 166–185; Eißfeldt 1934; Römer and de Pury, 2000, 35–40). Source critical studies operated with various understandings of Deuteronomistic redactions of the books of Judges, Samuel, and Kings, as well as prophetic books. Common to this relegation of material to a later redactor was the lack of value placed on the "late," "Deuteronomistic" additions (Duhm 1901). In the post-Noth developments of the DH hypothesis, discussed below, the emphasis moved to these redactional additions, impacted by tradition historical studies that, for example, pointed out the importance of the language of covenant in Deuteronomy (Moran 1963; Schmidt 1965; Wolff 1985; Thiel 1973, 1981).

Some scholars have labeled as "deuteronomic" material that pertained to and was influenced by Deuteronomy. That which had to do with a later "school" is called "Deuteronomistic." Nevertheless, these terms have not been used consistently and therefore become confusing. Sometimes the term "deuteronomic" has been applied to the book of Deuteronomy and "Deuteronomistic" to Joshua–Kings. The labels have been applied to sources, redactions, and authors. Even scholars taking a literary approach to the relationship of Deuteronomy to Joshua–Kings have applied the terminology of Deuteronomist, Deuteronomistic, and deuteronomic in various ways (Polzin 1980).

Two clusters of scholarly assumptions are foundational for Noth's DH hypothesis and many of its subsequent iterations. One centers on the idea of a historical religious reform under Josiah (2 Kgs 22–23) and involves identifying the law book found in the temple (2 Kgs 22:8) with some form of Deuteronomy. This position usually entails the dating of some form of Deuteronomy to the seventh century. Scholars understand the narratives involving Josiah (2 Kgs 22–23) as reflecting historical efforts to reform the cult according to the prescripts of

Deuteronomy. Others argue that Deuteronomy was composed during this period to justify the reforms of Josiah, if not the reforms of Hezekiah (Handy 1995; Albertz 2005). The historicity of a reform is assumed. Even scholars who see the reform of Josiah as fictional, or date the reform and/or Deuteronomy to a later period, usually relate it to a historical development that occasioned the need for such a narrative (Römer 2005, 49–56).

Through its identification with the book found by Josiah, therefore, Deuteronomy functions as a key to the literary history of the Bible. This in turn provided a cornerstone in the reconstruction of ancient Israelite history, thus the designation as "Archimedean point"—a point of reference for the reconstruction of the dates of origin for the traditions which make up the Pentateuch—given to Deuteronomy and its connection to Josiah. These assumptions are deeply linked with the problem of dating (Preuss 1982; Lohfink 1993; O'Brien 1995; Eynikel 1996, 7–31). One exception to the usual line of argument is Kratz, who does not connect the dating of Deuteronomy to Josiah's reform but thinks the connection between the two is secondary. He argues for the possibility of both a seventh-century date and an early exilic date for *Urdeuteronomium* but leans toward the latter (Kratz 2005, 131–132).

The other cluster concerns the idea of a Deuteronomistic author, school, or movement connected in some way to this reform. This author(s) or scribal school may either have been historically involved with the reform, have later been inspired by it, or have invented it to support the theology expressed in the unified historical work termed DH, which the author(s) wrote or successively edited.

These two sets of positions are now seriously under question, although they also continue to be alive and well: in academic textbooks, commentaries, and study Bibles, and through the assumptions and language that permeate discourse on Joshua–Kings and other books.

Since Noth, the idea of a unified "Deuteronomistic History" gained ground and has dominated scholarly discourse "until this day." Countless renderings and reconstructions of the compositional history of a unified work of history encompassing some form of Deuteronomy–Kings have been put forth (Römer 2005, 13–41). It was modified endlessly, yet Noth's thesis has become one of the most established axioms of biblical research, although there were a few who rejected parts of it (Eißfeldt 1965; Fohrer 1968, 193–195).

Post-Noth Developments

Scholars developed the DH hypothesis in two main directions following Noth. In the United States, the theory of two editions came to be widely accepted. The "double redaction" or "block" hypothesis departed from Noth by dating a first version of the DH to the seventh century. It solved the problem posed by the existence of both positive and negative views of the monarchy by proposing that the original narrative was later supplemented after the fall of Judah. First proposed by Heinrich Ewald already in the mid-nineteenth century, the main proponents of this idea are Frank Moore-Cross and Richard Nelson and their successors, often referred to as the "Cross School" or "Harvard School" (Römer and de Pury 2000, 35–38; Cross 1973, 274–289; Nelson 1981; Knoppers 1993–1994).

In Germany in particular, a second development of the DH hypothesis suggested several successive redactions of the DH. Often referred to as the "Göttingen School," it accepted the exilic dating of Noth but added more and more redactional layers. This direction disagrees with Noth mainly regarding his claim of a single author with very few additions (Smend 1971). From Noth's Dtr, Rudolf Smend distinguished a second redactor concerned with the law and called it DtrN (N = nomistic redactor). Smend called the first, basic historian DtrH (H = historian). With this elaboration, Smend agreed with Noth about dating the DH to the exilic period, and so disagrees with the Cross School on this point. Following Smend's model, scholars such as W. Dietrich and T. Veijola developed further criteria for distinguishing more redactional layers, including a prophetic redactor, DtrP (Dietrich 1972; Veijola 1975; Römer and de Pury 2000, 67–74).

A third tendency is that of a shrinking DH, which agrees with Noth's basic thesis of one single author in the exilic period but considers many blocks of text to be later additions. For example, Van Seters is in basic agreement with Noth in seeing the Deuteronomistic historian as a single author in the exilic period but argues that what he calls the "Court History" (2 Sam. 10–20; 1 Kgs 1–2) and the Elisha narratives were later, post-Deuteronomistic additions. A similar position is argued by McKenzie (Van Seters 1983; McKenzie 1991).

More recently, the idea of an even later Persian period diaspora redaction has gained ground. It combines the Göttingen School approach of several redactions with the idea of a later addition of prophetic materials in Kings from the "neo-Nothians" (Römer 2005, 31). According to Römer, the DH existed for a time as a unified work consisting of Deuteronomy–Kings, until Deuteronomy was severed from Joshua–Kings to be joined with the priestly work Genesis–Numbers to form the Pentateuch.

Despite the many developments of Noth's thesis, in general, the idea of a unified Deuteronomistic work of history replaced the source critical understanding of the genesis of Joshua–Kings (Westermann 1994). After a couple of decades, however, discussions that had begun to undermine the classical documentary hypothesis also came to have an impact on the DH hypothesis. Intense discussions about the relationship between the DH and the Pentateuch have led to more attempts to reconstruct the growth of texts and their redactions into larger units (Schmid 2006; Römer 2004; Schmitt 2004; Aurelius 2003; Kratz 2005). The DH came to be discussed within the larger context of the Primary History, or Enneateuch, to account for the compositional history of Genesis–Kings (Schmid 2006; Dozeman, Römer, and Schmid 2011). Although Deuteronomy may appear to have been ignored by the Pentateuchal studies which focused narrowly on the first four books, the Tetrateuch, these developments brought Deuteronomy back into the context of Pentateuch and Torah.

Among these developments that have impacted approaches to the DH is the tendency in Pentateuchal research to date the Yahwist to a much later date than in the original documentary hypothesis (Schmid 1976; Rendtorff 1980; Van Seters 1975). This led to renewed discussions regarding the relationship between the "Yahwist" and the "Deuteronomist," even to the point of equating the two (Rose 1981; Blum 1990) or posing that the Yahwist had been influenced by the Deuteronomist. Some scholars have suggested doing away with the Yahwist altogether (Dozeman and Schmid 2006; Ellens and Greene 2009).

The Pentateuch, it is proposed, is the product of a "debate," beginning in the exilic and into the Persian period, between two major "schools of thought" or scribal schools, the "Priestly" and the "Deuteronomistic" (Blum 1990; Römer 2005, 178–183; Otto 2007). This way of framing the issue seems to be a variant of the idea of a "nomistic" redaction of the

DH. It also involves ideas about the formation of the Pentateuch as the result of the combining of a D-composition and a P-composition, a "historical compromise" between priestly and the Deuteronomistic Schools, or a "post-Priestly," scribal reworking of the Tetrateuch and Deuteronomy (Blum 1990; Römer 2005, 178–183; Otto 2007).

The very idea of a DH has also been subjected to increasing criticism, as has the usefulness of the terminology associated with this hypothesis (Clements 2004, 83–95; Rösel 2009). A major problem involves determining criteria for "Deuteronomism." The phenomenon of "Deuteronomism" is pervasive, but it is described in so many different ways that the idea of a "Deuteronomist" stands in danger of losing its meaning. Already in the nineteenth century, the term "Deuteronomist" was being used in more than one way and did not always seem to have any clear link to the book of Deuteronomy, or the conceived source of Deuteronomy. The various types of redaction activity assigned to "Deuteronomist(s)" are not coordinated with one another either, creating confusion for contemporary and later scholars. Over one hundred years ago Sigmund Mowinckel, in describing what he called the *source C* of Jeremiah—much of what Duhm had defined as Deuteronomistic—identified its authors with the "canonizers" (Mowinckel 1914). This view is like the idea of "redactors." The main difference between Mowinckel's time, when these authors were looked down on, and the last forty to fifty years is the value assigned to these "later" phases of composition, which are now deemed much more interesting.

The myriad revisions of Noth's thesis in various directions are in themselves a testimony to its problems. Further, arguments have been raised against the unity of the DH and the claim that the work constitutes a "history." Already early on, Ernst Sellin and Georg Fohrer preferred to see Deuteronomistic redactions of individual books and did not accept the idea of a unified history (Forher 1968, 202–236), and Arthur Weiser maintained that each book had its own distinct history and that there was no unified DH, although he did acknowledge a Deuteronomistic "environment" (Weiser 1966). Würthwein (1994, 1–11) and Westermann (1994) both warned against the idea of a Deuteronomistic History, and Eynikel (1996, 363–364) and Knauf (2000, 388–398) have come to similar conclusions. In addition, scholars such as Norbert Lohfink have questioned the existence of what has been called the "Deuteronomistic Movement" (Lohfink 1995, 313–382). However, in spite of the periodic criticism of, and objections to, the concept of the DH and even its pronounced demise (Childs 1979, 235–238; Rendtorff 1986), the number of reaffirmations of the DH hypothesis as well as the continued debate about both its pros and cons testify to the fact of its survival (O'Brien 1989; Schearing and McKenzie 1999; Römer 2000; Auld 1999; Nelson 2005, 319–337; Witte et al 2006; Geoghehan 2006, 96–118). The number of publications on various aspects of a DH and the Deuteronomistic redactions of biblical books is overwhelming. The Deuteronomistic History has become ingrained in commentaries and textbooks. Even some of the attempts to critically assess it and present an alternative theory or method retain the terminology (Veijola 2003; Noll 2007; Hjelm 2004, 10–15). The idea of a DH is still very much alive, although "Deuteronomistic" means so many different things that it is in danger of losing meaning (Wilson 1999, 77).

The many variants of the DH hypothesis attempt to explain the genesis of the present form of Deuteronomy–Kings. However, as a secondary effect, these approaches have imposed constraints on the reading of these books. Are there other options for exploring the relationship between Deuteronomy and the books of Joshua, Judges, Samuel, and Kings?

Beyond the Deuteronomistic History Hypothesis: Reading Deuteronomy with Joshua–Kings

Final-form readings and synchronic approaches to Deuteronomy and its relationship to Joshua–Kings have also flourished in the last fifty years. The pervasiveness of the DH hypothesis is seen in that even scholars who choose a final-form approach have often chosen to employ its language. Polzin, for example, cites heuristic concerns as his reason for choosing the term "Deuteronomic history" (Polzin 1980, 12–24). His trilogy, starting with *Moses and the Deuteronomist: A Literary Study of the Deuteronomic History*, takes Deuteronomy–Kings as a literary whole and labels the narrator/writer the "Deuteronomist."

Polzin's literary, synchronic, narrative analysis is an early example of the so-called literary turn in biblical studies. Partly as a reaction to the atomization of the text brought about by source, form, tradition, and redaction criticism, biblical scholars began taking inspiration from literary approaches, especially from the 1970s onward. This led to the production of narrative analyses and intertextual and structuralist readings, as well as postmodernist theoretical approaches and methods derived from the humanities and social sciences (Moore 2016).

Because there is so little agreement about the compositional history of the DH, the discussion of any topic that relies on diachronic analysis can become extremely complicated and dense, even for nonspecialists within biblical studies. The fact that the criteria for dating separate sources, traditions, or redactional layers are always conjectural leads to different results depending on which reconstruction is chosen. Few who master the plethora of theories can juggle them deftly enough to communicate smoothly to those outside the specialty. To some scholars, the reconstructed literary and compositional history serves as one of the pieces of a puzzle to reconstruct the political, religious, and social history of the monarchies of Israel and Judah (Knoppers 1993–1994). To others, it serves as a tool for reconstructing the postmonarchic process of identity formation for what emerged as Persian and Hellenistic period Judaism, both within Yehud and in the Diaspora (e.g., Davies 1992, 1998). However, the fragmentation that has resulted from separation into sources, additions, and redactions makes it difficult to determine which text is being read and goes quite contrary to the way most readers do read. Because many of the hypothetical reconstructions of the compositional history now serve as givens in secondary discussions of specific topics and themes such as leadership, prophecy and the role of prophets, priesthood, divine election, worship, land, and restoration, many of the assumptions on which these discussions are based become invisible. The fact that the DH hypotheses have shaped the premises for the examination of these themes or subjects in ways that are easily obscured is a challenge and a problem for the construction of knowledge.

For example, I have argued that Deuteronomy's concept of "chosen place" has been the victim of a captivity of sorts (Thelle 2012). Presuppositions of the DH hypothesis, constructed through source critical and redaction critical paradigms, have determined how the concept of "chosen place" has been understood. I argued that it is necessary to redescribe this biblical concept without becoming ensnared by issues such as the dating of

Deuteronomy, the idea of a historical religious reform in the time of Josiah, or the role of "centralization" in scholarship on the DH hypothesis. Although usually brought up within discussions of literary dependence or compositional growth of the Pentateuch, the fact that the idea of a central sanctuary is present in other books of the Pentateuch is often underplayed in discussions of the uniqueness of Deuteronomy. Even Wellhausen pointed out that the view of sanctuary in the legislation of Exodus, Leviticus, and Numbers reflects a "centralized" understanding (Wellhausen 1905, 34, 39; Nihan 2004). But if read as a part of the Pentateuch, Deuteronomy's insistence on the cult site as Yahweh's "chosen" site becomes Moses's interpretation of an existing vision of this sanctuary in "the land."

Synchronic, final-form readings of Deuteronomy in relation to Joshua–Kings approach the text as it has been received and try to make sense of it. Contradictions, competing perspectives, outright anachronisms, and obscurities in the text might very well be a result of the compositional history, but that history is almost always irretrievable and will always remain hypothetical. Synchronic final-form readings do not have to explain how the text came to find its shape but rather attempt to explore what meanings may be elicited from a text, explain how a text can mean certain things, and account for how readers read. Such readings do pay heed to textual variants and do acknowledge and make choices concerning manuscript traditions such as the Septuagint (LXX) and Massoretic Text (MT), for example. Further, such processes of exploration are cumulative, dialectical, intertextual, and composite. These types of readings follow a story but also discern a narrative universe. Beyond the narrative hooks connecting whole books into a consecutive sequence like "after the death of Moses," "after the death of Joshua," "after the death of Samuel," there are deeper, symbolic and paradigmatic connections between the books and between larger sections of narrative. Therefore, final-form readings are concerned both with linear-narrative-chronological features of the text as well as with thematic, symbolic, and paradigmatic dimensions, intertextual allusions, and concepts of background. Although not primarily concerned with historical questions, literary approaches are not necessarily ahistorical (Britt 2016).

Because of Deuteronomy's place in the Pentateuch/Torah, reading Deuteronomy in relation to Joshua, Judges, Samuel, and Kings will mean reading them in the larger context of the Primary History, or the Torah and Nevi'im. The term "Former Prophets" does not carry any reference to the DH hypothesis and is therefore perhaps a better term for the collection Joshua–Kings. However, it brings in the concept of the Jewish canon, an ideological aspect that is not always considered by those who opt for this term. The term "First Story" has been used in literary approaches to designate the whole of Genesis–Kings (Gunn 2016).

Read sequentially in the canonical order, Deuteronomy presents the first written, oral interpretation of torah. Deuteronomy 1:5 presents what will follow as Moses *undertaking to make plain* or *clear* (*ho'il be'er*) "this law." This event, including the words that the character Moses speaks, constitutes the explication of "this law." It is preserved in written form and is designated and presented as a book. Deuteronomy 31:24 narrates the event that Moses writes down "all the words of this law in a book," the law that is announced as about to be explicated in 1:5. It is the first oral torah.

Identifying with the narrative audience of Moses's speech, the Israelites who stand at the threshold to the promised land, readers and listeners (or ideal audience) will follow both the narrator's and Moses's rhetorical pointers. As Moses recalls the events of the "fathers" in the wilderness, readers identify the laws, statutes, and ordinances that he lays out, or explicates, with the revelation that Moses received at Horeb/Sinai, as recorded in Exodus, Leviticus, and Numbers. They paradoxically stand with Moses "on that day" when the narrative Israelite audience—not their ancestors, according to Moses—received the Decalogue (5:3). When Moses presents the laws and instructions collected in Deuteronomy 12–26, readers have been told multiple times that this is the torah, the laws and ordinances that they (the Israelites) must keep "when you cross the Jordan to possess the land that Yahweh your God is giving you." This conditional framework is constitutive of Deuteronomy.

Deuteronomy functions in several ways as a crucial book that connects Genesis–Numbers and Joshua–Kings. One can see this hinge-function independently of a historical, compositional process, although Deuteronomy has been ascribed such a key role in most redaction historical explanation (Römer 2016, 127). The very liminality of Deuteronomy (i.e., the threshold nature of the book) makes it a hinge in several senses besides functioning as a narrative or redactional "connector." It is a connector of time; the narrative "now" of Deuteronomy is always in the present, on the plains of Moab, even when the narrative present occasionally shifts to a time when they are already in the land, practicing the laws. Deuteronomy points back to the time of the ancestors and to Egypt, forward to a future "in the land," and warns of a possible future expulsion from the land. It is a connector of space, between outside and inside the land, between Sinai and Moab, between Egypt and Canaan. Laid out by Moses, "this law" is presented on the threshold, as the future conquerors and possessors of Yahweh's promised inheritance gaze upon the land. It is framed by Moses, who must remain outside. It is given to a people with a specific, already troubled past, one which brings with it a commitment they have made to their God. Yet the validity of the stipulations of that covenant is consigned to a space beyond and a time in the future.

In addition to narrative and rhetorical pointers, Deuteronomy has Moses recount specific past events to his audience, the second-generation Israelites. Moses repeatedly calls his audience to remember that they were once "a slave in the land of Egypt," a memory that serves as a powerful motivator for the Israelites to adhere to Yahweh and rejoice in the festivals (5:15; 15:15; 16:3, 12; 24:18, 22). Moses's retelling of the events that readers will recall from accounts in Exodus include Yahweh leading the Israelites in the wilderness, events at Horeb/Sinai with the Decalogue, and the golden calf episode, among others. Events narrated in Numbers that Deuteronomy has Moses spin in a particular way include the spies' episode and the conquests in the Transjordan. These evocations of the past, now controlled by Moses through his narration (Caleb and Joshua, the only survivors who could have set Moses straight, don't), set the stage for the new life of the people with the Law, in the land and without Moses. Looking back with the admonition "remember, do not forget" transforms the past by directing the audience to look forward.

Deuteronomy points forward specifically to the book of Joshua, where everything is done "as Yahweh had commanded by Moses." Joshua and his role as the one who will lead the people into the land is referenced numerous times (1:38; 3:28; 31:7–8, 14, 23; 34:9). The ritual prescribed in Deuteronomy (27) is fulfilled in Joshua (Josh. 8:31–36), which reports on its enactment.

Moses' spin on these past events has the possible outcome of leaving readers sympathizing with the Israelites. Moses is manipulative, blaming them for past wrongs without telling them of mitigating circumstances (spies' mission). He even blames the Israelites for his own punishment of not being allowed to enter the land. The privileged readers know all of this, yet the powerful tug of Moses' rhetoric and the narrator's presentation of his words as *torah* have a deep and persuasive effect. The idea that the land must be occupied and the inhabitants driven out is a major theme in Deuteronomy. It is the prime condition for the validity of everything that Moses is instructing them about the law, "when you enter the land and live in it . . . then you shall" (11:31–32). The fulfillment of this condition is the first major theme of the Former Prophets, taking up the majority of Joshua. In Deuteronomy and Joshua, the success of the Israelite tribes in possessing the land and dispossessing—if not slaughtering—the former inhabitants is predicated upon the Israelites' adherence to Yahweh. This overall impression remains despite ambivalence concerning the success of the settlement in Joshua (a theme greatly expanded in Judges).

One narrative thread that weaves connections between Deuteronomy and the books before and after it (in the narrative chronology) features Caleb son of Jephunneh. One of the "good" spies, he defends the favorable report about the land (Num. 13:30; 14:6–9). He is spared death and allowed to enter the land with Joshua (Num. 14:24, 30, 38). In Moses' recounting of the episode in Deuteronomy, Caleb's fidelity to Yahweh is given as the reason for this, without any detail, implying perhaps that his actions and speech in Numbers are judged by Moses to represent fidelity (Deut. 1:36). Moses does not mention the ten spies instigating the opposition to the plan. If relying on Moses' retelling in Deuteronomy, therefore, the second-generation on the plains of Moab is left to accept Moses' judgment on Caleb's character, unless one assumes other knowledge on their behalf. Joshua and Judges include what readers encounter as follow-up on Caleb's legacy, when these books narrate his settling of the territory of Judah. Caleb defeats the Anakim (who had frightened the spies in Numbers) and settles in Hebron, recorded as its own special episode in Joshua (14:6–15). The first tribe to have its settlement-story told, the description of Judah's boundaries (Josh. 15:1–12) is sandwiched between this and another Caleb episode (Josh. 15:13–19). The second episode involves Caleb, his nephew Othniel, and Caleb's daughter Achsah. Offered by Caleb as a bride for whomever attacks and settles Kiriath-Sepher, Achsah negotiates for herself a territory that includes springs (recalling Genesis episodes that combine marriage deals and wells). Even though the first notes signaling the incomplete conquest show up soon after (Josh. 15:63), the episode is recapped in Judg. 1:9–15 as a paradigmatically successful settlement narrative.

As a parallel to the Caleb episodes in Joshua, the land allotment to the tribe of Joseph (Ephraim) becomes the narrative junction for a short episode about the daughters of Zelophehad (Josh. 17:3–6). This takes up a narrative strand from Num. 27 and 36, invoking once more the theme of women as guarantors of land, contingent upon their agreeing to specific marriages which ensures that the land does not leave the tribe (a theme present also in Ruth). Together with the Caleb episodes, they exemplify the inextricable connection between women, tribal land, and the survival of the tribe, a theme that becomes paramount in Judg. 20–21.

According to Josh. 11:16–23, 21:43–45, and 22:1–6, the conquest, wiping out of inhabitants, and settlement are a complete success. But the book also leaves plenty of ambiguity as to the fulfillment, in scattered notices of people remaining in the land, as well as in the warnings against intermarrying (Josh. 23:7, 12–13). The unfulfilled mission of dispossessing the inhabitants of the land is the setting for Judges. Joshua may be contradict itself about the success of the conquest and settling, but Judges is clear that portions of land failed to be settled completely and there are towns where the inhabitants were not driven out.

How does this situation relate to the preconditions for Yahweh's protection and loyalty set down in Deuteronomy? Deuteronomy's precondition for the practice of the laws and ordinances is that the Israelites possess the land and drive out or annihilate the inhabitants and their cult. Judges systematically unveils the result of the conquest and settling: the tribes had not fulfilled the ḥerem, they had not driven out or annihilated the indigenous populations after all (Judg. 1:21–36).

In Judg. 2:1–5, a theophany reminiscent of Genesis occurs before an assembly of the people, where the angel of Yahweh reminds them of the covenant and accuses them of not having obeyed his command. As a result, Yahweh will not keep up his promise of driving out the nations. Instead, they will now be a snare and an adversary. In an ironic reversal of Deuteronomy's precondition for the institution of the Law, the lingering presence of the inhabitants of the land now becomes a handy explanation for a new situation (2:11–3:6). This portion of Judges shores up the ambiguities in Joshua by explaining that the people were loyal until the time of Joshua's death. This style of "reinterpretation" is not that different from Moses' representation of the events of the past to the Israelites on the plains of Moab.

In some sense, the rationalizations of Judg. 2:20–3:6 represent responses to the rigidity of Deuteronomy and the programmatic nature of the accounts of conquest and settlement in Joshua. These verses achieve the effect of abrogating Deuteronomy's conditionality while also providing a new interpretation that can deal with the admitted failure to do "as Yahweh had commanded by Moses." Judges deftly lays out explanations for the perpetual threat of apostasy, first experienced before the entry into the land (Num. 25), and combines them with the rationale that it was in fact God who purposely did not drive out all the inhabitants of the land (Judg. 2:20–22), in spite of his previous promises to do so. In this way, Judges combines rebellion and apostasy, deep issues in Exodus–Deuteronomy, with the "problem" of the incomplete conquest. The name of Moses is invoked in 3:4 as one of the few mentions within Judges, designating the "commandments of Yahweh" (*miṭvot yhwh*) as those which he "commanded their [referring to the successive generations of Israelites] ancestors by the hand of Moses."

The ingenious splicing of key strands at the beginning of Judges buttresses the rationale for its narrative cycles. It also smooths over the pivot that takes place, from the threat of foreign gods (Egypt) and departure from Yahweh (Baal Peor) to the Canaanite threat from within the land and the much closer "others." These include the Moabites, Midianites, Ammonites, and Philistines, as well as religious competition from the Baals and the Asherahs, the gods of the Canaanites, which soon becomes endemic. The theme of incorrect worship of Yahweh, represented by the Golden Calf episode, comes up in Judges too. The Israelite tribes were supposed to eliminate these cultic threats (Deut. 12), they were supposed to annihilate the Canaanites. Since they did not and have not, their existence continues to be one of mitigating disaster.

In 1–2 Kings the Baals, Asherahs, and the abhorrent Canaanite practices become the main threat, although "outer" threats from Aram, Assyria, Egypt, and eventually Babylonia also frame the religio-political stage. The institution of kingship is the new tool that is supposed to secure the preconditions for keeping the law (for example by securing "rest from enemies," and building a temple). And, as we know, the kings consistently fail to eradicate Baal, Ashera worship, as well as illicit Yahwistic cultic practices.

Ironically, for all the emphasis on obeying Yahweh and not abandoning him throughout Judges, there is no mention of *torah* or *sepher hatorah*. In Judges, the emphasis is on loyalty to Yahweh over other gods, on idolatry, focused on the threat of the "Baals and the Asheras/Ashtorets." Obedience and adherence to Yahweh are not ever explicitly connected to the concept of Torah or to Moses. The exceptions might be the key mentions of the *miṭvot yhwh* describing the ancestors as having obeyed (Judg. 2:17, and 3:4, which invokes the name of Moses). The book of the law that Deut. 31:24 and Josh. 23:6 had spoken of does not appear to serve a role, although the prohibition against other gods is front and center (Judg. 2:11–15, 19; 3:12; 4:1; 6:1; 10:6; 13:1). The illicit methods of divination so strictly prohibited in Deut. 18:11–12 are not of great concern to Judges either but do emerge or appear to be assumed in 1 Samuel 28.

Although not explicitly identified as such, the Decalogue is alluded to in the narrative of Micah and his mother (Judg. 17) in a not-so-subtle way. The narrative showcases theft, bearing false witness, dishonoring parents, and taking the name of Yahweh in vain. It also includes installing a non-Levitical priest, although the narrative also reports the inclusion of an actual Levite, who happens to be wandering, looking for work. The tribe of Dan then steals and carries off the shrine, and it is reported that Moses's grandson and his sons remained priests there until the captivity (under Assyria?). The contested *ketib* mention of Jonathan ben Gershom ben Moshe implicates Moses and *torah* in a crushing way: the destroyer of a molten metal idol has a grandson who ministers to another one! The mention of Shiloh as the presumably legitimate cult center offers a link here to the polemic against the cult site of Dan in 1 Kings 12, complementing what reads as a searing, ironic commentary on egregious breaches of Decalogue and cultic ritual in practice.

Intriguingly, however much Moses and his role as lawgiver looms in the Pentateuch, aside from Joshua he barely makes an appearance in the following books. Joshua mentions Moses's name more often than any book (fifty-eight times) except Exodus and Numbers, even more than Deuteronomy. Joshua's authority comes from his mission of fulfilling what "Yahweh had commanded by Moses," and he himself is portrayed as a mini-Moses of sorts: God promises to be with him as he was with Moses (Josh. 1:5), and the people promise to obey him as they did Moses (Josh. 1:17), which might not seem so comforting, considering how much they rebelled against Moses. As Moses did, Joshua sends out a spy mission. Then, Joshua leads the people across a body of water that piles up to let them cross over, told extensively and explicitly connected to the Exodus event (Josh. 4:23); and they celebrate Passover (Josh. 5:10). The Israelites stand in awe of Joshua, just as they had stood in awe of Moses (Josh. 4:14); and mirroring Moses's burning bush experience, Joshua experiences a theophany where he is commissioned and told that he is standing on holy ground (Josh. 5:13–15). In the battle against Ai, Joshua uses his sword as Moses used his staff. Joshua fulfills the ritual prescribed in Deuteronomy 27 when he builds an altar and writes a copy of (a second) "the *torah* of Moses" (Josh. 8:32 [8:30–35 follow 9:2 in the LXX]). Finally, Joshua mediates a divine speech to all the tribes recapping key events from the past, including the ancestral narratives, and puts forward the conditions of the covenant with Yahweh (Josh. 24:1–14), paralleling Moses's covenant closing and the narration of writing of the law in Deuteronomy 29–30 and 31.

The character Moses, the law, book of the law, or Law of Moses are rarely referenced in Judges, Samuel, or Kings. In these books, adherence to Yahweh and obedience to him are couched in other language, such as "doing what is right in the eyes of Yahweh." The few occurrences are connected to behavior of the royal figures, which is interesting considering that the one positive role that Deuteronomy ordains for the hypothetical monarch pertains to having "this law" written down, keeping it with him, and reading it (17:18–20).

In his speech to Solomon (1 Kgs 2:3), David counsels the future king to follow the ways of Yahweh in the *sepher hatorah*. Read as coming from the mouth of David, this sounds quite ironic. Although David is never reported to have followed "other gods," he nowhere appears to care about specific ordinances, and violates three of the ten commandments in one chapter (2 Sam. 11). Moreover, even though he is favored by Yahweh and "chosen" by him, apostasy or the lure of "other gods" is not a theme in the David story, as it is in the narratives of most of the kings who follow him, and the judges who precede him, except Samuel, of course.

David's words to Solomon, framed in what is usually determined to be Deuteronomistic language, also mark the point in the overarching narrative where this type of conditional language takes a turn away from focusing on the protection of the *people*, as in Deuteronomy, Joshua, Judges, Samuel, or even 1 Kgs 6:12–13. In 1 Kgs 2:2–4, the language focuses on protecting the "line of David" on the throne. Even though David is speaking to Solomon about his role as monarch, which may partially explain this, it is striking that protection of the people is not mentioned. Further, David's pretty words quickly move on to concerns of *Realpolitik*, when he basically orders the murder of specific individuals who are threats to his dynasty.

A transition from the emphasis on protection of the people to protection of the dynasty of David is perhaps anticipated in Samuel's speech warning against kingship, where both king *and* people are specified (1 Sam. 12:14–15). This is preceded by the warnings of 1 Sam. 8:11–17, which do not speak of any kind of protection. Solomon's apostasy (1 Kgs 11) is in breach of the fealty to Yahweh required and constitutes breach of the covenant according to Deuteronomy. Yet, as in the promise mediated by Nathan (2 Sam. 7), the dynasty of David will still be protected, though Solomon's son loses most of the land. It is intriguing that David, the star king, charges his successor to keep Yahweh's "statutes, commandments, ordinances, and testimonies, as it is written *batorat moshe*," just at the point where concepts of election, so strong in Deuteronomy, are applied to David and his royal line, and to Jerusalem, the chosen city (Thelle 2012).

This application of divine election to David and the city in Kings, so carefully forged in 1 Kgs 8:15–16 and anticipated in 2 Sam. 7, indicates a different utilization of the power of divine election than that found in Deuteronomy, which emphasizes the people and "the place." The reference to that which is written in the "law of Moses" (1 Kgs 2:3) connects back to the opening of Joshua, where the book of the law of Moses is conceived as a guideline for success, as well as a guarantor of it. David's invocation of it in 1 Kgs 2:3 also points forward to the law book in 2 Kgs 22 and gives import to the idea that this book had been disregarded or lost, as that narrative implies. David's advice to Solomon was ignored. Yet, David is held up throughout 1–2 Kings as the measuring stick for evaluating the monarchs' truthfulness to Yahweh, and some measure up, even though the law book of Moses appears to have been forgotten.

In the mixed evaluation of Jehu, this perhaps most zealous pro-Yahweh king nevertheless is judged as having been "not careful to follow the law of Yahweh the God of Israel with all his heart" (2 Kgs 10:31). The reason was that he kept Jeroboam's calves, which of course alludes to Exodus (Exod. 32) and Deuteronomy (9), and echoes language of Kings (1 Kgs 12). The law of Yahweh (no Moses here) was the yardstick for the king whose name most pithily testifies to his loyalty, yet he failed. And unlike for Solomon and other Judahite kings, no reference to David can mitigate for a Northern monarch, although Jehu's descendants are given four generations on the throne.

The only time in Kings that "book of the law of Moses" refers to a specific law occurs in the evaluation of Amaziah (2 Kgs 14:6). It refers to the prohibition of punishment of children for the crimes of parents (Deut. 24:16), a practice which incidentally does not appear to apply to Yahweh.

In the lengthy ideological exposition on the reasons for the fall of Israel (2 Kgs 17), the people are accused of not following "the law that I commanded your ancestors and that I sent to you by my servants the prophets" (2 Kgs 17:13). Not a "book of the law here, and not" the law of Yahweh or "the law of Moses," but one mediated by prophets. The understanding of the role of prophets as mediators of *torah* signals a view that prophecy (as reflected in the books of the Nevi'im) incorporates a process of interpreting or mediating the *torah* (Mal. 3), consistent with Moses's activity in Deuteronomy.

Later in the section concerning those who were brought in to inhabit Samaria after the deportation of the Israelites, in a reversal of the theme of possession and settlement of the land we read, "They did not know the law of the god of the land (*mishpat ehohei ha'aretz*)" (2 Kgs 17:26). This phrase is repeated three times here, also after the report of the Assyrian king sending a priest to settle in Bethel and teach them the correct ways of worship. They end up worshiping Yahweh, and "other gods" as well, and do not worship Yahweh correctly. They are condemned for not following the "laws, ordinances, and *torah* that Yahweh commanded the sons of descendants of Jacob" (2 Kgs 17:34, 37). By applying the expectation of *torah*-adherence to non-Israelite individuals living in the land, these accusations tie obedience to *torah* closely to the land. As such, this is in line with Deuteronomy. The emphasis is on how the inhabitants of Samaria worship "to this day" (2 Kgs 17:34, 41), by drawing a strong analogy to the behavior of the Israelites which the text condemns so strongly. In other words, the present inhabitants are just as incorrigible as the Israelites before them, and obedience appears to be unattainable. The expulsion of Israel from the land has not cleansed it.

The evaluation of Manasseh (2 Kgs 21:2–8) quotes what is reported as Yahweh's speech to David and Solomon in the past, speaking of the temple and Jerusalem in terms Deuteronomy applies to the "chosen place." Manasseh is accused of having placed an image of Asherah in the temple, the house of special status in the city that has divinely protected status because of David. This evaluation contrasts the worst of the Judean kings with the "chosen" David and with Solomon, the builder of the temple (and the one who is punished for his idolatry that leads to the split of the kingdom). In addition to marshalling these themes so central to 1–2 Kgs as a whole, the speech goes on to cite the conditional promise of safety in the land if they adhere to Yahweh and act "according to all the law that my servant Moses commanded them." (2 Kgs 21:8; Thelle 2012, 41–56). That concern is fundamental to Deuteronomy.

The Josiah narrative must achieve simultaneously a preservation of Josiah's legacy as the king who did everything according to "the words of the law written in the book," and "all the law of Moses" (2 Kgs 23:24, 25) yet now also refute the notion that correct royal behavior could save the people. There is not even an appeal to David, so that neither chosen dynasty nor law-abiding, loyal king can mitigate for Yahweh's wrath at the sins that have piled up, supposedly because of Manasseh. In a sense, the concept of the Law of Moses now trumps the ideology of David's chosenness.

The bookend references to *sepher hatorah* in the Former Prophets (Josh. 1:8; 2 Kgs 22:8, 11) have been important to redaction historical approaches that see these as editorial, theological framing devices for the DH. In a canonical perspective the books of the Nevi'im as a whole are framed by the mention of both the *torat Moshe* as well as the reference to Horeb and Elijah in Mal. 3:23–24). In a narrative and intertextual perspective these references orient the books of the Former and Latter Prophets in relation to one another as well as to the Pentateuch, as collections and as a comprehensive story.

The allusions to the Law and Prophets in Mal. 3:23–24 appear to leave an opening for viewing *torah* and prophecy (or Torah and Nevi'im) in a way that allows for future interpretation (Thelle 2021). In this canonical, intra-biblical perspective, prophecy is to interpret *torah*. In 2 Kings 22, the *sepher hatorah* provides the guide for judging the religious and moral status quo of the people. In narrative hindsight, the judgments on the kings of Israel and Judah that have preceded this episode find their measuring stick in relation to the role of David and in relation to Deuteronomy, and the few other references to the term *torah* in Joshua-Kings come into a wider perspective. Deuteronomy and the Torah as a whole thus fit in as well. Deuteronomy starts the program, it initiates Torah as prophecy. It looks forward, and is always in the present.

Ideally, what can be read following, or with, Deuteronomy is quite open. Deuteronomy's referents to the future can adapt to any number of scenarios. The Samaritan community reads the Pentateuch without the Former Prophets or any other Scripture and identify as "heirs" of the Pentateuchal story. The Ethiopic Beta Israel's *Orit*, or *Octateuch*, contains the Pentateuch plus Joshua, Judges, and Ruth, and possibly facilitates an emphasis on the uniquely Ethiopian kingdom history. Joshua–Kings, which came to be conceived as the collection referred to as Prophets/Former Prophets, is only the more dominant of several narratives that latches onto Deuteronomy as part of the Torah/Pentateuch.

This situation underscores the ideal, prescriptive, and future-facing nature of Deuteronomy in relation to Joshua–Kings. Deuteronomy is a rhetorically powerful example of an interpretative practice, that itself became authoritative. Through its portrayal of Moses' explication of "this law," Deuteronomy gives authority both to Moses as interpreter, to the actual content of the law, and to the process by which Deuteronomy itself becomes *torah*. The reader of Deuteronomy is always standing at the threshold of the land and is repeatedly reminded of this throughout the book. Reading Joshua–Kings with Deuteronomy, "these words" resonate, often in dissonance, often in harmony, sometimes in unison, and always as a creative counterpoint.

Bibliography

Albertz, R. "Why a Reform Like Josiah's Must Have Happened." In *Good Kings and Bad Kings*, edited by L.L. Grabbe, pp. 27–46. LHBOTS 393/European Seminar in Historical Methodology, 5. London: T & T Clark, 2005.

Auld, G. A. "The Deuteronomists and the Former Prophets, or What Makes the Former Prophets Deuteronomistic?" In *Those Elusive Deuteronomists: "Pandeuteronomism" and Scholarship in the Nineties*, edited by L. S. Schearing and S. L. McKenzie, pp. 116–126. JSOTSup 268. Sheffield: Sheffield Academic Press, 1999.

Aurelius, E. *Zukunft jenseits des Gerichts: Eine redaktionsgeschichtliche Studie zum Enneateuch*. BZAW, 319. Berlin: de Gruyter, 2003.

Blum, E. *Studien zur Komposition des Pentateuch*. BZAW, 189. Berlin: de Gruyter, 1990.

Britt, B. M. "Remembering Narrative in Deuteronomy." In *The Oxford Handbook of Biblical Narrative*, edited by Dana Nolan Fewell, pp. 157–167. Oxford: Oxford University Press, 2016.

Childs, B. S. *Introduction to the Old Testament as Scripture*. Philadelphia: Fortress Press, 1979.

Clements, R. E. 2004. "The Former Prophets and Deuteronomy–A Re-examination." In *God's Word for Our World, Volume I: Biblical Studies in Honor of Simon John De Vries*, edited by J. Harold Ellens, Deborah L. Ellens, Rolf P. Knierim, and Isaac Kalimi, pp. 83–95. JSOTSup, 388. London: T & T Clark International.

Cross, F. M. *Canaanite Myth and Hebrew Epic: Essays in the History of the Religion of Israel*. Cambridge: Harvard University Press, 1973.

Davies, P. R. *In Search of "Ancient Israel."* JSOTSup, 148. Sheffield: JSOT Press, 1992.

Davies, P. R. *Scribes and Schools: The Canonization of Hebrew Scriptures*. Library of Ancient Israel. Louisville: Westminster John Knox Press, 1998.

Dietrich, W. *Prophetie und Geschichte: Eine redaktionsgeschichtliche Untersuchung zum deuteronomistischen Geschichtswerk*. FRLANT, 108. Göttingen: Vandenhoeck & Ruprecht, 1972.

Dozeman, T. B., T. C. Römer, and K. Schmid, eds. *Pentateuch, Hexateuch, or Enneateuch? Identifying Literary Works in Genesis through Kings*. Ancient Israel and Its Literature, 8. Atlanta: SBL, 2011.

Dozeman, T. B., and K. Schmid, eds. *A Farewell to the Yahwist? The Composition of the Pentateuch in Recent European Interpretation*. SBL Symposium Series, 34. Atlanta: SBL, 2006.

Driver, S. R. *A Critical and Exegetical Commentary on Deuteronomy*. International Critical Commentary. Edinburgh: T & T Clark, 1903.

Duhm, B. *Das Buch Jeremia*. HAT, 11. Tübingen, Germany: J.C.B. Mohr (Paul Siebeck), 1901.

Eißfeldt, O. *Einleitung in das Alte Testament: unter Einschluss der Apokryphen und Pseudepigraphen. Entstehungsgeschichte des Alten Testaments*. Tübingen: Mohr Siebeck, 1934.

Eißfeldt, O. *The Old Testament: An Introduction: Including the Apocrypha and Pseudepigrapha, and Also the Works of Similar Type from Qumran: The History of the Formation of the Old Testament*. 3rd ed. Translated by Peter R. Ackroyd. New York: Harper and Row, 1965.

Ellens, J. H., and J. T. Greene, eds. "What Happened to the Yahwist? Reflections after Thirty Years: A Collegial Conversation between Rolf Rendtorff, David J.A. Clines, Allan Rosengren, and John Van Seters." In *Probing the Frontiers of Biblical Studies*, pp. 39–66. Princeton Theological Monograph Series. Eugene: Pickwick, 2009.

Eynikel, E. *The Reform of King Josiah and the Composition of the Deuteronomistic History*. OTS, 33. Leiden: Brill, 1996.

Fohrer, G. *Introduction to the Old Testament: Initiated by Ernst Sellin, Completely Revised and Rewritten by Georg Fohrer*. Nashville: Abingdon, 1968.

Geoghegan, J. C. *The Time, Place, and Purpose of the Deuteronomistic History: The Evidence of "Until This Day."* BJS, 347. Providence: BJS, 2006.

Gunn, D. M. "Telling and Retelling the Bible's First Story." In *The Oxford Handbook of Biblical Narrative*, edited by Dana Nolan Fewell, pp. 95–108. Oxford: Oxford University Press, 2016.

Handy, L. K. "Historical Probability and the Narrative of Josiah's Reform in 2 Kings." In *The Pitcher Is Broken: Memorial Essays for Gösta W. Ahlström*, edited by S.W. Holloway and L.K. Handy, pp. 252–275. JSOTSup, 190. Sheffield: Sheffield Academic Press, 1995.

Hjelm, I. *Jerusalem's Rise to Sovereignty: Zion and Gerizim in Competition*. JSOTSup, 404/ Copenhagen International Seminar, 14. London: T & T Clark, 2004.

Knauf, E. A. "Does "Deuteronomistic Historiography" (DH) Exist?" In *Israel Constructs Its History: Deuteronomistic Historiography in Recent Research*, edited by A. de Pury, T. Römer and J.-D. Macchi, pp. 388–398. JSOTSup, 306. Sheffield: Sheffield Academic Press, 2000.

Knoppers, G. N. *Two Nations under God: The Deuteronomistic History of Solomon and the Dual Monarchies*. 2 vols. HSM, 52–53. Atlanta: Scholars Press, 1993/1994.

Kratz, R. *The Composition of the Narrative Books*. Translated by J. Bowen. London: T & T Clark International, 2005.

Lohfink, N. "Recent Discussion on 2 Kings 22–23: The State of the Question." In *A Song of Power and the Power of Song: Essays on the Book of Deuteronomy*, edited by D. L. Christensen, pp. 36–61. Sources for Biblical and Theological Study. Winona Lake: Eisenbrauns, 1993.

Lohfink, N. F. "Gab es eine deuteronomistische Bewegung?" In *Jeremia und die "deuteronomistische Bewegung,"* edited by W. Groß, pp. 313–382. BBB, 98. Weinheim: Betz Athenäum, 1995.

McConville, J. G. "The Old Testament Historical books in Modern Scholarship." *Themelios* 22 (1997): 3–13.

McKenzie, S. L. *The Trouble with Kings: The Composition of the Books of Kings in the Deuteronomistic History*. VTSup, 42. Leiden: Brill, 1991.

Montgomery, J. A., and H. S. Gehman, eds. *A Critical and Exegetical Commentary on the Book of Kings*. ICC. Edinburgh: T & T Clark, repr., 1986.

Moore, S. D. "Biblical Narrative Analysis from the New Criticism to the New Narratology." In *The Oxford Handbook of Biblical Narrative*, edited by Dana Nolan Fewell, pp. 27–50. Oxford: Oxford University Press, 2016.

Moran, W. L. "The Ancient Near Eastern Background of Love of God in Deuteronomy." *Catholic Biblical Quarterly* 25 (1963): 77–87.

Mowinckel, S. *Zur Komposition des Buches Jeremia*. Videnskapsselskapets skrifter II. Hist.-filos. Klasse. Kristiania: Jacob Dywad, 1914.

Nelson, R. D. *The Double Redaction of the Deuteronomistic History*. JSOTSup, 18. Sheffield: JSOT Press, 1981.

Nelson, R. D. "The Double Redaction of the Deuteronomistic History: The Case is Still Compelling." *Journal for the Study of the Old Testament* 29, no. 3 (2005): 319–337.

Nihan, C. "The Holiness Code between D and Some Comments on the Function and Significance of Leviticus 17–26 in the Composition of the Torah." In *Das Deuteronomium zwischen Pentateuch und deuteronomistischem Geschichtswerk*, edited by E. Otto and R. Achenbach, pp. 81–122. FRLANT, 206. Göttingen: Vandenhoeck & Ruprecht, 2004.

Noll, K. "Deuteronomistic History or Deuteronomic Debate? (A Thought Experiment)." *Journal for the Study of the Old Testament* 31, no. 3 (2007): 311–345.

Noth, M. *Überlieferungsgeschichtliche Studien*. Schriften der Königsberger Gelehrten Gesellschaft. Geisteswissenschaftliche Klasse, 18. Halle: Niemeyer 1943.

Noth, M. *The Chronicler's History*. JSOTSup, 50. Sheffield: JSOT Press, 1987.

Noth, M. *The Deuteronomistic History*. JSOTSup, 15. Sheffield: JSOT Press, 1991.

O'Brien, M. A. *The Deuteronomistic History Hypothesis: A Reassessment*. OBO, 92. Freiburg: Vandenhoeck & Ruprecht, 1989.

O'Brien, M. A. "The Book of Deuteronomy." *CRBS* 3 (1995): 95–128.

Otto, E. "Scribal Scholarship in the Formation of Torah and Prophets: A Postexilic Scribal Debate between Priestly Scholarship and Literary Prophecy—The Example of the Book of Jeremiah and Its Relation to the Pentateuch." In *The Pentateuch as Torah: New Models for Understanding Its Promulgation and Acceptance*, edited by G. N. Knoppers and B. M. Levinson, pp. 171–184. Winona Lake: Eisenbrauns, 2007.

Paul, J. M. "Hilkiah and the Law (2 Kings 22) in the 17th and 18th Centuries: Some Influences on W.M.L. de Wette." In *Das Deuteronomium: Entstehung, Gestalt und Botschaft*, edited by N. Lohfink, pp. 9–12. BETL, 68. Leuven: Leuven University Press, 1985.

Paul, J. M. *Het Archimedisch Punt van de Pentateuchkritiek: Een historisch en exegetish Onderzoek naar de Verhouding van Deuteronomium en de Reformatie van Koning Josia* (2 Kon. 22–23). The Hague: Uitgeverij Boekencentrum B.V., 1988.

Polzin, R. *Moses and the Deuteronomist: A Literary Study of the Deuteronomic History. Part I: Deuteronomy, Joshua, Judges*. New York: Seabury, 1980.

Preuss, H. D. *Deuteronomium*. EdF, 164. Darmstadt: Wissenschaftliche Buchgesellschaft, 1982.

Rendtorff, R. *The Old Testament: An Introduction*. Philadelphia: Fortress Press, 1986.

Rendtorff, R. *The Problem of the Process of Transmission in the Pentateuch*. JSOTSup, 89. London: JSOT Press, 1980.

Römer, T. C. "Cult Centralization in Deuteronomy 12: Between Deuteronomistic History and Pentateuch." In *Das Deuteronomium zwischen Pentateuch und deuteronomistischem Geschichtswerk*, edited by E. Otto and R. Achenbach, pp. 153–167. FRLANT, 206. Göttingen: Vandenhoeck & Ruprecht, 2004.

Römer, T. C. *The Future of the Deuteronomistic History*. BETL, 147. LeuvenŁ: Peeters, 2000.

Römer, T. C. "The Narrative Books of the Hebrew Bible." In *The Hebrew Bible: A Critical Companion*, edited by J. Barton, pp. 109–132. Princeton: Princeton University Press, 2016.

Römer, T. C. 2005. *The So-called Deuteronomistic History: A Sociological, Historical and Literary Introduction*. London: T & T Clark.

Römer, T. C., and A. de Pury. "Deuteronomistic Historiography (DH): History of Research and Debated Issues." In *Israel Constructs Its History: Deuteronomistic Historiography in Recent Research*, edited by A. de Pury, T.C. Römer, and J.-D. Macchi, pp. 24–141. JSOTSup, 306. Sheffield: Sheffield Academic Press, 2000.

Rose, M. *Deuteronomist und Jahwist. Untersuchungen zu den Berührungspunkten beider Literaturwerke*. ATANT, 67. Zürich: Theologischer Verlag, 1981.

Rösel, H. "Why 2 Kings 17 Does Not Constitute a Chapter of Reflection in the 'Deuteronomistic History.'" *Journal of Biblical Literature* 128, no. 1 (2009): 85–90.

Schmid, H. H. *Der sogenannte Jahwist: Beobachtungen und Fragen zur Pentateuchforschung*. Zürich: Theologischer Verlag, 1976.

Schearing, L.S., and S.L. McKenzie, *Those Elusive Deuteronomistis: The Phenomenon of Pan-Deuteronomism*. JSOTSup 268. Sheffield: Sheffield Academic Press, 1999.

Schmid, K."Buchtechnische und sachliche Prolegomena zur Enneateuchfrage." In *Auf dem Weg zur Endgestalt von Genesis bis II Regnum: Festschrift Hans-Christoph Scmitt zum 65. Geburtstag*, edited by M. Beck and U. Schorn, pp. 1–14. BZAW, 370. Berlin: de Gruyter, 2006.

Schmidt, W. H. "Die deuteronomistische Redaktion des Amosbuches: Zu den theologischen Unterschieden zwischen dem Prophetenwort und dem Sammler." *ZAW* 77 (1965): 168–193.

Schmitt, H. C. "Dtn 34 als Verbindungsstück zwischen Tetrateuch und deuteronomistischen Geschichtswerk." In *Das Deuteronomium zwischen Pentateuch und deuteronomistischem Geschichtswerk*, edited by E. Otto and R. Achenbach, pp. 180–192. FRLANT, 206. Göttingen: Vandenhoeck & Ruprecht, 2004.

Smend, R. "Das Gesetz und die Völker: Ein Beitrag zur deuteronomistischen Redaktionsgeschichte." In *Probleme biblischer Theologie: G. von Rad zum 70. Geburtstag*, edited by H. W. Wolff. Munich: Chr. Kaiser, 1971.

Thelle, R. I. *Approaches to the Chosen Place: Accessing a Biblical Concept*. LHBOTS, 564. New York: T & T Clark International, 2012.

Thelle, R. I. "The Minor Prophets' Relation to the Torah and Former Prophets." In *The Oxford Handbook of the Minor Prophets*, edited by J. O'Brien. Oxford: Oxford University Press Handbooks Online, 2021.

Thiel, W. *Die deuteronomistische Redaktion von Jeremia 1–25*. WMANT, 41. Neukirchen-Vluyn: Neukirchener, 1973.

Thiel, W. *Die deuteronomistische Redaktion von Jeremia 26–52*. WMANT, 52. Neukirchen-Vluyn: Neukirchener, 1981.

Van Seters, J. *Abraham in History and Tradition*. New Haven: Yale University Press, 1975.

Van Seters, J. *In Search of History: Historiography in the Ancient World and the Origins of Biblical History*. New Haven: Yale University Press, 1983.

Veijola, T. 1975. *Die ewige Dynastie: David und die Enstehung seiner Dynastie nach der deuteronomistischen Darstellung*. Toimituksia—Suomalaisen Tiedeakatemian, Annales Academiae Scientiarum Fennicae: Sarja-Ser. B, 193. Helsinki: Suomaleinen Tiedeakatemia.

Veijola, T. "Deuteronomismusforschung zwischen Tradition und Innovation (III)." *TRu* 68 (2003): 1–44.

Weinfeld, M. "Deuteronomy–The Present State of the Inquiry." *Journal of Biblical Literature* 86 (1967): 249–262.

Weinfeld, M. *Deuteronomy 1–11: A New Translation with Introduction and Commentary*. AB, 5. New York: Doubleday, 1991.

Weinfeld, M. *Deuteronomy and the Deuteronomic School*. Oxford: Oxford University Press, 1972. Reprinted Winona Lake: Eisenbrauns, 1992.

Weiser, A. *Einleitung in das Alte Testament*. 6. improved ed. Göttingen: Vandenhoeck & Ruprecht, 1966.

Wellhausen, J. *Die Composition des Hexateuchs und der historischen Bücher des Alten Testaments*. Berlin: Georg Reimer, 1899.

Wellhausen, J. *Prolegomena zur Geschichte Israels*. 6th ed. Berlin: Georg Reimer, 1905.

Westermann, C. *Die Geschichtsbücher des Alten Testaments: Gab es ein deuteronomistisches Geschichtswerk? Neudrucke und Berichte aus dem 20. Jahrhundert*, 87. Gütersloh: Chr. Kaiser Gütersloher Verlagshaus, 1994.

Wilson, R. R. "Who Was the Deuteronomist? (Who Was Not the Deuteronomist?): Reflections on Pan-Deuteronomism." In *Those Elusive Deuteronomists: "Pandeuteronomism" and Scholarship in the Nineties*, edited by L. S. Schearing and S. L. McKenzie, pp. 64–82. JSOTSup, 268. Sheffield: Sheffield Academic Press, 1999.

Witte, M., K. Schmid, D. Prechel, and J. C. Gertz, eds. *Die deuteronomistische Geschichtswerke: Redaktions- und religionsgeschichtliche Perspektiven zur "Deuteronomismus"—Diskussion in Tora und Forderen Propheten*. BZAW, 365. Berlin: de Gruyter, 2006.

Wolff, H. W. *Joel und Amos*. BKAT, 14. Neukirchen-Vluyn: Neukirchener, 1985.

Wurthwein, E. "Erwägungen zum sog. deuteronomistischen Geschichtswerk: Eine Skizze." In E. Wurthwein, *Studien zum deuteronomistischen Geschichtswerk*, pp. 1–11. BZAW, 227. Berlin: de Gruyter, 1994.

CHAPTER 21

DEUTERONOMY, HOSEA, AND THE THEORY OF NORTHERN ORIGINS

BILL T. ARNOLD

Who Began the Conversation?

THE theory explored in this chapter is the notion that Deuteronomy, or a significant early portion of the book, originated in the north sometime prior to the fall of Samaria to the Assyrians in 722 BCE. This alleged northern origin is thought to explain the close connection between themes and phrases in Deuteronomy and the northern prophet Hosea of the eighth century BCE.[1]

A closely related variation of the proposal is the view that Deuteronomy was composed in Judah but by refugees from Israel who brought the agenda of Deuteronomy and Hosea with them after the fall of Samaria and perhaps developed it further while in exile in the south.

The development of the proposal tracks certain other developments in the history of scholarship on the Hebrew Bible.[2] The nineteenth-century consensus on Pentateuchal origins concluded that the sociopolitical background of Deuteronomy was Josiah's reforms, whether as the instigating program or the ensuing effect of those reforms, and little further speculation was offered by the scholarship regarding Deuteronomy's origins. The crystallization of that consensus by Julius Wellhausen assumed a three-stage diachronic development: (1) Ur-Deuteronomy (12–26*); (2) two accretions developed independently of each other, first, 1–4*, 12–26*, and 27*, and second, 5–11*, 12–26*, and 28–30*; and (3) a conflation of these two editions.[3] The consensus seldom gave any thought to northern origins for these materials, even though the Elohist—with which Deuteronomy has many affinities—originated in the north.

Scholars long have observed the close connection between themes and phrases in Deuteronomy and Hosea, so that Deuteronomy could be taken as "the spiritual heir of Hosea."[4] Such connections, however, had not necessitated, in and of themselves, a theory of northern origins for Deuteronomy.

Scholarly investigation of Deuteronomy changed in the early twentieth century when, among others, Adam C. Welch argued that the Deuteronomic Code showed affinities with the northern kingdom of Israel and, in fact, originated in one of the leading sanctuaries of the north, such as Shechem, Samaria, or Bethel.[5] Welch insisted upon a close association between Hosea and Deuteronomy, although he believed an early Deuteronomic Code had influenced the prophet rather than vice versa. Such assertions began a period of intense debate in the 1920s, which has been called the "Battle over Deuteronomy."[6] Issues at stake were disputes over Josiah's reforms, cult centralization, and the age of Deuteronomy. Welch's assumptions that the law antedated Amos and Hosea were vigorously refuted, along with his assumption that centralization was not prevalent in the earliest Deuteronomic Code.[7]

The question of the northern origins of Deuteronomy was advanced considerably by the classic study of Albrecht Alt, who focused on parallels between Hosea and a proto-Deuteronomy or *Urdeuteronomium*, which was a northern document later carried south by refugees after the fall of Samaria in 722 BCE.[8]

The notion of a proto-Deuteronomy came to play a significant part in the scholarship because Deuteronomy is itself clearly a later, Judahite (or even later Judean) product. But the quest for origins (northern or otherwise) is unavoidably tied to the concept of an early form because Deuteronomy has clearly grown through successive accretions marked by a series of superscriptions, leaving clues to how the book evolved.[9] For Alt, the theology of kingship in Deuteronomy was characteristically Hosea, and impossible in Judah with its dynastic succession.

Others have revised and modified this approach. For Ronald E. Clements, the authors of Deuteronomy were "heirs of the religious traditions of the Northern Kingdom," probably Levites, associated with Shechem or Bethel, who were now refugees in the south after the fall of Samaria.[10] This approach can assume northern origins for a Deuteronomic "movement" connected to a significant number of refugees from the north arriving in Jerusalem, and it continues to have many advocates.

Alexander Rofé concluded that northern refugees arrived in Jerusalem "with a notable literary legacy," which he defines as "covenant traditions and songs now found in Deuteronomy, as well as historical traditions preserved in the historical books and in Hosea."[11] Dominant themes were cult centralization, an anti-monarchial theology, the kingship of YHWH, and the central role of Shechem. Then, in the early seventh century BCE, the heirs of this legacy, now finding shelter in Judah and in "the homes of the king's high officials," became devotees instead of the Davidic dynasty and transferred their theology of centrality to Jerusalem.[12]

The assumption that northern, proto-Deuteronomic traditions made their way to Jerusalem can also be applied to specific theologies, such as the exodus tradition as a normative, constitutive event, in light of evidence that in Judah, by contrast, Zion theology with its exclusive focus on David and Jerusalem were primary.[13] In this approach, much emphasis has been placed on the theory of northern refugees in seventh-century Judah as heirs to the prophetic traditions of the eighth century.

Ernest W. Nicholson, after considering the connections between Deuteronomy and the Elohist as evidence of northern origins, highlighted Deuteronomy's affinities with Hosea.[14] For Nicholson, the connections between Hosea and Deuteronomy are to be explained as deriving from "the same source—the teaching of the prophetic party in northern Israel."[15] The idea that Hosea and Deuteronomy are both dependent in various degrees upon a common northern tradition is a variation on the northern tradition approach, and it has the advantage of not relying necessarily on a theory of refugees living in or near Jerusalem.[16] The location of the borrowed themes vaguely in "the prophetic party" of the north, however, contained within it certain inconsistencies and problems, so much so that Nicholson himself came to revise his views, arguing instead for a provenance of Deuteronomy among exiles from Judah living in Babylonia.[17]

The conviction that Hosea was somehow a forerunner to a northern proto-Deuteronomy and the subsequent Deuteronomic movement was advocated most persuasively by Hans Walter Wolff. As early as 1956, Wolff reasoned that certain aspects of Hosea's teaching could not have been standard among prophets, but could only have originated through his contacts with a circle of Levites.[18] He argued further that these Levites were probably associated with the sanctuary at Shechem after being expelled by Jeroboam I (925–905 BCE) from the sanctuaries at Bethel and Dan (1 Kgs 12:31; 13:33). Wolff's comments in his Hosea commentary on the "numerous connections" between Hosea and Deuteronomy are frequently quoted in the secondary literature.

> Entire complexes of thought characteristic of Deuteronomic paraenesis occur first in Hosea. Thus, we find reminiscences of the exodus from Egypt, of divine guidance through the wilderness, and of the entry into the arable land, combined with the themes of Israel's satiation, presumption, and forgetting of Yahweh. In addition, there is the struggle against Israel's political alliances; the manner in which תּוֹרָה (tôrâ) is spoken of; Yahweh as Israel's "teacher"; Yahweh's "love"; "redemption"; the genuine prophet who is "with God"; "brotherhood"; the *maṣṣēbôth* of the Canaanites; "grain, new wine, and olive oil."[19]

Wolff believed the direction of influence was clear, and that Hosea was indeed "one of the fathers of the early Deuteronomic movement."[20]

Many others have weighed in on this topic, although the differences between them and the broad strokes with which I have painted this portrait are often differences by degree only. Before turning to a brief summary of the current state of the question, I offer here a reflection on the problem of assessing redactional activity on Hosea, which is a critical preliminary question that must be addressed.

Scholars now often assume the themes and phrases in Deuteronomy that Wolff argued were borrowed from Hosea are actually "Deuteronom(ist)ic."[21] It is thought that Wolff's position presumed a simplistic scribal transmission of the prophetic utterances, which no doubt involved a lengthy process. It may be just as reasonable to presume, it has been pointed out, that Hosea was the result of subsequent Deuteronom(ist)ic redaction(s) by Judean scribes post-586 BCE.

Wolff, however, included a detailed, and it seems likely to me, quite convincing, transmission history for Hosea.[22] He believed Hosea's three self-contained transmission complexes (first, 1:2–6, 8–9, and 2:1–3:5; second, 4:1a–11:11bβ; and third, 12–14) were "already fixed in writing during the prophet's lifetime," which is precisely the point of the criticism. It presumes too early in the traditions-history process that Hosea was a literary object. But he also proposed four redactional levels, spanning in time from early in the Deuteronomic movement down to the exile. The first two involved traditions handed down by prophets in Israel, and the last two by redactors in Judah. And yet the first three were also activities done in Hosea's lifetime by his contemporaries; only the last one was later, applying the prophet's accusations against Israel to Judah. What is remarkable in his reconstruction, whether or not one allows that it holds up under closer scrutiny, is that Wolff avers that all the transmission steps correspond to the literary connections between Hosea and Deuteronomy. In other words, the redactional processes that eventuated in our current canonical Hosea were conducted by Deuteronomic and (during the exile), Deuteronomistic redactors, so that the themes and phraseology of Hosea and Deuteronomy are interlocking and interconnected. So it was Hosea's circle of contemporaries—thought by Wolff to be Levitical priests—who "became oriented towards Judah or even took up residence there as a result of the attacks" upon them at the time of Israel's downfall, and eventually became "the forerunners of the Deuteronomic movement."[23]

In my view, Wolff's rather sophisticated reconstruction of the similarities of thought and phraseology between the two books carries more explanatory power to explain their similarities than a view that alleges Hosea was finally edited late in a post-Deuteronomistic process. There are simply too many connections between the two, so that Hosea is "threaded with deuteronomic ideas" so completely that a late post-Deuteronomistic redaction would have been more thorough than one can imagine.[24]

WHAT IS THE STATUS OF THE CONVERSATION?

The Alt-Wolff explanation is currently one of the dominant theories regarding a northern context for proto-Deuteronomy. It would be misleading, however, to suggest that this approach is a genuine consensus because many scholars are not convinced that Hosea influenced the Deuteronomic movement, nor that Deuteronomy itself had origins in the north. Currently, then, the quest for the origins of the earliest form of Deuteronomy falls along a continuum.

On one end of the spectrum, some scholars continue to hold to a reconstruction that has Deuteronomy originating in an early form in Israel, highlighting its affinities with the Elohist, the Elijah narratives, and especially Hosea.[25] Near this end of the continuum, a few scholars assume Deuteronomy developed in Judah, composed by royal scribes of Hezekiah and Josiah, although with older strands of a Shechem ceremony and a Gilgal tradition.[26] In this vein, some have proposed that the immediate frame of the legal core (11:26–30; 27:4–8, 11–13) is the remnant of an older Shechem tradition incorporated into Deuteronomy.[27] Still others allow for refugees from the north after 722 BCE, which, it is assumed, gives explanation to the connections between Deuteronomy and Hosea.[28] Indeed, it has been argued recently that, despite the trend among scholars of Hosea, it is entirely likely that his career continued long after 722 BCE, and in fact, much of the core of the present book of Hosea was composed while he lived in Judah around 700 BCE.[29] It has also been claimed that a post-722 BCE influx of refugees from Israel led to "a new consciousness for shared brotherly cohesion," which inspired collection of family law and social cohesion.[30]

Scholars unconvinced that movement southward could have occurred so early have postulated that the Bethel sanctuary continued to serve for perhaps two centuries after the fall of Samaria and functioned as a conduit for northern traditions into Persian Yehud.[31] Reconstructions linking Deuteronomy to refugees from Israel immigrating to Judah, however, must be cautious because of a recent debate about such a migration. Nadav Na'aman questions the theory, but Israel Finkelstein defends it.[32]

Just as intense has been the debate on whether or not the reforms of Josiah are connected to a pre-exilic Deuteronomy.[33] Recent investigations have also suggested that some traditions in Deuteronomy (2:1–3:29) were much more independent of the parallel accounts in Numbers than previous scholarship, and suggested instead that they offer a view of events that have origins in the northern Transjordan.[34] This approach has much to commend it, especially as a more indirect way of explaining literary and thematic connections with Hosea and, to a lesser extent, Amos, since it may also have had Transjordanian connections.

The assumption that a migration of "Levitical priests" from the north as precursors to the Deuteronomic reforms has been offered to explain the distinction between these priests, who may have had affinities with the scribes who wrote Deuteronomy, as distinct from "the priests and the Levites" of Chronicles.[35] It may also be that Hosea appears to express the perspective of his kin group in a public forum, which is directed at the royal administration of Israel, using characteristic phrases and themes of that kin group pervasively throughout the book.[36]

On the opposite end of the continuum are scholars who consider Deuteronomy to have developed in Judah, typically assuming a series of redactions in the exilic and postexilic period by scribes in Jerusalem expressing ideas native to Judah. This approach essentially reverses the direction of influence and dates the connections with Hosea much later, envisioning a series of late Deuteronom(ist)ic redactions of Hosea and other biblical books, which itself went through a process of updating.

The postexilic Deuteronomy theory has influenced the canonical themes and phraseology of a post-Deuteronomistic expansion of Hosea.[37] To this way of thinking, the direction of influence is from Deuteronomy to Hosea at a late stage of redaction, although there is essentially no systematic connection between the two, leaving no evidence of northern origins for the former. It has also been asserted that the only geographically specific references to the north—the Gerizim and Ebal passages (11:26–30; 27:1–26)—were late insertions by "Yahwistic Samarians" into an older version of Deuteronomy.[38] Indeed, communication between north and south was not a "one-off" occurrence in the late eighth century, but some have argued that "literary traditions from Samaria to Judah" was an ongoing reality long after the fall of Samaria.[39]

Among scholars who assume late Deuteronom(ist)ic redactional activity in Hosea to explain the connections, some have objected recently that the northern theory as formulated in the 1970s was flawed by scholars who assumed "the basic literary integrity of Deuteronomy and the works to which it was being compared, such as Hosea."[40] Especially noteworthy is the objection that Hosea itself, assuming that it was composed in Israel, was not ultimately a literary object until much later. In this case, Hosea traditions were received, revised, and transmitted by scribes in Judah many years later. Thus, it can be argued, that the "Deuteronomisms in Hosea . . . stem from the hands of Judean scribes who revised the prophetic works in light of deuteronomic or Deuteronomistic theology, most likely following 586 BCE."[41]

Simply put, given the many themes and phrases shared by Hosea and Deuteronomy, and assuming also that the origins of Hosea are to be sought in northern Israel in the late eighth century BCE, then the only possible conclusion is that Deuteronomy has been influenced in the early seventh century, or slightly later, by the older prophetic text. Inserting into one's argument from the outset the assumption that Hosea was extensively edited by

Deuteronom(ist)ic or post-Deuteronom(ist)ic scribes much later predetermines the outcome of the question.

Perhaps one way of eliminating such circular reasoning is to give greater attention to the inscriptional evidence. Such potentially important, but often overlooked, evidence comes from the paleographic details of Hebrew in northern Israel when compared to writing in Judah. Johannes Renz concluded, after an investigation of letter typology, that after the last quarter of the eighth century BCE, almost all Israelite types of the former northern kingdom continued in Judah, at times even typologically advancing.[42] It is tempting to assume that northern scribes—with their culture, training, and perhaps traditions—were thus integrated into the royal court and scribal culture of Judah. Yet the evidence is obviously limited, and while it may well be that this was the continuation of the Old Hebrew script intentionally created in a nationalistic impulse in the fledgling Israelite kingdom, which then continued in Judah, it hardly proves a northern origin for Deuteronomy.[43] Indeed, we have evidence of a reduced but nevertheless continuing Israelite presence in and around Samaria after 722 BCE, enough to suggest that "the Assyrian campaigns did not have utterly transformative effects in northern Israel."[44]

Caution is also in order because it appears that scribes from both Israel and Judah were trained in the same techniques as early as the late ninth century BCE, most likely sponsored by official state polities in both cases, and that deliberate cooperation between Israel and Judah continued so that both biblical law and history became possible by the eighth century.[45] Regardless of specific details, it appears that both north (including the Transjordan territories) and south shared an artisanal scribal culture in the eighth century BCE, which certainly would have made easier any transition from Hosea to Deuteronomy.

What Is Trending in the Conversation?

Any progress on the relationship between Hosea and Deuteronomy must address a methodological problem that continues to prohibit a definitive resolution to the question. If one decides a priori that (1) a Deuteronomic movement generated almost entirely new theological themes, phrases, and lexical expressions in a given period of time—such as the late seventh century BCE, or the exilic, or postexilic period—and further that (2) those themes and expressions did not occur in earlier Israelite texts, then ex hypothesi (3) any of those same themes or expressions occurring in canonical Hosea must necessarily have been the result of a later post-Deuteronom(ist)ic redactional process. In this way, the result of one's investigation will be predetermined, and one will naturally conclude that eighth-century Hosea is not closely related to Deuteronomy, and therefore we have little or no evidence of northern origins for the latter.

In critiquing the approach, I choose not to challenge its apriority because all redaction critics must begin somewhere; to some degree, all redaction criticism involves a degree of circularity. However, there are at least two additional problems here. First, one must call into question the confidence in our reconstruction of Deuteronomy itself. The degree of certainty in our redaction-critical decisions is disproportionate to the amount of speculation and theorizing required to reach them. This is not to abandon the enterprise altogether but to acknowledge that, while Deuteronomy shows numerous signs of layering and accretions, we are unable to date precisely when those accretions were added. Indeed, I have argued elsewhere that we have evidence to support the eighth-century date for a proto-Deuteronomy, and subsequent editions by Hezekiah and Josiah.[46] The themes and expressions of this Deuteronomic movement were certainly not created ex nihilo, and the connections with Hosea remain compelling, as does the possibility of a northern origin for a proto-Deuteronomy.

Second, the degree to which one finds traces of Deuteronom(ist)ic thought, or the amount of literary and thematic connection between Hosea and Deuteronomy, is a matter of varying opinion. Are these connections "traces" only—touches of Deuteronomism—or is Hosea more substantially filled with them so as to be pervasive throughout, and therefore intricately connected to Deuteronomy? While a thorough revision of all the data is impossible here, suffice it to say that I believe Hosea exhibits little that can be identified as genuine Deuteronom(ist)ic redactional activity, by which I mean late, post-Deuteronomistic redaction. Furthermore, recent work has led to a more cautious appreciation for just how dull are our instruments and how inadequate the lumber for building a thorough reconstruction of compositional theories.[47]

All future work on defining the precise nature of the connections between Hosea and Deuteronomy must move beyond merely noting common phraseology or lexical connections to examine what has turned out to be a more complex situation than has been previously investigated.[48] Scholars have given considerable attention recently to identifying more precisely what we have called here "connections" between texts, and they have now refined our understanding of the differences between influence, allusion, and quotation, including specific criteria to determine the relationship.[49] While it has been recognized now for over a century that Hosea and Deuteronomy are closely "connected," we have not adequately explored the nature of those connections, nor the deep-level, and, in my view, likely shared common traditions that lead to both genres.

Here I offer a few cursory comments on one particular text of Hosea as a case study that must, in my view, be included in this discussion, and which I believe supports the notion that a northern origin is likely for the earliest traditions now contained in Deuteronomy.

> Put a trumpet to your mouth—
> Like a vulture over the House of YHWH;
> Because they have transgressed My covenant
> and been faithless to My teaching. (Hos 8:1)[50]

The imagery of the "eagle/vulture" (*nešer*) is used positively in Deuteronomy (32:11), of YHWH hovering over Israel and bearing them away to safety during their dangerous wilderness journey (Exod 19:4). If Hosea's use of the imagery is dependent upon a common shared tradition, it has been flipped upside down to envision a threatening YHWH or perhaps surrogate enemy like Assyria ominously circling the prey—the house of YHWH.[51] Like Deuteronomy, Hosea never refers directly to Jerusalem or its temple (unless here), and interpreters often assume this reference is to the Promised Land as YHWH's estate (Hos 9:3).[52]

In Hosea (Hos 8:1b), the parallelism is revealing because it requires the connotation "rebel against" for the idiom *pāšaʿ* + *ʿal*, in light of the word doublet with *ʿbr*, "transgress" the covenant. It has long been observed that this idiom for violating the covenant (*ʿbr* + *barît*) is distinctively Deuteronomistic language.[53]

Perhaps even more significantly for our purposes here, "my covenant" (bərîtî) and "my tôrâ" (tôrātî) are synonymously parallel, equating YHWH's covenant with his teaching (significantly, in the singular).[54] The use of tôrâ in the singular in Hosea (Hos 4:6; 8:12) should not be overlooked as insignificant when compared to its use in Deuteronomy, where "this law" becomes for the first time a single concept to denote the totality of divine laws, or rather in the singular, the divine will for Israel (1:5). This is one of the most distinctive innovations of Deuteronomy, when compared to parallels in the Tetrateuch, where tôrâ always denotes one teaching among others (Lev 6:2), rather than a crystallized single new concept—that of religious law. In this way, Deuteronomy's use of tôrâ is closer to Hosea than to the legal materials preceding it in the Tetrateuch.

Furthermore, the use of "covenant" and "tôrâ" in synonymous parallelism is close to the identification of the covenant with the law itself found in the Deuteronomic sermon identifying the covenant with the Ten Words (4:13). The Torah here is likely the Ten Words and "other similar material," making it likely that Hosea innovated the notion of a "theological" covenant, and making all arguments that Hosea (Hos 8:1) was a later addition contrived and unnecessary.[55] Hosea assumes that the covenant being rejected by the people of YHWH had a written component—that is, an inscribed instruction.[56]

The verse illustrates the intractable problems of determining the direction of influence between Hosea and Deuteronomy. So, for example, the focus on a national covenant with Israel has been taken to be a concept formulated in the mid-seventh century or later, and therefore this verse is taken as a Deuteronom(ist)ic redaction of Hosea.[57] In this way, Hosea's influence on Deuteronomy is essentially nil, and there is little evidence for a theory of northern origins. However, the notion that "covenant" as a theological innovation of the reforms of Josiah is not established, and a perfectly sensible argument can be made that Hosea developed his marriage metaphor, precisely on the basis of covenant theology, whether or not the term "covenant" was at work in every case.[58]

Furthermore, on the assumption that the Deuteronomic Code was dependent upon the Covenant Code (Exod 20:23–23:33) and, to a lesser extent, the surrounding narrative account (Exod 19-24)—in which the notion of covenant was combined for the first time with criminal, civil, and ritual law—then one may easily assume that covenant theology was at work among those related to eighth-century Hosea.[59] Thus, a likely scenario that explains all the relevant evidence is that a somewhat provincial understanding of YHWH's covenant with Israel (Exod 19-24) was at home in the traditions of Israel in general and in Hosea in particular, especially since many of the themes of the eighth-century prophets appear to be addressed in the Covenant Code.[60] This covenant theology then received in the seventh century its full expression among the Deuteronomic reformers. Those reformers, it seems only logical, were influenced most and best by Hosea and perhaps other northern traditions, adding several features, primary among them the reimagining of YHWH's covenant on the model of a Neo-Assyrian treaty document.[61]

The next block of material reflects a strident opprobrium against the making of kings and princes.

> They have made kings, but not with My sanction;
> They have made princes, but not of My choice.
> With their silver and gold
> They have made themselves images,

> To their own undoing.
> He rejects your calf, O Samaria!
> I am furious with them!
> Will they never be capable of purity?
> For it was Israel's doing;
> It was only made by a joiner,
> It is not a god.
> No, the calf of Samaria
> shall be reduced to splinters! (Hos 8:4–6)

The prophet's disdain for kings and princes finds full-throated expression here because they make idols, which may well reflect Canaanite royal ideology imported into the northern kingdom's political life.[62] Parallel *hiphil* expressions, "made kings" (*himlîkû*) and "made princes" (*hēśîrû*),[63] unequivocally condemn Israel's many royal figures, the burden of which is their undoing, as the corresponding nouns (*melek* and *śārîm*) make clear (Hos 8:10). This is, of course, a quite general condemnation of royal ideology, without providing details. Was Hosea condemning kingship in general, including the Davidic line in Judah or just the way in which the people of Israel were participating in acclamation processes that led to multiple dynasties in the north? While we cannot answer these questions, the text is clear that the problem with Israelite kings is that they did not have YHWH's sanction (they were not "from" YHWH), nor were they of his choice (YHWH did not "know" them).

Deuteronomy's "law of the king" (17:14–20) is much studied, but little consensus has emerged. The law contributes to an encompassing vision of the people of YHWH under a "constitutional theocracy," in which the knowledge of the *tôrâ* is "democratized" by means of a pervasive culture of learning that reaches the king himself.[64] In this understanding, Israel's king need not be a descendant of David, although he must be a fellow Israelite. Other prerequisites are listed, but primary among them is the insistence that the king of Israel must be an exemplary student of the *tôrâ*, supervising its preservation through Levitical copies, learning to read it himself and constantly, and living by its precepts (17:18–20). This may surely and naturally be taken as an extrapolation of Hosea's objection that Israel's kings were not sanctioned or chosen by YHWH. Deuteronomy responds by allowing that a monarch may be set over Israel, like those of the nations around them, except that this king is one "whom YHWH your God will choose" (17:15). The law then proceeds to clarify what YHWH's choice implies.

As a possible extrapolation of the prophetic admonishment, now stated positively, the Deuteronomic Code expresses a qualified acceptance of monarchy. It seems unlikely, I think, even allowing for the possibility of layers of late Deuteronom(ist)ic reconceptualization of kingship, to postulate a royal ideology at home in the early Second Temple period that did not insist on Davidic lineage.[65] It seems eminently more likely that this law of the king stands historically and ideologically between an older criticism of monarch at home in the prophetic circles of Israel and the later Deuteronomic movement.[66] This places the law between the older north Israelite traditions that were opposed to kingship and the Deuteronomistic traditions of the exilic period that glorified the Davidic line.

Furthermore, the law's subtle warning against a king who acquires large quantities of silver and gold for himself (17:17) may well have in view Hosea's loathing of the use of silver for the production of *'ăṣabbîm*—images of false gods (Hos 8:4b; *DCH* 6:526; *HALOT* 2:865;

LXX *eidōla*). Hosea is ambiguous whether the king himself or the Israelites are guilty of using silver for the manufacture of idols. But the immediate literary proximity of kings and the abuse of silver is at least suggestive for Deuteronomy (17:17). The prophet's scathing "He rejects your calf, Samaria," speaks of the bull image as a "male calf" or "young bull" (*'ēgel* Hos 8:5–6), which appears to draw on northern traditions common with the Elohist (Exod 32:4, 8, 19, 24, 35), most likely referring scornfully to Jeroboam's original heresy at Bethel.[67] The irrational dependence upon idolatry, leading to exile among the nations, is a theme that continues into the next block of material in Hosea (Hos 8:1-14), and which also has much in common with Deuteronomy.

A final text excoriates Israel for its multiplication of altars and the rejection of *tôrâ*.

> For Ephraim has multiplied altars—for guilt;
> His altars have redounded to his guilt:
> The many teachings I wrote for him
> Have been treated as something alien.
> When they present sacrifices to Me,
> It is but flesh for them to eat:
> YHWH has not accepted them.
> Behold, He remembers their iniquity,
> He will punish their sins:
> Back to Egypt with them!
> Israel has forgotten his Maker;
> And built temples
> (And Judah has fortified many cities).
> So I will set fire to his cities,
> And it shall consume their fortresses. (Hos 8:11–14)

Any casual reading of this pericope reveals a striking number of lexical and ideological connections with Deuteronomy. While this opening statement is clearly not a call for cult centralization, the prophetic critique of multiple altars (*mizbəḥōt* Hos 10:1, 8; 12:12) is nevertheless clear and likely a forerunner to Deuteronomy's call for centralization (12:1–31), as an agenda for the rest of Deuteronomic law.[68]

More striking still, from the perspective of comparison with Deuteronomy, is the reference to "the many teachings" that YHWH wrote for Israel (Hos 8:12a). The phrase is difficult, and the text of MT (*Qere*) is *rubbê tôrātî* ("the numerous things of my *tôrâ*"), which could just as easily be taken as plural "laws" (*tôrōtî*) with no consonantal emendation.[69] However, the plural form "my laws" is not necessary since the nomen regens, "multitude" (whether *Qere* or *Kethiv*), connotes plurality of the substantive clause, and *tôrâ* in Hosea is a singular concept elsewhere (Hos 4:6; 8:1, 12).[70] Wolff states categorically that Hosea's concept of Torah as the entire "knowledge of God" inaugurates a comprehensive understanding that was later presupposed by Deuteronomy.[71] While it is impossible to determine what "the multitude of my *tôrâ*" might have been, the prophetic critique alleges that even an authoritative written text would be distorted into something strange in ancient Israel, and therefore rejected.[72]

In conjunction with the innovative and distinctive use of *tôrâ* in Hosea and Deuteronomy, the prophet's notion that YHWH wrote (or will write; the prefix form *'ektāb* is either preterite or future) the *tôrâ* for Ephraim is also striking. The theme of writing and written communication is prominent in Deuteronomy, reflected in (a) YHWH's writing of the Ten Words on two stone tablets (4:13; 5:22; 9:10; 10:1–4); (b) the command to write certain precious words upon one's doorposts and gates (6:9; 11:20); (c) the mandate for the ideal Deuteronomic king to have a copy of the *tôrâ* written in the presence of the Levitical priests (17:18); (d) the provision for a written certificate of divorce (24:1, 3); and finally, (e) the theme builds to a crescendo (27–31), where the verb "write" (*ktb*) occurs twelve times, often in conjunction with *tôrâ* or "book" (*sēper*).[73] If one assumes that this tradition (Hos 8:12) is original to the prophetic collection, rather than a late Deuteronom(ist)ic redaction, then the likelihood of influence from the eighth-century Hosea to the Deuteronomic reformers finds in this expression another connection.

A further lexical connection to consider is the contrast in Hosea (Hos 8:13–14) between YHWH's remembering (*yizkōr*) of Israel's iniquity, on the one hand, and Israel's forgetting (*wayyiškaḥ*) its Maker, on the other hand. The contrasting themes of remembering (*zkr*) and forgetting (*škḥ*) are taken up and elaborated in Deuteronomy (Deut 8:12–14; Hos 13:6).[74] The warning "back to Egypt with them (Hos 8:13)" recurs in both Hosea (Hos 9:3; 11:5) and Deuteronomy (17:16; 28:68) as another shared theme as well as the appeal so central to Hosea's pervasive message to "return" (*šwb*) to YHWH (Hos 6:1 passim; Deut 4:29–30).[75]

All these themes found in Hosea (Hos 8:1–14)—covenant, *tôrâ*, monarchy, idolatry, cult centralization, "remembering" and "forgetting," the writing of *tôrâ*, and more—are essential to the Deuteronomic agenda. The concentration of themes and lexical connections between Hosea and Deuteronomy are suggestive that it could even have been a handbook, something like a "Bible" or sacred text inspiring the early Deuteronomic reformers. Moreover, the chapter is a relatively self-contained unit, which is integrally bound to a larger discourse extending through Hosea (Hos 4:1–11:12) and, indeed, to the book as a whole.[76] This makes it less likely, in my view, that the whole of this chapter has been significantly expanded by a late Deuteronom(ist)ic redaction sufficient to explain all these connections. Moreover, the mention of "Judah" (Hos 8:14), like other references to Judah (Hos 1:7; 4:15; 5:5; 6:11), are perfectly natural if, as I believe is likely, Hosea himself lived as many as twenty years after 722 BCE and finished his career in Judah attempting to explain what went wrong in Israel.[77] Such an approach explains the conceptual connections between Hosea and Deuteronomy; as Hos 2:4-25 may be said to be "a merger of the tradition of hortatory prose with Hosea's prophecy,"[78] Deuteronomy is then a legal or priestly extrapolation of Hosea's message.

CONCLUSION

The connections between Deuteronomy and Hosea can hardly be denied, although scholars differ on whether the connections are essential or incidental; that is, whether they are deep-level contacts reflecting an historical relationship, or whether they might be merely surface-level or phraseological links as a result of shared cultural background, or perhaps owing to late redactional insertions. One's decisions about the direction of influence between these two books, and the timing of such influence, will predetermine one's answer to the question of Deuteronomy's origins, whether in Israel or Judah.

On the one hand, current understandings of transmission processes also contribute to the impasse. If one presumes a composition theory that confidently involves a multilayered redaction history, resulting in numerous literary strands in proto-Deuteronom(ist)ic, Deuteronom(ist)ic, and post-Deuteronom(ist)ic redactional strata of the Pentateuch and the several books related to Deuteronomy, and that Hosea itself evinces such layers from late post-Deuteronomistic redacting, then the questions addressed in this chapter are essentially unanswerable.

If, on the other hand, Hosea evinces a certain literary integrity, as has been suggested here, which cannot be explained by appealing to late redactional changes, then we have a different outcome. And since Deuteronomy's legal core (12:1–26:19) can stand alone without its narrative frames (1:1–11:32; 27:1–34:12), yet those frames themselves cannot be read alone, it follows that the legal core is older. And if older, it stands to reason that Deuteronomy's legal core may indeed have been influenced by the tradents who preserved and completed the composition of Hosea. In this likely scenario, it seems to me, the theory that explains the most data and answers more questions than it raises is that proto-Deuteronomy (at least) originated in Israel, or in Judah by northern tradents.

Notes

1. I thank my students Chelcent Fuad and Aaron Woods for their assistance with an early version of this chapter.
2. Cynthia Edenburg and Reinhard Müller, "A Northern Provenance for Deuteronomy? A Critical Review," *Hebrew Bible and Ancient Israel* 4 (2015): 148–161, esp. 148.
3. Julius Wellhausen, *Die Composition des Hexateuchs und der historischen Bücher des Alten Testaments*, 3rd ed. (Berlin: Georg Reimer, 1899), 193.
4. S. R. Driver, *A Critical and Exegetical Commentary on Deuteronomy*, ICC 5 (Edinburgh: T. & T. Clark, [1895]1965), xxvii; Moshe Weinfeld, *Deuteronomy and the Deuteronomic School* (Oxford: Clarendon Press, 1972), 366–370; Francis I. Andersen and David Noel Freedman, *Hosea: A New Translation with Introduction and Commentary*, AB 24 (Garden City: Doubleday, 1980), 131–132; and Hans-Jürgen Zobel, "Hosea und das Deuteronomium: Erwägungen eines Alttestamentlers zum Thema 'Sprache und Theologie,'" *Theologische Literaturzeitung* 110 (1985): 14–24.
5. Adam C. Welch, *The Code of Deuteronomy: A New Theory of Its Origin* (London: J. Clarke & Co., Limited, 1924), 190–192 and 193–220; and see Gary N. Knoppers, "The Northern Context of the Law-Code in Deuteronomy," *Hebrew Bible and Ancient Israel* 4 (2015): 162–183, and Ernest W. Nicholson, *Deuteronomy and Tradition* (Philadelphia: Fortress Press, 1967), 58–82.
6. Walther Baumgartner, "Der Kampf um das Deuteronomium," *Theologische Rundschau* 1 (1929): 7–25.
7. Baumgartner, "Kampf," 21–22. Welch believed Deut 12:1–7 was a late insertion, and that the book generally did not prescribe centralization; Welch, *Code of Deuteronomy*, 55–62.
8. Albrecht Alt, "Die Heimat des Deuteronomiums," in *Kleine Schriften zur Geschichte des Volkes Israel, Vol. 2* (München: Beck, 1953), 2:250–275, esp. 272–275. Followed by many in the field, most notably Gerhard von Rad, *Studies in Deuteronomy* (Chicago: H. Regnery Co, 1953), 60–69.
9. Paul Kleinert, *Das Deuteronomium und der Deuteronomiker: Untersuchungen zur alttestamentlichen Rechts- und Literaturgeschichte* (Bielefeld: Velhagen & Klasing, 1872), 166–168; cf. Reinhard G. Kratz, "The Headings of the Book of Deuteronomy," in

      Deuteronomy in the Pentateuch, Hexateuch, and the Deuteronomistic History, ed. Konrad Schmid and Raymond F. Person, FAT/II 56 (Tübingen: Mohr Siebeck, 2012), 31–46.
10. Ronald E. Clements, "Deuteronomy and the Jerusalem Cult Tradition," *Vetus Testamentum* 15 (1965): 300–312, here 300.
11. Alexander Rofé, *Deuteronomy: Issues and Interpretation* (London: T&T Clark, 2002), 8.
12. Rofé, *Deuteronomy*, 8–9. Similarly, see Moshe Weinfeld, "The Emergence of the Deuteronomic Movement: The Historical Antecedents," in *Das Deuteronomium: Entstehung, Gestalt und Botschaft*, ed. Norbert Lohfink, BETL 68 (Leuven: University Press, 1985), 76–98.
13. Yair Hoffman, "A North Israelite Typological Myth and a Judaean Historical Tradition: The Exodus in Hosea and Amos," *Vetus Testamentum* 39 (1989): 169–182, esp. 181–182.
14. Nicholson, *Deuteronomy and Tradition*, 70.
15. Nicholson, *Deuteronomy and Tradition*, 76–79.
16. Cf. Andersen and Freedman, *Hosea*, 131; and J. Andrew Dearman, *The Book of Hosea*, NICOT (Grand Rapids: Eerdmans, 2010), 39.
17. Ernest W. Nicholson, *Deuteronomy and the Judaean Diaspora* (Oxford: Oxford University Press, 2014), 10 and 74–100.
18. Hans Walter Wolff, "Hoseas geistige Heimat," *Theologische Literaturzeitung* 81 (1956): 83–94; repr. *Gesammelte Studien* (Munich: Kaiser, 1964), 232–250, esp. 244–250.
19. Hans Walter Wolff, *Hosea: A Commentary on the Book of the Prophet Hosea*, trans. Gary Stansell, Hermeneia (Philadelphia: Fortress Press, 1974), xxxi; Wolff, "Hoseas geistige Heimat." Cf. Konstantin Zobel, *Prophetie und Deuteronomium: Die Rezeption prophetischer Theologie durch das Deuteronomium*, Beihefte zu Zeitschrift fur die alttestamentliche Wissenschaft 199 (Berlin: de Gruyter, 1992), 5–6, 49, and *passim*.
20. Wolff, *Hosea*, 226, and *passim* for his repeated assertions throughout the commentary that Deuteronomy has appropriated, expanded, and given new form to the older preaching of Hosea.
21. On the problem of the range of terms—proto-Deuteronomic, Deuteronomic, post-Deuteronomic, early-Deuteronomistic, Deuteronomistic, late-Deuteronomistic, post-Deuteronomistic, and now even simili-Deuteronomistic and anti-Deuteronomistic—see Hans Ausloos, *The Deuteronomist's History: The Role of the Deuteronomist in Historical-Critical Research into Genesis-Numbers*, Oudtestamentische studiën 67 (Leiden: Brill, 2015), 259–285 and 335–336.
22. Wolff, *Hosea*, xxix–xxxii, for what follows.
23. Wolff, *Hosea*, xxii and xxxi.
24. The way the prophet's discourses are "threaded with Deuteronomic ideas" has led to another possibility that the themes and phraseology shared by Hosea and Deuteronomy were already authoritative in the north in the eighth century BCE; Andersen and Freedman, *Hosea*, 75. While this cannot be ruled out as impossible, it is even more theoretical than the late redaction theory.
25. For example, T. C. Vriezen and A. S. van der Woude, *Ancient Israelite and Early Jewish Literature*, trans. Brian Doyle (Leiden: Brill, 2005), 263. Cf. also Patrick D. Miller, Jr, *Deuteronomy*, IBC (Louisville: John Knox Press, 1990), 5; Jack R. Lundbom, *Deuteronomy: A Commentary* (Grand Rapids: Eerdmans, 2013), 29.
26. Moshe Weinfeld, *Deuteronomy 1–11: A New Translation with Introduction and Commentary*, AB 5 (New York: Doubleday, 1991), 1–84.
27. Rofé, *Deuteronomy*, 7–9 and 100–101; and cf. Weinfeld, *Deuteronomic School*, 366.
28. For example, Richard D. Nelson, *Deuteronomy: A Commentary*, OTL (Louisville: Westminster John Knox, 2002), 7.

29. Heath D. Dewrell, "Yareb, Shalman, and the Date of the Book of Hosea," *Catholic Biblical Quarterly* 78 (2016): 413–429, esp. 423–424.
30. Konrad Schmid, *A Historical Theology of the Hebrew Bible*, trans. Peter Altmann (Grand Rapids: Eerdmans, 2019), 225. Schmid especially highlights Deut 21:15–21; 22:13–29; 24:1–4; and 25:5–10 in this category, contrasted with only one individual stipulation in the Covenant Code (Exod 22:16–17).
31. Joseph Blenkinsopp, "Bethel in the Neo-Babylonian Period," in *Judah and the Judeans in the Neo-Babylonian Period*, ed. Oded Lipschitz and Joseph Blenkinsopp (Winona Lake: Eisenbrauns, 2003), 93–107; Ernst Axel Knauf, "Bethel: The Israelite Impact on Judean Language and Literature," in *Judah and the Judeans in the Persian Period*, ed. Oded Lipschitz and Manfred Oeming (Winona Lake: Eisenbrauns, 2006), 291–349.
32. Nadav Na'aman, "Sojourners and Levites in the Kingdom of Judah in the Seventh Century BCE," *Zeitschrift für altorientalische und biblische Rechtsgeschichte* 14 (2008): 237–279; and Nadav Na'aman, "Dismissing the Myth of a Flood of Israelite Refugees in the Late Eighth Century BCE," *Zeitschrift für die alttestamentliche Wissenschaft* 126 (2014): 1–14; Israel Finkelstein, "Migration of Israelites into Judah after 720 BCE: An Answer and an Update," *Zeitschrift für die alttestamentliche Wissenschaft* 127 (2015): 188–206; and see Knoppers, "Northern Context," 182n59.
33. Philip R. Davies, "Josiah and the Law Book," in *Good Kings and Bad Kings*, ed. Lester L. Grabbe, Library of Hebrew Bible/Old Testament studies 393:5 (London: T&T Clark International, 2005), 65–77; compared with Rainer Albertz, "Why a Reform Like Josiah's Must Have Happened," in the same volume (27–46).
34. Daniel E. Fleming, *The Legacy of Israel in Judah's Bible: History, Politics, and the Reinscribing of Tradition* (New York: Cambridge University Press, 2012), 114–132.
35. Karel van der Toorn, *Scribal Culture and the Making of the Hebrew Bible* (Cambridge: Harvard University Press, 2007), 89–96; and Diether Kellermann, לֵוִי, *Theological Dictionary of the Old Testament* 7:483–503. Some would speculate further that the Levites of the north, with origins in the Elide priesthood, eventually came into conflict with Aaronides and Zadokites of the south; Deborah W. Rooke, *Zadok's Heirs: The Role and Development of the High Priesthood in Ancient Israel* (Oxford: Oxford University Press, 2000), 52–62.
36. Stephen L. Cook, *The Social Roots of Biblical Yahwism*, Studies in biblical literature, Society of Biblical Literature 8 (Atlanta: Society of Biblical Literature, 2004), 67–120 and 231–266.
37. Gale A. Yee, *Composition and Tradition in the Book of Hosea: A Redaction Critical Investigation*, SBLDS 102 (Atlanta: Scholars Press, 1987), 305–313; Martti Nissinen, *Prophetie, Redaktion und Fortschreibung im Hoseabuch: Studien zum Werdegang eines Prophetenbuches im Lichte von Hos 4 und 11*, AOAT 231 (Kevelaer: Butzon & Bercker, 1991), 336–350. See further Nicholson, *Deuteronomy and the Judaean Diaspora*, 88–90; Ehud Ben Zvi, *Hosea*, FOTL 21A/1 (Grand Rapids: Eerdmans, 2005), 12–19 and 30–31; and James M. Bos, *Reconsidering the Date and Provenance of the Book of Hosea: The Case for Persian-Period Yehud*, LHB/OTS 580 (London: T&T Clark, 2013), 130–163.
38. Knoppers, "Northern Context," 169–177.
39. Gary N. Knoppers, *Jews and Samaritans: The Origins and History of Their Early Relations* (Oxford: Oxford University Press, 2013), 45–70.
40. Edenburg and Müller, "Northern Provenance," esp. 154–155.
41. Edenburg and Müller, "Northern Provenance," 155.
42. Johannes Renz, *Schrift und Schreibertradition: Eine paläographische Studie zum kulturgeschichtlichen Verhältnis von israelitischem Nordreich und Südreich*, ADPV 23

(Wiesbaden: Harrassowitz, 1997), 46 and 51–52; and cf. Johannes Renz and Wolfgang Röllig, *Handbuch der althebräischen Epigraphik*, 3 vols. in 4 (Darmstadt: Wissenschaftliche Buchgesellschaft, 1995), II/1.95–208.

43. On the Old Hebrew script, see Christopher A. Rollston, *Writing and Literacy in the World of Ancient Israel: Epigraphic Evidence from the Iron Age*, Society of Biblical Literature, Archaeology and biblical studies 11 (Leiden: Brill, 2010), 42–44. Caution is needed with this evidence for a variety of reasons; cf. Fleming, *The Legacy of Israel in Judah's Bible*, 300–303.
44. Knoppers, *Jews and Samaritans*, 28–42, here 29. On so-called Israelian Hebrew, see Gary A. Rendsburg, "The Strata of Biblical Hebrew," *Journal of Northwest Semitic Languages* 17 (1991): 81–99, esp. 87–92; cf. also Rollston, *Writing and Literacy*, 109.
45. Christopher A. Rollston, "Scribal Education in Ancient Israel: The Old Hebrew Epigraphic Evidence," *The Bulletin of the American Schools of Oriental Research* 344 (2006): 47–74, esp. 67–68; Renz and Röllig, *Handbuch*, II/1.98–99; Seth L. Sanders, *The Invention of Hebrew* (Urbana: University of Illinois Press, 2009), 122–133 and 157–168.
46. Bill T. Arnold, "Number Switching in Deuteronomy 12–26 and the Quest for Urdeuteronomium," *Zeitschrift für Altorientalische und Biblische Rechtsgeschichte* 23 (2017): 163–180, esp. 178–180.
47. For example, cf. Raymond F. Person and Robert Rezetko, "Introduction: The Importance of Empirical Models to Assess the Efficacy of Source and Redaction Criticism," in *Empirical Models Challenging Biblical Criticism*, ed. Raymond F. Person and Robert Rezetko, AIL 25 (Atlanta: Society of Biblical Literature Press, 2016), 1–35.
48. James Robson, "The Literary Composition of Deuteronomy," in *Interpreting Deuteronomy: Issues and Approaches*, ed. David G. Firth and Philip S. Johnston (Downers Grove: IVP Academic, 2012), 19–59, esp. 48–49.
49. For example, David M. Carr, "Method in Determination of Direction of Dependence: An Empirical Test of Criteria Applied to Exodus 34,11–26 and Its Parallels," in *Gottes Volk am Sinai: Untersuchungen zu Ex 32–34 und Dtn 9–10*, ed. Matthias Köckert and Erhard Blum, Veröffentlichungen der Wissenschaftlichen Gesellschaft für Theologie 18 (Gütersloh: Gütersloher Verlagshaus, 2001), 107–140. Cf. also Geoffrey David Miller, "Intertextuality in Old Testament Research," *Currents in Biblical Research* 9 (2011): 283–309.
50. Unless otherwise noted, translations throughout are the author's, occasionally tied to the NJPS.
51. Interestingly, Deuteronomy's long list of curses also flips the imagery; cf. 28:49.
52. Andersen and Freedman, *Hosea*, 486; Dearman, *Hosea*, 217.
53. Besides here in 8:1, cf. Hos 6:7, and Deut 17:2, Josh 23:16; Judg 2:20; 2 Kgs 18:12; cf. Weinfeld, *Deuteronomic School*, 367.
54. Mayer I. Gruber, *Hosea: A Textual Commentary*, Library of Hebrew Bible/Old Testament studies 653 (New York: Bloomsbury T&T Clark, 2017), 340.
55. A. A. Macintosh, *A Critical and Exegetical Commentary on Hosea*, ICC (Edinburgh: T&T Clark, 1997), 293.
56. Dearman, *Hosea*, 218 and 231.
57. For the argument that covenant theology is a Josianic development, see Lothar Perlitt, *Bundestheologie im Alten Testament*, Wissenschaftliche Monographien zum Alten und Neuen Testament 36 (Neukirchen Vluyn: Neukirchener Verlag, 1969), 4–6 and 146–152.
58. Dearman, *Hosea*, 50–59 and 217–218.
59. Bernard M. Levinson, *Deuteronomy and the Hermeneutics of Legal Innovation* (New York: Oxford University Press, 1997); Benjamin Kilchör, *Mosetora und*

Jahwetora: Das Verhältnis von Deuteronomium 12–26 zu Exodus, Levitikus und Numeri, Beihefte zur Zeitschrift für altorientalische und biblische Rechtsgeschichte 21 (Wiesbaden: Harrassowitz Verlag, 2015).

60. Frank Crüsemann, "Das Bundesbuch—Historischer Ort und Institutioneller Hintergrund," in *Congress Volume, Jerusalem 1986*, ed. J. A. Emerton, Vetus Testamentum Supplements 40 (Leiden: Brill, 1988), 27–41, esp. 40–41.
61. Jan Joosten, "Covenant," in *The Oxford Handbook of Biblical Law*, ed. Pamela Barmash (Oxford: Oxford University Press, 2019), 7–18, esp. 15–16.
62. Andersen and Freedman, *Hosea*, 492.
63. The only occurrence of the H-stem of this root, *śrr* I, "appoint a ruler; set up a prince" (*Dictionary of Classical Hebrew* 8:199; *Hebrew and Aramaic Lexicon of the Old Testament* 3:1363).
64. Dominik Markl, *Gottes Volk im Deuteronomium*, Beihefte zur Zeitschrift für altorientalische und biblische Rechtsgeschichte 18 (Wiesbaden: Harrassowitz, 2012), 307.
65. For example, Reinhard Müller, "Israel's King as *Primus Inter Pares*: The 'Democratic' Re-conceptualization of Monarchy in Deut 17:14–20," in *Leadership, Social Memory, and Judean Discourse in the Fifth-Second Centuries BCE*, ed. Diana V. Edelman and Ehud Ben Zvi, Worlds of the Ancient Near East and Mediterranean (Sheffield: Equinox, 2016), 57–76.
66. Alexander Rofé, "Ephraimite versus Deuteronomistic History," in *Storia e tradizioni di Israele: Scritti in Inore di J. Alberto Soggin*, ed. Daniele Garrone and Felice Israel (Brescia: Paideia, 1991), 221–235, esp. 228–229; reprinted in *Reconsidering Israel and Judah: Recent Studies on the Deuteronomistic History* (G. N. Knoppers and J. G. McConville, eds.; Winona Lake: Eisenbrauns, 2000), 462–474.
67. Cook, *Social Roots*, 252–254.
68. Andersen and Freedman allow that "centralization of the cult might appear the most logical next move" for prophetic critique; *Hosea*, 508.
69. Following LXX, Aquila, Syriac, and Vulgate. It is also just as likely that the phrase is conditional, "Though I write for him the multitude of my instructions" (NRSV).
70. Wolff, *Hosea*, 133; Dearman, *Hosea*, 227; Macintosh, *Hosea*, 325; *contra* Andersen and Freedman, *Hosea*, 509.
71. Wolff, *Hosea*, 138.
72. Dearman speculates that the prophet may have known and referred in this statement to the Book of the Covenant, the Deuteronomic Code, the Holiness Code, or less likely, even to a collection of Hosea's own prophecies; cf. Dearman, *Hosea*, 231.
73. Deut 27:3, 8; 28:58, 61; 29:19[20], 20[21], 26[27]; 30:10; 31:9, 19, 22, 24. Jean-Pierre Sonnet, *The Book within the Book: Writing in Deuteronomy*, Biblical Interpretation Series 14 (Leiden: Brill, 1997).
74. Weinfeld, *Deuteronomic School*, 367–368; cf. also Michael Carasik, *Theologies of the Mind in Biblical Israel*, StBibLit 85 (New York: Peter Lang, 2005), 188–196.
75. Weinfeld, *Deuteronomic School*, 369.
76. Andersen and Freedman, *Hosea*, 482–483.
77. Dewrell, "Yareb," 424. Dewrell makes the excellent point that his context in Judah around 700 BCE explains Hosea's continued invective against the shrine at Bethel, as though the people of the north had incredibly failed to learn their lesson (Hos 4:15; 5:8; 10:5,15; 12:4; 13:2).
78. Andersen and Freedman, *Hosea*, 131.

CHAPTER 22

DEUTERONOMY AND JEREMIAH

MARK LEUCHTER

Who Began the Conversation?

OVER roughly a century of modern critical scholarship, no consensus has been reached on the questions that attend the matter of Deuteronomy's relationship to the book of Jeremiah. There has never been agreement on how to date Deuteronomy, how to identify its authors' social and theological background, whether anything can be said about the historical Jeremiah's relationship to these authors, or even if the book of Jeremiah and its contributors have much to do with the historical prophet of the same name. To be sure, virtually all critical scholars recognize that the relationship exists—the book of Jeremiah has far more Deuteronomistic language than any other prophetic book, and the superscription assigns its contents to the same historical period in which we are told that Deuteronomy came to public attention (Jer 1:1–2; 2 Kgs 22:8–11). But beyond this very basic point of agreement, the opinions spread out as far and wide as the nations who departed from the Tower of Babel.

While the views regarding the Deuteronomy–Jeremiah relationship are varied, the positions regarding the origins, provenance, and social setting for the composition of Deuteronomy are somewhat easier to summarize. Of course, many arguments have been advanced ranging from Late Bronze Age authorship (Berman 2011) to Hellenistic-era shaping (Gmirkin 2017) and all points in between, but most scholarly models tend to fall into three primary categories. The first of these is that the work is a late monarchic composition appearing during the reign of King Josiah and produced by elite Jerusalemite scribes of the seventh century BCE. The second is that the work is primarily exilic, penned by Judahite scribes in exile, and developed by those same scribal circles during the Persian period. Third, though less commonly argued, is that Deuteronomy is early monarchic and northern in its compositional origins and was transmitted to Judah (in substantial form) following the fall of the north in 721 BCE. In what follows I will adopt a perspective that largely matches the first opinion, but with some adjustments. As I will discuss further later, Deuteronomy should be viewed as a repository of late monarchic traditions deriving from the time of Josiah (642–609 BCE), with a substantial edition of the book emerging at this time (Leuchter 2007). Yet this edition became a theological curriculum that continued to grow in subsequent eras, and the book of Jeremiah shows signs of influence and interaction with Deuteronomy during various phases in its development. With this understanding in mind, we shall turn to a consideration of how scholars have attempted to account for the Deuteronomy–Jeremiah relationship, and how those attempts have evolved over roughly a century of critical research.

It was with Bernard Duhm's commentary that the book of Jeremiah was first truly subjected to a careful literary analysis, resulting in a model that partitioned it into three principle sources, with only a relatively small amount of material—all poetic—assigned to the prophet and the rest siphoned off and regarded as simply tertiary scribal additions (Duhm 1901). Building on Duhm, Sigmund Mowinckel's approach to the book similarly identified major source-critical distinctions (poetry in Source A, prose narrative in Source B, prose "sermons" in Source C, and an independent poetic anthology in Jer 30–31 in Source D); Source C contained the close connections to Deuteronomy's language (Mowinckel 1914). Yet like Duhm, Mowinckel did not regard the C material as any notable reflection of Jeremiah's actual teachings. In his view, the divinely inspired material—and thus the "authentic" prophetic utterances—were restricted to the poetry in the A source, with Baruch's contribution in the B material providing a lesser yet still valuable narrative context. Thus, despite the clear connection to Deuteronomy's language, Mowinckel's argument relegated the C material to the margins of the book of Jeremiah, an obstacle in the attempt to recover the genuine teachings and message of the great prophet himself.

Like many scholars of their era, Duhm and Mowinckel built their arguments on several assumptions concerning literary genres and theological perspectives that no longer enjoy acceptance in critical scholarly work. The first was the priority given in the study of prophetic texts to tease out the *ipsissima verba* of the prophet, which diminished the importance of material in these texts that appeared to derive from elsewhere. With the goal of recovering what these scholars believed were the actual words of the prophets, the other passages in these prophetic works were little more than fat to be trimmed, devoid of real significance. The second assumption was that "genuine" prophecy was to be identified with poetry, while prose material was later and inauthentic; the Deuteronomistic passages were placed in a decidedly less significant category.

Mid-twentieth-century scholarship saw some advances but still utilized the basic source-critical model. J. Phillip Hyatt argued that while the prophet no doubt knew the book of Deuteronomy (in some form), his message stood in contradistinction to it, and the secondary scribes who developed the Jeremiah traditions attempted to "claim" Jeremiah for their own literary and ideological enterprise through adding Deuteronomistic material into their collection of prophetic texts (Hyatt 1942). Hyatt's argument was a major step forward as it attempted to penetrate the social and cultural reality of the scribes themselves, positing their own acceptance of Deuteronomy and the theological and intellectual tradition it heralded. John Bright, by contrast, revisited the question of source-critical provenance: while he recognized the formal distinctions between poetry and prose, his analysis of the prose sermons led him to the conclusion that some of these texts may well have derived from the prophet himself, or were at lease closely connected to the prophet's own preaching. The literary style, he proposed, was a matter of convention: the language of the prose sermons reflected the way that literate figures in Jeremiah's era expressed themselves in writing (Bright 1951), a position he continued to advance in his subsequent commentary on the book (Bright 1965).

The direction of research changed, however, in the 1970s and 1980s, beginning with an essay by James Muilenberg (1970) and followed by Gunther Wanke's monograph (1971), each taking very different approaches to the question of Baruch b. Neriah's contribution to the book of Jeremiah. Muilenberg attempted to situate Baruch in the context of a "scribal era" and take seriously how that cultural context would have affected the way someone like Baruch may have conceived of his charge as a transmitter of prophetic legacies. Wanke looked carefully at the material typically assigned to Baruch (Mowinckel's "B source") and discerned within it multiple stages of redactional growth that could not be credited to a single historical scribe in an overly simplistic or reductive manner. While neither scholar devoted much attention to the prophet Jeremiah's real or imagined interaction with the book of Deuteronomy, their work established renewed attention to material that had long been considered less significant in the study of the book of Jeremiah and brought scribes and their methods to the forefront of research.

Around the same time, Ernest Nicholson published a monograph (1970) that directed attention to the prose "sermons" in the book of Jeremiah (Mowinckel's C source). Nicholson argued that exilic Deuteronomists composed them to extend the themes of God speaking through prophets to those enduring the difficulties of forced migration away from their homeland. Nicholson also argued that though the sermons derived from preachers living among exiled Judahites in Babylon, the sermons were based on genuine teachings of the prophet; this was a departure from Bright's position, who considered Jeremiah as a possible contributor to some of the sermons, but who did not see the anonymous scribes behind the rest of this material as developing the prophet's actual teachings in a systematic manner. Nicholson's position, by contrast, posited a closer ideological relationship between the exilic Deuteronomists who composed these sermons and the prophet himself. Still, Nicholson assumed a linear direction of influence from Jeremiah to the exilic Deuteronomists; the scribes, in his view, still privilege the prophet with the one-up position and are beholden in their own work to the prophet's message and stature.

This perspective changed dramatically with the publication of a major monograph on the Deuteronomistic tradition by Moshe Weinfeld (1972). In this work, Weinfeld examined the role played by scribes throughout the ancient Near East and the strong points of contact between those scribal traditions and the rhetorical and linguistic features in the book of Deuteronomy. A major portion of Weinfeld's monograph was devoted to the Deuteronomistic material—both "sermons" and narratives—in the book of Jeremiah as part of this nexus of scribal discourse. Weinfeld understood this material as deriving from the late exilic period and classified it as an extension of the concepts in Deuteronomy and the Deuteronomistic History, a tradition that he saw originating among royal Jerusalemite scribe-sages (rather than Levites, the position argued by Rad [1953] and others). In this, he stood in general agreement with many of his predecessors that these texts were less the legacy of the prophet and more the work of subsequent scribal redactors. But from Weinfeld's perspective, this work was no less significant to the formation of the book and indeed to the development of ideas in Israelite religion than the poetic oracles he credited to the prophet himself.

Weinfeld's work was somewhat of a watershed moment in the study of the relationship between Jeremiah and Deuteronomy. He proposed that the prophetic book in its conceptual substance was ultimately the work of the scribes, not (just) the prophet after whom it was named, and a flurry of groundbreaking scholarship followed in the wake of Weinfeld's monograph. Winfried Thiel (1973) revisited the approaches of Hyatt in his careful study of passages in Deuteronomy, arguing for a thoroughgoing Deuteronomistic redaction not only of the prose but also the poetry in the book of Jeremiah. In the same year, Helga Weippert's monograph tackled the same textual material but argued that lexical particularities point not to a thoroughgoing Deuteronomistic appropriation and redaction of the Jeremiah traditions but the opposite: that the prose and poetry originated from the prophet's own ministry and showed the prophet's own contributions (Weippert 1973). In this, Weippert's discussion revived that of Bright that this circle of writers drew from a common linguistic idiom from which the Deuteronomists also drew.

Thiel and Weippert thus adopted opposite perspectives on the "language" of Deuteronomy and its authors. An attempt to break this impasse is reflected in the work of Jack R. Lundbom (1975), who drew attention to compositional methodologies that considered features beyond the strictures of locution. Lundbom utilized rhetorical-critical methods to identify units of material comprised of both poetry and prose. For Lundbom, some of these units were the result of scribes who adapted received material, but others stemmed from the prophet himself and carry the same distinct rhetorical profile evident in the book of Deuteronomy. Lundbom sought not to diminish the value of redaction-critical studies but to qualify and broaden the ways in which the source material could be considered, observing that a prophet like Jeremiah (and the scribal supporters of his day) could alternate modalities of expression in both poetry and prose while forming single and cohesive units of literary discourses. In this case, the influence of Deuteronomy was something that affected both the formation of prophetic oracles stemming from the historical Jeremiah as well as the handiwork of subsequent scribes who shaped the prophet's written oracles.

Karl-Friederich Pohlmann (1978) took up the issue of Deuteronomy and Deuteronomistic influence in Jeremiah from a rather different direction. Pohlmann argued that the book of Jeremiah (especially the historiographic material) was the result of extended redaction during the Persian period (539–332 BCE) reflecting two primary perspectives, namely, that of groups who valued the experience of exile and diaspora under Babylon (586–539 BCE) and that of groups who emphasized the experience of those with connections to the homeland during this era. Pohlmann's criteria was not based on Deuteronomistic language or ideas but, rather, how those words and concepts were applied to the communal themes of continuity in the land versus forced migration and dislocation. Pohlmann's dating of this material to a primary postexilic context accounts for expressions common in Deuteronomy evident in both authorial emphases collected in the book of Jeremiah, as Deuteronomy had become a common tradition by that time which disparate and competing groups could draw from and apply to serve their respective agendas. Pohlmann's work presumed that the Deuteronomistic impulses in the work were secondary and temporally distant from the prophet's own life and time, and simply a matter of linguistic lemmas that could be easily deployed as evidenced in other late texts (Pohlmann 1978, 16–18).

The major commentaries that emerged in the 1980s reflect the retrenchment of these different and seemingly mutually exclusive approaches to the Deuteronomy–Jeremiah connection. William Holladay's commentaries (1986, 1989) approached the book with the view that the prophet Jeremiah and his close circle of supporters knew and depended upon Deuteronomy in their activity and the texts that resulted from it. Holladay, in fact, suggested that many of the prose sermons in the book were produced in conscious awareness of Deuteronomy's call for the septennial public reading of the law (Deut 31:9–13) and were consequently crafted to coincide with such readings (Holladay 1989, 29–35). On the other end of the spectrum, Robert Carroll (1986) saw much Deuteronomistic ideology and language in the book of Jeremiah, but virtually nothing therein originating in the late monarchic era with the prophet or his scribal supporters. He assigned the overlaps to Persian-period redactors/writers and argued that the book itself gives us no way to recover reliable historical information about the era with which it is concerned.

Standing somewhere in between Holladay and Carroll is the encyclopedic commentary of William McKane (1986; the second volume was published in 1996 but is an extension of the first), who saw much Deuteronomistic material in the early compositional layers of the book. But McKane also saw the book's confusing and apparently ad-hoc structure as an indication of its redactional expansion developed over many centuries. McKane coined the term "rolling corpus" to describe this process (1986: xlix–l), where existing passages inspired later scribes to add new exegetical material, inspired not only by the language and style of the extant Jeremiah traditions they inherited but by the language and style of the Deuteronomistic literature they also knew. McKane's model drew attention to the nature of Deuteronomistic language and themes in the book as a deeply complicated phenomenon not easily ascribed to a simple line of dependence or influence from one corpus of text or texts to another.

What Is the Status of the Conversation?

The state of contemporary work on the Deuteronomy–Jeremiah relationship is in some ways as varied as the views discussed earlier. By the end of the twentieth century, something of a consensus had emerged that the Deuteronomistic language and themes in the book of Jeremiah were indeed the result of the contribution of Deuteronomistic thinkers and writers who shaped the book in the wake of the titular prophet's activity. However, disagreement on the meaning of the term "Deuteronomistic" created a new set of obstacles (see further discussion in Schearing and McKenzie 1999), and scholars remained divided over the provenance, duration, scope, and purpose of the Deuteronomistic literature, which consequently affected approaches to the Deuteronomistic valences within the book of Jeremiah.

More recent research on Deuteronomy and Jeremiah has also been characterized by a sharper break on matters of dating the composition of texts. Most North American scholars have tended to follow Weinfeld's model in one form of another in seeing the presence of Deuteronomistic language and ideology in Jeremiah, placing the principle development of this material in a late monarchic-through-exilic context. This has also been strongly informed by the influence of Frank Cross's theory regarding a pre-exilic Deuteronomistic tradition developing during the reign of Josiah (Cross 1973, 274–289; building, of course, on Martin Noth's original theory [1943]). The book of Jeremiah is often characterized as a repository of prophetic oracles following shortly after this period and extending into the early years of the exile strongly related to this tradition. Examples of this approach can be found in work by David Noel Freedman (1993, 47–48), Richard E. Friedman (1995), Marvin Sweeney (1996), and Baruch Halpern (2003), to name but a few. By contrast, others have opted to see the "Deuteronomistic" development of the Jeremiah tradition as obtaining primarily in the Persian period. From this perspective, Deuteronomistic theology may have had its roots in the late monarchic period, but the production of complex textual works deploying advanced and sophisticated methods of scribal hermeneutics are more credibly placed in a Persian context. This position has been championed (in rather different ways, it should be noted) by Konrad Schmid (1996), Eckart Otto (2007), Raymond Person (2002), Thomas Romer (1999, 2000), and Christl Maier (2002).

Both scholarly camps, however, carry problematic assumptions. As already discussed, the Deuteronomistic scribal group should not be seen as royal in orientation but as operating beyond the reach and interests of the royal court, a position that scholars who align closely with the Weinfeld and Cross traditions have generally not taken into consideration. While there can be no doubt that royal scribes produced literary materials that left an impression on the Deuteronomistic texts and the book of Jeremiah (Schniedewind 2004), studies in recent years by Lauren Monroe (2011) and Daniel Fleming (2013) have made strong cases for situating the development of some literary traditions well beyond the reach of the royal hierarchy. These studies are supported by epigraphic evidence and social-scientific factors that point to decentralized outlets for text production *alongside* central, monarchic scribal institutions throughout most of the Iron Age in Israel and Judah (Byrne 2007; Sanders 2009; Malena 2014). In this case, the prophetic protests against the royal establishment in the book of Jeremiah do not necessarily break with the ideology of the Deuteronomists or their literary achievements. The Deuteronomistic features of the book of Jeremiah fall within the range of discursive trends evident in Deuteronomy and the Deuteronomistic History, both of which may have originated during the late monarchic period, but not (strictly speaking) as pro-monarchic texts at the hands of royal scribes with a royal agenda.

The foregoing carries implications for the arguments that the Deuteronomistic development of the Jeremiah tradition took place primarily in the Persian period. These arguments often rest on the view that Judahite or early Jewish scribes could only have produced such learned scribal works under the auspices of a grand imperial cultural superstructure, a position that is difficult to maintain for a few reasons. First, while it is most certainly the case that the Persian period ushered in a new type of intellectual culture that strongly affected Jewish scribes in Jerusalem (and elsewhere), the view that the rhetorical and hermeneutical sophistication in the book of Jeremiah could only have obtained in such a setting discounts the possibility that Judahite writers in the late monarchic or exilic periods could have developed their own learned, sophisticated scribal works. Mesopotamian texts and scribal methods influenced Judahite writers well before the end of the monarchic era (Aster 2007; Machinist 1983; Levinson 2004), and the Deuteronomistic works utilizing these advanced methods are most plausibly situated (substantially) in the late monarchic period as well on internal rhetorical grounds (Leuchter 2010; Na'aman 2006). That Judahite writers of the late monarchic or exilic eras could not have developed their own sophisticated texts in conversation with scribal trends they encountered through Mesopotamian imperialism does not stand up to critical scrutiny; it neglects evidence suggesting monarchic-era scribal culture flourishing in Jerusalem and beyond during the monarchic period (Richelle 2016).

Second, the type of engagement with Mesopotamian scribal trends we encounter in the Deuteronomistic and Jeremianic corpora is quite distinct from what we find in Jewish scribal works that can be confidently dated to the Persian period. In those works, we encounter the collection of ideologically and linguistically distinct materials onto single scrolls, and the diversity of the sources was left in plain sight to highlight their distinctiveness (Sanders 2014). I have argued elsewhere that the reason for this is to be found in the adoption of Aramaic script, language, and hermeneutics that were promulgated among the scribal castes of the Persian empire. In this scribal culture, the diversity of source material was deliberately highlighted to demonstrate that retextualization of Hebrew language texts in Aramaic script somehow transcended their earlier distinctions (Leuchter 2017b). The Deuteronomistic texts do not evidence this intellectual ethos, and this also applies to the Deuteronomistic passages in the book of Jeremiah. If these passages were primarily composed in the Persian period, we should find a greater diversity of linguistic sources woven into these discourses, which is not the case; the prose style of Jeremiah is remarkably consistent. Moreover, the book of Jeremiah repeatedly draws attention to the multiplicity of Jeremiah traditions circulating in antiquity beyond the fixed boundaries of the book itself (Sharp 1997, 508–509), which stands far afield from Persian-period scribal constructs like the Pentateuch (ca. 450 BCE) or the Book of the Twelve (ca. 350 BCE). Both clearly use earlier and independent sources, but the existence of those sources beyond the material boundaries of those books receives no attention or allusion whatsoever.

Finally, there is the linguistic evidence of the book: while Deuteronomistic language could, of course, be annexed by Persian-era scribes, the concentration and distribution of this language within the book of Jeremiah far outweigh other types of traditional or conventional linguistic forms that Persian-period writers would have known. We must consider this alongside recent studies into the culture and practice of scribes in Israel and the ancient Near East more generally. The conventions of scribal culture were such that writers in the Persian period would have digested a wide variety of linguistic sources and reproduced written works bearing the rhetorical and lexical hallmarks of so broad a literary enculturation (Carr 2005; 2011, 13–101). While linguistic criteria alone may not serve as a conclusive basis for dating a text's composition or development, the sociolinguistic factors would lead us to see far more evidence of other types of linguistic convention represented in the "Deuteronomistic" sections of the book of Jeremiah if those sections were indeed composed during the Persian period. That this is not the case suggests an earlier and more limited scribal circle standing behind the book's development. Persian-period additions and shaping can most certainly be identified in the book (e.g., the MT plus in Jer 33, 14–26), but its principle composition and redaction should be placed in the late monarchic and exilic periods (Hornkohl 2014). The argument that the learned scribal dimensions of the book demanded the intellectual resources of Persian imperialism ignores these important considerations, and unfortunately perpetuates assumptions held by late nineteenth-/early twentieth-century biblical scholars that were informed by cultural and theological biases about Jewish scribes.

The foregoing points challenge the a priori assumptions that the contents of the book of Jeremiah primarily derive from a Persian-period context, but even among those scholars who do see much earlier material therein, emphases have changed in recent years. While scholars recognize the presence of Deuteronomistic discourse in the work, the focus has rested more on how that discourse has been applied and, more significantly, by whom. Building on earlier studies, Carolyn Sharp (2003) and Dalit Rom Shiloni (2013, 198–252) have directed critical attention to the diversity of social perspectives preserved in the book that draw from Deuteronomistic concepts, noting that the book of Jeremiah contains material that alternately advocates for *golah*/exilic communities, on the one hand, and communities bound to the homeland, on the other. The presence of these distinct voices within the book points to the circulation of the prophet's teachings among different groups, both of which equally knew and applied Deuteronomistic language and concepts in making their respective cases for identity and legitimacy. This proposal may support the idea of Deuteronomy as an intellectual tradition rather than the ideology of a cohesive and limited scribal group, but it may also suggest changes within a single cohesive group over time catalyzed by the turbulence of neo-Babylonian imperialism.

To this end, Nathan Mastnjak (2016) has contributed significantly to the discussion by noting that the book of Jeremiah evidences a shift in the perception of the social status of Deuteronomy as a text. Mastnjak observes that references to Deuteronomy in a variety of the poetic oracles view the work as a source of "prestige," while references in passages that are widely regarded to be from the hands of (later) Deuteronomistic redactors assume Deuteronomy to be a "classic." The former uses Deuteronomy to lend greater rhetorical weight to the discourse, while the latter presupposes its place as an authoritative and binding literary tradition. These distinctions might signal how Deuteronomy was perceived by different curators of the Jeremiah traditions and indicate a change in the character of the scribal group to which they belonged. Alternately they may represent discursive strategies used to address wider audiences whose perceptions and presumptions about Deuteronomy were in flux (presumably in the very last years of the monarchy and the period of the exile).

If the latter is the case, then the question is not whether the curators of the Jeremiah traditions changed how they perceived Deuteronomy's textuality (which from the outset was composed not solely for prestigious purposes but as a cosmic text; Leuchter 2017a, 164–177). Rather, it relates to the preservation and applicability of Jeremiah's literary legacy in connection to a binding, authoritative Deuteronomistic tradition under uncertain and turbulent social circumstances. Reckoned differently, the distinctions between references to Deuteronomy as a prestige text versus authoritative classic have to do with the writers' social location in a society facing the possibility of destruction. It may for this reason that Deuteronomy's binding nature as a written text is highlighted in the contributions of (exilic) Deuteronomistic scribes to the book of Jeremiah alongside the similar authoritative textuality of their own literary efforts (e.g., Jer 36:32). Ancient accounts of the production of textual testimonies are intimately linked to the concept of death and the desire to transmute one's living voice (*nefesh*; Vayntrub, forthcoming). The increased focus on Deuteronomy's textual authority in the book of Jeremiah may reflect this same type of anxiety on a larger ethnographic level. Indeed, the pervasive focus on writing and writers in the book of Jeremiah (Eggleston 2016) ties into this very idea, with the engagement of Deuteronomy functioning as a gauge for increased social anxiety among the Judahite audience during and after the Babylonian conquest.

What Is Trending in the Conversation?

These more recent trajectories in the study of textuality, writing, language, and social identity recommend different approaches to the study of the Deuteronomy–Jeremiah relationship. First, advances in the understanding of how scribes accessed and digested a wide spectrum of sources calls into question proposed distinctions between Deuteronomy, the

Deuteronomistic History, and the Deuteronomistic valences in the book of Jeremiah. All these literary works should be traced to a common (Levite) scribal group working in the late seventh century BCE, whose members continued to develop these works during the exilic era (see further Leuchter 2017a, 156–161). It is better to define the "Deuteronomistic" tradition as a network of sources, memories, themes, and genres that were textualized by a cohesive and distinct circle of writers; among these genres is prophecy, with the book of Jeremiah standing out as the prime example. The presence of strong Deuteronomistic currents within the book does not point to a "Jeremiah group" of Deuteronomists working at odds with a "Deuteronomistic History group" of scribes but to the Deuteronomists' interest in prophetic oracles alongside legal and narrative sources.

Consequently, the often-noted absence of Jeremiah from the Deuteronomistic History should not be evidence of a "break" between the writers behind Jeremiah and other Deuteronomists (pace Römer 2000). Rather, the turning of Deuteronomistic attention to the genre of prophecy led to the Jeremiah tradition as the principal vehicle for their ideology during the exile; this in turn influenced the subsequent exilic redaction of the Deuteronomistic History which possesses important hermeneutical points of contact with the book of Jeremiah (Leuchter 2008, 180–184). The prophet Jeremiah may not be in the final version of the Deuteronomistic History, which indicates that the principal version of that work was completed sometime before the prophet's own renown was firmly established. But the echoes of the book of Jeremiah can surely be sensed in the passages therein which developed during the latter decades of the exile, with similar influence found in Deuteronomy as well (Brettler 1999; see further later). Such hermeneutical and rhetorical connections obviated the need to write Jeremiah into the Deuteronomistic historiography as the (growing) book bearing his name was part of a larger intertextual Deuteronomistic curriculum (Leuchter 2015).

All of this affects how we may look again at the complicated question of the Deuteronomy-Jeremiah relationship with a different set of critical tools. Rather than simply looking at issues of language or themes, we should consider some larger conceptual tropes or presuppositions that speak to common worldviews shared between the works, with implications for mutually affective literary influence. It is reasonable to see Deuteronomy as the point of departure, as most commentators would agree that some form of Deuteronomy existed at the outset of Jeremiah's prophetic activity. As such, we may identify influence in a number of passages in the book that draw from it; among these are the references to Deut 15 in the manumission narrative in Jer 34, the reliance upon the covenant ceremony in Deut 27 and the covenant discourse in Jer 11, and the reference to the divorce legislation in Deut 24 in Jer 3:1. Not all of these (and other) moments appeal to Deuteronomy in quite the same way (Mastnjak 2016), but the allusions or references are either explicit or nearly so. Nevertheless, the relationship goes beyond mere verbal allusions or literary dependence (though that is an important factor, as we will see later), as both works flesh out unique social, mythological, and theological paradigms.

The first paradigm we should consider is the materiality of written texts containing sacral discourse and their social location. A variety of witnesses throughout the biblical record align with the common ancient Near Eastern dynamic that kept sacred texts within the depths of a temple and within the reach of its priestly scribes. These texts were typically accessible only to the priests and factored into a process that ended in priestly oral instruction. In such a dynamic, revelation in the public sphere was a matter of oral performance or teaching, with texts functioning behind the scenes (as it were) in an esoteric setting. Deuteronomy completely and consistently flips the script on this process in virtually all its compositional/redactional layers. Oral teaching is an essential component of its contents as witnessed in passages such as Deut 1:5 and 17:8–13, but these passages subordinate oral teaching or performance to textuality: the oral instruction described in the latter is ratified through its eventual inclusion into a written corpus, and the former is presented as a textual report of an oral episode. Elsewhere, Deuteronomy emphasizes that its contents (in some form or another) should be inscribed in a variety of locations, on a variety of materials, and for a variety of purposes. Finally, all these witnesses to the materiality of Deuteronomy's contents are identified as ways to maintain cosmic order, preventing social corrosion and maintaining the integrity of the ethnos through its accessibility (Leuchter 2017a, 175–177).

Textuality in Deuteronomy exerts a strong influence on the materiality of written prophetic oracles in the book of Jeremiah. The direction of influence here is suggested by the type of references to materiality: Deuteronomy's authors attempt to argue for the legitimacy of textual materiality as essential to revelation, while Jeremiah's authors presuppose it. More than any other prophetic book, the book of Jeremiah expressly connects its prophetic oracles not only to textual transmission but to textual origination. To be sure, many oracles reflect oral modalities of performance, but key passages within the book point to those oracles as grouped into collections characterized by material textual boundaries. One thinks, for example, of the famous *Letter to the Exiles* (Jer 29:5–7), which is noted in Jer 29:4 to have once been an independent literary source that could be carried by a royal officer on a diplomatic mission. Indeed, Jer 29 manages to transform other once-independent written sources into prophetic revelation through their retextualization into the Jeremiah traditions, which looks ahead to the opening of the following oracular unit (Jer 30–31) that expressly identifies its contents as part of a scroll (Jer 30:2).

It cannot be accidental that these oracles lead into the episode of Jer 32 that highlights the materiality of a land-deed document as the basis for revelation (Jer 32:6–15), or that all of this builds into arguably the most important episode in the entire book of Jeremiah, that is, the production, destruction, and reproduction of the so-called *Urrolle* in Jer 36. Within this episode, the materiality of the scroll is just as significant as the contents of the oracles written upon it (Jer 36:2, 4, 17–18, 21–24, 32). All these passages are situated in the center of the book of Jeremiah, establishing them as the rhetorical anchor for the oracles and narratives surrounding them. The implication is that the materiality of the book itself is essential to its revelatory message, and that the very act of its textual production holds the key to its theological meaning and function. Such a concept that would have been tremendously important to the exilic audience for whom the principal form of the book was ultimately shaped, but also to more limited groups of literati in the last decades of the monarchy who initially produced, collected, transmitted, and served as the audiences for its oracles.

This leads us to a second point, namely, that the audiences for the oracles in the book of Jeremiah were diverse both in terms of population demographics (Crouch 2017) and social/cultic setting well beyond contexts where material texts were stored or consulted. The book itself stresses this at strategic points, beginning with the call narrative in the book's opening chapter. Jeremiah is identified in Jer 1:5 as a "prophet to the nations" (*goyyim*); though the term eventually comes to mean the nations surrounding Judah (as evidenced by the "Oracles against the Nations" in MT Jeremiah 46–51), the term applies very well to the variety of lineage groups *within* Judah (Fleming 2013, 272) that comprised Jeremiah's early audiences in the late monarchic period. This is expanded a few verses later in Jer 1:10, where the prophet's audiences are not just lineage groups but the "kingdoms" (*mamlakhot*) that rise and fall. This, too, may relate to foreign kingdoms, but it also addresses the political circumstances characterizing monarchic culture and society in late seventh and early sixth centuries BCE Judah that saw much discourse on the fate of the former northern kingdom of Israel and speculation on what this meant for the Davidic monarchy. The developing book of Jeremiah surely addressed exilic audiences reflecting on their own traumatic experiences through the consultation of written works, but these earlier monarchic-era audiences would have encountered some of the book's contents in a very different form, namely, as part of the oral culture surrounding the living Jerusalem cult.

It is a mistake to imagine that the Jerusalem cult was solely the province of Aaron priests emulating the language and concepts that would find their way into the Pentateuch's P traditions, or that the Deuteronomists had little connection to or interest in it. Surely there was a distinctively Aaronide-priestly cultic tradition, but the Jerusalem cult was a centrifugal force in late monarchic Judah's social and economic world (Steiner 2003), and it would be in or adjacent to such a setting that texts like Deuteronomy would be studied, rehearsed, and debated among the literati alongside the Aaron traditions and other texts, foreign and domestic (Quick 2017, 159–178). If some of Jeremiah's oracles were delivered in Jerusalem during this same time, then they, too, became part of this eclectic discourse. That Jeremiah's oracles (both prose and poetry) so regularly contain Deuteronomistic language may be credited to their origination or performance in a cultic-social space that also included the reading and rehearsal of Deuteronomy. It is clear from multiple sources in the book of Jeremiah that the prophet's oracles were delivered in the context of temple gatherings and spaces, and Deuteronomy repeatedly emphasizes that its contents should factor into cultic settings as well. This dovetails with recent scholarship on scribal culture and the complex relationship between orality and textuality governing the composition and transmission of textual corpora; as much as discrete textual sources established a basis for oral rehearsal, oral settings and rehearsals invariably affect the way that those discrete textual works were reproduced (Carr 2011, 13–101).

This also calls into question the assignment of the various sources in Jeremiah to strict temporal or geographical categories. Many prose oracles may well stem from exilic scribal hands (and there is often rhetorical or ideology evidence in these texts to reinforce such a view), but others may have developed within the context of the Jerusalem cult where prose text traditions were part of the sacral-curricular ether shared by diverse scribal groups. Here Holladay's proposal that the prose oracles align in part with the septennial reading of Deuteronomy legislated in Deut 31:9–13 (Holladay 1989, 29–35) should be reconsidered with a significant adjustment. It may not be that the prose oracles in the book of Jeremiah were composed alongside septennial readings, as the seven-year trope connects to mythological motifs more than to programmatic intent (Leuchter 2017a, 175–176). But if Deuteronomy was part of a wider oral-intellectual culture characterizing the late-monarchic Jerusalem cult, then the recitation and study of its contents invariably influenced the formation of the early prophetic contents of the book of Jeremiah—both prose *and* poetry. Just as significantly, the shared language and themes in Jeremiah and Deuteronomy may reflect how the performance of the prophetic oracles in the same cultic/social space affected the development of the (still-forming) book of Deuteronomy.

A telling piece of evidence for this can be found in the undeniable relationship between the Song of Moses (Deut 32) and Jeremiah's oracles (Holladay 2004). Most scholars have viewed the former as a source for the prophetic locution in the latter, which is reasonable if the Song of Moses does indeed originate in an era before the late monarchic period (as is often argued; see Sanders 1998, 432). More recently, though, Mastnjak has observed that one lexical commonality shared by the Song of Moses and Jeremiah's oracles points in the opposite direction, with the oracles serving as the source material. Mastnjak concludes that the Song of Moses in its entirety should thus be viewed as a relatively late, learned-scribal work rather than an early liturgical poem (Mastnjak 2016, 224–225). But the oral-textual dynamic described earlier suggests a different way to account for the evidence; that is, the textual transmission of the old Song of Moses was affected by the way it was utilized *alongside* Jeremiah's oracles in an oral-cultic setting. That is, the language of Jeremiah's oracles found their way into the performance of the older liturgical poem because both were part of a Deuteronomistic stream of cultic discourse operative in late-monarchic Jerusalem; a scribe steeped in this discourse interpolated language from one into the other precisely because the Song of Moses was performed in the same social and ritual space as the oracles of Jeremiah.

Such a reconstruction accounts for the specific literary features that Mastnjak notes while also accounting for the more widespread reliance on the Song of Moses throughout the book of Jeremiah, aligning with common observations regarding the antiquity of the Song of Moses more generally (on linguistic and conceptual grounds). The old poem influenced the curators of the Jeremiah traditions, but the Jeremiah traditions clearly served as a prism through which the old poem was eventually refracted as it was textualized in subsequent iterations. This sheds some light on the complexity in the Deuteronomy–Jeremiah relationship insofar as it reveals that a model limited to some sort of linear dependence of one on the other cannot be easily sustained. In some cases, Deuteronomy's influence on the formation of the book of Jeremiah may be confidently asserted, while in others a more cautious consideration of phenomenological and sociological factors is required. But this also illuminates another crucial feature shared between Deuteronomy and Jeremiah, and that is the prominent authority of scribes and the explicit veneration of the scribal craft as a matter of cosmic significance. Deuteronomy highlights this in several ways, chief of which is in its characterization of Moses. Though Deuteronomy does not overtly identify Moses as a scribe (*soper*), it uses scribal language to describe his activity from the outset of the work. Moses "explicates" the (written) *torah* (Deut 1:5; Schaper 2007), and the language in Deut 4:44–45 suggests that the torah Moses "establishes" in Israel is an exegetical recombination of various written collections (*edot, huqqim, mišpatim*). Moses's own scribal activity recommences in a more explicit manner toward the end of the book in Deut 31:22–24, where he writes down what he has taught Israel in the preceding chapters. Yet as the opening canto of Deuteronomy (in its pre-exilic form) notes, YHWH's revelation and Moses's teaching are a binary pair; in Deut 5:4–5, Moses's intermediation somehow facilitates the *direct* revelation of the Decalogue, establishing that all of Moses's teachings are to be viewed as divine in origin, including their preservation in written form.

But it is ultimately the Levites—to whom Moses entrusts this written teaching—who emerge most prominently as a scribal caste in Deuteronomy. Deuteronomy makes the written *torah* accessible throughout the land and even empowers lay Israelites to write copies for themselves (Deut 6:9; 11:20; 17:18–19), but the production, transmission, reading, and teaching of the public and authoritative versions of this written *torah* are firmly placed in the hands of Levites. It is not only to them that Moses entrusts the copy he writes in Deut 31; it is the Levites who oversee the covenant ceremony in Deut 27 where a public copy of the *torah* is written at Mt. Ebal (or, in some manuscript versions, Mt. Gerizim), suggesting that it is they who write the public copy in question. It is also Levites who are implicitly presented as teachers and explicators of the written *torah* akin to the model established by Moses (Deut 16:18–20; 17:8–13), and it is the Levites who read the official versions of the *torah* in the septennial ceremony described in Deut 31:9–13 (Leuchter 2017a, 176–180). This constellation of episodes blurs the distinctions between the Levites within the book of Deuteronomy and the Levite authors who composed it in the late seventh century BCE and who redacted it in subsequent decades. Consequently, when Deut 18:18 refers to the divine word placed in the mouth of a Mosaic prophet—which could characterize the entirety of Moses's speech in Deuteronomy—it becomes a cipher for the very same divine word entrusted to Levite scribes, expressed through their textual and pedagogical activity (van der Toorn 1996, 355–356).

The presentation of scribes in the book of Jeremiah is entirely in step with this characterization of scribes. The most prominent, overt example of this is a brief passage in Jeremiah 36, where the scribe Baruch makes abundantly clear that the divine word in the prophet's mouth (Jer 1:9; cf. Deut 18:18) has been directly and perfectly transmuted into the scroll he has produced (vv. 17–18). More generally, Jer 36 is a sort of ground zero for the connection to scribes as presented in Deuteronomy. Just as Deuteronomy blurs the typological lines between Moses and the Levites as scribes, so, too, does Jeremiah 36 blur the boundaries between Jeremiah the prophet and Baruch the scribe on typological grounds. YHWH commands the prophet to write his oracles (Jer 36:1–3), while Jeremiah has Baruch actually produce the scroll (Jer 36:4); some scholars view this as evidence that Jeremiah was illiterate or that writing was somehow beyond or beneath him as a prophet, but this misses the rhetorical effect of seeing a divine command to the prophet fulfilled by the scribe. Jeremiah 36 presupposes the Deuteronomic dynamic where Levite scribes take on the mantle of Mosaic *torah* authority, equating scribes with prophets.

This in fact ties into the trend in Mesopotamian culture where scribes and prophets were intermingled. While one might argue that Deuteronomy and Jeremiah tap into this trend independently of each other, the fact that scribes throughout the book of Jeremiah are repeatedly cast in a manner that recalls Levites in Deuteronomy (Leuchter 2008, 105–107) indicates that the Jeremiah tradition accesses this larger scribal-revelation trend through the Deuteronomic paradigm. It is not likely that all the Levites of the late monarchic era were Deuteronomists, and the biblical record contains evidence suggesting fissions within the ranks of Levites from the end of the monarchic period to the early Persian period (Schaper 2000). Yet within Deuteronomy and Jeremiah, they are "made over" in such an image, and this does seem to affect how later generations of Levites were characterized in other biblical and extra-biblical sources (Van der Toorn 2007, 89–96). The predominance of the Jeremiah tradition among the *golah* community of the Persian period may have been the conduit for this broader reimagining of Levites as scribal authorities.

Another feature that both Deuteronomy and the Jeremiah tradition share is a unique concept of Israel's ethnicity and its relationship to the land. A variety of factors in the last quarter of the seventh century BCE affected Deuteronomy's concept of Israel as a people: the end of a century of neo-Assyrian imperialism, the presence of descendants of northern refugees from the fallen northern kingdom alongside a generation of hinterland reintegration by native Judahites, and most significantly, the purge of the countryside cult by Josiah as part of his effort to centralize power in Jerusalem (2 Kgs 23). This last event did great damage to the kinship structures of hinterland lineages organized in large part around ancestral rites and shrines (Halpern 2003), calling into question the genetic connection between these social groups and their ancestral estates. At the same time, this also moved the hinterland lineages into a conceptual space closer to that of the northern refugees who had long been separated from their own ancestral lands. Deuteronomy responds to these conditions in a number of ways, applying kinship language to the entire population (see further Crouch 2014, 113), making the written *torah* the exclusive source for cultic ideology (rather than local or lineage-based religious systems), and even stressing that Israel's ethnic/communal identity originated independently of the land. To a degree, this may be traced to the resident-alien worldview held by Deuteronomy's authors (Levites of northern heritage), but it was woven into Deuteronomy's rhetoric at a time when such a worldview became a potential option for coping with uncertain social and political conditions.

The Jeremiah tradition takes up this same issue by supporting it but also offering a, sometimes explicit, critique. The focus on a diverse population within Judah informs many of the early oracles in the book (Crouch 2017), but the theme also surfaces throughout Jeremiah 26–45, where clan/lineage affiliations are regularly highlighted when individuals are named. The authors of these materials draw attention to the fractures within the Judahite population in the waning years of the monarchy, suggesting the on-the-ground social atomism that Deuteronomy's authors attempted to remedy (Leuchter 2009). Nevertheless, even as these chapters shed light on the fractures within Judahite society, they advocate for a galvanizing ideology rooted in Deuteronomy's ideology, including strong allusions to Deuteronomy itself. Jeremiah 26 revisits the prophet's famous Temple Sermon (widely recognized by scholars as an oracle steeped in Deuteronomistic language and thought) and goes on to establish Jeremiah's place within a recognized tradition of authoritative prophecy consistent with Deut 18:15–18; the critique of Judah's kings throughout the ensuing chapters repeatedly hinges upon the circumscription of monarchs in Deut 17:14–20 as a proviso for maintaining their royal hegemony in the land (Deut 17:20); the gathering of the postdestruction Judahite community at Mizpah is prefaced by the application of Deuteronomic terms to Gedaliah's role as Nebuchadnezzar's appointed governor (Jer 40:7//Deut 31:12), establishing that the terms of the Deuteronomic covenant continue to apply even when these populations are forcibly relocated to nonancestral territory.

Most prominent in this regard is Jeremiah's oracular language in the dialogues between him and the fleeing Judahite remnant community, which uses Deuteronomy's covenant language to affirm the basis for the group's religious and ethnic identity (Jer 42). Jeremiah's audience in these chapters has lost not only their connection to their ancestral lands or their monarchic-era political home; they have returned to Egypt, the place or force that had threatened to "un-make" Israel throughout the latter's corporate lifespan. Yet even here, their identity as a collective group remains viable in the prophet's view so long as they pay heed to his decidedly Deuteronomistic oracle. Adherence to Deuteronomy's covenant ideology is the basis for identity and communal integrity, and rejection of it is grounds for their dissolution (Jer 44). This overrides ethnic connections to ancestral land—an idea that undergirds many oracles in the first part of the book as well, which should be assigned on sociological grounds to the resident-alien worldview of both the Deuteronomists and the writers behind the book of Jeremiah (Leuchter 2017a, 161–164).

This last consideration leads us to one final question: to what degree did the book of Deuteronomy influence the historical Jeremiah himself? This is a loaded question, to be sure, because many of the assumptions harbored by scholars in past days about the historicity of the prophet cannot be sustained. With few exceptions, scholars recognize that some historical prophet named Jeremiah relates to the book bearing his name to one degree or another. Yet what we encounter in the book of Jeremiah is primarily the picture of a remembered figure rather than an uninflected presentation of an historical person. Jeremiah is certainly remembered within the book bearing his name as a prophet steeped in Deuteronomy's language and ideas; this may be because an early form of Deuteronomy directly influenced him or because the prophet's own lineage roots (a Levite of northern heritage; Jer 1:1) overlap so strongly with those of the authors of Deuteronomy (as noted earlier). Many researchers rightly argue that the influence of Deuteronomy in both prose and poetic materials assigned to the prophet arises in large part from the exilic redaction of originally independent material. Indeed, due caution is warranted in making any assignments of any passages to the historical prophet. Even the relationship noted earlier between the Song of Moses and Jeremiah's oracles cannot be taken as specific proof that Jeremiah knew or used Deuteronomy: it is possible that the prophet's original teachings were transmitted later by Deuteronomistic scribes (Carr 2005, 148–149). It is also possible that even if the Song of Moses did influence the historical Jeremiah, this may not have to do with its place within the book of Deuteronomy but its renown as an old liturgical tradition (Thiessen 2004).

But one consideration does give us reason to think that the historical Jeremiah did take some direct influence from Deuteronomy during his period of activity, and that is the sheer volume of Deuteronomistic language in the book bearing his name. There is by far more Deuteronomistic material in the book of Jeremiah than in any other prophetic book. This material derives primarily from writers other than the prophet Jeremiah, but even this indicates an understanding of the prophet held by those writers, and a comparison with the book of Hosea is telling. The connections between Deuteronomy, the Deuteronomists, and Hosea have been observed by many scholars, and one might imagine that in the late seventh century BCE or during the exile, the Deuteronomists would have turned to so potent a prophetic tradition to anchor their own developing theology and worldview. Yet Hosea exhibits relatively little Deuteronomistic reworking, expansion, or shaping. The simple fact that the Deuteronomists took on the Jeremiah tradition as so potent a literary vehicle for their ideology points to a perception among ancient audiences that the prophet Jeremiah was amenable to Deuteronomistic thinking and known to have engaged the contents of Deuteronomy in his own performances and teachings.

The Deuteronomistic redaction of the book of Jeremiah may therefore build upon an extant and unique connection between the prophet himself and Deuteronomy's ideas and expressions that other prophetic figures of the period did not share. One thinks, for example, of the clear relationship between Deut 18:18 and Jer 1:9 (found nowhere else in the Hebrew Bible), the biographical material abstracted from a variety of passages that makes Jeremiah a kinsman of members of the Deuteronomistic scribal circle (McBride 2009; van der Toorn 1996, 371), and the prophet's own words in the letter to the exiles that exegetically apply locution from Deuteronomy (Berlin 1984). Notable also is that Jer 36—the sole instance in all prophetic literature that describes how a prophetic book originated—is structured so closely upon the discovery of Deuteronomy narrated in 2 Kgs 22–23 (Isbell 1978). Even if this is a matter of (exilic) literary design, it speaks to broader perceptions regarding the prophet Jeremiah's written oracles in an earlier form as obtaining as holy writs under the rubric of Deuteronomy (so also the implications of the "until this day" locution in Jer 36; see Geoghegan 2006, 159–164). It is not unreasonable to propose that, in some way, Deuteronomy had a direct effect on the prophet's own self-perception and sense of purpose, and this effect was remembered, stylized, and amplified in the subsequent growth of the book.

Bibliography

Aster, Shawn Zelig. 2007. "The Image of Assyria in Isaiah 2:5–22: The Campaign Motif Revisited." *JAOS* 127:249–278.

Berlin, Adele. 1984. "Jeremiah 29:5–7: A Deuteronomic Allusion." *HAR* 8:3–11.

Berman, Joshua. 2011. "CTH 133 and the Hittite Provenance of Deuteronomy 13." *JBL* 130 (1): 25–44.

Brettler, Marc Zvi. 1999. "Predestination in Deuteronomy 30:1–10." In Schearing and McKenzie, 171–188.

Bright, John. 1951. "The Date of the Prose Sermons of Jeremiah." *JBL* 70:15–35.

Bright, John. 1965. *Jeremiah*. New Haven: Yale University Press.

Byrne, Ryan. 2007. "The Refuge of Scribalism in Iron I Palestine." *BASOR* 345:1–31.

Carr, David. 2005. *Writing on the Tablet of the Heart: Origins of Scripture and Literature*. Oxford: Oxford University Press.

Carr, David. 2011. *The Formation of the Hebrew Bible: A New Reconstruction*. Oxford: Oxford University Press.

Carroll, Robert. 1986. *Jeremiah: A Commentary*. OTL. London: SCM Press.

Cross, Frank Moore. 1973. *Canaanite Myth and Hebrew Epic*. Cambridge: Harvard University Press.

Crouch, Carly. 2014. *The Making of Israel*. VTSup. Leiden: Brill.

Crouch, Carly. 2017. "Playing Favorites: Israel, Judah, and the Marriage Metaphor in Jeremiah 3." Paper presented at the Annual Meeting for the Society of Biblical Literature.

Duhm, Bernhard. 1901. *Das Buch Jeremia*. Tübingen: Mohr.

Eggleston, Chad L. 2016. *"See and Read Hear All These Words": Concepts of the Written in the Book of Jeremiah*. Winona Lake: Eisenbrauns.

Fleming, Daniel. 2013. *The Legacy of Israel in Judah's Bible*. Cambridge: Cambridge University Press.

Freedman, David Noel. 1993. *The Unity of the Hebrew Bible*. Ann Arbor: University of Michigan Press.

Friedman, Richard E. 1995. "The Deuteronomistic School." In *Fortunate the Eyes That See*, edited by A. B. Beck et al., 70–80. Grand Rapids: Eerdmans.

Geoghegan, Jeffrey C. 2006. *The Time, Place of Purpose of the Deuteronomistic History: The Evidence of "Until This Day."* BJS. Providence: Brown University.

Gmirkin, Russell E. 2017. *Plato and the Creation of the Hebrew Bible*. London: Routledge.

Halpern, Baruch. 2003. "Late Israelite Astronomies and the Early Greeks." In *Symbiosis, Symbolism, and the Power of the Past*, edited by W. G. Dever and S. Gitin, 323–352. Winona Lake: Eisenbrauns.

Holladay, William. 1986. *Jeremiah*, Vol. 1. Hermeneia. Minneapolis: Fortress Press.
Holladay, William. 1989. *Jeremiah*, Vol. 2. Hermeneia. Minneapolis: Fortress Press.
Holladay, William. 2004. "Elusive Deuteronomists, Jeremiah, and Proto-Deuteronomy." *CBQ* 66 (2004): 55–77.
Hornkohl, Aaron. 2014. *Ancient Hebrew Periodization and the Language in the Book of Deuteronomy: The Case for a Sixth-Century Date of Composition*. SSLL. Leiden: Brill.
Hyatt, J. Phillip. 1942. "Jeremiah and Deuteronomy." *JNES* 1:156–173.
Isbell, Charles. 1978. "2 Kings 22:3–23:24 and Jeremiah 36: A Stylistic Comparison." *JSOT* 8:33–45.
Leuchter, Mark A. 2007. "Why Is the Song of Moses in the Book of Deuteronomy?" *VT* 57:295–317.
Leuchter, Mark A. 2008. *The Polemics of Exile in Jeremiah 26–45*. Cambridge: Cambridge University Press.
Leuchter, Mark A. 2009. "The 'Prophets' and the 'Levites' in Josiah's Covenant Ceremony." *ZAW* 121:312–347.
Leuchter, Mark A. 2010. "The Sociolinguistic and Rhetorical Implications of the Source Citations in Kings." In *Soundings in Kings*, edited by K-P. Adam and M. Leuchter, 119–134. Minneapolis: Fortress Press.
Leuchter, Mark. 2015. "The Exegesis of Jeremiah in and beyond Ezra 9–10." *VT* 65 (1): 62–80.
Leuchter, Mark A. 2017a. *The Levites and the Boundaries of Israelite Identity*. Oxford: Oxford University Press.
Leuchter, Mark A. 2017b. "The Aramaic Transition and the Redaction of the Pentateuch." *JBL* 136:249–268.
Levinson, Bernard. 2004. "Is the Covenant Code an Exilic Composition? A Response to John Van Seters." *In Search of Pre-exilic Israel: Proceedings of the Oxford Old Testament Seminar*, edited by John Day, 272–325. LHBOTS. London: T&T Clark.
Lundbom, Jack R. 1975. *Jeremiah: A Study in Ancient Hebrew Rhetoric*. Missoula: Scholars Press.
Machinist, Peter. 1983. "Assyria and Its Image in the First Isaiah." *JAOS* 103:719–737.
Maier, Christl. 2002. *Jeremia als Lehrer der Tora: Soziale Gebote des Deuteronomiums in Fortschreibungen des Jeremiabuches*. FRLANT. Göttingen: Vandenhoeck & Ruprecht.
Malena, Sarah. 2014. "Fertile Crossroads: The Growth and Influence of Interregional Exchange in the Southern Levant's Iron Age I-II Transition, Examined through Biblical, Epigraphic, and Archaeological Sources." PhD diss., University of California, San Diego.
Mastnjak, Nathan. 2016. *Deuteronomy and the Emergence of Textual Authority in Jeremiah*. FAT. Tübingen: Mohr-Siebeck.
McBride, Samuel Dean. 2009. "Jeremiah and the Levitical Priests of Anathoth." In *Thus Says the Lord: Essays on the Former and Latter Prophets in Honor of Robert R Wilson*, 179–96. New York.
McKane, William. 1986. *A Critical and Exegetical Commentary on Jeremiah*, Vol. 1. ICC. Edinburgh: T & T Clark.
Monroe, Lauren. 2011. *Josiah's Reform and the Dynamics of Defilement*. Oxford: Oxford University Press.
Mowinckel, Sigmund. 1914. *Zur Komposition des Buches Jeremia*. Oslo: Jacob Dybwad.
Muilenberg, James. 1970. "Baruch the Scribe." In *Proclamation and Presence*, Fs. G.H. Davies, edited by J. I. Durham and J. R. Porter, 215–238. London: SCM Press.

Na'aman, Nadav. 2006. Nadav Na'aman, "The Temple Library of Jerusalem and the Composition of the Book of Kings." In *Congress Volume 2004*, edited by Andre Lemaire, 129–152. VTSup. Leiden: Brill.

Nicholson, Ernest. 1970. *Preaching to the Exiles: A Study of the Prose Tradition in the Book of Jeremiah*. Oxford: Blackwell.

Noth, Martin. 1943. *Überlieferungsgeschichtliche Studien I*. Halle: Max Niemeyer, 1943.

Otto, Exckart. 2007. "Scribal Scholarship in the Formation of Torah and Prophets: A Postexilic Scribal Debate between Priestly Scholarship and Literary Prophecy—The Example of the Book of Jeremiah and Its Relation to the Pentateuch." *The Pentateuch as Torah: New Models for Understanding its Promulgation and Acceptance*, edited by B. M. Levinson and G. K. Knoppers, 171–184. Winona Lake: Eisenbrauns.

Person, Raymond. 2002. *The Deuteronomistic School: History, Social Setting, and Literature*. Atlanta: SBL, 2002.

Pohlmann, Karl-Friederich. 1978. *Studien zum Jeremiabuch: Ein Beitrag zur Frage Nach der Entstehung des Jeremiabuches*. FRLANT. Göttingen: Vandenhoeck & Ruprecht.

Quick, Laura. 2017. *Deuteronomy 28 and the Aramaic Curse Tradition*. OTRM. Oxford: Oxford University Press.

Rad, Gerhard von. 1953. *Studies in Deuteronomy*. Studies in Biblical Theology. London: SCM.

Richelle, Matthieu. 2016. "Elusive Scrolls: Could Any Hebrew Literature Have Been Written Prior to the Eighth Century BCE?" *VT* 66:1–39.

Römer, Thomas. 1999. "How Did Jeremiah Become a Convert to Deuteronomistic Ideology?" In Schearing and McKenzie, 189–199.

Römer, Thomas. 2000. "Is There a Deuteronomistic Redaction in the Book of Jeremiah?" In *Israel Constructs Its History: Deuteronomistic Historiography in Recent Research*, edited by A. de Pury et al., 399–421. JSOTSup. Sheffield: Sheffield Academic Press.

Rom-Shiloni, Dalit. 2013. *Exclusive Inclusivity: Identity Conflicts between the Exiles and the People Who Remained (6th–5th Centuries BCE)*. LHBOTS. New York: Bloomsbury T&T Clark.

Sanders, Paul. 1998. *The Provenance of Deuteronomy 32*. OTS. Leiden: Brill.

Sanders, Seth. 2009. *The Invention of Hebrew*. Urbana: University of Illinois Press.

Sanders, Seth. 2014. "What If There Aren't Any Empirical Models for Pentateuchal Crtiticism?" In *Contextualizing Israel's Sacred Writings: Ancient Literacy, Orality and Literary Production*, edited by B. B. Schmidt, 281–304. Atlanta: SBL Press.

Schaper, Joachim. 2000. *Priester und Leviten im achämenidischen Juda: Studien zur Kult- und Sozialgeschichte Israels in persischer Zeit*. FAT. Tübingen: Mohr Siebeck.

Schaper, Joachim. 2007. "The 'Publication' of Legal Texts in Ancient Judah." In *The Pentateuch As Torah: New Models for Understanding Its Promulgation and Acceptance*, edited by B. M. Levinson and G. K. Knoppers, 225–236. Winona Lake: Eisenbrauns.

Schearing, Linda S., and McKenzie, S. L. 1999. *Those Elusive Deuteronomists: The Phenomenon of Pan-Deuteronomism*. JSOTSup. Sheffield: Sheffield Academic Press.

Schmid, Konrad. 1996. *Buchgestalten des Jeremiabuches: Untersuchungen zur Redaktions- und Rezeptionsgeschichte von Jer 30–33 im Kontext des Buches*. WMANT. Neukirchen: Neukirchener Verlag.

Schniedewind, William. 2004. *How the Bible Became a Book: The Textualization of Ancient Israel*. Cambridge: Cambridge University Press.

Sharp, Carolyn J. 1997. "Take Another Scroll and Write: A Study of the LXX and the MT of Jeremiah's Oracles against the Nations." *VT* 47:487–516.

Sharp, Carolyn J. 2003. *Prophecy and Ideology in Jeremiah: Struggles for Authority in the Deutero-Jeremianic Prose*. OTS. London: T & T Clark.

Steiner, Margarete Laura. 2003. "The Evidence from Kenyon's Excavations in Jerusalem: A Response Essay." In *Jerusalem in Bible and Archaeology: The First Temple Period*, 347–363. Atlanta: Society of Biblical Literature.

Sweeney, Marvin. 1996. "Jeremiah 30–31 and King Josiah's Program of National Restoration and Religious Reform." ZAW 108:569–583.

Thiel, Winfriend. 1973. *Die deuteronomistische Redaktion von Jeremia 1–25*. WMANT. Neukirchen: Neukirchener Verlag.

Thiessen, Matthew. 2004. "The Form and Function of the Song of Moses (Deuteronomy 32:1–43)." *JBL* 123:401–424.

Van der Toorn, Karel. 1996. *Family Religion in Ancient Babylonia, Syria and Israel*. Leiden: Brill.

Van der Toorn, Karel. 2007. *Scribal Culture and the Making of the Hebrew Bible*. Cambridge: Harvard University Press.

Vayntrub, Jacqueline E. 2020. "Ecclesiastes and the Problem of Transmission in Biblical Literature." In *Scribes and Scribalism*, edited by Mark Leuchter. New York: T & T Clark.

Wanke, Gunter. 1971. *Untersuchungen der Sogennante Baruchschrift*. BZAW. Berlin: De Gruyter.

Weinfeld, Moshe. 1972. *Deuteronomy and the Deuteronomic School*. Oxford: Clarendon.

Weippert, Helga. 1973. *Die Prosareden des Jeremiabuches*. BZAW. Berlin: de Gruyter.

SECTION V

RECEPTION HISTORY OF DEUTERONOMY

CHAPTER 23

DEUTERONOMY IN THE TEXTS FROM THE JUDEAN DESERT

ARIEL FELDMAN

Who Began the Conversation?

PRIOR to discovery of the ancient Jewish texts widely known as the Dead Sea Scrolls (DSS), students of Deuteronomy had two medieval Hebrew texts of this book at their disposal: the Masoretic Text (MT) and the Samaritan Pentateuch (SP). The DSS revealed Hebrew manuscripts of Deuteronomy predating the earliest copies of the MT and SP by more than one thousand years. Moreover, these scrolls brought to light a wealth of previously unknown literary works engaging Deuteronomy. Thus, the DSS offer an unprecedented window into the transmission and reception of this book in the Second Temple period (538 BCE–70 CE).

Several studies explore the impact of Deuteronomy on the DSS. In an early overview of the evidence, Julie A. Duncan in the *Encyclopedia of the Dead Sea Scrolls* (2000) observes that it was "a popular book at Qumran, rivaled only by the *Psalms*." Within the larger corpus of the DSS dealing with Deuteronomy, she identifies several subgroups: biblical manuscripts, *tefillin* and *mezuzot*, excerpted texts, and nonbiblical compositions. Duncan notes that though Qumran copies of Deuteronomy, spanning a period of some three hundred years, are numerous, the textual evidence they yield is slim, as the majority are very fragmentary. Mapping the various manuscripts and their affinities with the previously available witnesses of Deuteronomy, MT, SP, and Septuagint (LXX), she highlights their tendency to slightly expand the text, often under the influence of parallel verses. Duncan counts some two hundred variants in the twenty-eight Qumran copies of Deuteronomy and suggests that half of them are preferable readings. She also emphasizes the significance of the excerpted texts and *tefillin* and *mezuzot*—all reflecting a personal use of Deuteronomy—as important textual witnesses. Duncan concludes her survey with a brief discussion of several nonbiblical compositions using this book, both sectarian and nonsectarian: the *Temple Scroll,* the *Damascus Document, 4QFlorilegium* (4Q174), and *4QTestimonia* (4Q175).

In a slightly later study—"Reading Deuteronomy in the Second Temple Period" (2005)—Sidnie White Crawford also seeks to gauge the impact of Deuteronomy on the DSS. Like Duncan, she highlights the high number of the Qumran manuscripts of Deuteronomy as an indication of this book's "importance ... in the life and thought of the Qumran community." Unlike Duncan, however, White Crawford places the excerpted texts of Deuteronomy as equals within the large subgroup of Qumran copies of this book, affirming that despite their excerpted nature they are biblical manuscripts. While agreeing with Duncan that some of the DSS copies of Deuteronomy from Qumran align with the MT, LXX, and SP, White Crawford doubts whether the majority of the DSS manuscripts can be classified vis-à-vis these textual traditions due to their fragmentary nature. Like Duncan, she notes the "expansionistic" aspect of Deuteronomy in the DSS, well-illustrated by multiple instances of harmonization. Such modifications by no means undermine the authoritative status of these texts. For such "expansionistic" tendencies are attested to in the many "special-use" DSS manuscripts, such as *tefillin* and *mezuzot,* as well as in the text that Samaritans selected as the base of their Pentateuch. Finally, she briefly considers the use of Deuteronomy in the *4QReworked Pentateuch* and the *Temple Scroll.* White Crawford concludes that while "Deuteronomy may be termed the 'second law,'" it "clearly had attained first place in Second Temple Judaism."

In addition to underscoring the significance of the DSS for the study of Deuteronomy's reception in antiquity, these and several other surveys of the reception of Deuteronomy in the DSS—like Ulrich Dahmen in "Das Deuteronomium in Qumran als umgeschriebene Bibel" (2003); Timothy H. Lim in "Deuteronomy in the Judaism of the Second Temple Period" (2007); and David Lincicum, *Paul and the Early Jewish Encounter with Deuteronomy* (2010)—establish a general pattern of inquiry into Deuteronomy's impact on the Scrolls. Thus, they helpfully divide the relevant texts into two broad categories, "biblical" and "nonbiblical" or, less anachronistically, "scriptural" and "nonscriptural." Within the first category, they identify several subgroups, such as excerpted texts, while in the second they distinguish between texts reflecting a distinct worldview of a particular religious community (or communities), commonly labeled "sectarian," and those that may have originated within the wider circles of Second Temple Judaism, "nonsectarian." None of these classifications adopted here are meant to be rigid. Rather, they should serve as a general map guiding the reader through the complexities of a highly diverse DSS corpus. Also, these studies reveal some of the issues in the current study of Deuteronomy in the DSS. For instance, different evaluations of some of the copies of Deuteronomy raise a question as to whether the established method of classifying manuscripts by comparing them with the MT, LXX, and SP serves the evidence well. In fact, the following survey of the "biblical" DSS copies of Deuteronomy points to several recently proposed alternatives. Moreover, whereas the earlier overviews of Deuteronomy in the DSS favor "biblical" manuscripts, later studies attempt to incorporate more of the "nonbiblical" texts, paying close attention to their assumed sectarian or nonsectarian origins. Though a detailed treatment of all such texts would exceed the limits of the present survey, it offers a substantial sample of various kinds of uses of Deuteronomy in the "non-biblical" DSS. First, however, it takes a close look at the biblical manuscripts containing Deuteronomy.

What Is the Status of the Conversation?

The precise count of the manuscripts of Deuteronomy found in the Judean Desert remains debatable. First, it is often impossible to determine whether a fragment preserving a few words from Deuteronomy represents a full-fledged copy of this book. Second, there are several texts resisting a clear-cut classification. One case in point are the so-called *4QReworked Pentateuch* (4QRP) scrolls, categorized as biblical manuscripts by some and as rewritten Bible texts by others. There are also the excerpted Deuteronomy texts. Some of them (4QDeut^{b,k1,n,q}) are often included in the lists of the DSS copies of Deuteronomy. Others, such as *tefillin* and *mezuzot*, though similar in scope, are not. Third, several fragments of Deuteronomy are suspected of being forgeries. In an attempt to provide as broad an overview of the evidence as possible, the following list includes all of them—seventy-three texts in total—arranged by the location where they have been presumably found.

Khirbet Qumran (59)
Cave 1 (3)
1QDeut^a (1Q4; 30–1 BCE)
1QDeut^b (1Q5; 50 BCE –30 CE or 30–1 CE)
Tefillin
1QPhyl (1Q13)
Cave 2 (3)
2QDeut^a (2Q10; 50 BCE)
2QDeut^b (2Q11; Herodian hand)
2QDeut^c (2Q12; late Herodian hand)
Cave 4 (47)
Deuteronomy only
Hebrew:
4QDeut^a (4Q28; 175–150 BCE)
4QDeut^b (4Q29; 150–100 BCE)
4QDeut^c (4Q30; 150–100 BCE)
4QDeut^d (4Q31; 125–75 BCE)
4QDeut^e (4Q32; 50–25 BCE)
4QDeut^f (4Q33; 75–50 BCE)
4QDeut^g (4Q34; 25–1 BCE)
4QDeut^h (4Q35; 50–1 BCE)
4QDeut^i (4Q36; 100–50 BCE)
4QDeut^j (4Q37; 50 BCE)
4QDeut^{k1} (4Q38; 30–1 BCE)
4QDeut^{k2} (4Q38a; 30–1 BCE)
4QDeut^{k3} (4Q38b; 50 CE)
4QDeut^m (4Q40; 50–1 BCE)
4QDeut^n (4Q41; 30–1 BCE)
4QDeut^o (4Q42; 75–50 BCE)
4QDeut^p (4Q43; 75–50 BCE)
4QDeut^q (4Q44; 50–1 BCE or beginning of the first century CE)
4QpaleoDeut^r (4Q45; 75–50 BCE)
4QpaleoDeut^s (4Q46; 250–200 BCE)
4QDeut^t (4Q38c)
4QDeut^u (4Q38d; 150 BCE)

Greek:
4QLXXDeut (4Q122; 200–150 BCE)
Deuteronomy along with other books of the Torah
4QRP[b] (4Q364; 75–50 BCE)
4QRP[c] (4Q365; 75–50 BCE)
4QRP[d] (4Q366; 75–50 BCE)
Tefillin (mid-second century BCE–first century CE)
4QPhyl A (4Q128)
4QPhyl B (4Q129)
4QPhyl C (4Q130)
4QPhyl D (4Q131)
4QPhyl G (4Q134)
4QPhyl H (4Q135)
4QPhyl I (4Q136)
4QPhyl J (4Q137)
4QPhyl K (4Q138)
4QPhyl L (4Q139)
4QPhyl M (4Q140)
4QPhyl N (4Q141)
4QPhyl O (4Q142)
4QPhyl P (4Q143)
4QPhyl Q (4Q144)
4QPhyl S (4Q146)
Mezuzot
4QMez A (4Q149; second–first centuries BCE)
4QMez B (4Q150; first century CE)
4QMez C (4Q151; 50–1 BCE?)
4QMez D (4Q152; first century BCE)
4QMez E (4Q153)
Cave 5 (1)
5QDeut (5Q1; 200–150 BCE)
Cave 6 (1)
6QpapDeut? (6Q3)
Cave 7 *(1)*
Greek
7QLXXDt (=7Q6, 7Q7, 7Q9)
Cave 8 (2)
Tefillin and Mezuzot
8QPhyl (8Q3; first century CE)
8QMez (8Q4; Herodian hand)
Cave 11 (1)
11QDeut (11Q3; 50 BCE)
Other Sites (5)
MurDeut (Mur 2; before 66 CE)
XḤev/SeDeut (XḤev/Se 3; 50–68 CE)
MasDeut (Mas 1043/a-d; Mas 1c; early Herodian formal hand)
Tefillin
Mur 4
XḤev/SePhylactery (XḤev/Se 5)
Fragments of Unknown Provenance (3)
Tefillin

XQPhyl 1-3 (50–1 CE)
Likely Forgeries (6)
The Schøyen Collection:
MS 5214/1 (4Q[?]Deutl, DSS E108, DSS F.Deut5)
MS5214/2 (4Q[?]Deut2, DSS E109, DSS F.Deut6)
The Asuza Pacific University Collection:
E153 (F.Deut1) and E154 (F.Deut2)
The Southwestern Baptist Theological Seminary Collection:
E163 (F.Deut3) and E164 (F.Deut4)

With an exception of two manuscripts in Greek, all other texts listed here are in Hebrew. Two of them, including the earliest copy of Deuteronomy (4QpaleoDeut^s), are inscribed in paleo-Hebrew script. Many of these scrolls might have contained Deuteronomy alone, while three manuscripts (4Q364–366, 4QRP^{b,c,d}) clearly include other books of the Torah.

There is not a single complete scroll of Deuteronomy in this list. In fact, very few are well preserved. For example, 4QDeut^c preserves no more than 120 verses from nineteen chapters. Still, fragmentary as they are, these scrolls yield a rich trove of readings. Most of these have been long available in the MT, LXX, and SP. One example is the well-known reading "the Most High ... fixed the boundaries of the peoples according to the number of *the sons of God*" (32:8) in 4QDeut^j (cf. LXX). The MT and SP have "the Most High ... fixed the boundaries of the peoples according to the number of *the sons of Israel*." Others, such as the equally often cited six-couplet wording of Deuteronomy (32:43) in 4QDeut^q (cf. the four couplets of the MT and the eight of the LXX), are unique. To evaluate the contribution of these readings, a few words should be said about the previously available MT, SP, and LXX of Deuteronomy.

In an attempt to identify discrete features of the MT Deuteronomy, scholars point to a few readings suggesting a theologically motivated revision. The reading "Ebal" (27:4) in MT, instead of "Gerizim" of the Old Greek (as evidenced by the Old Latin) and SP, may imply an anti-Samaritan polemic. At the same time, the MT seems to reflect an anti-polytheistic stance. "When the Most High ... fixed the boundaries of the peoples according to *the sons of God*" (32:8; 4QDeut^j; LXX) is replaced in MT with "When the Most High ... fixed the boundaries of the peoples according to the number of *the sons of Israel*." Similarly, instead of "Praise, o *Heavens,* his people, *worship him all sons of God*" (32:43; 4QDeut^a; LXX), the MT reads "Praise, o *nations,* his people." On a larger scale, while the MT, SP, and LXX all harmonize verses by changing, adding, and omitting details, the MT appears to be the least harmonized of the three texts.

A well-known feature of the SP is the transposition of parallel passages from Deuteronomy back into Exodus and Numbers. In SP Deuteronomy itself, however, there are only few instances of such transpositions (2:7; 10:6–7; 14). The SP also harmonizes more verses than MT, but less than LXX. While all these appear to have originated in a Jewish text of Deuteronomy adopted by the Samaritans, a few others are commonly believed to reflect the particular worldview of this community. Thus, an additional commandment in the Decalogue (5:18 SP) stipulates an establishment of worship on Mt. Gerizim. Also, unlike MT and LXX which use "the place that God will choose," SP reads "the place that God has chosen." Finally, SP has "Gerizim" (27:4), whereas the MT and most LXX manuscripts read "Ebal." Recently, several studies challenged the attribution of these readings to the "Samaritan layer" of SP and argued that they are original to Deuteronomy.

The LXX Deuteronomy is often described as a literal rendering of the Hebrew. Therefore, its many deviations from the MT and SP are likely to reflect variant readings. These include a partial reversal of the order of the Decalogue (5:17–18), a substantially longer wording of certain passages (6:4, cf. Papyrus Nash; 23:18; 26:9–10; 32:43), and many harmonized verses.

The DSS copies of Deuteronomy are routinely assessed according to their similarities to or differences from the MT, LXX, and SP. The most comprehensive classification of the Qumran copies of Deuteronomy along these lines has been produced by Armin Lange in *Textual History of the Bible* (2017). His analysis excludes several manuscripts as either too fragmentary or unclassifiable and leaves out all the *tefillin* and *mezuzot*. For what is left, he suggests the following categorization:

Proto-MT: 4QDeut[e], 4QDeut[d], MasDeut
Close to LXX: 4QDeut[q]
Close to both MT and SP: 4QDeut[d], 4QDeut[f], 4QDeut[i], 4QDeut[o], 5QDeut
Nonaligned: 1QDeut[h], 4QDeut[b], 4QDeut[c], 4QDeut[h], 4QDeut[j], 4QDeut[k1], 4QDeut[k2], 4QDeut[n], 4QpaleoDeut[r], 4QRP[b], 4QRP[c], 4QRP[d]

What Is Trending in the Conversation?

While identifying similarities and differences between the newly discovered DSS and long-available versions like the MT, SP, and LXX is crucial, this and similar methods of classification have several disadvantages. First, taking much later texts as a point of departure renders the comparison anachronistic. Second, it privileges the MT, SP, and LXX over all other texts. To avoid these shortcomings, several alternative approaches to classifying DSS biblical manuscripts have been developed. One method highlights the fact that certain books are attested in several literary editions and evaluates the manuscript evidence accordingly. Another approach seeks to situate a given manuscript within two major scribal trends evident in the DSS. Andrew Teeter points out in *Scribal Laws: Exegetical Variation in the Textual Transmission of Biblical Law in the Late Second Temple Period* (2014) that these two have been described as "free" or "careful," "conservative" or "interventionist," and "exact" or "facilitating."

Can these two approaches be applied specifically to the DSS copies of Deuteronomy? The lists of biblical books attesting to multiple literary editions tend to exclude Deuteronomy. Apparently, even the SP does not qualify as a discrete edition of this book, especially if much of the so-called Samaritan layer precedes Samaritan appropriation of the text. Still, there is at least one DSS manuscript that may reflect a distinct edition of Deuteronomy, *4QReworked Pentateuch*[b] (4Q364). This scroll, preserving a considerable amount of Deuteronomy, features a juxtaposition of 2:8–14 with Num 20:17–18 as in the SP, a unique reordering of the text (frag. 26b, e, col. ii), multiple instances of longer wording (10:11; 11:23; 14:26; 11:6), and other noteworthy divergences from the known versions (1:17; 2:30–3:2; 10:6–7). As to the grouping of the manuscripts according to these two scribal trends, it seems that very few Qumran copies of Deuteronomy exhibit "an exact" approach to the text (one candidate would be 4QDeut^g), while many seem to belong with the "facilitating" one.

A special word needs to be said about the so-called excerpted texts. Four DSS manuscripts of Deuteronomy are commonly described as such:

4QDeut^n (4Q41): 8:5–10; 5:1–29, 31–6:1
4QDeut^j (4Q37): 5:1–11, 13–15, 21–33; 6:1–3; 8:5–10; 11:6–10, 12, 13; 11:21?+Exod 12:43–44; 12:46–13:5; Deut 32:7–8
4QDeut^q (4Q44): 32:9–10?, 37–43
4QDeut^kl (4Q38): 5:28–32; 11:6–13; 32:17–18, 22–23, 25–27

Passages included in these scrolls appear also in *tefillin* and *mezuzot* and/or are featured in later Jewish liturgy. Hence, as was mentioned earlier on, it is often assumed that they were intended for a personal devotional use.

Tefillin and *mezuzot* themselves are also excerpted biblical texts. Rabbinic sources require Exod 13:1–16; Deut 6:4–9; 11:13–21 for *tefillin;* and Deut 6:4–9; 11:13–21 for *mezuzot*. While some of the *tefillin* and *mezuzot* match these later rabbinical requirements, others include longer passages from Exodus (12:43–13:16) and Deuteronomy (5:1–6:9; 10:12–11:21). One peculiar slip of *tefillin* (4QPhyl N) contains Deut 32:14–20, 32–33.

Tefillin and *mezuzot* exhibit textual phenomena familiar from other DSS copies of Deuteronomy. There are harmonized verses, especially in the Decalogue, such as the reason for observing the Sabbath (4QPhyl G; 8QPhyl; 4QMez A), paraphrase (11:8, 12 [8QPhyl]), additions (5:1 [4QPhyl G]; 5:31[4QPhyl H]; 11:7 [8QPhyl]), and abbreviations (5:32–6:1 in 4QPhyl A, B, J; 4QMez C). Many of the excerpted scrolls reflect the aforementioned "facilitating" approach to the text.

Finally, a mention should be made of the two so-called pre-Samaritan DSS copies of Exodus and Numbers transposing passages from Deuteronomy into these two books. Since it is highly unlikely that these scrolls were produced by Samaritan scribes, they are labeled "pre-Samaritan" or "proto-Samaritan." As such, these two are also an important witness to the text of Deuteronomy:

4Q22 (4QpaleoExod^m; 100–25 BCE):
Deut 1:9–16 is introduced after Exod 18:24 (col. 19)
5:24–27 is introduced in Exod 20:19 (col. 21)
9:20 is added in Exod 32:10 (col. 38)
4Q27 (4QNum^b; 50–1 BCE):
Deut 2:9, 17–19 is appended to Num 21:11 (Deut 2:9) and 21 (Deut 2:17–19) (col. 13)
2:24 is appended to Num 21:20 (col. 13)
3:21 is appended to Num 27:23 (col. 21)
3:24–25, 26b-28 is appended to Num 20:13 (col. 11)

There are also two nonbiblical DSS following such a pre-Samaritan text of Exodus. In *4QTestimonia* (4Q175 5–8) a quotation from Exod 20:21 juxtaposes Deut 5:28–29 and 18:18–19, as in the SP. Similarly, *4QReworked Pentateuch^a* (4Q158 6 7–9) places Deut 5:28–29; 18:18–20+22 next to Exod 20:21 and Deut 5:30–31 after Exod 20:17.

All in all, the scrolls surveyed so far contain the following passages from Deuteronomy (Table 23.1):

Table 23.1. Deuteronomy in the Biblical Dead Sea Scrolls

Deuteronomy	Scroll
1:1-6, 17-28, 32-33, 45-4:1-6, 17-33, 45-46	4Q364
1:1-17, 22-24, 29-39, 41, 43-46	4QDeut^h
1:4-5	11QDeut
1:7-9	2QDeut^a
1:8?	4QpaleoDeut^f
1:9, 11, 13	1QDeut^b
1:9-16	4QpaleoExod^m 19
1:22-25	1QDeut^a
1:45?	4QpaleoDeut^r
2:1-6, 28-30	4QDeut^h
2:8	4QDeut^o
2:8-9, 12-14	4Q364
2:9, 17-19	4QNum^b 13
2:24	4QNum^b 13
2:28-30	11QDeut
2:29-30	4QDeut^c
2:30-37	4Q364
3:1-2	4Q364
3:14-29	4QDeut^d
3:18-22	4QDeut^m
3:18-23	4Q364
3:21	4QNum^b 21
3:24	4QDeut^e
3:24-25, 26b-28	4QNum^b 11
3:25-26	4QDeut^c
4:1	4QDeut^d
4:1, 13-17, 31-32	4QDeut^c
4:24-26	4QDeut^f
4:30-34	4QDeut^o
4:31-34	4QDeut^h
4:32-33	4QDeut^m
4:43, 47, 49	1QDeut^a
4:49	4QDeut^i
5:1	4QDeut^i
5:1-2, 4-11, 13-31	4QPhyl B
5:1, 3, 5, 8-10, 12-14, 27-32	4QPhyl A
5:1, 4, 5, 8, 9, 11, 14, 16	4QPhyl O
5:1-5, 8-9?	4QDeut^o
5:1-9, 11-17, 21-25, 27	1QPhyl
5:1-11, 13-15, 21-33	4QDeut^j
5:1-14	8QPhyl
5:1-18, 20-32	4QPhyl J
5:1-21	4QPhyl G
5:1-33	4QDeut^n; XQPhyl
5:7-9, 11-18, 21-24	4QPhyl L
5:11, 13-14, 16 (?)	4QMez A
5:22-33	4QPhyl H

Table 23.1. Continued

Deuteronomy	Scroll
5:24-27	4QpaleoExod^m 21
5:27-33	4QMez C
5:28-29; 18:18-19	4Q175 5-8
5:28-29; 18:18-20, 22	4Q158 6
5:28-32	4QDeut^{k1}
5:30-31	4Q158 7-9
5:33	4QPhyl M
6:1	4QDeut^n
6:1-2	DSS 108
6:1-3	4QDeut^j
6:1-5	4QPhyl H, M
6:1, 3, 5, 7, 9	4QMez C
6:1-9	8QPhyl; XQPhyl
6:2-3	4QPhyl A, B, J
6:4-9	4QPhyl C; Mur 4; XHev/Se 5
6:4-11	4QDeut^p
6:5-6	4QMez B
6:5-7	4QMez D
6:6-7	4QPhyl I
6:7-9	4QPhyl O
7:2-7, 16-25	4QpaleoDeut^r
7:3-4	4QDeut^c
7:12-16, 21-26	4QDeut^e
7:15-24	5QDeut
7:18-22	4QDeut^m
7:22-26	4QDeut^f
8:1-7, 10-11, 15-16	4QDeut^e
8:1-5	4QDeut^c
8:2-5	F.153 F.Deut1
8:2-14	4QDeut^f
8:5-20	5QDeut
8:5-10	4QDeut^{j,n}
8:8-9	1QDeut^b
8:18-19	1QDeut^a
9:1-2	5QDeut
9:4-7, 21-23	XHev/Se 3
9:6-7	4QDeut^f
9:6-7, 12-18, 22-24, 27-29	4Q364
9:7 or 16:3	1QDeut^a
9:10	1QDeut^b
9:11-12, 17-19, 29	4QDeut^c
9:12-14	4QDeut^g
9:20	4QpaleoExod^m 38
9:21	4QDeut^h
9:25-29	F.163 F.Deut3

(continued)

Table 23.1. Continued

Deuteronomy	Scroll
9:27-28	1QDeut[a]
10:1	F.163 F.Deut3
10:1-2, 5-8	4QDeut?
10:1-3	MurDeut
10:1-4, 6-7, 10-13, 22	4Q364
10:8-12	2QDeut[c]
10:11-12	4QpaleoDeut[r]
10:12, 14-15	4QDeut[l]
10:12, 15-18, 20	4QMez C
10:12-19	XQPhyl
10:12-22	4QPhyl A, J, K; 8QMez; 8QPhyl
10:14, 16, 18, 20, 22	4QMez B
10:17-18, 21-22	1QPhyl
10:22	4QPhyl P
11:1-2	4QMez B
11:1-2, 6-9, 23-24	4Q364
11:1-3, 18-20	4QPhyl P
11:1-3?, 5?, 6-21	8QPhyl
11:1, 8-12	1QPhyl
11:1-12	4QPhyl J, K
11:1-15, 17-21	4QPhyl A
11:1-21	8QMez
11:2-3	MurDeut
11:3, 9-13, 18	4QDeut[c]
11:4	4QLXXDeut
11:4, 13, 15-18	4QPhyl Q
11:6-13	4QDeut[k1]
11:6-10, 12-13, 21?	4QDeut[j]
11:10	1QDeut[a]
11:13, 14, 16, 17, 19, 21	4QPhyl D
11:13-15, 17-19, 21	4QPhyl I
11:13-21	4QPhyl C; Mur 4; XḤev/Se 5
11:17-18	4QMez E
11:19-21	4QPhyl S
11:27-30	1QDeut[a]
11:28, 30-32	4QpaleoDeut[r]
11:30-31	1QDeut[b]
12:1, 2-5, 11-12, 22	4QpaleoDeut[r]
12:11-14	F.164 F.Deut4
12:14	1QDeut[a]
12:18-19, 26, 30-31	4QDeut[c]
12:25-26	MurDeut
12:31	4QDeut[t]
13:1	4QDeut[t]
13:1-6, 8, 13-14	1QDeut[a]

Table 23.1. Continued

Deuteronomy	Scroll
13:5-7, 11-12, 16	4QDeut^c
13:19	4QpaleoDeut^r
14:1, 2-4, 19-22, 26-29	4QpaleoDeut^r
14:14-16, 18, 20-21	4Q366
14:21, 24-25	1QDeut^a
14:24-26	4Q364
14:28-29	4QDeut^t
14:29 or 15:2	MurDeut
15:1-4, 15-19	4QDeut^c
15:1 or 2	MurDeut
15:5-6, 8-10	4QpaleoDeut^r
15:14-15	1QDeut^b
16:2-3, 6-11, 20-22	4QDeut^c
16:4, 6-7	1QDeut^a
16:19?	7Q6 1
17:1-5, 7, 15-20	4QDeut^c
17:5-6?	4QpaleoDeut^r
17:12-15	2QDeut^b
17:16	1QDeut^b
17:17-18	4QDeut^f
18:1	4QDeut^c
18:6-10, 18-22	4QDeut^f
19:2-3	4QpaleoDeut^r
19:3, 8-16	4QDeut^{k2}
19:13-15	4QDeut^f
19:20-21	4Q365
19:21	4QDeut^h
20:1	4Q365
20:1-6	4QDeut^f
20:6-19	4QDeut^{k2}
20:9-13	4QDeut^i
20:19	7Q6 2+7Q9
21:4-12	4QDeut^f
21:8-9	1QDeut^b
21:8-9? or 30:7-8?	4QpaleoDeut^r
21:23	4QDeut^i
22:1-9	4QDeut^i
22:3-6	4QpaleoDeut^r
22:12-19	4QDeut^f
23:6-8, 12-16, 22-26	4QDeut^i
23:7, 12-15	4QpaleoDeut^r
23:18-20	4QDeut^g
23:21-26	4QDeut^f
23:22-26	4QDeut^{k2}
23:26	4QDeut^a
24:1-8	4QDeut^a

(continued)

Table 23.1. Continued

Deuteronomy	Scroll
24:1	4QDeut^l
24:1-3	4QDeut^{k2}
24:2-7	4QDeut^f
24:5, 10-16	1QDeut^b
24:16-22	4QDeut^g
25:1-5, 14-19	4QDeut^g
25:3-9	4QDeut^f
25:13-18	1QDeut^b
25:19	4QDeut^{k2}
26:1-5	4QDeut^g
26:1-5, 18-19?	4QDeut^{k2}
26:14-15	4QpaleoDeut^s
26:18-19	4QDeut^f
26:19	4QDeut^c; 6QpapDeut?
27:1?	4QDeut^{k2}
27:1-2, 24-26	4QDeut^c
27:1-10	4QDeut^f
27:4-6	F.154 F.Deut2
28:1-14, 18-20, 22-25, 29-30, 48-50, 61	4QDeut^c
28:15-18, 20	4QpaleoDeut^r
28:15-18, 33-36, 47-52, 58-62	4QDeut^o
28:21-25, 27-29	4QDeut^g
28:44-48	1QDeut^b
28:67-68	4QDeut^l
29:2-5	4QDeut^f
29:9-20	1QDeut^b
29:17-19	4QDeut^c
29:22-25	4QDeut^o
29:24-27	4QDeut^b
30:3-14	4QDeut^b
30:16-18	4QDeut^{k3}
30:19-20	1QDeut^b
31:1-10, 12-13	1QDeut^b
31:9-11	4QDeut^h
31:12	4QDeut^l
31:16-19	4QDeut^c
31:29	4QpaleoDeut^r
32:1-3	4QDeut^b
32:3	4QDeut^c
32:5-9	DSS F.109, DSS F.Deut6
32:6-8, 10-11, 13-14, 33-35	4QpaleoDeut^r
32:7-8	4QDeut^j
32:9-10?, 37-43	4QDeut^q
32:14-20, 32-38	4QPhyl N
32:17-18, 22-23, 25-27	4QDeut^{k1}
32:17-29	1QDeut^b
32:20-21	5QDeut
32:22-23?	7Q7

Table 23.1. Continued

Deuteronomy	Scroll
32:39-43	4QDeut^q
32:46-47	MasDeut
33:1-2	4QDeut^l; 5QDeut
33:2-8, 29	4QpaleoDeut^r
33:8-22	4QDeut^h
33:12-19, 21-24	1QDeut^b
33:17-24	MasDeut
33:29	4QDeut^h
34:1	4QpaleoDeut^r
34:2-6	MasDeut
34:4-6, 8?	4QDeut^l

NONBIBLICAL SCROLLS

The DSS have also yielded an abundance of nonbiblical texts using Deuteronomy. These uses can be broadly divided, following Devorah Dimant's "Use and Interpretation of Mikra in the Apocrypha and Pseudepigrapha" (1990), into "expositional" and "compositional." The English translation of the nonbiblical DSS here follows Michael O. Wise, Martin G. Abegg, and Edward M. Cook, *The Dead Sea Scrolls: A New Translation* (2005).

Expositional Uses

Expositional uses of Deuteronomy include a few cases where the DSS engage this book utilizing external markers of exegesis. One example comes from a nonbiblical text featuring an actualizing *pesher-type* exegesis of a poem, Moses's Song (32:1–43), which was apparently understood as prophetic. The *Damascus Document* (CD 8:9–12; 19:22–23) accuses the opponents of the group of failing to "separate from the people," "arrogantly throwing off all restraint," and "living by wicked customs." To support this accusation, it cites: "Their wine is venom of snakes, the cruel poison of vipers (32:33)," introducing it by a formula "of which God had said." Next, CD identifies the "snakes," "wine," and "poison of vipers" with "the kings of the Gentiles," "their customs," and "the chief of the kings of Greece."

Explicit quotations from Deuteronomy also belong here. Though they do not include a formal exposition, it "is expressed by the rhetorical or narrative use of the biblical elements" (Dimant 1990). In the DSS, explicit quotations from Deuteronomy can be found in legal contexts. Arguing against polygamy, CD turns to Deuteronomy's laws on kingship (17:14–20). It quotes "and he shall not have many wives" (17:17a), introducing it with a formula: "and of the prince it is written" (CD 4:20–5:6; 4Q269 3 2; 6Q15 1 1–3). Next, CD goes on to explain why the exemplary King David had many wives despite this prohibition. It claims that David "did not read the sealed book of the Torah which was in the Ark (of the Covenant)."

Explicit quotations also occur in admonitions. The paraenetic section of CD (8:14-15; 19:27–28) quotes Deuteronomy (7:8; 8:5), introducing these verses with the formula "as Moses said (to Israel)." The exhortatory epilogue of the sectarian *Miqṣat Maʿase ha-Torah* (4QMMT C 12–16) selectively quotes 31:29, "For I know that after my death you will surely act corruptly, turning aside from the way that I have commanded you. In time to come trouble will befall you." It is preceded by the phrase "and it is also written that." Deuteronomy 30:1-2 (influenced by 4:29–30) comes next, introduced as "and it is writ[ten]."

Liturgical texts also employ explicit quotations from Deuteronomy. Thus, a prayer found in the sectarian *War Scroll* (1QM 10:2–5) cites 20:2–5 outlining the High Priest's address to the troops. It is introduced by the phrase "he taught us from of old through all our generations, saying" and preceded by another explicit quotation from 7:21–22 introduced as what "he (Moses) told us."

4QTestimonia (4Q175), often understood as a sectarian selection of messianic proof-texts, presents a peculiar case. An excerpted text of sorts, it contains four paragraphs, each being a quotation, though no introductory formulae are used. The first one comes from Exod 20:21 (lines 5–8). As noted earlier, the scroll relies here on a pre-Samaritan text of Exodus juxtaposing verses from Deuteronomy (5:28–29; 18:18–19). The third quotation (33:8–11), referring, among other things, to the Urim and Thummim, reads "and they shall cause your ordinances to shine from Jacob" (33:10; cf. LXX). This reading can be understood in light of traditions associating Urim and Thummim with the precious stones embedded in the High Priest's garments, suggesting that the divine answer was provided by means of light emitted by the stones.

Compositional Uses

While expositional uses of Deuteronomy introduce and/or interpret it, in compositional uses for Dimant (1990) "the biblical element is subservient to the independent aim and structure of its new context." The many types of intertextuality placed in this category include rewritings, implicit quotations/allusions, references to a figure or an event, pseudepigraphy, and a literary model.

Rewritings

Several fragmentary DSS engage Deuteronomy quite extensively (e.g., *4QOrdinances* [4Q159]; *Apocryphon of Moses* [1Q29, 4Q375–376, 4Q408]). However, only *Words of Moses* and *Temple Scroll*, both non-sectarian works, are sufficiently preserved to qualify as rewritings thereof.

The *Words of Moses* is extant in two copies, 1Q22, and a single fragment from Cave 4. It begins with a series of divine instructions to Moses delivered on the very day on which Moses began his farewell address to Israel (1:3). Outlining what he should do and say, YHWH's injunctions suggest an attempt to model the setting of the farewell on the Sinai revelation. The address itself adopts the structure of Deuteronomy: an exhortation is followed by an exposition of laws. The legal section begins with the laws of the Sabbatical year, fusing precepts found in Exodus 23, Leviticus 25, and Deuteronomy 15 (col. 3:1–7). Next the scroll turns to the Day of Atonement (cols. 3:9–4), a topic absent from Deuteronomy. While the rest of the text is lost, it is possible that *Words of Moses* is a selective rewriting of biblical laws aligned with the Jewish calendar, from the month of Tishre onward.

The composite literary work known as the *Temple Scroll* is available in several copies. Beginning with a rewriting of Exodus (34:1–35) and encompassing some 540 Pentateuchal commandments, its best-preserved copy (11QT^a; 11Q19) concludes with a section labeled the "Deuteronomic Paraphrase" (cols. 51–66). This section depicting YHWH speaking in the first person appears to come from the hand of the *Temple Scroll* redactor. Its placement at the end of the composition imitates the structure of the Pentateuch with Deuteronomy being its final book. The "Deuteronomic Paraphrase" in the *Temple Scroll* covers much of the Deuteronomic Code (12–26), with a notable exception of Deuteronomy's teachings on the Sabbatical year (15:1–18).

Embedded in the "Deuteronomic Paraphrase" is a distinct literary unit labeled the "Law of the King" (11QT^a 56:12–59:21). It expands on Deuteronomy's regulations pertaining to the royal office (17:14–20), introducing a detailed treatment of the royal bodyguard, royal advisors, king's wife, permitted versus required war, and blessings and curses on the king and his people (28:1–68).

Three further fragmentary copies of the *Temple Scroll* preserve parts of the "Deuteronomic Paraphrase": 11QT^b (11Q20) 26 ii and 30 parallels 11QT^a 51:5–17; 54:19–21; a newly identified 5Q21 parallels 11QT^a 66:2–8 with variations in readings suggested by the surviving text and the extant spacing; and, more importantly, 4QT^b (4Q524) features an additional material from Deuteronomy (18:1–4; 22:11; 25:5–9).

Implicit Quotations and Allusions

The DSS also yield many implicit quotations and allusions to Deuteronomy. The criteria for differentiating between the two are far from clear. Hence the following selection presents them together grouped according to the literary contexts in which they appear.

Legal exposition. CD stipulates that one's daughter should not be given away to someone who is "unfit for her" (4Q267 7 13; 4Q269 9 2–3; 4Q270 5 16–17; 4Q271 3 9–10). This ruling alludes to Deuteronomy's prohibition of mixing seeds and kinds (22:9–11). A similar application of this passage, this time with a reference to a union between priests and women outside the household of Aaron appears in 4QMMT B 75–82. Allusions to Deuteronomy occur also in non-sectarian legal texts. The laws identifying the true prophet (13:2–6; 18:15–20) are alluded to in one of the manuscripts of the *Apocryphon of Moses* (4Q375 1 a+b). Another copy of this *Apocryphon* (4Q376) points to laws regulating a siege of an enemy city (20:10, 12; 3:2). *4QOrdinances* (4Q159) deals with a forming of a court (17:9, frags. 2–4 +8 3–6), a prohibition of cross-dressing (22:5, frags. 2–4+8 6–7), an indictment of a wife for not remaining a virgin until her marriage (22:13–21, frags. 2–4 +8 8–10), and provisions for the poor (23:25–26; 24:19–21, frags. 1 ii +9 3–5). Multiple allusions to Deuteronomy can also be found in the *Temple Scroll* (11QT^a), in the columns preceding the "Deuteronomic Paraphrase":

14:1–2 (11QT^a 48:7–10): cutting oneself and making a baldness
14:2–3 (11QT^a 48:6–7): unclean foods
14:18 (11QT^a 48:1): unclean animals

14:21 (11QT^a 48:5-7): selling unclean animals to Gentiles
14:23-26 (11QT^a 43:13-15): bringing the tithe to the Temple
16:7 (11QT^a 17:9): Passover regulations
23:11? (11QT^a 45:7): nocturnal emission
23:13 (11QT^a 46:13-14; 11Q20 12:24-25): the location of the latrines (cf. also 1QM 7:7)

Hymns, blessings, and prayers. A prayer in the *War Scroll* (1QM 11:5) calls for God's help alluding to 8:17. Another sectarian text, the *Thanksgiving Hymns* (1QH^a 5:33), invokes a divine promise from 28:46. A non-sectarian collection of prayers, *Words of the Luminaries*, features multiple allusions to Deuteronomy. One of these prayers (4Q504 17:4-6 [1-2 iv (recto) 4-6]) refers to YHWH's choice of Jerusalem (7:6, 8), while another (4Q504 16 [1-2 iii] 7-9) alludes to YHWH disciplining Israel like a parent disciplines a child (8:5) and lists the punishments (28:59). Moses's Song (32:1-43) is featured in multiple prayers and hymns, both sectarian and non-sectarian (32:2, 1Q34^{bis} 1+2 3; 32:11, 4Q504 6 7-8; 32:22, 1QH^a 4:25; 4Q491 10 ii 17; 32:42, 1QM 12:11-12; 19:4; 4Q492 1 4).

Admonitions. An admonition in the CD describes the Israelites' sins in the desert (1:27; CD 3:8) and refers to sinners as "a people wandering in counsel, for there is not insight in them" (32:28; CD 5:17; 4Q266 3 ii 4-5). A nonsectarian exhortation (4Q370 [4QAdmonFlood] 1 i 1-2; MasAdmonFlood) refers to the ingratitude of those who lived before the flood for the abundance of food (8:10).

Pesher. Several sectarian texts employ a *pesher-type* or actualizing exegesis using Deuteronomy as a secondary or an auxiliary text. One example is the interpretation of Nathan's oracle to David (2 Sam 7:10-14; 1 Chr 17:9-12) in *4QFlorilegium* (4Q174 1-2, 21 i 3-4). Citing Deuteronomy (23:3-4), it identifies "congregation of the Lord" (23:3-4) with the "house" (2 Sam 7) and expands the list of those banned from the eschatological Temple to include foreigners and proselytes.

Pesher-type allusions. Multiple sectarian texts allude to scriptural passages through a lens of a pesher-type exegesis. Thus, the phrase "boundary shifters," borrowed from Deuteronomy (27:17; 19:14) and Hosea (5:10), is used in CD to describe opponents of the Qumran community as violating boundaries of the covenant (5:20 [4Q267 2 4]; 19:15-16).

Historical summaries. One historical summary (4Q461 [4QNarrative B] 1 3) uses Deuteronomy to describe the Israelites' slavery in Egypt (26:6), while another (4Q226 [4QpsJub^b] 4 1) alludes to it (31:3) to describe the commissioning of Joshua. Yet another summary (4Q390 [4QapocrJer C^e] 1 9) utilizes Deuteronomy (31:17-18) to depict Israel's apostasy during the seventh Jubilee since the devastation of the land.

Miscellaneous. Among the many other DSS texts alluding to Deuteronomy are the scrolls concerned with the book of Joshua. One (4QJosh^a 1) uses Deuteronomy (8:34-35) to explain two excerpts from Joshua (Josh 4:18; 5:2-7). It suggests that the reading of the Torah took place as the Israelites crossed the Jordan. A scroll rewriting the book of Joshua (4Q378 3 ii+4 11; 14) refers to people's mourning for Moses (34:8) and uses Deuteronomy (31:7-8) to expand on the Transjordanian tribes' response to Joshua (Josh 1:17). Another rewritten Joshua text (4Q379 3 i 6) recasts the fall of Jericho in light of a legislation pertaining to an idolatrous city (13:17), as does also *4QCommentary on Genesis* A (4Q252 3:1-6) in its story of Sodom and Gomorrah. A third text recasting the book of Joshua, *4QProphecy of Joshua* (4Q522 9 ii 7-9), uses Deuteronomy (33:11-12; 26:15) in Joshua's prophetic speech describing Zadok's future service at the Temple.

Finally, several phrases from Deuteronomy recur in the DSS. Whether allusions or literary motifs, these include "to remove foreskin of one's heart" (10:16) in 1QpHab 11:13; 4Q434 1 i 4; "to stiffen one's neck" (10:16) in 4Q182 1 2; 4Q506 131-132 13; "(to walk in) stubbornness of one's heart" (29:18) in CD 2:17; 1QS 1:6; 4Q390 1 12; "the place the Lord your God will choose" (12:5 and *passim*) in 4Q375 1 i 8; 4QMMT B32; 4Q504 1-2 iv 4; "to urge disloyalty" (13:6) in CD 5:2 (=4Q267 2 5); 4Q270 2 ii 14; 11QT^a 54:15; "God hides his face" (31:17, 18; 32:30) in CD 1:3 (=4Q266 2 i 8; 4Q268 1 11); 4Q390 1 9-11; 11QT^a 59:7.

Of much interest is the frequent use of the terms "hidden" and "revealed" from Deut 29:29. The sectarian scrolls utilize them to convey the notion of an ongoing revelation. In some texts this is a revelation of divine mysteries, involving theology, cosmology, and eschatology (1QH^a 19:20 [4Q427 1 1]; 26:15 [4Q427 7 i 19]; 4Q268 1 7). Elsewhere, "hidden" and "revealed" stand for legal matters. The "revealed" are the commandments given to the entirety of Israel at Sinai (cf. CD 5:5), whereas the "hidden" stands for legal precepts disclosed only to Qumran community (1QS 1:9; 5:11–12; 8:11–12; CD 3:13–14). Still, under the influence of Ps 19:13, these two terms may also describe intentional and unintentional sins, as seems to be the case in one of the liturgical texts (4Q508 [4QPrFetes^b] 4 2). The two later usages are closely related and are, in fact, interlinked in the Community Rule (1QS 5:11–12).

References to Figures and Events

Since Deuteronomy reiterates events from Exodus and Numbers, it is often difficult to determine whether a given text points to a figure or an event as described in Exodus and Numbers or to their secondary use by Deuteronomy. One such example is the appointment of officers by Moses (Exod 18:21, 25; Deut 1:15) in the rewritten Joshua text (4Q378 [4QapocrJosh^a] 3 ii 6-8). Likewise, the references to "the curses of his covenant" (CD 1:17; 4Q266 2 i 17) and "the blessings and curses" written in the "bo[ok of Mo]ses" (4QMMT C 20–21) point to either Deuteronomy (28:1–58) or Leviticus (Lev 26:14–46). Similarly ambiguous is the aforementioned appellation the "bo[ok of Mo]ses," which, along with the "sealed book of the Torah" (CD 5:2), might be the only explicit reference to Deuteronomy as a whole in the DSS, though it may also stand for the Pentateuch.

Pseudepigraphy

Multiple DSS feature Moses as a speaker (e.g., 2Q21 [2QapocrMoses?] 1 4-6). Whether it is the Moses in Deuteronomy or the Moses in Exodus or Numbers is unclear. One exception is the aforementioned *Words of Moses*, which assumes the dominant voice of Moses in Deuteronomy.

Literary Models

On a macro-level, several DSS seem to follow the juxtaposition of a parenesis with a legal exposition in Deuteronomy. For instance, CD opens with an extensive admonition followed by legal material. 4QMMT reverses the order. It begins with an exposition of the laws introduced as "these are some of the rulings" (1:1; B 1) and concludes with an exhortation alluding to the covenantal blessings and curses. This pattern is adopted also in the "Law of the King" of the *Temple Scroll* (11QT^a 56:12–59:21).

On a micro-level, the sectarian ceremony of the renewal of the covenant in the *Community Rule* is modeled on the depiction in Deuteronomy of a ceremony featuring an alternating pronouncement of blessings and curses (Deut 27–28; cf. also 11:26–29). The *Community Rule* transforms this one-time event into an annual ceremony incorporating quotations and allusions to multiple scriptural passages, including Deuteronomy (1QS 1:16–2:25; 4Q256 2–3; 4Q257 2; cf. also 5Q11). Thus, the call to the participants to "bring all the knowledge, powers and possessions into the Community of God" (1QS 1:11–13; cf. 3:3) points to "You shall love the Lord your God with all your heart, and with all your soul, and with all your might" (6:5), whereas the curse on the person entering the covenant with an intent to violate it (1QS 2:11–18) is based on "All who hear the words of this oath and bless themselves, thinking in their hears, 'We are safe even though we go our own stubborn ways'" (29:18–20).

Deuteronomic Ideas

This overview of the influence of Deuteronomy on the nonbiblical DSS would be incomplete without noting at least some of the nonverbal affinities between Deuteronomy and the DSS. For instance, there are texts that take up a legal topic discussed by Deuteronomy, such as the rules of testimony (19:15–19), but do not use the language of Deuteronomy (CD 9:16–10:3; 4Q266 8 iii 3; 4Q270 6 iv 11–15). Moreover, multiple DSS mirror themes and ideas from Deuteronomy.

Of the dominant recurring themes in Deuteronomy, one is the covenant between YHWH and Israel. Covenant and covenant loyalty are highly prominent in the sectarian DSS. The Qumran community perceived itself to be bound by a unique renewed covenant with YHWH, elect within Israel who went astray. Deuteronomy also calls for a centralization of the sacrificial worship in a place that YHWH will choose. By extension, multiple DSS highlight the unique status of Jerusalem. Both sectarian (e.g., 4QMMT B 29–31, 59–62) and non-sectarian scrolls (e.g., 4Q522 9 ii; *Temple Scroll*) share a deep concern with its purity. Deuteronomy highlights the divine gift of the land, possession of which depends on obedience. Many DSS feature the Promised Land, its riches (4Q378 11), boundaries (1QapGen 21:15–20), and purity (4Q522 9 i). Deuteronomy emphasizes the importance of learning and teaching, a concern shared by many scrolls (e.g., CD 15:14; 1QS 3:13; 9:13; 1QSa 1:7). Finally, Deuteronomy requires obedience to YHWH's laws, an expectation pervading the entire DSS corpus.

CONCLUSION

Deuteronomy is more than abundantly represented among the scrolls found in the Judean Desert and especially in the caves near Khirbet Qumran. This matches the plethora of uses of Deuteronomy in a wide variety of texts found among the DSS. Covering the entire spectrum of intertextual phenomena, its language, structure, and ideas permeate a wide range of nonbiblical scrolls, from legal codes, to liturgy, to admonitions, to rewritings. The preoccupation with Deuteronomy is shared by both sectarian and nonsectarian scrolls. For the community (or communities) reflected in the former texts, Deuteronomy is first and foremost a book of Moses and a source of YHWH's law. Yet it is also a text through which community's past, present, and future are interpreted, a book evoked in communal ceremonies and prayers, and a piece of Torah worn on one's body daily as *tefillin*.

Bibliography

Dahmen, Ulrich. "Das Deuteronomium in Qumran als umgeschriebene Bibel." In *Das Deuteronomium*, edited by Georg Braulik, 269–309. OBS. Frankfurt am Main: Peter Lang, 2003.

Dimant, Devorah. "Use and Interpretation of Mikra in the Apocrypha and Pseudepigrapha." In *Mikra*, edited by Martin J. Mulder, 379–419. CRINT 2.1. Assen: van Gorcum, 1990.

Duncan, Julie A. "Deuteronomy, Book of." In *Encyclopedia of the Dead Sea Scrolls* 1:198–202. Oxford: Oxford University Press, 2000.

Lange, Armin. "Ancient, Late Ancient, and Early Medieval Manuscript Evidence." In *The Hebrew Bible: Volume 1B; Pentateuch, Former and Latter Prophets*, edited by Armin Lange and Emanuel Tov, 23–59. Textual History of the Bible. Leiden: Brill, 2017.

Lim, Timothy H. "Deuteronomy in the Judaism of the Second Temple Period." In *Deuteronomy in the New Testament*, edited by Maarten J. J. Menken and Steve Moyise, 6–26. London: T&T Clark, 2007.

Lincicum, David. *Paul and the Early Jewish Encounter with Deuteronomy*. Tubingen: Mohr Siebeck, 2010.

Teeter, David Andrew. *Scribal Laws: Exegetical Variation in the Textual Transmission of Biblical Law in the Late Second Temple Period*. FAT 92. Tubingen: Mohr Siebeck, 2014.

von Weissenberg, Hanne. "Deuteronomy at Qumran and in 4QMMT." In *Houses Full of All Good Things: Essays in Memory of Timo Veijola*, edited by Juha Pakkala and Martt Nissinen, 520–537. Helsinki: Finnish Exegetical Society, 2008.

White Crawford, Sidnie. "Reading Deuteronomy in the Second Temple Period." In *Reading the Present in the Qumran Library*, edited by Kristin de Troyer and Armin Lange, 127–140. Atlanta: SBL, 2000.

CHAPTER 24

DEUTERONOMY IN THE NEW TESTAMENT

MICHAEL LABAHN

INTRODUCTION

LIKE Jews of the period, the New Testament (NT) and its literary sources appreciate Deuteronomy as part of the Torah of Moses (Kreuzer 1998, 71). In nearly every NT writing, quotations from Deuteronomy, generally following its interpretation in the Greek Septuagint (LXX), are important. As parallels between the Old and New Testaments show, Deuteronomy was mostly used next to the prophets, especially Isaiah, and the Psalms. Indirect literary, linguistic, and theological influences including narrative structural elements of Deuteronomy in the NT are shaped by their particular understandings of Christ, worship of the one God, love for God and neighbor, the law as God's life-enhancing will, the figure of Moses, his liberation song, cultic orders, and many other motifs. Deuteronomy is also a source for the theological convictions of early Christian theologians and their technique of rereading and interpreting Deuteronomy resembling Jewish interpretations of Deuteronomy during that period. The most reliable traces of use are in quotations from Deuteronomy, so we will concentrate our discussion of these quotations.

Deuteronomy in the New Testament edited by Maarten Menken and Steve Moyise provides a methodologically sound overview by various experts on particular NT writings. In addition to the introductory overview of Deuteronomy in Second Temple Judaism, the contributions deal with NT quotations from Deuteronomy in Mark, Matthew, Luke-Acts, John, Romans, Galatians, 1-2 Corinthians, the Pastoral Letters, Hebrews, and Revelation (Moyise and Menken 2007).

THE DECALOGUE

Linking the NT to Deuteronomy cannot ignore the Decalogue, the *Shema* (Mark 12:29–31; John 5:19–47) and the great commandment (de Vos 2016; Lee 2020; Baron 2022). Evidence for the use of the Decalogue can be found in most of the NT writings.

We start with few examples of the re-use of the decalogue in NT. Mark quotes the second table of the Decalogue as: "You shall not murder. You shall not commit adultery. You shall not steal. You shall not bear false witness. You shall not defraud. Honor your father and mother" (Mark 10:19) without clearly identifying either Exodus or Deuteronomy as its source. The possessive "your mother" used in Mark (Mark 7:10) creates parallels with Deuteronomy (Deut. 5:16) as well as Exodus (Exod. 20:12, 21:17) and Leviticus (Lev. 20:9). The Decalogue in the Gospel of Mark follows the order in the Masoretic text (MT), rather than the order in the LXX, and moves the command to honor parents to the end of the list. "Das Gebot, Vater und Mutter zu ehren, steht betont am Ende, weil es im Kontext um die Gestaltung von Familienbeziehungen geht" (Söding 2022, 294). Mark (Mark 10:22) also refers to "defrauding" instead of "coveting" although he does acknowledge the dangers of greed or desire (Gundry 1993, 553).

Paul quotes the Decalogue twice in Romans where a knowledge-guiding function is ascribed to the law distinguishing between sin and desire (Rom. 7:7; Deut. 5:2). Moreover, it is often unclear whether the NT is referring to the Decalogue in Deuteronomy (Deut. 5:6–20) or in Exodus (Exod. 20:12–16) or simply to an individual commandment. A well-known example comes from Romans: "What then should we say? That the law is sin? By no means! Yet, if it had not been for the law, I would not have known sin. I would not have known what it is to covet if the law had not said, 'You shall not covet.'" (Rom. 7:7 NRSV). Even if these words are exactly from the Decalogue (Ciampa 2007, 105), the marked reference to the law is part of a broadening of horizons in which the law assumes a more comprehensive role.

Similarly, Paul's teaching, "'You shall not commit adultery; You shall not murder; You shall not steal; You shall not covet'; and any other commandment, are summed up in this word, 'Love your neighbour as yourself'" (Rom. 13:9 NRSV), may refer to Deuteronomy (Deut. 5:17–19. 21; Lev. 19:18). It certainly represents a basic biblical teaching that love fulfills the law (Rom. 13:8, 10). Paul, however, modifies the order of the commandments in Deuteronomy. The same order appears in the Gospel of Luke (Luke 18:20). Changes in the order of the commandments in MT also appear in the Letter of James (James 2:11) where the prohibition of adultery precedes the prohibition of murder (Carson 2007, 1001–1002). The NT may not have made these revisions but may simply be using an alternative Hebrew or Greek tradition for Deuteronomy.

The significance of the Decalogue in the NT is not surprising, but the question arises whether the evidence can be ascribed to a literary use of Deuteronomy or Exodus or simply represent a reference to cultural memory. "Modifikationen im Wortlaut und die wechselnde Reihenfolge der zitierten Dekaloggebote erklären sich am besten durch die Aufnahme unterschiedlicher liturgischer oder katechetisch-didaktischer Überlieferung" (Sänger 2007a, 283).

The various uses and reuses of Deuteronomy discussed in research reveal divergent modes of reception. Whether the Decalogue has the same special position (*Sonderstellung*) in the NT as it has in Judaism remains unclear (Stemberger 1989, 91). "Trotz seiner relativ schmalen Bezeugung in der frühjüdischen Literatur darf man davon ausgehen, daß der Dekalog für weite Kreise eine Art Orientierungsrahmen bildete" (Sänger 2007a, 276).

The *Shema*

Deuteronomy is of major importance for the development of theological reflections in both Jewish and early Christian groups, and its reception is important for understanding how Christianity and Judaism separated from one another. For example, that Jesus in the NT became part of the divine unity (John 10:30) and an object of human love so that his commandments need to be observed (John 14:15) demonstrates how traditional and new readings of the *Shema* merged to establish an eschatological *Shema* (John 17:21). "The Johannine Shema is thus both apologetic and polemical; it explicates Jesus's unique relation to God and condemns those Jews who fail to recognize the unity of Father and Son" (Baron 2018, 205).

An important protagonist to be considered is Jesus himself, whose reception of Deuteronomy in his proclamation of the kingdom of God cannot be ignored. Since his teaching is preserved in the NT and Jesus's reference to Deuteronomy is a precondition for the early Christian use of the Old Testament (OT), we have to take it into consideration here. Above all, the great commandment appears as a central text of ethics in the context of Jesus's proclamation of the kingdom of God. The combination of *Shema* (Deut. 6:4–5) and the commandment to love one's neighbor (Lev. 19:18) is not unprecedented in Jewish tradition. Whether the combination is a common synopsis of the Decalogue, however, is questionable (Allison 1994, 273).

Q: The Temptation of Jesus

The Q sayings are an early Christian, semibiographical document used by the Gospels of Matthew and Luke. Q knows Deuteronomy well (Allison 2000, 72). Keeping the importance of quotations in mind, the temptation story of Jesus plays a crucial role (Q 4:1–13). First, its narrative setting complies with the exodus events described in Deuteronomy: forty years in the desert (Deut. 2:7, 29:5; Exod. 16:35) and forty days of Moses on Mount Horeb (Deut. 9:9, Exod. 34:8) correspond to the forty-day fasting of Jesus in the desert (Q 4:1–2). The temptation motif is also reminiscent of Deuteronomy (Deut. 8:2). Jesus and the devil both quote the OT in their arguments, and the three quotations of Jesus can be attributed to Deuteronomy (Labahn 2010, 255–264).

Once, Jesus quotes only the negative protasis: "man does not live by bread alone" (Deut. 8:3; Q 4:4) stressing that God lets Israel suffer from hunger in the desert (Labahn 2010, 256). Then he quotes "Do not put the Lord your God to the test" (Deut. 6:16). And, finally, "The Lord your God you shall fear; him you shall serve" (Deut 6:13). There are parallels in Deut 5:9, Ex 20:5 stressing the call for obedience in the Decalogue, and to Ex 34:14, 4 Kgds 17:35–36. Consequently, studies interested in the relationship of Christology and theology consider the love of God in Deuteronomy (Deut. 6:5) to be the link between the three different temptations (Gerhardsson 1966, 77). Jesus in Q argues "mit den zentralen Texten des Dtn, indirekt mit Dtn 4 und 5 und d.h. mit dem Dekalog, und direkt mit Dtn 6, wo mit dem Schema Israel das sog. Hauptgebot steht (Dtn 6,4f. bzw. 6,4-9)" (Michel 2011, 77). Such an interpretation captures the fact that the temptation of Jesus is about exclusive worship of God, which Jesus as the one who has come and as the Son of God (Q 3:16, 3:22, 4:3, 4:9, 10:22) exemplifies. Nonetheless, the three temptations emerge as a complex network of intertextuality, which would be too limited by an exclusive reference to Deuteronomy (Deut. 6:5).

Let us look at the interpretation of the third temptation of Jesus. The insertion of the μόνῳ (alone) is not necessarily reminiscent of Deut 6:4-5, but underscores the contrast to the devil's offer of universal dominion (πάσας τὰς βασιλείας). As many researchers assume, due to the position of the temptation narrative, Deuteronomy gives importance to understanding the will of God. Because of its connection with Jesus as the significant teacher on whose proclamation Q is based, however, trust and worship of the only true God is transferred to obedience to Jesus. The assumption that these allusions including reference to Exodus and Leviticus underline a new Exodus typology including Jesus's similarity to Moses can hardly be verified (Allison 2000, 69–73).

The Gospels of Matthew and Luke (Matt. 4:10; Luke 4:8) have, in turn, influenced the tradition of Deuteronomy (Deut. 6:13, 10:30) in Codex A LXX (Wevers 1995, 120).

The Letters to the Corinthians

One focus of NT studies is on the Pauline letters (Ciampa 1998; Wisdom 2001; Wagner 2006; Bekken 2007; Lincicum 2010; Waters 1996). Despite differences in detail, these studies present Paul as a theologian who draws his teaching from the OT but develops his own interpretations often dependent on Jewish readings (Lincicum 2008).

In Paul's letters to the Corinthians, the use of texts and literary structures from Deuteronomy, predominantly from its laws, is connected with sermons. "Paul, like Moses, seeks to spell out for the new people of God the theological and ethical consequences of the act of salvation that is an exodus" (Rosner 2007, 119). Overall, however, only a few unambiguous quotations from Deuteronomy can be verified. The expulsion formula "cut off the wicked one from among you" (1 Cor. 5:13) is found in Deuteronomy (Deut. 13:16, 17:7, 19:19, 21:21, 21:24, 24:7) sometimes with the phrase "from Israel" (Deut. 17:12, 22:22) but neither is related to a particular source text. "There is good evidence that the contexts of all six appearances of the Deuteronomy expulsion formula in their original contexts have exerted an influence on Paul's instruction across the chapter" (Rosner 2007, 122). Although Paul makes a powerful point by this reference to Deuteronomy (Zeller 2009, 209), a quotation formula is missing.

The rule about feeding a working ox (Deut. 25:4) in 1 Corinthians (1 Cor. 9:9; 1 Tim. 5:18) is introduced as a quotation, unequivocally and quite artfully. The Pauline text deviates in using οὐ κημώσεις instead of οὐ φιμώσεις whereby old manuscripts (Papyrus 46, Sinaiticus, A, C, etc.) already read the reference as a quotation and correct the Pauline text using the LXX. In a radical and almost singular way, Paul allegorically appropriates the individual instruction protecting the animal in order to justify his financial recognition. According to Paul, the heralds of the word are singled out in relation to the animal (and to the wording of the Torah) because of their end-time function (1 Cor. 9:10–12).

There is an unmarked quotation from Deuteronomy (Deut. 19:15) in 2 Corinthians (2 Cor. 13:1) that shows multiple problems. Without a quotation formula, the order is used as a self-evident legal principle. In announcing his third journey as an expression of his apostolic authority, Paul appeals to three witnesses (Thrall 2000, 874) or, more likely, the double announcement of his severe appearance (Bultmann 1976, 243) comes into question. The reference substantiates Paul's claimed authority in a polemical context of his correspondence.

Other forms of reception also play a significant role in the Letters to the Corinthians (1 Cor. 8:1–14) (Rosner 2007, 126–133) even though the reference to Deuteronomy (Deut. 6:4) is not always certain.

THE LETTER TO THE GALATIANS

Galatians (Gal. 3:10, 13) conspicuously focus on the subject of the curse in Deuteronomy (Deut. 21:23, 27:25). The law is rhetorically used against appeals to the "works of the law" (Gal. 3:1–14). The target text "For all who rely on the works of the law are under a curse" (Gal. 3:10 NRSV) is justified by the source text "Cursed be anyone who does not uphold the words of this law by observing them" (Deut. 27:26 NRSV). According to Paul, life comes from faith (Gal. 3:11) in contrast to the model of the law (Lev. 18:5). In the model of faith, Christ has become a curse on behalf of believers, which is again justified with Deuteronomy: "anyone hung on a tree is under God's curse" (Deut. 21:23 NRSV). Jewish arguments against early Christians considered the cross as a curse which clearly labeled Jesus "as falscher Prophet, Volksverräter (vgl. Deut 13,2ff.) und Gotteslästerer (1Sam 11,7)" (Sänger 2007b, 103). These target texts are not quotations but adaptations to counter those arguments. The adaptations are linguistically shaped by Deuteronomy's wider context and by Jewish exegesis. It needs to be "understood ... by the incorporation of language from later texts dealing with the curse and by other Jewish understandings" (Ciampa 2007, 102–103). The two source texts are used in opposite directions, the first against fulfilling the commandments of the law, the second to justify life by faith. Deuteronomy (Deut. 27:26) curses insufficient keeping of the law, leading exegetes to see the reference text in contradiction to the Pauline usage highlighting a "conflict between the wording of the quotation and Paul's statement in the first part of the verse" (Stanley 2004, 123–124). "The phrase 'the words of this law' could have proved ambiguous for those who were not familiar with the broader context of the passage, but 'all the things written in the book of the law' makes clear that what is in view is obedience to the whole of the Mosaic law" (Cowan 2020, 223).

THE LETTER TO THE ROMANS

Several target texts in the Letter to the Romans find their source in Deuteronomy, next to the re-use of the Decalogue. Romans appeals to Deuteronomy (Deut. 30:11–14) as a proof text for the idea of righteousness based on faith (Rom. 10:6–8) although Romans adapts the wording of this source text (Seifrid 1985; Koch 1986, 185–186; Hübner 1993, 314; Ciampa

2007, 108–109). This source text speaks of the immediacy of Torah to the people of God. The target text in Romans reads Deuteronomy in a Christological manner where the life-giving God is immediately close not in the law, but in the life-giving Christ. "Paul can read Deut 30:11-14 to mean the presence of God's word in the community of God's people empowers the obedience to faith" (Hays 1989, 163).

Romans (Rom. 10:19) adapts a speech of Moses addressed to Israel using third-person verbs from Deuteronomy (Deut. 32:21) into a speech of Paul to the followers of Jesus using second-person verbs. Romans contrasts the condemnation of the preaching of Paul by the Jews with the acceptance of his preaching by the Gentiles. Consequently, God will make the Jews who reject Jesus jealous of the Gentiles who accept him (Hübner 1984, 97; Stanley 2008, 143–144).

Paul then reflects on God's promise to Israel (Rom. 11:1–36) with the idea of the holy remnant. He lapses into a sharply polemical tone about the Jews who reject Jesus which he justifies with a quotation from Deuteronomy, "the Lord has not given you a mind to understand, or eyes to see, or ears to hear" (Deut. 29:4 NRSV), into which he inserts the "sluggish spirit" from Isaiah (Isa. 29:10 NRSV). "God gave them a sluggish spirit, eyes that would not see and ears that would not hear" (Rom. 11:8 NRSV).

In the last part of Romans, there are two quotations from the song of Moses (Deut. 32:1–43). In a section about love in everyday life, for example, Romans (Rom. 12:19) inserts a free translation of a speech by God in Deuteronomy (Deut. 32:35) to justify the renunciation of human vengeance in favor of God's final judgment. The quotation in Romans—"Vengeance is mine, I will repay, says the Lord"—corresponds to Jewish exegetical tradition and is linguistically close to the Hebrew version לִי נָקָם וְשִׁלֵּם—"Vengeance is mine, and recompense" (Ciampa 2007, 112–113). With regard to the reading in Symmachus, one can think of a Hebrew or a Greek source text, but a definitive identification of a source remains speculative, since Romans adapted its source text.

The Letters to Timothy

The Letters to Timothy show fewer traces of Deuteronomy, perhaps due to their brevity (Häfner 2007, 136) or to their unique way of interpreting the OT (2 Tim. 3:14–17; Häfner 2000). Quotations and allusions to Deuteronomy in Timothy often already appear in other letters so that the sources for these target texts may be the letters of Paul rather than Deuteronomy (Häfner 2007, 141).

Timothy justifies its explanation about the elders' right to wages (1 Tim. 5:18) with "you shall not muzzle an ox while it is treading out the grain" (Deut. 25:4 LXX). Although introduced by a citation formula, the word order has been changed so that the elders are directly equated with the ox and, like the ox, are entitled to compensation from their ministry. As in the Gospel of Luke (Luke 10:7 NRSV), Deuteronomy stands next to a word of Jesus as scriptural authority for the teaching on elders in Timothy.

Timothy may justify the protection of an official from false accusations (1 Tim. 5:19), using a legal instruction on witnesses in Deuteronomy (Deut. 19:15). The relationship of the target text to its source, however, remains unclear (see list by Häfner 2007, 146).

The Gospel of Mark

The three synoptic gospels contain direct quotations, allusions, and other forms of reception. The Gospel of Mark finds Deuteronomy already in its sources. Central is Jesus's commandment to love, which combines the *Shema* (Deut. 6:4; Mark 12:29) and the great commandment (Deut. 6:5; Mark 12:30) with the commandment to love one's neighbor (Mark 12:31; Lev. 19:18). "You shall love the Lord your God with all your heart, and with all your soul, and with all your mind, and with all your strength" (Mark 12:30 NRSV) differs slightly from LXX version of Deuteronomy, changing and expanding the list of body parts called on to love God.

The answer of the scribe in the Gospel of Mark (Mark 12:32–33) is reminiscent of Deuteronomy (Deut. 4:35) and other OT traditions (2 Sam. 7:22; 1 Kgs. 19:19; Isa. 37:20, 45:5). The inner ability to love in his answer differs from Jesus's use of Deuteronomy (Deut. 6:5–6) and Leviticus (Lev. 19:18).

Sadducees set a trap for Jesus (Mark 12:19) using Deuteronomy (Deut. 25:5–6). Despite the use of a quotation formula—"Moses wrote . . ."—the Sadducees freely quote his teaching on levirate marriage (Deut. 24:1, 3). Consequently, the target text is not a quotation (*pace* Moyise 2007, 27), but still exciting insofar as in this dispute (Mark 10:1–12), a dialogue about the interpretation of Moses's commandments on marriage is conducted. Here, the commandment from Deuteronomy is opposed by the direct will of God (Gen. 38).

Apart from the use of "the Lord your God will raise up for you a prophet like me from among your own people; you shall heed such a prophet" (Deut. 18:15 NRSV) in the Gospel of Mark (Mark 9:4, 7) or motifs from Deuteronomy in the end-time speech (Mark 13:1–37), the precise identification of the source texts in the Gospel of Mark remains difficult (Marcus 1993, 83; Moyise 2007, 38–39). The quotations can be found in discussions and are used as authority by both positive and negative characters in the gospel. The appeal to Deuteronomy is thus an authority in the Gospel of Mark, the value of which results from the respective narrative context and through the respective speaker. Set in the right context, especially through Jesus, Deuteronomy articulates the will of God.

The Gospel of Matthew

Matthew and Luke adopt the quotations from their sources Mark and Q. There are also quotations from their special traditions. Beginning with Matthew, the three texts from Q are included in the account of Jesus's temptation (Matt. 4:1–11). Matthew adds appropriately from LXX "but with every word that comes out of the mouth," which shows understanding of the Gospel of Matthew that "Jesus is the Son of God by obeying his Father, from his exemplary fulfilment of the commandments from Deuteronomy until his death on the cross" (Menken 2007, 49). In addition, there is a further focus on the six "You have heard . . . but I say to you" antitheses in the Gospel of Matthew (Matt. 5:21–48), which the gospel takes at least partially from its sources maybe even the preaching Jesus.

1	Matt 5:21	Deut 5:17 (or Exod 20:13)	Decalogue
2	Matt 5:27	Deut 5:18 (or Exod 20:14)	Decalogue
3	Matt 5:31	free rendition of Deut 24:1, 3 cf. Mark 10:11-12; Matt 19:9	
4	Matt 5:33	possible reference texts: Deut 5:11, 20; 23:22 and others	
5	Matt 5:38	Deut 19:21 (or Exod 21:24; Lev 24:20)	
6	Matt 5:43	possible reference texts: Deut 7:2; 20:16; 23:4, 7 (without a literal match).	

The affinity of the six antitheses with material from Deuteronomy suggests that the reference was used intentionally. Jesus's authority as an eschatological teacher of the interpretation of Torah expresses God's will articulated in Deuteronomy in eschatological time in a new and intensified manner: "So to Matthew, the Torah with all its details is of importance, but its governing principle is love or mercy" (Menken 2007, 52).

Another quote from a variant source is the teaching on an unrepentant sinner (Matt. 18:15–18). If a one-on-one admonition is not sufficient, a conversation with two or three members of the community is suggested, taking up the word of the two or three witnesses from Deuteronomy (Deut. 19:15b) with minor adjustments to the context. If the quote was added by the Gospel of Matthew, the focus shifts from the willingness to forgive to the willingness to repent (Menken 2007, 54). Otherwise, the source for the quotations are the Gospel of Mark and are thus found in teaching and controversial scenes with various protagonists including Jesus.

Quotations from the Decalogue the teachings on divorce (Deut. 24:1, 3; Matt. 19:7) and the great commandment (Deut. 6:5; Matt. 22:37) are edited according to linguistic style of the Gospel of Matthew (Menken 2007, 53, 55–56, 57).

The *Shema* in the Gospel of Matthew (Matt. 22:37b; Luke 10:27; against Mark 12:29) is distinguished from the commandments, so that the omission of the *Shema* there represents more of a specification than a "tightening" or "Straffung" (Luz 1997, 271).

The teaching on the levirate in the Gospel of Matthew (Matt. 22:24) references both Deuteronomy (Deut. 25:5) and Genesis (Gen. 38:8), but is not a quotation (Luz 1997, 263). The "You shall not steal" expansion of the Decalogue in the Gospel of Mark (Mark 10:19) is omitted in the Gospel of Matthew (Matt. 19:18). These instructions in Deuteronomy are recognized as rules of life, but at the same time they are inserted into Matthew's own theology through interpretation and intensified through the hermeneutics of love and the idea of better justice.

The Gospel of Luke

Target texts in the Gospel of Luke are also taken from source texts in Q and Mark (Rusam 2003, 2). The Gospel of Luke (Luke 10:25–28) probably does not take the combination of quotations from Deuteronomy (Deut. 6:5) and Leviticus (Lev. 19:18) from the Gospel of Mark (Mark 12:28–31), but from an alternative source (Fitzmyer 1985, 877–878). Both quotations are put together without the *Shema* (Deut. 6:4), although Jesus characterizes them as "written in the law" (Luke 2:23, 10:26) in contrast to the Gospel of Mark. The Gospel of Luke is not concerned with the great commandment (Mark 12:28; Matt 22:36, 22:38), but with eternal life.

Therefore, the gospel deals with deeds that lead to an ethically effective life before God. The keyword "neighbor" in the parable of the good Samaritan (Luke 10:29–37) is closely connected with Deuteronomy and interprets what such love of God and neighbor means. "Dabei wird mit Hilfe des Stichworts πλησίον das Gebot der Nächstenliebe exemplifiziert und interpretiert" (Rusam 2003, 114): Regarding the use of the Decalogue about the right deed to attain eternal life (Luke 18:18–27), the gospel, despite its social-ethical tendency, deletes the addition "you shall not steal" in the Gospel of Mark (Mark 10:19).

The Gospel of Luke (Luke 18:20) follows Deuteronomy (Deut. 5:17–20) and corrects the order of the prohibitions of adultery and murder in the Gospel of Mark (Rusam 2003, 118–119). The Gospel of Luke finds a positive twist by the willingness to place oneself fully in God's loving service by giving up one's possessions (Luke 12:33, 14:33, 18:21).

References to the Sabbath in the NT like healings on the Sabbath (Luke 23:56) and Sabbath observance radically reinterpret the understanding of these commandments for the followers of Jesus. Similarly, "Whoever comes to me and does not hate father and mother, wife and children, brothers and sisters, yes, and even life itself, cannot be my disciple" (Luke 14:26 NRSV) radically reinterpets the understanding of the commandment to honor one's parents in Judaism.

The NT not only quotes individual passages from Deuteronomy but also adapts large literary motifs like the well-known travel motif in the Gospel of Luke (Luke 9:51–19:51). Some scholars have attempted to prove not only individual allusions but also a direct influence from Deuteronomy on this travelog based on common content and vocabulary resemblance of literary structure as well as on motif of wandering and their understanding of a portrait of Jesus as a prophet like Moses (Swartley 1994). For Christopher F. Evans, the NT text emerged from sermons on Deuteronomy (C. F. Evans 1955). In contrast, Craig A. Evans defines the reception as "infrequent and slight" (C. A. Evans 1993, 132). Moessner (1983, 1997) offers a thematic approach to the reception of Deuteronomy in the travel sections, although he may not accurately represent the theology of Deuteronomy (Pao and Schnabel 2007, 314). Although individual motifs in the Lucan travelog can be traced back to Deuteronomy and although all these studies open our mind for the wealth of OT motifs in Luke, we should follow the critical assessment by Denaux: "it seems difficult to maintain that the book of Dt functioned as the model of Luke's Gospel or the Lukan Travel Narrative" (Denaux 1997, 280).

Acts of Apostles

The Acts of Apostles have a striking interest in the expectation of the prophet from Deuteronomy (Deut. 18) which is the only quotation from Deuteronomy found in Peter's speech after the healing of the lame man (Acts 3:22–23) and in Stephen's speech (Acts 7:37). The two target texts are connected. Peter's missionary speech (Acts 3:11–26) is composed from traditional elements (Bock 1987, 191–192; Marshall 2007, 547). The target texts in Acts reflect the way Deuteronomy appears in an early Christian testimony (Albl 1999, 191–195; Holtz 1968, 71–81). Moses, who announced Jesus's coming, shares Jesus's fate in a way, anticipating and thus confirming it (Acts 7:37). The text is a shortened variation of Moses said, "The Lord your God will raise up for you from your own people a prophet like me. You must listen to whatever he tells you" (Acts 3:22–23) so that a Christological interpretation emerges, in which the coming of Christ corresponds to the word of Moses (Rese 1969, 76–77). The Christologically interpreted events of the fate of Moses in Deuteronomy typologically refer to the fate of Jesus, as his word about the prophet himself represents prophecy aimed at obedience. "Auch illustriert das Zitat . . . die Person des Mose und ermöglicht dem Leser die Analogie zwischen Mose und Jesus selbst herzustellen" (Rusam 2003, 138).

THE GOSPEL OF JOHN

"Deuteronomy is one of the most important sources for the Gospel of John" (Labahn 2017a, 210). Because there is only one free quotation, allusions, narrative, and argumentative or thematic traces are of great importance such as the call to love God, which in the Gospel of John also includes love for his Son and revealer Jesus (Beutler 1998a; Popkes 2005, 294–296). "Der eigentliche Schwerpunkt der Verwendung des Alten Testaments liegt . . . bei den sehr viel zahlreicheren Anspielungen und der Übernahme alttestamentlicher Motive" (Hengel 1989, 282).

The Gospel of John (John 8:17) uses the motif of two witnesses (Deut. 19:1) who, in the gospel, become Jesus and his Father (John 19:19). The gospel (John 5:31–34) understands the law as a witness for Jesus (Labahn 2017a, 213–214). The gospel freely uses at least two source texts in Deuteronomy (Deut. 17:6; 19:15) and perhaps one in Numbers (Num. 35:30).

The Gospel of John (John 8:54) also alludes to or quotes Deuteronomy (Deut. 6:4) where Jesus identifies his father who bears witness to him with the one whom his opponents refer to as "He is our Lord." Jesus asks his adversaries to seek only the glory that comes from "who alone is God" (John 5:44). In the Gospel of John, the belief in the one God is a basic axiom, albeit in the form that this God can only be found in his only-begotten Son (John 1:18). These allusions are concentrated on the testimony of the law for Jesus (John 5–7) especially the duration of the illness of the paralytic (Labahn 2017a, 215–224).

THE LETTER TO THE HEBREWS

The reception of Deuteronomy in the Letter to the Hebrews is controversial concerning number and character of the references. There are at least four explicit OT quotations in Hebrews (Heb. 10–13), three of which come from Deuteronomy (Deut. 31–32; Steyn 2007, 153–154; Allen 2008, 44–71). This makes the song of Moses particularly influential for an understanding of the letter (Gheorghita 2003, 95).

The first quotation (Heb. 1:5–14) is in a series emphasizing the superiority of God's Son over the angels alluding to Deuteronomy (Deut. 32:43 LXX; Odes 2:43) which contains a longer and partially different text than the MT. This source text also appears at Qumran (4QDeutq; Lange 2009, 99–100) so that the Letter to the Hebrews (Heb. 1:6b) together with LXX testifies a Hebrew text that differs from MT (Wevers 1995, 533). In the NT text, the praise of God in the song of Moses becomes an eschatological perspective in Christ (Deut. 31:29) for those who benefit from salvation in him and to their response.

Also, action-related is another quotation from Deuteronomy (Deut. 32:35-6) in Hebrews (Heb. 10:30). In this speech, which calls on converts to avoid any future sin, the Jesus appropriates the words of Moses (Steyn 2007, 157). Again, different source texts for this target text have to be considered, but it is "closer to the Hebrew and the Syro-Hexapla fragment."

Other explicit quotations from Deuteronomy (Deut. 9:16, 31:6 and a probable allusion Deut 17:6) appear in Hebrews (Heb. 10:28, 12:21, 13:5). These target texts use motifs relating to Moses, the covenant, and cultic topics from Deuteronomy and elsewhere in the OT. "Our author applied his knowledge from Deuteronomy in an informative and a normative manner in the light of the exalted Son and the implications for the Christian community" (Steyn 2007, 168).

Deuteronomy is also in the background of the exhortation to keep its audience as wandering community on the path of obedience to God's word, but it is too far reaching to understand the Letter to the Hebrews as a "new" Deuteronomy (Allen 2008).

THE REVELATION TO JOHN

The Revelation to John is filled with references to Deuteronomy including the Decalogue (Rev. 9:20-21). By taking up elements from the song of Moses (Deut.32:1-43) and the song celebrating the saving at the Red Sea (Exod. 15:1-21) in Revelation (Rev. 6:10, 10:5-6, 15:5, 16:5, 19:2)—not in each case it is evident which song is alluded to or if a direct dependence can be proved—it shows correspondence "des richtenden und rettenden Handelns Gottes während des Exodus aus Ägypten und seines eschatologischen Gerichts über die Feinde der bedrängten christlichen Gemeinde" (Tilly 2009, 463).

The content of the Revelation to John is protected by the formula: "if anyone takes away from the words of the book of this prophecy, God will take away that person's share in the tree of life and in the holy city, which are described in this book" (Rev. 22:19). As in Deuteronomy (Deut. 4:2, 12:32), the content of the Revelation to John is inalterable. "Die auf der Deuteronomiumsseptuaginta basierende Warnung . . . markiert als Lektüreanweisung den Anspruch des gesamten letzten Buches der christlichen Bibel, den kleinasiatischen Gemeinden das von Gott in Christus gestiftete eschatologische Heil zu verkünden und sie zugleich vor dem ständigen Assimilationsdruck . . . zu bewahren" (Tilly 2005, 238-239). No other NT book is as textually fixed as Revelation. With this outrageous claim, Revelation turns itself into a new authoritative Christian document whose acceptance can decide about life and death of its readers who are instructed to act accordingly (Labahn 2013). Reference to Deuteronomy helps to underscore the claim of being God's eschatological revelation, who acts as judge and liberator for a church following God and his son, the Lamb.

REREADING DEUTERONOMY IN THE NT

Next to the citations of Deuteronomy mentioned above, there are further modes of rereading Deuteronomy in NT, as allusions, echoes, and so on. With Deuteronomy, the NT shares the confession of the one God and the love for him and the human neighbors.

In discussion with and sometimes against Deuteronomy, the NT takes up the challenge of integrating the confession of Christ into the confession of the one God. Deuteronomy is reread, so to speak, into a Deuteronomy as read by Early Christians. Whether the context of the rereadings, quotations, or allusions to Deuteronomy in the NT which some scholars conclusively identify, is that much recalled, however, seems doubtful to me. Many have rightly shown that the NT use of Deuteronomy must be read against the background of the Jewish reception of Deuteronomy. Thus, the NT is connected to Deuteronomy, but also reinterprets Deuteronomy, and thus remains at a distance from the contemporary Jewish understanding of Deuteronomy which has to be considered within the discussion of the parting of Judaism and Christianity. Both share the worship of the one God and the great concern of love for God and man, as well as including ethical orientation taken from the Decalogue as indication of the goodwill of God and the experience of God's judgment and liberation, as in the song of Moses.

The question of the textual form of source texts used in the NT target texts is of great importance. NT citations do not always represent an accurate depiction of its source in Deuteronomy, but reread it within the NT context. For the most part, a Greek text is source for the NT, but then the question arises as to whether the NT text might possibly have different or even better variant source than the LXX. For example, the more horizontal image "beyond the sea" in Deuteronomy (Deut. 30:13 NRSV) which appears as a vertical image "descend into the abyss" (Rom. 10:7 NRSV) in the NT may be from a Targum translation of Deuteronomy in Aramaic (Dunn 1988, 606). In my opinion, some NT uses of Deuteronomy are more likely to be expressions of creative reinterpretations by a target text which reflects its own understanding of its source text.

There is a general consensus that allusions must be verifiable, but there is still dissent about the question how to define an allusion. Although without adequate linguistic evidence, scholars often reference NT traditions (Matt. 17:5, 21:10; Mark 9:7; Luke 7:16, 9:35; Acts 3:22–23) which call on Christians to "listen to" Jesus because he is a "prophet like Moses" (Deut. 18:15–18). "The Markan transfiguration narrative [Mark 9:7] identifies Jesus this prophet-like-Moses" (Marcus 1993, 81; Pao and Schnabel 2007, 299). Whether the Gospel of John (John 1:21, 45, 5:46, 6:14, 7:40) alludes to the "prophet like Moses" tradition in Deuteronomy (Köstenberger 2007, 419–420), or not, depends on one's definition of an allusion.

"Our law does not judge people without first giving them a hearing to find out what they are doing" (John 7:51 NRSV) "harks back to texts such as Deut 1:16-17; 17:4; 19:18" (Köstenberger 2007, 456), but this does not mean more than thematic convergences. The linguistic connotations of "judge" and "law" in Deuteronomy and the Gospel of John, for example, are not sufficient to definitively identify the source text (Labahn 2007). The less linguistic and content-related evidence for a source text, the less certainty of an allusion can be expected, especially if there are multiple influences of different source texts. Sometimes, when multiple OT sources (Deut. 9:23; Num. 14:11; Ps. 78:22, 32) for NT texts like "Master (δέσποτα), now you are dismissing your servant in peace" (Luke 2:29 NRSV) or "so we see that they were unable to enter because of unbelief" (Heb 3:19 NRSV) make a definitive identification of their source difficult, often determined as "biblical language" (Rusam, 2003, 54–56, 78), it might be better to speak of "recollections ... of prominent concepts" (Guthrie 2007, 921). If the relationship is, for example, an unbelief motif, it is not simply an allusion but a motif whose source text cannot exactly be determined.

The "be without fear" motif in a NT target text like "Keep alert, stand firm in your faith, be courageous, be strong. Let all that you do be done in love" (1 Cor. 16:13) may echo or allude to a source text in Deuteronomy "Be strong and bold; have no fear or dread of them, because it is the Lord your God who goes with you; he will not fail you or forsake you" (Deut. 31:6-7). Rarely, however, can a source text in Deuteronomy of a NT figure of speech or a motif be clearly identified. Similarly, attempts to find a source text in Deuteronomy (Deut. 1:9-17) for a target text in the NT (1 Cor. 6:1-6) methodically built only on linguistic correspondences is an instructive example. With only a general reference to "Exod 18/Deut and related passages" identifying Deuteronomy as a source text remains too daring (Ciampa and Rosner 2007, 711).

There is some popularity in understanding NT passages as literarily built according to a blueprint along OT texts. For example, reading 1 Corinthians (1 Cor. 10:14-21) as a Christian *midrash* on Deuteronomy (Deut. 32:17-21) is a difficult thesis (Hanson 1974, 115). Identifying a target text in the NT as a sermon or midrash does not do justice to the literary character of NT narratives. Thus, at least as far as the synoptics are concerned, they cannot be traced back to Christian sermons but must be regarded as elaborate narratives based on tradition and sources. If the traces of possible source texts in Deuteronomy are sometimes inconspicuous or inconsistent, then doubts about the use of OT blueprints for the design of such sections are appropriate. It is therefore a definite step forward when, a more reflective, differentiating methodology for analyzing influences is used (Evans 1993, 137-138).

Conclusions

To refine the relationship between Deuteronomy and the NT will require meticulous, detailed study not only of the intertextual play of both texts, but also in identifying allusions, echoes, images, motifs, and literary models. Even if the results of where the NT makes direct use of Deuteronomy remain controversial, the importance of Deuteronomy for the theological discourse of the NT has been well researched. Nonetheless, a lot of future work is still necessary in multiple areas of research to produce a comprehensive description of the relationship between Deuteronomy and the NT.

Bibliography

Albl, Martin C. *"And Scripture Cannot Be Broken": The Form and Function of the Early Christian Testimonia Collections*. Supplements to Novum Testamentum 96. Leiden: Brill, 1999.

Allen, David M. *Deuteronomy and Exhortation in Hebrews. A Study in Narrative Re-Presentation*. Wissenschaftliche Untersuchungen zum Neuen Testament 2/238. Tübingen: Mohr Siebeck, 2008.

Allison, Dale C. "Mark 12:28-31 and the Decalogue." In *The Gospels and the Scriptures of Israel*. Edited by Craig Evans and W. Richard Stegner, pp. 270-278. Journal for the Study of the New Testament Supplement Series 104. Sheffield: Sheffield Academic Press, 1994.

Allison, Dale C. *The Intertextual Jesus. Scripture in Q*. Harrisburg: Trinity Press International, 2000.

Baron, Lori. *The Shema in John's Gospel*. Wissenschaftliche Untersuchungen zum Neuen Testament. Reihe 2/574. Tübingen: Mohr Siebeck, 2022.

Baron, Lori. "The Shema in Mark and John and the Parting of the Ways." In *The Ways That Often Parted: Essays in Honor of Joel Marcus*. Edited by Lori Baron, Jill Hicks-Keeton, Matthew Thiessen, pp. 187–210. Early Christianity and Its Literature 24. Atlanta: SBL Press, 2018.

Bekken, Per Jarle. *The Word Is Near You: A Study of Deuteronomy 30:12-14 in Paul's Letter to the Romans in a Jewish Context*. Beihefte zur Zeitschrift für die neutestamentliche Wissenschaft 144. Berlin: de Gruyter, 2007.

Beutler, Johannes. "Das Hauptgebot im Johannesevangelium." In *Studien zu den johanneischen Schriften*. Edited by Johannes Beutler, pp. 107–120. Stuttgarter Biblische Aufsatzbände 25. Stuttgart: Katholisches Bibelwerk, 1998a.

Bock, Darrell L. *Proclamation from Prophecy and Pattern. Lucan Old Testament Christology*. Journal for the Study of the New Testament 12. Sheffield: JSOT Press, 1987.

Bultmann, Rudolf. *Der zweite Brief an die Korinther*. Vandenhoeck and Ruprecht, 1976.

Ciampa, Roy E. "Deuteronomy in Galatians and Romans." In *Deuteronomy in the New Testament*. Edited by Steve Moyise and Maarten J. J. Menken, pp. 99–117. Library of New Testament Studies 358. London: T & T Clark, 2007.

Ciampa, Roy E. *The Presence and Function of Scripture in Galatians 1 and 2*. Wissenschaftliche Untersuchungen zum Neuen Testament. Reihe 2/102. Tübingen: Mohr Siebeck, 1998.

Ciampa, Roy E., and Brian S. Rosner. "The Structure and Argument of 1 Corinthians: A Biblical/Jewish Approach." *New Testament Studies* 52 (2006): 205–218.

Ciampa, Roy E., and Brian S. Rosner. "1 Corinthians." In *Commentary on the New Testament Use of the Old Testament*. Edited by G. K. Beale and D. A. Carson, pp. 695–752. Grand Rapids: Baker Academics, 2007.

Carson, D. A. "James." In *Commentary on the New Testament Use of the Old Testament*. Edited by G. K. Beale and D. A. Carson, pp. 997–1013. Grand Rapids: Baker Academics, 2007.

Cowan, J. Andrew. "The Curse of the Law, the Covenant, and Anthropology in Galatians 3:10-14: An Examination of Paul's Use of Deuteronomy 27:26." *Journal of Biblical Literature* 139 (211–229): 2020.

Crowe, Brandon. *The Obedient Son: Deuteronomy and Christology in the Gospel of Matthew*. Beihefte zur Zeitschrift für die neutestamentliche Wissenschaft, 188. Berlin: de Gruyter, 2012.

Denaux, Albert. "Old Testament Models for the Lukan Travel Narrative. A Critical Survey." In *The Scriptures in the Gospels*. Edited by Christopher M. Tuckett, pp. 271–305. Bibliotheca Ephemeridum Theologicarum Lovaniensium 131. Leuven: Peeters, 1997.

Dunn, James D. G. *Romans 9-16*. Word Biblical Commentary 38B. Dallas: Word Books, 1988.

Evans, Craig A. "Luke 16.1-18 and the Deuteronomy Hypothesis." In *Luke and Scripture: The Function of Sacred Tradition in Luke-Acts*. Edited by Craig A. Evans and James A. Sanders, pp. 121–139. Minneapolis: Fortress Press, 1993.

Evans, C. F. "The Central Section of St. Luke's Gospel." In *Studies in the Gospels: Essays in Honour of R.H. Lightfoot*. Edited by D. E. Nineham, pp. 37–53. Oxford: Blackwell, 1955.

Fitzmyer, Joseph A. *The Gospel According to Luke X-XXIV. A New Translation with Introduction and Commentary*. The Anchor Bible 28A. Garden City: Doubleday, 1985.

Gheorghita, Radu. *The Role of the Septuagint in Hebrews. An Investigation of its Influence with Special Consideration to the Use of Hab. 2:3–4 in Heb 10:37–38*. Wissenschaftliche Untersuchungen zum Neuen Testament. Reihe 2/160. Tübingen: Mohr Siebeck, 2003.

Gerhardsson, Birger. *The Testing of God's Son. (Matt 4:1-11 & par). An Analysis of an Early Christian Midrash*. Lund: CWK Gleerup, 1966.

Gundry, Robert Horton. *Mark: A Commentary on His Apology for the Cross*. Grand Rapids: Eerdmanns, 1993.

Guthrie, George H. "Hebrews." In *Commentary on the New Testament Use of the Old Testament*. Edited by G. K. Beale and D. A. Carson, pp. 919–995. Grand Rapids: Baker Academics, 2007.

Häfner, Gerd. "Deuteronomy in the Pastoral Epistles." In *Deuteronomy in the New Testament*. Edited by Steve Moyise and Maarten J. J. Menken, pp. 136–151. Library of New Testament Studies 358. London: T & T Clark, 2007.

Häfner, Gerd. *"Nützlich zur Belehrung" (2 Tim 3,16). Die Rolle der Schrift in den Pastoralbriefen im Rahmen der Paulusrezeption*. Herders biblische Studien 25. Freiburg im Breisgau: Herder, 2000.

Hanson, Anthony Tyrell. *Studies in Paul's Technique and Theology*. London: SPCK, 1974.

Hays, Richard B. *Echoes of Scripture in the Letters of Paul*. New Haven: Yale University Press, 1989.

Hengel, Martin. "Die Schriftauslegung des 4. Evangeliums auf dem Hintergrund der urchristlichen Exegese." *Jahrbuch für biblische Theologie* 4 (1989): 249–288.

Holtz, Traugott. *Untersuchungen über die alttestamentlichen Zitate bei Lukas*. Texte und Untersuchungen zur Geschichte der altchristlichen Literatur 104. Berlin: Akademie-Verlag, 1968.

Hübner, Hans. *Biblische Theologie des Neuen Testaments. Band 2: Die Theologie des Paulus*. Göttingen: Vandenhoeck & Ruprecht, 1993.

Hübner, Hans. *Gottes Ich und Israel. Zum Schriftgebrauch des Paulus in Römer 9-11*. Forschungen zur Religion und Literatur des Alten und Neuen Testament 136. Göttingen: Vandenhoeck & Ruprecht, 1984.

Koch, Dietrich-Alex. *Die Schrift als Zeuge des Evangeliums. Untersuchungen zur Verwendung und zum Verständnis der Schrift bei Paulus*. Beiträge zur historischen Theologie. Band 69. Tübingen: Mohr Siebeck, 1986.

Köstenberger, Andreas J. "John." In *Commentary on the New Testament Use of the Old Testament*. Edited by G. K. Beale and D. A. Carson, pp. 415–512. Grand Rapids: Baker Academics, 2007.

Kreuzer, Siegfried. "Die Sache auf das Wort gebracht. Sprache und Wirkung des Buches Deuteronomium von der joschijanischen Reform bis zu den Reformatoren." In *Am Anfang war das Wort*. Edited by Albrecht Grözinger and Johannes von Lüpke, pp. 56–80. Veröffentlichungen der Kirchlichen Hochschule Wuppertal. Neue Folge 1. Neukirchen-Vluyn: Neukirchener Verlag, 1998.

Labahn, Michael. "Living Word(s) and the Bread of Life" In *What We Have Heard From the Beginning: The Past, Present, and Future of Johannine Studies*. Edited by Thatcher, Tom, pp 59–62. Waco: Baylor University Press, 2007.

Labahn, Michael. "'Das Buch dieser Prophetie'—die Schriften Israels und die Schrift des Sehers. Überlegungen zur Schrifthermeneutik der Johannesoffenbarung." In *The Scriptures of Israel in Jewish and Christian Tradition. Essays in Honour of Maarten J.J. Menken*. Edited by Bart J. Koet, Steve Moyise, and Jospeh Verheyden, pp. 265–283. Supplements to Novum Testamentum 148. Leiden: Brill, 2013.

Labahn, Michael. *Der Gekommene als Wiederkommender. Die Logienquelle als erzählte Geschichte*. Arbeiten zur Bibel und ihrer Geschichte 32. Leipzig: Evangelische Verlagsanstalt, 2010.

Labahn, Michael. "Deuteronomy in John." In Michael Labahn, *Ausgewählte Studien zum Johannesevangelium. Selected Studies in the Gospel of John. 1998-2013*. Edited by Antje Labahn, pp. 209-228. With an Introduction by Gilbert Van Belle. Biblical Tools and Studies 28. Leuven: Peeters, 2017a.

Labahn, Michael. "'It's Only Love'—Is That All? Limits and Potentials of Johannine 'Ethic'—A Critical Evaluation of Research." In Michael Labahn, *Ausgewählte Studien zum Johannesevangelium. Selected Studies in the Gospel of John. 1998-2013*. Edited by Antje Labahn, pp. 115-154. With an Introduction by Gilbert Van Belle. Biblical Tools and Studies 28. Leuven: Peeters, 2017b.

Lacomara, Aelred. "Deuteronomy and the Farewell Discourse (Jn 13:31-16:33)." *The Catholic Biblical Quarterly* 36 (1974): 65-84.

Lee, John J. R. *Christological Rereading of the Shema (Deut 6.4) in Mark's Gospel*. Wissenschaftliche Untersuchungen zum Neuen Testament. Reihe 2/533. Tübingen: Mohr Siebeck, 2020.

Lincicum, David. *Paul and the Early Jewish Encounter with Deuteronomy*. Wissenschaftliche Untersuchungen zum Neuen Testament. Reihe 2/284. Tübingen: Mohr Siebeck, 2010.

Lincicum, David. "Paul's Engagement with Deuteronomy: Snapshots and Signposts." *Currents in Biblical Research* 7, no. 1 (2008): 37-67.

Luz, Ulrich. *Das Evangelium nach Matthäus. 3. Teilband Mt 18-25*. Evangelisch-Katholischer Kommentar zum Neuen Testament I/3. Zürich: Benziger, 1997.

Marshall, I. Howard. "Acts." In *Commentary on the New Testament Use of the Old Testament*. Edited by G. K. Beale and D. A. Carson, pp. 513-606. Grand Rapids: Baker Academics, 2007.

Marcus, Joel. *The Way of the Lord: Christological Exegesis of the Old Testament in the Gospel of Mark*. Edinburgh: T&T Clark, 1993.

Menken, Maarten J. J. "Deuteronomy in Mathew's Gospel." In *Deuteronomy in the New Testament*. Edited by Steve Moyise and Maarten J. J. Menken, pp. 42-62. Library of New Testament Studies 358. London: T & T Clark, 2007.

Michel, Andreas. "Die Versuchung bzw. Erprobung Jesu in Mt 4,1-11. Anmerkungen zum Thema Christologie und Deuteronomium." In *Erinnerung an Jesus. Kontinuität und Diskontinuität in der neutestamentlichen Überlieferung. Festschrift Rudolf Hoppe*. Edited by Ulrich Busse, Michael Reichardt, and Michael Theobald, pp. 73-85. Bonner Biblische Beiträge 166. Göttingen: V&R Unipress, 2011.

Moessner, David P. *Lord of the Banquet. The Literary and Theological Significance of the Lukan Travel Narrative*. Philadelphia: Trinity Press, 1997.

Moessner, David P. "Luke 9:1-50: Luke's Preview of the Journey of the Prophet like Moses of Deuteronomy." *Journal of Biblical Literature* 102 (1983): 575-605.

Moyise, Steve. "Deuteronomy in Mark's Gospel." In *Deuteronomy in the New Testament*. Edited by Maarten J. J. Menken and Steve Moyise, 27-41. Library of New Testament Studies 358. London: T & T Clark, 2007.

Moyise, Steve, and Maarten J. J. Menken, eds. *Deuteronomy in the New Testament*. Library of New Testament Studies 358. London: T & T Clark, 2007.

Pao. David W., and Eckhard J. Schnabel. "Luke." In *Commentary on the New Testament Use of the Old Testament*. Edited by G. K. Beale and D. A. Carson, 251-414. Grand Rapids: Baker Academics, 2007.

Popkes, Enno Edzard. *Die Theologie der Liebe Gottes in den johanneischen Schriften. Zur Semantik der Liebe und zum Motivkreis des Dualismus*. Wissenschaftliche Untersuchungen zum Neuen Testament. Reihe 2/197. Tübingen: Mohr Siebeck, 2005.

Rese, Martin. *Alttestamentliche Motive in der Christologie des Lukas*. Studien zum Neuen Testament 1. Gütersloh: Gütersloher Verlagshaus Mohn, 1969.

Rosner, Brian S. "Deuteronomy in 1 and 2 Corinthians." In *Deuteronomy in the New Testament*. Edited by Steve Moyise and Maarten J. J. Menken, pp. 118–135. Library of New Testament Studies 358. London: T & T Clark, 2007.

Rosner, Brian S. "The Function of Scripture in 1 Cor 5,13b and 6,16." In *The Corinthian Correspondence*. Edited by Reimund Bieringer, pp. 513–518. Bibliotheca Ephemeridum Theologicarum Lovaniensium 125. Leuven: Peeters, 1996.

Rusam, Dietrich. *Das Alte Testament bei Lukas*. Beihefte zur Zeitschrift für die neutestamentliche Wissenschaft und die Kunde der älteren Kirche 112. Berlin: de Gruyter, 2003.

Sänger, Dieter. "Tora für die Völker—Weisungen der Liebe." In *Von der Bestimmung des Anfangs. Studien zu Jesus, Paulus und zum frühchristlichen Schriftverständnis*, pp. 266–301. Neukirchen-Vluyn: Neukirchener Verlagshaus 2007a.

Sänger, Dieter. "Verflucht ist jeder, der am Holze hängt" (Gal 3,13b). Zur Rezeption einer frühen antichristlichen Polemik." In *Von der Bestimmung des Anfangs. Studien zu Jesus, Paulus und zum frühchristlichen Schriftverständnis*, pp. 99–106. Neukirchen-Vluyn: Neukirchener Verlagshaus, 2007b.

Seifrid, Mark A. "Paul's Approach to the Old Testament in Romans 10:6-8." *Trinity Journal* 6 (1985): 3–37.

Söding, Thomas. *Das Evangelium nach Markus*. Theologischer Handkommentar zum Neuen Testament 2. Leipzig: Evangelische Verlagsanstalt, 2022.

Stanley, Christopher. *Arguing with Scripture: The Rhetoric of Quotations in the Letters of Paul*. New York: T&T Clark, 2004.

Stanley, Christopher. *Paul and the Language of Scripture: Citation Technique in the Pauline Epistles and Contemporary Literature*. Society for New Testament Studies Monograph Series 74. Cambridge: Cambridge University Press, 2008.

Stemberger, Günter. "Der Dekalog im frühen Judentum." In *Jahrbuch für Biblische Theologie* 4. Edited by Martin Ebner et al., pp. 91–103. Neukirchen-Vluyn: Neukirchener Verlag, 1989.

Steyn, Gert J. "Deuteronomy in Hebrews." In *Deuteronomy in the New Testament*. Edited by Steve Moyise and Maarten J. J. Menken, pp. 152–168. Library of New Testament Studies 358. London: T & T Clark, 2007.

Swartley, Willard M. *Israel's Scripture Traditions and the Synoptic Gospels: Story Shaping Story*. Peabody: Hendrickson, 1994.

Thrall, Margaret E. *A Critical and Exegetical Commentary on the Second Epistle to the Corinthians vol. 2 Commentary on II Corinthians VIII-XIII*. International critical commentary on the Holy Scriptures of the Old and New Testaments 34. Edinburgh: T & T Clark, 2000.

Tilly, Michael. "Die Offenbarung des Johannes und das Moselied (Dtn 32)." In *Beiträge zur urchristlichen Theologiegeschichte*. Edited by Wolfgang Kraus, pp. 453–464. Beihefte zur Zeitschrift für die neutestamentliche Wissenschaft 163. Berlin: de Gruyter, 2009.

Tilly, Michael. "Textsicherung und Prophetie. Beobachtungen zur Septuaginta-Rezeption in Apk 22,18f." In *Studien zur Johannesoffenbarung und ihrer Auslegung. Festschrift Otto Böcher*. Edited by Friedrich Wilhelm Horn and Michael Wolter, pp. 232–247. Neukirchen-Vluyn: Neukirchener Verlag, 2005.

Vos. Jacobus Cornelis de. *Rezeption und Wirkung des Dekalogs in jüdischen und christlichen Schriften bis 200 n.Chr.* Ancient Judaism and Early Christianity 95. Leiden: Brill, 2016.

Wagner, J. Ross. "Moses and Isaiah in Concert: Paul's Reading of Isaiah and Deuteronomy in the Letter to the Romans." In *"As Those Who are Taught". The Interpretation of Isaiah from the LXX to the SBL.* Edited by Claire Mathews McGinnis and Patricia K. Tull, pp. 87–105. Society of Biblical Literature Symposium Series 27. Atlanta: Society of Biblical Literature, 2006.

Waters, Guy Prentiss. *The End of Deuteronomy in the Epistles of Paul.* Wissenschaftliche Untersuchungen zum Neuen Testament. Reihe 2/211. Tübingen, Germany: Mohr Siebeck, 2006.

Wevers, John William. *Notes on the Greek Text of Deuteronomy.* Septuagint and Cognate Studies 39. Atlanta: Scholars Press, 1995.

Wisdom, Jeffrey R. *Blessing for the Nations and the Curse of the Law. Paul's Citation of Genesis and Deuteronomy in Gal 3.8-10.* Wissenschaftliche Untersuchungen zum Neuen Testament. Reihe 2/133. Tübingen: Mohr Siebeck, 2001.

Zeller. Dieter. *Der erste Brief an die Korinther.* Kritisch-exegetischer Kommentar über das Neue Testament 5. Göttingen: Vandenhoeck & Ruprecht, 2009.

CHAPTER 25

DEUTERONOMY AND EARLY RABBINIC JUDAISM

JOEL GEREBOFF

Who Began the Conversation?

Early Rabbinic Judaism (70–500 CE) was a period of intense intellectual and pastoral creativity that crafted an enduring cultural identity for Jews. The following chapter focuses on the reception of Deuteronomy in three significant collections of writings from the period: *Tosefta*, *Mishnah*, and *Sifre Devarim*.

The *Tannaim* were teachers like 'Aḳabya b. Mahalaleel, Gamaliel of Jabneh, Ṭarfon, Simeon b. Gamaliel, Nathan ha-Babli, and Polemo. Their traditions or midrash which offer theological explanations of and pastoral applications for both narrative and legal traditions in the Bible, were preserved in *Tosefta* and *Mishnah*. Their midrash on Deuteronomy itself is preserved in the *Sifre Devarim*. The intention of these writings is not to interpret Deuteronomy, but to bring Deuteronomy into a conversation with a complex of nonbiblical traditions.

I will focus on how *Tosefta*, *Mishnah*, and *Sifre Devarim* handle Deuteronomy in general, rather than how they treat specific legal issues like tithes (14:22–29), holy days (16:1–17), household discipline (21:18–21), divorce (24:1–4), or the levirate (25:5–10).

There are scholarly analyses of the *Sifre Devarim*; however, there is no systematic examination of the overall influence of Deuteronomy on writings in Early Rabbinic Judaism. Instead, scholars have focused on the history and range of views on specific legal issues in Deuteronomy. The *Tannaim* treat Deuteronomy only as part of their overall interpretation of Exodus, Leviticus, and Numbers.

Since this chapter focuses on Early Rabbinic scholarship of Deuteronomy itself as an entire document, I will not comment upon these more focused academic studies. In general, other than discussions of the midrash devoted to Deuteronomy, scholarship on the treatment of Deuteronomy in Early Rabbinic Judaism is best understood in terms of several overarching issues. What is the relationship between exegetically derived and formulated law and laws generally phrased in a casuistic formulation and lacking rationales or supporting texts from the Bible? Is Early Rabbinic midrash coherently framed, "authored" and then intentionally redacted works, or anthology of various traditions. Is midrash better understood as a driving force in the Bible itself or as an independent historical and rhetorical product of Early Rabbinic Judaism? Which midrash developed in the "school" of Aqiva ben Joseph (50–32 CE) and which in the school of Ishmael Ben Elisha (90–135 CE)?

I will not explain the reception of Deuteronomy by the *Amoraim*—students, teachers, judges, and preachers in Palestine and Babylon between 200 and 500 CE—who provided legal analyses and homilies not only on Deuteronomy but also on other teachings which were eventually preserved in the *Talmud*. Their hermeneutics, their genres, and the historical periods when these traditions evolved are much too complex.

I also will not explain the reception of Deuteronomy in the *Targums* or in prayers. *Targums* are interpretative translations of the Bible from Hebrew into Aramaic; prayers often stitch together biblical verses with a common theme. Although the practice of synagogue-based translations of passages read from the Torah is noted in several works from the first century onward, little is known about the early synagogue practice of Torah reading. Most importantly, synagogues predate the emergence of rabbis and appear to have been outside of their purview for some time. Flesher and Chilton provide a rich overview of current research on Targums (Flesher and Chilton 2011). Examples of studies of the various Targums on Deuteronomy, including how the translations relate to midrash on legal traditions, include Moshe Bernstein (2002), David Lincicum (2010), and Avigdor Shinan (1994).

Similarly, tracing the actual development of Jewish prayer faces the challenge of determining which prayers, if any, may have been routine in late Second Temple and after the destruction of the Temple by the Romans in 70 CE. Although scholarship on various devotional practices is intriguing, the scholarship on liturgy is too vast to include its reception of Deuteronomy here.

Well-known examples of how the midrash of the *Tannaim* on Deuteronomy (6:4–9) inspired Jewish devotions are *Shema*, *tefillin*, *tsitsit*, and *mezuzah*. The *tefillin* are small leather boxes containing scrolls with passages from Exodus (13:1–16) and Deuteronomy (6:4–9; 11:13–21), which are tied to the foreheads and on one arm with leather thongs when Jews pray on weekdays. The *tsitsit* are tassels attached to the corners of the shawls, which Jews wear when they pray. *Mezuzah* are small containers for scrolls with passages from Deuteronomy (6:4–9; 11:13–21), which Jews attach to the door jamb of their homes.

Sarit Kattan Gribetz (2015) analyzes the way in which several documents from the Second Temple era, as well as descriptions in later texts from *Mishnah*, understand the *Shema* (6:4–9). Most interestingly, she shows that most do not associate the *Shema* with liturgy. Ruth Langer (2018) refers to the Nash Papyrus, *tefillin* from Qumran, and descriptions of Jesus reciting the *Shema* but concludes, "None of this external evidence reflects a liturgical unit where Jews recite this biblical text regularly or within a ritual context" (Langer 2018, 156).

WHAT IS THE STATUS OF THE CONVERSATION?

Jeffrey H. Tigay (1996) in the introduction to his Jewish Publication Society commentary on Deuteronomy emphasizes the impact of this biblical book on rabbinic Judaism. Tigay states, "Deuteronomy helped shape many of the fundamental aspects of Jewish belief and practice that are still followed today. Fully two hundred of the traditional 613 commandments are based on Deuteronomy. One of the most far reaching influences of the book was achieved through the interpretation of 17:11 by means of which the rabbis found warrant to create new laws when necessary, and not only to interpret the Torah" (xxvii). Deuteronomy's contribution to Jewish worship, especially in the daily recitation of the *Shema*, two of whose three paragraphs are from Deuteronomy (6:4–9; 11:13–21). In addition, phrases from Deuteronomy are woven into other portions of Jewish prayer, including into the Passover Haggadah. Moreover Deuteronomy "shaped the very form of Jewish worship. Deuteronomy sought to free religion from excessive attachment to sacrifice and priesthood and to encourage rituals that teach love and reverence for God to every Israelite" (Tigay 2008, xxviii). Furthermore, "Deuteronomy is the source of the idea that religious life should be based on a sacred book, and hence of the obligation of all Jews, not only an elite class, to learn the Torah and to teach it to their children" (xxviii). Finally, Tigay speaks of the impact of Deuteronomy on Jewish theology, especially the notion of monotheism that it asserts passionately. Bernard M. Levinson offers a similar overview and observes that "Deuteronomy is also a deeply traditional text that, more than any other book of the Bible, provides the foundation of Judaism" (2018, 61). In what follows I will detail more pointedly the contributions of scholarship to tracing the connections to Deuteronomy in the earliest strata of rabbinic literature.

WHAT IS TRENDING IN THE CONVERSATION?

A much-debated issue regarding rabbinic Judaism is the relationship between halakhic midrash and extra-legal traditions, laws or "traditions" that are formulated without explicit reference to or support from biblical texts. The question seeks to determine what may have been the original way law was authorized in rabbinic Judaism. Azzan Yadin-Israel observes that the question assumes "that there exists a discrete rabbinic or proto-rabbinic Judaism, whose relationship with *Midrash* or *Halakah* [laws not derived from biblical verses] can be traced over time." He goes on to note that no definitive answer has emerged and "that this is ultimately a failure to account for the significant synchronic differences within the tannaitic corpus" (2006, 35). Yadin-Israel goes on to distinguish the relationship to scripture and the varying hermeneutics of Aqiva and the hermeneutics of Ishmael. In the end, *Mishnah*, which is traditionally seen aligned with the approach of Aqiva, or what is seen as the "school of Aqiva," does not interpret laws from the Bible, but at best, episodically anchors its legal interpretations to the Bible. In the end, in some cases laws are tightly connected to the Bible, while in other writings from Early Rabbinic Judaism they are independent of the Bible. At present, this is the dominant scholarly position that sees both interpretations of biblical traditions and views of other sources of authority evident in Second Temple period. The latter may include ancestral traditions that are asserted to be passed on, often orally, for many centuries. H. L. Strack and Gunter Stemberger provide a good overview of the discussion of the relationship between Mishnah and midrash (Strack and Stemberger 1996, 126–129). Accordingly, I first will look more carefully at scholarship on *Mishnah, Tosefta,* and *Sifre Devarim.*

A good amount of scholarly effort during the past twenty-five years has focused upon Mishnah. Such studies go beyond important lower critical work or studies of individual laws, tractates, or tracing the relationship between statements in Mishnah and Second Temple works. Christine Hayes offers reflections on a series of papers published in 2008 that were delivered at a session of the SBL in 2006. Hayes notes two methodological commonalities and then maps respective views of these papers on three key issues in Mishnah studies. She notes that all four papers study Mishnah but do not isolate it from other rabbinic and nonrabbinic texts. Second, all these studies approach Mishnah synchronically, and they "turn from philological-historical study either partially or wholly. They read Mishnah as a literary text, rhetorical text or performance, focusing on genre, style, structure and a wide range of literary features" (Hayes 2008, 291). Hayes then identifies three contested issues in Mishnaic studies to which these studies contribute, and which ultimately are central to determining the nature of Mishnah. These issues are whether Mishnah is the product of strong, intentional redaction; the purpose of Mishnah—whether it is a law code, a loose anthology of sources, or a pedagogic manual; the relationship of Mishnah to other tannaitic texts and how to pursue comparative studies. Hayes underscores that her effort was to map the state of Mishnaic studies and not to propose a synthesis. "The time for synthesis is not now, not when we have just escaped from the pitched battles, between one-size-fit-all theories that seek to flatten and homogenize our data" (Hayes 2008, 296). Amram Tropper lays out the importance of literary approaches and notes that historical analyses must take seriously the literary features of Mishnah (2010), as do Strack and Stemberger (1996, 133–139) and David C. Kraemer (2006).

While there is much about Mishnah that remains in dispute, what is evident is that Mishnah is not presented as a commentary on the Bible. Biblical verses are not the organizing framework for Mishnah, and such verses appear only episodically in *Mishnah*. *Mishnah* is organized by topics like Sabbath, oaths, and tithes. *Mishnah* contains many anonymous legal statements, generally lacking any explanatory rationales, as well as conflicting opinions and disputes among sages. *Mishnah* itself (Hagiga 1:8) speaks of its tenuous relationship to the Bible. "[Some rules] hover in the air and have naught to support them; [some] are mountains hanging by a hair, for the [teaching of] scripture [thereon] is scanty and the rules many; [some] have that which supports them." As Kraemer observes, "Whatever the relative distribution of Mishnah's law in these three categories, the mere willingness of Mishnah to admit this variety of relationships tells us much about the reception of the Bible in Early Rabbinic Judaism. What it says is that, as far as the rabbis were concerned, while the Bible was 'authoritative,' it was not necessary" (2014, 36). *Mishnah* "writes with scripture," but it does not portray itself as deriving from it. While from time to time *Mishnah* explicitly cites the Bible [though some of these may be later additions to the text], and while other parts of *Mishnah* presume various rules in the Bible, the actual statements in Mishnah stand on their own, without any support provided for such rules. Some scholars take the statement of the transmission of Torah, "Moses received Torah at Sinai and passed it to" that appears in an idiosyncratic tractate (Avot [1:1]) as the authorizing view underlying *Mishnah*, a notion of oral transmission from Sinai of views not found in the written text; other scholars claim that *Mishnah* presumes a looser theory of oral traditions, not going back to Sinai, or simply see Mishnah taking for granted its own authority to lay out legal views. But what of the role of overt citations of the Bible in *Mishnah*?

Several recent studies, for example, Alexander Samely (2002), Kraemer (2014), and Stemberger (2013) analyze the handling of the Bible in *Mishnah*. These scholars underscore that ultimately it is *Mishnah* that picks and chooses which verses, or more often portions of verses from the Bible, it seeks to cite. The redactor of *Mishnah* determines what is cited and how it is deployed in the text. The redactor uses bits and pieces of the Bible to creatively underscore the ideas of *Mishnah*. Kraemer labels this an "aggressive reading of scripture." No evident pattern characterizes the choices of which verses are explicitly cited and which are assumed, but not introduced into *Mishnah*.

Mishnah cites more than 100 verses from Deuteronomy, the largest number for the five books of the Torah. Most come from the Deuteronomic Code (12:1–26:26). Many from other sections of Deuteronomy are connected to legal issues, like the *Shema*, flogging, or idol worship. Virtually all legal issues spoken of in Deuteronomy are topics discussed in *Mishnah*. That *Mishnah* comments for the most part exclusively on these portions of Deuteronomy is not surprising given the legal nature of *Mishnah*. Deuteronomy as a collection of laws is vital to *Mishnah*, but one would need to examine each law case by case to trace how Mishnah understands and treats these laws. Sometimes, *Mishnah* does little more than restate biblical laws; in other cases it radically revises them or expresses a rule that results from a harmonization of differing biblical verses pertaining to the issue.

Similarly, how the positions of *Mishnah* compare with those of other Second Temple exegetical interpretations and uses of these biblical views must be examined one by one. As Stemberger observes, "While much work has been done on the history of individual exegetical traditions, the history of exegetical approaches and methods and lines of continuity and change between the Second Temple period and after 70 is still considerably less explored. Much remains to be done" (2013, 194). Returning to Hayes's comments, I can restate that in the end it is the character of *Mishnah*, its rhetorical quality, its literary traits, and its performative aspects that shape how *Mishnah* relates to the Bible and to Deuteronomy in particular.

In terms of *Tosefta*, its handling of the Bible is the same as that of *Mishnah*. *Tosefta* is not organized around biblical verses. Like the study of *Mishnah*, much work has been done in the past decades on the overall character of this document and its relationship with Mishnah. Tropper (2010) reviews the various theories of that relationship (Strack and Stemberger 1996, 152–155; Mandel 2006; Brody 2014).[1] One view sees *Tosefta* as redacted after *Mishnah* with its individual tradition postdating Mishnah and serving as a commentary on that earlier work. A second model takes note of discrepancies between the two works and claims that *Tosefta* contains independent parallels. These traditions derive from independent sources. Finally, a third model, one advanced more recently, is the "edited parallel model." According to this view, *Tosefta* and *Mishnah* have a complex set of interrelationships—at times *Tosefta* preserves an earlier version of a tradition that *Mishnah* simplifies. *Tosefta* does include a larger number of biblical citations than *Mishnah*, with those from Deuteronomy again being the most extensive. Again, most of the verses come from the Deuteronomic Codes, and verses from other sections are generally treated as teaching law. In the end *Tosefta* writes with Deuteronomy, and it would require analyzing its discussion of specific rules to see how it understands that biblical book.

Compared with *Mishnah* and *Tosefta*, the three known halakhic midrash on Deuteronomy—*Sifre Deuteronomy*, *Mekhilta Devarim*, and *Sifre Zutta Devarim*—focus on Deuteronomy itself, though selectively and within the approach and goals of each of those works.[2] Citations from Deuteronomy also appear in the halakhic midrash on Exodus, Leviticus, and Numbers, consistent with the rabbinic view that scripture forms one unified document that illuminates itself. These three midrashim on Deuteronomy, along with the other halakhic midrash in Early Rabbinic Judaism, have been the subject of much research in past years. The discovery of the Cairo Genizah has greatly advanced the textual criticism of these works. Menahem Kahana (2005) has catalogued all these Genizah fragments and has published new editions of several halakhic midrash. In addition to this invaluable work of lower criticism that is built upon detailed philological and grammatical studies, and that often trace the development of exegetical traditions, Kahana (2006) has presented a detailed overview of the general study of halakhic midrash. His work makes evident both largely accepted as well as disputed aspects of scholarship on these sources. He endorses the view proposed by David Zvi Hoffman (1908–1909) at the beginning of the twentieth century that the various halakhic midrash can be assigned to "two schools," that of Aqiva and that of Ishmael.[3] These respective groups of commentaries differ in terms of the names of sages mentioned in each, their hermeneutical principles and methods, and their technical terminology. Only several of these midrash survived as documents after the Middle Ages with the others being lost. But based on citations in other rabbinic works, and now on the Genizah materials, scholars have reconstructed, with varying degrees of success, some of the other midrash. At present the assertion that the midrash can be assigned to Aqiva or Ishmael or even to "schools" associated with each figure has been challenged, and a modified approach is to note that there are clear distinctions in terms of the aforementioned features between those works that since the time of Hoffman were labeled as works of the schools of Aqiva of Ishmael.

Jay Harris (1992, 2006) challenges the division according to the schools of Ishmael and Aqiva, or at least he questions the significance this notion had among rabbinic circles until the late nineteenth century. Yadin-Israel (2004, 2014) modifies the formulation of Hoffman and details differences in approach between the midrash assigned to Aqiva and Ishmael. Paul Mandel (2017, 276–282) presents an alternative view to that of Yadin Israel, whom he critiques, of the respective positions of the midrash of Aqiva and Ishmael on the relationship between extra-biblical legal traditions and the interpretation of scripture. These comments flow out of Mandel's analysis of the word *darash*, arguing that in early traditions it signifies instruction on a legal issue and only in the second century CE is it used to label biblical exegesis. Strack and Stemberger (1996, 247–275) provide a general introduction to halakhic midrash as well as each of the individual documents.

Moreover, these differences appear in the legal sections of the respective midrash, as they do seem to derive from the same source for their more limited sections that focus upon nonlegal portions of Exodus and Deuteronomy.[4]

Only *Sifre Deuteronomy* was transmitted after the medieval period. As with other all the halakhic midrash, there is large agreement that the major redaction of these works took place in the third century CE, and they all, but in varying degrees, cite selections from Mishnah. Like other rabbinic sources, however, additional revisions were made to these works over the course of their subsequent transmission. There is far more research on a work assigned to the school of Aqiva than on the other two documents. *Sifre Zutta* was reconstructed by Kahana (1994, 2002) from citations in a Karaite work and is a different from *Sifre Deuteronomy*. Hoffman's edition of this midrash was also based primarily upon citations in medieval biblical commentaries and several Genizah fragments known to him at the beginning of the twentieth century. Kahana has subsequently published other Genizah fragments and, along with others, has critiqued much of Hoffman's work. To make clear its connection to the approach of Ishmael, Kahana refers to this midrash as *Mekhilta Devarim*.

Herbert Basser (2004) also presents an overview and illustration of midrash from Early Rabbinic Judaism and a critique of Kahana's work on *Mekhilta Devarim* (1990).[5] I focus our discussion on scholarship on *Sifre Deuteronomy*, situating it within some broader trends in the study of halakhic midrash.

Sifre Deuteronomy covers only certain sections of Deuteronomy (1:1–30; 3:23–29; 6:4–9; 11:10–26:15; 31:14; 32:1–32). Kahana (1996, 95) remarks, "The principles that guide the redactors of *Sifre Deuteronomy* in including exposition on these sections is unclear." Louis Finkelstein published a critical edition of this midrash in 1939 in Berlin, but he produced an eclectic text combining readings from different manuscripts with the variants listed in the critical notes. The work has been critiqued, and serious scholarship on *Sifre Deuteronomy* must not rely on Finkelstein's text but must examine all the readings as well as more recently published Genizah fragments. *Sifre Deuteronomy* is a composite work. Scholarship on this midrash has included analyses of specific *pisqaot*, units within the midrash, and some larger studies of either the work as a whole or of many sections of it. To better appreciate these studies, it is helpful to provide a few comments relating to the broader study of midrash in general. I focus on matters of the definition of midrash and methods for its study, including comparative analyses.

Carol Bakhos essay (2006), "Methodological Matters in the Study of Midrash," a piece in her edited volume, *Current Trends in the Study of Midrash*, provides a rich discussion of the interconnections between divergent ways scholars define "midrash" and the correlative methodological approaches to its study. She reviews in this essay work by leading scholars, including Yonah Fraenkel, Jacob Neusner, David Stern, Daniel Boyarin, James Kugel, and Marc Hirshman. She sets her task as "an attempt to focus on how issues related to defining midrash are not only bound up with broader methodological issues but serve to exemplify the complexity of notions such as contextual limits and scholarly vantage points" (Bakhos 2006, 161). After examining the development of definitions in contextualized reading, she explores how the fissure between treating midrash as either a literary or a historical phenomenon has plagued midrash studies over recent decades. In the end she critiques an approach that only focuses upon the exegetical aspects of midrash, or that traces the history of a midrash or that sees midrash as a closed literary universe. Instead, she advocates for the position of cultural poetics. As she puts in, "Current studies, certainly those emerging from the school of New Historicism, add the need for historians to re-conceptualize the role literary artifacts play within the historical horizon, and at the same time the need for readers of texts to appreciate the ways in which literature enmeshes and is enmeshed within the fabric of culture." In adopting this approach, one "constructs a more complexly integrated paradigm for understanding the inextricably bound relationship between the literariness of a text and its role in culture, society and history" (Bakhos 2006, 179–182). One can thereby identify how internal factors within the interpreted text and the history of its interpretation, as well as external forces, such as historical context including the location of the imagined group who stands behind and is the audience of midrash, contributed to the formulation of midrash.

Steven D. Fraade has stood at the forefront of scholars who have advanced a clear statement of methodological principles for the study of midrash. Next I will take up his work on *Sifre Deuteronomy*. Here I note his views on how to engage in what is often termed "comparative midrash." Fraade has focused much of his work on systematically comparing the corpora of different texts of biblical exegesis stemming from the Second Temple period through Early Rabbinic Judaism. These include the diverse works among the Dead Sea Scrolls, especially those works that are uniquely sectarian, the writings of Josephus, Philo, and rabbinic documents. In an essay first presented at a conference on rabbinic perspectives on Dead Sea Scrolls, Fraade lays out four guiding principles. These include, first, noting both similarities and dissimilarities; second, not simply counting the differences and similarities. Both are illuminating. Third, "In comparing and contrasting the two textual corpora, I need to attend not only to contents, but also to their textual forms, hermeneutical strategies and rhetorical functions; that is not only to the shared traditions, but to the morphological means by which those traditional understandings of the Bible are performatively both connected to the Bible and communicated to their respective studying communities." Fourth, in comparing treatments of the same text, we should resist connecting them in a direct linear development but through analogical comparison and contrast (Fraade 2006, 44–45). Such an approach characterizes his work, including his many studies of *Sifre Deuteronomy*. But before discussing his contributions, we note briefly other scholarship devoted to this rabbinic document.

Examinations of *Sifre Deuteronomy* appear in the course of many studies of different aspects of rabbinic law and biblical exegesis. For example, books on levirate marriage, tithing, or cities of refuge will introduce passages from *Sifre Deuteronomy* and other rabbinic treatments of those sections of Deuteronomy. These studies are far too numerous to mention. Several articles have dealt only with one or two *pisqaot* of *Sifre Deuteronomy*. These include publications by Deborah Barer (2017), Fraade (1986, 2007, 2011, 2017), Amit Gevaryahu (2017), Chaya Halberstam (2014), Marc Hirshman (2009), Shlomo Naeh and Aharon Shemesh (2013), David Rothstein (2017), and Adiel Schremer (2017). These studies vary in their methodology, assumptions, and specific issues they explore. Together they provide insights into the engagement of Early Rabbinic Judaism with Deuteronomy.

Several works have addressed larger sections of *Sifre Deuteronomy* and offer general observations on the work. These include works by Hammer (1986), Neusner (1987b), Basser (1984), and Fraade (1991). Hammer and Neusner both have translated *Sifre Deuteronomy* using the Finkelstein text, with Hammer in his endnotes referring to significant variants in several manuscripts. Jaffee at present is working on a translation of *Sifre Deuteronomy* that captures its oral performative quality. He has published a brief example and discussed his overall assumptions and goals. His approach recognizes that these midrash are not records of spoken discourse. "Rather they are archly literary, carefully constructed so as to convey to their rabbinic audience the experience of receiving 'Torah'" (Jaffee 2014, 144).[6]

Hammer covers briefly such matters as the relation of midrash in Early Rabbinical Judaism to *Mishnah*, the origin and structure of *Sifre Deuteronomy*, its interpretive methods and formulas and basic homiletical themes and ideas. About this last topic Hammer underscores that *Sifre Deuteronomy* begins with rebuke (1:1), which ends with reconciliation and words of comfort. He also catalogs its several specific themes: first, the importance of the people of Israel; second, Israel is beloved and will be redeemed and the nations who have dealt cruelly with her are condemned; third, Jacob serves as the prototype of Israel; fourth, the personality of Moses; fifth, the merits of the land of Israel; sixth, God's gracious nature and judgment of peoples and individuals; eighth, human relationships; and ninth, the Torah as an antidote to evil. Hammer thus presents a list of themes, and since his primary goal is to present a translation with brief textual and explanatory notes, his work is not a systematic study of *Sifre Deuteronomy* or its relationship with Deuteronomy.

Jacob Neusner in his translation and analysis of *Sifre Deuteronomy* presents a study of its rhetorical, logical, and topical programs. This work is part of Neusner's larger effort to characterize the core documents of Early Rabbinic Judaism and then in turn engage in comparative and historical explorations. He acknowledges that that *Sifre Deuteronomy* is a composite work with no single author. But he asserts that he will show it makes "a coherent statement in both form and proposition, it exhibits a cogent character, therefore, derives from a considered set of decisions of a rhetorical, logical and topic order, and it flows, derives from an authorship, a collectivity of consensus about this particular writing" (Neusner 1987a, 4). In a later essay, Neusner (2004) describes *Sifre Deuteronomy* as pursuing a diverse topical program in order to demonstrate a few fundamental propositions. He then notes four principal topics that encompass the document's proposition. First, the covenant between Israel and God; second, the history of Israel and the nations; third, Israel, the community, and its governance; fourth, the structure of intellect in laws and the Law. While all scholars of Early Rabbinic Judaism appreciate the fundamental changes Neusner brought to the study of Judaism and rabbinic texts and history, his overall approach to analyzing each rabbinic document has been generally seen as faulty. Examples of such critiques are Bakhos (2006), Boyarin (1992), Fraade (2009), and Hauptman (2009). Among the criticisms are his inattention to the intricacies of exegesis, his criteria for discerning programs within each document, and his lack of attention to the intertextuality among rabbinic traditions.

Basser has authored several works on midrash and on *Sifre Deuteronomy*. His 1984 published dissertation presents a translation and commentary on Moses's farewell address (32:1–23) in *Sifre Deuteronomy*. His goal is "to portray the process whereby a Tannaitic midrash which comments upon a poetic part of the Pentateuch assumes its present form. The translation and commentary may serve to introduce the major methods and themes of a Tannaitic midrash on a poetic section of The Bible (stressing Israel's historic election, present suffering, and future redemption) to those who are not familiar with the Rabbinic method of making acoustic shifts in words of The Bible to reveal unsuspected references to Covenant, Torah and the Messianic Era" (Basser 1984, 1). His translation is largely based on Finkelstein, and his commentary deals with scriptural, textual, linguistic, and exegetical matters. His underlying assumption is that "despite its wide extent and diversity, rabbinic literature shows a surprising unity in its ideas. Its various parts seem to have exerted a mutual influence on one another, and a clear line of historical development is not evident" (Basser 1984, 2). Although Basser recognizes individual traditions have a history to their formulation, transmission, and revision, he argues that the entire corpus of rabbinic literature may be consulted to parse any text in *Sifre Deuteronomy*. In many instances Basser appeals to a good deal of texts from the Second Temple era, literature antecedent to rabbinic texts. In a review of Fraade's *From Tradition to Commentary*, Basser critiques him for failing to trace the development of exegetical traditions as well as his not drawing upon the entire corpus of midrash to understand *Sifre Deuteronomy* (1993). Fraade's detailed response to this critique draws out their divergent assumptions about the background for the formation of rabbinic traditions and documents and the methods for discerning them (1994). For Fraade, it is necessary "to understand a particular rabbinic text in relation to the particular cultural and historical context in which it assumed its present overall form so as to first function as a rhetorical work of continuous commentary." While not denying that some rabbinic traditions may draw upon an earlier history of interpretations, his "method rests on the need to recognize that these histories are different from one another and while mutually illuminating and intersecting need to be kept distinct" (Fraade 1994, 243).

These comments point to the goals and approach of Fraade's own work on *Sifre Deuteronomy*. Indeed, Fraade has published numerous books and articles that closely analyze rabbinic traditions and documents in terms of their hermeneutical, historical, and rhetorical features and settings. Rather than treating traditions in isolation from the document in which they appear, and also after having engaged in detailed discussions of philology, text criticism, and comparison for interpretive purposes with comments on the relevant biblical sections in other nonrabbinic and rabbinic works, Fraade seeks to make sense of a document as constructed work with an audience who itself in part is constructed through its interaction with the document. When he compares various documents, he identifies how they treat biblical materials—do they, for example, rewrite the Bible, or do they cite and comment upon it?

In *From Tradition to Commentary*, Fraade sets forth differences in the approach to the Bible among texts from Qumran, Philo, Josephus, and *Sifre Deuteronomy*. This method has characterized his work throughout his career. This book focuses upon certain sections from *Sifre Deuteronomy*, those dealing with Torah, Torah study, and sages; thus, it does not claim to be a commentary or an analysis of the substance of the entire book. Using a method attentive to both literary-exegetical concerns and historical factors, he lays out how *Sifre Deuteronomy* rather than being a topical treatise is a dialogical commentary. *Sifre Deuteronomy* seeks to engage its readers, students of rabbinic Torah, in a conversation between the biblical text and a range of rabbinic comments and their own socio-historical circumstances. Through this process students enact the text through their sorting, combining, and discussing the collection and thereby they perform and enact themselves. "The purpose of *Sifre Deuteronomy* is to engage dialogically its ancient rabbinic students in its reconstructive and redemptive work of its interpretation." Fraade's rich approach underscores how *Sifre Deuteronomy* not only interprets Deuteronomy and rabbinic comments on that work, but more so, how it has the students transform themselves in the process. Fraade offers a rich analysis of the exegetical and rhetorical dimensions of this *Sifre Deuteronomy* that perhaps best makes evident how this midrash exemplifies processes through which early rabbis formed themselves as students of and makers of Torah. Fraade's concluding comments capture the interaction of these rabbinic sages with Deuteronomy. He states, "Rabbinic engagement with Torah as covenantal 'song' is to be found as much in rabbinic texts of scriptural interpretation as in the intended study and interpretation of those rabbinic texts themselves. The study in and of itself is a performative religious experience of Divine presence and redemptive expectation. The rabbinic Torah is a multivocal song to be dialogically, and socially performed" (Fraade 1991, 163). It is by this means that Deuteronomy becomes rabbinic Torah.

In this paper I do not discuss the place of Deuteronomy in two other genres of early rabbinic writings, Targumim and liturgical texts. The field of Targum studies intersects with the study of rabbinic documents and Targumim in their final form are rabbinic works. The practice of synagogue based translation of passages read from the Torah is noted in a number of works from the first century onwards. However, there is much that is unknown about early synagogues and practices of Torah reading. Most importantly, synagogues predate the emergence of rabbis and appear to have been outside of their purview for some time. Similarly, tracing the actual development of Jewish prayer faces the challenge of determining which prayers, if any, may have been routine in late Second Temple and post destruction periods. The scholarship on liturgy is vast and I will not discuss the place of texts from Deuteronomy in it. Flesher and Chilton provide a rich overview of current research on Targum. Examples of studies of the various Targumim on Deuteronomy, including how the translations relate to statements in halakhic midrash include: Bernstein, Grossfeld, Hayward, Lincicum, Maher, Shinan. In terms of liturgy, Gribetz analyzes the way in which several documents from the Second Temple era, as well as descriptions in later texts from Mishnah, understand Deuteronomy 6:4-9, the *shema*. Most interestingly, she shows that for most of the works, the texts is not associated with liturgy. Langer (2018:156) refers to the Nash Papyrus, *tefillin* from Qumran and descriptions of Jesus reciting Deut 6:4-5, but concludes, "None of this external evidence reflects a liturgical unit where Jews recite this biblical text regularly or within a ritual context."

Notes

1. Additional overview of Tosefta and its relationship to Mishnah are Strack and Stemberger (1996, 152–55), Mandel (2006), and Brody (2014).
2. Numerous citations from Deuteronomy also appear in the halakhic midrash on the books of Exodus, Leviticus and Numbers, consistent with the rabbinic view that scripture forms one unified document that illuminates itself.
3. See Yadin (2006, 37) for such a reframing of the notion of the school of Aqiva and Ishmael.
4. Jay Harris (1992, 2006) challenges the division according to the schools of Ishmael and Aqiva, or at least he questions the significance this notion had among rabbinic circles until the late nineteenth century. Yadin (2004, 2006, 2014) modifies the formulation of Hoffman and details differences in approach between the midrash assigned to Aqiva and Ishmael. Mandel (2017, 276–82) presents an alternative view than Yadin's, whom he critiques, of the respective positions of the midrash of Aqiva and Ishmael on the relationship between extra biblical legal traditions and the interpretation of scripture. These comments flow out of Mandel's (2017) analysis of changes in the meaning of the word *darash*, arguing that in early traditions it signifies instruction on a legal issue and only in the second century CE is it used to label biblical exegesis. Strack and Stemberger (1996, 247–75) provide a general introduction to halakhic midrash as well as each of the individual documents.
5. Basser (2004) also presents an overview and illustration of Midrash Tannaim, and in Basser 1990 a critique of aspects of Kahana's work on Mekhilta Deut.
6. Jaffee at present is working on a translation of *Sifre Deuteronomy* that captures its oral performative quality. He has (2014) published a brief example and discussed his overall assumptions and goals. His approach recognizes that these Midrashic documents are not records of spoken discourse. "Rather they are archly literary, carefully constructed so as to convey to their rabbinic audience the experience of receiving 'Torah'" (Jaffee 2014, 144).

Bibliography

Bakhos, Carol. 2006. "Methodological Matters in the Study of Midrash." In *Current Trends in the Study of Midrash*, edited by Carol Bakhos, 161–185. Leiden: Brill.

Barer, Deborah. 2017. "Reading Midrash as Theological Practice." In *Religious Studies and Rabbinics: A Conversation*, edited by Elizabeth Shanks Alexander and Beth A. Berkowitz, 82–104. New York: Routledge.

Basser, Herbert. 1984. *Midrashic interpretations of the Song of Moses*. New York: Peter Lang.
Basser, Herbert. 1990. *In the Margins of the Midrash: Sifre Ha'azinu Texts, Commentaries, and Reflections*. Atlanta: Scholars Press.
Basser, Herbert. 1993. "Fraade, *From Tradition to Commentary*." *Jewish Quarterly Review* 84: 82–90.
Basser, Hebert. 2004. "Midrash Tannaim." In *Encyclopedia of Midrash Volume I*, edited by Jacob Neusner and Alan Avery-Peck, 510–20. Leiden: Brill.
Bernstein, Moshe. 2002. "The Aramaic Versions of Deuteronomy 32: A Study in Comparative Targumic Theology." In *Targum and Scripture: Studies in Aramaic Translation and Interpretations in Memory of Ernest G. Clarke*, edited by Paul V.M. Flesher, 29–52. Leiden: Brill.
Boyarin, Daniel 1992. "On the Status of Tannaitic Midrashim." *Journal of the American Oriental Society* 112: 455–65.
Brody, Robert. 2014. *Mishnah and Tosefta Studies*. Jerusalem: Magness Press.
Cohen, Shaye J. 2007. "The Judaean Legal Tradition and the Halakhah of the Mishnah." In *Cambridge Companion to the Talmud and Rabbinic Literature*, edited by Charlotte Elisheva Fonrobert and Martin S. Jaffee, 121–43. Cambridge: Cambridge University Press.
Crawford, Sidney White. 2005. "Reading Deuteronomy in the Second Temple Period." In *Reading the Present in the Qumran Library: the Perception of the Contemporary by Means of Scriptural Interpretations*, edited by Kristin De Troyer and Armin Lange, 127–40. Atlanta: Society of Biblical Literature.
Fraade, Steven D. 1986. "Sifre Deuteronomy 26 (ad. Deut. 3:22): How Conscious the Composition." *Hebrew Union College Annual* 54: 245–301.
Flesher, Paul V.M. and Chilton, Bruce. 2011. *The Targums: A Critical Introduction*. Leiden: Brill.
Fraade, Steven D. 1991. *From Tradition to Commentary: Torah and its Interpretation in Midrash Sifre to Deuteronomy*. Albany: State University of New York.
Fraade, Steven D. 1994. "Response to Herbert Basser." *Jewish Quarterly Review*. 84: 237–47.
Fraade, Steven D. 2004. "Deuteronomy in Sifre to Deuteronomy." In *Encyclopedia of Midrash, Volume I.*, edited by Jacob Neusner and Alan Avery-Peck, 54–59. Leiden: Brill.
Fraade, Steven. 2006. "Looking for Narrative Midrash at Qumran." In *Rabbinic Perspectives: Rabbinic Literature and the Dead Sea Scrolls: Proceedings of the Eighth International Symposium of the Orion Center for the Study of the Dead Sea Scrolls and Associated Literature, 7-9 January, 2003*, edited by Steven D. Fraade, Aharon Shemesh & Ruth A. Clements, 43–66. Leiden: Brill.
Fraade, Steven D. 2007. "Rabbinic Midrash and Ancient Jewish Biblical Interpretation." In *Cambridge Companion to the Talmud and Rabbinic Literature*, edited by Charlotte Elisheva Fonrobert and Martin S. Jaffee, 99–120. Cambridge: Cambridge University Press.
Fraade, Steven D. 2009. "Jacob Neusner as Reader of the Mishnah, Tosefta, and Halakhic Midrashim." *Henoch* 31: 259–71.
Fraade, Steven D. 2011. "Deuteronomy and the Polity in the Early History of Jewish Interpretation." Reprinted in Steven D. Fraade, *Legal Fictions: Studies of Law and Narrative in the Discursive Worlds of Ancient Jewish Sectarians and Sages*, 211–26. Leiden: Brill.
Fraade, Steven D. 2011. "Rewritten Bible and Rabbinic Midrash as Commentary." Reprinted in Steven D. Fraade, *Legal Fictions: Studies of Law and Narrative in the Discursive Worlds of Ancient Jewish Sectarians and Sages*, 381–98. Leiden: Brill
Fraade, Steven D. 2011. "'The Torah of the King' (Deut 17: 14–20) in the *Temple Scroll* and Early Rabbinic Law." Reprinted in Steven D. Fraade, *Legal Fictions: Studies of Law and Narrative in the Discursive Worlds of Ancient Jewish Sectarians and Sages*, 285–319. Leiden: Brill.

Fraade, Steven D. 2017. "'If a Case is Too Baffling for You to Decide...' (Deut 17: 8–13): Between Constraining and Expanding Judicial Autonomy in the Temple Scroll and Early Rabbinic Scriptural Interpretation." In *Sibyl, Scriptures, and Scrolls, John Collins at Seventy, Volume I*, edited by Joel Baden, Hindy Najman and Eibert Tigchelaar, 409–31. Leiden: Brill.

Goldberg, Abraham. 1983. "The School of Rabbi Aqiba and the School of Rabbi Ishmael in Sifre Deuteronomy Pericopes 1–54." *Te'udah* 3: 9–16 (Hebrew).

Goldsmith, Simcha. 2013. "Were There Really *Midreshei Halakhah*?" *Hebrew Union College Annual* 84–85: 25–47.

Gribetz, Sarit Kattan. 2015. "The Shema in the Second Temple Period: A Reconsideration." *Journal of Ancient Judaism* 6: 58–84.

Gruber, Mayer I. 2009. "Rewritten Deuteronomy in 1QS and in m. Sotah 7:5. In *Mishneh Torah: Study in Deuteronomy and Its Cultural Environment in Honor of Jeffrey H. Tigay*, edited by Nili Sacher Fox, David A. Glatt-Gilad, and Michael J. Williams, 139–55. Winona Lake: Eisenbrauns.

Gvaryahu Amit. 2017. "Twisting Words: Does Halakhah Really Circumvent Scripture?" *Journal of Jewish Studies* 68, 260–83.

Halberstam, Chaya. 2014. "Justice without Judgment: Pure Procedural Justice and the Divine Courtroom in *Sifre Deuteronomy*. In *The Divine Courtroom in Comparative Perspective*, edited by Ari Mermelstein and Shallom E. Holtz, 49–68. Leiden: Brill.

Halberstam, Chaya. 2017. "Partial Justice: Law and Narrative in Sifre Deuteronomy." In *The Faces of Torah: Studies in the Texts and Contexts of Ancient Judaism in Honor of Steven Fraade*, edited by Michal Bar-Asher Siegal, Tzvi Novick, and Christine Hayes, 309–21. Göttingen: Vandenhoeck & Ruprecht.

Hammer, Reuben. 1986. *Sifre: A Tannaitic Commentary on the Book of Deuteronomy*. New Haven: Yale University Press.

Harris, Jay M. 1992. "Modern Studies of Midrash Halakhah: Between Tradition and Wissenschaft." In *The Uses of Tradition: Jewish Continuity in the Modern Era*, edited by Jack Wertheimer, 261–77. New York: Jewish Theological Seminary.

Harris, Jay M. 2006. "Midrash Halachah." In *The Cambridge History of Judaism, Vol. 4: Late Roman-Rabbinic Period*, edited by Steven T. Katz, 336–68. Cambridge: Cambridge University Press.

Hauptman, Judith. 2009. "Jacob Neusner's Methodological Contributions to the Study of Rabbinic Text." *Henoch* 31: 271–83.

Hayes, Christine. 2008. "What is (The) Mishnah? Concluding Observations." *Association for Jewish Studies Review* 32: 291–97.

Hirshman, Marc. 2009. *The Stabilization of Rabbinic Culture, 100 C.E.-350 C.E.* New York: Oxford University Press.

Hoffmann, David. 1908–09. *Midrasch Tannaim zum Deuteronomium*. Berlin: Defus T. H. Ittskoyski.

Jaffee, Martin S. 2014. "'The Weaver of Midrash in Performance': Notes to an Oral-Performative Translation of Sifre Devarim." In *Jacob Neusner: A Legacy of Learning: Essays in Honor of Jacob Neusner*, edited by Alan J. Avery Peck, 142–61. Leiden: Brill.

Kahana, Menahem. 1985. "New Fragments of the Mekhilta on Deuteronomy." *Tarbiz* 54: 485–551 (Hebrew).

Kahana, Menahem. 1986. "Citations of the Deuteronomy Mekilta Ekev and Ha'azinu." *Tarbiz* 56: 19–59 (Hebrew).

Kahana, Menahem. 1987. "Pages of the Deuteronomy Mekhilta on Ha'azinu and Wezot HaBerakhah." *Tarbiz* 57: 165–201 (Hebrew).

Kahana, Menahem. 1994. "Citations from a New Tannaitic Midrash to Deuteronomy and Their Relation to Sifre Zutta." *Proceedings of the Eleventh World Congress of Jewish Studies. Division C, Volume 1: Rabbinic and Talmudic Literature*, 23–30. Jerusalem: World Union of Jewish Studies (Hebrew).

Kahana, Menahem. 2002. *Sifre Zutta on Deuteronomy: Citations from a New Tannaitic Midrash*. Jerusalem: Hebrew University (Hebrew).

Kahana, Menahem. 2002. "The Tannaitic Midrashim." In *The Cambridge Genizah Collection: Their Contents and Significance*, edited by Stefan C. Reif, 59–73. Cambridge: Cambridge University Press.

Kahana, Menahem. 2005. *Genizah Fragments of Halakhic Midrashim*. Jerusalem: Magness Press.

Kahana, Menahem. 2006. "The Halakhic Midrashim." In *The Literature of the Sages, Volume 2*, edited by Shemuel Safrai, 3–105. Assen: Van Gorcum.

Kraemer, David. 2006. "The Mishnah." In *The Cambridge History of Judaism, Vol. 4*, edited by Steven T. Katz, 299–315. Cambridge: Cambridge University Press.

Kraemer, David. 2014."The Rabbinic Reception of the Bible: A Study in Complexity". *Journal of the Bible and Its Reception* 1: 29–46.

Langer, Ruth. 2018. "New Directions in Understanding Jewish Liturgy." In *Early Judaism: New Insights and Scholarship*, edited by Frederick E. Greenspahn, 147–73. New York: New York University Press.

Levinson, Bernard M. 2018. "Introduction to Deuteronomy." In *Engaging Torah: Modern Perspectives*, edited by Walter Homolka and Aaron Panken, 61–76. Cincinnati: Hebrew Union College Press.

Lincicum, David. 2010. "Later Trajectories of Interpretation: Sifre and Targums." In *Paul and the Early Jewish Encounter with Deuteronomy*, David Lincicum, 184–92. Tubingen: Mohr Siebeck.

Mandel, Pau. 2006. "The Tosefta." In *The Cambridge History of Judaism, Vol. 4*, edited by Steven T. Katz, 316–35. Cambridge: Cambridge University Press.

Mandel, Paul. 2017. *The Origins of Midrash: From Teaching to Text*. Leiden: Brill.

Naeh, Shlomo and Shemesh, Aharon. 2013. "Deuteronomy 19: 15–19 in the Damascus Document and Early Midrash." *Dead Sea Discoveries* 20: 179–99.

Neusner, Jacob. 1987a. *Sifre to Deuteronomy: An Analytical Translation*. Atlanta: Scholars Press.

Neusner, Jacob. 1987b. *Sifre to Deuteronomy: An Introduction to the Rhetorical, Logical and Topical Program*. Atlanta: Scholars Press.

Rothstein, David. 2017. "Women in the Public Sphere: Positions of Sipre Deuteronomy Viewed Against the Matrix of the Hebrew Bible and Other Rabbinic Text." *Zeitschrift fur Altorientalische und Biblischen Rechtsgeschichter* 23: 279–94.

Ruiten, J.T. A. G. M. van. 1994. "The Use of Deuteronomy 32:39 in Monotheistic Controversies in Rabbinic Literature." In *Studies in Deuteronomy in Honour of T. C. J. Labuschagne on the Occasion of his 65th Birthday*, edited by F. Garcia Martinez, A. Hilhorst, J.T.A.G.M. van Ruitten and A.S. van der Woulde, 223–41. Leiden: Brill.

Samely, Alexander. 2002. *Rabbinic Interpretation of Scripture in the Mishnah*. Oxford: Oxford University Press.

Schremer, Adiel. 2017. "'Most Beautiful of Women': Story and History in Sifre Deuteronomy." In *The Faces of Torah: Studies in the Texts and Contexts of Ancient Judaism in Honor of Steven Fraade*, edited by Michal Bar-Asher Siegal, Tzvi Novick, and Christine Hayes, 529–43. Göttingen: Vandenhoeck & Ruprecht.

Shinan, Avigdor. 1994. "The Aggadah of the Palestinian Targums of the Pentateuch and Rabbinic Aggadah: Some Methodological Consideration." In *The Aramaic Bible: Targums in their Historical Context*, edited by D.R. G. Beattie and M. J. McNamara, 203–17. Sheffield: Journal for the Study of the Old Testament Press.

Stemberger, Gunter. 2013. "From Inner-Biblical Interpretation to Rabbinic Exegesis. In *New Cambridge History of the Bible*, edited by John Paget and Joachim Schaper, 190–217. Cambridge: Cambridge University Press.

Strack, H. L. and Stemberger, Gunter. 1996. *Introduction to the Talmud and Midrash*. Minneapolis: Fortress Press.

Tigay, Jeffrey H. 1996. *The JPS Torah Commentary Deuteronomy*. Philadelphia: Jewish Publication Society.

Tropper, Amram. 2010. "The State of Mishnah Studies." In *Rabbinic Texts and the History of Late-Roman Palestine*, edited by Martin Goodman and Philip Alexander, 91–116. Oxford: The British Academy.

Yadin, Azzan. 2004. *Scripture as Logos: Rabbi Ishmael and the Origins of Midrash*. Philadelphia: University of Pennsylvania Press.

Yadin, Azzan. 2006. "Resistance to Midrash? Midrash and Halakhah in the Halakhic Midrashim." In *Current Trends in the Study of Midrash,*" edited by Carol Bakhos, 35–58. Leiden: Brill.

Yadin-Israel, Azzan. 2014. *Scripture and Tradition: Rabbi Akiva and the Triumph of Midrash*. Philadelphia: University of Pennsylvania Press.

CHAPTER 26

DEUTERONOMY AND ISLAM

JOHN KALTNER

Who Began the Conversation?

A one-of-a-kind palimpsest was accidentally discovered in 2018. Christie's Auction House had recently put up for sale what appeared to be fragments from a Qur'an manuscript that were dated to the eighth century CE. Upon examining images of the fragments, Éléonore Cellard of the Collège de France soon realized that there was much more there. Underneath the Arabic text she was able to make out lettering of a different sort, and after further analysis she identified it as a Coptic translation of a portion of Deuteronomy that was probably written in the seventh century CE.

Qur'an palimpsests are not very common, and this one is the only example of Arabic writing on top of non-Arabic writing, as well as the only manuscript in which the Qur'an is written over a biblical text. The remarkable find was heralded by the media, and the palimpsest sold for nearly six times its estimated value of one hundred thousand British pounds (Cellard 2017–2018).

This chapter adopts a different approach toward Deuteronomy than the others in this volume. It does so because there has been very little previous scholarship on the topic of Islam and Deuteronomy. Passages from Deuteronomy have sometimes been cited by Muslims, and this has usually been done for apologetic purposes in order to support Islamic beliefs without engaging Deuteronomy in a sustained and thorough way. The reception history of Deuteronomy in Islam is therefore quite limited and lacks the substance and depth it has in Judaism and Christianity. Nonetheless, there are some important and intriguing connections between Islam and Deuteronomy that should be acknowledged and will be considered here. The palimpsest just mentioned serves as a useful metaphor in this regard—like those fragments, when the Islamic tradition is considered from a certain perspective, we can discern features and aspects of it that indicate a certain, if sometimes difficult-to-notice, connection with Deuteronomy.

The Bible in Islam

This situation is not unique to Deuteronomy since there has not been a great deal of engagement with the Bible on the part of Muslims, and much of what does exist has been polemical or apologetic in nature. This is primarily due to Islam's view of the Bible and the relationship of the Old Testament and the New Testament to the Qur'an. According to Islamic teaching, the word of Allah was revealed to earlier peoples through a succession of prophets, many of whom are biblical figures like Abraham, Moses, and Jesus. The message all those prophets received and passed on to their people was the same—that they should worship only Allah in complete submission (*islām* in Arabic). Islam maintains that the followers of the prior prophets did not accurately preserve the revelation they received, and this led to the need for a final prophet who would deliver the word of Allah in its correct form. That final prophet was Muhammad (ca. 570–632 CE), and the message he brought is contained in the Qur'an. Muslims therefore believe the Bible is a tainted text that has been superseded by the Qur'an.[1] Some Islamic scholars are familiar with the Bible and cite it on occasion, but most Muslims have had little contact with the Jewish and Christian scriptures.[2]

Perhaps the closest the Qur'an comes to quoting the Bible is a parallel to Psalms (Ps 37:29). "We wrote in the Psalms, as We did in [earlier] Scripture: 'My righteous servants will inherit the earth'" (Q 21:105).[3]

Elsewhere, the Qur'an refers to biblical figures and traditions frequently, with approximately thirty individuals identified by name in both the Bible and the Qur'an.[4] Whenever the Qur'an relates a story that is also in the Bible, however, it interprets it in a way that Islamizes it.

In the four chapters that recount the flood story, Noah, for example, speaks only one time when he curses the offspring of his son Ham (Gen 9:25–27). Because Noah is considered a prophet in Islam, he has more of a voice in the Qur'an, where he is shown warning and encouraging his people to heed his advice and turn to Allah (Q 11:25–49).

A similar shift in presentation can be seen in the way Jesus is described in the Qur'an. Islam teaches that nothing in creation should be associated with Allah because doing so would compromise the divine unity, so the Christian beliefs in the Trinity and incarnation are challenged in the Qur'an to the point that even Jesus himself denies them (Q 5:116–118).

A rare example of a Muslim scholar who cited the Bible for nonpolemical purposes was Ibrahim b. Umar b. Hasan al-Biqā'ī (d. 1480), who wrote a commentary on the Qur'an and a later treatise explaining and justifying his use of the Bible in that commentary. Unlike most other Muslim scholars, al-Biqā'ī directly quoted the Bible rather than paraphrasing or summarizing it. His main purpose in doing so was to draw upon the Bible to fill in the gaps in the Qur'an's versions of biblical stories. He justified his use of the Bible in this way because Muhammad often referred to the Bible. Al-Biqā'ī did not consider the entire Bible to be a reliable record of divine revelation, but he maintained that even biblical traditions considered by Muslims to be fabricated could be cited as long as they were identified as such. Virtually all the biblical traditions al-Biqā'ī quotes are narratives, and so Deuteronomy does not play an important role in his work. Nonetheless, it is a fascinating example of Muslim use of the Bible that led to the inclusion of portions of the biblical corpus in the vast body of Islamic commentary on the Qur'an that is known as *tafsīr* (Saleh 2008).[5]

What Is the Status of the Conversation?

Deuteronomy in Islam

Deuteronomy has sometimes attracted the attention of scholars and other Muslims due to a few passages it contains in which the words of YHWH to Moses are interpreted as endorsing a central teaching of Islam. "I will raise up for them a prophet like you from among their own people; I will put my words in the mouth of the prophet, who shall speak to them everything that I command" (18:18; cf. 18:15).[6] Muslim scholars have considered this verse to be a prediction of the coming of Muhammad, who will bring the revelation of Allah to Muslims in the Qur'an. Deuteronomy is read in this way to validate the belief that Muhammad was the last of a series of prophets sent by Allah who were all given a divine message to communicate to their contemporaries. In this way, Deuteronomy is important in Islamic theology because it supports and legitimates its understanding of prophecy, including the Qur'an's claim that Muhammad is mentioned in the prior scriptures as "the unlettered prophet they find described in the Torah that is with them, and in the Gospel" (Q 7:157).[7]

Lazarus-Yafeh (1992, 104) lists some of the Muslims who have cited the verses in Deuteronomy 18 as references to Muhammad, including 'Ali b. Rabban (ninth century CE), Ibn Qutayba (ninth century CE), al-Birūnī (tenth/eleventh centuries CE), and Ibn Ḥazm (eleventh century CE). The important role the book of Deuteronomy and these passages in particular have played in Muslim scholarship can be seen in the index of Adang's and Schmidtke's work on Islamic reception of the Bible (2019, 475–480). Deuteronomy is the most frequently cited biblical book by the scholars they have studied, and "The LORD your God will raise up for you a prophet like me from among your own people; you shall heed such a prophet" (18:15) and "I will raise up for them a prophet like you from among their own people; I will put my words in the mouth of the prophet, who shall speak to them everything that I command" (18:18) are far and away the most commonly discussed passages by those scholars.

Another passage from Deuteronomy that has been interpreted in a similar way by Muslims contains the opening words of the Blessing of Moses imparted on the Israelites before he died. "The Lord came from Sinai and dawned from Seir upon us; he shone forth from Mount Paran" (33:2a). Muslim commentators have claimed that this verse symbolically speaks of how Judaism (Sinai) and Christianity (Seir) will eventually be superseded by Islam (Mount Paran).[8] The association of Sinai with Judaism is clear enough, but Muslim scholars had to engage in some creative interpretation in order to have one of the other two place names convey the meaning they desired. Seir is usually located south of the Dead Sea in the region of Edom or northern Arabia, but it was now identified as a mountain or town farther north in the area of Nazareth, which was closely associated with Jesus. Paran is also in the south, and its location in Arabia is what enabled Muslim scholars to identify it with Islam.

An example of Muslim use of Deuteronomy for apologetic purposes can be seen in a letter written by the Muslim polymath Muhammad b. Abi Talib al-Dimashqi (d. 1327 CE) to Christians in Cyprus in 1321. His letter was a response to a message sent to him by an anonymous Christian attempting to explain Christian attitudes toward Muhammad and how the Qur'an supports Christianity. In answer to the writer's claim that Muhammad arrived on the scene unannounced, al-Dimashqi cites the Blessing of Moses (33:1–5) to claim otherwise. "You know what is meant by Sinai is Moses and the Torah, since Sinai was the mountain of direct address, that what is meant by Seir is Christ and the Gospel, since Seir is the town of Nazareth, and that what is meant by the mountains of Paran is Muhammad and the Qur'an, since Paran is Mecca and the mountains of Paran are those of the Hijaz" (Tieszen 2015, 199). Al-Dimashqi then goes on to quote Deuteronomy's instructions on prophets (18:18) to make the case for Muhammad's legitimacy as a prophet.

> You know that the people of Israel have no brothers except Isma'il, and that no one has arisen among the people of Isma'il and the people of Kedar who upheld the general law and the supreme revealed law in the way that Moses did except Muhammad. And since it is stated in the Torah, "A prophet like Moses will not come from among the people of Israel," God said, "I will raise up a prophet from your brothers," not saying, "from you" so as not to contradict his own words. Hence our Prophet rose up from the people of Isma'il. God's word was in his mouth, and he delivered it orally for he was illiterate, he had not studied, he could not write, and he had not gone on journeys for anyone to think he had studied on a journey.
> (Tieszen 2015, 199–200)

The same reliance on Deuteronomy to support Muhammad's status as a prophet has carried on into modern times, as seen in the work of the Egyptian reformer Rashid Rida (d. 1935). He maintained that several biblical texts predict the coming of the prophet of Islam, and paramount among these is Deuteronomy (18:18). Countering Christian claims that Deuteronomy is referring to Jesus, Rida argued that the term "prophet" is different from that of " messiah," which Jesus is given in both the New Testament and the Qur'an, so God's words to Moses about a future figure could only be a reference to the prophet of Islam (Seferta 1985, 11–13).

Connections between Deuteronomy and Islam have been posited in various ways, many of which have centered on the relationship between Deuteronomy and the Qur'an. Approximately twenty-five of the nearly one thousand entries in the five-volume *Encyclopaedia of the Qur'ān* (McAuliffe 2001–2006) refer to Deuteronomy. These references typically do not suggest that the Qur'an is dependent upon Deuteronomy as a source, but rather they cite biblical texts that somehow relate to or help to explain parts of the Qur'an. For example, the similarity between Qur'an passages that endorse a *lex talionis* form of justice and Deuteronomy (19:21) is noted.

Some entries propose that the Qur'an is familiar with or referring to an event recorded in the Bible. For instance, "Polemic and Polemical Language" suggests that Q 2:72–73 alludes to Deuteronomy (21:1–9) stipulating how the Israelites are to atone for the unsolved murder of a person whose body is found in a field. "When you [Israelites] killed someone and started to blame one another—although God was to bring what you had concealed to light—We said, 'Strike the [body] with a part of [the cow]': thus God brings the dead to life and shows His signs so that you may understand." As is often the case, the Qur'an lacks the detail of Deuteronomy and so not every element of the latter is in the former. Nonetheless, the wider literary context of the Qur'an strongly suggests that it is an Islamic interpretation of Deuteronomy.

A recent work presents an English translation of the Qur'an that includes notes and commentary in those places where some association with the Bible or biblically related literature is proposed, and Deuteronomy is cited almost one hundred times in those comments (Reynolds 2018). In some cases, the connections are tenuous or too general to be of significance. For example, according to this commentary, the command to the Children of Israel to remember God's blessings (Q 2:40) "may follow from" the way YHWH asks the Israelites to remember the divine favors they have received in Deuteronomy (5:15; 7:18; 8:18; 15:15; 16:12) and elsewhere in the Bible (Reynolds 2018, 40–41). Similarly, the admonition against killing children (Q 6:137) is "in conversation with" Deuteronomy (12:31) when it condemns child sacrifice (Reynolds 2018, 242–243). It is difficult to establish with certainty that the Qur'an is intentionally responding to Deuteronomy, but they and other examples highlight the fact that the Qur'an has some intriguing connections with Deuteronomy. These many connections are not evidence that demonstrates the Qur'an is dependent on Deuteronomy, but the presence of so many parallels indicates that some sections of the Qur'an sound like Deuteronomy.

The Qur'an (Q 2:93) contains an interesting possible citation of a phrase from Deuteronomy that has been commented on by some non-Muslim scholars. "Remember when We took your pledge, making the mountain tower above you, and said, 'Hold on firmly to what We have given you, and listen to [what We say].' They said, 'We hear, and we disobey,' and through their disbelief they were made to drink [the love of] the calf deep into their hearts." The passage, likely alluding to the golden calf episode recounted in Exodus (Exod 32:1–35), describes the Israelites' inability to remain faithful to the covenant YHWH made with them. Their insolence is expressed in their response "we hear, and we disobey" (Arabic, *sami'nā wa 'aṣaynā*). That Arabic phrase is similar to a Hebrew phrase in Deuteronomy (5:27), where Moses reminds the people about what they said to him at Mt. Sinai when YHWH gave them the law. "Go near, you yourself, and hear all that the Lord our God will say. Then tell us everything that the Lord our God tells you, and we will listen and do it." The Israelites' final few words ("we will listen and do it") in Hebrew (*šəma'nû və'āśînû*) are etymologically very close to what they say in Arabic in the Qur'an, but the meaning is the exact opposite because of the different senses of the Hebrew and Arabic verbs. Their statement of compliance and obedience in Deuteronomy is a declaration of defiance and disobedience in the Qur'an. At the end of the same chapter, a similar phrase is found on the lips of believers (Q 2:285), only this time the second verb is slightly different and translates as "we hear, and we obey" (*sami'nā wa aṭa'nā*).

The first non-Muslim scholar to note the resemblance here between Deuteronomy and the Qur'an was Hirschfeld, who suggested in a 1902 publication that Muhammad mistakenly heard or read the Hebrew due to its closeness to the Arabic, which is now reflected the first time the parallel appears in the Qur'an (Q 2:93). When Muhammad realized his error, he corrected it the second time the parallel appears in the Qur'an (Q 2:285; Hirschfeld 1902, 108–109).

More recently, Firestone has argued that Muhammad did not make a mistake, but he was engaging in a practice that had a long and honored history in pre-Islamic Arabian poetry and rhetoric by taking a satirical swipe at the Jewish community with which he had been at odds because they refused to accept him as a prophet. In this way, Muhammad presented the Israelites in the Bible and the Jews in Muhammad's own day as uttering the same negative comment that expressed their disobedience both at Mt. Sinai with Moses and during his own time among them in Medina (Firestone 1997, 442–446).

Taking a somewhat different approach to argue for the relevance of Deuteronomy for the Qur'an, Saleh discerns a frame in the earliest sections of the Qur'an from Mecca parallel with Deuteronomy. He maintains that their presentation of Muhammad's mission is based on a Jewish paradigm of prophecy (Saleh 2018).[9] According to Saleh, the Islamic use of the paradigm differs from Deuteronomy in that Muhammad was presenting a "deuteronomistically-inflected" religion (Saleh 2018, 82) that did not express concern for the fate of Israel. Saleh describes the punishment stories of the Qur'an—he prefers the term "messengership stories"—as the Deuteronomistic Universal Frame that was reworked to better fit Muhammad's situation as an individual prophet in the desert who had no formal ties to Judaism or Christianity. This new framework is designed around a series of prophets or messengers who were sent to different peoples in order to offer them guidance and to warn them of punishment if they failed to obey. This broad outline maps quite well to the paradigm from Deuteronomy that is found in various early Jewish and Christian contexts, and it provides the theological background that explains Muhammad's career and preaching during the early Meccan period.

In Saleh's view, a key difference between the frames in the Qur'an and in Deuteronomy is the universality of the former. In the Qur'an the paradigm is not limited to Israel but includes all of humanity with prophets from various peoples being sent by Allah. Another significant distinction that changes the theological impact and meaning is that in the biblical tradition the prophets are killed but in the Islamic one they are saved and vindicated, along with those Allah chooses to rescue. In the Qur'an (Q 21:9), Allah comes to the assistance of the messengers. "We fulfilled Our promise to them (the messengers) in the end: We saved them and those We wished to save, and We destroyed those who exceeded all bounds." The universality of the Qur'an's presentation of the pattern is apparent in its inclusion of several Arabian, but non-Jewish, messengers who play the same role as their biblical counterparts. Hūd is sent to the people of ʿĀd, Ṣāliḥ to those of Thamūd, and Shuʿayb to the inhabitants of Madyan, and in each case their audience refuses to heed their message and is destroyed as a result (Q 53:50–54; 89:6–14). In this way, Muhammad's prophetic career is presented as part of an established universal divine plan. "This Qur'anic recasting of human history on deuteronomistic lines was essential to the coherency of Muhammad's ministry as part of a cosmic plan that had a meaning regardless of how it was perceived by his audience. Deuteronomistic history was the basis of his ministry" (Saleh 2018, 87). Saleh believes that the Qur'an's use of the pattern of warning followed by rejection and punishment that is found throughout the Deuteronomistic History reflects the influence of Judaism in the Arabian environment in which Islam emerged and developed.

What Is Trending in the Conversation?

Deuteronomistic Inflection Points

Drawing upon and further extending Saleh's idea that the Qur'an recasts human history along the lines of Deuteronomy, this section identifies several points of contact between the Qur'an and Deuteronomy regarding how God is understood in the two works. The intention is not to suggest that the Qur'an is somehow drawing from or dependent upon Deuteronomy, but rather to explore how Muhammad's presentation of Islam as a "deuteronomistically-inflected" religion, to use Saleh's term, might include how Allah is viewed in the Qur'an.

An aspect of the divine nature mentioned in Deuteronomy and central to Islam is the idea that God has spoken to other key figures in the past. This can be seen in Deuteronomy's identification of YHWH as the covenant partner of the ancestors of ancient Israel: "It is not because of your righteousness or the uprightness of your heart that you are going in to occupy their land; but because of the wickedness of these nations the LORD your God is dispossessing them before you, in order to fulfill the promise that the LORD made on oath to your ancestors, to Abraham, to Isaac, and to Jacob" (9:5 cf. 4:1; 7:12). The three patriarchs Abraham, Isaac, and Jacob are among the prophets frequently mentioned in the Qur'an whom Allah sent to warn their people, and it sometimes uses the terminology of oath or promise found in Deuteronomy to designate the special relationship that existed between YHWH and the Israelites (Q 2:40, 47, 83; 5:12; 20:80). In this way, Deuteronomy highlights YHWH's ongoing engagement with humanity that is at the heart of the Islamic view of the history of prophecy and the interaction of the divine with humans.

Islam is an aniconic religion that avoids all representations of Allah due to the belief that Allah does not have a body and therefore cannot be physically depicted. Deuteronomy acknowledges this same aspect of the divine nature in its recollection of how the Israelites experienced YHWH. "Then the LORD spoke to you out of the fire. You heard the sound of words but saw no form; there was only a voice" (4:12). A few verses later, Deuteronomy recognizes that YHWH's lack of a physical form contains a built-in danger in that it runs the risk of causing the people to create images that are then associated with YHWH. "Since you saw no form when the LORD spoke to you at Horeb out of the fire, take care and watch yourselves closely, so that you do not act corruptly by making an idol for yourselves, in the form of any figure—the likeness of male or female, the likeness of any animal that is on the earth, the likeness of any winged bird that flies in the air, the likeness of anything that creeps on the ground, the likeness of any fish that is in the water under the earth" (4:15–18; cf. 4:23–26; 5:8; 17:2–3; 27:15). This is another point of contact between Deuteronomy and the Qur'an which warns against ascribing divinity to created objects.

Islam forbids idolatry because it teaches that the unity and oneness of Allah (*tawhīd*) is Allah's defining quality. This is seen in the first part of the profession of faith that is recited three times during each of the five daily calls to prayer that is meant to express Allah's greatness ("There is no God but Allah"). It is also a theme found repeatedly throughout the Qur'an. "Truly, your God is one" (Q 37:4). The most serious sin a person can commit is to engage in *shirk*, or association, whereby one associates something from creation with Allah in a way that violates the divine unity (Q 6:22; 10:28; 31:13).

Shirk can take different forms, including polytheism, the worship of idols, and ascribing divinity to someone or something in the created world. According to the Qur'an, association is the only sin that Allah will not forgive (Q 4:48). While the Qur'an denounces such practices, it typically does not go into detail regarding precisely what sort of objects idolaters worship (Q 22:30). An exception to this can be seen in some of the passages about Abraham, the prototypical Muslim, who rejected the polytheism that was practiced by his father and other contemporaries. In one story he refuses to worship the sun, moon, and stars and thereby implicitly follows the Deuteronomistic teaching that one should not be led astray and bow down to the heavenly bodies (Q 6:74–79). Other traditions describe how

Abraham turned his back on and sometimes destroyed the idols and figures that his father and others worshipped (Q 19:41-50; cf. 21:51-71; 26:69-89; 37:83-98).[10]

Despite the divine transcendence that such a lack of physicality might imply, both the Qur'an and Deuteronomy maintain that Allah and YHWH somehow remain close to humanity. Although the Qur'an considers Allah to be completely other and unlike human beings, some passages speak of an intimate closeness between the two that has encouraged mystics to suggest a connection between humanity and divinity that borders on heresy for others. For example, the Qur'an (Q 50:16) presents an image of the relationship between Allah and humans that appears to allow for no separation between the two. "We created man—We know what his soul whispers to him: We are closer to him than his jugular vein." A similar sense of nearness is mentioned in Deuteronomy which refers to the law, perhaps suggesting that it is observance of the law that allows the people to experience their closeness to YHWH. "For what other great nation has a god so near to it as the LORD our God is whenever we call to him? And what other great nation has statutes and ordinances as just as this entire law that I am setting before you today?" (4:7-8).

The sense of divine closeness in Deuteronomy and the Qur'an is reinforced through the anthropomorphisms they sometimes employ when referring to YHWH and Allah. Sometimes Deuteronomy describes YHWH engaged in human-like activities.[11] "But in spite of this, you have no trust in the LORD your God, who goes before you on the way to seek out a place for you to camp, in fire by night, and in the cloud by day, to show you the route you should take" (1:32-33). Others mention some of the divine body parts, like feet, hands, and eyes. "Because the LORD your God travels along with your camp, to save you and to hand over your enemies to you, therefore your camp must be holy, so that he may not see anything indecent among you and turn away from you" (23:14).

Elsewhere references are made to the face of YHWH. "Never since has there arisen a prophet in Israel like Moses, whom the LORD knew face to face" (34:10; cf. 5:4). Other anthropomorphisms ascribe human emotions like jealousy to YHWH. "For the LORD your God is a devouring fire, a jealous God" (4:24). In several passages, YHWH is presented as a divine warrior who leads the Israelite troops into battle and fights on their behalf against the enemy. "Know then today that the LORD your God is the one who crosses over before you as a devouring fire; he will defeat them and subdue them before you, so that you may dispossess and destroy them quickly, as the LORD has promised you" (9:3; cf. 3:22; 20:2-4).

Similar anthropomorphisms are also found in the Qur'an. Although the Qur'an teaches that Allah is unlike human beings, anthropomorphisms are not uncommon in the Qur'an and the proper way to interpret these passages was an especially controversial issue during the early centuries of Islam.[12] An example can be seen in "All that remains is the face of your Lord, full of majesty, bestowing honor" (Q 55:27: cf. 2:115; 28:88; 30:38; 76:9). Likewise, when Allah orders Noah to build the ark, he is told to do so "under Our (watchful) eyes" (Q 11:37; cf. 23:27; 52:48; 54:13-14).

The divine hand is mentioned on occasion. "Those who pledge loyalty to you (Muhammad) are actually pledging loyalty to God Himself—God's hand is placed on theirs" (Q 48:10a cf. 3:73; 5:64). There are also allusions to Allah hearing and speaking throughout the text. Similarly, there are references in the Qur'an to the throne of Allah (Q 40:15), where Allah is described as "the Lord of the throne" (cf. Q 9:129; 23:116; 43:82).

Many Muslim commentators maintain that these and other examples of anthropomorphisms in the Qur'an should be read metaphorically and are not meant to be taken literally. Some have argued that "the face of Allah" refers to the divine essence, in contrast to the divine attributes that are described in the so-called ninety-nine names of God.[13] In the same way, when the eyes of Allah are referred to, they describe the protection that Allah provides for the created world. Similarly, passages that mention the divine hand are simply acknowledging Allah's power over humanity and the world.

Others have suggested that the anthropomorphisms should be read literally, but we have no way of knowing what they mean because the human experience and understanding of these terms is completely inadequate to comprehend what their significance is on the divine level. These and similar anomalies in the Qur'an that are impossible for humans to understand have sometimes been interpreted through appeal to the Arabic phrase *bila kayf*, which means "without (knowing) how," as a way of claiming that some dimensions of Allah's existence remain a mystery to human beings.[14] Within the history of biblical interpretation, there is a similar tendency to interpret anthropomorphisms metaphorically and symbolically rather than literally, and so what might appear to be a key difference between Deuteronomy and Islamic views of Allah is not as significant as it first seems.

No quality is more closely identified with Allah in Islam than mercy. Two of the most commonly cited names for Allah by Muslims are the "Merciful One" (*al-rahmān*) and the "Compassionate One" (*al-rahīm*). Each of the Qur'an's 114 chapters but one begins with the phrase "In the name of Allah, the merciful, the compassionate," and the Qur'an is full of references to human beings experiencing divine forgiveness and mercy regardless of whatever shortcomings they possess or sins they may have committed.[15] The Qur'an's account of the golden calf episode provides an example (Q 7:148–154). The outline of the plot follows closely that of Exodus with one notable exception—unlike Exodus, every human character in the Qur'an experiences divine forgiveness for their offenses after they seek Allah's mercy. While the biblical version of events ends in a fragmented fashion with all the participants alienated from one another and from YHWH, the Qur'an's story is one of healing and reconciliation that is grounded in divine mercy.[16]

The law is an important part of the background of the golden calf story. According to Exodus (Exod 32:1–33:6), the events take place in the immediate aftermath of Moses receiving the law, and by worshipping the image of the calf the Israelites are guilty of violating the central legislation against taking other gods besides YHWH. The Qur'an communicates the message that even in the face of such disregard for the divine will, Allah is ready to forgive those who acknowledge their mistake and ask for mercy. In Exodus, the story of the golden calf does not impart this same lesson, but Deuteronomy does when it encourages people to reorient themselves toward the divine will and experience forgiveness. "In your distress, when all these things have happened to you in time to come, you will return to the LORD your God and heed him. Because the LORD your God is a merciful God, he will neither abandon you nor destroy you; he will not forget the covenant with your ancestors that he swore to them" (4:30–31; cf. 32:36). In this passage the important Islamic concept of divine mercy is moved to the fore by reminding people that they will come to know the compassion of YHWH if they return to following the law.

An additional aspect of Islam's view of the divine nature that is referred to in Deuteronomy is God's uniqueness.[17] The first half of the Muslim profession of faith succinctly expresses this belief—"There is no god but Allah!"

Deuteronomy imparts the same message in a passage that stresses the close nexus between YHWH's uniqueness and the law. "So, acknowledge today and take to heart that the

LORD is God in heaven above and on the earth beneath; there is no other. Keep his statutes and his commandments, which I am commanding you today for your own well-being and that of your descendants after you, so that you may long remain in the land that the LORD your God is giving you for all time" (4:39–40; cf. 32:39). The passage's statement that "the LORD is God in heaven above and on the earth beneath; there is no other" echoes the Muslim profession of faith, and the reminder immediately after it to keep YHWH's statutes and commandments can be read as a necessary outcome or result of the divine uniqueness. YHWH's status as the one and only God legitimates the law and underscores the importance of following it.

Many of the passages already discussed indicate the role of YHWH and Allah as a lawgiver is a further dimension of the deity's identity that Deuteronomy and the Qur'an both acknowledge, and their shared agreement on that role can be seen in the similar vocabulary they employ to describe it. In both cases, the language of a path or way is used to explain how the law should function for people. It is meant to point them in a certain direction, keep them on the straight and narrow, and lead them to a destination that the deity has determined for them.[18] In Deuteronomy exhortations to follow the law are sometimes found in close proximity to references to the path one should travel. "But you, stand here by me, and I will tell you all the commandments, the statutes and the ordinances, that you shall teach them, so that they may do them in the land that I am giving them to possess. You must therefore be careful to do as the LORD your God has commanded you; you shall not turn to the right or to the left. You must follow exactly the path that the LORD your God has commanded you, so that you may live, and that it may go well with you, and that you may live long in the land that you are to possess" (5:31–33). The law of YHWH is the path of YHWH, and only those who adhere to it can experience the reward that awaits those who successfully navigate the journey. "The LORD will establish you as his holy people, as he has sworn to you, if you keep the commandments of the LORD your God and walk in his ways" (28:9; cf. 8:6; 10:12–13; 26:16–17).

In the Qur'an the same association between law and a path or way is also present. The common Arabic word for law (*sharīʿah*) originally described "the path one takes to reach a water source."[19] Its meaning was eventually extended to include the law, and this sense can be seen in a verse in the Qur'an that contains a term etymologically related to *sharīʿah* that is immediately followed by a word describing the way Allah expects Muslims to follow. "We have prescribed a law (*shirʿah*) and a way for each of you. If God had willed, He could have made you one community, but He tests you through what He has given you. So, race one another in doing good deeds. All of you will return to God, and He will explain to you what you differed about" (Q 5:48b).

Each community has its own law and way of life. The first half of the verse, not cited here, makes it clear that the text is talking about Muslims and the People of the Book, particularly Jews and Christians. It reminds Muhammad that the Qur'an confirms the Bible, while at the same time acknowledging the differences that exist between Muslims and the People of the Book.[20] The implication is that each group should follow the law, or way, that has been given to it and leave judgment up to God.

This overview demonstrates that some of the most significant aspects of the understanding in the Qur'an of the divine nature are also present in Deuteronomy, including an ongoing relationship with humans throughout history, close proximity to humanity despite a lack of physicality, an abundance of mercy, and uniqueness that legitimates the role of

YHWH and Allah as lawgiver. Consequently, it can be argued that Saleh's observation that the Qur'an has a "deuteronomistically-inflected understanding of the history of prophecy" might be extended to include its view of God.

The palimpsest that was mentioned in the opening section of this chapter is a fitting image with which to close it. Those fragments on which the text of the Qur'an is superimposed over a portion of Deuteronomy nicely illustrate some of the contours of the relationship between Deuteronomy and the Qur'an discussed here. Deuteronomy has sometimes been read in a predictive way that supports the Qur'an's views of itself and its prophet. In this reading, Deuteronomy forms the basis upon which the Qur'an is built, just as the Coptic text of the manuscript is the foundation on which the Arabic is written. But the palimpsest can be viewed in another way, one that sees a more fluid relationship between the two texts. In this reading, they bleed into and inform one another as each text attempts to articulate its own message while also becoming part of the other. The points of contact between Deuteronomy and the Qur'an treated here suggest that the latter way of reading opens up new ways of thinking about the relationship between the two.

Notes

1. The Arabic term commonly used to describe the corruption of pre-qur'anic revelations is *taḥrīf*. A number of Qur'an passages are cited by Muslim scholars as the basis of this charge (for example, Q 2:79–80 and 3:75–78), which can take the form of either a physical alteration of the text of the Bible or a distorted interpretation of its meaning. See Saeed (2002) for a discussion of *taḥrīf*.
2. Outside the Qur'an, most Muslims are exposed to biblical figures through the Stories of the Prophets (*qiṣaṣ al-anbiyā'*), collections of traditions that recount the lives of important individuals of the past. One of the most well-known is that of al-Kisā'ī compiled in the twelfth century CE (al-Kisa'i 1997).
3. The edition of the Qur'an quoted throughout is that of Abdel Haleem 2004. The Qur'an regularly uses first-person plural forms to refer to Allah in a way similar to what is sometimes found in the Bible (cf. Gen 1:26).
4. See Kaltner and Mirza (2018) for an overview of how these biblical figures are presented in the Qur'an and other Islamic literature.
5. Another scholar who made frequent use of the Bible in his study of the Qur'an a century before al-Biqā'ī was Ibn Barrajān, as explained in Casewit (2016).
6. All biblical quotations in English in this chapter are taken from the New Revised Standard Version. Firestone (2016, 16) notes the similarity between Deut 18:15 and Q 3:81: "God took a pledge from the prophets, saying, 'If, after I have bestowed Scripture and wisdom upon you, a messenger comes confirming what you have been given, you must believe in him and support him.'"
7. Other passages in the Qur'an function in a similar way. When Abraham and his son Ishmael build the "House of God," the Ka'ba toward which Muslims turn five times a day in prayer, they ask that Allah will send them a teacher from "among themselves," an allusion to Muhammad (Q 2:127–129). In another passage Jesus prays for the coming of a figure he calls Ahmad, which is a form of the name Muhammad (Q 61:6).
8. Among the Muslim scholars who offered this interpretation of Deut 33:2a are al-Māwardī (tenth/eleventh centuries CE), Yāqūt al-Hamawī (twelfth/thirteenth centuries CE), and

Ibn Taymiyya (thirteenth/fourteenth centuries CE); see Lazarus-Yafeh (1992), 109. Firestone (2016, 13) notes that Muslim polemicists of the medieval period claimed that Jews had moved to Arabia because they believed texts like Deut 33:2 indicated a prophet would emerge in the area.

9. Scholarship on the Qur'an commonly distinguishes between those chapters of the Qur'an that come from the time that Muhammad was in Mecca (ca. 610–622) and those from the period after he made the migration or *hijrah* to Medina (ca. 622–632).
10. See Hawting (1999) on the theme of idolatry in Islam. The idolatry of Abraham's father and people is not mentioned in the book of Genesis, but it is a theme in some Jewish nonbiblical literature. See, for example, *Genesis Rabbah* 38:13; *Apocalypse of Abraham* 4:3-6; and *Jubilees* 12:2-3.
11. A study of some of the biblical anthropomorphisms of the deity is found in Smith (2014).
12. Anthropomorphism in Islam and the other monotheistic religions is the topic of Shah (2012).
13. The ninety-nine names of Allah are a set of attributes that identify qualities the deity possesses, like mercy, knowledge, and forgiveness. Most of them have their basis in the Qur'an, and invocation of them is a common practice in Muslim prayer.
14. One of the earliest proponents of this concept was the theologian al-Ashari (d. 936), who cited it in response to the rationalist Mu'tazila school of thought.
15. The only chapter in the Qur'an that does not begin in this way is the ninth, and it is commonly thought that it is missing there because the ninth chapter was originally part of the eighth one and was separated from it at a later point in time.
16. For an analysis of how the golden calf episode has been interpreted in Judaism, Christianity, and Islam, see Pregill (2020).
17. Chapter 112 of the Qur'an, *Surat al-Ikhlāṣ*, presents a concise description of the deity's inimitability. "Say, 'He, is God the One, God the eternal. He begot no one nor was He begotten. No one is comparable to Him.'"
18. This function of the law in Deuteronomy is discussed in Miller (2013). An overview of Islamic law is provided in Hallaq (2009).
19. Badawi and Abdel Haleem (2008), 481.
20. The term "People of the Book" appears in approximately thirty verses in the Qur'an, and it refers to those groups who were given a written revelation from Allah prior to the time of Muhammad. See Albayrak (2008).

Bibliography

Abdel Haleem, M. A. S., trans. 2004. *The Qur'an: A New Translation*. Oxford: Oxford University Press.

Adang, Camilla, and Sabine Schmidtke. 2019. *Muslim Perceptions and Receptions of the Bible: Texts and Studies*. Atlanta: Lockwood Press.

Albayrak, Ismail. 2008. "The People of the Book in the Qur'an." *Islamic Studies* 47, no. 3: 301–325.

Badawi, Elsaid M., and Muhammad Abdel Haleem. 2008. *Arabic-English Dictionary of Qur'anic Usage*. Leiden: Brill.

Casewit, Yousef. 2016. "A Muslim Scholar of the Bible: Prooftexts from Genesis and Matthew in the Qur'an Commentary of Ibn Barrajān of Seville (d. 536/1141)." *Journal of Qur'anic Studies* 18, no. 1: 1–48.

Cellard, Éléonore. 2017–2018. "Une nouvelle contribution à l'histoire du Coran en Égypte au VIIIe siècle: le palimpseste copto-coranique." *La lettre du Collège de France* 44. http://journals.openedition.org/lettre-cdf/4325.

Firestone, Reuven. 1997. "The Failure of a Jewish Program of Public Satire in the Squares of Medina." *Judaism* 46, no. 4:439–452.

Firestone, Reuven. 2016. "The Problematic of Prophecy." *Journal of the International Qur'anic Studies Association* 1: 11–22.

Hallaq, Wael B. 2009. *An Introduction to Islamic Law.* Cambridge: Cambridge University Press.

Hawting, G. R. 1999. *The Idea of Idolatry and the Emergence of Islam: From Polemic to History.* Cambridge: Cambridge University Press.

Hirschfeld, Hartwig. 1902. *New Researches into the Composition and Exegesis of the Quran.* London: Royal Asiatic Society.

Kaltner, John, and Younus Y. Mirza. 2018. *The Bible and the Qur'an: Biblical Figures in the Islamic Tradition.* London: Bloomsbury.

al-Kisa'i, Muhammad ibn 'Abd Allah. 1997. *Tales of the Prophets.* Translated by Wheeler M. Thackston, Jr. Chicago: KAZI Publications.

Lazarus-Yafeh, Hava. 1992. *Intertwined Worlds: Medieval Islam and Biblical Criticism.* Princeton: Princeton University Press.

McAuliffe, Jane Dammen, ed. 2001–2006. *Encyclopaedia of the Qur'ān.* 5 vols. Leiden: Brill.

Miller, Patrick D. 2013. "'That You May Live': Dimensions of Law in Deuteronomy." In *Concepts of Law in the Sciences, Legal Studies, and Theology,* edited by Michael Welker and Gregor Etzelmüller, 137–157. Tübingen: Mohr Siebeck.

Pregill, Michael E. 2020. *The Golden Calf between Bible and Qur'an: Scripture, Polemic, and Exegesis from Late Antiquity to Islam.* Oxford: Oxford University Press.

Reynolds, Gabriel Said. 2018. *The Qur'ān and the Bible.* New Haven: Yale University Press.

Saeed, Abdullah. 2002. "The Charge of Distortion of Jewish and Christian Scriptures." *The Muslim World* 92: 419–436.

Saleh, Walid A. 2008. "A Fifteenth-Century Muslim Hebraist: Al-Biqā'ī and His Defense of Using the Bible to Interpret the Qur'ān." *Speculum* 83, no. 3: 629–654.

Saleh, Walid A. 2018. "The Preacher of the Meccan Qur'an: Deuteronomistic History and Confessionalism in Muḥammad's Early Preaching." *Journal of Qur'anic Studies* 10, no. 2: 74–111.

Seferta, Yusuf H. R. 1985. "The Prophethood of Muḥammad in the Writings of Muḥammad 'Abdu and Rashīd Riḍā'." *Hamdard Islamicus* 8, no. 2: 11–29.

Shah, Zulfiqar Ali. 2012. *Anthropomorphic Depictions of God: The Concept of God in Judaic, Christian and Islamic Traditions.* Herndon: The International Institute of Islamic Thought.

Smith, Mark S. 2014. *How Human Is God?: Seven Questions about God and Humanity in the Bible.* Collegeville: Liturgical Press.

Tieszen, Charles. 2015. *A Textual History of Christian-Muslim Relations.* Minneapolis: Fortress Press.

CHAPTER 27

DEUTERONOMY IN AFRICAN-AMERICAN CHRISTIANITY

STEPHEN BRECK REID

Who Began the Conversation?

From "Talking Book" to Freedom Narratives

DEUTERONOMY provides a keystone between the Pentateuch and the Deuteronomistic history (Judges through Kings). African interpretation of Deuteronomy begins in North Africa from 180 to 203 CE, where church fathers like Tertullian in his *Contra Judaeos* and Augustine in his *Contra Faustum Manichaeum* commented on Deuteronomy.[1] The fall of the Roman Empire provided a context for Constantinople over Rome. The Arab conquest of Africa diminished the African interpretation of Deuteronomy.[2]

African American interpretation of Deuteronomy fits into three periods. Each demonstrated a nexus of competences.

The first period describes the rise of biblical interpretation of Deuteronomy by kidnapped Africans enslaved in North America who spoke no English and would eventually embrace the King James Version (KJV) as the authoritative word of God. This section will also examine some precritical interpretations of Deuteronomy by people from Africa and the African diaspora. These individuals recount their journey from enslavement to freedom by interpreting passages from Deuteronomy to build a bridge between Deuteronomy and the social location of enslaved Africans.

Early Autobiographies and Sermons on the Struggle toward Freedom

The freedom narratives create a bridge between Deuteronomy to the social location of enslaved Africans. Consistently these stories point to barriers to reading, on the one hand, and the nature of the Bible as a talking book, on the other. Already in the 1990s, black theology understood the importance of these once named "slave narratives" and precritical biblical interpretation and theology.[3] Now, even mainstream biblical scholars and theologians recognize their importance.[4]

One barrier to reading was the English language and literacy. Many Africans were literate in native languages as well as Arabic, but not English.

Public policies supporting chattel slavery were another barrier. The enslavement of Africans remained a debated topic in the common square. Many states also enacted laws that made it illegal to teach African slaves how to read.

The debated nature of chattel slavery generated literature. Nineteenth-century European American fiction, like *Uncle Tom's Cabin* (1852) by Harriet Beecher Stowe and *Huckleberry Finn* (1884) by Mark Twain, romanticized enslavement.

Subsequently, twentieth-century fiction by both European American authors like *The Confessions of Nat Turner* (1967) by William Styron and African American authors like *Beloved* (1987) by Toni Morrison offered a different picture of enslaved persons.

The first-person freedom narratives chronicled the resistance to white supremacy from the eighteenth century to the nineteenth century in the United States. Freedom narratives gave a voice to often-marginalized people, but their readers were primarily European Americans. For these readers in the North, narratives like *Twelve Years a Slave* (1853) by Solomon Northup pulled back the curtain and revealed the brutality of chattel slavery.

Emerson B. Powery and Rodney S. Sadler Jr. replace the term "slave" with "formerly enslaved." They replaced the widely used label "slave narratives" with "freedom narratives."[5] From the perspective of European American readers, these were slave narratives, but from the perspective of their African American writers, these were freedom narratives. Mahalia Jackson points to the process in her song "How I Got Over." Freedom narratives are stories about how enslaved Africans "got over," how they moved to freedom.

Most freedom narratives focus on two different passages from Deuteronomy (6:4–9; 31:6). There are only occasional references to the Deuteronomic Code (15:12–17) or the Covenant Code (Exod 21:2–16) which address slavery but receive little attention in the freedom narratives.

The Greatest Commandment in the New Testament (Mark 12:29–30) echoes the Shema (Deut 6:4–9)—the most referenced tradition from Deuteronomy in the freedom narratives.

Formerly enslaved persons often considered the Shema to be a touchstone of integrity. Three writers—Aaron, known only by his first name, Jared Maurice Arter, and Bishop Lucius Henry Holsey—work substantively with the Shema itself. Boyrereau Brinch, J. Vance Lewis, and Major James Wilkerson interpret the Shema using its parallel in the New Testament. Wilkerson used the New Testament parallel to Deuteronomy as a bulwark against the institution of slavery.[6] Aaron and Holsey both connect the Shema with the laws on slaves in Deuteronomy (15:1–14). Aaron connected the laws on slaves with "When you come into the land that the LORD your God is giving you, you must not learn to imitate the abhorrent practices of those nations" (18:9).[7]

Light and Truth of Slavery: Aaron's History (1845) is a series of essays on slavery, politics, and religion, rather than an autobiography. We know little more of his life than that he was enslaved for a time and then became an itinerant bondsman. He made the point that Deuteronomy and especially the Shema are a charter for a Christian nation. The laws of slavery in Deuteronomy (15:1–14; 23:15–16) and Leviticus (Lev 25:8–55) stipulate manumission after six years. He argues that a country like the United States that so abhors monarchy should not support slavery.[8]

Jared Maurice Arter was born on January 27, 1850, in Jefferson County, West Virginia, into enslavement. At age nine he witnessed John Brown's raid on Harper's Ferry. Arter's master at the time worked at the arsenal that Brown attacked. After emancipation in 1863 his family moved to Washington, DC. In 1873 he became a Baptist and then earned his bachelor's degree from Pennsylvania State College and served as instructor at Virginia Theological Seminary and College.

Arter frames his discussion of public service with a poem:

> Joy is duty, so with golden lore
> The Hebrew rabbis taught in days of yore.
> And happy human hearts heard their speech
> Almost the highest wisdom man [sic] can reach.[9]

In the section titled "Life of Complete Service to Christ," Arter connects the Shema to the teaching of Jesus without an explicit reference to the synoptic gospels (Matt 22:37; Luke 10:27; Mark 12:30–31). Rather he moves to the story of the woman who anoints the feet of Jesus (Mark 14:3–8; Matt 26:6–14). Many African American interpreters, including Arter, blend the Shema with its parallel in the New Testament. Arter demonstrates knowledge of British history when he writes, "The Christian must have power with God and man [sic]. Bloody Mary is reported to have said: I fear the prayers of John Knox more than all the armies of Europe."[10] During his baccalaureate sermon to the Cairo High School in 1901, Arter uses Deuteronomy as a moral foundation to argue that "morality is the vestibule of religion."[11]

Bishop Lucius Henry Holsey was born in July 3, 1842, near Columbus, Georgia. His mother, Louisa, was an enslaved African and his father, James Holsey, was her enslaver. At the death of James Holsey, Lucius was enslaved by Holsey's cousin, T. L. Lynn, in Hancock County, Georgia. A few days before his own death, Lynn told Holsey to select his next enslaver. Holsey selected Richard Malcolm Johnston, a planter and educator, who later took a position as an English professor at the University of Georgia in Athens. Holsey worked for Johnston as a house slave, carriage driver, and gardener. He lived with that family in Athens from 1857 until the abolition of slavery.

Holsey did not go to school. His early collection of books included two Webster's blue spellers, a common dictionary, John Milton's *Paradise Lost*, and a Bible. He was able to buy these by collecting and selling rags to a junk house in the city.

Holsey married Harriet Turner, an enslaved fifteen-year-old, on November 8, 1862. She lived in the home of Bishop George Foster Pierce of the Methodist Episcopal Church, now the United Methodist Church. The Methodist Episcopal Church survived several schisms. When the African American Methodist Church split from the Methodist Episcopal Church, the Methodist Episcopal Church decided to create a new denomination, the Colored Methodist Episcopal Church, now the Christian Methodist Episcopal (CME) Church.

Holsey became a Methodist and eventually served as the fourth bishop of the CME Church. He served in that position for almost fifty years. Harriet and Lucius had fourteen children. Nine survived. Johnston gave Holsey land in Hancock County near Sparta Georgia, where Holsey farmed and ran a boarding house named "Rockby Academy." Harriet Holsey did laundry for the students at the academy.

When Holsey sought ordination in 1868 with the blessing of Bishop Pierce, Holsey was assigned to the Hancock circuit in Georgia. Holsey was selected as a delegate to the first

General Conference of the CME Church, South. During the conference Holsey was appointed to the Trinity CME Church in Augusta, Georgia. Holsey was elected bishop in 1873 when he was thirty years old. The family of eleven lived in a two-room house with a coal stove for heat.

Bishop Holsey with other leaders of the Methodist Episcopal Church South and the CME Church founded Paine College in Augusta, Georgia; Lane College in Jackson, Tennessee; the Holsey Normal and Industrial Academy; a secondary school in Cordele, Georgia; and the Helena B. Cobb Institute for Girls in Barnesville, Georgia. During 1891–1904 he compiled and published *Songs of Love and Mercy*. Holsey also served as editor-in-chief of the periodical *The Gospel Trumpet*, the church paper.

The following excerpt is taken from Holsey's autobiography. "The Unity of Christianity" demonstrates his interpretation of the Shema.

> "Hear, O Israel, the Lord thy God is one Lord," and so it might be said, "Hear, all ye religions of the nations and ages, the Lord thy God is one God and one Father." From him all truth must come, since he is "the only true God," and the only One in the universe that can dictate to the will and conscience and moral and religious proclivities of men and angels, and whatever other intelligences may reside in his dominions. All truth is from God and must lead to God. Every thread and line and living cable that ramifies and thrills the living entities, though sometimes hidden and broken and covered with the débris and scoria of the wear and tear of the centuries, will take us back to God, the great Original, chaining all to the rock-ribbed mountains of the eternal shore. If there were ten thousand religions, and ten times ten thousand forms of worship, to be true and beneficial to mankind, they must all point to God and own him as the true and only proper and rightful object of prayer, praise and adoration. "All things are yours," to lead you to God and plant you on the solid rock of truth and the eternal shore.[12]

The depiction of the deity "dictates" four things: (1) will, (2) conscience, (3) moral and religion "proclivities," and (4) intelligences. Each of these elements played a major role in the theological and moral discourse. Holsey welded these elements of human character to the one true God. Holsey gestures again to the divine origin of "truth" that comes from and ever returns "back to God, the great Original."

Holsey does not describe the scourges of slavery but rather points to the way that history functions: "sometimes hidden and broken and covered with the debris and scoria of wear and tear of the centuries." In other words, the flotsam and jetsam of life and history can obscure the "truth." Bishop Holsey also begins with Matthew: "On these two commandments hang all the law and the prophets" (Matt 22:40) and then turns to Deuteronomy (6:5) as a marker for the centrality of God's law as the foundation of human civilization.[13]

Major James Wilkerson, born into enslavement in Virginia, subsequently purchased his freedom in New Orleans, Louisiana, in 1835. He also purchased the freedom of his mother, who lived in Petersburg, Virginia. Wilkerson claims that his background includes links to the Bengal of Africa, the Anglo-Saxons of Europe, and the Powhattan of America. A pastiche of ethnic hybridity of Wilkerson, African, Anglo-Saxon, and Native American heritage marks something that will be characteristic of African American identity and the style of interpretation model. Like Arter and Holsey, Wilkerson was also a member of the clergy. He served the Methodist Episcopal Church until 1838 when he joined the African Methodist Episcopal Church (AME) in Ohio as a missionary throughout the West and

South. He served in Indianapolis and then Baltimore. By the end of his autobiography he is contemplating ministry travel to Havana.[14]

Wilkerson connects the "peculiar Divine Institution" of chattel slavery with the crucifixion, "and so nail said traffic, with all of its inexpressible horrors, on the cross of Christ."[15] In 1837 John C. Calhoun, a pro-slavery U.S. Senator from South Carolina, gave a speech arguing that "the peculiar institution of the South" had allowed enslaved African and African Americans to become "so civilized and so improved, not only physically, but morally and intellectually."[16] The phrase became a shorthand for subsequent endorsements of slavery. In contrast, when Wilkerson binds the words of the Shema from Deuteronomy lifted up by Jesus (Luke 10:27) to the crucifixion, he indicts chattel slavery and appeals for restorative justice.

Boyrereau Brinch was born in west Africa in 1742, kidnapped at age sixteen, and first enslaved as a sailor in the British navy. In the French Indian Wars (1756–1763), he enlisted in the Connecticut militia. He received an honorable discharge and emancipation (1783). Brinch became blind. He told his story to Benjamin Prentiss, an abolitionist journalist who published the volume as *The Blind African Slave* (1810). Brinch remembers a walk on the ship when the abject conditions prompted a poem and reflection on Matthew (7:7–12) and Luke (10:25–37) which parallel the Shema.[17] Once again Brinch appeals to the New Testament as an exhortation to compassion. He died in Georgia, Vermont, on April 20, 1827.

John Dixon Long was another minister of the Methodist Episcopal Church. He was born in New Town, Maryland, on September 26, 1817. His father was a former sea captain. His mother, Sally Laws Henderson Long, was a devout member of the Methodist Episcopal Church. His mother died in 1828 and his father in 1834. Long, then, supported his two sisters and brother. He moved to Philadelphia in 1856, only to be disappointed by the level of support for slavery in the city.

Long writes, "We poor slaves can't read, and how do we know what the Bible says! Bitter experience . . . " Like Wilkerson, Long referred to the New Testament use of Deuteronomy as a charter for freedom.[18]

Thomas Quigly, a Methodist minister from Pennsylvania, brought charges against Long for his abolitionist work in the Philadelphia Methodist Episcopal Conference at the 1858 General Conference, but the charges were dropped. Long died in Philadelphia in 1894.[19]

J. Vance Lewis wrote in his autobiography that he was born in Louisiana. His family decided to remain on the plantation after the Emancipation Proclamation (1863). He started his studies at Leland University and then, after serving as a teacher and principal to save money, Lewis made his way to Lincoln University in Pennsylvania, an unnamed school in Ann Arbor, Michigan, and the Chicago College of Law. He was admitted to the bar on November 22, 1897, and practiced law in Michigan, Illinois, and Texas. He moved to Houston and set up a successful practice. He was indicted for "irregularities" and suspended during the investigation. Lewis used the time to travel in Europe lecturing on race relations. When the case was resolved, he faced death threats because of his prominence.

Lewis argues that there is a trajectory in history. He construes the statement "It is not good for a person to be alone" (Gen 2:18) as a divine indication that humans need associations that become governments. A key resource for political practice is "religion." Good government, according to Lewis, is defined by Deuteronomy and validated, according to Lewis, by Jesus, who shows a way forward in human civilization. Even Christopher Columbus's adventures from Spain serve divine behest to convert the natives to Christianity.[20]

Only the entrepreneur, Elleanor Eldridge, focused on "Be strong and bold; have no fear or dread of them, because it is the Lord your God who goes with you; he will not fail you or forsake you" (31:16). She uses Moses's words of encouragement as a divine authorization. Eldridge herself was not afraid to stand alone for the sake of the right. So it is not surprising that her lone voice would include a passage which others left aside.

Elleanor Eldridge was probably born in Warwick, Rhode Island. Her maternal grandmother, Mary Fuller, was probably Narragansett, a Native American people in Rhode Island. Her father, Thomas Prophet, was the grandson of a man kidnapped at the mouth of the Congo River. Mary Fuller, using some of her family's land holdings, purchased the enslaved Thomas Prophet. Her daughter married Robin Eldridge, the father of Elleanor Eldridge.

Illness and reverses in real estate deals left her in financial straits. Frances Harriet Whipple Green McDougall (1805–1878), an abolitionist writer who was also from Rhode Island, helped Eldridge to publish three editions of her memoirs to earn her own living and recoup the real estate losses.

Eldridge characterizes her courage in the face of legal conflicts with a combination of statements from Deuteronomy and other biblical traditions.[21] Deuteronomy served as an epigram to her life story, as it did for other formerly enslaved persons.

The preponderance of treatments of Deuteronomy in the freedom narratives gravitate to the Shema. Some writers fuse Deuteronomy and its subsequent use in the sayings of Jesus. Deuteronomy's laws on slaves (15:1–14) receive some attention. The arguments consistently assume that the United States as a Christian country would follow the precept set forth in Deuteronomy, especially where Jesus validates them as the greatest commandments. Deuteronomy also provided exhortation to courage and perseverance.

What Is the Status of the Conversation?

From the Harlem Renaissance to Civil Rights Preaching

Zora Neale Hurston (1891–1960) from the Harlem Renaissance and Martin Luther King Jr. (1929–1968) of the civil rights movement both focus on the plot of Deuteronomy more than particular words. Both in their own manner appropriate Moses as a model leader for African Americans, bridging Deuteronomy and African American tropes and aesthetics.

Zora Neale Hurston was born in Notasulga, Alabama, on January 7, 1891, but her family moved to Eatonville, Florida, in 1894. Eatonville was a Negro enclave in segregated Florida, one of the first all-black towns incorporated in the United States. Her father, John Hurston, a Baptist preacher and sharecropper, was elected mayor of Eatonville in 1897. He was called as pastor of Macedonia Missionary Baptist Church, the largest in the town (1902).

Her third novel, *Moses, Man of the Mountain* (1939), was published by Lippincott. Previously she published a short story in the African American literary journal *Challenge* (September 1934) titled "The Fire and the Cloud," which "describes a dead and ascending Moses as half man, half god." While she was still at Columbia in 1935, Hurston worked on the project with funding from the Rosenwald Foundation. She sent a draft to Lippincott in the spring of 1935. She told a friend in December 1935 she was working on a novel about Moses.[22]

"Hurston attempts nothing less than to kidnap Moses from Judeo-Christian tradition, claiming that his true birthright is African and that his true constituency is Afro-American."[23] Hurston perceived the special relationship between the figure of Moses and African American tradition. The imagining of Moses was simultaneously a reimagining of a group of people. The "freedom" of Moses prefigured African American freedom through the aesthetics. "The chosen people image demonstrates how the slave created their own imaginative mental world, secure from a degraded status."[24] Hurston uses biblical material as well as *The Antiquities of the Jews* by Flavius Josephus (37–100 CE).[25]

Hurston did not consider the novel a success.[26] Several factors contribute to this assessment. The novel lacks strong women characters. "In *Moses*, Zipporah is simply left at home."[27] The depiction of Moses also suffers from indecision. "She is never quite sure if the outsider Moses is black or white, an uncertainty lending confusion to his racial statements."[28]

The final chapter in *Moses, Man of the Mountain* recounts Moses on Mount Nebo and Pisgah. The people asked: "When are we crossing over?"[29] This gestures toward a theme in the novel, crossing over a metaphor of transformation and actualization. Moses is a liberator but only in a restricted sense. "He had found out that no man may make another free. Freedom was something internal."[30] Hurston understands freedom as self-expression even in the context of oppression. "Hurston makes fun of slave mentality" that mistakes freedom as an entity that can be given.[31] The melancholy haunts Moses. "Responsibility had seemed too awful to them time and again."[32] The question that opens the chapter faces the reader at every page. "So Israel was at the Jordan in every way."[33]

The prominent theme of decision occurs again with Hurston's interpretation of Deuteronomy. "Moses sat on the peak of Pisgah, looking both ways in time."[34] Here Hurston takes the geographical spatial elements of the passage and transforms them into temporal elements as well. "It was a sight such as the world had never seen before."[35] One last task for Moses was to construct his own tomb on Mount Nebo. The place of his burial would be a persistent mystery. Here Hurston seems to follow the biblical narrative. Hurston makes this more unclear than the biblical text. The novel ends with an enigmatic observation. "Then he turned with a firm tread and descended the other side of the mountain and headed back over the years."[36]

King and the Southern Christian Leadership Conference (SCLC) then organized the Poor Peoples Campaign (1968), planning another march on Washington. The sanitation workers striking in Memphis, however, asked King and SCLC for help in their nonviolent protest. On April 3, 1968—the eve of his assassination—a weary King delivered his "I See the Promised Land" speech at the Bishop Charles Mason Temple in Memphis, the headquarters of the Church of God in Christ, an African American denomination.

King sets the scene for the speech with a hypothetical panoramic view of history. God takes King to a place for this panoramic view and asks him, "What age would you like to live in?" The mental flight begins in Egypt through the Sea of Reeds to the Promise Land, but he asserts he would not stop there. Time and event after time and event, he punctuates each with the phrase "I would not stop there." Even the Emancipation Proclamation did not tempt King. He would not stop there. He says, "I would turn to the Almighty and say, 'If you will let me live for a few years in the middle of the twentieth century I will be happy.'"[37]

King stops at this point and observes that this is a strange statement to make because the world it "all messed up." He suggests that the pharaoh had a strategy to subvert the pleas for freedom from the Hebrew slaves, a strategy of dissension in the ranks to the enslaved. King then pivots and says, "When the slaves get together."[38] The theme of unity occurs in Deuteronomy, but King does not seem to refer to Deuteronomy to buttress his point here.

Embedded in the speech is the recurring phrase "All we say to America is, 'Be true to what you said on paper.'"[39] The hermeneutical move here harks back to a move in the freedom narratives such as those by Arter and Holsey. The theological underpinnings of the United States gave rise to core documents and values often violated in order to oil the mechanism of race-based capitalism, whether chattel slavery or Jim Crow.

The speech concludes with the most famous section, where King refers to being on the mountaintop. King says God had allowed him to go up "from the plains of Moab to Mount Nebo to the top of Pisgah that is across from Jericho" (34:1–4) and see the Promise Land. King takes the spatial reference and transforms it into a temporal one. Once again, King trades in a trope that has been part of African American biblical hermeneutics from an early period. The assassination of King made the speech prescient and thereby emblazoned it on the landscape of speeches in the United States for years to come.

Hurston and King used the narrative of Deuteronomy rather than the text of Deuteronomy. Hurston's Moses saw more than one mountaintop, Sinai as well as Nebo and Pisgah. Each one shaped him and his legacy. King focused on the Pisgah. Both writers, however, invited the reading community to a self-assessment, a call to action and actualization.

WHAT IS TRENDING IN THE CONVERSATION?

Readings after the Mountaintop

The post–civil rights interpreters receive another competence: the ability to move from the scaffold of African American location, tropes, and aesthetics and receive international and North American scholarship. In my own research, I move between the scaffold of African American locations, tropes, and aesthetics and the scaffold of European and North American scholarship. Bennett uses the scaffold of critical race theory (CRT) and critical legal theory (CLT) to interrogate the biblical text and scholarship.

In *Experience and Tradition: A Primer in Black Biblical Hermeneutics* (1990), I treat Deuteronomy briefly. After a short discussion of Exodus, I treat the entire book of Deuteronomy through a succinct discussion of one sermon on a small historical credo in Deuteronomy (26:4–9). I call this small historical credo an "AME Thanksgiving."

Two events shaped the origin of the African Methodist Episcopal (AME) Church. First, the AME Church grew out of the Free African Society (FAS) established by Richard Allen, Absalom Jones, and other free Africans in Philadelphia in 1787 as a self-help organization. Second, members of St. George Methodist Episcopal Church took communion segregated by race: European Americans first and then African Americans. When Richard Allen took communion with the European members, the ushers expelled him. This marked a breaking point for Allen and Jones. The rehearsal of history became a staple in AME Church practice.

Robert A. Bennett proposes that black theology and the North American biblical theology share a common scaffolding.[40] I make a similar move in my discussion of the small historical credo. Five elements from European and North American historical critical studies shape my reading. I work with four elements of the European and American scholarship.

First, I adopt the form-critical and tradition-historical work of Gerhard von Rad[41] and Martin Noth[42] looked for what today one would call the "metanarrative that shaped the Pentateuch and the Deuteronomistic History." Von Rad treats the small historical credo as an iconic, poetic, and cultic fragment. "The role of ritual and worship is to call the believer to a decision and to undergird that decision time and again."[43] These would form the *kerygma* of religious speech.

Second, I employ the proposals of the biblical theology movement as exemplified in George Ernest Wright who argued that the recital of salvation history organized ancient Israel and Judah.[44]

Third, I accept the theory that the origin of Deuteronomy in Israel migrated with the exiled priests and scribes from Samaria.[45]

Fourth, I follow the "decision" existentialist interpretation of Rudolf Bultmann and von Rad.[46]

Wright emphasized the role of recital of history—the typological reading of the exodus-conquest narrative in the United States from the colonial period to the present.[47] In a different context, Carter G. Woodson heralded the importance of rehearsing "Negro" history. The preaching of the civil rights movement traded in analogies between the civil rights movement and the movement from slavery to freedom in the Bible.

From colonial times to the present, interpreters in the United States have used the narrative of Israel and Judah as a lens to explain the fate of the United States.[48] Often these exhibit an American exceptionalism. African American denominations such as the CME Church and the AME Church respond to American racism with African American exceptionalism.[49] The call to decision parallels the move to decision in the traditional African American preaching model.[50]

Harold V. Bennett was the first African American scholar of the modern era to focus on Deuteronomy. After receiving an MDiv from the Interdenominational Theological Center, Bennett completed a PhD at Vanderbilt University. He published a revision of his dissertation on Deuteronomy (14:22–29; 26:12–15).[51] These texts mandate the allocation of grain, fruit, wine, and meat in biblical communities.

Two questions loom large for Bennett: (1) Were these stipulations followed? and (2) Would they have been helpful for the widows, strangers, and orphans they were supposedly to support? Bennett begins with the scaffolding of European and American scholarship and presents the historical-critical framework and the relevant history of research. "Conventional scholarship contends that Deut 14:22–29 and 26:12–15 worked to the advantage of and rectified the conditions of the *almanah*, *ger*, and *yatom*."[52] The historiographic and legal assumptions of this conventional wisdom depend on Enlightenment theories and legal theory that misunderstand "the role of law in ancient Israel" as well as contemporary law.

In my research, I speak out of civil rights discourse; Bennett builds on CRT and CLT, which began in the seventies in law schools. CRT is a movement that challenges the ability of conventional legal strategies to deliver social and economic justice and specifically calls for legal approaches that take race into consideration. CLT criticizes not only particular legal rules but also the social institutions which perpetuate patterns of injustice and dominance in the United States. CRT and CLT argue that that despite the law's claims to distribute power justly and equitably, it does not. Instead, the law provides an unjust and inequitable use of power by wealthy European American men.

CRT and CLT share two central interests. First, they outline how the regime of white supremacy and the subordination of people of color function in the United States. "The second is a desire not merely to understand the vexed bond between law and racial power but to *change* it."[53] Another element involves the rejection of the prevailing notion of "neutral" and "objective" scholarship. Rather, it emerges from contested and inevitably political conversations. CRT and CLT present a watershed in African American interpretation of Deuteronomy in that it has "a deep dissatisfaction with traditional civil rights discourse."[54] Bennett brings CRT and CLT to bear on these questions.

The insights about the role and function of law in contemporary settings for Bennett call for a new appreciation of the social and political context that gave rise to Deuteronomy. The law today as in antiquity links one's social features and one's socioeconomic location. He invites a re-evaluation of legal effectiveness and its impact on the regulated vulnerable social subgroups. Bennett argues against conventional wisdom about these laws. "We contend that the ethical position in Deuteronomy 14:22–29 and 26:12–15 were responses to issues that the drafters of these codes sought to prevent or restrain."[55]

The categories widow (*almanah*), stranger (*ger*), and orphan (*yatom*) share a common trait, the absence of a protection of an adult male. A clue to the special interest of the Deuteronomic Code may come from its call for centralization of worship "in the place that [the deity] chooses" (*bammaqom asher yibhar* 14: 23a+24b). Centralization produced a victimization of the widow, the stranger, and the orphan. Support from the households in their villages now gives way to more distant resources in the cultic center. The inclusion of the stipulation Deuteronomy compels the vulnerable to perceive this as an expression of divine will. According to Bennett, Deuteronomy's call for the centralization of worship cloaked the self-interests the YHWH-alone cult.[56]

The pernicious nature of these stipulations becomes obvious with the references to the triennial tithes. The language "so that they might eat their fill within your towns" (26:12b) indicates the protracted indigence of the widow, stranger, and orphan who receive only periodic assistance. Furthermore, the same tithing pattern conveys a false sense of hope for the widow, stranger, and orphan. "Working with the assumption that peasants simply did not have much food left after taking care of their daily obligations, Deuteronomy 14:22–29 and 26:12–15 simply become romantic legal injunctions."[57]

Bennett begins his treatment of Deuteronomy in the *Africana Bible* with two poems: "Mother to Son" by Langston Hughes and "The Negro National Anthem" by James Weldon Johnson. Each poem rehearses the challenges of African American life and the resilience of the community in struggle.[58] He uses these poems from the Harlem Renaissance to shed light on African American existence. More than that, they provide a North Star for African American hermeneutics in general and Deuteronomy in particular. The poems point to the hermeneutical horizon of Bennett that begins with the view from the underdog. The challenge Bennett makes methodologically provokes readers to see problems in biblical solutions that disadvantage the underdog. The African American church, according to Bennett, must bring forth the perspective of the underdog to the forefront of claims from social-service agencies ancient and contemporary as it assesses these institutions.

Conclusion

The interpretation of the freedom narratives pays attention to the language of Deuteronomy to locate the social existence of enslaved Africans. The use of the material from Zora Neale Hurston (Harlem Renaissance) and Martin Luther King Jr. (civil rights movement) picks up more on the narrative plot of Deuteronomy rather than the poetics. Bennett and Reid focus on the historical and close reading of the Hebrew text. This history of reception lifts several lessons. The earliest strata of texts make two claims. First, the depiction of Deuteronomy as primarily focused on the Shema: "Hear Oh Israel" is seen as an exhortation to complete allegiance to God. Second, a structure of the debate will claim that the United States as a Christian nation requires living according to the Bible, including admonitions for enslaved persons. The reception history would indicate reading Deuteronomy as a freedom narrative.

Notes

1. Geoffrey D. Dunn, trans., *Tertullian* (New York: Routledge, 2004); Roland J. Teske, Maureen Tilley, and Boniface Ramsey, trans., *Augustine's Doctrinal Writings: A Translation for the 21st Century*, 9 vols. (New York: New York City Press, 1995).
2. David E. Wilhite, *Ancient African Christianity: An Introduction to a Unique Context and Tradition* (London: Routledge, 2017).
3. Dwight N. Hopkins and George Cummings, eds., *Cut Loose the Stammering Tongue: Black Theology in the Slave Narratives* (Maryknoll: Orbis, 1992); Dwight N. Hopkins, *Shoes That Fit Our Feet: Sources for a Constructive Black Theology* (Maryknoll: Orbis, 1993); Dwight N. Hopkins, *Down, Up, and Over: Slave Religion and Black Theology* (Minneapolis: Fortress, 2000).
4. Gerald O. West, ed., *Reading Other-Wise: Socially Engaged Biblical Scholars Reading with Their Local Communities*, Semeia Studies 62 (Atlanta: SBL Press, 2007).
5. Emerson B. Powery and Rodney Steven Sadler, *The Genesis of Liberation: Biblical Interpretation in the Antebellum Narratives of the Enslaved* (Louisville: Westminster John Knox, 2016), 1.
6. James Wilkerson, *Wilkerson's History of His Travels & Labors, in the United States, as a Missionary in Particular, that of Union Seminary, in Franklin Ohio. Since He Purchased His Liberty* (Columbus, 1861), 27.
7. English translations throughout are from the New Revised Standard Version (1989).
8. Aaron, *The Light and Truth of Slavery: Aaron's History* (Worcester, 1845), 33.
9. Jared Maurice Arter, *Echoes from a Pioneer Life* (Atlanta: A.B. Caldwell Publishing Company, 1922), 102–103.
10. Arter, *Echoes from a Pioneer Life*, 103.
11. Arter, *Echoes from a Pioneer Life*, 90.
12. Lucius Henry Holsey, *Autobiography, Sermons, Addresses and Essays of Bishop L.H. Holsey, DD* (Atlanta: Franklin, 1898), 194f.
13. Holsey, *Autobiography*, 195.
14. Meredith Malburne, https://docsouth.unc.edu/neh/wilkerson/summary.html

15. Major James Wilkerson, *Wilkerson's History of His Travels & Labors, in the United States, As a Missionary, in Particular, That of the Union Seminary, Located in Franklin Co., Ohio, Since He Purchased His Liberty in New Orleans, La. &c.* (Columbus, 1861), 33.
16. John C. Calhoun, "Speech on the Reception of Abolition Petitions, Delivered in the Senate, February 6th, 1837," in *Speeches of John C. Calhoun, Delivered in the House of Representatives and in the Senate of the United States*, ed. Richard R. Cralle (New York: D. Appleton, 1853), 625–633.
17. Boyrereau Brinch and Benjamin F. Prentiss (Benjamin Franklin), *The Blind African Slave, or Memoirs of Boyrereau Brinch, Nick-named Jeffrey Brace. Containing an Account of the Kingdom of Bow-Woo, in the Interior of Africa; with the Climate and Natural Productions, Laws, and Customs Peculiar to That Place. With an Account of His Captivity, Sufferings, Sales, Travels, Emancipation, Conversion to the Christian Religion, Knowledge of the Scriptures, &c. Interspersed with Strictures on Slavery, Speculative Observations on the Qualities of Human Nature, with Quotation from Scripture* (St. Albans: Printed by Harry Whitney, 1810).
18. John Dixon Long, *Pictures of Slavery in Church and State; Including Personal Reminiscences, Biographical Sketches, Anecdotes, etc. etc. with an Appendix, Containing the Views of John Wesley and Richard Watson on Slavery* (Philadelphia, 1857), 127.
19. John Dixon Long, https://www.wikiwand.com/en/John_Dixon_Long
20. J. Vance Lewis, *Out of the Ditch: A True Story of an Ex-Slave* (Houston: Rein & Sons, 1910), 126.
21. Elleanor Eldridge, *Memoirs of Elleanor Eldridge* (Providence: B.T. Albro, 1838), 100f.
22. Robert E. Hemenway, *Zora Neale Hurston: A Literary Biography* (Chicago: University of Illinois, 1977), 256.
23. Hemenway, *Zora Neale Hurston*, 257.
24. Hemenway, *Zora Neale Hurston*, 259.
25. Morris, "Hurston's *Moses, Man of the Mountain*," 315.
26. Robert J. Morris, "Zora Neale Hurston's Ambitious Enigma: Moses, Man of the Mountain," *College Language Association Journal* 40 (March 1997): 308.
27. Morris, "Hurston's *Moses, Man of the Mountain*," 319.
28. Hemenway, *Zora Neale Hurston*, 260.
29. Zora Neale Hurston, *Moses, Man of the Mountain* (Chicago: University of Illinois Press, 1984), 338.
30. Hurston, *Moses, Man on the Mountain*, 344.
31. Hemenway, *Zora Neale Hurston*, 268.
32. Hurston, *Moses, Man on the Mountain*, 345.
33. Hurston, *Moses, Man on the Mountain*, 347.
34. Hurston, *Moses, Man on the Mountain*, 343. This anticipates the rhetorical move Martin Luther King Jr. will make in his speech "I See the Promised Land."
35. Hurston, *Moses, Man of the Mountain*, 344.
36. Hurston, *Moses, Man of the Mountain*, 351.
37. Martin Luther King Jr., "I See the Promised Land," in *Testament of Hope: The Essential Writings of Martin Luther King Jr.*, ed. James M. Washington (San Francisco: Harper & Row, 1986), 280.
38. King, "I See the Promised Land," 280f.
39. King, "I See the Promised Land," 282.
40. Robert A. Bennett, "Biblical Theology and Black Theology," *Journal of the Interdenominational Theological Center* 3, no. 2 (Spring 1976): 1–16.

41. Gerhard von Rad, "The Form Critical Problem of the Hexateuch," in *The Problem of the Pentateuch and Other Essays* (New York: McGraw-Hill, 1966), 1–78.
42. Martin Noth, *History of Pentateuchal Traditions* (Englewood Cliffs: Prentice Hall, 1972); Martin Noth, *The Deuteronomistic History* (Sheffield: Journal for the Study of the Old Testament Press, 1981).
43. Stephen Breck Reid, *Experience and Tradition: A Primer in Black Biblical Hermeneutics* (Nashville: Abingdon, 1990), 73.
44. G. Ernest Wright, *God Who Acts: Biblical Theology as Recital* (Chicago: H. Regnery, 1952). See also Brevard Childs, *Biblical Theology in Crisis* (Philadelphia: Westminster Press, 1970).
45. E. W. Nicholson, *Deuteronomy and Tradition* (Philadelphia: Fortress Press, 1967), 58–82.
46. Rudolf Bultmann, "Man under Faith," *Theology of the New Testament* 1: 302 (New York: Charles Scribner's Sons, 1955), 301.
47. George Ernest Wright, *Biblical Theology and Recital* (Chicago: H Regnery, 1952).
48. Conrad Cherry, ed., *God's New Israel, Religious Interpretations of American Destiny* (Chapel Hill: University of North Carolina Press, 1998).
49. Cornel West, *Prophesy Deliverance: An Afro-American Revolutionary Christianity* (Philadelphia: Westminster Press, 1982), 70.
50. Kenyatta R. Gilbert, *The Journey and Promise of African American Preaching* (Minneapolis: Fortress, 2011), 7.
51. Harold V. Bennett, *Injustice Made Legal: Deuteronomic Law and the Plight of Widows, Strangers, and Orphans in Ancient Israel* (Grand Rapids: Wm B Eerdmans, 2002).
52. Harold V. Bennett, "Triennial Tithes and the Underdog: A Revisionist Reading of Deuteronomy 14:22–29 and 26: 12–15," in *Yet with a Steady Beat: Contemporary U.S. Afrocentric Biblical Interpretation*, ed. Randall C. Bailey (Atlanta: Society of Biblical Literature, 2003), 11.
53. Kimberlé Crenshaw, Neil Gotanda, Gary Peller, and Kendall Thomas, eds., *Critical Race Theory: The Key Writings That Formed the Movement* (New York: New Press, 1995), xiii.
54. Crenshaw, *Critical Race Theory*, xiv.
55. Bennett, "Triennial Tithes," 13–14.
56. Bennett, "Triennial Tithes and the Underdog," 14–15.
57. Bennett, "Triennial Tithes and the Underdog," 16–17.
58. Harold V. Bennett, "Deuteronomy," in *The Africana Bible: Reading Israel's Scriptures from Africa and the African Diaspora*, ed. Hugh R. Page, Jr. et al. (Minneapolis: Fortress, 2010), 100–101.

Bibliography

Aaron. *The Light and Truth of Slavery: Aaron's History*. Worcester, 1845.

Arter, Jared Maurice. *Echoes from a Pioneer Life*. Atlanta: A.B. Caldwell Publishing Company, 1922.

Bennett, Harold V. "Deuteronomy." In *The Africana Bible: Reading Israel's Scriptures from Africa and the African Diaspora*, edited by Hugh R. Page, Jr. et al. Minneapolis: Fortress, 2010.

Bennett, Harold V. *Injustice Made Legal: Deuteronomic Law and the Plight of Widows, Strangers, and Orphans in Ancient Israel*. Grand Rapids: Wm B. Eerdmans, 2002.

Bennett, Harold V. "Triennial Tithes and the Underdog: A Revisionist Reading of Deuteronomy 14:22–29 and 26: 12–15." In *Yet with a Steady Beat: Contemporary U.S. Afrocentric Biblical Interpretation*, edited by Randall C. Bailey, 7–18. Atlanta: Society of Biblical Literature, 2003.

Bennett, Robert A. "Biblical Theology and Black Theology." *Journal of the Interdenominational Theological Center* 3, no. 2 (Spring 1976): 1–16.

Bennett Jr., Lerone. *Before the Mayflower: A History of the Negro in America, 1619–1962.* Chicago: Johnson, 1962.

Boyrereau, Brinch, and Benjamin F. Prentiss (Benjamin Franklin). *The Blind African Slave, or Memoirs of Boyrereau Brinch, Nick-named Jeffrey Brace. Containing an Account of the Kingdom of Bow-Woo, in the Interior of Africa; with the Climate and Natural Productions, Laws, and Customs Peculiar to That Place. With an Account of His Captivity, Sufferings, Sales, Travels, Emancipation, Conversion to the Christian Religion, Knowledge of the Scriptures, &c. Interspersed with Strictures on Slavery, Speculative Observations on the Qualities of Human Nature, with Quotation from Scripture.* St. Albans: Printed by Harry Whitney, 1810.

Bultmann, Rudolf. "Man under Faith." *Theology of the New Testament* 1: 302. New York: Charles Scribner's Sons, 1955.

Calhoun, John C. "Speech on the Reception of Abolition Petitions, Delivered in the Senate, February 6th, 1837." In *Speeches of John C. Calhoun, Delivered in the House of Representatives and in the Senate of the United States*, edited by Richard R. Cralle, 625–633. New D. Appleton, 1853.

Cherry, Conrad, ed. "Front Matter." In *God's New Israel*, i–vi. Religious Interpretations of American Destiny. Chapel Hill: University of North Carolina Press, 1998. www.jstor.org/stable/10.5149/9780807866580_cherry.1

Childs, Brevard. *Biblical Theology in Crisis.* Philadelphia: Westminster Press, 1970.

Crenshaw, Kimberlé, Neil Gotanda, Gary Peller, and Kendall Thomas, eds. *Critical Race Theory: The Key Writings That Formed the Movement.* New York: New Press, 1995.

Dunn, Geoffrey D., trans. *Tertullian.* New York: Routledge, 2004.

Eldridge, Elleanor. *Memoirs of Elleanor Eldridge.* Providence: B.T. Albro, 1838.

Gilbert, Kenyatta R. *The Journey and Promise of African American Preaching.* Minneapolis: Fortress, 2011.

Hemenway, Robert E. *Zora Neale Hurston: A Literary Biography.* Chicago: University of Illinois, 1977.

Holsey, Lucius Henry. *Autobiography, Sermons, Addresses and Essays of Bishop L.H. Holsey, DD.* Atlanta: Franklin, 1898.

Hopkins, Dwight N., *Down, Up, and Over: Slave Religion and Black Theology.* Minneapolis: Fortress, 2000.

Hopkins, Dwight N., *Shoes Rhat Fit Our Feet: Sources for a Constructive Black Theology.* Maryknoll: Orbis, 1993.

Hopkins, Dwight N., and George Cummings, eds. *Cut Loose the Stammering Tongue: Black Theology in the Slave Narratives.* Maryknoll: Orbis, 1992.

King Jr., Martin Luther. "I See the Promised Land." In *Testament of Hope: The Essential Writings of Martin Luther King Jr.*, edited by James M. Washington, 279–288. San Francisco: Harper & Row, 1986.

Long, John Dixon. *Pictures of Slavery in Church and State; Including Personal Reminiscences, Biographical Sketches, Anecdotes, etc. etc. with an Appendix, Containing the Views of John Wesley and Richard Watson on Slavery.* Philadelphia, 1857.

Morris, Robert J. "Zora Neale Hurston's Ambitious Enigma: Moses, Man of the Mountain." *College Language Association Journal* 40, no. 3 (March 1997): 305–335.

Nicholson, E. W. *Deuteronomy and Tradition*. Philadelphia: Fortress Press, 1967.

Noth, Martin. *The Deuteronomistic History*. Sheffield: Journal for the Study of the Old Testament Press, 1981.

Noth, Martin. *History of Pentateuchal Traditions*. Englewood Cliffs: Prentice Hall, 1972.

Powery, Emerson B., and Rodney S. Sadler Jr. *The Genesis of Liberation: Biblical Interpretation in the Antebellum Narratives of the Enslaved*. Louisville: Westminster John Knox, 2016.

Reid, Stephen Breck. *Experience and Tradition: A Primer in Black Biblical Hermeneutics*. Nashville: Abingdon, 1990.

Vance, Lewis, J. *Out of the Ditch: A True Story of an Ex-Slave*. Houston: Rein & Sons, 1910.

von Rad, Gerhard. "The Form Critical Problem of the Hexateuch." In *The Problem of the Pentateuch and Other Essays*, 1–78. New York: McGraw-Hill, 1966.

Teske, Roland J., Maureen Tilley, and Boniface Ramsey, trans. *Augustine's Doctrinal Writings: A Translation for the 21st Century*. 9 vols. New York: New York City Press, 1995.

West, Cornel. *Prophesy Deliverance: An Afro-American Revolutionary Christianity*. Philadelphia: Westminster Press, 1982.

West, Gerald O., ed. *Reading Other-Wise: Socially Engaged Biblical Scholars Reading with Their Local Communities*. Semeia Studies 62. Atlanta: SBL Press, 2007.

Wilhite, David E. *Ancient African Christianity: An Introduction to a Unique Context and Tradition*. London: Routledge, 2017.

Wilkerson, James. *Wilkerson's History of His Travels & Labors, in the United States, as a Missionary in Particular, that of Union Seminary, in Franklin Ohio. Since he Purchased his Liberty*. Columbus, 1861.

Wright, G. Ernest. *God Who Acts: Biblical Theology as Recital*. Chicago: H. Regnery, 1952.

CHAPTER 28

LATIN AMERICAN LIBERATION THEOLOGY AS A RESPONSE TO DEUTERONOMY

MERCEDES GARCÍA BACHMANN

Who Began the Conversation?

Before the Conversation: Postcolonial Latin America?

A conversation leading to a mutual conversion between Deuteronomy and its readers in Latin America is no more than fifty years old. What is postcolonial Latin America and why would it matter enough to ensure a chapter in such a distinguished volume? This is no minute issue and, certainly, one this writer has been pondering.

Most Spanish-speaking Latin Americans would take "Latin America" to mean, like themselves, Spanish speakers or, the most, Portuguese speakers. This continent, however, also includes some countries which do not speak either language; or at least some islands are still under British colonial rule. We could also speak of US military bases in the continent, but the point is made that "postcolonial Latin America" is not easily defined. These lands mean also home for many nations within those countries, which have managed to keep their indigenous languages, despite being ignored or persecuted by the majorities that benefitted from colonization by European empires. Colonization benefits go from large economic advantages, such as land ownership, to seemingly minor issues, such as belonging to the majority culture or never having to face legal or health instances in a foreign, ignorant, or hostile hegemonic milieu.

At least in my country, Argentina, another benefit of colonization is the financial and symbolic state support of Roman Catholicism by the Constitution. An example of this symbiosis is the discussion during 2018 of a law to legalize abortion in certain circumstances. These discussions evidenced that even in matters of public concern and of women's bodies' autonomy, religious convictions and threats play a key role. Not only that: they were valid means to impose religious groups' values, whose spokespersons are in the vast majority male and patriarchal, on a nation with diverse population in many aspects.

It is a case study because also Deuteronomy ties together these three aspects, the political, the societal/community, and religious ideas about YHWH's will for the people. Also long-standing, although not certainly now considered original, interpretations of Deuteronomy are institutionalized in the ethical and political policies of Catholic Christianity, and Christianity is still regarded by many as the continent's religion. One thing is clear: reading Deuteronomy's urging to be one nation with one God in my context is a challenge!

Postcolonial Latin America Starts Talking to and with Deuteronomy

Considering the central role of cult centralization, it is surprising how little Deuteronomy has appealed and still appeals to Latin American biblical scholars. Many of our resources are produced at grassroots levels, and we lack centralized repositories of journals, and thus it is hard to track regional sources. Still, books and articles on Deuteronomy in Latin America are few.[1] In these pages I will try to share and assess what has been and is being produced by scholars living in Spanish-speaking countries and Brazil. Since my interest is on a Latin American reading, bibliographical references to sources from other parts of the world will be made, but not discussed.

I venture to state that, as often, there is no single starting point for autochthonous biblical studies in this continent. On the one hand, shortly after the Second Vatican Council (1962-1965), Pope Paul VI convened a Latin American conference of bishops in Medellín, Colombia (1968). This meeting is the birth certificate of liberation theology. On the other hand, Protestants were seeking their own identity between their European origins, their Latin American identities, and their bigger sister, Roman Catholicism. The Medellín documents identify the poor of the continent—the vast majority of whom was at the time Roman Catholic—with the Church. The contribution of Protestants lies especially in that they started from their context, from which they read the Scriptures and did theology. Their methodology, still largely used, consists of *ver-juzgar-actuar*: the socio-analytical mediation raises issues concerning systemic poverty (*ver* = see), the hermeneutical mediation seeks God's pertinent word for these situations (*juzgar* = discern), and the practical mediation leads to engagement in the political arena (*actuar* = take action).[2] Within this new church, what is called *lectura popular de la Biblia*—people's reading of the Bible—in ecclesial base communities blossomed. Meantime, Protestant churches had started to prepare their first indigenous biblical scholars. These scholars—mostly men—came back to Latin America, with graduate degrees earned abroad in the early 1980s. Roman Catholics and Protestants identified with the poor started to meet and read the Bible together and with local folks.

Even though none of these scholars focused on Deuteronomy, they deserve our appreciation for opening the way to what we are able to produce today, with a particular worldview, which could be generally labeled Latin American liberation theology. They built bridges between theological studies in Europe or the United States and Latin America, taught at different places for decades, produced a good number of books and articles, directed several theses and dissertations, were active in founding or keeping alive biblical journals, and, in general, parented critical, ecumenical, Liberation biblical studies in Latin America.

Although there are a few female theologians who belong to this pioneering generation of Latin American scholars, they did not teach Bible in the recognized schools—if they could get permission to teach theology at all—and, in general, worked more on pastoral issues, literature, languages, or pedagogics; or in base communities, religious high schools, and places other than universities or seminaries. Ana Flora Anderson—the only female named!—) appears often when reference is made to the first Latin American Christian biblical scholars in Brazil. It has been difficult to identify her own contribution, since she does not seem to have published much on her own. I will mention four Old Testament scholars and only paint a few brushstrokes about each one.

José Severino Croatto was from Argentina. He studied in Rome and the Holy Land. He was Roman Catholic but taught at the Protestant seminary in Buenos Aires (ISEDET) from 1975 until his death in 2004. Croatto specialized in Semitic languages, Genesis, Isaiah, hermeneutics, and the phenomenology of religion. It would not be an exaggeration to state that he left disciples throughout the whole continent, for each one of us who studied at ISEDET was deeply influenced by him.[3]

Of about the same period is Armando J. Levoratti, also from Argentina, who studied also in Rome and in Chicago. Levoratti was related to the Roman Catholic seminary in La Plata, Argentina, from 1960 until his death in 2016. In the last decades he oversaw the edition of several large Latin American biblical commentaries. In the 1980s Levoratti accomplished the titanic deed of translating the whole Old Testament into what became "the Argentinean version" of the Bible. In recent years, many of us, Roman Catholic and Protestant Latin American younger scholars, were invited by Levoratti to revise that earlier translation and provide updated study notes and introductions.[4]

Another scholar long related to and identified with Latin America is George V. Pixley, who grew up in Nicaragua from Baptist missionary parents. As far as I know, he has not written on Deuteronomy. Pixley published a history of Israel as seen from the poor, with a few references to Deuteronomy and the Deuteronomistic history.[5] Walter Brueggemann includes him as a Central American liberation theologian. According to Brueggemann, Pixley considered his best book that on Exodus.[6] He died in 2023.

The last name to mention here is that of Milton Schwantes, from Brazil, who did his PhD in Heidelberg, on the right of the poor in the prophets, a love he never abandoned. He taught at the Lutheran and Methodist seminaries in Brazil, from 1978 to his death in 2012. Schwantes has a long history as a father figure, formally advising students in their dissertation stages and more informally in fostering biblical studies in the continent. According to Fabio Almeida, together with Ana F. Anderson, Carlos Mesters, José Comblin, and Gilberto Gorgulho, Milton was one of these first scholars to come back with a graduate degree and start liberation theology biblical studies.[7]

After finishing graduate studies, all these scholars took up again grassroots-level work in their own communities, along with teaching at seminaries. They kept a balance between sound academic scholarship, engaged community work, teaching, and mentoring younger generations. In the political turmoil of the 1960s and 1970s, Deuteronomy was not central for any of these theologians but, at best, part of a larger set of texts and themes, such as land reform, God's preference for the poor, and increasing exploitation of people by capitalism. This same trend continues today: for most of us in Latin America, writing comes together with—often after—grassroots work. This grassroots, pastoral work still determines our interests and often also our possibilities. Most of us find it a luxury to engage in research for the sake of research and not for the sake of concrete peoples' needs—or we write out of particular invitations from scholars of the North-Atlantic academic world, as happens to be what brings me, with gratitude, to explore what might be a Latin American view on Deuteronomy.

What Is the Status of the Conversation?

After that pioneering generation, conversation between Deuteronomy and Latin America started to develop very timidly in our lands. Brazil has a comparatively large number of students doing graduate studies abroad in Germany, Rome, or the United States, who still teach or have recently retired in several universities in their own country. Georg Braulik, Eckart Otto, Frank Crüsemann, and Norman Gottwald have all mentored Latin American scholars of Deuteronomy. In this section I will refer to scholars who have contributed to a postcolonial Latin American theology of liberation and who have, in that conversation, dealt with pertinent themes, and thus I will share snippets of conversation topics between Deuteronomy and Latin American biblical scholars.

Concern for the Poor

Reviewing scholars' production, it has become apparent that concern for oppressed and despised groups, either in socioeconomic—"the poor"—or, more recently, cultural terms—"the Other"—is one of the most important engines for scholars engaged in liberation theology on this continent.[8]

Concern for gender oppression is also key for change on this continent, as will become clear when we review recent conversations. Heteronormative and cisgender groups are key producers of "Others" in our societies. Even though Deuteronomy does not address gender in a thorough way, it takes part of this conversation and keeps promoting a binary worldview. For instance, some women are grouped with children and animals as passive objects to be protected as Israelites. Some women are to be taken or destroyed (3:6-7, 19; 20:14). A different example of gender bias is legislation where the only subject of actions is the male. He takes additional wives, and then prefers one over the other (21:15-17).

Gender is not the only binary category in Deuteronomy. Israel and the nations from whom they are to take over the land are one of the overarching binaries (1:1-3:29).

If we are to speak of leading scholars, one name we cannot miss is that of Haroldo Reimer, because of his own work, mainly on the Pentateuchal legislation and Amos. He has written on the different sabbatical laws allowing impoverished Israelites to attain their freedom again on the Jubilee year.[9] Reimer is a disciple of Frank Crüsemann, as may be seen, for instance, in his adoption of Crüsemann's concentric structure of the Deuteronomistic Code.

According to Reimer and Crüsemann, around the center of the code (19:1-21:9), which deals with issues of life/death, we find the laws concerning tithing (14:22-26; 26:12-15).

The whole code is "prefaced by 12:1–14:21, also very important symbolically, as it sets the condition of holiness and avoidance of idolatry that will color the whole book."[10] This is an important insight because holiness and idolatry are not perceived only as religious adherence, but as markers of ethical decisions for or against the most needed among Israel. This link between ethical and cultic aspects of life is also explored by other scholars, as we will see. Reimer's study is also significant for us because here we can see how a concern for justice merges with concern for ecojustice, a theme he has been contributing to in the last decades.

Another scholar from this intermediate generation, Carlos A. Dreher, believes Deuteronomy stems from peasants and prophets from the northern kingdom of Israel. Studying the last two laws which allow people to eat from the neighbor's grapes or grain if hungry (23: 25–26 [Eng. 24–25]), Dreher notes how interlinked kings' power, laws, and YHWH are. These interrelationships could work to bring peasants back to slavery or to protect them:

> Together with YHWH's uniqueness and demand for one only place of worship, Deuteronomy strives to avoid the impoverishment and subsequent enslavement of farmworkers. Fight against idolatry reflects this intention. Only YHWH, who took you out of Egypt, from the house of slavery, can guarantee that farm workers, ever more constrained to pay taxation, will survive. [...] The power of weapons, international commerce, and luxurious life at court had their utmost expressions under [Solomon, Ahab, and Jeroboam II]. These things bring the people back to Egypt. Therefore, it is necessary to limit the king's power (17, 14–20).[11]

Pedro Kramer, who earned his PhD in 1999, wanted to find "the interdependence between the liturgical and the socio-economic legislation and not to show it as a kind of juxtaposition or as two co-existing areas."[12] His contention is that the legislator intended to "finish with the reality of social classes and excluded, marginalized, impoverished, and oppressed people through his legal code in Dt 12–28." In his view, the vision of a society without poor (5:1–33) has been made explicit and complemented by new legislation (12–28).[13] Kramer notes that "the dt legislator [...] sets up these two pericopes [26:1–11 and 12–13] as a closing molding to Dt 14,22–29."[14] While the same commandment to share the triennial tithe opens and closes this block (26:12–13), the prescribed ritual in the temple precincts involves an oath of having "annihilated (driven away) from my house the holy and given it to the Levite, the resident-alien, the orphan, and the widow" (26:3).[15]

One of the few women who have entered this discussion is Patricia Pizzorno, who wrote her master's thesis on the concept of blessing in selected texts from the Pentateuch.[16] She notes that Deuteronomy wants to see not social classes, but "brothers." I concur with her perception that the legislators of Deuteronomy wanted to stress the idea of siblings from each household sharing with siblings in need from the abundance of YHWH's gifts, particularly through the prescribed festivals.[17] Even though using "brother" for someone who is not kin is for most people today strange if not suspect of evangelical jargon, the idea of seeing the other in need as kin could be one of Deuteronomy's contributions to our broken world.

Preoccupation with the "brother in need" has been one of the engines that moved scholarship on Deuteronomy in this part of the Americas. This should not come as a surprise, since liberation theology, with its Marxist analysis of social processes, has left its imprint on theological studies in the continent.

In the same line, another contribution comes from a scholar from Costa Rica, José Enrique Ramírez Kidd, who wrote his PhD dissertation on the Hebrew term גר *gēr* ("resident alien") in the Bible. Obviously, this is not a work only on Deuteronomy; still, he offers much important information on our book, for Deuteronomy cares for the *gērîm*—resident aliens. Ramírez Kidd shows the term has several meanings depending of factors such as whether it appears alone or in the triad "resident alien, orphan, widow." There are also differences when it is used as verb or as noun, in the Deuteronomic Code, the Holiness Code, and so on. I found particularly pertinent his conclusion that the appearance of the triad is the legislators' effort to promote solidarity in times of political turmoil:

> The combination of the noun גר with the pair "widow–orphan" in the laws given on behalf of the triad. "גר–orphan–widow," is a novelty of Deuteronomy which brought together persons who were in a similar situation of need. The inclusion of the widow and the orphan in these laws can be explained in relation to the increasing urbanisation which took place in Israel during the Iron IIb period (900–700 BC). Formerly the provision for the needs of widows and orphans was a family matter, there was no need for legal measures to provide for them. Such measures became necessary only when the old forms of solidarity were substituted by individualism and orphans and widows lost the natural support of their families. The emergence of the noun גר as a legal term is related to the need for a generic nominal term to designate in the laws, the status of immigrants settled in Israel after the fall of Samaria in 721 BC. This term attempts to preserve Israel's identity in situations of political turmoil, in which immigrants were to be accepted as having similar rights and duties as those of the native citizens. This noun functioned, on the one hand, as an internal boundary between the native members of the Israelite community and those newly accepted and, on the other hand, as a sort of external boundary of the community in relation to other immigrants, whose religious practices were commonly perceived as a threat to their own material security and religious purity.[18]

Out of the same concerns, my own dissertation touched briefly on Deuteronomy.[19] My interest is on poor female workers and how texts appraise them. Male and female workers are conspicuous throughout the whole Bible, but there is hardly any substantial amount of data in any single book. Within the Deuteronomistic History frame, I dealt with some laws in Deuteronomy, especially on slavery (5:14–21; 15:12–18; 16:9–15; 23:16–17), on the captive wife (21:10–14), and on a prostitute's fee to the temple (23:18 [Eng. 19]).

Most Latin American scholars study the large issues in Deuteronomy, such as its probable origin, the worship of YHWH alone, the concern for hungry peasants and for the causes of hunger, but not within an encompassing study of the whole book.

To confirm the panorama already painted, let me finish this section by stating that the only scholar who has entered a conversation with the whole book of Deuteronomy is Edesio Sánchez Cetina, a scholar from Mexico. In his annotated bibliography, he states about one of his sources: "Not a biblical commentary, but an introduction to Latin American reality from a Christian perspective. It is of great importance for reading the Bible from the social-historic Latin American context."[20] Again, in Sánchez Cetina's bibliography, one may see that most of what has been produced on this continent responds to particular concerns, that is, theses and articles on the Ten Commandments, the Sabbath, poverty, or ecology, rather than books on Deuteronomy as a whole.

A Noteworthy Scarcity: Female Scholars

So far, few female scholars in Latin America have had a conversation leading to a mutual conversion with Deuteronomy. There are several reasons for this scarcity.

First, one should not imagine large numbers of universities and scholars, because that is not this continent's reality. Very few countries have divinity schools in their universities, and most theological schools are privately administered; and from these, the majority belongs to the Roman Catholic Church—yet another residue of our colonial history. Although several Pentecostal and other evangelical groups grew in the last decades, most of these churches are suspicious of academic theology. Mainstream Protestant churches have or had theological schools, either on their own or with other sister churches; but again, we should not imagine many.

A second reason for the scarcity of women in dialogue with Deuteronomy is the scarcity of women in the Latin American academic world in general and in areas such as Bible or systematic theology. We could spend pages on reasons and excuses; let us just use the shortcut "patriarchy" to explain it.

Also, like most of our male colleagues, those of us who are engaged in Old Testament studies have touched on Deuteronomy as we argued some other issue, rather than concentrate on the whole book. For instance, Elizabeth Cook (Steike), from Guatemala, teaches at the Universidad Bíblica Latinoamerica in Costa Rica. She has written only one article on Deuteronomy, and it is on the water crisis.[21]

The acute observation of Milton Schwantes might apply here. Asked for the reasons to have postponed for years translating his dissertation into Portuguese, he answered: "We don't love ourselves much; we have introjected fragmentation and therefore we do not value much what we produce."[22] Here we could learn from Deuteronomy, in that it sets Israel at the center of YHWH's favor out of sheer favor and not out of any merit (4:37–39; 6:1–25; 10:14–15).

WHAT IS TRENDING IN THE CONVERSATION?

Ever Classic and Ever Pertinent: Social Justice

Is it possible to read Deuteronomy both as imperial propaganda and as concerned with the oppressed? Yes. Both the oppressor and the oppressed find traditions in Deuteronomy to interpret their own social agendas. This is no surprise, since the Bible suffers a hermeneutical process by which it becomes independent from its author's (or authors') intention for creating it. Deuteronomy is, itself, proof of such variety in hermeneutical processes! As so many other biblical texts, Deuteronomy has been used both to oppress and to liberate, to speak of love and to remark on separation. The very concept of a covenant conjures up both the idea of equity or partnership and the idea of imposition, depending on how power is negotiated between the partners. Not only that: in evaluating a covenant our own ideology also plays a role. For instance, today poor countries' governments generate enormous debts with the International Monetary Fund and the World Bank. Apart from being predators, the fact that a large part of those moneys goes to corrupt pockets and not to the country's development makes them ethically highly problematic. Yet not only are they legal in the international arena, but some of the people who are to pay dearly for moneys they will not get would say, "We have to honor our debts." Indeed, covenants must be fulfilled or its sanctions fall upon the culprit (28:15–68).

Treaties impose obligations; the degree to which they benefit the weaker partner makes all the difference in how they should be evaluated. This is where Deuteronomy may be read as life-giving. Quite the contrary to most present-day covenants we are subjected to, YHWH offers a covenant of love and liberation rather than abuse of its weaker partner, Israel (7:6–8). All the same, Israel—rulers and people—is to keep its part of the bargain and take care of its resident aliens, orphans, widows, Levites, and dependents and keep away from other deities. Many Latin American scholars have accepted the claim that Josiah's reform was a cry for liberation from Assyrian bondage, wrapped in exodus language, for instance, in the reason for a sabbatical rest (5:12–15) and in YHWH's claim to be Israel's only lord (16:1–7).

Deuteronomy in the Bible today may have evolved in as many as six socioeconomic settings between 1200 and 332 BCE. This long span partly explains why one may interpret Deuteronomy in so many ways; why there are laws in favor of life for the poor and laws that call for massive killings.[23] Politics and religion come together and affect community when the Passover celebration is seen in the light of people's oppression under an earthly power opposite to YHWH. This becomes an important motif for our continent, in which life with enough food, a better redistribution of resources, and dignity is much needed. Yet we do not face foreign colonial rule from which to liberate our countries, but rather theft and/or poisoning of natural resources; economic sanctions that cause hunger and poverty over countries and peoples; neoliberal financial policies deepening the chasm between rich and poor; internal corruption; and increasing involvement of religious conservative groups in state politics.

> How to rescue this subversive memory of the Passover celebration in order to feed the Latin American peoples' struggles for liberation? What image, what understanding of God is conveyed to the people of our continent? What interests are played behind the scenes when attempts are made to manipulate Latin American people's religion?[24]

Deuteronomy's command to observe Passover for YHWH and Passover's potential for liberation raise a warning at a time when religious groups throughout the continent are claiming political power. These religious groups, however, belong to conservative denominations and are consciously or unconsciously allied to the neoliberal agenda. They stand opposite to liberation theology, with its option for the oppressed and against oppressive systems and in general attribute merits or maladies to individual moralistic behavior, not to systemic injustice.

One example of misuse of texts against the poor may be the treatment of the law on tithes. As noted by several scholars, the annual tithe is to be taken to the sanctuary by every family and be eaten there by that whole extended family and others in need (14:22–29).[25] Today, however, giving an institution the tenth of one's income has become a mark of being a Christian in several churches and pseudo-churches. While discernment of how to convert Deuteronomy's "tithe of your grain, your new wine, and your oil" (12:17) to money is certainly arduous, at this point I would not argue for or against it as such. What concerns me is that, when used by preachers of the "prosperity gospel"—of whom there are too many on this continent—it means large amounts of money coming to organizations that have no interest whatsoever in social justice in exchange for promises of material individual prosperity for the giver. A biblical teaching on justice within the covenantal framework is turned into a law expected to be blindly obeyed by exploitative religion.[26] In the continent with a deep gap between rich and poor, redistribution of wealth is an issue Deuteronomy can teach us about; yet it requires far more than endowing churches and pseudo-churches with monetary tithes.

While Kramer's interest lies in how, by relating the ritual laws to the socioeconomic laws, the legislator sought to prevent social inequality and inclusion of the poor in the system, another scholar from Brazil, Fábio Py Murta de Almeida, shows that justice is much more than sharing tithes. He deals with the commandment to keep the Sabbath and concludes that the return to "you" (6:15) is a homogenizing element showing the real interest of the legislator. This "you" is not the slave or the foreigner—or even the son!. This "you" is a landed peasant who meets at the gates with other landed peasants— the 'am ha'aretz or "people of the land"—and who owns and cares for his means of production. A bonus of the commandment is rest for slaves and foreigners, but the law is not concerned with them but with the owners' interests, namely, the land and the means of production.[27]

Not every partner in this dialogue with Deuteronomy is an easy goer. Fernando Candido seeks to bring to attention discordant elements --"collisions of memories"—within "the rhetorical contract" that is Deuteronomy. In his words:

> I evaluate the particularity of each struggle to encourage a subaltern agenda that promotes the social justice of recognition and redistribution. The "abominable and per/verted alliance" intra-Deuteronomy proposes a radically democratic communitarian ethos (i) in favor of an open culture to the Other and (ii) against authoritarian pyramidal structures. Therefore, I note that these dual tactics place the imperial values of hierarchy and subtraction [sic] of the "Deuteronomic brotherhood" in the community's debate.[28]

All these scholars are concerned with those excluded by the socioeconomic and the religious systems and those who, in the name of YHWH, exclude these or those, namely, the hegemonic groups of followers of YHWH, those whom the Torah addressed as "you" in Deuteronomy and those who read Deuteronomy today. While Kramer thinks of the socioeconomic poor – Levites, slaves, widows—Almeida explores the system's self-preservation, and Candido is concerned with the many representations of people as perverted or as "Other." Kramer and Pizzorno emphasize the brother; Almeida emphasizes the "you" of the law, and Candido deconstructs the abominable. At a time when everything seems to exacerbate divisions among us, the chance to read Deuteronomy against its own superficial logic of binary separations—we over against them, Israel over against Canaan, holy over against abominable, landed peasant over against slave, and so on—may help us see many-colored peoples. Again: Deuteronomy is not about laws, but about a covenant with a people, and the more included in "the people" the better! The concept of "people" in Deuteronomy, however, is ambiguous. Women are sometimes included but at other times, such as when the people go to war or when it comes to the sign of belonging to the covenant—circumcision—they are not included.[29]

A Newer Concern: Migration and Human Trafficking

That migration and human trafficking are today noticed on the international arena only requires reading the newspapers: North Africans trying to get to Italy and Cubans to the United States by boat; Syrians seeking refuge in Europe and the Americas; Colombians and Venezuelans migrating to other Latin American countries; Central American caravans walking to the US border; and these very days, countries closing their borders because of pandemic spread of virus. The list could go on and on, with ever-new subjects and objects of hospitality or rejection.

Élio Gasda notes that "Migrants and refugees are one of the most shocking phases of global capitalism. Leaving one's own country has become the only way to escape violence and death."[30]

Lília Dias Marianno, from Brazil, reflects on migration in the Bible and in today's world.[31] This is not a new phenomenon, though, as the Bible amply attestso. The Americas have been a fertile land for refugees and migrants since colonial times. Thus, care for the immigrant and the refugee is a key theological issue in Deuteronomy and in our own times and locations.

Another manifestation of migration is trafficking human beings against their own interests or rights, by coercion or deceit, for the purpose of economic gain for the trafficker/s.[32] Although it has become one of capitalism's ugliest faces, it is not new and it did not become a crime until relatively recently. Biblical authors knew it from their own experience of war, piracy, indebtedness, or plain need of cheap (for the owners) human resources. Recently, a few biblical resources on migration and trafficking have appeared in journals from the region and elsewhere.[33]

A Newer Concern: Ecology

Haroldo Reimer has broadened the dialogue with Deuteronomy both by encouraging some of his students and by raising up himself another topic, that of ecology. Here I would like to bring in Eveline Moreira de Morales's work on eco-centric values in several texts (20:19–20; 22:6–7; 23:13–15).[34]

A Newer Concern: YHWH's Oneness and Today's (Inter) Religious Concerns

Although it does not seem to stem from the earlier generation, in recent years one of the core Deuteronomic texts, the *Shema'* (6:4–9), has been the subject of different analyses.[35] I have located at least four theses dealing with the *Shema'* presented at different schools. In order of age, the first one, by Nelvi Ceolin, is an appropriation of the text for building a culture of peace.[36] The second one belongs to Joerley de Oliveira Cruz, who aims to move from Deuteronomy's One (Hebrew *'ehād*) to the Trinity.[37] More recently, Douglas Oliveira dos Santos produced, under the direction of Ivoni Richter Reimer, an analysis of current

Christian concepts of monotheism stemming from translations of two OT texts into the LXX.[38] Finally, mention should be made of Julio Cárdenas Arenas, who compares a text from the NT and one from the Qur'an seeking interreligious dialogue (6:4).[39] These are new, still tentative developments of interreligious dialogue in a continent claimed to be Christian and Roman Catholic at that.

While my interest does not lie in current interreligious dialogues with Islam, one question does interest me, namely, the Deuteronomic tension between valid religion and other forms of ritual or spirituality, which for Deuteronomy are abominable. Usually female practices fall within the heterodoxy hardly tolerated by orthodoxy. And, conversely, orthodoxy sides with patriarchal interests.

We Have Homework! Women and Deuteronomy

Perhaps Deuteronomy's totalitarian view on one nation under one God at one temple has discouraged women to deal much with it—although, frankly, female scholars have dealt with much more misogynistic texts. I have been able to mention a few works by female scholars, but Deuteronomy seems to be low among female liberation or feminist scholars' preferences.

One reason may be the fact that, to create a covenantal frame and strengthen group identity, Deuteronomy deleted women's memories and religious practices. As a result, it is hard to use Deuteronomy as a mirror for our own experiences. I started with a case study of how the Roman Catholic and conservative evangelical churches wrongly sought control of the sexual and reproductive choices of women, especially abortion. Deuteronomy unashamedly takes for granted God's involvement in Israel's politics. The Torah was given directly by YHWH (4:44–45; 27:1–8), the king is to read Torah daily (17:18–20), and so on. Today many believe the church should not interfere in state legislation imposing its beliefs on a population in which there are not only people from other denominations and faiths, but also many nominal members of their own constituencies who do not feel represented by such meddling. Initially, I wanted to state that these are huge differences between both contexts, mine and Deuteronomy's. On second thought, however, I wonder how much I was buying into Deuteronomy's ideology of unity: How are we to know to what extent women felt comfortable with a system that imposed so many restrictions on them, not only in the name of the state but of their only God (YHWH 'eḥād) as well? How much did families and women from the religious periphery really follow Deuteronomy's program? To what extent did they bypass it in their daily faith journey and liturgical practice?

In summary, Deuteronomy and Latin American biblical scholars have conversed with each other and have undergone conversion because of such conversations. That the biblical text has the potential to convert us does not need much explanation within churchgoers or theological people. That Latin American scholars make Deuteronomy's conversion possible might not be self-evident. I mean it in two ways. First, in order to have a conversation, both partners must listen to each other, and such listening brings in possible changes (or at least, respect for the dialogue partner). Secondly, a text becomes the object of multiple readings and in that sense, when read from Latin America, it becomes a different Deuteronomy, so to speak, from an African, European, queer, or any other Deuteronomy.

Notes

1. Many of us publish regularly in *Revista de Interpretación Bíblica Latinoamericana (RIBLA)*, which intends to offer substantial, yet located, scholarship. It would be too long to list every contribution by the scholars I mention, although I have allowed myself a few references from each. *RIBLA* is available online, https://www.centrobiblicoquito.org/ribla/.
2. See, for instance, Miguel A. Ferrando, "La interpretación de la Biblia en la Teología de la liberación, 1971–1984," *Vida y Pensamiento* 50 (2009): 75–92 (78–80 and 81–82 on the most read biblical books). On Liberation theology, see Vasilios Dimitriadis, "Gustavo Gutiérrez: Liberation Theology for a World of Social Justice and Just Peace," *Journal of Ecumenical Studies* 54, no. 3 (2019): 431–441; John Dear, S. J., "Gustavo Gutierrez and the Preferential Option for the Poor," *National Catholic Reporter*, November 8, 2011, https://liberationtheology.org/library/National_Catholic_Reporter_-_Gustavo_Gutierrez_and_the_preferential_option_for_the_poor_-_2011-11-09.pdf; Leonardo and Clodovis Boff, "A Concise History of Liberation Theology," https://liberationtheology.org/library/a-concise-history-of-liberation-theology.pdf.
3. José Severino Croatto, *El hombre en el mundo I: Creación y designio. Comentario a Génesis 1* (Buenos Aires: La Aurora, 1974); *Crear y amar en libertad. Estudio de Génesis 2:4–3:24* (Buenos Aires: La Aurora, 1986); *Exilio y sobrevivencia. Tradiciones contraculturales en el Pentateuco* (Buenos Aires: Lumen, 1997); *Isaías: La palabra profética y su relectura hermenéutica, I: 1–39: El profeta de la justicia y de la fidelidad* (Buenos Aires: La Aurora, 1989); *Isaías. La palabra profética y su relectura hermenéutica, II: 40–55: La liberación es posible* (Buenos Aires: Lumen, 1994); *Imaginar el futuro. Estructura retórica y querigma del Tercer Isaías* (Buenos Aires: Lumen, 2001); *Experiencia de lo sagrado y tradiciones religiosas. Estudio de fenomenología de la religión* (Estella: Verbo Divino, 2002).
4. *El Libro del Pueblo de Dios* (Madrid: Paulinas, 1980), https://www.vatican.va/archive/ESL0506/_INDEX.HTM. *La Biblia. Libro del Pueblo de Dios* (Estella: Verbo Divino, 2015).
5. George V. Pixley, *Historia sagrada, historia popular: Historia de Israel vista desde los pobres* (San José: DEI, 1989), https://archive.org/details/historiasagradahoopixl.
6. Walter Brueggemann, *Theology of the Old Testament: Testimony, Dispute, Advocacy* (Minneapolis: Fortress, 2005). George V. Pixley, *Éxodo, una lectura evangélica y popular* (Mexico: Casa Unida de Publicaciones, 1983).
7. Milton Schwantes, *O direito dos Pobres* (São Leopoldo: Oikos/Editeo, 2013); *Sentenças e Provérbios: sugestões para a interpretação da Sabedoria* (São Leopoldo: Oikos, 2009); *As monarquias no Antigo Israel—Um roteiro de pesquisa histórica e arqueológica* (São Leopoldo/São Paulo: Centro de Estudos Bíblicos/Edições Paulinas, 2006); *A terra não pode suportar suas palavras—Amós 7,10. Reflexão e estudo sobre Amós* (São Paulo: Paulinas, 2004); see also Fabio Py Murta de Almeida, "A contemporaneidade dos estudos de Deuteronômio 5,12–15," *Observatório da Religião* 1 (2015): 73–95 (89). I am greatly indebted to Almeida for providing me bibliography on the history of research, especially in Brazil. See Ana Flora Anderson and Gilberto Gorgulho, "O Cântico dos Cânticos: O amor erótico e o projeto do povo irmão," in *Profecia e esperança. Um tributo a Milton Schwantes*, ed. Carlos A. Dreher, Erny Mugge, Iria Hauenstein, and Isolde R. Dreher (São Leopoldo: Oikos, 2006), 337–344 (337).
8. *RIBLA*'s first three volumes (1988) deal with people's reading of the Bible, violence in relation to power and oppression, and God's option for the poor as hermeneutical option. See also Magali do Nascimento Cunha, "The Liberating Awareness: God's Call to Transformation of Racial Injustice," *Ecumenical Review* 72, no. 1 (2020): 48–61, https://

doi.org/10.1111/erev.12487, where she combines the "Ver–Juzgar–Actuar" method with the World Council of Churches' "Pilgrimage of Justice and Peace" approaches.
9. Haroldo Reimer, "Un tiempo de gracia para recomenzar. El año sabático en Éxodo 21,2–11 y Deuteronomio 15,1–18," *RIBLA* 33 (1999): 31–47; "Leyes y relaciones de género. Notas sobre Éxodo 21,2–11 y Deuteronomio 15,12–18," *RIBLA* 37 (2000): 116–127; "Sobre pájaros y nidos. Mirada ecológica en leyes del Deuteronomio," *RIBLA* 39 (2001): 33–43; "Textos sagrados e educação ambiental," *Fragmentos de Cultura* 13 (2003): 133–154; *Toda criação. Bíblia e Ecologia* (São Leopoldo: Oikos, 2006).
10. Reimer, "Sobre pájaros y nidos," 35. Translations are mine, unless otherwise stated.
11. Original: "Junto a la unicidad de Yahvéh y de la exigencia por su culto en un solo lugar, el Deuteronomio busca evitar el empobrecimiento y la consecuente esclavización del campesinado. El combate a la idolatría es reflejo de esto. Unicamente Yahvéh, que te sacó de Egipto, de la casa de servidumbre, es capaz de garantizar la sobrevivencia del campesinado, cada vez más duramente obligado a tributar. [. . .] La fuerza de las armas, el comercio internacional y el lujo en la corte, tuvieron sus máximas expresiones bajo estos reyes. Son cosas que llevan al pueblo de vuelta a Egipto. Por eso es preciso limitar el poder del rey (Dt. 17, 14–20)." Carlos A. Dreher, "Las uvas del vecino," *RIBLA* 14 (1993): 23–39 (30).
12. Pedro Kramer, "Origem e legislação de Deuteronômio: programa de uma sociedade sem empobrecidos e excluídos" (PhD diss., Escola Superior de Teologia [EST], São Leopoldo, 1999), 283. Kramer published his dissertation with the same title in 2006, but it is out of print. I thank the EST library and my colleague Marcia Blasi's kindness in copying and sending me chapters 4–5 of Kramer's dissertation. He compared works by Georg Braulik (also referred to as Braulik-Lohfink, Roman Catholic scholars related to the University of Vienna), Eckart Otto (from the Evangelical school of theology at the Ludwig-Maximilian University in Munich), and Frank Crüsemann (Theological school at Bethel, Germany).
13. Kramer, "Origem," 284.
14. Kramer, "Origem," 286.
15. See also Pedro Kramer, "Estrangeiro, órfão e viúva na legislação deuteronômica," *REMHU, Revista Interdisciplinar da Mobilidade Humana* 18, no. 35 (2010): 247–264.
16. Pizzorno, "'Yo estaré contigo y te bendeciré': aproximación al concepto de bendición en el Antiguo Testamento" (Master's thesis, São Leopoldo: Escola Superior de Teología, 2009), 94–108; "'No debe haber necesitado en medio de ti . . .' (Dt 15.4): Dimensión social de la bendición en el libro del Deuteronomio," *Protestantismo em Revista* 23 (Sept.–Dec. 2010): 85–91, http://revistas.est.edu.br/index.php/PR. As far as I have been able to find out, she is Uruguayan.
17. Pizzorno, "Yo estaré contigo y te bendeciré," 101.
18. José Enrique Ramírez Kidd, *Alterity and Identity in Israel: The ger in the Old Testament* (Berlin: De Gruyter, 1999), 131. Ramírez Kidd earned his PhD at the University of Hamburg.
19. Mercedes L. García Bachmann, *Women at Work in the Deuteronomistic History* (Atlanta: SBL Press, 2013).
20. Edesio Sánchez Cetina, *Deuteronomio. Introducción y comentario* (Comentario Bíblico Iberoamericano; Buenos Aires: Kairós, 2002), 510–511, referring to Gregorio Iriarte's *Para comprender América Latina. Realidad socio-política* (Estella: Verbo Divino, 1991); see also "Paz en la Biblia," *RIBLA* 74 (2017): 55–73.
21. Elizabeth Cook (Steike), "La lluvia de Yahvé y la vida en la tierra: un diálogo entre Génesis y Deuteronomio," *Vida y Pensamiento* 26 (2006): 43–71. I thank Elsa Tamez for this reference; Tamez herself, a leading biblical scholar, has not worked on Deuteronomy.
22. Haroldo Reimer, "Não há *dabar* sem contexto: Apontamentos sobre hermenêutica bíblica em Milton Schwantes," *Caminhos* (Goiânia) 11, no. 2 (2013): 246–259 (250).

23. Shigeyuki Nakanose, "Para entender el libro del Deuteronomio ¿Una ley a favor de la vida?," *RIBLA* 23 (1996): 168–184 (169–177). Nakanose, who is from Japan but has spent much of his life in Brazil, wrote his dissertation on Josiah's Passover (*Josiah's Passover: Sociology and the Liberating Bible* (Maryknoll: Orbis, 1993).
24. Kramer, "Origem," 289.
25. Kramer, "Origem," 262; Eduardo Paulo Stauder, "O dízimo como prática comunitária e solidária: uma leitura histórico-crítica de Deuteronômio 14,22–29" (Master's thesis, Universidade Metodista de São Paulo, São Bernardo do Campo, Brazil, 2007), 102.
26. Kramer, "Origem," esp. 283–307; Leopoldo Cervántes-Ortiz, "La llamada 'Teología de la Prosperidad': Un análisis teológico introductorio y crítico," *Vida y Pensamiento* (UBL) 39, no. 2–40, no. 1 (2019–2020): 175–210 counters Deut 26:11–13 and 8:15–18, with their communitarian emphasis, to Prosperity Theology's individualistic propaganda. See also Pedro Triana, "Un proyecto de solidaridad, justicia social y resistencia. Una [sic] estudio a partir de Deuteronomio 15,1–18," https://revtriana.wordpress.com/2011/11/17/un-proyecto-de-solidaridad-justicia-social-y-resistencia/; "Palabras para tempos de crises" I–IV, https://revtriana.wordpress.com/2011/08/30/palavras-para-tempos-de-crises/; Claudete Beise Ulrich, "O dízimo no Antigo Testamento," http://www.luteranos.com.br/textos/dizimo-no-antigo-testamento.
27. Fabio Py Murta de Almeida, "Uma ecologia refém do poder econômico: Leitura exegética sócio-econômica de Deuteronômio 5,12–15" (Master's thesis, Methodist University of São Paulo, São Bernardo do Campo, Brazil, 2007), esp. 92–125; see also his "Coisas de criança. Uma leitura do terceiro mandamento," *Revista de Cultura Teológica* 14, no. 55 (2006): 61–82.
28. Fernando Candido da Silva, "Uma aliança abominável e per/vertida? Anotações subalternas sobre o arquivo deuteronômico" (PhD diss., Universidade Metodista de São Paulo, São Bernardo do Campo, Brazil, 2011), ix (English abstract, by Candido).
29. Mercedes L. García Bachmann, "Deuteronomy," in *Global Bible Commentary*, ed. Daniel Patte et al. (Nashville: Abingdon, 2004), 54–55.
30. Élio Estanislau Gasda, "O estrangeiro na Bíblia en a comunidade cristã," in *Migrações, refúgio e comunidade cristã. Reflexões pastorais para a formação de agentes*, ed. Carmem Lussi and Roberto Marinucci (Caminhos; Brasilia: CSEM/São Paulo: PAULUS, 2018), 51–60 (51).
31. Lília Dias Marianno, "La ley y los 'fuera-de-la-ley'. Los encuentros y desencuentros entre la ley y los migrantes en el antiguo Israel," *RIBLA* 63 (2009): 45–53. See also Lussi and Marinucci, *Migrações, refúgio e comunidade cristã* (note 30); M. Daniel and R. Carroll, "Welcoming the Stranger: Toward a Theology of Immigration in Deuteronomy," in *For Our Good Always: Studies on the Message and Influence of Deuteronomy in Honor of Daniel I. Block*, ed. Jason S. DeRouchie, Jason Gile, and Kenneth J. Turner (Winona Lake: Eisenbrauns, 2013), 441–461; Reimer, "Sobre pájaros y nidos," 36–42.
32. See United Nations Office on Drugs and Crime, https://www.unodc.org/unodc/en/human-trafficking/index.html.
33. Years ago, Ms. M. Amelia Sosa noticed at a workshop how Naomi's command to Ruth, "Go and he will tell you what to do" resembles how many girls are constrained into prostitution. In an African context, Fulata Lusigu Moyo, "'Traffic Violations.' Hospitality, Foreignness, and Exploitation: A Contextual Biblical Study of Ruth," *JFSR* 32, no. 2 (2016): 83–94, esp. 87–93; Élio Estanislau Gasda, "'Arrancadlos de la mano de los inicuos'

(Sal 82,4): Mirada ético-teológica de la trata de seres humanos," *Theologica Xaveriana* 63, no. 175 (2013): 87–111.
34. Eveline Rachel Moreira De Morais, "A Bíblia na educação ambiental. A contribuição dos textos ecocêntricos do Antigo Testamento" (Master's thesis, Goiânia: Pontifícia Universidade Católica de Goiás [Brazil], 2008). Reimer, "Sobre pájaros y nidos," 36–42.
35. Notice also that the *Shema´* is one of the key texts in the early stages of African American production; see Stephen Breck Reid's chapter in this volume.
36. Nelvi Jorge Ceolin, "Ouvir e amar a Javé. Dt 6,4–9: Um caminho para a cultura de paz" (Master's thesis, Porto Alegre [Brazil]: Pontifícia Universidade Católica do Rio Grande do Sul, 2006).
37. Joerley Orlando de Oliveira Cruz, "Javé é único (*´ehad*) em Dt 6,4–9" (Master's thesis, Universidade Metodista de São Paulo [Brazil]: São Bernardo do Campo, 2011).
38. Douglas Oliveira dos Santos, "O Deus traduzido: Uma análise das traduções a partir de Josué 24:15 e Deuteronômio 6:4" (Master's thesis, Goiânia: Universidade Católica de Goiás, 2016).
39. Julio César Cárdenas Arenas, "Lectura pragmalingüística de Dt 6.4, Mc 12.29b y Corán 112.1 para el diálogo interreligioso" (Medellín: Universidad Pontificia Bolivariana [Colombia], 2016).

Bibliography

Almeida, Fabio Py Murta de. "Coisas de criança. Uma leitura do terceiro mandamento." *Revista de Cultura Teológica* 14, no. 55 (2006): 61–82.

Almeida, Fabio Py Murta de. "Uma ecologia refém do poder econômico: Leitura exegética sócio-econômica de Deuteronômio 5,12-15." Master's thesis, Universidade Metodista de São Paulo (Brazil): São Bernardo do Campo, 2007.

Almeida, Fabio Py Murta de. "A contemporaneidade dos estudos de Deuteronômio 5,12-15." *Observatório da Religião* 1, no. 2 (2015): 73–95.

Anderson, Ana Flora, and Gilberto Gorgulho. "O Cântico dos Cânticos: O amor erótico e o projeto do povo irmão." In *Profecia e esperança. Um tributo a Milton Schwantes*, edited by Carlos A. Dreher, Erny Mugge, Iria Hauenstein, and Isolde R. Dreher, 337–344. São Leopoldo: Oikos, 2006.

Beise Ulrich, Claudete. "O dízimo no Antigo Testamento." http://www.luteranos.com.br/textos/dizimo-no-antigo-testamento.

Boff, Leonardo, and Clodovis Boff. "A Concise History of Liberation Theology." https://liberationtheology.org/library/a-concise-history-of-liberation-theology.pdf.

Brueggmann, Walter. *Theology of the Old Testament: Testimony, Dispute, Advocacy*. Minneapolis: Fortress, 2005.

Cárdenas Arenas, Julio César. Lectura pragmalingüística de Dt 6.4, Mc 12.29b y Corán 112.1 para el diálogo interreligioso. Medellín: Universidad Pontificia Bolivariana (Colombia), 2016.

Carroll R., and M. Daniel. "Welcoming the Stranger: Toward a Theology of Immigration in Deuteronomy." In *For Our Good Always: Studies on the Message and Influence of Deuteronomy in honor of Daniel I. Block*, edited by Jason S. DeRouchie, Jason Gile, and Kenneth J. Turner, 441–461. Winona Lake: Eisenbrauns, 2013.

Ceolin, Nelvi Jorge. Ouvir e amar a Javé. Dt 6,4–9: Um caminho para a cultura de paz. Master's thesis, Porto Alegre [Brazil]: Pontifícia Universidade Católica do Rio Grande do Sul, 2006.

Cervántes-Ortiz, Leopoldo. "La llamada 'Teología de la Prosperidad': Un análisis teológico introductorio y crítico." *Vida y Pensamiento* (UBL) 39, no. 2–40, no. 1 (2019–2020): 175–210.

Cook (Steike), Elizabeth. "La lluvia de Yahvé y la vida en la tierra: un diálogo entre Génesis y Deuteronomio." *Vida y Pensamiento* 26 (2006): 43–71.

Croattio, José Severino. *El hombre en el mundo I: Creación y designio. Comentario a Génesis 1.* Buenos Aires: La Aurora, 1974.

Croattio, José Severino. *Crear y amar en libertad. Estudio de Génesis 2:4–3:24.* Buenos Aires: La Aurora, 1986.

Croattio, José Severino. *Isaías: La palabra profética y su relectura hermenéutica, I: 1–39: El profeta de la justicia y de la fidelidad.* Buenos Aires: La Aurora, 1989.

Croattio, José Severino. *Isaías. La palabra profética y su relectura hermenéutica, II: 40–55: La liberación es posible.* Buenos Aires: Lumen, 1994.

Croattio, José Severino. *Exilio y sobrevivencia. Tradiciones contraculturales en el Pentateuco.* Buenos Aires: Lumen, 1997.

Croattio, José Severino. *Imaginar el futuro. Estructura retórica y querigma del Tercer Isaías.* Buenos Aires: Lumen, 2001.

Croattio, José Severino. *Experiencia de lo sagrado y tradiciones religiosas. Estudio de fenomenología de la religión.* Estella: Verbo Divino, 2002.

Cunha, Magali do Nascimento. "The Liberating Awareness: God's Call to Transformation of Racial Injustice." *Ecumenical Review* 72, no. 1 (2020): 48–61, doi:10.1111/erev.12487.

Dear, John, S. J. "Gustavo Gutierrez and the Preferential Option for the Poor." *National Catholic Reporter*, November 8, 2011, https://liberationtheology.org/library/National_Catholic_Reporter_-_Gustavo_Gutierrez_and_the_preferential_option_for_the_poor_-_2011-11-09.pdf.

Dimitriadis, Vasilios. "Gustavo Gutiérrez: Liberation Theology for a World of Social Justice and Just Peace." *Journal of Ecumenical Studies* 54, no. 3 (2019): 431–441.

Dreher, Carlos A. "Las uvas del vecino." *RIBLA* 14 (1993): 23–39.

Ferrando, Miguel A. "La interpretación de la Biblia en la Teología de la liberación, 1971–1984." *Vida y Pensamiento* 50 (2009): 75–92.

García Bachmann, Mercedes. "Deuteronomy." In *Global Bible Commentary*, edited by Daniel Patte et al., 52–63. Nashville: Abingdon, 2004.

García Bachmann, Mercedes. *Women at Work in the Deuteronomistic History*. Atlanta: SBL Press, 2013.

Gasda, Élio Estanislau. "'Arrancadlos de la mano de los inicuos' (Sal 82,4): Mirada ético-teológica de la trata de seres humanos." *Theologica Xaveriana* 63, no. 175 (2013): 87–111.

Gasda, Élio Estanislau. "O estrangeiro na Bíblia en a comunidade cristã." In *Migrações, refúgio e comunidade cristã. Reflexões pastorais para a formação de agentes*, edited by Carmem Lussi and Roberto Marinucci, 51–60. Serie Caminhos. CSEM/São Paulo: Paulus, 2018.

Kramer, Pedro. "Origem e legislação de Deuteronômio: programa de uma sociedade sem empobrecidos e excluídos." PhD diss., Escola Superior de Teologia (EST), São Leopoldo (Brazil), 1999.

Kramer, Pedro. "Estrangeiro, órfão e viúva na legislação deuteronômica." *REMHU, Revista Interdisciplinar da Mobilidade Humana* 18, no. 35 (2010): 247–264.

Marianno, Lilia Dias. "La ley y los "fuera-de-la-ley." Los encuentros y desencuentros entre la ley y los migrantes en el antiguo Israel." *RIBLA* 63 (2009): 45–53.

Moreira de Morais, Eveline Rachel. "A Bíblia na educação ambiental. A contribuição dos textos ecocêntricos do Antigo Testamento." Master's thesis, Pontifícia Universidade Católica de Goiás: Goiânia (Brazil), 2008.

Moyo, Fulata Lusigu. "'Traffic Violations.' Hospitality, Foreignness, and Exploitation: A Contextual Biblical Study of Ruth." *JFSR* 32, no. 2 (2016): 83–94.

Nakanose, Shigeyuki. *Josiah's Passover: Sociology and the Liberating Bible.* Maryknoll: Orbis, 1993.

Nakanose, Shigeyuki. "Para entender el libro del Deuteronomio. ¿Una ley a favor de la vida?" *RIBLA* 23 (1996): 168–184.

Oliveira Cruz, Joerley Orlando de. Javé é único (*'ehad*) em Dt 6,4–9. Master's thesis, Universidade Metodista de São Paulo [Brazil]: São Bernardo do Campo, 2011.

Oliveira Dos Santos, Douglas. "O Deus traduzido. Uma análise das traduções a partir de Josué 24,15 e Deuteronômio 6,4." Master's thesis, Pontifícia Universidade Católica de Goiás: Goiânia (Brazil), 2016. http://tede2.pucgoias.edu.br:8080/handle/tede/3470.

Pixley, George V. *Éxodo, una lectura evangélica y popular.* México: Casa Unida de Publicaciones, 1983.

Pixley, George V. *Historia sagrada, historia popular: Historia de Israel vista desde los pobres.* S. José de Costa Rica: DEI, 1989. https://archive.org/details/historiasagradahoopixl.

Pizzorno, Patricia. "Yo estaré contigo y te bendeciré": aproximación al concepto de bendición en el Antiguo Testamento. Master's thesis. São Leopoldo: Escola Superior de Teología, 2009.

Pizzorno, Patricia. "No debe haber necesitado en medio de ti . . . " (Dt 15.4): dimensión social de la bendición en el libro del Deuteronomio." *Protestantismo em Revista* 23 (sept.dec. 2010): 85–91. (Online journal of the Núcleo de Estudos e Pesquisa do Protestantismo da Escola Superior de Teologia—EST, São Leopoldo, RS, Brazil.

Ramírez Kidd, José Enrique. *Alterity and Identity in Israel: The ger in the Old Testament.* Berlin: De Gruyter, 1999.

Reimer, Haroldo. "Un tiempo de gracia para recomenzar. El año sabático en Éxodo 21,2–11 y Deuteronomio 15,1–18." *RIBLA* 33 (1999): 31–47.

Reimer, Haroldo. "Leyes y relaciones de género. Notas sobre Éxodo 21,2–11 y Deuteronomio 15,12–18." *RIBLA* 37 (2000): 116–127.

Reimer, Haroldo. "Inclusão e resistência—Anotações a partir do Deuteronômio." *Estudos Bíblicos* (Petrópolis) 72 (2001): 11–20.

Reimer, Haroldo. "Sobre pájaros y nidos. Mirada ecológica en leyes del Deuteronomio." *RIBLA* 39 (2001): 33–43.

Reimer, Haroldo. "Textos sagrados e educação ambiental." *Fragmentos de Cultura* 13 (2003): 133–154.

Reimer, Haroldo. *Toda criação. Bíblia e Ecologia.* São Leopoldo: Oikos, 2006.

Reimer, Haroldo. "Não há dabar sem contexto: Apontamentos sobre hermenêutica bíblica em Milton Schwantes." *Caminhos* (Goiânia) 11, no. 2 (2013): 246–259.

Sánchez Cetina, Edesio. *Deuteronomio. Introducción y comentario.* Comentario Bíblico Iberoamericano. Buenos Aires: Kairós, 2002.

Sánchez Cetina, Edesio. "Paz en la Biblia." *RIBLA* 74 (2017): 55–73.

Schwantes, Milton. *A terra não pode suportar suas palavras—Amós 7,10. Reflexão e estudo sobre Amós.* São Paulo: Paulinas, 2004.

Schwantes, Milton. *As monarquias no Antigo Israel—Um roteiro de pesquisa histórica e arqueológica.* São Leopoldo: Centro de Estudos Bíblicos/Edições Paulinas, 2006.

Schwantes, Milton. *Sentenças e Provérbios: sugestões para a interpretação da Sabedoria.* São Leopoldo: Oikos, 2009.

Schwantes, Milton. *O direito dos Pobres.* São Leopoldo: Oikos/Editeo, 2013.

Siqueira, Tércio Machado, "El mesianismo y su contraposición con Deuteronomio (17,14–20)." *RIBLA: Revista de Interpretacion Bibica Latinoamericana* 60 (2008): 139–146.

Stauder, Eduardo Paulo. "O dízimo como prática comunitária e solidária: uma leitura histórico-crítica de Deuteronômio 14,22–29." Master's thesis. São Bernardo do Campo: Universidade Metodista de São Paulo, 2007.

Triana, Pedro. "Un proyecto de solidaridad, justicia social y resistencia. Una [sic] estudio a partir de Deuteronomio 15, 1–18." Blog, November 17, 2011, https://revtriana.wordpress.com/2011/11/17/un-proyecto-de-solidaridad-justicia-social-y-resistencia/.

Triana, Pedro. "Palabras para tempos de crises." https://revtriana.wordpress.com/2011/08/30/palavras-para-tempos-de-crises/.

Zabatiero, Júlio Paulo Tavares. "Em busca de uma economia solidária—Dt 14,22–15,23: resistência popular e identidade social." *Estudos Bíblicos* (Petrópolis) 84 (2004): 9–21.

CHAPTER 29

DISABILITY IN DEUTERONOMY AND ITS RECEPTION

SARAH J. MELCHER

WHO BEGAN THE CONVERSATION?

FIRST, we'll explore how ancient interpreters understood disability and Deuteronomy. Infertility was viewed as a disability in ancient times as reflected within interpretations of Deuteronomy. According to the *Babylonian Talmud* (*ta'anit* 2a) and Rabbi Johanan, there are three keys over which the Holy One retains sole jurisdiction: the key of rain, the key of childbirth, and the key of resurrection of the dead. In developing this theme, the passage cites Deuteronomy 28:12 to support the idea that the Holy One controls the rain. The passage cites Genesis 30:22, in which God opens Rachel's womb to develop the idea that God controls childbirth. *Ta'anit* (8a–b) cites Deuteronomy 11:17 and then associates a lack of rain with the inability to give birth, stating, "When the heavens are closed up so that neither dew nor rain falls, it is similar to a woman who is in labor but who cannot give birth."[1] Later, the same passage compares the term "closed up" (*'atsirah*) in reference to rain to "closed up" (*'atsirah*) in reference to a woman's infertility or the inability to give birth. Following after, the idea of YHWH "remembering" (*peqidah*) is applied to both rain and childbirth, so that if YHWH "remembers" the earth, it will rain (Ps 65:10). If YHWH "remembers" a woman, she will conceive and give birth (Gen 21:1). Likewise, "bearing" can refer to rain falling on the earth or to a woman giving birth.

Saadia ben Joseph Gaon (1993, 882/892–942) in his Torah commentary on Deuteronomy (7:12) emphasizes the conditional nature of its covenant, describing the blessings of the covenant as a "reward for listening" (*Torat Chaim Chumash* ע). The blessings of Deuteronomy 7:12–16 promise that there will be no infertility among the people who adhere to the covenant stipulations or among their animals. An implication of this interpretation is that someone who is infertile has violated the covenant.

Samuel ben Meir (1085–1158), also known as Rashbam, states that if the current generation fails to keep YHWH's commandments, then the blessing does not apply, but if a later generation is faithful to the covenant, they will be rewarded accordingly (7:12) (*Torat Chaim Chumash* ע). Later in his commentary, he focuses on the basic Hebrew form (*'aqar*) signifying male infertility, showing a particular concern with the vowel pattern (7:14) (*Torat Chaim Chumash* עא).

Deuteronomy (8:1) also makes bearing children conditional upon fulfilling the stipulations of the covenant as Moses has conveyed them. It states, "You shall faithfully observe all the instruction that I enjoin upon you today, that you may live and increase, enter and possess the land that YHWH promised on oath to your ancestors." To be fertile, to bear children, is a reward for observing YHWH's instruction. Obadiah ben Jacob Sforno (1475–1550) identifies three categories of transient values: having children, living into old age, and accumulating wealth. He contends that abiding by YHWH's commandments can result in achieving all three. YHWH does not offer only eternal life, but a successful, fulfilling life on earth. Sforno then agrees that abiding by God's commandments can help with fertility (*Torat Chaim Chumash* עד).

According to Shlomo Yitzchaki (1040–1105), also known as Rashi, the focus is on completing every commandment, not just doing a part of it (*Torat Chaim Chumash* עד). Abraham Ibn Ezra also highlights the necessity of keeping all the commandments (*Torat Chaim Chumash* עד).

However, Moses ben Nahman (1194–1270), also known as Ramban, again emphasizes fertility, stating that keeping all the commandments will result in the Israelites being fruitful in the womb, on the soil, and among the domesticated animals (8:1) (*Torat Chaim Chumash* עד).

Of course, ancient approaches to disability are concerned with the bodily metaphors that are used in the Bible, like those employed in Deuteronomy. One metaphor is used in Deuteronomy numerous times to connote people's rebelliousness or stubbornness, that of a "stiff-necked" people (9:6, 13; 10:16). Sforno claims that it is impossible to be righteous and "stiff-necked" simultaneously. He describes the "stiff-necked" as people who follow their own inclinations and priorities rather than accepting the yoke of YHWH's commandments. For Sfrono, the stiff-necked are unable to turn around and face their teacher, because the neck is too stiff (9:6) (*Torat Chaim Chumash* פ). When speaking about the phrase: "Then, cut away the foreskin about your hearts and stiffen your necks no more (10:16)," Sforno compares cutting away the "foreskin" of the heart to removing prejudices and realizing the errors in perceiving the world that were based on false pretenses. Being stiff-necked keeps one from truly recognizing the Creator and the evil act that turning away represents (*Torat Chaim Chumash* צ-צא).

Deuteronomy (23:1–8) explicitly excludes from the "congregation of YHWH" anyone whose testicles are crushed or whose penis has been cut off. If infertility is a disability, this may explain the exclusion. Rashi quickly makes the connection between the missing penis and the inability to beget children. He also states that semen needs to flow uninterrupted (*Torat Chaim Chumash* קצז). The Babylonian Talmud Tractate *Yebamot* (70) stipulates that a man whose testicles are damaged or whose penis is cut off may not eat of the *Terumah* offering. *Sifrei Devarim* regards the penis being cut off as the more serious condition since it cannot be healed and thus there can be no regeneration (*Sifrei Devarim* 247).

What Is the Status of the Conversation?

In this second section, I'll review some recent interpretations by biblical scholars of Deuteronomy and its perception of disability.

Jeremy Schipper cites Deuteronomy (7:14–15) in a larger section where he argues that infertility was treated as a disability in biblical, ancient Near Eastern, and rabbinic literature (Schipper 2006). Moses conveys YHWH's covenant faithfulness, which includes the promise that no human being or animal would be infertile in the Promised Land. The language links infertility closely with sickness and disease. Schipper argues convincingly that infertility was regarded as a disability in the Near Eastern context in antiquity.

Schipper also studies Deuteronomy's prohibition against misdirecting a blind person (27:18). In addition, by means of a thorough word study of Hebrew terms following the *qittēl* pattern, Schipper makes the case that disability was a "meaningful conceptual category in the ancient world" (Schipper 2006, 67).

In Rebecca Raphael's treatment of Deuteronomy, she discusses its emphasis on the senses (Raphael 2008). Like Hector Avalos, she stresses Deuteronomy's focus on the auditory (see Avalos 2007). In addition, she speaks of Deuteronomy's tendency to present other gods—those of the surrounding, non-Israelite nations (4:28; 5:7; 6:14; 7:4; 8:9; 11:16; 13:2+6; 17:3; 18:20; 28:14; 29:26; 30:17; 31:18+20)—as persons with disabilities, while YHWH is portrayed as a person without disabilities. In fact, she argues that Deuteronomy is dependent upon physical terms in order to represent YHWH (Raphael 2008, 40).

Raphael suggests that we can better understand Deuteronomy's conception of YHWH if we compare how it describes other gods. First, other gods are described as idols, as the work of human artifice. As she states, "Thus, Deuteronomy's language for the concept of idolatry not only emphasizes but links terms for foreignness, materiality, and artifactuality" (Raphael 2008, 41). She argues that the sarcasm present about idols in Deuteronomy probably influenced the exilic and postexilic prophets and their treatment of idols. Deuteronomy mocks physical representations. These idols cannot use the senses. They cannot hear, see, eat, or smell.

Conversely, YHWH can exercise those senses. In other words, the other gods are individuals with disabilities, while Israel's YHWH is not. While Deuteronomy does not describe YHWH directly, it uses the idols and their disabilities to describe YHWH. In contrast to them, YHWH speaks in a superlative manner and acts in a superlative manner, while other gods lack efficacy (Raphael 2008, 43). Deuteronomy makes the point repeatedly that objects of wood and stone have no senses. According to Raphael, the nature of YHWH is constructed by representing other gods as people with disabilities. They lack functioning senses, but YHWH can see, hear, and speak. Deuteronomy exalts what can be heard but cannot be seen. Nevertheless, YHWH uses all the senses.

Pointedly, no image is used to describe YHWH, in keeping with the prohibition against visual representations (5:8). YHWH is represented in Deuteronomy only in auditory theophanies. Deuteronomy emphasizes hearing as the preferred means of receiving YHWH's teaching. As Raphael notes, Deuteronomy makes a strong connection between idolatry and disability/disease (28:1–68).

Raphael draws an important and perceptive conclusion. Because of Deuteronomy's insistence that the legitimate way of receiving communication from YHWH is through hearing, Deaf people are effectively excluded. For Deuteronomy, Deaf people cannot acquire YHWH's teaching legitimately (Raphael 2008, 47).

In *Disability in the Hebrew Bible: Interpreting Mental and Physical Differences*, Saul M. Olyan generally refers to Deuteronomy only in passing (Olyan 2008, 182–183). However, his discussion of genital damage (23:1–8) and mental illness (28:28–29) in Deuteronomy is more extensive.

Deuteronomy does not use the common Hebrew term *mûm* for "disability"—translated by Olyan as "defect"—but teaches that men with genital damage are excluded from the "assembly of YHWH," which Olyan interprets as meaning that men with genital damage may not enter the sanctuary. Deuteronomy usually refers to the "Tent of Meeting" (31:14), but it probably reflects the later reality of the "Jerusalem Temple" (Olyan 2008, 11, 136n36). Drawing upon Isaiah (56:3)—which seems to contradict Deuteronomy (23:1–8)—Olyan believes the concern leading to exclusion is the inability to reproduce (Olyan 2008, 33). Olyan notes the apparent necessity to keep these men away from the divine presence (Olyan 2008, 35). According to Olyan, Deuteronomy (23:1–8) also excludes the uncircumcised—the Ammonites and the Moabites. Israelite males who are uncircumcised have violated the covenant and will be punished by the extinction of their lineage. In my opinion, this is significant since circumcision was commonly practiced in the ancient Near East as a fertility ritual.

Olyan points out that divine curses in Deuteronomy (28:28–29) punish people who violate the covenant with "madness, blindness, and bewilderment" (Olyan 2008, 73). Adherence to the covenant is very central to Deuteronomy. As Olyan observes, mental disability, like blindness, is portrayed as a covenantal curse (28:28) (Olyan 2008, 71). Likewise, those violating the prescriptions of the covenant are threatened with a life that will never prosper and they are promised oppression and robbery, without anyone to save them (28:29). Olyan suggests that Deuteronomy teaches that people with disabilities will have to be dependent upon more powerful members of the community who may take advantage of them. This is one case in which disability is denigrated through negative associations. For Olyan, the issue with disability for Deuteronomy is that it engenders weakness and dependency.

Olyan published a later essay, "The Ascription of Physical Disability as a Stigmatizing Strategy in Biblical Iconic Polemics," which treats, in part, Deuteronomy's handling of human-made idols (Olyan 2011). He discusses Deuteronomy's tendency to denigrate idols by attributing physical disability to them. They cannot see, smell, eat, or hear (4:28).

Modern interpreters also emphasize the conditional nature of the promise of fertility. According to *Unscrolled: 54 Writers and Artists Wrestle with the Torah*, fertility is one of the rewards of fertility, health, and agricultural prosperity that people receive because of maintaining the covenant (Bennett 2013, 311).

Another modern perspective is offered in *The Torah: A Women's Commentary* (Eskenazi and Weiss 2008). For Deuteronomy (9:6), Israel has already proven rebellious, which is expressed in the phrase "stiff-necked people." The metaphor "circumcise the foreskin of your hearts" (10:16) refers to the removal of any emotional blocks that keep people from adhering to YHWH's teachings and that compel them to exhibit rebellious behavior (Eskenazi and Weiss 2008, 2699).

A difficulty with the use of the metaphor "stiff-necked" is attributing a moral lack to a physical feature. For those who have a problem with mobility of the neck, this can be a hurtful metaphor. Disability studies have made it clear that associating a moral failure with a physical feature can be used to denigrate people with disabilities.

Don C. Benjamin suggests that Deuteronomy disqualifies certain types of individuals from being a part of the assembly of YHWH (23:2–9), including eunuchs who have served as advisors to the rulers of other countries (Est 1:10). The basis for their exclusion is not a physical disability, but their previous social status (Benjamin 2015, 150).

Jack R. Lundbom in his commentary on Deuteronomy initially points out that Deuteronomy is describing conditions that prevent men from begetting children (Lundbom 2013, 643). He also maintains that the "assembly of YHWH" is a gathering of all the adult Israelite males (Lundbom 2013, 646). Therefore, an Israelite priest with genital damage was not permitted to approach YHWH's altar (Lundbom 2013, 644). As Candida R. Moss and Joel S. Baden point out, to be excluded from the Jerusalem Temple meant "separation from the heart of Israelite society" (Moss and Baden 2015, 13; Moss and Schipper 2011).

WHAT IS TRENDING IN THE CONVERSATION?

Hector Avalos has noted that Deuteronomy is "audiocentric," meaning that Deuteronomy privileges "hearing, listening, and heeding" as means of gathering information and communicating (Avalos 2007). Deuteronomy's valuation of hearing is evident, with the Hebrew root *shama‘* ("he hears") used with a frequency second only to Isaiah and Jeremiah. In Deuteronomy (1:16–17) "hearing" is valued to achieve justice for members of the community. Magistrates are instructed to listen carefully to those who come before them for a decision. The decision should be impartial with the magistrate hearing all parties fairly, whatever their station in life.

Yet hearing is at the root of being in right relationship with YHWH. Listening works both ways. YHWH is depicted as hearing the people, and they are exhorted to listen to YHWH's instruction. YHWH is described as hearing the people's complaint (1:34). Later in Deuteronomy (1:43), Moses grumbles that the people did not listen when he conveyed YHWH's warning to them. Of course, at times, YHWH does not hear the people when they cry out (1:45). Moses maintains that YHWH would not listen to him when he made his case for seeing the Promised Land (3:26). Elsewhere (9:19), Moses recalls the occasion when he appealed to YHWH not to destroy the people and YHWH "listened" (10:10). Of course, Moses remembers another occasion when the people did not listen to YHWH (9:23). Later (18:15–16), Moses indicates that another prophet will be sent after Moses's death and the people are exhorted to listen to the words of YHWH that the prophet conveys. YHWH indicates that the people will be held accountable if they fail to listen to the words of the prophet (18:19). The obituary of Moses (34:9) indicates that the people "heeded" the words of Joshua, the prophet who succeeded Moses. The people are also urged to "heed" the words of their parents or suffer dire consequences (21:18–21).

Happily, YHWH would not listen to Balaam when he attempted to curse the Israelites (23:6). Yet YHWH did hear the Israelites when they cried out in Egypt (26:7).

Perhaps the most crucial usage of the Hebrew root *shama‘* is to exhort the people to follow YHWH's statutes and ordinances (4:1, 10; 5:1; 12:28; 15:5; 27:9–10; 28:1–2). Early in Deuteronomy, the importance of hearing YHWH's voice in order to follow divine commandments and rules is made clear by Moses: "YHWH spoke to you out of the fire; you heard the sound of words but perceived no shape— nothing but a voice. He declared to you the covenant that he commanded you to observe, the Ten Commandments; and he inscribed them on two tablets of stone. At the same time YHWH commanded me to impart to you the statutes and ordinances for you to observe in the land that you are about to cross into and occupy" (4:12–14). If the people fail to follow YHWH's voice, and do not observe the commandments, they will perish (8:20). The people are exhorted to listen to the saga about the nations being dispossessed of the land (9:1).

The intensive form of the root *shama'* occurs where the people are assured of a fruitful homeland if they listen intently to YHWH's commandments (11:13). If the people hearken to YHWH's instruction, it will result in blessing, but if they do not, then curses will be actualized (11:27–28).

Of course, like other biblical passages, Deuteronomy denigrates idols for their inability to see and hear: "There you will serve gods, made by human hands, wood and stone, which cannot see or hear or eat or smell" (4:28). While the metaphor is intended to disparage inanimate objects, the argument that idols cannot see or hear, however, potentially ridicules people with disabilities. It is worth noting, that if people who have turned away from the YHWH of Israel return to YHWH and listen to YHWH's voice, then the covenant still stands, and YHWH will remember the commitments inherent in that covenant (4:30–31). Elsewhere (13:3–4), the people are cautioned against "listening" to the voices of any prophet who would lead them to worship other gods.

Of course, the people of YHWH were concerned about hearing the voice of YHWH directly: "For who of all flesh ever heard the voice of the living YHWH speak out of the fire, like us, and lived? Go closer and hear all that YHWH our God says, and then you tell us everything that YHWH our God tells you, and we will listen and do it" (5:23–24). In this passage, they try to persuade Moses to listen to YHWH directly on their behalf, so that they do not have to take the risk to do so themselves. Later, YHWH praises the people for their request and promises to convey to Moses all the instructions so that he might in turn reveal them to the people (5:28).

Deuteronomy famously exhorts Israel to hear YHWH and to observe YHWH's instructions, especially in the Shema which commands Israel to keep the words of YHWH in their hearts. The people are to teach these words to their children. They are to recite YHWH's words when they are away and when they are at home; when they lie down and when they arise. The people are even instructed to "Bind them as a sign on your hand and let them serve as an emblem on your forehead; inscribe them on the doorposts of your house and on your gates" (6:8–9).

At the root of the relationship between YHWH and the people is the spoken word and the hearing of that word. Speaking and hearing was how this divine–human relationship was cultivated and maintained. Of course, the emphasis on hearing the spoken word of YHWH as the means to right relationship is problematic for those with a hearing impairment. A recent article by Mike Gulliver and William John Lyons makes the case that the audio-centric tendencies of Deuteronomy do not mean that Deaf people were not able to assume priestly duties nor would they have been prevented from contributing significantly to agricultural pursuits (Gulliver and Lyons 2018). They suggest that even in ancient times there was the possibility that Deaf people formed communities where signing was the primary means of communication.

One blessing in Deuteronomy (7:12–16) is particularly important for any critical analysis of Deuteronomy on disability. In this short subsection, the conditional nature of YHWH's covenant is reiterated. If the people of YHWH carefully observe YHWH's rules, YHWH will maintain the covenant faithfully, the one promised to the ancestors. Part of YHWH's commitment includes the fecundity of humans, grain, wine, oil, cattle, sheep, and goats. YHWH will "bless you and multiply you" who keep the covenant, specifically with the fruitfulness of their bodies and the fruitfulness of their land. No one in the land will be infertile, neither male nor female (Weinfeld 1991, 373).

On the one hand, Moss and Baden argue that the word 'aqar (7:14) may refer to male impotence rather than infertility. They note that infertility in the Bible is usually perceived as a problem attributed to the female in the relationship (Moss and Baden 2015, 38). Jeffrey H. Tigay, on the other hand, interprets the phrase 'aqar wa'aqarah as "sterile male or female" (Tigay 1996, 89). Given that both terms are parallel to one another, "sterile male or female" makes the most sense. The feminine form of the word is most often understood as "infertile woman" (Koehler Baumgartner 2001, 874). Ronald Clements argues strongly that the promise of human fertility is to be understood in the context of the covenant in Deuteronomy (Clements 1998, 351).

Deuteronomy also makes the increase of human beings conditional, stating, "You shall faithfully observe all the instruction that I enjoin upon you today, that you may live and increase and be able to possess the land that YHWH promised on oath to your fathers" (8:1; 13:18; 30:16). Being fertile is necessary to humankind's increase.

Just a few verses later (8:5), the discipline that YHWH provides is compared to that given by a father to his son. Following closely on the heels of the promise of "increase," the implication, then, is that YHWH may use infertility and lack of increase to discipline the people of YHWH. The language of "blessed shall be the fruit of your womb" (28:4) and "YHWH will make you abound in prosperity in the fruit of your womb" (28:11) certainly implies fertility. This fertility extends to the animals and the crops as well. This fertility, of course, is conditional on abiding by YHWH's statutes and commandments. Conversely, any failure to follow the covenant stipulations can result in the loss of fertility (28:18).

We will explore here some of the metaphors in Deuteronomy that may have implications for those who have a disability. Often Deuteronomy illustrates its theological positions in physical terms, using metaphors of the body. For example, a repeated motif occurring in Deuteronomy is the injunction to "walk in his ways" (8:6; 10:12; 11:22; 19:9; 26:17; 28:9; 30:16). The metaphor implies that one should order one's life to follow YHWH's precepts fully. The expression "walk in his ways," however, is a metaphor envisioning people who are physically mobile. It depicts Moses urging the people of YHWH to take physical action in order to be obedient to YHWH.

Also, Moses tells the people of YHWH that the presence of YHWH in their midst prevented their clothes from wearing out and their feet from swelling (8:4; 29:4). The implication is that YHWH prevented the people from wear and tear on their bodies as they wandered in the wilderness. Modern readers with disabilities might ask: "Why doesn't God keep us from having swollen feet?"

Another example of a physical metaphor is: "Every spot on which your foot treads shall be yours (11:24)," to convey the divine gift of land. If one's foot does not tread upon the land, does that negate the divine gift? People with mobility disabilities might feel excluded from this promise.

Deuteronomy portrays following a path as a metaphor for being faithful to YHWH's statutes and commandments. It also uses the metaphor of "straying from the path" to convey failure to adhere to YHWH's precepts (5:29-30; 8:12, 16; 10:12; 11:22). People receive divine blessings by following the right path but bring divine curses upon themselves by straying from that path (11:27-28).

Deuteronomy's instructions on prophets—"As for that prophet or dreamer of dreams, he shall be put to death; for he spoke falsely against YHWH your God—who brought you out from the land of Egypt and who redeemed you from the house of bondage—to make you stray from the path that YHWH your God commanded you to walk. Thus, you will purge evil from your midst (13:6)"—illustrate more implications of the "path" metaphor. Prophets occupied an elevated status among the people of YHWH. This prophet, however, is causing people to turn away from their YHWH and to worship other gods. YHWH had commanded the people to follow the path. Here the prophet has encouraged someone in an extreme way to "stray from the path" YHWH has chosen.

Later, Deuteronomy (13:7-12) explores the example of a close family member leading the reader to worship other gods. These verses make it even clearer that to "stray from the path" is to turn away from YHWH.

In another scenario, Deuteronomy teaches that if a city or town goes astray from YHWH, then there are very serious consequences (13:13-19). In that case, the people are to destroy that city or town—"Let nothing that has been dedicated stick to your hand, in order that YHWH may turn from his blazing anger and show you compassion, and in his compassion multiply you as he promised your fathers on oath" (13:18). Deuteronomy stipulates that sticking to YHWH's path and being faithful to YHWH are prerequisites for fertility and having your family increase. The nations are thrust from the path of the people of YHWH into the Promised Land because they had behaved wickedly (9:4). Indeed, the nations strayed from YHWH's path before the people of YHWH arrived in the plains of Moab (9:12, 16).

An interesting issue is the relationship between the people's holiness and the states of being that compromise that holiness. Deuteronomy makes the point that the people of YHWH are holy—"For you are a people consecrated to YHWH your God: YHWH your God chose you from among all other peoples on earth to be his treasured people" (14:2). Upon those who have been made holy, there are numerous obligations. They are obliged to adhere to a particular diet, to give a tenth of crops and livestock, and to set aside a portion of the tithe for those at risk or on the margins of the community.

Deuteronomy (15:4-11) admonishes the people of YHWH to care for the needy and to be generous or suffer the consequences. Sociological studies in disability show that disability and poverty go hand in hand. Some reports suggest that persons with disabilities are twice as likely to be poor. The implications of Deuteronomy (14:4-11; 24:14-15) are that the people of YHWH should be generous to those who are poor as a result of their disability.

Deuteronomy gives specific instructions about offering a tithe:

> You shall consecrate to YHWH your God all male firstlings that are born in your herd and in your flock: you must not work your firstling ox or shear your firstling sheep. You and your household shall eat it annually before YHWH your God in the place that YHWH will choose. But if it has a defect, lameness or blindness, any serious defect, you shall not sacrifice it to YHWH your God. You may eat it in your settlements, the unclean and the clean together, just

like the gazelle and the deer. Only you must not partake of its blood; you shall pour it out on the ground like water. (15:19–23)

The firstling from the flock or herd may not be offered as a sacrifice—a consecrated offering—if it has any serious defect, blindness, or lameness. So anything offered before YHWH must be free of defect. Elsewhere, Deuteronomy states more broadly that the people of YHWH should not sacrifice an ox or a sheep that has a serious defect, because the practice "is abhorrent to YHWH your God" (17:1). The implication is that an animal with a defect is not worthy of being offered to YHWH.

Another metaphor that has implications for people with disabilities is an instruction dealing with the appointment of magistrates and officials (16:19–20). It cautions judges against taking a bribe "for bribes blind the eyes of the discerning and upset the plea of the just" (16:19b). Of course, the intent of the cautionary statement is to suggest that a bribe affects the judgment of a judge and makes it difficult to render a fair decision. Just people may not be able to obtain a fair verdict if bribery has occurred. Although the intent of the statement is to prohibit bribery, it also implies that people who are blind are not able to make a discerning or fair judgment. Through a disability lens, this is an unacceptable premise. Yet the instruction makes the community's well-being and their ability to occupy the land contingent upon their pursuit of justice.

Of course, disability is sometimes the result of an injury. If another person causes a disabling injury, Deuteronomy holds the perpetrator accountable, contending that the punishment should fit the crime—"Your eye must not show pity: life for life, eye for eye, tooth for tooth, hand for hand, foot for foot" (19:21).

Interestingly, Deuteronomy (22:8) requires someone building a new house to make a parapet for the roof in order to prevent someone falling from it. In this case, the people of YHWH are to act in such a way as to prevent injury to others. Certainly, people with disabilities would celebrate any attempt to prevent injury.

As mentioned earlier, Deuteronomy prohibits a man with genital damage from entering the assembly of YHWH (23:1–8). This verse occurs with other prohibitions against certain parties entering the assembly: people born of incestuous unions or their offspring as well as the Moabites and the Ammonites. The passage offers a rationale for the exclusion of the Moabites and Ammonites, but none for men with genital damage. It is possible that the reason for excluding them has to do with their perceived disability, but it may very well have to do with their inability to reproduce. It is worth noting that individuals who are Edomites or their descendants are to be included in the congregation of YHWH.

Deuteronomy (24:1–4) also teaches that if a married woman is divorced by her first husband, then she may remarry, but if the second husband either divorces her or dies, the first husband may not remarry her because "she has been defiled" (*huttamma'ah* hitpael perfect 3fs). Though several translations use the language that the remarriage would bring sin upon the land, the Hebrew, in my opinion, could use language of defilement as in the previous case of the hitpael 3fs. An English translation of the hif'il imperfect 2ms might read "you shall defile." In context it would read "You must not defile the land that YHWH your God is giving you as a heritage."

Deuteronomy 25:11–12 attempts to protect men from genital damage. If two men get into a fight and one's wife tries to help her husband by seizing the other man's genitals, she is to be severely punished by having her hands cut off. The punishment is undertaken by the community.

In the annual tithe offering, a family is to bring their produce to the central sanctuary where they consume their food (26:12–15). Every third year, the tithe was distributed locally to the poor, to the widow, the stranger, and the orphan. Given what was said earlier about the connection between persons with disabilities and poverty, this provision will help people with disabilities.

Some curses in Deuteronomy have implications for its understanding of disability. For example, anyone who would misguide a blind person will be cursed (27:18). The curses in chapter 27 reflect a range of disabilities.

"YHWH will make pestilence cling to you, until he has put an end to you in the land that you are entering to possess. YHWH will strike you with consumption, fever, and inflammation, with scorching heat and drought, with blight and mildew; they shall pursue you until you perish" (28:21–22). This curse presents YHWH as retaliating against those who do not follow the commandments, inflicting the disobedient with serious disease.

The curses continue: "YHWH will strike you with the Egyptian inflammation, with hemorrhoids, boil-scars, and itch, from which you shall never recover. YHWH will strike you with madness, blindness, and dismay. You shall grope at noon as a blind man gropes in the dark; you shall not prosper in your ventures, but shall be constantly abused and robbed, with none to give help" (28:27–29). These curses suggest physical disabilities from which people will not recover, depicting the deity as inflicting disability as a punishment for disobedience.

Similarly, covenant disobedience triggers a divine response in 28:35: "YHWH will afflict you at the knees and thighs with a severe inflammation, from which you shall never recover—from the sole of your foot to the crown of your head." The diseases and physical maladies are those that will afflict not only the desert generation before Moses but also their offspring who stray from the covenant (28:59–61; 29:21).

Conclusion

Today few people with disease or disabilities attribute their disease or disability to the hand of God, especially as a punishment. Many who have a disability are understandably reluctant to attribute their condition to a deity. Most people with disabilities and their companions or advocates would prefer to think that disability affects people in a random way, having nothing to do with sinfulness or disobedience. Disability has nothing to do with a person's worthiness or the depth of one's piety.

From the ability to bear children to the ability to live a faithful life before God, Deuteronomy portrays all abilities and other blessings as coming from the hand of God. All are contingent upon people's faithfulness to God's covenant requirements. This can be a perspective which excludes some people.

Also difficult are those passages that prescribe some form of exclusion from the site of worship or from the community. People with disabilities today are striving for greater inclusion. They want the obstacles to full inclusion to be removed, and they want to be regarded fully as welcome, valued members of the community.

The exploration of Deuteronomy's audio-centric emphasis has also led to insights about how people with disabilities may be unintentionally excluded through a community's preoccupations with how to approach the deity properly. The preoccupation with "hearing" and "heeding" the word of YHWH can exclude those who are hearing impaired or those who use visual means to connect with God.

Further biblical study with sensory criticism (Avalos et al. 2007) and from a disability studies perspective is strongly advised. This article does suggest the value of such studies and indicates some areas for further research, but clearly more in-depth studies would be valuable.

Note

1. All translations in this essay are my own.

Bibliography

Avalos, H. 2007. "Introducing Sensory Criticism in Biblical Studies." In *This Abled Body: Rethinking Disabilities in Biblical Studies*, edited by H. Avalos, S. J. Melcher, and J. Schipper, 47–59. Atlanta: Society of Biblical Literature.

Avalos, H., S. J. Melcher, and J. Schipper, eds. 2007 *This Abled Body: Rethinking Disabilities in Biblical Studies*. Atlanta: Society of Biblical Literature.

Benjamin, D. C. 2015. *The Social World of Deuteronomy: A New Feminist Commentary*. Eugene: Cascade Books.

Bennett, R., ed. 2013. *Unscrolled: 54 Writers and Artists Wrestle with the Torah*. New York: Workman Publishing.

Clements, R. E. 1998. "The Book of Deuteronomy: Introduction, Commentary, and Reflections." In *The New Interpreter's Bible*, vol. 2, 271–538. Nashville: Abingdon Press.

Eskenazi, T. C., and A. L. Weiss, eds. 2008. *The Torah: A Women's Commentary*. New York: URJ Press and Women of Reform Judaism.

Gaon, Saadia. 1993. *Commentary on Deuteronomy in Torat Chaim Chumash*. Jerusalem: Mossad Harav Kook.

Gulliver, M., and W. J. Lyons. 2018. "Conceptualizing the Place of Deaf People in Ancient Israel: Suggestions from Deaf Space." *Journal of Biblical Literature* 137, no. 3: 537–553.

Koehler, L., and W. Baumgartner. 2001. *The Hebrew and Aramaic Lexicon of the Old Testament*. Vol. 1. Leiden: Brill.

Lundbom, J. R. 2013. *Deuteronomy: A Commentary*. Grand Rapids: William B. Eerdmans.

Moss, C. R., and J. S. Baden. 2015. *Reconceiving Infertility: Biblical Perspectives on Procreation and Childlessness*. Princeton: Princeton University Press.

Moss, Candida R., and Jeremy Schipper, eds. 2011. *Disability Studies and Biblical Literature*. New York: Palgrave Macmillan.

Olyan, S. 2008. *Disability in the Hebrew Bible: Interpreting Mental and Physical Differences*. New York: Cambridge University Press.

Olyan, S. 2011. "The Ascription of Physical Disability as a Stigmatizing Strategy in Biblical Iconic Polemics." In *Disability Studies and Biblical Literature*, edited by C. R. Moss and J. Schipper, 89–102. New York: Palgrave Macmillan.

Raphael, R. 2008. *Biblical Corpora: Representations of Disability in Hebrew Biblical Literature.* New York: T & T Clark.

Schipper, J. 2006. *Disability Studies and the Hebrew Bible: Figuring Mephibosheth in the David Story.* New York: T & T Clark.

Sifrei Devarim, Sefaria: A Living Library of Jewish Texts. https://www.sefaria.org/Sifrei_Devarim.247?lang=bi.

Tigay, Jeffrey H. 1996. *The JPS Torah Commentary. Deuteronomy.* Philadelphia: The Jewish Publication Society.

Weinfeld, M. 1991. *Deuteronomy 1–11: A New Translation with Introduction and Commentary.* Vol. 5. The Anchor Yale Bible. New Haven: Yale University Press.

CHAPTER 30

DEUTERONOMY IN THE LGBTQIA+ COMMUNITY

DAVID TABB STEWART

Introduction

WHAT is it that LGBTQIA+ criticism and interpretation can unearth in Deuteronomy that other approaches have not?[1] What can LGBTQIA+ approaches add to, or subtract from, consensus views of this text? LGBTQIA+ interpretation is more than a cluster of vernacular readings—it is a form of reader response criticism. That is, it privileges particular readers and what they might see that others miss. The lenses offered by LGBTQIA+ perspectives bring to the fore a set of topics and questions: What does the Bible say about the body, about gender, about sex, and about sexuality? What does it say about relationships between heavenly beings, humans, and animals—relations up and down the "ladder of being" (e.g., idolatry as metaphorical adultery)? How do biblical statements about these things compare to "what nature teaches" or what actual human lives might reveal? Should we speak of one gender or sexual "system" or are there several "systems" or foci? Does biblical evidence reveal discrete idea sets in putative sources or only one landscape of these matters? To answer these questions, and others, LGBTQIA+ interpreters are free, like other interpreters, to consider contexts literary, historical, and cultural; the text's tradents; and history of reception—not just to examine a few isolated prooftexts of "terror." They stand holding the magnifying glass of the reader, not on the queer object of the reader's gaze but holding the glass as a queer subject who can place themselves within the text and claim it all. In this regard, queer readers may exercise their imagination, and like midrashists of old, fill in the textual gaps with their own stories, or playfully deconstruct texts or graft them together.

Texts of Interest

If, for the sake of argument, one allows Deuteronomy's division into four layers following the proposal of Eckart Otto (2012, 231–257) with some modifications from Daniel Block

(2015, 182), one can associate sets of texts with each. Thus, the first layer (Deut. 12–26, 28) is "Josianic," the legal material usually labeled "D" or "Deuteronomic," which revises the "Book of the Covenant" at Exodus 21–23. To this, the blessings and curses of chapter 28 can be added. Our texts of interest include Deut. 22:5 (so-called cross-dressing); 22:13–29 (marriage, divorce, accused virgin, adultery, betrothal, rape); 23:1 (22:30, Eng.; incest with father's former wife); 23:2 (23:1, Eng.; crushed testes; cutoff penis); 23:11–14 (23:10–13, Eng.; nocturnal emissions); 23:18–19 (23:17–18, Eng.; so-called cultic prostitution); 28:59–62; 29:21; 32:24 (pestilence and plague).

Three Deuteronomistic layers (Dtr) follow: the second layer (Deut. 5–11), the "Horeb Redaction," includes: Deut. 5:17 (v. 18 Eng.; no adultery). The third layer (Deut. 1–4, 29–30), the "Moab Redaction," includes Deut. 30:9 (promise of prosperous wombs). The fourth layer (Deut. 27, 31– 34), the final post-exilic additions, including the cursing liturgy in chapter 27 and other poems, offers Deut. 27:20–23 (covenant curses rejecting incest and bestiality); 32:24 (plague as a divine arrow); and 33:11(Moses praying that God would smite the loins of the tribe of Levi's foes). The relevant topical material is thinner in the Deuteronomistic layers than in "D" itself.

Within this material, a queer interpreter might notice that:

(1) The sexual system in Deuteronomy is not precisely that of the Holiness Code (H) or other Priestly texts (P) in Leviticus, or for that matter, what emerges from the Genesis Yahwist/Elohist (JE) stories, and indeed shows some shading between its Deuteronomic (D) and Deuteronomistic (Dtr) layers. That is, texts from different putative sources reveal "tensions" between their treatments or, perhaps, developments. For instance, Deuteronomy modifies the purity system, associated with sexual behavior and other matters.

(2) The Deuteronomic gender system contrasts with that of H, P, and JE in Genesis, when it pejorizes the partial and complete eunuch. This also stands in contrast to Isaiah 56:1–8 (part of the haftarah read with Deut. 31 and on public fast days). This passage presents righteous, Sabbath-keeping eunuchs promised a divine inheritance. Likewise, it contrasts to Jeremiah's reception of the divine command to be asexual (16:2). However, the creation of a castrate may be implied in Moses's call for divine punishment on tribal Levi's foes (Deut. 33:11). Another "prooftext of terror" allegedly condemning "cross-dressing" (Deut. 22:5) also stands in contrast to the Jeremiah who prophesies that God "has created a new thing on earth: a woman encompasses a man" (31:22, NRSV).

(3) The interpretation of other Deuteronomic "prooftexts of terror" rely on interpretative myths that understand Deuteronomy 23:18–19 (vv. 17–18, Eng.) as cultic prostitution (and ultimately take these verses as anti-gay); and the threatened judgments of plagues particularly aimed at HIV/AIDS and other "gay" diseases in the LGBTQIA+ community.

Prior interpretations of these passages sometimes appear to rely on impressionistic readings or reader assumptions taken as normative and, thus, not in need of ideological disclosure or examination. In this regard, the parade example is the common interpretation of Deuteronomy 23:18–19. That this must refer to cultic prostitution has been the foregone conclusion by many readers of Frazer's Golden *Bough*.[2]

Deuteronomic Sexual System in Biblical Comparison

Within the Pentateuch, there appears to be six major biblical species of sexual transgression: adultery, incest, bestiality, sex—literal or metaphoric—with divine or other numinal beings such as angels or ghosts, menstrual sex, and *zenût* (root z-n-h), or "lechery, whoredom." This last term is used to refer to prostitution and heterosexual fornication (Deut. 22:21), including that done by men leading to idolatry (Num. 25:1). Thus *zenût* is also attracted toward the category of "adultery" (root n-ʔ-p, Hos. 4:12-14) and used metaphorically for numinal sex (i.e., idolatry) (Lev. 20:5; Deut. 31:16). One could also ask if adultery, as the parade case of sexual misbehavior, is sometimes a synecdoche subsuming *zenût* and all other forbidden sex. Does it sometimes stand for the whole? Or is *zenût* the overarching genus?

What may be surprising is that the treatments of sex (and sexuality) are handled somewhat differently within the putative sources JE, P, H, D and its Dtr editors. Thus, another question: Are differences a matter of simple supplementation, suggesting that all sexual misbehaviors are to be read together as a continuous set? That is, are they part of a giant "playing field," with equal importance, as suggested by the famous codifications of biblical law in Maimonides's *Mishneh Torah* (1170–1180) or Joseph Karo's *Shulkhan Arukh* (1565)? Or, should each biblical treatment stand alone? Are differences then to be smoothed over and suppressed, or should differences be privileged and even similarities treated as different because of local context? Does near or distant context trump when extracting meaning? Or, if differences arise from rule swap-outs in subsequent texts, do they also show a development of ideas? Obviously, all these questions bear on interpretation and so preface the question: How is the Deuteronomic/Deuteronomistic sexual system different?

Incest

For instance, incest is alluded to in three stories in Genesis: a possibility of male-on-male incest between Ham and Noah suggested by the language of "uncovering nakedness," the story of Lot and his daughters, and the story of Reuben and Bilhah (Gen. 35:22, 49:4). Leviticus tremendously elaborates this with its ten commandments against incest (Lev. 18:7–16), with its incipit that covers the nuclear family (Lev. 18:6 read with 21:2–3), and in two instances of quasi-incest, with the two-women rules (Lev. 18:17–18). Leviticus 20:21, the verse that so troubled Henry VIII, even undermines levirate marriage for a widowed sister-in-law. This is followed by penalties ranging in severity from death to childlessness (Lev. 20:11–14, 17, 20–21). In particular, male-male incest is picked up implicitly in the nuclear family as above, the male central figure (EGO) with his father (Lev. 18:7–8) and his paternal uncle explicitly (Lev. 18:14). As I have argued elsewhere, Leviticus 18:22, and especially 20:13 within its in-law context, extends the male prohibition to the same range of male-female incest (see Stewart 2006, 2017, 2020). Female-on-female incest is never mentioned.

In Deuteronomy's arguably post-exilic Deuteronomistic layer, prohibitions of incest with stepmother (27:20), sister and half-sister (27:22), and mother-in-law (27:23) implicitly include the mother, reasoning from minor cases to major. The three explicit prohibitions are reinforced by the anathemas of the covenantal cursing liturgy (Deut. 27:15–26). Deuteronomy 23:1/22:30 (Eng.) forbids marrying a father's [former] wife. "Former" is supplied by translators to clarify that the mother, or current stepmother, is not in view (already forbidden), or current concubine (already condemned in the Reuben-Bilhah story). She must be either a widowed wife or a divorced wife (Tigay 1996, 209). Deuteronomy thus forbids a different levirate marriage than Leviticus (i.e., son with father's former wife). Perhaps Deuteronomy also forbids here EGO's sexual relations with the widowed or abandoned concubine. The Deuteronomistic literature, after all, takes up the cases of misused, widowed concubines: Absalom with the ten concubines of his father David (2 Sam. 16), and Adonijah's attempt to take Abishag, the widowed concubine of David (1 Kings 2).

Bestiality

Adam's task of naming the animals proved useless as a mate search: "for Adam no fitting helper was found" (Gen. 2:20). Thus, we are set up for concern about animal-human sex. The Covenant Code forthrightly forbids sex with animals (or probably more specifically, with quadrupeds or domestic livestock, as *běhēmâ* can convey meaning on several different taxonomic levels—species, genus, phylum) and prescribes the death penalty (Exod. 22:19). Further, Leviticus 20:15–16 specifies death for man, woman, *and beast*. This follows Leviticus 18:23's quite graphic commandments: "With respect to any livestock, do not place your penis in it to defile yourself" (my translation). Leviticus 18:23b, at the climax of Leviticus 18's concatenation of sexual reprobation, prohibits a woman standing in front of a beast as *tebel* or "confusion." This might allude to sexualized folk tales about Eve and the serpent (biblically, a quadruped at first). But if it were possible, Leviticus 20:16 pushes the envelope even further by using different verbs. The woman "approaches" the livestock or quadruped "to lie down with it" showing intent and action. Here we arrive at the parade sexual behavior by women that is forbidden in the Hebrew Bible—not lesbianism by the way, which is never mentioned anywhere. Kinsey found female bestiality to be almost nonexistent except in the imagination (Kinsey et al. 1953, 505, 509). Rather, Kinsey found that such behavior was most often exhibited by teenage boys and livestock workers (Kinsey, Pomeroy, and Martin 1948, 670–671, 674). As for Deuteronomy, it simply condemns sexual relations with livestock by another covenantal curse (27:21).

Numinal and Menstrual Sex

Deuteronomy pays no attention to the "sons of *elohim*" with the "daughters of men" (Gen. 6), or the men of Sodom's desire for angelic beings (Gen. 19), or the condemnation of "passing seed to Molekh" (Lev. 18:21; 20:1–5) where "seed" is a double entendre (literally semen or, metaphorically, children offered to an idol), or *zenût* with ghosts (Lev. 20:6). Instead, Deuteronomy condemns consulting ghosts by the technology of *ʾōb wĕyiddĕʿōnî* and seeking oracles from the dead (Deut. 18:11).

Deuteronomy does not take up the wash-up-and-wait purity rules associated with the emission of semen in heterosexual relations (Lev. 15:19). Neither does Deuteronomy take up the menstrual sex prohibition (Lev. 18:19) or its "cutoff" penalty (i.e., the failure of one's posterity) (Lev. 20:18–19). Deuteronomy mentions no sexual discharges except pollution by nocturnal emission of soldiers in the military encampment (a Dtr text, Deut. 23:11–14; vv. 10–13, Eng.). Traditional rabbinic interpretation takes the "anything untoward" of Deuteronomy 23:10 as covering all sorts of ritual pollutions and moral misfires (Tigay 1996, 213–214).

The underplay of "numinal" and menstrual sex and sexual pollution shows a kind of demythologization of prohibited sex in Deuteronomy's sexual system. However, the attachment of covenantal curses to three forms of incest and bestiality might be seen as an opposite move. Though these ritual curses echo the ancient Near Eastern treaty genre, especially Hittite suzerain treaties, they are different from Job's self-curses in his oath of clearance (Job 31) and the famous "negative confessions," or "declaration of innocence before the gods of the Tribunal," in the *Egyptian Book of the Dead* (ch. 125). Rather, the "amens" to each of the curses (Deut. 27: 20–23) resonate with the "amen, amen" to the curse the suspected adulteress, or *sotah*, accepts in the ritual for jealousy (Num. 5:22). Nevertheless, Deuteronomy lacks the contagion "magic" of Numbers where the written curses are dissolved into the "water of bitterness" that the woman drinks. The Deuteronomic curses are spoken aloud but not materially consumed.

Adultery: Heterosexual Texts of Terror?

Adultery is the "great sin" in ancient Egypt (Rabinowitz 1959) and at Ugarit (Moran 1959) and in Genesis 20:9. Genesis addresses seven boundary cases of potential adulteries: the three wife-sister stories (Abraham and Sarah, Isaac and Rebekah, with Pharaoh, and Abimelech), two slave stories (Abraham and Hagar, Joseph and Potiphar's wife), a possible but not certain rape by Shechem of Dinah (Feinstein 2014, 77), and Tamar bat-Shua posing as a *qĕdēšâ* to accost her father-in-law so that he would perform his levirate duties. Triangulating from these cases suggests that adultery is (1) consensual sex, (2) consummated between a married woman and a man other than her husband, (3) where both have agency, and (4) her paramour knows she is married. The relationship is *not* symmetrical: A married man may have an extramarital relationship as long as the other woman is not married. "A husband had an exclusive right to his wife; a wife might share her husband with his other wives and did not have an exclusive right to him" (Tigay 1996, 71). Moreover patrilineal inheritance of property also necessitated certainty that the child of a wife was the child of her husband, or her *levir*, to raise up an inheritor for the deceased. Thus both the apodictic commands against adultery at Sinai/Horeb (Exod. 20:14) and the command on the Moabite plain (Deut. 5:17, v. 18 Eng.) would reasonably draw on this view from Genesis. But H offers more specificity, forbidding relations with the fellow citizen's wife (*ʾēšet-ʿămîtĕkā*, Lev. 18:20) to avoid "pollution," but specifying the death penalty for adultery with a man's wife (*ʾēšet-ʾîš*, Lev. 20:10a) who is a neighbor's wife (*ʾēšet-rēʿēhū*, Lev. 20:10b), for both man and woman. This could implicitly cover the *ʾēšet-gēr*, or wife of the resident alien. However, the "designated" or promised slave woman (*šipḥâ neḥĕrepet*), who has relations with someone other than her intended, is not punished (she is presumed to have no agency), though her rapist who also does *not* die, must offer an expensive ʾāšām sacrifice (Lev. 19:20–22). No recompense is paid to the slave master by the rapist, although he has taken the virginity of the slave; nor is there recompense to the slave woman herself.

Thus, while Deuteronomy retains the generality of the Sinaitic command (Deut. 5:17, v. 18, Eng.), it expands the death penalty beyond the circle of the neighbor's wife (and leaves out the problem of ritual and moral pollution with the fellow citizen's wife). The parade command at Deuteronomy 22:22 prescribes death for relations with *any other* man's wife (ʾiššâ bĕʿūlat-baʿal), for both man and woman. Moreover, Deuteronomy defines relations with virgin women who are betrothed (Deut. 22:23–27) and so secured by a bride-price, as adultery, *extending the coverage* of the law in a second way. When a man "lies with" a virgin in the city, she is guilty of adultery unless she cries out at her rape (vv. 23–24), perhaps like Tamar bat-David (2 Sam. 13:19). The woman taken by force in the mountains is presumed to have cried out and so faces no penalty (vv. 25–27). Without reference to the slave case in H, it also takes up concerns about virgin women wrongly (Deut. 22:13–19) and rightly accused (Deut. 22:20–21) of sex before betrothal or marriage, preserving patriarchal rights to the father's missed bride-price when his daughter has been raped (Deut. 22:28). The rapist must marry, and never divorce, the raped girl (v. 29). She is *not* asked what she thinks. This particular law also seems to take into account the Deuteronomistic story of Tamar bat-David who, at the verge of rape by her half-brother Amnon, requests marriage (2 Sam. 13:8–17). However, no biblical text here deals with the rape of a married woman unlike Hittite law no. 197 (Hoffner 1997), though one might argue *a fortiori* that she is covered.

Coming to punishments for adultery, where H prescribes the death penalty (Lev. 20:10), the mode of execution is not specified but presumed by most commentators to be stoning. Thus Deuteronomy 22:21–22 seems to be read *into* Leviticus. The girl found guilty of fornication is stoned in v. 21. By *a fortiori* reasoning, traditional commentators argue the same penalty applies to adulterers. But P has an entirely different solution in Numbers 5:11–31, the ritual for jealousy. By placing on the head of the suspected adulteress the "meal offering of remembrance," giving her the "water of bitterness" to drink, and vocalizing an imprecation with the woman's "Amen," the spell is induced to enter her. Proof of her guilt is shown either by the prolapse of her internal organs (womb and vagina) or a miscarriage (i.e., a ritually induced abortion). If none of this happens, and she can "retain seed," she is absolved. Neither H nor D makes space for this trial by ordeal.[3]

In summary, and taking Deuteronomy as a stand-alone text, the analysis above shows within Deuteronomy a narrowed field of incest prohibitions, and one new forbidden relationship within the entire field of biblical incest concerns the husband's former wife. Minimal incest and bestial rules are enforced by covenantal curses. No interest is shown in numinal or menstrual sex. Seminal emissions are only a concern in the war camp. Adultery as a sexual crime is greatly enlarged to include all men's wives and the betrothed. In addition, the death penalty extends to "questionable" rapes in the city and the wife found not to be a virgin upon marriage. In Deuteronomy, adultery shows up in its foundational and Deuteronomistic layers (in an extended sense in the family texts of Deut. 21:19–25:19 for D and the general command in Deut. 5:17 for Dtr-Horeb). On the basis of Hosea 4:13–14 read with Deut 22:21, Phyllis Bird argues that "fornication and adultery" are "the most serious of women's offenses" as "an attack on men's honor" (1997b: 232 and n. 41). Thus, D does not reinforce the notion in H (Lev. 18 and 20) of women having intercourse with animals as their parade sexual misbehavior.

Sexuality in Deuteronomy

The reduced interest of Deuteronomy in the other categories of sexual behavior—incest, bestiality, numinality, and menstrual sex—raises the question as to whether the category of adultery is meant to stand for all forbidden sex. This might be the conclusion if all of the sex texts across putative biblical documents were read together. By expanding its adultery rules to cover the betrothed and its penalties to cover virgins, Deuteronomy may be moving that way. After all, many incests could also be adulteries, and the focus on in-law cases and restriction of the levirate are in that direction too.

The heteronormativity of Deuteronomy is reinforced by its silence on female-female, intersex, or male-male sexual relations. Fulfilling the prime directive (to reproduce, multiply, and fill the earth (Gen. 1:28, 9:1, 7), and its associated concern for fertility, is only really supported by the rejection of bestiality. The silence about forbidding menstrual relations (a practice that pushes heterosexual relations into times of fertility) may leave sex during menstruation available for "natural" birth control. The patriarchal concern for producing progeny known to be the father's supports the hedging-in of sex through adultery, incest, and virginity rules. The "sexuality" of Deuteronomy is not so much "heterosexuality" of the modern world (as many heterosexual behaviors are forbidden and there is no opposite here) or the binary sexualities of "permitted" and "forbidden," often found in the ancient world (Foucault 1:37–38, 106, 2:25, 27, 30–32). Rather, it offers something more like Foucault's notion of "sanguinity," the "sexuality" that preserves bloodlines and unites suitable families (Foucault 1:69, 109).

The bloodline concern comes front and center with the *mamzer*: "No one misbegotten (*mamzer*) shall be admitted into the congregation of the Lord" (Deut. 23:3 (23:2, Eng.). The meaning of *mamzer* is not certain, but its context suggests either the offspring of illicit relations, as in the incest of Deuteronomy 23:1 (22:30, Eng.), or relations with a foreigner like the Ammonite or Moabite mentioned in v. 4 (23:3, Eng.), or possibly the fruit of prostitution (Tigay 1996, 211). As argued below, same-sex relations are mostly, if not totally, ignored.

DEUTERONOMIC GENDER SYSTEM IN BIBLICAL COMPARISON

If in the twenty-first century we approach gender in terms of cisgender (mental gender and body parts at birth agree), transgender (mental gender and body parts from birth disagree), and nonbinary (neither mental gender nor, in some cases, body parts conform to the gender poles), we gain some sense of the complexity of gender. But neither ancient Israel nor the Tannaim and Amoraim who sought to interpret and reason with biblical law were stuck in binarisms. In Genesis chapter two, we can already see three genders: *hāʾādām* the androgyne, cut into two parts and refashioned as *ʾiššâ* and *ʾîš*, the former named Ḥawwah (Eve), and the latter named Adam (Boyarin 1995, 35–46). Nature itself teaches us that as many as 2 percent of human beings are "intersex," though not fully bigendered.[4] Some such persons would fall under the halakhic category of "eunuch under the sun" (*sārîs hammâ*, "a born eunuch with a penis but without viable testes or other sexual maturation by age twenty." See m.Yeb. 8:4), as opposed to a "eunuch made so by a human" (*sārîs ʾādām*, a eunuch by cutting off testes, penis, or both; see Maimonides, *Mishneh Torah* (*Marriage* 2:13-14). The rabbis in *Mishnah Arakhin* (1:1) and many other places refer to *four* genders when grappling to apply biblical laws *that are gendered* (e.g., in Leviticus 27:1–7) (P). *M. Arakhin* takes up the issue of the fines associated with retracting a vow that gives a person to God—a girl or boy, or a woman or man. Some biblical laws, of course, are not specific to gender and so apply to everyone—but these are not. The operative question of the rabbis here seems to be: How do you apply gender-specific laws to people who are neither male nor female? The solution is that the law does *not* apply to the *ʾandrôgînôs*, the Mishnaic Hebrew term for "androgyne" borrowed from Greek, and the *ṭumṭum*, the "person of unknown gender," or "one whose genitals are hidden by a skin flap." Their reasoning follows a sort of matrix algebra: (+male/-female = male); (+female/-male = female); (+male/+female = *ʾandrôgînôs*); (-male/-female = *ṭumṭum*). Jewish halakhot add the two types of eunuchs above, plus the *ʾāylônît*, "a ram-like woman with no breasts, etc." (*Mishneh Torah: Marriage* 2:6), as gender phenomena for as many as seven genders in modern counts.

Leviticus 27:8 (P) may hint at one other possible solution, though couched as an exception for the poor, "But if one cannot afford the equivalent, he shall be presented before the priest, and the priest shall assess him . . ."—here assessing an affordable fine. In Leviticus chapters 13 and 14 (P), priests also evaluate the symptoms of scale disease, the degree of mold in cloth and houses, and so on. Thus, one can imagine how the cases of intersex persons drew attention, first from circumcisers (*mohelim*) and then, ultimately, from priests who, when the intersex persons were brought to them, exempted them from laws specific to men and women.

Deuteronomy, as seen above, has its own share of gendered laws, specific to family inheritance, misbehavior of sons, marriage, rape, accused virgin girls, nocturnal emissions, and so on. Two laws in Deuteronomy take up this problem. Deuteronomy 22:5 mentions the "instruments" appurtenant to males and females. Second, injuries to genitals, unlike in Leviticus 21:20 where the concern is restricted to priests, Deuteronomy 23:2 (23:1, Eng.) takes these as an issue for all Israelite castrates.

Deuteronomy 22:5: Cross-Dressing?

The history of the reception of Deuteronomy 22:5 has been vexed in the modern era. The New Jewish Publication Society (NJPS) translation reads:

> A woman (*ʾiššâ*) must not put on man's apparel (*kĕlî-geber*),
> Nor shall a man (*geber*) wear woman's clothing (*śimlat ʾiššâ*);
> For whoever does these things is abhorrent to the Lord your God (*tôʿăbat-YHWH*).

This is not unlike nearly all English translations except Young's Literal Translation (YLT) which manages to use the plural "habiliments" for *kĕlî* (sg.), suggesting something like "characteristic apparatus." Rabbinic Hebrew uses the plural, *kĕlē* for "clothing" (Tigay 1996, 200) but the plural in biblical Hebrew does not (e.g., 1 Sam. 21:6, "vessels"). Thus, "apparel" or "clothing" is not quite right for the first arm of the verse. The normal meaning in biblical Hebrew is "implement" or "vessel," and *Targum Onkelos* translates it as *zên haggeber*, "weapon" or "armor of a man."[5] My translation is more hyperliteral and closer to the syntax:

(1) [A] Do not have [B] the weapon-of-a-strong-man [C] on a woman;
(2) [A'] Do not wear, [C'] O strong man, [B'] a garment-of-a-woman,
(3) because it is an abhorrence of the Lord your God, whoever does these.

This clarifies that there are two apodictic laws and a motive clause. Most commentators appear to read *back* the phrase *śimlat ʾiššâ* into *kĕlî-geber*, ignoring the semantic difference between *ʾîš* and *geber*,[6] and that *śimlat* and *kĕlî* are both singular. Most also miss the possible vocative, "O strong man." A vocative in "clause-medial position," which partitions off the beginning clause constituent, "seems to highlight the informational status of the initial constituent." The back end of the clause also receives "rhetorical highlighting" (Miller 2010, 356–358). Thus, "O strong man" highlights the *different* information in the first and third constituents of the second clause from those of the first clause, "a garment cannot be worn," rather than "an instrument or weapon held or placed."

The NJPS and most English translations *do* show the parallelism inherent in the first two arms of the verse, but not what it actually looks like. The patterns of words and phrases in the first arm is: (A) command verb, (B) things appurtenant to a person, but (C) not appurtenant to another person. The second arm rearranges these as A', C', B'. The verse also appears to emphasize the man (Brenner 1997, 145 n. 52; Guest 2006, 233), as the woman is not the grammatical subject of the first clause. Note how this happens: centering "strong man" in the second clause highlights him as an appositive to the commanded subject, "you," setting him up as the identified subject of direct address.

Thus, collapsing these features of the texts, stressing symmetry and synonymy, and erasing variegation leads to the easy, yet anachronistic, assertion that this is about cross-dressing and homosexuality. Gagnon does this in *The Bible and Homosexual Practice* without any exegesis of this particular verse in his six mentions (2001, 109, 119, 135, 156, 311, 438). A polemic does not answer the questions the verse raises: What are the "instruments" of a "strong man"? Why use the fancier term, *geber*? What is possibly intended here?

Tigay (1996, 200, 383) collects, and others add, possible rationales for these two prohibitions:

(1) transvestism, as gender-blurring, would violate the law of forbidden mixtures (*kilʾayīm*; see Lev. 19:19 and Deut. 22:9–11 and below);
(2) a disguise for heterosexual males to gain access to women's areas for fornication (Rashi; Ibn Ezra also argues the inverse, that women would change to men's clothes for promiscuity with men);
(3) as a source of sexual stimulation;
(4) as homosexual role-playing that blurs sexual boundaries (Frymer-Kensky 1989, 97);
(5) as a practical complication to maintaining ritual purity (*m. Kelim*);
(6) as part of "pagan" rites or magical practices (see Hoffner 1966; Nissinen 1998);
(7) as "blurring-of-the-order-of-creation" (Davidson 2007); who bolsters it with
(8) a structuralist literary argument.

Explanations (2), (3), and (4) depend on eisegesis that sexualizes the passage not supported by the base text itself as noted above. Rationales (2) and (4) involve what we might call "cruising" in the present day. Transvestism, as a subterfuge for heterosexual sex ((2)), is an example of a practice read into a text where there is no biblical story that would corroborate the gesture. Likewise, rationales (3) and (4) appear to be homiletical "applications" without any other confirmation in biblical narrative, and indeed (4) looks like a backformation from the hetero/homosexual binary. The medieval commentators saw the main crime as heterosexual while some contemporary readers see the main crime as homosexual.

As for rationale (5), one could argue that *Kelim*, the very Mishnah that deals with gear that becomes ritually polluted by exposure to semen or menstrual blood (Kelim 1.5), has Deuteronomy 22:5 (and probably also 23:11–14 on nocturnal emissions) in view. In its elaboration of the purity system, it discusses the potential ritual uncleanness of a spinner's coil and the knob of a spindle (Kelim 11.6), weapons of war (11.8), a sword (13.1), and a quiver (16.8). If the "potency of a woman with a discharge transcends that of a man with a discharge" (1.4), a practical problem for warfare arises from trading gear or clothing back and forth (uncleanness is communicated by contact and carrying, 1.3)—affecting both, but perhaps the *geber* the most.

Of the remainder, (1) and (7) + (8) are versions of the problem of mixtures, and (6) is the problem of non-Israelite rites or magic practices. These two problems appear to be the strongest biblical explanations on offer. However, I will argue that this last point, which is consistent with the rejection of idolatry in the law and prophets, and the strong rejection of magical practices by Deuteronomy, is the most likely.

Davidson, in *Flame of Yahweh*, argues the strongest version of the mixture problem by linking his "blurring-of-the-order-of-creation" rationale to a literary argument. "The natural order of creation which divided humanity into male and female" is corrupted, he argues (Davidson 2007, 171). He invokes Genesis, nature, and the rationale of *kīl'ayīm* simultaneously. However, we have already seen that the "natural order" gives us intersex people, and the "natural order of creation" in Genesis chapter two gives us three models of a human: androgyne, male, and female. Do not intersex people continue the divine image of the androgyne, as male and female together, or like the *ṭumṭum*, a person of hidden gender, just as the divine gender is hidden (Exod. 33:22–23)? Thus, Davidson really leaves us with the problem of *kīl'ayīm* alone.

Davidson develops support for his thesis by adding a literary argument based on Steven Kaufman's analysis of the structure of Deuteronomy as a whole, and particularly of Deuteronomy 22:5–12, where he sees a chiasmus (X-structure). The chiastic structure of Deuteronomy 22:5–12, in his view, is formed by repeated topics: the first arm, (A) v. 5, dress; the second, (B) vv. 6–7, animals; (C) v. 8, house; (C') v. 9, field; (B'); v. 10, animals; and the final arm, (A') vv. 11–12 clothing. Note that vv. 9–11 deal with the principle of *kīl'ayīm* mixing two seeds interplanted in vineyards (v. 9), yoking two kinds of plow animals (v. 10), and wearing linsey-woolsey cloth (linen + wool, v. 11). He does not treat the tassels of v. 12. "By means of this arrangement, the law against "cross-dressing" is placed in chiastic parallel with the laws against forbidden mixtures" (172 n. 143). His position has the virtue of using part of the near context of Deuteronomy 22:5.

However, three issues work against the literary structural argument before examining the question of *kīl'ayīm* proper. The chiastic arms are only parallel if the details of the arms are conflated into topics, and v. 12, which may also be a case of *kīl'ayīm* (Milgrom 2000, 1662–1663), is left out. Chiasmus, as an X-structure, is a focusing trope that privileges its central position. Here it must then be (C) and (C'), the parapet of a house and a second planting in a vineyard. The double focus does not make sense. Further, arms (B) and (C) are not about *kīl'ayīm*, while (C'), (B'), and v. 11 (A') are. The "chiasm" is not balanced. Based on the analysis above, verse 5 (A) is, at best, only partially about clothing. Finally, the notion of the chiasm overlooks the Masoretic paragraph markings. Verse 6 is preceded by a *petucha*, signifying that what follows is independent and not intimately connected to the preceding paragraphs. Verse 5, and the paragraphs before, are themselves preceded by *setumaot*, indicating "what is closed," that is, what is connected. Thus, according to the Massoretes, verse 5 is connected to what is before but independent of what is after. There is no chiasmus here.

With respect to the principle of *kīlʾayīm*, Nelson argued, "mixtures seen as violating or blurring natural or social boundaries were thought to generate impurity (Lev. 19:19)." Thus for Nelson, failing to differentiate gender boundaries, as alleged in Deuteronomy 22:5, is forbidden as something *tôʿēbâ*, "repugnant" (2004, 267–268). However, this argument confuses the categories of "purity" and "holiness" (Lev. 19:19 is part of the Holiness Code and is *not* part of the Purity Code in Lev. 11–15). Moreover, "purity/impurity" (*ṭāhŏr/ṭūmʾâ*) language is not used in Leviticus 19:19, or in Deuteronomy 22:5 or 22:9–12.

Nevertheless, for many commentators the problem of "mixtures" becomes mixed up with the problem of "impurity." These two categories are not a union set and do not intersect. This is not a minor confusion either. The mixed linsey-woolsey cloth, also known as *šaʿaṭnēz*, is not forbidden because it is impure[7] but because it is sanctified, that is, set apart for the priests' garments, the high priest's turban (Exod. 28:6, 28:37, 39, 39:29), and the tabernacle's inner curtains (Exod. 26:1), as first argued by Josephus and more recently by Milgrom (2000, 1662–1663). Milgrom also points out that the rule against sowing a second seed in a vineyard (Deut. 22:9) will sanctify (*yiqdaš*) the yield. Indeed, the tassels of Deuteronomy 22:12 may also have been made of *šaʿaṭnēz*, and so sanctified. As Milgrom argues: "The tassels, then, are an exception to the Torah's general injunction against wearing garments of mixed seed.... The resemblance to the priest's turban and other priestly clothing is no accident" because it reminds the wearer that they can also participate in that sanctity (Milgrom 2000, 1663–1664). Thus, if *kīlʾayīm*'s principle of sanctification is operative in Deuteronomy 22:5, surely this does not lead to the conclusion desired by Davidson. But are the gender inversions "holy" in some sense? Do gender changes then set aside trans* people as special to God? The answer could be "yes."

That gear swapping might lead to "sanctification," or divine set-aside, does appear in non-Israelite religious contexts. Nissinen argues, "both castration and cross-dressing were signs of devotion to an alien deity" (1998, 43). Nissinen discusses the example of the goddess Ishtar/Inanna's cultic functionaries, *assinnūtu, kurgarūtu, and kuluʾūtu*:

> Their duties consisted of ecstatic dance, music, and plays. They dressed up and wore makeup like a woman, and they carried masks and weapons, which they used in their dances and plays. According to the Neo-Sumerian *Hymn of Iddin-Dagan* to *Inanna*, they played an important role in the New Year's festival in which they proceeded before Inanna dressed as androgynes. Their typical gear was a spindle (*pilaqqu*)—a feminine symbol—but they also bore swords and other cutting weapons. (1998, 30)

However, Hoffner provides the most important arguments here that have not been adequately answered. He argues that, in ancient Israel, "the symbols of virile manhood were the bow and arrow, and those of womanhood the spindle or distaff and the characteristically feminine garments" (1966, 329) based on David's lament for Saul and Jonathan (2 Sam. 1:22), to which we might add the sword from the same verse.[8] Proverbs 31:19 references the spindle, as does 2 Samuel 3:29. This symbolization mimics the proscriptions of Ugaritic and

Hittite texts as well as Luwian hieroglyphic evidence from the neo-Hittite principalities in ancient Syria. In the Ugaritic tale of Aqhat, where bow and arrows made by the divine smith, Kathar-wa-Khasis, are requested by the goddess Asherah. "Aqhat reminds her that the bow is for men, and in particular for heroes, but not for women" (Hoffner 1966, 330, 333; II Aqhat VI 39–40). Indeed, Asherah herself holds the spindle in a Hittite version of the Canaanite myth of Elkunirša (p. 330 and n. 24). The holding of the spindle by men implies a loss of masculine strength and is part of an exculpatory curse laid on Joab and his descendants. David uses this to clear himself of wrongdoing over the death of Abner (2 Sam. 3:28–29). Of course, self-curses made in fealty to the covenant are already part of Deuteronomy (Deut. 27:15–26).

Hoffner asks the critical question: "Why . . . would an ancient man or woman wish to wear the attire or symbols of the opposite sex?" (333). He suggests some of the rationales above: a sexual practice like homosexuality item (4) but adds that this could be said more directly; a cultic practice in veneration of a bi-gendered deity—of which there are some examples including Shaushga at Yazilikaya in Hatti-land, and Ishtar with a beard (333–334). Hoffner opts for the late second millennium BCE . . . "ritual curse forms which utilize the external symbols of masculinity and femininity to maintain, restore, or eradicate the sexual potency of oneself or one's enemy" (334). By sympathetic magic—in particular, the principle of reversal, *contraria contrariis*—"the client [serves] as a kind of living dressmaker's dummy upon whom the practitioner could interchange the symbols which, accompanied by the proper spells, would effect the desired result." His conclusion: "The biblical prohibition [in Deut. 22:5] is characteristically elliptical and makes no mention of motive, but simply describes the outward motions of the practice" (334). Thus, the prohibition of this magic practice echoes the general rejection of seven kinds of magic at Deuteronomy 18:10–11 and the demythologization apparent in the Deuteronomic sexual system.[9] The practice is not sanctifying but its opposite—desanctifying.

The presumptive translation of Deuteronomy 22:5 as "cross-dressing" seems so obvious to the modern reader and perhaps to the translator too, as a "dynamic equivalent." However, the gratuitous sexualization of this verse does no one a favor, though the argument above does seem to save the text for patriarchy—something that *is* found in biblical law. What is specifically condemned in Deuteronomy 22:5 is not gender play or gender swapping per se but rather gender play in service to magic-for-ill or to another god.

Thus, we come to the third arm of Deuteronomy 22:5, where the two magical practices are declared *tôʿăbat-YHWH*, "an abhorrence of YHWH." What is abhorrent to God, biblically speaking? *Tôʿēbâ* appears 117 times in nominal form, 17 times in Deuteronomy, and the root appears 22 times as a verb and once so in Deuteronomy.[10] In Deuteronomy, *tôʿēbâ*, refers nine times to idolatry, three times to magic practice (Deut. 22:5 would make four), and once to alleged cultic prostitution (see below).[11]

One problem with difficult biblical passages is to get all the data to fit together. A first glimpse of a possible pattern tempts one to stop. It seems to suffice, but is it optimal? A follow-up question should be asked. Could one reorder the data into a different pattern? The ancient rabbis made an effort to collect interpretations and then "turn them, and turn them again" to see how they worked. To see another pattern takes imagination—even a queer imagination.

Deuteronomy 23:2 (Heb.)//23:1 (Eng.): The Eunuch?

The second difficult passage for constructing gender in Deuteronomy is the eunuch verse. They have either crushed testes (*pĕṣûʿa-dakkāʾ*) or their "spiller" or "penis" has been cut off (*karût šŏpkâ*). What gender is such a eunuch? Does how this happened make a difference? For one might be born this way, and Soughers (2018) points out that one in 1,500–2,000 children is visibly intersex at birth. Such may become a "eunuch" by sex-reassignment surgery as a child, without consent, or as a consenting adult. Prisoners and slaves were candidates for unchosen castration in the ancient world—in our day, trans* people choose sex-reassignment surgery. More common in the modern era are vasectomies, cutting and sealing the tubes carrying sperm. This form of "male birth control" could be viewed functionally as a castration. In the Hellenistic period, some castrated themselves for religious purposes (Tigay 1996, 386 n.24). Thus, if Deuteronomy 22:5 speaks of male and female genders, Deuteronomy 23:2 recognizes the existence of nonbinary gendered people.

All these cases can be accommodated by the modern category of transgender that encompasses all those with gender-marking changes to their bodies, or who feel incongruences between their bodies and their inner gender, or who experience gender fluidity, or understand themselves to be nonbinary. Transgender is the complement of cisgender, which includes males and females who do not experience ambiguities between their bodies and felt gender but rather congruence. Transgender people could be sorted into the additional gender categories implicit and explicit in the biblical texts and developed by the early rabbis discussed above.

From a queer perspective, here is the problem: No one with the two conditions (crushed testes; cutoff penis) "shall be admitted to the congregation of the Lord." Tigay argues, "It is not clear that this law applies to all who have these conditions or only to those who acquired them voluntarily" (1996, 210). If so, does this mean expulsion or restriction for "choosers" with respect to their community? Ibn Ezra asserted that not being "admitted to the congregation" meant castrated people could not marry a Jewish woman. Thus, he seems to perceive that the problem for the community was no seed for reproduction. However, in Israelite times, the "congregation" seems to have been a site of citizenship and communal participation for adult males (Tigay 1996, 209–210), and nonparticipation would be disenfranchising to women and all sorts of eunuchs.

Thus, Deuteronomy 23:2, as it stands, reads as transphobic, especially for a male transitioning to a female. If it were the last biblical word, its most generous interpretation, limiting it to "choosers," still excludes—including catching some "snipped" heterosexual males and adult intersex people in its net. Even though a female transitioning to a male is not contemplated in Deuteronomy 23:2, they might also be excluded on the same basis of inability to deliver seed. In Deuteronomy 33:11, Moses even calls for tribal Levi's foes to be struck in their loins (*yādāyw*), making clear this is perceived as a punishment.

Nevertheless Trito-Isaiah and Jeremiah seem to offer correctives to all this—and so perhaps offer the earliest biblical commentary on Deuteronomy 23:2. At Isaiah 56:3b–5:

> Let not the eunuch (*hassārîs*) say, / I am a withered tree."
> For thus said the Lord: / As for the eunuchs (*sārîsîm*) who keep my sabbaths,
> Who have chosen what I desire / And hold fast to my covenant—
> I will give them in my house / And within my walls,

> A monument (*yād*) and a name / Better than sons and daughters.
> I will give them an everlasting name / Which shall not perish (yikārēt, "be cut off").

Thus Isaiah brings to the table Sabbath- and covenant-keeping eunuchs who will have a "penis" or "loin" (*yād*), metaphorically a "monument," and a name which will not be "cut off"—something better than sons and daughters. Isaiah appears to collect key *Leitworter* from Deuteronomy 23:2 and 33:11. If we turn to a Deuteronomistic narrative, Nathan-melech the eunuch lives "in My house," that is, the precincts of the Jerusalem Temple (2 Kgs. 23:11). How can Nathan-melech live there if not part of the community? Ebed-melech, the eunuch, rescues Jeremiah from the pit (Jer. 38:7–12) and God remembers and names "them" (Jer. 39:15–18). To this list, one could add the righteous eunuchs named in Esther: Hegai, Hattah, and Harbona (Esth. 2:3, 14–15, 4:5, 7:5). What would these eunuchs be allowed to do? Isaiah 56:6-7 suggests that collectively with foreigners they may pray at, and bring sacrifices and offerings to, the Temple.

Jeremiah also speaks of something else: "How long will you waver, O faithless daughter? For the Lord has created a new thing on the earth: *a woman encompasses a man*" (Jer. 31:22 (emphasis added). Although no one really knows what this means, a queer person may offer a midrash: This new creation on earth is a transgender person, someone transmasculine or transfeminine. Or even this: If *hāʾādām* was a male, as some argue, from whom a woman was surgically removed by God (and so the man surrounds the woman in a sense), is the new divine creation the opposite, a woman—a new Eve—who contains the man?

Prooftexts of Terror?

Although several of the texts above might be taken as sexual "texts of terror" for hetero- and bisexual people, and some might attempt to use Deuteronomy 22:5 and 23:2 (23:1, Eng.) to terrorize people who are transgender, intersex, or lesbian through invented applications, there remains another class of difficult texts in Deuteronomy. These texts are specifically applied by some interpreters to all gay people or generalized to all sexual or gender minorities.

Deuteronomy 23:18–19 (17–18, English): Homosexual Cultic Prostitution?

The idea of homosexual cult prostitution, wielded as an accusation against LGBTQIA+ people, takes as a "prooftext" Deuteronomy 23:18–19 (vv. 17–18, Eng.):

> No Israelite woman (*běnôt Yiśrāʾēl*) shall be a cult prostitute (*qědēšâ*),
> Nor shall any Israelite man (*běnê Yiśrāʾēl*) be a cult prostitute (*qādēš*).
> You shall not bring the fee (*ʾetnan*) of a whore (*zônâ*) or the pay (*měḥîr*) of the dog (*keleb*)
> Into the house of the Lord your God in fulfillment of any vow (*neder*),
> For both are abhorrent to the Lord your God (*tôʿăbat-YHWH*).
>
> (NJPS)

Nothing suggests here that a *qādēš*, if he were a cult prostitute, is not servicing women as would be expected if this were about theogamy. Is there such a thing in ancient Israel, and if so, how did we get to the polemical reading of male homosexual prostitute? How does the reliance on synonymous parallelism as an interpretative trope play in understanding the noun pairs, *qĕdēšâ* and *qādēš*, *'etnan* and *mĕḥîr*, *zônâ* and *keleb*? In this case, do the word pairs decode each other's meaning? Of course, parallelism is not only synonymous but often extends ideas, or even pairs opposites. Finally, does the diagnostic term *tôʿēbâ*, and especially its use in Deuteronomy, help illuminate the passage as a whole?

One can see in Targum Onkelos, a third century CE Aramaic translation of the Hebrew, a similar effort to make sense by finding a contemporaneous application:

> A woman of the daughters of Israel shall not become the wife of a slave,
> And no man of Israel shall marry a bondwoman.
> You shall not bring the fee of a whore or the exchange of a dog
> Into the sanctuary of the Lord your God in fulfillment of any vow,
> For both are remote before the Lord your God.
>
> (Drazin 1982, 214)

The issue of slavery is imported to v. 18, and *qĕdēšâ* and *qādēš* are understood as "wife of a slave" and "husband of a slave." The topic of slavery appears in the adjacent verses, vv. 16–17, and are taken to provide context. One suspects this "marriage" is understood as fornication because they could not be properly married. Perhaps Onkelos sees the parallels as metonymic and so allowing the comparison. Abravanel (1437–1508) also does *not* understand these two "prostitutes" as involved in the *cultus* but rather as those that follow armies (i.e., military prostitutes). This view would coordinate with the concern for seminal emissions in the war camp (Deut. 23:11–14).

However, the surface meaning of *qĕdēšâ* and *qādēš* would be "holy female or male worker," or "sanctuary/temple worker," as the dictionaries and more than fifty years of cognate research into Akkadian *qadištu* and Ugaritic *qadišu* suggest (DeGrado 2018, 9, 11, 13). As DeGrado further argues: "The simplest interpretation of Deut 23:18 is that the [*qĕdēšâ*] and the [*qādēš*] are types of cultic functionaries" and "no biblical passage explicitly refers to cultic prostitution" (2018, 20, 23). Gruber (1983, 1986, 1988), who laid much of the groundwork for this conclusion, does think that Deuteronomy 23:18 specifically describes two kinds of individuals, a female adulterer, perhaps influenced by Onkelos' translation, and a male cultic functionary (1983, 173–176).[12]

To use the terms ironically, or as a euphemism, is a secondary move in semantic development. The key texts for this are Genesis 38:15, 21–22 and v. 24. Judah first sees a woman with her face covered and takes her as a *zônâ* (v. 15). Tamar bat-Shua herself understood the setup as she carefully disguises herself (v. 14). When Judah sends his friend to inquire later about the whereabouts of the woman he had met, the Adullamite asks delicately after the *qĕdēšâ*, the villagers answer: "There is no *qĕdēšâ* here." He duly reports this to Judah, using the same term, *qĕdēšâ*. Thus, everyone has plausible deniability—something that is lost if the *qĕdēšâ* is always a *zônâ*. When Tamar bat-Shua begins to show, she is reported to Judah in v. 24 as having "played the harlot [*zāntâ*]" and thus become pregnant by *zĕnûnîm*, "harlotries." Note that Judah's perspective, though framing the story, is independent of the villagers' perspective. The point here is that the two terms may be made synonymous by reader/hearers after the story-event, but the terms are not automatically synonymous here.

If they are, it spoils the humor of the story. That the *qĕdēšâ* is not always a *zônâ* is suggested when the *qādēš* of Deuteronomy 23:18 does not parallel with *zōnê*, a perfectly good masculine term at Hosea 4:14.

DeGrado argues that over time the *Wortfeld* of *qĕdēšâ*, though not at first including "prostitute," becomes extended by a pejoration process to include it (2018, 18). In contrast to scholars who take an all-or-nothing approach—the term always meaning "prostitute and not priestess" or "priestess and not prostitute"—DeGrado suggests that the context determines whether it means "prostitute" or "priestess" but never the two at the same time (2018, 12, 21).

The argument that the *qĕdēšâ* and *qādēš* must be something more than a class of sanctuary functionaries like Nathan-melekh builds on the assumption that Tamar bat-Shua actually was a prostitute, not just called one. It does not consider the subtlety of her disguise and the subtlety of her plan to take Judah as her levir. Once this interpretative domino has fallen, all else follows. The fee of a *zônâ* must be the fee of the *qĕdēšâ*. The *qādēš* is assumed to have a price and everyone knows that dogs are homosexual. The parallelistic pattern is seductive.

However, there are other biblical data available to consider. Hosea 4:13–14b (NJPS) mentions the sacrifice of a *qĕdēšâ*:

(13) They (regularly) sacrifice [*yĕzabbēḥû*] on the mountaintops
And (regularly) offer (up in smoke) [*yĕqaṭṭĕrû*] on the hills . . .
That is why their daughters fornicate [*tîznēnâ*]
And their daughters-in-law commit adultery! [*tĕnāʾapnâ*]
(14) I will not punish their daughters for fornicating [*tîznēnâ*] Nor their daughters-in-law for committing adultery [*tĕnāʾapnâ*];[13] For they themselves turn aside with whores [*hazznôt*]
And (regularly) sacrifice [*yĕzabbēḥû*] with prostitutes [*haqqĕdēšôt*].

As DeGrado notes, "the cultic activities frame a description of illicit sexual acts" (i.e., fornication and adultery), and the "metaphor of adultery" here should "be read in the light of Hosea's broader condemnation of non-Yahwistic worship" (2018, 32–33).

The *qĕdēšâ* offers a sacrifice with an "adulterous" non-YHWH worshipping lover, or perhaps like Hannah assists in the sacrificial slaughter of her own votive offering (1 Sam. 1:25; Pl. of *š-ḥ-ṭ*). This supports the notion of the *qĕdēšâ* as a cultic functionary in an Israelite context. Such a *qĕdēšâ* would need to be clean of sexual discharges, as the woman in Proverbs 7:14 implies, having brought her votive peace offering already. However, if *qĕdēšôt* are cultic functionaries, they are not necessarily from the tribe of Levi, and this could be a part of the problem.

Deuteronomy makes quite a business over not neglecting, and so stressing the importance of, the "Levitical priests" (a coinage of Deuteronomy) and the Levites (eighteen times). The Levites stand to minister before God (18:7), carry the Ark of the Covenant (31:25), and eat the sacrifices (Deut. 18:1). They are to declare with a loud voice the covenantal curse: "Cursed be anyone who makes an idol or casts an image, anything abhorrent to the Lord (*tôʿăbat-YHWH*)" (27:14–15)—echoing the final phrase of Deuteronomy 23:19 above. Stressing the correct tribe for cultic requirements suggests others, non-Levitical workers and their practices, may have inserted themselves into Israelite worship. Such outsider functionaries become a suitable target in the Josianic reform:

He deposed the idolatrous priests whom the kings of Judah had ordained to make offerings in the high places at the cities of Judah and around Jerusalem; those also who made offerings to Baal, to the sun, the moon, the constellations, and all the host of the heavens.

(2 Kgs. 23:5)

This deposing also included the *qadēšîm* (2 Kgs. 23:7; see also 1 Kgs. 14:24; 15:12; 22:47) who are cultic functionaries but never associated with sexual activity despite the translators (Gruber 1983; Bird 1997a; DeGrado 2018, 20–21).

Theogamy?

Some readers of the biblical accounts have postulated that theogamy, or the "fertility cult hypothesis," is in view. The king and the goddess have sex to insure fertility in the land; cultic prostitution imitates and extends this fertility magic. This notion of cultic prostitution in the ancient Near East and among the "Semites" was popularized in the late nineteenth century by Sir James Frazer in *The Golden Bough*. In his extended exposition of the "King and Queen of the Wood" associated with the sacred grove at Lake Nemi south of Rome he asserts that the goal of the fertility goddess and her mate was to demonstrate their own fertility and so promote the fertility of the earth, animals, and humans. He argues that

> dramatic weddings of gods and goddesses . . . were carried out as solemn religious rites in many parts of the ancient world; hence, there is no intrinsic improbability in the supposition that the sacred grove at Nemi may have been the scene of an annual ceremony of this sort. Direct evidence that it was so there is none, but analogy pleads in favor of the view.[14]

Notice that Frazer nicely discloses his circular method: (1) the fertility practice occurs many places but there is no evidence for it here; (2) similarities among such practices allow an analogization of these to represent a singular practice; and so (3) to project it upon the empty screen of Nemi (and ancient Israel). Some chapters later, he connects rites associated with theogamy to the ancient Israelites:

> The Phoenician kings reigned at Citium . . . the Chittim of the Hebrews . . . Naturally, the Semitic colonists brought their gods with them from the motherland. They worshipped Baal of the Lebanon who may have been Adonis, and . . . they initiated the rites of Adonis and Aphrodite, or rather Astarte.[15]

Cultic prostitution is attached to theogamous rites as a kind of apotropaic fertility magic:

> In Cypress, it appears that before marriage all women were formerly obliged by custom to prostitute themselves to strangers at the sanctuary of the goddess, whether she went by the name of Aphrodite, Astarte, or what not. Similar customs prevailed in many parts of Western Asia. Whatever its motive, the practice was clearly regarded . . . as a solemn religious duty performed in the service of that great Mother Goddess of Western Asia whose name varied, while her type remained constant, from place to place.[16]

The payment to the prostitute was forwarded as an offering to the temple, hence, the possible match with Deuteronomy 23:18–19. While this model of cultic prostitution explains opposite-sex cultic prostitution, it cannot explain same-sex prostitution. The embedded assumption that theogamy is a kind of universal explanation that obtains in ancient Israel must be rejected for lack of evidence.

Dogs

One also notices that *keleb*, "dog," is taken literally in Onkelos. Drazin argues that all three Targumim are "paralleling the understanding in Sifre and b. Temurah 29a, 30a: 'if one has exchanged a lamb for a dog'" (Drazin 1982, 215 n.20). As the Targumim are earlier texts, it suggests that the earliest understanding was literal—a sacrificial lamb could not be swapped with a dog or value of one for the other. Likewise, Rashi and Ibn Ezra understood *keleb* as a literal dog. When Abravanel suggests, "dogs are the lowliest of all animals," he seems to explain why dogs are the animal mentioned in a trade of sacrificial animals. Puppies were used in Hittite healing rituals, so the idea that dogs could be used in religious ceremonies is available in the ancient Near East.

Some moderns see dogs as symbolic of "homosexuals" because of the animals' supposed observable behaviors. However, what dog behaviors does the Hebrew Bible actually feature? In its seventeen references, dogs are known for their great appetites, eating mangled meat, dragging away and eating human corpses, licking blood, and prowling about the city at night presumably to find food. Thus the Israelite experience with dogs, beyond helpers to shepherds implied in Job 30:1, is that they run in unsupervised packs, similar to what I saw once in a Guatemalan village. A man there said "Our dogs run free, not like yours" referring to the United States. Similarly, dogs in the New Testament (NT) eat food thrown from tables and lick sores. Thus, "Do not give what is holy to the dogs" (Matt. 7:6). Pack behavior is also referred to in Psalm 22:17 (v. 16, Eng.): "Dogs surround me / a pack of evil ones closes in on me," and in NT exhortations (Phil. 3:2; Rev. 22:15). In two gospels, dogs are analogized to Canaanites (i.e., gentiles). In another fourteen Hebrew Bible verses, "dog" in the singular also functions as a pejorative as in "dead dog," "dog's head," or the question, "Am I a dog?" In *Sirach*, a dog is analogized to the poor and a "headstrong wife." However, nowhere else are dogs a pejorative for homosexual or their alleged sexual behaviors mentioned.

Thus, when looking at the biblical contexts for *keleb* there is really no basis for jumping to the conclusion that this must be a male homosexual prostitute. "Homosexuality" is not a category in ancient Israel and the term was not even invented until the nineteenth century. While a dog could be part of a ritual in the ancient Near East, in Israel its habits of eating mangled flesh, corpses, and blood, would disqualify the animal for sacrifice if it were not already disqualified as the wrong kind of quadruped (Deut. 14:3–8).

Thus, when considering votive offerings of an animal, it must be an "animal that may be brought to the Lord" (Lev. 27:9). Such may not be exchanged for one better or worse (Lev. 27:10). If it is an unclean animal, like a dog, "that may not be brought as an offering to the Lord," it must be presented to the priest who assesses its value (Lev. 27:11–12) and can potentially be ransomed (Lev. 27:27) by paying the assessment. However, Deuteronomy does *not allow* this Priestly workaround for an unclean animal. No equivalent assessment of the *měḥîr*, value or price, of the dog is permitted as a substitute.

Thus, if two sorts of extra-Israelite or non-Levitical and idolatrous sanctuary functionaries and two types of votive offerings are forbidden, the verses *are* about the *cultus*. It is not about cultic prostitution or idolatry per se but about the infusion of unpermitted practices into Israelite worship. There has been a breakdown concerning who can be Temple functionaries (only Levitical priests and Levites). There is a second breakdown of the purity system in sacrifice (no unclean animal equivalents and no offerings of prostitution fees potentially or symbolically polluted by sexual discharges). This is what is tôʿēbâ.

Collecting these observations, and deploying them in a more literal translation of Deuteronomy 23:18–19:

> There shall not be a (non-levitical, non-Yahwistic) sanctuary worker (*qĕdēšâ*) among the daughters of Israel;
> There shall not be a (non-levitical non-Yahwistic) sanctuary worker (*qādēš*) among the sons of Israel.
> Do not bring a fee of a *zônâ* or value of a dog
> (into) the "house of YHWH your God," for any vow,
> Because it is an "abhorrence of YHWH your God, i.e. both of them are.

Diseased Body or "Plague System"

The LGBTQIA+ community, along with the Jewish community, has been sensitized to the idea that plagues can be blamed on, or thought of as punishments for, minority communities and their behaviors (same-sex relations; not converting to Christianity). Deuteronomy has three places (28:59, 61; 29:21; 32:4) where plague judgments are threatened. In addition, any behavior that is declared *tôʿăbat-YHWH*, the Deuteronomic reproach in two passages used to condemn the LGBTQIA+ community (Deut. 22:5; 23:18–19), is additionally covered by the covenantal curse at Deuteronomy 27:26 "Cursed be he who does not uphold the terms of this Teaching and observe them." The problem for the LGBTQIA+ community is that diseases that first appear, or mostly appear in this community, especially among gay men, are seen as the wrath of God falling in judgment. "The Lord will bring upon you all the diseases and plagues, *kŏl ḥŏlî wĕkŏl-makkâ*, "that are not mentioned in the Book of Teaching, until you are wiped out" (Deut. 28:61). This summing up *et cetera* could include any other disease not yet imagined in the text. HIV/AIDS, Monkey pox, COVID 19, all could fit into this continuation list. Deuteronomy 28:59 imagines in the *makkôt zarʿe* and *makkôt gedolôt*, "strange and great plagues," all the diseases precipitated by siege warfare (28:49–62): typhus, typhoid, scurvy, intestinal diseases, and dysentery as suggested by Tigay who follows Abravanel (272 n. 93, 397). At Deuteronomy 29:21, Tigay understands *makkôt* as a metaphor for any natural disasters (281). The "continuing plague (*rešep*)" and "deadly pestilence (*qeteb*)" that is possibly smallpox (Deut. 32:24), along with the *makkôt* of chapters 28–29, are covenant-generated punishments. Specifically, they threaten ancient Israelites who vex God by unrepentant idolatry (32:21). Thus, when one generalizes these punishments to any people, for any lawbreaking, how should we then explain children and heterosexual adults with HIV or any disease mentioned above or not yet thought of? Thus, we are left with the question of how to apply justly these verses and the consideration of theodicy.

STANDING WITHIN DEUTERONOMY

Queer analysis offers a correction to the misprision of texts often used to condemn LGBTQIA+ people. This analysis suggests that the primary concerns of Deuteronomy in these "texts of terror" are idolatry and related magical practices. However, to correct problematic readings also erases notice of the lives of LGBTQIA+ people, although the attention was negative. Trans*, intersex, and asexual people might find themselves in Deuteronomy 23:2; lesbians, gays, and bisexuals, in this reading, are not singled out in Deuteronomy, although bisexuals are implicitly covered in the many rules for heterosexuals. However, we are all addressed, straight and queer alike, by Deuteronomy 16:20: "Justice, justice you shall pursue, that you may thrive."

Notes

1. The letters of LGBTQIA+ abbreviate "Lesbian, Gay, Bisexual, Transgender, Queer, Intersex, Asexual, and others." That any of these terms represent distinct identities is not always the case. Whereas "Queer" sometimes encompasses all of these terms, or functions as an identity itself, Queer theory holds open a space for the unthought-of "Other." The plus sign (+) points at other "identities" such as "eunuch," "gender fluid," "gender nonbinary," "Two Spirit" (a cover term for more than 150 indigenous/First Nations' lexica with differing semantic fields), Indigiqueers, etc.; "Transgender," sometimes rewritten as "trans*," also connotes a cluster of possibilities indicated by the asterisk ("transgender," "transsexual," "transfeminine," "transmasculine," etc.). "Intersex" covers seventeen or so bodily syndromes—and is not an identity for most. One might think about all these labels as indicating a three-dimensional space limned by three axes: biological sex (chromosomal, anatomic, and physiological), gender, and sexuality. The various terms describe points, ranges, and clusters of possibilities in that universe. For instance, Kinsey's studies suggested a range of sexualities between exclusive heterosexuality (position 0 in his scheme) and exclusive homosexuality (position 6). His hypothesis did not exhaust the thinking on this point.
2. Frazer began publishing his first volume of *The Golden Bough* in 1890. By 1915 his work extended to 12 volumes. The abridged edition published in 1963, based on the first abridged edition of 1922, is cited herein.
3. These, and somewhat similar observations by Ellens (2008), could be taken up by neo-documentarian debates, suggesting the generativity of LGBTQIA+ interpretation.
4. Thus not a full androgyne or, in more antiquated language, "hermaphroditic" but rather "pseudo-hermaphroditic."
5. Drazin 1982, 204–205 and 205 n.4; Tigay 1996, 210: "The three Targumim reflect the opinion of R. Eliezer b. Yaakov in the Sifre and b. Nazir 59a: 'a woman may not go to war in armor.'" See also Gen. 27:3 when Isaac says to Esau "Take your gear (*kēlêkâ*), your quiver and your bow."
6. This noun form can indicate "strength" (Job 38:3) and not simply "man" as the related verb, *gbr* "be mighty," suggests.
7. Barr has made the case that we have two distinct category sets with two possible intersections: "not holy :: holy" and "(ritually) impure :: pure." Things pure can also be holy or not; things impure cannot be holy, but not all things 'unholy' or 'common' are impure (1973, 123).
8. Hoffner adds 2 Sam. 22:35, 2 Kgs. 13:15–19, Hos. 1:7, and Ps. 127:4–5. See also Gen. 27:3.
9. Or, anti-Canaanite legislation as suggested by Anderson (2004, 31–32, nn. 65, 70) and earlier commentators (e.g., Phillips 1973, 145, 156–157).

10. One hundred thirty-nine times overall in the Tanakh. By contrast *tôʿēbâ* appears only six times in Leviticus, five times in chapter 18 where all forbidden sexual behaviors in the chapter are diagnosed as *tôʿēbâ* (thus in order, incest, menstrual sex, adultery, passing seed to Molekh, stressed for male-male incest, and bestiality) and once in chapter 20 (male-male incest). The key incest crime in Leviticus is father + son such that even mother + son is read as uncovering the nakedness of the father.
11. Idolatry at Deut. 7:25, 7:26 (2x), 12:31, 13:15, 17:4, 20:18, 27:15, 32:16; magic: 18:9, 18:12 (2x) + 22:5; one each for so-called cultic prostitution (23:19), eating unclean animals (14:3), sacrificing an animal with a *mûm* (17:1), remarrying a divorced wife after she had remarried (24:4), and dishonest weights and measures (25:16).
12. See also Goodfriend 1992 for an accessible summary of Gruber's research. Note that Beatrice Brooks (1941) also called attention to the idea that these cult functionaries were not necessarily prostitutes.
13. The uses, similarities, and differences of the roots *z-n-h* and *n- ʾ-p* have been discussed above. Their *Wortfelder* intersect but the terms are not synonymous.
14. James George Frazer, "Chapter XII: The Sacred Marriage" (1922), in *The Golden Bough*, abridged ed. (New York: Macmillan, 1963), p. 162.
15. James George Frazer, "Chapter XXXI: Adonis in Cypress" (1922), in *The Golden Bough*, abridged ed. (New York: Macmillan, 1963), p. 383.
16. Ibid., p. 384.

Bibliography

Anderson, Cheryl B. *Women, Ideology, and Violence: Critical Theory and the Construction of Gender in the Book of the Covenant and the Deuteronomic Law*. JSOT Suppl. 394. London: T & T Clark, 2004.

Barr, James. "Hebrew Lexicography." In *Studies on Semitic Lexicography*. Edited by Pelio Fronzaroli, pp. 103–126. Florence: Istituo di Linguistica e di lingua orientali, Università di Firenze, 1973.

Bird, Phyllis A. "The End of the Male Cult Prostitute: A literary, Historical, and Sociological Analysis of Hebrew *Qādēš-Qědēšim*." In *1995 Congress Volume*. Supplements to Vetus Testamentum. Edited by J. A. Emerton, pp. 37–80. Leiden: Brill, 1997a.

Bird, Phyllis A. "'To Play the Harlot': An Inquiry into an Old Testament Metaphor." In *Missing Persons and Mistaken Identities: Women and Gender in Ancient Israel*, pp. 219–236. Minneapolis: Fortress Press, 1997b.

Block, Daniel I. "Deuteronomic Law." In *The Oxford Encyclopedia of the Bible and Law*. Edited by Brent A. Strawn, pp. 1:182–194. Oxford: Oxford University Press, 2015.

Boyarin, Daniel. *Carnal Israel: Reading Sex in Talmudic Culture*. Berkeley: University of California Press, 1995.

Brenner, Athalya. *The Intercourse of Knowledge: On Gendering Desire and Sexuality in the Hebrew Bible*. Biblical Interpretation Series 26. Leiden: Brill, 1997.

Brooks, Beatrice A. "Fertility Cult Functionaries in the Old Testament." *Journal of Biblical Literature* 60 (1941): 227–253.

Davidson, Richard M. *Flame of Yahweh: Sexuality in the Old Testament*. Peabody: Hendrickson, 2007.

DeGrado, Jessie. "The *qdesha* in Hosea 4:14: Putting the (Myth of the) Sacred Prostitute to Bed." *Vetus Testamentum* 68 (2018): 8–40.

Drazin, Israel. *Targum Onkelos to Deuteronomy*. New York: Ktav, 1982.

Egyptian Book of the Dead: The Book of Going Forth by Day: Being the Papyrus of Ani. Translated by Raymond O. Faulkner; commentary by Ogden Goelet, Jr.; edited by Eva von Dassow. San Francisco: Chronicle Books, 1998.

Ellens, Deborah L. *Women in the Sex Texts of Leviticus and Deuteronomy: A Comparative Conceptual Analysis*. LHBOTS 458. New York: T & T Clark, 2008.

Feinstein, Eve Levavi. *Sexual Pollution in the Hebrew Bible*. Oxford: Oxford University Press, 2014.

Foucault, Michel. *The History of Sexuality: An Introduction*. Vol. 1: *The History of Sexuality*. Translated by Robert Hurley. New York: Vintage Books, 1990.

Frazer, James George. *The Golden Bough* (1922). Abridged ed. Repr., New York: Macmillan, 1963.

Frymer-Kensky, Tikva. "Law and Philosophy: The Case of Sex in the Bible." *Semeia* 45 (1989): 89–102.

Gagnon, Robert A. J. *The Bible and Homosexual Practice: Texts and Hermeneutics*. Nashville: Abingdon, 2001.

Goodfriend, Elaine Adler. "Prostitution." In *The Anchor Bible Dictionary*. Edited by David Noel Freedman, pp. 5:505–510. New York: Doubleday, 1992.

Gruber, Mayer I. "Hebrew *Qedēšāh* and Her Canaanite and Akkadian Cognates." *Ugarit Forschungen* 18 (1986): 133–148.

Gruber, Mayer I. "The *Qedēšāh*: What Was Her Function?" *Běʾēr Šebaʿ* 3 (1988): viii, 45–51. [Hebrew].

Gruber, Mayer I. "The *Qādēš* in the Book of Kings and in Other Sources." *Tarbiz* 52, no. 2 (1983): v, 167–76. [Hebrew].

Guest, Deryn. "Deuteronomy." In *The Queer Bible Commentary*. Edited by Deryn Guest, Robert E. Goss, Mona West, and Thomas Bohache, pp. 122–143. London: SCM Press, 2006.

Hoffner, Harry Angier, Jr. *The Laws of the Hittites: A Critical Edition*. Documenta et Monumenta Orientis Antiqui 23. Leiden: Harrassowitz, 1997.

Hoffner, Harry Angier, Jr. "Symbols for Masculinity and Femininity: Their Uses in Ancient Near Eastern Sympathetic Magic Rituals." *Journal of Biblical Literature* 85 (1966): 326–334.

Kinsey, Alfred C., Wardell B. Pomeroy, Clyde E. Martin, and Paul H. Gebhard. *Sexual Behavior in the Human Female*. Philadelphia: W. B. Saunders, 1953.

Kinsey, Alfred C., Wardell B. Pomeroy, and Clyde E. Martin. *Sexual Behavior in the Human Male*. Philadelphia: W. B. Saunders, 1948.

Ladin, Joy. "Torah in Transition." *Trans Torah* (2008-2023). Accessed July 28, 2022. https://www.transtorah.org.

Maimonides [Rambam]. *Mishneh Torah*.1170-1180. Accessed January 9, 2023. https://www.sefaria.org/texts/Halakah//Mishneh Torah.

Milgrom, Jacob. *Leviticus 17-22: A New Translation with Introduction and Commentary*. The Anchor Bible 3A. New York: Doubleday, 2000.

Miller-Naudé, Cynthia L. "Vocative Syntax in Biblical Hebrew Prose and Poetry: A Preliminary Analysis." *Journal of Semitic Studies* 55 no. 2 (2010): 347–364.

Miqraʾot gedolot [*The Commentator's Bible*]: *Devarim*. Edited, translated, and annotated by Michael Carasik. Philadelphia: Jewish Publication Society, 2015.

Moran, W. L. "The Scandal of the 'Great Sin' at Ugarit." *Journal of Near Eastern Studies* 18 (1959): 280–281.

Nelson, Richard D. *Deuteronomy: A Commentary*. Old Testament Library. Louisville: Westminster John Knox Press, 2004.

Nissinen, Martti. *Homoeroticism in the Biblical World: A Historical Perspective*. Minneapolis: Fortress, 1998.

Otto, Eckart. *Deuteronomium 1-11, Erster Teilband: 1.1-4.43*. Herders Theologischer Kommentar zum Alten Testament. Freiburg: Herders, 2012.

Phillips, Anthony. *Deuteronomy*. Cambridge: Cambridge University Press, 1973.

Rabinowitz, Jacob J. "The 'Great Sin' in Ancient Egyptian Marriage Contracts." *Journal of Near Eastern Studies* 18 (1959): 73.

Soughers, Tara K. *Beyond a Binary God: A Theology of Trans* Allies*. New York: Church Publishing, 2018.

Stewart, David Tabb. "Indigenous Categories of Sexuality in Biblical Law." In *Sexuality and Tora*. Library of Hebrew Bible/Old Testament Studies. Edited by Bruce Wells, pp. 20-47. Bloomsbury: T & T Clark, 2020.

Stewart, David Tabb. "Leviticus." In *The Queer Bible Commentary*. Edited by Deryn Guest, Robert E. Goss, Mona West, and Thomas Bohache, pp. 77-104. London: SCM Press, 2006.

Stewart, David Tabb. "LGBTI/Queer Hermeneutics and the Hebrew Bible." *Currents in Biblical Research* 15, no. 3 (June 2017): 289-314.

Tigay, Jeffrey H. *Deuteronomy*. The New JPS Torah Commentary. Philadelphia: Jewish Publication Society, 1996.

Index

For the benefit of digital users, indexed terms that span two pages (e.g., 52–53) may, on occasion, appear on only one of those pages.

Tables and figures are indicated by *t* and *f* following the page number

Abba, Raymond, 227–228
Achenbach, Reinhard, 295
African-American Christianity
    abolitionism and, 434, 436–437
    Africana Bible and, 441
    AME (African Methodist Episcopal Church) and, 439–440
    American exceptionalism and, 440
    Civil Rights Movement and, 437–439
    Covenant Code and, 433
    critical legal theory (CLT) and, 439–441
    critical race theory (CRT) and, 439–441
    cult centralization and, 441
    Deuteronomic Code and, 433, 441
    Emancipation Proclamation and, 436–438
    Free African Society and, 439
    Freedom Narratives and, 432
    Harlem Renaissance and, 437–439
    Harper's Ferry and, 434
    Jesus and, 436
    Moses and, 437–438
    Poor Peoples Campaign and, 438–439
    SCLC (Southern Christian Leadership Conference) and, 438–439
    Shema and, 433, 435, 437
    slavery and, 433, 436
    stranger, fatherless, and widow and, 441
    white supremacy and, 441
Aharoni, Yohanan, 118–119
Albright, William F., 74–75, 152, 154, 160, 226
Allen, Richard, 439
Alt, Albrecht
    amphictyony and, 260
    case and apodictic law, 43
    Decalogue and, 43
    Hosea and, 258, 331
    Immigration Paradigm and, 152, 154
    origins of Deuteronomy and, 258
    Urdeuteronomium and, 270
Amoruso, Francesco, 154
amphictyony, 152, 258, 260, 270
Anderson, Ana Flora, 449
Anderson, Cheryl, 194
Arbino, Gary P., xiii
archeology and *maqom*. *See also maqom;*
    space theory and *maqom*
    Arad and, 118–120, 124–126
    bamot and, 113–119, 122–126
    Beersheba and, 118–120, 124–126
    Beth Shemesh and, 118, 122
    Bull Site of Manasseh and, 122–124
    City of David and, 116, 121
    cult centralization and, 113–114, 119, 123–124
    cult corners and, 117, 119, 123
    dating and, 112–119, 121, 124–126
    decommissioning of structures and, 118–120, 124
    Hazor and, 117–118, 122
    Herod's Temple and, 114
    Hezekiah and Josiah and, 113–114, 119–120
    household sanctuaries and, 123
    Jerusalem and, 113, 120–122
    Lachish and, 117–119, 122, 124–125
    Levantine temple types and, 115–116
    maqommim and, 112–113, 116–119
    Megiddo and, 117–118, 120, 122
    Moses and, 113
    Mt. Ebal and, 113, 122
    open-air sites and, 122
    origins of Deuteronomy and, 114, 126
    cultic sites outside Jerusalem and, 113, 117–121

archeology and *maqom* (*cont.*)
    Shiloh and, 113, 117, 121–122, 126
    Tel Burna and, 122
    Tel Dan and, 118
    Tel Moza and, 122, 125–126
Archimedean point, Deuteronomy as, 256, 313–314
Arnold, Bill T., xiii, 138
Arter, Jared Maurice, 434
Astruc, Jean, 255
Augustine, 75, 150, 432
Avalos, Hector, 467, 469

Ba'al, 257, 321, 493
Babylonian Exile, 50, 209, 212–213
Babylonian Talmud, 255, 465–466
Bach, Alice, 193
Bachmann, Mercedes Garcia, 194
Baden, Joel S., 38, 469, 471
Bakhos, Carol, 410
bamot, 113–119, 122–126
Barer, Deborah, 411
Barrett, Lisa Feldman, 142
Basser, Herbert, 410–412
Bellwood, Peter, 156
Benett, Robert A., 439–440
Benjamin, Don C., 39, 469
Bennett, Harold, 193, 244, 440
Berge, Kåre, 212
Bergsma, John, 38
Berlin, Adele, 192
Berman, Joshua, 35
Black Church. *See* African-American Christianity
Blenkinsopp, J., 211, 292–293
blessings and curses
    Covenant Code and, 61
    covenant curses, 81, 478
    Covenant with Abraham and, 66
    Decalogue and, 43, 50
    disability and, 468, 472, 474
    Esarhaddon's Succession Treaties (EST) and, 59–64, 64–65t, 68
    futility curses, 63–64, 68
    Hezekiah and Josiah and, 60
    as instruments of social control, 57
    monotheism and, 81
    Moses and, 66
    New Testament and, 390
    Sefire treaties and, 63–67, 63t, 67t
Block, Daniel I., 82, 477–478
Boer, Roland, 276–277
Boyrain, Daniel, 410
Braulik, Georg, 47, 76, 79, 99, 197–198, 236
Brenner, Athalya, 193, 195
Bright, John, 152
Brinch, Boyrereau, 433, 436
Brown, John, 434
Brueggemann, Walter, 169

Calhoun, John C., 436
Calvin, John, 150–151
Cambridge Platonists, 73–74
Candido, Fernando, 455
Carmichael, Calum, 39
Carr, David M., 292, 293
Carroll, Robert, 350
Carsten, Janet, 244–245
Cellard, Eleonore, 419
Champollion, Jacques-Joseph, 113
Chapman, Stephen, 168
Chilton, Bruce, 405, 413–414
Christianity. *See also* African-American Christianity; Jesus; New Testament
    Decalogue and, 46
    early Christianity, 150, 390
    Islam and, 419–420, 422, 424
    Judaism and, 74, 77, 210, 388, 397
    monotheism and, 74, 77
    Pharisees and, 210
    war and, 150–151
Civil Rights movement, 437–439
Claassens, S. J., 40
Claburn, W. Eugene, 120
Clarke, Edward Daniel, 113
Clements, Ronald E., 259, 270, 331, 471
Code of Hammurabi, xiii, 33, 45
Comte, Auguste, 74
Cook, Edward, 379
Cook, Elizabeth, 453
Cook, Stanley Arthur, 114
Covenant Code
    African-American Christianity and, 433
    blessings and curses and, 61
    Code of Hammurabi and, 37
    code or covenant and, 34–39

cult centralization and, 4
Decalogue and, 37
Deuteronomic Code and, 36–40, 236, 240
Hezekiah and Josiah and, 258–259, 264
Hosea and theory of northern origins and, 337–338
LGBTQIA+ community and, 480
monotheism and, 79
Moses and, 7
Near Eastern law and, 19
Pentateuch and, 289–290
scribes and, 208
stranger, fatherless, and widow and, 236, 240
Crawford, Sidnie White, 368
critical legal theory (CLT), 244, 439–441
critical race theory (CRT), 439–441
Croatto, José Severino, 449
Cross, Frank Moore, 224, 245, 350
Crouch, C.L., 39
Crüsemann, Frank, 450
cult centralization
African-American Christianity and, 441
archeology and *maqom* and, 113–114, 119, 123–124
Covenant Code and, 4
Deuteronomic Code and, 441
DTH (Deuteronomistic History) and, 313, 318
Hexateuch and, 297–298
Hezekiah and Josiah and, 257
Hosea and theory of northern origins and, 331, 339–340
Liberation Theology and, 448
literary history and, 4–8
monotheism and, 84–85
Pentateuch and, 290–291, 297–298
priests and Levites and, 224, 228–229
women and, 193
curses. See blessings and curses
Cyrus the Great/Cyrus II, 276

Dahmen, Ulrich, 231, 368
Darby, Erin, 39
Darius I, 276–277
Daube, David, 39
Dead Sea Scrolls, 367, 379, 411. See also Dead Sea Scrolls

Decalogue
authority of, 44, 47–48
case and apodictic law and, 43
Code of Hammurabi and, 45
code or covenant and, 34–35, 37
correlations between the laws of Deuteronomy and, 48, 48t
curses and, 43, 50
Deuteronomic Code and, 37
DTH (Deuteronomistic History) and, 322
Elohist and, 42–43
Esarhaddon's Succession Treaties (EST) and, 45–46
finger of Yahweh and, 45
form-criticism and, 43
Golden Calf and, 50–51
Hosea and theory of northern origins and, 340
I Am formula and, 45–46
idolatry and, 49–51
Jeremiah and, 357
Dead Sea Scrolls and, 371
Moab Covenant and, 50
monotheism and, 7, 49–50, 80
Moses Wilhelm Shapira and, 42–43
New Testament and, 386–387, 393, 396
Pentateuch and, 9–10
Sitz im Leben of, 43–44
stone tablets and, 44
DeGrado, Jessie, 491–492
Deuteronomic Code
authorship of, 42, 151, 255–258, 313, 346–347
African-American Christianity and, 433, 441
code or covenant and, 36–40
Covenant Code and, 36–39, 236, 240
cult centralization and, 441
dating of 112–119, 121, 124–126, 151, 313–315, 350–352. See also archeology and *maqom*
Decalogue and, 37
early Rabbinic Judaism and, 408
Hosea and theory of northern origins and, 331, 337
Liberation Theology and, 450–452
monotheism and, 84–85
Near Eastern law and, 18–20, 25–26
origins of Deuteronomy, 5, 114, 126, 151, 256–261, 269–270, 293–294, 330, 440

Deuteronomic Code (*cont.*)
   stranger, fatherless, and widow and, 236, 240, 242, 244
Deuteronomistic History (DTH)
   Caleb and, 320–322
   compositional history of, 317
   Cross, Frank Moore, 314
   cult centralization and, 313, 318
   dating of Deuteronomy and, 313, 315
   David and, 322–323
   Decalogue and, 322
   documentary hypothesis and, 315
   Former Prophets and, 313, 318, 324–325
   Göttingen School and, 314–315
   Hezekiah and Josiah and, 313–314, 318, 324
   Jeremiah and, 354
   Joshua-Kings and, 313–325
   Manasseh and, 324
   Moses and, 318–322
   Noth, Martin and, 312–314
   Pentateuch and, 315–316, 318, 322
   Persian diaspora and, 315
   scribes and, 314–316
   sefer hatorah and, 321–325
   source criticism and, 313
   space theory and, 104–105
   tradition history and, 312
   Urdeuteronomium and, 312–313
Dever, William G., 120
de Wette, Wilhelm Martin Leberecht
   authorship of Deuteronomy and, 256
   DTH (Deuteronomistic History) and, 313
   Hezekiah and Josiah and, 113–114, 256
   maqom and, 113–114
   Mosaic authorship of Deuteronomy and, 151, 256
   origins of Deuteronomy and, 151, 256, 269–270
   Sefer Torah and, 256
   Urdeuteronomium and, 269–270
DH *See* Deuteronomistic History (DTH)
Dimant, Devorah, 379–380
al-Dimashq, Muhammad ibn Abi Talib, 421–422
disability
   Babylonian Talmud and, 465
   bodily metaphors and, 471–472
   bribery and, 473
   care for the needy and, 472
   covenant disobedience and, 474
   curses and, 468, 472, 474
   genital damage and, 466–469, 473–474
   holiness and, 472
   idolatry and, 467, 470
   infertility as, 465–467
   mental illness and, 468
   Moses and, 466
   remarriage and, 473
   tithes and, 472–473
   Yahweh and, 467–472
Documentary Hypothesis, 302
Douglas, Mary, 211
Drazin, Israel, 494
Dreher, Carlos A., 451
Driver, Samuel R., 74, 256
Duhm, Bernhard, 316, 347
Duke, Rodney, 228
Duncan, Julie A., 367

early Rabbinic Judaism
   Aqiva and Ishmael and, 409
   Dead Sea Scrolls and, 411
   Deuteronomic Code and, 408
   halakhic midrash and, 406
   Mekhilta Devarim and, 408–410
   midrash and, 410
   Mishnah and, 404–408
   Second Temple and, 408
   Shema and, 405–406, 408
   Sifre Deuteronomy and, 408–413
   Sifre Devarim and, 404–406
   Sifre Zutta and, 408–409
   Tannaim and, 404–405, 414
   Tosefta and, 404, 408
economics. *See* socio-economics
Edenburg, Cynthia, 194
Eilberg-Schwartz, Howard, 154
Eldridge, Elleanor, 437
Ellens, Deborah, 194
Emancipation Proclamation (1863) and, 436–438
Emerton, John, 227
EST *See* Esarhadon's Succession Treaties
Ewald, Heinrich, 42, 270, 314
Exum, J. Cheryl, 193
Eynikel, E., 316
Ibn-Ezra, R. Abraham, 255

Faust, Avraham, 276
Fensham, Charles, 236
Finkelstein, Israel, 333
Finsterbusch, Karin, 48, 83, 196
Firestone, Reuven, 423
Fitzpatrick-McKinely, Anne, 39
Fleming, Daniel, 351
Flesher, Paul, 413–414
Fohrer, Georg, 316
Former Prophets, 9, 168–170, 225–226, 313, 318, 324–325
Foster, Benjamin, 155
Fraade, Steven D., 410–413
Fraenkel, Yonah, 410
Frankena, Rintje, 35–36, 59–61
Free African Society, 439
Freedom, David Noel, 350

Garroway, Kristine, 237
Gasda, Élio, 456
Gender and 139-140, 450, 483-490
genital damage, 466–469, 473–474
George, Mark K., 96
Gevaryahu, Amit, 411
God. *See* monotheism; Yahweh (YHWH)
Golden Calf, 50–51, 256, 261–262, 321, 427
Good Samaritan, 393
Göttingen School, 314–315
Gottwald, Norman K., 152
Gramsci, Antonio, 155
Gribetz, Sarit Kattan, 405–406
Gulliver, Mike, 470
Gunkel, Hermann, 43

Halberstam, Chaya, 411
Halpern, Baruch, 350
Hammer, Reuben, 411
Harlem Renaissance, 437–439
Harper's Ferry (1859) and, 434
Harris, Jay, 409
hate. *See* love and hate
Hayes, Christine, 407
Ḥazm, Ibn, 421
Hempel, Johannes, 257
Hengel, Martin, 209
Herzog, Ze'ev, 118–119, 124
Heschel, Abraham Joshua, 172

Hexateuch
  composition, 294–298
  cult centralization and, 297–298
  Deuteronomy and, 151, 154
  Leviticus and, 295–298
  Numbers and, 294–295
  Pentateuch and, 292–298
  Priestly Tradition (P), 294, 298
  war and, 151, 154, 157, 159–161
Hezekiah and Josiah
  amphictyony and, 260
  Assyria and, 263–264
  Ba'al and, 257
  Babylonian Talmud and, 255
  blessings and curses and, 60
  Covenant Code and, 258–259, 264
  Deuteronomy and, 313–314, 318, 324
  Golden Calf and, 261–262
  Hosea and, 258–263
  Jehu and, 262–263
  Jeremiah and, 346–347, 350
  Leviticus and, 258–259, 261
  LGBTQIA+ community and, 492–493
  maqom and, 113–114, 119–120
  Moses and, 170
  origins of Deuteronomy and, 257–264
  priests and Levites and, 223–225, 258–259, 261
  scribes and, 212
  tithes and, 257
  war and, 151
  Yahweh and, 262
Hiebert, Paula S., 238
Hirschfeld, Hartwig, 423
Hirshman, Marc, 410, 411
History of Religions School, 119
Hittite treaties, 33–37, 137
Hoffman, David Zvi, 409
Hoffner, Harry, 487–488
Hogue, Timothy, 45
Holiness Code and, 157, 238–240, 295–296, 452, 487
Holladay, John S., Jr., 123, 275
Holladay, William, 349–350
Holscher, G., 270
Holsey, James, 434–435
Holsey, Lucius Henry, 434

INDEX

Hossfeld, Frank-Lothar, 43
Houten, Christiana van, 239
Huldah, 165, 168–170
Hurowitz, Victor Avigdor, 121
Hurston, Zora Neale, 437
Hurtado, Larry W., 78
Hyatt, J. Phillip, 347

Islam
   aniconism of, 425
   anthropomorphism and, 426–427
   Christianity and, 419–420, 422, 424
   Golden Calf and, 427
   idolatry and, 425
   Jesus and, 420–422
   messenger stories and, 424
   Moses and, 421–422
   Muhammad and, 420–422, 423–424
   Noah and, 420
   People of the Book and, 428
   polytheism and, 425–426
   prophets and, 421–422, 424
   sharī'ah and, 428
Israel. *See also* Jerusalem
   Assyria and, 263–264
   cult centralization and, 181
   Islam and, 423
   non-Israelites and, 184
   Shema and, 180
Isserlin, Benedikt S., 160

Jacobs, Sandra, xi, xiii
Jay, Nancy, 198
Jeremiah
   Aaron and, 356
   Baruch b. Neriah and, 348
   Book of the Twelve and, 352
   Decalogue and, 357
   Deuteronomy and, 350–351, 352
   Hezekiah and Josiah and, 346–347, 350
   Hosea and, 360
   land-deeds and, 355
   Levites and, 357–358
   Mesopotamian scribes and, 351–352, 358
   Moses, and, 165–166, 169, 171–172
   Pentateuch and, 352
   Persia and, 351
   Samuel and, 168–169

   Song of Moses and, 357–360
Jerusalem. *See also* cult centralization; *maqom*; priests and Levites
   as chosen place, 324
   destruction of, 50, 96–98
   election formula and, 105
   Holy of Holies and, 46, 51
   maqom and, 104–105, 113, 120–122
   space theory and, 104–105
   Temple and, 5, 46, 51, 113–126, 223–225, 260–264, 324
Jesus
   African-American Christianity and, 436
   commandment to love and, 392
   Islam and, 420–422
   Shema and, 388, 392–394, 405, 434–437
Jonker, Louis, 276–277
Josephus, 438
   Dead Sea Scrolls (DSS)
   Community Rule and, 383–384
   Damascus Document and, 368, 379–380
   Decalogue and, 371
   Deuteronomy and, 374–379t
   4QReworked Pentateuch and, 368–369, 372–373
   4QTestimonia and, 368, 373, 380
   Moses and, 383
   Song of Moses and, 379
   Temple Scroll and, 380–382
   War Scroll and, 382
   Words of Moses and, 380–381

Kahana, Menahem, 409–410
Kamlah, Jens, 121
Kaufman, Stephen A., 47, 486
Kaufmann, Yehezkel, 75
Kawashima, Robert, 192
Kelle, Brad E., 153
Kennett, R. H., 270
Kenyon, Kathleen, 116
Kidd, José Enrique Ramírez, 452
King, Martin Luther, Jr., 437
Kinsey, Alfred, 480
Kitchen, Kenneth, 35, 113
Knafl, Anne K., xiii
Knauf, Ernst Axel, 119, 316
Knierim, Rolf, xi

Kraemer, David C., 407
Kramer, Pedro, 451, 455
Kratz, Reinhard, 314
Kruse, Joachim J., 301
Kuenen, Abraham, 74, 113
Kugel, James, 410

Lambert, David A., 81, 143
Landsberger, B., 19
Lapsley, Jacqueline, 138
law. *See* Covenant Code; Decalogue; Deuteronomic Code; Near Eastern law
Lawrence, Paul, 35
Lazarus-Yafeh, Hava, 421
Lefebvre, Henri, 95–97
Lemkin, Raphael, 157–158
Lemos, T. M., 153
Levinson, Bernard, 35–36, 39, 61–62, 208–209, 301, 406
Levirate Law, 243–244, 247
Levoratti, Armando J., 449
Lévy, Edmond, 40
Lewis, J. Vance, 433, 436
LGBTQIA+ community
  adultery and, 481–482
  apotropaic magic and, 493–494
  bestiality and, 480
  bloodlines and, 483
  Covenant Code and, 480
  cross-dressing and, 484–488
  diseased body and, 494–495
  dogs and, 494–495
  eunuchs and, 483–484, 489–490
  gender binary and, 483–490
  genital damage and, 489
  heteronormativity and, 483
  cult prostitution and, 490–495
  idolatry and, 486, 495–496
  incest and, 479–480
  literary structural argument and, 486–487
  Mishnah Arakhin and, 484
  Mishneh Torah and, 479, 484
  plagues and, 494–495
  purity rules and, 481, 486–487
  queer analysis and, 478, 489, 495–496
  reader response criticism and, 477
  texts of terror and, 481–482
  votive offerings and, 494–495

Liberation Theology
  Deuteronomy and, 450–452
  Holiness Code and, 452
  Latin America and, 447
  prosperity gospel and, 455
  resident alien, orphan, widow and, 452
  Second Vatican Council and, 448
  Shema and, 456–457
Lipka, Hilary, 194
literary history
  Deuteronomy and, 4–8
  Covenant Code and, 4–8
  cult centralization and, 4–8
  Decalogue and, 9
  Moses and, 6–11
  Pentateuch and, 9
  scribes and, 212–213
  secularization and, 6
  Shema and, 7
  torāh and, 3
Lohfink, Norbert, 46, 99
Long, John Dixon, 436
love and hate
  El Amarna letters and, 136–137
  Elephantine Papyri and, 140–141
  Esarhaddon's Succession Treaties (EST) and, 136
  Gender relations and, 139–140
  marriage and, 140
  sexual intercourse and, 140
Löw, Martina, 97–98
Lundbom, Jack R., 39, 349, 469
Lynch, Matthew, xiii
Lynn, T. L., 434
Lyons, William John, 470

MacDonald, Nathan, 76–77
Maier, Christl M., 96, 351
Malešević, Siniša, 154–155
Mandel, Paul, 409
Manning, Patrick, 156
maqom. See also archeology and *maqom*; space theory and *maqom*
  administration of justice and, 101–102
  centralization formula and, 103–104
  Deuteronomistic History (DTH) and, 104–105
  Feast of Tabernacles and, 102

maqom (cont.)
   functions of, 100
   Jerusalem and, 104–105
   Moses and, 102
   Mt. Gerizim and, 105–106
   Passover and, 101
   Thirdspace, 107–108
   Torah and, 102
Marianno, Lilia Dias, 456
Mastnjak, Nathan, 353, 357
Mayes, Andrew, 196
Mazar, Amihai, 118–123
Mbuwayesango, Dora, 199–200
McBridge, S. Dean, Jr., 163
McCarthy, Dennis J., 35, 60
McConville, J. Gordon, 76, 193, 228
McDougall, Harriet Whipple Green, 437
McKane, William, 350
Mendenhall, Geroge E., 34, 59, 152
Menken, Maarten, 386
Middle Assyrian Laws, 37
Milgrom, Jacob, 295–296
Miller, Patrick D., 78–79
Miller, R. D., 39
Mirguet, Francoise, xiii
Moberly, R. W. L., 76, 84
monotheism
   anachronism and, 77
   ban on images and, 76
   Cambridge Platonists and, 73–74
   Covenant Code and, 79
   cult centralization and, 84–85
   Decalogue and, 7, 49–50, 80
   Deuteronomic Code and, 84–85
   The Enlightenment and, 76
   ethical monotheism, 74–75
   History of Religions and, 76–77
   idolatry and, 75, 80–81
   intermarriage and, 84
   other gods and, 76, 78–86, 85t
   Religionsgeschichtliche Schule and, 74
   Shema and, 82–83
   Song of Moses and, 78, 84–85
   Yahweh and, 77–78, 80, 80t, 85–87, 85t
Monroe, Lauren, 351
Moore-Cross, Frank, 314
Moran, William, 137, 195
More, Henry, 73–74

Morris, E. F., 160
Morrow, William, 36
Moses. *See also* Decalogue; Song of Moses
   African-American Christianity and, 437–438
   Deuteronomy and, 42, 151, 313
   Covenant Code and, 7
   Dead Sea Scrolls (DSS) and, 383
   death of, 7, 34, 299–300
   Deuteronomistic History (DTH) and, 318–324
   Elijah and, 165, 169–170
   Elisha and, 169–170
   farewell speeches of, 3, 11, 34, 37–38
   former prophets and, 168–170
   Hezekiah and Josiah and, 170
   Hosea and, 166–167, 170–171
   Huldah and, 170
   Islam and, 421–422
   Jeremiah and, 165–166, 169, 171–172
   Jesus and, 394–397
   Malachi and, 172–173
   maqom and, 102, 113
   monotheism and, 75–81
   New Testament and, 391
   Pentateuch and, 42, 255–256, 290
   Prophets and, 167
   Samuel and, 163, 166, 168–170
   Tetrateuch and, 167–168
Moss, Candida R., 469, 471
Mowinckel, Sigmund, 43, 316, 347
Moyise, Steve, 386
Muilenberg, James, 348

Na'aman, Nadav, 119, 333
Naeh, Shlomo, 411
Najman, Hindy, 6, 210
Nam, Roger, 275, 278
Near Eastern law
   Covenant Code and, 19
   Deuteronomy and, 18–20, 25–26
   Nippur Homicide Trial and, 21–22
Near Eastern treaties, 23–24, 133–137, 259
Nelson, Richard, 314
Neusner, Jacob, 410–412
New Testament. *See also* Pentateuch
   Christology and, 388–389
   Corinthians and, 389–390

curses and, 390
Decalogue and, 386–387, 393, 396
Deuteronomy and, 387
early Christianity and, 390
Galatians and, 390
Hebrews and, 395–396
Jesus and, 388–389
John and, 395
Luke and, 393–394
Mark and, 392, 394
Matthew and, 392–393, 393*t*
Moses and, 391
Q source and, 388–389
Revelation and, 396
Romans and, 390–391
Sadducees and, 392
Shema and, 388, 392–393
Timothy and, 391
wages and, 391
Nicholson, E. W., 259–261, 270, 331–332, 348
Nihan, Christophe, 107, 270–271
Nikolsky, Ronit, 139
Nippur Homocide Trial, 21–22
Northup, Solomon, 433
Noth, Martin. *See also* Deuteronomistic History (DTH)
    amphictyony and, 260
    tradition history and, 312

Oestreicher, Theodor, 120, 257
Oliveira dos Santos, Douglas, 456–457
Olson, Dennis T., 3, 47
Olsson, C., 155
Olyan, Saul M., 468
origins of Deuteronomy, 5, 114, 126, 151, 256–261, 269–270, 293–294, 330, 440
orphans. *See* stranger, fatherless, and widow
Osterhammel, Jürgen, 156
Oswald, Wolfgang, 43
Otto, Eckart, 35–36, 48, 99, 300, 351, 477–478
Otto, Rudolph, 165
Owen, D. I., 22

Pappe, Ilan, 154
Paul VI, 448
Pentateuch
    authorship of, 42, 255–256, 290
    compositional history of, 43–44, 269–271, 294–298

Covenant Code and, 289–290
cult centralization and, 290–291, 297–298
Hexateuch and, 292–294
Deuteronomistic History (DTH) and, 315–316, 318, 322
Deuteronomy and, 256, 297–298, 313–314
Esarhaddon's Succession Treaties (EST) and, 290–291
Genesis and, 293
Hexateuch and, 292–298
Holiness Code and, 295–296
inheritance and, 292, 294–295
Jeremiah and, 352
land of milk and honey and, 295–297
Moses and, 42, 255–256, 290
non-D materials and, 291–294
Numbers and, 294–295
Pentateuch and, 293–294, 298–301
P source (Priestly Tradition) and, 294–298
priests and Levites and, 290–291, 295–298
Samaritan Pentateuch, 45, 103–104, 367
scribes and, 297–298
Torah and, 298–299
Perlitt, Lothar, 170
Person, Raymond, 351
Philo of Alexandria, 47, 210
Pixley, George V., 449
Pizzorno, Patricia, 451
Pohlmann, Karl-Friedrich, 349
Polzin, R., 317
Poor Peoples Campaign (1968), 438–439
Powery, Emerson B., 433
Prentiss, Benjamin, 436
Pressler, Carolyn, 193
priests and Levites
    cult centralization and, 224, 228–229
    cultic officials and, 230
    Hezekiah and Josiah and, 223–225, 258–259, 261
    Julius Wellhausen and, 222–227
    Levitical priests, 45, 101, 166, 216, 222–227, 230–231, 261, 290–291, 297–298, 303, 333–334, 340, 492–494
    Micah and, 224
    Numbers and, 221–223
    Pentateuch and, 290–291, 295–298
    tribe of Dan and, 226
Prophet, Thomas, 437
Prophets. *See* Islam; Moses

Puukko, Antti Filemon, 257
Py Murta de Almeida, Fabio, 455

Quigly, Thomas, 436
Qutayba, Ibn, 421

Rabban, Ali b., 421
Rabbinic Judaism. *See* early Rabbinic Judaism
Radner, K., 23
Ramos, Melissa, 36
Raphael, Rebecca, 467–468
Ravenhill, Philip, 57
redaction criticism, 312, 317, 335–336
Reeder, Caryn, 194
Reich, Ronny, 121
Reimer, Haroldo, 450
Reimer, Ivoni Richter, 456–457
Renz, Johannes, 211, 335
Rhyder, Julia, 297–298
Richter, Sandra L., 112, 122
Richter-Devroe, Sophie, 154
Rida, Rashid, 422
Robinson, Edward, 114
Rofé, Alexander, 331
Rollston, Christopher, 207
Romer, Thomas, 351
Rom-Shiloni, Dalit, 352
Rossi, Benedetta, 300
Roth, Martha T., 19, 21, 40
Rothstein, David, 411
Routledge, Bruce, 155
Ruane, Nicole, 198
Russell, Stephen C., xiii

ben Joseph, Sa'adia, 465
Sadler, Rodney S., Jr., 433
Saleh, Walid, 423–425, 429
Samely, Alexander, 407
Samuel, H., 231
ben Meir, Samuel (Rashbam), 466
Sánchez Cetina, Edesio, 452
Schaper, Joachim, 76, 209, 213
Schipper, Jeremy, 467
Schmid, Konrad, 137, 291, 299–300, 351
Schniedewind, William, 209
Schremer, Adiel, 411
Schultz, Friedrich Wilhelm, 47
Schwantes, Milton, 449, 453
Schwarz, Baruch J., 297

scribes
 Babylonian Exile and, 212–213
 Covenant Code and, 208
 culture of, 210–215
 hermeneutics and, 208–209
 Hezekiah and Josiah and, 212
 as informational elite, 213
 Jeremiah and, 347–358
 nationalism and, 207
 Pentateuch and, 297–298
 script creation and, 207
 specific activities of, 208
 training of, 206
 utopian vision and, 212
 writing and, 214–215
 Yahweh as scribe and, 214–215
Sefer Hatorah, 321–325
Sefer Torah, 254, 256
Sefire treaties, 37, 63–67, 63*t*, 67*t*
Sellin, Ernst, 316
Shapira, Amnon, 196
Shapira, Wilhelm H, 42
Sharp, Carolyn, 352
Shema
 African-American Christianity and, 433, 435, 437
 early Rabbinic Judaism and, 405–406, 408
 Israel and, 180
 Jesus and, 388, 392–394, 405, 434–437
 Liberation Theology and, 456–457
 literary history and, 7
 monotheism and, 82–83
 New Testament and, 388, 392–393
Shemesh, Aharon, 411
Shiloh, Yigal, 116
Short, Damien, 158
Shukron, Eli, 121
Shulkhan Arukh, 479
Sifrei Devarim, 466
Simon, Richard, 255
Sinai pericope, 293
Smend, Rudolf, 315
Sneed, Mark, 193–194, 244
socio-economics
 agricultural production and, 272–273
 coinage and, 277–278
 cult centralization and, 275–276
 currency and, 274–275

Elisha and, 274–275
Hezekiah and, 270, 273, 275
Hosea and, 274–275
household economics and, 272–273
industrialization and, 275
Iron period 271-276
Jerusalem and, 276–277
moneyless taxation and, 278–279
Neo-Assyrian Empire and, 273, 275–276
new economic zones and, 274
Persian Period (539-332 BCE) and, 276–278
Philisto-Arabian coins and, 277
public architecture and, 274
Samaria and, 277
Sitz im Leben and, 269
Urdeuteronomium and, 269–273, 278–280
Soja, Edward, 95–97
Song of Moses
    Dead Sea scrolls and, 379
    Jeremiah and, 357–360
    monotheism and, 78, 84–85
Sonnet, Pierre, 208
Soughers, Tara, 489
Southern Christian Leadership Conference (SCLC), 438–439
space theory
    administration of justice and, 101–102
    centralization formula and, 103–104
    Deuteronomistic History (DTH) and, 104–105
    gates and, 100
    Jerusalem and, 104–105
    Lamentations and, 96
    Henri Lefebvre and, 95–97
    Mt. Gerizim and, 105–106
    perceived space and, 95–97
    sociology of space and, 97–98
    Soja and, 95–97
    Thirdspace and, 96, 107–108
    Torah and, 102
Spengler, Oswald, 213
Spinoza, Baruch, 255
Stack, George, 150
Stackert, Jeffrey, 35, 39
Stager, Lawrence, 224
Stemberger, Gunter, 407, 409
Stern, David, 410
Steuernagel, Carl, 256

Strack, H. L., 407, 409
stranger, fatherless, and widow
    African-American Christianity and, 441
    Covenant Code and, 236, 240
    Critical Legal Theory (CRT) and, 244–245
    fatherless people (orphans) and, 237–238
    strangers and, 239
    widows and, 238–239
    Deuteronomic Code and, 236, 240, 242, 244
    feastal calendar and, 245–246
    females as, 240–241, 241t
    gleaning and, 242
    Holiness Code and, 240
    household lists and, 245
    judicial procedure and, 241–243
    kinship and, 244–248, 247f
    Levirate and, 243–244, 247
    Sabbath and, 242
    tithe and, 243
Sweeney, Marvin, 350

Taggar-Cohen, Ada, 35
Tal, Josef, 97
Teeter, David Andrew, 372
Ten Commandments. *See* Decalogue
Tertullian, 432
Thiel, Winfried, 349
Tigay, Jeffery H., 270, 273, 405, 471, 485
tithes, 4–5, 112–113, 221–222, 229, 243–244, 257, 273, 279, 291, 454–455, 472–473
Torah. *See* early Rabbinic Judaism; Pentateuch
Torah of the King, 258
Tsai, D. Y., 23
Turner, Harriet, 434
Turner, Victor H., 246

Uehlinger, Christoph, 119
Urdeuteronomium, 5, 7, 10–11, 231, 256, 269–273, 278–280, 290–291, 312–313, 331
Ussishkin, David, 119

Van der Toorn, Karel, 207–209, 212–213
Van Seters, John, 209
Vaux, Roland de, 113
Veijola, Timo, 209
von Rad, Gerhard, 75, 152, 258–260, 270, 440

INDEX

Wanke, Gunther, 348
war
  biblical materials and, 153–154
  Christianity and, 150–151
  colonialism and, 156–159
  Conquest Paradigm and, 154
  The Enlightenment and, 151
  genocide and, 153–154, 157–158
  hegemony and, 155, 159
  Hexateuch and, 151, 154, 157, 159–161
  Hezekiah and Josiah and, 151
  holy war (*herem*) and, 152–153
  Peasant Revolt and, 152, 154
  The Reformation and, 150–151
  Settler Colonialism and, 156–159
  violence and, 154–155
  war and, 155
  Yahweh Alone motif and, 159
Wegner, Judith, 194
Weinfeld, Moshe, 35–36, 59–60, 270, 348–349
Weippert, Helga, 349
Weiser, Arthur, 316
Welch, Adam Cleghorn, 122, 257–258, 273, 331
Wellhausen, Julius
  authorship of Deuteronomy and, 256
  cult centralization and, 313
  Decalogue and, 43
  Documentary Hypothesis and, 313
  maqom and, 113
  monotheism and, 74, 78
  origins of Deuteronomy and, 269–270, 330
  priests and Levites and, 222–223, 226
Wells, Bruce, 18–20, 22, 37, 39–40
Westbrook, Raymond, 22, 140, 247
Westermann, Claus, 58, 316
Wette, W. M. L. de, 113
widows. *See* stranger, fatherless, and widow
Wilkerson, James, 433, 435
Williamson, H. G. M., 170
Wilson, Ian, 100

Wilson, Robert R, 169–171
Wiseman, D. J., 35
Wolfe, Patrick, 159
Wolff, Hans Walter, 258–259, 332–333, 339
women. *See also* stranger, fatherless, and widow
  absence of individual rights and, 191–193
  controlling sexual access to, 192–193
  cult centralization and, 193
  female circumcision and, 200
  Hannah and, 197
  land rights and, 191–192
  Liberation Theology and, 449, 451, 455, 457
  Miriam and, 191
  social and legal status of, 191–193
Wright, David P., 37
Wright, George Ernest, 227, 440
Wright, G. R. H., 115
Wurthwein, E., 316

Yadin-Israel, Azzan, 406
Yahweh (YHWH). *See also* monotheism
  anthropomorphism of, 426–427
  categorical supremacy of, 77–78, 85–87, 85t
  intimacy of Moses with, 165
  Islam and, 425–428
  Liberation Theology and, 456–457
  oneness of, 76, 79, 82–84, 456–457
  as scribe, 214–215
  throne of, 96, 262
  uniqueness of, 76–87
  unity of, 7, 10, 83
  war and, 159
  Yahweh Alone motif, 159
Yasur-Landau, Assaf, 159–160
Yitzchaki, Shlomo (Rashi), 466
Younger, K. Lawson, Jr., 159–160

Zhakevich, Philip, 211